INDIAN PSYCHOLOGY

INDIAN PSYCHOLOGY

Volume II

Emotion and Will

Jadunath Sinha

MOTILAL BANARSIDASS
INTERNATIONAL
DELHI

Reprint Edition : Delhi, 2023
Second Edition : Calcutta, 1958

ISBN : 978-81-96123-68-0 (3 Vols. Set)

Also available at
MOTILAL BANARSIDASS INTERNATIONAL
H. O. : 41 U.A. Bungalow Road, (Back Lane) Jawahar Nagar, Delhi - 110 007
4261/3 (basement) Ansari Road, Darya Ganj, New Delhi - 110 002
203 Royapettah High Road, Mylapore, Chennai - 600 004
12/1A, 2nd Floor, Bankim Chatterjee Street, Kolkata - 700 073
Stockist : Motilal Books, Ashok Rajpath, Near Kali Mandir, Patna - 800 004

Printed in India
MOTILAL BANARSIDASS INTERNATIONAL

To my deceased Wife

CONTENTS

CONTENTS

CONTENTS

BOOK II

The Psychology of the Alaṅkāra

CHAPTER VII

CHAPTER VIII

CHAPTER IX

IIP. = *Introduction to Indian Philosophy* (Jadunath Sinha), The Modern Press, Agra, 1949.

IPC. = *Indian Psychology: Cognition*, Vol. I, (Jadunath Sinha), S.P.H., 1958.
JTBG. = Prameyadīpikā (Jayatīrtha) on BG., G.P.P., 1938.
KA. = Kāvyādarśa (Daṇḍin).
Kaṭh. = Kaṭha.
KK. = Kiṣkindhyākāṇḍa.
KPD. = Kāvyapradīpa.
KPK. = Kāvyaprakāśa (Mammaṭa), Jīvānanda's edition, Calcutta, 1897.
KR. = Kaṇādarahasya (Śaṅkaramiśra), Ch.S.S., No. 231.
KS. = Kāvyānuśāsana (Hemacandra), Bombay, 1938.
KS.,AC. = Alaṅkāracandrikā on KS., Bombay, 1938.
K.S.S. = Kashi Sanskrit Series, Benares.
KSV. = Viveka on KS., Bombay, 1938.
KV. = Kiraṇāvalī (Udayana), Benares, Saṁvat, 1941.
LR. = Locanarocanī (Jīva Goswāmī) on UNM., Berhampur, Śaka, 1885.
Māṇḍ = Māṇḍūkya.
Mait. = Maitrāyaṇī.
MB. = Mitabhāṣiṇī (Mādhava Sarasvatī) on SP., V.S.S., 1893.
MBG. = Madhusūdana's commentary on BG., edited by Pūrṇānanda Sen Gupta, Benares, 1885.

MPK. = Kāvyaprakāśa (Mammaṭa), Jīvānanda's edition, Calcutta, 1897.
Muṇḍ. = Muṇḍaka.
NBG. = Nīlakaṇṭha's commentary on BG.
NBh. = Nyāyabhāṣya (Vātsyāyana) on NS., Jīvānanda's edition, Calcutta, 1919.
NBS. = Nārada Bhaktisūtra, Calcutta, Bengali year, 1361.
NDP. = Nāṭyadarpaṇa (Rāmacandra and Guṇacandra), G.O.S.
NK. = Nyāyakandalī (Śrīdhara) on PBh., V.S.S., 1895.
NKL. = Nyāyakalikā (Jayanta Bhaṭṭa), S.B.T., 1925.
NKS. = Nyāyakusumāñjali (Udayana), Benares, 1913.
NKSP. = Nyāyakusumāñjaliprakāśa (Vardhamana) on NKS., Benares, 1912.
NM. = Nyāyamañjarī (Jayanta Bhaṭṭa), V.S.S., 1895.
NNP. = Nyāyanivandhaprakāśa (Vardhamāna), BI., 1911.
NS. = Nyāyasūtra (Gautama), Jīvānanda's edition, Calcutta, 1919.
NSA. = Nyāyasiddhāñjana (Veṅkaṭanātha), Benares, 1901.
NSAG. = Abhinavabhāratī (Abhinava Gupta) on NTS., G.O.S., 1956.
NSār. = Nyāyasāra (Bhāsarvajña), B.I., 1910.
NSM. = Nyāyasiddhāntamañjarī (Jānakīnātha), Benares, 1916.
N.S.P. = Nirṇaya Sāgar Press, Bombay.
NSV. = Nyāyasūtravṛtti (Viśvanātha) on NS., Jīvānanda's edition, Calcutta, 1919.

NTD. = Nyāyatātparyadīpikā (Jayasiṁhasūri) on NSār., B.I., 1910.
NTS. = Nāṭyaśāstra (Bhāratamuni), G.O.S., 1956.
NV. = Nyāyavārtika (Uddyotakara) on NBh., B.I., 1893.
NVTP. = Nyāyavārtikatātparyapariśuddhi (Udayana), B.I., 1911.
NVTT. = Nyāyavārtikatātparyaṭīkā (Vācaspati Miśra), V.S.S., Benares, 1898.
PBh. = Praśastapādabhāṣya on VS., V.S.S., 1895.
PK. = Pañcāstikāya (Kundakunda Svāmī), Bombay, Saṁvat, 1972.
PKS. = Pañcāstikāyasamayasāra („).
PKV. = Pañcīkaraṇavārtika (Sureśvara), K.S.S., 1923.
POP. = Path of Purity (E.T. of Buddhaghoṣa's Viśuddhimagga), P.T.S.,
PP. = Prakaraṇapañcikā (Śālikānātha Miśra), Ch.S.S., 1903-04.
PR. = Pratāparudrīyayaśobhūṣaṇa (Kumārasvāmī).
PRA. = Prameyaratnārṇava (Bālakṛṣṇa Bhaṭṭa), Ch.S.S., No. 97.
Pras. = Praśna.
PS. = Prītisandarbha (Jīva Goswāmī) edited by Prāṇa Kiśora Goswāmī.
P.T.S. = Pali Text Society, London.
PY. = Padayojanikā (Rāmatīrtha) on US., G.P.P., 1917.
RBG. = Rāmānuja's commentary on BG., G.P.P., 1938.

RBS. = Rāmānuja's commentary (Śrībhāṣya), on B.S., edited by Durga Charana Sāṁkhya—Vedātatīrtha, Calcutta, Bengali years, 1318-22.
RBTC. = Rāmānuja-bhāṣya-tātparya-candrikā (Vedāntadeśika Veṅkaṭanātha) on RBG., G.P.P., 1938.
RG. = Rasagaṅgādhara (Jagannātha Paṇḍita), N.S.P., 1947.
RGBG. = Rāghavendra's commentary on BG., G.P.P.
RKBG. = Rāmakaṇṭha's commentary on BG., N.S.P., 1943.
RP. = Ratnāpaṇa (Vidyābhuṣaṇa) on PR.
RS. = Rasārṇavasudhākara (Śiṅga Bhūpāla), T.S.S., 1916.
SAS. = Sarvārthasiddhi (Veṅkaṭanātha) on TMK., Benares, 1900.
SB. = Śaṁkarabhāṣya.
S.B.E. = Sacred Books of the East.
SBG. = Śaṁkarabhāṣya on BG., Poona, 1916.
SBS. = Śaṁkarabhāṣya on BS., Poona, 1918.
S.B.T. = Sarasvatī Bhavan Text, Benares.
ŚD. = Śāstradīpikā (Pārthasārathi Miśra), Benares, Saṁvat, 1964.
SDP. = Sāhityadarpaṇa (Viśvanātha Kavirāja), Jīvānanda's edition, Calcutta, 1934.
SDPJ. = Jīvānanda's gloss on SDP., Calcutta, 1934.
SDPV. = Sāhityadarpaṇavṛtti (Rāmatāraṇa Tarkavāgīśa), Calcutta, 1934.
SDR. = Siddhāntaratna (Baladeva Vidyābhūṣaṇa), S.B.T., Part I, 1924; Part II, 1927.
SDS. = Ṣaḍdarśanasaṁgraha (Mādhavācārya), Kalyana—Bombay, Saṁvat, 1982.
SK. = Sāṁkhya Kārikā (Īśvara Kṛṣṇa), Jīvānanda's edition, Calcutta, 1911.
SKG. = Gauḍapāda's Bhāṣya on SK., 1911.
SKM. = Sāhityakaumudī (Vidyābhūṣana).
SM. = Siddhāntamuktāvalī (Viśvanātha), N.S.P., 1916.
SN. = Saṁyutta Nikāya.
SP. = Saptapadārthī (Śivāditya), V.S.S., 1893.
SPB. = Sāṁkhyapravacanabhāṣya (Vijñānabhikṣu), Benares, 1909.
S.P.H. = Sinha Publishing House, Calcutta-26.
SPS. = Sāṁkhyapravacanasūtra (Kapila), B.I., 1888.
SR. = Saṅgīta-Ratnākara (Śārṅgadeva), Ānandāśrama Press, Poona, 1897.
SrBG. = Śrīdharasvāmī's commentary on BG., edited by Kailāsa Chandra Sinha, Calcutta, Bengali Year, 1292.
SS. = Śāṇḍilyasūtra, Bombay, Saṁvat, 1960.
SS. = Sarvārthasiddhi (Pūjyapāda) on U.T.S., Kolhapur, Śaka, 1839.
SSār. = Sāhityasāra (Acyutarāya).
SS., BC. = Bhakticandrikā (Nārāyaṇa Tīrtha) on SS. (Śāṇḍilya), S.B.T., No. 9.
SSS. = Svapneśvara's commentary on SS., (Śāṇḍilya), Bombay, Saṁvat, 1960.
SSV. = Sāṁkhyasūtravṛtti (Aniruddha) on SPS., B.I., 1888-89.
SSVM. = Commentary on SSV., (Mahādeva Vedāntin), B.I., 1888.
STK. = Sāṁkhyatattvakaumudī (Vācaspati Miśra), Bombay, Saṁvat, 1969.
STS. = Sāhityasāra (Sarveśvarācārya), T.S.S., No. 160.
ŚV. = Ślokavārtika (Kumārila), Ch.S.S., 1898-99.
Śvet. = Śvetāśvatara.
TA. = Tarkāmṛta (Jagadīśa), Jīvānanda's edition, Calcutta, 1921.
Tait. = Taittirīya.
TASār. = Tattvārthasāra (Amṛtacandra Sūri), Calcutta, 1919.
TAS. = Tattvānusandhāna (Mahādevānanda Sarasvatī) on ACK., B.I., 1901.
TBBG. = Tātparyabodhinī (Śaṅkarānanda) on BG., G.P.P.
TBh. = Tarkabhāṣā (Keśavamiśra), Poona, 1924.
TC. = Tattvacintāmaṇi (Gaṅgeśa), B.I.
TCR. = Tattvacintāmaṇirahasya (Mathurānātha), B.I.
TCS. = Tattvacintāmaṇi (Gaṅgeśa), Śabda, B.I.
TDBG. = Tattvadīpana (Vallabha) on BG., G.P.P., 1938.
TDTV. = Tattvadīpikātātparyavṛtti (Jayasenācārya), N.S.P., Saṁvat, 1972.
TK. = Tarkakaumudī (Laugākṣi Bhāskara), N.S.P., 1914.
TMK. = Tattvamuktākalāpa (Veṅkaṭanātha), Benares, 1900.

TPBG. = Tattvaprakāśikā (Keśava Kāśmīrī) on BG., G.P.P.
TR. = Tārkikarakṣā (Varadarāja), Benares, 1903.
TR. = Tantrarahasya (Rāmānujācārya), G.O.S., 1923.
TRV. = Tattvārtharājavārtika (Bhaṭṭa Akalaṅka), Benares, 1915.
TS. = Tarkasaṁgraha (Annaṁbhaṭṭa), Bombay, 1912.
TSār. = Tattvārthasāra (Amṛtacandra Sūri), Calcutta, 1919.
T.S.S. = Trivandrum Sanskrit Series, Trivandrum.
TSV. = Tattvārthaślokavārtika (Vidyānandi Svāmī), N.S.P., 1918.
TV. = Tattvavaiśāradī (Vācaspati Miśra) on YBh.
UK. = Uttara Kāṇḍa.
UNM. = Ujjvalanīlamaṇi (Rūpa Goswāmī), Berhampur, Śaka, 1885.
UP. = Upaniṣad (Īśādiviṁśottaraśatopaniṣadaḥ), N.S.P., 1948.
US. = Upadeśasāhasrī (Śaṁkara), edited by D. V. Gokhale, G.P.P., 1917.
U.T.S. = Tattvādhigamasūtra (Umāsvāmī) edited by J. L. Jaini.
VCM. = Vivekacūdāmaṇi (Śaṁkara), Gītā Press, Gorakhpur, Saṁvat, 2013.
VMBG. = Varavaramuṇi's commentary on BG.
VMR. = Vidvadmanorañjanī (Rāmatīrtha Yati), N.S.P., 1925.
VNBG. = Viśvanātha Cakravartī's commentary on BG.
VP. = Vedāntaparibhāṣā (Dharmarājādhvarīndra), Bombay, Saṁvat, 1968.
VPS. = Vivaraṇaprameyasaṁgraha (Mādhavācārya Vidyāraṇya), V.S.S., 1893.
VS. = Vaiśeṣika Sūtra (Kaṇāda), Gujarati Press, Saṁvat, 1969.
VSB. = Vaiśeṣikasūtrabhāṣya (Candrakānta Tarkālaṅkāra), Gujarati Press, Saṁvat, 1969.
VSR. = Vedāntasāra (Sadānanda), Jacob's edition, N.S.P., 1925.
V.S.S. = Vizianagram Sanskrit Series, Benares.
VSU. = Upaskāra (Śaṅkara Miśra) on VS., Gujarati Press, Saṁvat, 1969.
VSV. = Vaiśeṣikasūtravivṛti (Jaya Nārāyaṇa) on VS., Gujarati Press, Saṁvat, 1969.
YBh. = Yogabhāṣya (Vyāsa) on YS., Benares, 1911.
YK. = Yuddha Kāṇḍa.
YMD = Yatipatimatadīpikā (Śrīnivāsa), B.S.S., 1907.
YMP. = Maṇiprabha (Rāmānanda Yati) on YS., B.S.S., No. 75, 1903.
YS. = Yoga Sūtra (Patañjali), Benares, 1911.
YSB. = Yogasūtrārthabodhinī (Nārāyaṇa Tīrtha), Ch.S.S., Nos. 154 & 159.
YSC. = Yogasiddhāntacandrikā (Nārāyaṇa Tīrtha), Ch.S.S., No. 154.
YSV. = Yogasūtravṛtti (Nārāyaṇa Tīrtha), Ch.S.S., No. 154.
YV. = Yogavārtika (Vijñānabhikṣu) on YBh., Benares, 1884.
YVS. = Yogavāsiṣṭha.

PREFACE

The first volume—*Indian Psychology: Cognition*—deals with the physical basis of perception, stages, kinds, and conditions of perception, theories of perception, perception of space, time, genus, cognition, and self, indefinite perception, illusion, hallucination, dream, abnormal perception, supernormal perception, memory, imagination, thought and language.

The second volume deals with body and self, degrees of consciousness, mental states, pleasure and pain, springs of action, desire and aversion, emotion, attention, volition, and voluntary and non-voluntary actions according to the different schools of Indian philosophy. Numerous commentaries on the *Bhagavad Gītā* are replete with subtle psychological analysis of different emotions by the Vedantists of different schools. Their views are given in the Vedantist account of emotions.

It deals with the psychology of Alaṅkāra and elaborately treats of the nature of the permanent emotional dispositions or sentiments, the accessory or transitory emotions, and their expressions, the nature of æsthetic enjoyment, and the kinds of æsthetic or dramatic sentiments. It draws its material from a large number of Sanskrit texts dealing with the æsthetic sentiments.

It elaborately deals with the various kinds of religious emotions and sentiments. It mainly draws its material from the *Bhagavad Gītā*, the *Bhāgavata*, Rūpa Goswāmī's *Ujjvalanīlamaṇi* and *Bhaktirasāmṛtasindhu*, and Jīva Goswāmī's *Prītisandarbha*, and leaves out the account of the other mediaeval and modern Indian saints in different Indian languages.

It deals with the nature of volition and voluntary action and its determining cause as mainly given in Gaṅgeśa's *Tattvacintāmaṇi* (Śabda). His arguments are subtle, involved, and couched in a language which is not easy of comprehension. His arguments for the Prābhākara Mīmāṁsaka and the Nyāya doctrines are faithfully summarized here.

"Emotion" is one of the most important subjects of investigation in modern psychology. This work will enable the students of western psychology to know about the Indian treatment of the subject.

The treatment of the various types of mystical experiences and the methods of inducing them is beyond the scope of this book. But the various kinds of religious emotions and sentiments described in it will give a glimpse into their nature.

The two volumes, it is hoped, will give a fairly comprehensive account of Indian Psychology, the material of which is scattered in numerous Sanskrit texts.

A major portion of this book was written in 1935-36 when I was on leave. It gives me a great relief that I have been able to finish it and bring it out despite my ill health.

I acknowledge my gratitude to Paṇḍita Chaṇḍī Charaṇa Tarkatīrtha who helped me read *Tattvachintāmaṇi* (Śabda), which is the chief source of the last chapter. I acknowledge my debt to Sir Brajendra Nath Seal, M.A., Ph.D., whose "Syllabus of Indian Philosophy" was of great help to me.

39, S. R. Das Road,
Calcutta-26, India,
6th August, 1961.

JADUNATH SINHA

BOOK I

CHAPTER I

BODY AND SELF

1. *The Gross Body*

The *Kaṭha Upaniṣad* declares: "The self conjoined with the sense-organs and mind (manas) is the experiencer (bhoktā). The self is like a person seated in a chariot; the body is the chariot; intellect (buddhi) is the driver; mind (manas) is the bridle; and the sensee-organs are the horses."[1] The mind is superior to the sense-organs; the intellect is superior to the mind. The self is superior to the intellect. There is nothing superior to the self.[2] The mind-body-complex is an organ of experience subordinate to the self, which is its agent. It is an instrument of knowledge, feeling and action. The self is the knower, the enjoyer, and the active agent. The body, the sense-organs, mind, and intellect exist for the self. But the self exists for itself. There is no reality beyond it. It is the supreme goal to be realized.[3] Evidently the self here is identified with the supreme Self (Brahman). Sometimes the body is described as the city of Brahman or Self (brahmapura). The Self that resides in the heart-ether in the city of Brahman is to be sought.[4]

The Upaniṣads generally think the heart-cave or heart-ether as the seat of the self. The *Chāndogya Upaniṣad* says: "Within this city of Brahman or body there is a small lotus-like place or heart, and within it a small internal space (antarākāśa) or heart-ether; that which resides within this small space is to be sought." "That self which is more minute than barley, mustard seed, and rice, and greater than the earth, the sky, and the heaven resides in the heart within the body."[5] "This self exists in the heart within the body."[6] The *Bṛhadāraṇyaka Upaniṣad* says: "This

[1] Ātmānaṁ rathinaṁ viddhi śarīraṁ ratham eva ca. Buddhiṁ tu sārathiṁ viddhi manaḥ pragraham eva ca. Indriyāṇi hayān āhuḥ. i, 3, 3-4

[2] Ibid, i, 3, 10-1.

[3] Puruṣān na paraṁ kiṁ cit sā kāṣṭhā sā parā gatiḥ. Ibid, i. 3, 11.

[4] Chānd. Up., viii, 1, 1-2.

[5] Ibid., viii, 1, 1-2; iii, 14, 3.

[6] Eṣa ātmā' ntarhṛdaye. Ibid., iii, 14, 3.

knowing self exists in the internal space within the heart."[7] The *Katha Upaniṣad* says: "A self-controlled person conquers joy and sorrow by knowing the self through spiritual illumination, which resides in the inmost recess of the heart-cave (guhā) as imperceptible, hidden and ancient or eternal."[8] "The self, which is subtler than the subtle and greater than the great, resides in the cavity of the heart."[9] The *Taittirīya Upaniṣad* says: "The immortal, conscious, pure self resides in the space or ether within the heart."[10] The next passage refers to the brain as the abode of the centres of the sense-organs and the centres of volitions and intellectual activities.[11] The *Śvetāśvatara Upaniṣad* says: "The internal self always resides in the heart of persons."[12]

The *Taittirīya Upaniṣad* describes five sheaths (kośa) of the self, viz. the bodily sheath, the vital sheath, the mental sheath, the intellectual sheath, and the blissful sheath. "Within this physical body which is made of food, there is another body composed of the vital force; the former is filled with the latter, which is like the form of a person. Within the vital body there is another body which consists of mind; the former is filled with the latter, which is like the form of a person. Within the mental body there is another body which consists of intelligence: the former is filled with the latter, which is like the form of a person. Finally, within this intellectual body there is another body which consists of bliss; the former is filled with the latter, which is like the form of a person."[13] These bodies are called the bodily sheath (annamaya kośa), the vital sheath (prāṇamaya kośa), the mental sheath (manomaya kośa), the intellectual sheath (vijñānamaya kośa), and the blissful sheath (ānandamaya kośa). They are also called the bodily self, the vital self, the mental self, the intellectual self, and the blissful self. These are different conceptions of the self.[14]

[7] Eṣa vijñānamayaḥ puruṣaḥ ya eṣo' ntarhṛdaya ākāśas tasmiñ chete. Bṛ. Up., ii, 1, 17. Ibid, v, 6, 1.

[8] Kaṭha. Up., i, 2, 12. Ibid, ii, 1, 12.

[9] Aṇor aṇīyān mahato mahīyān ātmāsya jantor nihito guhāyām. Ibid, i, 2, 20. Ibid, ii, 3, 17.

[10] Sa ya eṣo'ntar hṛdaya ākāśaḥ. Tasminnayaṁ puruso manomayaḥ. Amṛto hiranmayaḥ. Tait. Up., i, 6, 1. Hṛdi hyeṣa ātmā. Praś. Up., iii, 6.

[11] Tait Up., i, 6, 2.

[12] Antarātmā sadā janānāṁ hṛdaye saṁniviṣṭaḥ. Śvet. Up., iii, 13. Ibid, iii, 20; iv, 17.

[13] Tait. Up., ii, 2-5. Ibid, iii, 10, 5; Sarvasāra Up., 2; Tejobindu Up., iv, 75.

[14] Tait. Up., ii, 8; iii, 10, 5; Sarvasāra Up., 2; Tejobindu Up., iv, 75.

The *Maitrāyaṇī Upaniṣad* says: "The self is pure, holy, tranquil, infinite, eternal, and autonomous. It abides in its own greatness. It pervades, vitalizes, and moves the body."[15] The body depends upon the self for its activities. But the self is free, independent, autonomous (svatantra). The *Kaiṣītaki Upaniṣad* says: "The conscious self pervades the whole body, even as a razor is placed in a razor-case, or as fire is placed in an oven. The sense-organs depend upon the self, even as poor kinsmen depend upon a rich person."[16] The body is sometimes said to be a temple of God (devālaya). He creates, inspires, and impels the body, the mind (manas), life (prāṇa) and the sense-organs to perform their functions. Consciousness is not a function of the body. It is prior to the body, and its cause.[17]

The *Bhagavad Gītā* gives the following account of the relation of body and self. The body is mortal, but the self which is embodied in it is immortal. The body is born and dies. But the self is neither born nor dies. It is unborn, eternal, inexhaustible, ubiquitous, unmoving, and immutable. The self assumes a new body when its old body is worn out. The body, five cognitive organs, five motor organs, mind (manas), intellect (buddhi), and egoism are composed of purity or essence (sattva), energy (rajas) and inertia (tamas), which are effects of prakṛti. But the self is devoid of these guṇas. The objects of the world also are composed of these three guṇas. The guṇas act upon other guṇas. There is determinism in the realm of nature. The sense-organs are greater than their objects; mind (manas) is greater than the sense-organs which are controlled by them; intellect (buddhi) is greater than mind; self (ātman) is greater than intellect. Egoism (ahaṁkāra) also is mentioned. The self is beyond them all. It can control all the external sense-organs and the internal organs. It can steady the restless and distracted mind. The mind-body-complex is the not-self (kṣetra), while the self is its knower (kṣetrajña). The knower is absolutely different from the known. The self is devoid of the guṇas. But it experiences them through the mind-body-complex. The body is the organ of the self's action. Without it the self cannot act. The cognitive sense-organs, mind, intellect, and egoism are the organs of knowledge.

[15] II, 3.
[16] iv, 20. *A Constructive Survey of Upaniṣadic Philosophy*, pp. 133-4.
[17] Kena Up., i, 1-8; Maitreyī Up., ii, 1.

The motor sense-organs directed by the internal organs are the organs of action. The self is the master of the body. When it departs from the gross body, it takes the sense-organs, manas, buddhi and ahaṁkāra along with it. It leaves the gross body, and departs with the subtle body. Until it realizes its disembodied and non-empirical nature it cannot achieve liberation.[18] The *Mahābhārata* recognizes the influence of body and mind on each other. It asserts, that bodily disease is produced by mental disease, and that mental disease is produced by bodily disease.[19] It ascribes bodily diseases to the predominance of any of the bodily humours—flatulence, bile and phlegm—over the other two. It traces bodily health to the equipoise of the bodily humours. The mind is composed of purity or essence (sattva), energy (rajas) and inertia (tamas). When these are in a state of equilibrium, the mind is in a healthy condition. But when rajas and tamas predominate over sattva, it becomes diseased.[20]

Caraka keenly realizes the influence of mind on body. He asserts, that dejection is the main cause of the aggravation of a disease; that joy is the chief cause of its decrease; that grief is the principal cause of emaciation of the body; that contentment is the chief cause of its development; that depression is the main cause of its decay; and that carrying out resolution is the principal cause of its growth.[21] He mentions many psychical causes of insanity such as extreme timidity, perversion of sattva of the mind, commission of immoral actions, bewilderment of the mind owing to the aggravation of some disease, and being overwhelmed by lust, love, anger, avarice, joy, fear, grief, apprehension, anxiety and the like. When the mind is unhinged and intelligence lapses, the bodily humours are excessively provoked, attack the heart, obstruct the sensory currents that come to the heart, and bring about insanity. Insanity is the perversion of mind, intelligence, consciousness, knowledge, memory, sense-perception and efforts or actions. It involves illusion, hallucination, delusion, false reasoning, and maladjustment to the social environment.[22] Caraka describes lust, anger, fear, greed, delusion,

[18] BG., ii, 18, 20-22, 24-5, 45, 67; iii, 7, 27-8; v, 28; vi, 24, 34-5; vii, 13; xiii, 1, 3, 5-6, 14, 19-21; xiv, 19-20; xv, 7-9; xviii, 14.

[19] Śāntiparva, ch. xvi, 9.

[20] DHIP., ii, p. 419.

[21] CS., Lahore, 1940, i, 25, 40.

[22] Ibid, ii, 7, 4. Unmādaṁ monobuddhi-saṁjñā-jnāna-smṛti-bhakti-śīla-ceṣṭācāra-vibhramaṁ vidyāt. Ibid, ii, 7, 5.

joy, grief, apprehension, anxiety and the like as the psychical causes of epilepsy.[23] A person who has controlled his sense-organs is not afflicted by a disease. Temperance, dispassion for objects of enjoyment, generosity, impartiality, truthfulness, forgiveness, good company, good will, good speech, good action, purity of mind, clear understanding, true knowledge, austerities and meditation are the mental remedies for diseases.[24] Diseases caused by hostile persons through poison, fire, hurt and the like are due to the faults of the intellect (prajñāparādha). Perversions of the mind such as envy, grief, fear, anger, pride, hatred and the like are the faults of the intellect.[25] Thus Caraka agrees with Gautama in regarding emotions and passions as due to ignorance (mithyājñana). When the mind is tainted with energy (rajas) and inertia (tamas) which overpower purity (sattva), it has false knowledge. When it abounds in purity which overpowers rajas and tamas, it has true knowledge of reality, which destroys ignorance and consequent emotions and passions.[26] Caraka regards body and mind as the seat of diseases.[27] Cakrapāṇi asserts, that mind unrelated to a body is not the abode of a disease. A disease is due to three bodily humours—flatulence, bile and phlegm. Or, it is due to the excess of energy (rajas) and inertia (tamas) over purity (sattva) of the mind.[28] Health is the equilibrium of the bodily humours. Disease is the disequilibrium of these humours, which is painful.[29] Remedy consists in restoring their equipoise which is pleasant. A mental disease is due to the non-attainment of a desired object or the attainment of an undesired object. It is due to the non-fulfilment of strong desires.[30] Caraka anticipates Freud's theory that a mental disease is due to repressed desire.

Body, mind and self conjoined with one another form a psychophysical organism.[31] The sense-organs are included in the body. Intellect (buddhi) and egoism (ahaṁkāra) are included in the mind (manas). The self is conscious. It has consciousness

[23] Ibid, ii, 8, 4.
[24] Ibid, iv, 2, 43, 46-7.
[25] Ibid, 1, 7, 51-2.
[26] Ibid, iv, 2, 38.
[27] Śarīraṁ satvasaṁjñaṁ ca vyādhīnām āśrayo mataḥ. Ibid, i, 1, 55. Sattva = manas.
[28] Ibid, i, 1, 57.
[29] Vikāro dhātu-vaiṣamyaṁ sāmyaṁ prakṛtir ucyate.
Sukha-saṁjñakam arogyaṁ vikāro duḥkham eva ca.
Ibid, i, 9, 4.
[30] Mānasaḥ punar iṣṭasyālābhāl lābhāccāniṣṭasyopajāyate. Ibid, i, 11, 45
[31] Sattvam ātmā śarīraṁ ca trayam etat tridaṇḍavat. Ibid, i, 1, 46.

The self acquires consciousness in conjunction with the sense-organs.[41] It is without origin and end, eternal, immutable, and infinite or inexhaustible.[42] The mind (manas) is unconscious but active. The self is conscious and becomes active, though ubiquitous, in conjunction with manas. The mind acts when it is guided by the self. It cannot act without the self's guidance. The self feels pleasure and pain in its own body, but not in another's body, because it has acquired its body by its own merits and demerits. It is a knower of all entities. It is supersensible.[43] It transmigrates with a subtle body (ātivāhika deha) invested with merits and demerits. It is composed of the subtle elements of earth, water, light, air, and ether and manas. It is devoid of a visible form, and can be seen by yogins with a divine eye.[44]

The later Upaniṣads mention six bases of meditation or cakras. The *Haṃsa Upaniṣad* mentions seven cakras: (1) ādhāra, (2) svādhiṣṭhāna, (3) maṇipūraka, (4) anāhata, (5) viśuddha, (6) ājñā, and (7) brahmarandhra. They are situated at the roots of the suṣumnā nerve, the generative organ, the navel, the heart, and the throat, the middle of the eye-brows, and the top of the cerebrum. The *Yogacūḍāmaṇi Upaniṣad* describes the ādhāra cakra as of four petals, the svādhiṣṭhāna cakra as of six petals, the maṇipūraka cakra as of ten petals, the anāhata cakra as of twelve petals, the viśuddha cakra as of sixteen petals, the ājñā cakra as of two petals, and the sahasrāra cakra as of a thousand petals. The *Yogaśikhā Upaniṣad* also holds the same view. It describes the mūlādhāra cakra as the seat of the individual self (jīva), and the Serpent Power (kuṇḍalinī) or the Supreme Power (parā śakti). The *Dhyānabindu Upaniṣad* and the *Śāṇḍilya Upaniṣad* describe the maṇipūraka cakra as of twelve petals. The latter asserts that the individual self is invested with life in this base, and that it moves in it being impelled by virtues and vices. According to the *Haṁsa Upaniṣad,* the heart-lotus (anāhata cakra) has eight petals, and is the seat of the individual self (jīva, haṁsa). Desire for virtues, sleep, laziness, desire for cruel actions, desire for vices, play, volition for walking, etc., love, pleasure, appropriation of objects, and detachment are the mental functions which are governed by its petals. The *Dhyānabindu Upaniṣad* describes the anāhata cakra as of eight petals. The *Nṛsiṁhapūrvatāpanīya*

[41] Ibid, iv, 1, 54.
[42] Ibid, iv, 1, 59, 61.
[43] Ibid, iv, 1, 75, 79-83.
[44] Ibid, iv, 2, 21.

Upaniṣad also holds the same view. The *Amṛtanāda Upaniṣad* describes the heart-lotus to be composed of air. The *Nṛsiṁhapūrvatāpanīya Upaniṣad* describes the viśusdha cakra as of twelve petals and the ājñā cakra as of sixteen petals. The *Yogacūḍāmaṇi Upaniṣad* regards the svādhiṣṭhāna cakra as the seat of life (prāṇa). The *Haṁsa Upaniṣad* describes (7) brahmarandhra as the seat of Brahman, Paramātman, or Supreme Self. The *Saubhāgyalakṣmī Upaniṣad* also regards it as the parabrahmacakra. It mentions (8) tālucakra and (9) ākāśa cakra in addition to the seven cakras mentioned above. The tālucakra is situated at the root of the palate near the uvula. There is a flow of nectar here as the result of meditation on it. It has twenty two petals. The ākāśa cakra is a lotus of sixteen petals facing upward. It is above the brahmarandhra and the seat of unobstructed intuitive experience of 'all is Brahman'.[45]

The Tantras speak of the cakras as centres of meditation. They are extremely subtle vital forces and centres of consciousness existing in suṣumnā in the spinal cord. They are not plexuses which surround it. The following cakras are mentioned. (1) The mūlādhāra cakra is the root of the suṣumnā nāḍī midway between the anus and the root of the genitals. It exists in the spinal cord which forms its axis. It has four red petals facing downward. It is made of earth. It is the seat of dormant cosmic energy (kuṇḍalinī) which sustains the phenomenal world and maintains the embodied existence of the individual self (jīvātman) by inspiration and expiration. It is the seat of parā vāk. It is the seat of a massive pleasurable sensation and voluminous organic sensation of repose. Its four petals are said to be connected with the four kinds of bliss, viz., supreme bliss (parānanda), innate bliss (sahajānanda), bliss of meditation (yogānanda), and bliss of a hero (vīrānanda) as the result of meditation on it. (2) The svādhiṣṭhāna cakra is inside suṣumnā at the root of the genitals. It is of vermilion colour and made of water. It has six petals. It is the seat of sexual feelings, lassitude, stupor, cruelty, suspicion and contempt. It is also the seat of credulity, disdain, delusion and false knowledge. Meditation on it destroys lust, anger, greed, delusion,

[45] Haṁsa Up., 1-2; Bombay, 1948, p. 147; Amṛtanāda Up., 27; Dhyānabindu Up., 19, 26, 47, 49; Yogaśikhā Up., i, 168-75; v, 5-11; vi, 33; Nṛsiṁhapūrvatāpanīya Up., ch. v; Yogacūḍāmaṇi Up., 4-6, 11; Śāṇḍilya Up., ch. I, p. 411; Yogakuṇḍalī Up., ch. III, 9-11, p. 559; Saubhāgyalakṣmī Up., ch. III, 1-9, (Madras, 1925).

pride and envy and facilitates the acquisition of knowledge. (3) The maṇipūra cakra is inside suṣumnā in the spinal cord at the root of the navel. It is so called because it is made of fire (tejas) and lustrous like a gem (maṇi). It has ten petals. It is the seat of shame, treachery, jealousy, desire, sleep, sadness, worldliness, delusion, aversion and fear. It is connected with stupefaction also. Meditation on it gives a yogin the power to create and destroy. (4) The anāhata cakra is inside suṣumnā in the spinal cord at the root of the heart. It is so called because the yogins hear the sound of Śabda Brahma or Aum by meditating on it, which is not produced by the striking of two objects (anāhata). It is made of air. It has twelve petals. It is the abode of the individual self (jīva). It is the seat of egoistic emotions, hope, anxiety, doubt, remorse, conceit, egoism, etc. It is connected with arrogance, languor, covetousness, duplicity, indecision, discrimination and endeavour also. Meditation on it gives the yogin great wisdom, nobility, complete sense-control and inspired speech. Intense concentration on it makes the mind engrossed in thoughts of Brahman. (5) The viśuddha cakra is a spinal centre at the base of the throat. It is so called because the individual self becomes pure (viśuddha) by seeing the inner self (haṁsa) here. It is made of ether (ākāśa). It has sixteen petals. It regulates the larynx and other vocal organs. Meditation on this centre makes the yogin merciful to all, constant, gentle, steady, modest, courageous, forgiving, self-controlled, pure, free from greed, malice, pride and sorrow, and gives him knowledge of all śāstras without instruction, and of the Brahman. (6) The lalanā cakra is opposite the uvula with twelve petals. It is the seat of ego-altrustic emotions such as self-regard, pride, affection, grief, regret, respect, reverence, contentment, etc. (7) The ājñā cakra is situated between the eye-brows. It is so called because the yogin receives the command of the Master (guru) or Brahman here. It is made of prakṛti and the internal organs (antaḥkaraṇa) or manas, buddhi, ahaṁkāra and citta. It is the seat of the internal organ. It has two petals. Meditation on it makes the yogin all-knowing, all-seeing, versed in all śāstras, a benefactor of all, and realize his unity with Brahman. When the manas is dissolved in the ājñācakra by repeated meditation on Aum, the yogin becomes devoid of all attachment for worldly objects and attains the status of supermind (unmanī). This centre is the abode of uninterrupted bliss. Parama Śiva (the Absolute) manifests himself to the yogin in all his might. He lives here as well as in the sahasrāra.

Above the ājñācakra there are the minor centres called manas-cakra and somacakra. (8) The manas-cakra has six petals. It is the seat of the sensations of sound, heat and cold, colour, odour, taste, and dreams and hallucinations. The motor nerves (ājñāvahā nāḍī) carry motor impulses from the ājñācakra to the periphery. The sensory nerves such as the auditory (śabdavahā nāḍī), the tactual (sparśavahā nāḍī), the optic (rūpavahā nāḍī), the olfactory (gandhavahā nāḍī), the gustatory (rasavahā nāḍī), come in pairs from the special sense-organs to the manas-cakra. It also receives the manovahā nāḍī which carries centrally initiated presentations such as dreams and hallucinations. The five sensory nerves, in pairs, and the manovahā nāḍī carry the impulses to the six petals of the manas-cakra. (9) Above the manas-cakra there is the somacakra. It has sixteen petals. It comprises the centres in the middle of the cerebrum above the manas-cakra. It is the seat of compassion, gentleness, patience, renunciation, meditativeness, gravity, sincerity, resolution, determination, magnanimity, etc. It is the seat of altruistic emotions and volitional control. The viśuddha cakra, the ājñā cakra and the soma cakra are the seats of mercy, gentleness, patience, detachment, constancy, mirth, exaltation, rapture, humility, meditativeness, quietude, gravity, enterprise, imperturbability, magnanimity and concentration. The functions (vṛtti) of the lower cakras are all bad; those of the anāhata cakra are mixed; arrogance, covetousness and duplicity are bad. while hope, endeavour and discrimination are good. (10) Above the manas-cakra there is the sahasrāra cakra with a thousand petals. It is white and has its head downward. Within it there is the full moon inside which there is a triangle shining constantly like lightning. There is the great void inside it, in which Parama Śiva or Para Brahman resides. He is the Ātman of all beings. There is no difference between the individual self (jīvātman) and the Universal Self (paramātman). The yogin realizes oneness between them when he attains Parama Śiva who sheds a constant and profuse stream of nectar. He is the Master (guru). He destroys nescience (ajñāna) and delusion (moha). He can be attained by a great effort of meditation. Meditation on this centre releases the yogin from the bondage of virtue and vice which are the products of prakṛti and cannot be attributed to the self. His merits and demerits accumulated in his past births (sañcita karma) also are destroyed. His manas is dissolved, and he attains embodied release. He is never born again. He acquires complete power to execute his will and prevent what is contrary to his will. There is said to be a blissful union of Para (Śiva) and Parā (Śakti) inside the great void, which generates a continuous flow of nectar. The yogin experiences the bliss of this union.[46]

The cakras are subtle centres of consciousness. They are not plexuses or ganglia, though they are connected with them. They are invisible vital and psychic forces which cannot be observed by dissection. They are visible to the yogin only as a result of prolonged meditation. When he unites kulakuṇḍalinī or cosmic divine energy in the mūlādhāra with Parama Śiva in the sahasrāra, he realizes supreme bliss (ānanda). The lotuses with their petals bloom when kuṇḍalinī passes through them. The cakras are the manifestations of the cosmic divine life (prāṇaśakti).[47] The body is the microcosm of the macrocosm.

An excellent sound (nāda) is produced in the mūlādhāra cakra by the action of volition of the self on the vital air. It is called parā vāk. It ascends to the svādhiṣṭhāna cakra, unfolds itself and becomes paśyantī. It ascends to the anāhata cakra, is united with the intellect (buddhi) and becomes madhyamā. It ascends upward, reaches the viśuddha cakra in the throat and becomes vaikharī. From there it rises towards the head, spreads over the palate, the tongue, lips, teeth, the root of the tongue, etc., and produces articulate sounds.[48]

The *Bhāvanā Upaniṣad* mentions fourteen nerves (nāḍī): alambusā, kuhū, viśvodarī, varuṇā, hastijihvā, yaśasvatī, aśvinī, gāndhārī, pūṣā, śaṅkhinī, sarasvatī, iḍā, piṅgalā and suṣumnā.[49] The *Dhyānbindu Upaniṣad* mentions seventy two thousand nerves which are generated in the spinal cord below the navel and above

[46] Ṣaṭcakranirūpaṇa, verses 4, 14, 19, 22, 28, 30-38, 40, 42 and 43 and commentary; *Serpent Power*, Madras, 1953, pp. 117-63; B. N. Seal: *The Positive Sciences of the Ancient Hindus*: Jñānasaṁkalanī Tantra; Saṅgītaratnākara; KR., p. 43; VSU., v, 2, 14, Mahānirvāṇa Tantra, Tarkālaṅkāra's commentary.

[47] *Serpent Power*, 1953, p. 161.

[48] Ṣaṭcakranirūpaṇaṭīkā, 11. Prapañcasāratantra, Calcutta, 1914, ch. II, 43.

[49] Bombay, 1948, p. 548.

the anus. Of them, the ten nerves, e.g., iḍā, piṅgalā, suṣumnā, gāndhārī, hastijihvā, pūṣā, yaśasvinī, alambusā, kuhū and śaṅkhinī are important. Iḍā is to the left; suṣumnā is in the middle, and piṅgalā is to the right. They are the most important nerves which carry vital forces.[50] The *Yogaśikhā Upaniṣad* mentions fifteen nerves, e.g., iḍā, piṅgalā, suṣumnā, gāndharī, hastijihvā, pūṣā, alambusā, śūrā, viśvodarī, sarasvatī, rākā, śaṅkhinī, kuhū, vāruṇī and citrā. Gāndhārī and hastijihvā rise from the nābhicakra to the two eyes. Pūṣā and alambusā rise from it to the two ears. Śūrā rises from it to the middle of the eye-brows. Viśvodarī takes in four kinds of food. Sarasvatī rises to the tip of the tongue. Rākā drinks water, sneezes and collects phlegm. Saṅkhinī rises from the throat and courses downward. It takes the essence of food and collects it in the head. Three nerves run from the navel downward. Kuhū excretes stool. Vāruṇī discharges urine. Citrā carries semen downward. Suṣumnā rises from the mūlādhāra cakra upward to the sahasrāra cakra. It is called brahmanāḍī between the mūlādhāra cakra and the ājñā cakra. Iḍā runs upward on the left of suṣumnā to the left nostril. Piṅgalā runs upward on the right of suṣumnā to the right nostril. They carry breath and inhale and exhale.[51] The *Varāha Upaniṣad* mentions suṣumnā, alambusā, kuhū, vāruṇī, yaśasvinī, piṅgalā, pūṣā, payasvinī, sarasvatī, śaṅkhinī, gāndhāri, iḍā, hastijihvā and viśvodari, which rise from the nāḍīcakra. Suṣumnā runs from mūlādhāra cakra to the brahmarandhra at the crown of the cerebrum and closes the aperture with its mouth. It is between iḍā and piṅgalā.[52] The *Śāṇḍilya Upaniṣad* describes fourteen nāḍīs. Suṣumnā runs from the root of the spinal cord upward to brahmarandhra. Iḍā is on its left. Piṅgalā is on its right. Sarasvatī is on its back. Kuhū is on its side. Vāruṇī is between yaśasvinī and kuhū. Payasvinī is between pūṣā and sarasvatī. Yaśasvinī is between gāndhārī and sarasvatī. Alambusā is inside the trunk (kanda). Kuhū runs on the right of suṣumnā downward to the anus. Vāruṇī runs below and above kuṇḍalinī. Yaśasvini and saumyā run downward to the toes. Iḍā runs upward to the left nostril. Piṅgalā runs upward to the right nostril. On the back of iḍā, gāndhārī runs upward to the left eye. On the back of piṅgalā, pūṣā runs upward to the right eye.

[50] 50-6; p. 288.
[51] V, 16-27; pp. 467-8.
[52] V, 23-30, 67; pp. 613-5.

Sarasvatī runs upward to the root of the tongue. Śaṇkhinī runs upward to the left ear. Payasvinī runs upward to the right ear. Alambusā runs upward and downward from the root of the anus.[53]

The Nyāya regards the gross body as the vehicle of experience, the self as the experiencer, the sense-organs as the organs of experience, and objects as objects of experience.[54] The body is the abode of voluntary actions and the sense-organs, and the vehicle of the experience of pleasure and pain produced by external objects in intercourse with the sense-organs.[55] The human body is composed of earth because it is endued with smell, colour, solidity and the like. Earth is its inherent cause. Some consider it to be composed of earth, water and light because it has odour, viscidity and heat. Some think it to be composed of earth, water, light and air because it has inhalation and exhalation as well. Some regard it as composed of earth, water, light, air, and ether because it has odour, moistness, digestion, breath, and porousness.[56] The semen and the ovum of the parents are the material cause of the body. The conjunction of the parts is its non-inherent cause. The soul's merits and demerits are its auxiliary cause.[57] God is its efficient cause because he supervises the soul's merits and demerits which are insentient and incapable of producing their effects without his guidance. The merits and demerits which produce a body are different from those which destroy it.[58] Some merits and demerits, which ripen and bear fruits, are exhausted, and bring about the death of a body. Other merits and demerits which have not yet matured bring about the birth of a body in order to produce their fruits through it in the form of enjoyments and sufferings.[59] The self cannot experience pleasure and pain without a body.[60] It is born out of the elements under the influence of merits and demerits.[61] If it were born

[53] Ch. I, 15; pp. 411-2.

[54] Ātmā bhoktā. Tasya bhogāyatanaṁ śarīram. Bhogasādhanānīndriyāṇi. Bhoktavyā indriyārthāḥ. NBh., i, 1, 9.

[55] Ceṣṭendriyārthāśrayaḥ śarīram. NS., i, 1, 11. NBL., i, 1, 11.

[56] NS., NBh., NSV., iii, 1, 28.

[57] Karmanimittā śarīrotpattiḥ. NBh., iii, 2, 70-1.

[58] Yo'ḍṛṣṭaḥ śarīropasarpaṇahetuḥ, sa evāpasarpaṇaheturapīti na. NBh., iii, 2, 75.

[59] Vipākasaṁvedanāt karmāśayakṣave śarīrapātaḥ prāyaṇam; karmāśayāntarcca punarjanma. NBh., iii, 2, 76.

[60] NBh., iii, 2, 73.

[61] Adṛṣṭakāritā bhūtebhyaḥ śarīrotpattiḥ. NBh., iii, 2, 73.

independently of them, it would not die. Its death is due to the exhaustion of the merits and demerits which produced it.[62]

The self is the agent of experience and action. It is the knower, enjoyer and actor. Its body is the organ of knowledge, feeling and action. It is subordinate to the self which is its agent. The self acquires the knowledge of external objects through the sense-organs which are parts of its body. It feels pleasure and pain produced by external objects acting on the sense-organs. It produces voluntary actions in the body, which are conducive to the attainment of good and the rejection of evil. The body is the seat of voluntary actions which are due to the volitions of the self.[63] The body acts on the self in producing sensuous knowledge and feeling. The self acts on the body in producing voluntary actions. The Nyāya advocates the theory of interaction between self and body.

The Vaiśeṣika also regards the body as the vehicle of the experience of pleasure and pain (bhogādhiṣṭhāna) like the Nyāya. and believes in the theory of interaction.[64] An action in a hand is produced by the conjunction of the self with the hand and a volition of the self.[65] The conjunction of the hand with the self is the non-inherent cause of bodily action. A volition of the self is its efficient cause. The body and its hand are its inherent cause.[66] The self produces desire; desire produces effort or volition; volition produces bodily action; bodily action produces movement in an external object.[67] This clearly proves that the self acts on the body. The body also acts on the self in producing perception. The self comes into contact with manas. Manas comes into contact with an external sense-organ. An external sense-organ comes into contact with an object. Then the perception of the object is produced. The sense-organ, which is a part of the body, produces perception in the self through the fourfold contact. The self is the inherent cause of perception; the self-mind-contact is its non-inherent cause. The sense-object-intercourse is its efficient cause.[68] Thus the Vaiśeṣika believes in inter-actionism.

[62] Bhūtamātrāt tu karmanirapekṣāt śarīrotpattau kasya kṣayāt śarīrapātaḥ prāyaṇam? NBh., iii, 2, 76.

[63] Hitāhitaprāptiparihārayogyavyāpārādhikaraṇaṁ śarīram. NM., p. 474. NKL., pp. 5-6.

[64] VSU., iv, 2, 5.

[65] Ātmasaṁyoga-prayatnābhyāṁ haste karma. v, 1, 1.

[66] VSU., v, 1, 1.

[67] VSV., v. 1, 1; BhP.

[68] VSV., viii, 1, 3.

But it gives pre-eminence to the self which it regards as an agent (kartā) and experiencer (bhoktā), while it regards the body as its vehicle of experience (bhogāyatana) and organ (karaṇa). The self enjoys and suffers through the body, which is its instrument subordinate to it. The Vaiśeṣika agrees with the Nyāya in its view of the nature of the gross body and its relation to the self.

The Sāṁkhya regards the gross body as a modification of the five elements—earth, water, light, air and ether.[69] Earth is its principal ingredient because it is in excess over the other four constituents.[70] The body is the seat of the sense-organs.[71]

Life force (prāṇa) does not produce the gross body because it is the common function of the sense-organs. Life cannot exist when they are destroyed because it is a function of them.[72] So it cannot produce a body in a dead body because the sense-organs are absent from it.[73] But life is the instrumental cause of the gross body as it is directed by its master, the self, for its experience. The self, being immutable and inactive, cannot directly act upon the constituents of the gross body, but can do so through the instrumentality of life, which is its instrument.[74] It experiences pleasure and pain through its gross body on account of merits and demerits acquired in the previous births.[75]

The self is different from the body. The self is the knower, while the body is the known object. The self is unmodifiable, while the body is modifiable. The self exists for itself, while the body exists for the self.[76] The body, the vehicle of experience, is formed when the empirical self guides its constituents through life for its experience in conformity with its merits and demerits.[77] So the conjunction of the constituents of the gross body with the empirical self invested with merits and demerits is the cause of the construction of the body, which is an organ of its experience.[78] Merits and demerits are the qualities of egoism (ahaṁkāra) which is an internal organ. They are not qualities of the transcendental self which is devoid of guṇas. The empirical self (jīva) limited

[69] Pāñcabhautiko dehaḥ. SPS., iii, 17.
[70] SPB., iii, 19; v, 112. [71] Ibid, v, 103.
[72] Karaṇavṛttirūpaprāṇaḥ karaṇaviyoge na tiṣṭhati. SPB., v, 113.
[73] Ibid, v, 113. [74] Ibid, v, 114-5.
[75] Ibid, v. 123. [76] Ibid, vi, 2.
[77] Bhoktur adhiṣṭhānād bhogāyatananirmāṇam. Ibid, vi, 59.
[78] Siddham adṛṣṭavad-ātmasaṁyoga-rūpeṇādhiṣṭhānasya bhogopakaraṇa-nirmāṇa-hetutvam. Ibid, vi, 61.

by egoism is different from the transcendental self which is not limited by egoism.[79] The merits and demerits which remain dormant during dissolution are activated at the time of creation, and produce an appropriate body for the experience of the empirical self.[80]

The relation of the self to its body as the knower and the known is due to non-discrimination (aviveka). Pañcaśikha traces the relation of 'I' and 'mine' to non-discrimination which persists in the form of an impression (vāsanā). Some Sāṁkhyas trace it to the subtle body which is the organ of experience of pleasure and pain.[81]

The Sāṁkhya regards the body, the sense-organs, mind (manas), intellect (buddhi) and egoism (ahaṁkāra) as evolutes of prakṛti constituted by sattva, rajas and tamas. The three internal organs are essentially one and called buddhi in the Yoga. There is interaction between mind (buddhi) and body in perception and volition. But there is no interaction between body or mind and self. The self is conscious. The mind (buddhi) is unconscious. When an object acts on the mind through the body and its sense-organs, a mental mode (vṛtti) assumes its form. The mode is unconscious, but it is intelligized by a reflection of the self on the transparent mind which abounds in sattva. This is the view of Vācaspati Miśra. But Vijñānabhikṣu maintains, that the self's reflection on a mental mode is reflected back on the self when it has experience of the mode. He believes in double reflection. while Vācaspati believes in single reflection. According to Vijñānabhikṣu, there is a kind of parallelism between an unconscious mental mode and a conscious experience of the self; there is no interaction between mind or body and self[82]

The Advaita Vedānta regards the gross body as composed of the five quintupled elements under the influence of the merits and demerits acquired in the previous birth. It is the gross organ of waking experience.[83] The five external sense-organs are produced by the five elements distributively with the predominance of sattva. The auditory organ is produced by ether; the tactual organ, by air; the visual organ, by light; the gustatory organ,

[79] Ibid, vi, 63. [80] SSV., iii, 6.
[81] SPS., SPB., vi, 67-9.
[82] *Indian Psychology: Cognition*, pp. 232-6.
[83] Pañcīkṛtebhyo bhūtebhyaḥ sthūlebhyaḥ pūrvakarmaṇā. Samutpannam idaṁ sthūlaṁ bhogāyatanam ātmanaḥ. VCM., 90.

by water; and the olfactory organ, by earth. The four internal organs—mind (manas), intellect (buddhi), egoism (ahaṁkāra), and memory (citta)—are produced by the five unquintupled elements collectively with the predominance of sattva. Doubt is the function of manas. Determination is the function of buddhi. Self-sense is the function of ahaṁkāra. Recollection is the function of citta. The five motor organs—the vocal organ, the prehensive organ, the locomotive organ, the excretive organ, and the generative organ—are produced by the five elements distributively with the predominance of rajas. The sense-organs and motor organs are insentient, and produce their effects under the guidance of a conscious self.[84] The five vital airs—prāṇa, apāna, vyāna, udāna and samāna—are produced by the five unquintupled elements collectively with the predominance of rajas.[85] The gross body is a manifest phenomenon (sthūla prapañca) devoid of ontological reality.[86]

The Advaita Vedānta, like the Sāṁkhya-Yoga, regards the body, the sense-organs, mind (manas), intellect (buddhi), egoism (ahaṁkāra), and memory (citta) as modifications of nescience (avidyā) composed of sattva, rajas and tamas. The four internal organs are essentially one, and called the internal organ. The mind is unconscious but translucent as sattva predominates in it. There is interaction between mind (antaḥkaraṇa) and body. But there is no interaction between mind and self (ātman). The conscious self is reflected on the mind or its mode and intelligizes it. It erroneously regards the mental mode as its quality due to superimposition (adhyāsa). The Advaita Vedānta view resembles Vācaspati Miśra's view.

According to the Sāṁkhya, life is not physical (bhautika) force, but the common function of all sense-organs. It is sustained by the powers of the sense-organs.[87] Vijñānabhikṣu regards it as the common function of the three internal organs—manas, buddhi and ahaṁkāra. The five kinds of vital forces—prāṇa, apāna, udāna, samāna, and vyāna—are the modes of the internal organs.[88] They are figuratively spoken of as airs (vāyu) because

[4] VSR., pp. 17-8; VP., p. 358.
[5] VP., p. 359; Subodhinī on VSR., p. 19; VSR., p. 19.
[6] Pancīkaraṇavārtikābharaṇa, 36.
[7] SSV., SSVM., V, 113.
Prāṇaścāntaḥkaraṇasyaiva vṛttibhedaḥ. SPB., iii, 9.

of their motions.[89] Some regard them as particular kinds of airs, which operate through a function of the internal organ in the form of a vital effort (jīvanayoniprayatna). But Vijñānabhikṣu urges that this view is wrong because desire and other modes of manas and agitation of life produced by them should abide in the same substrate, viz. manas.[90] Īśvarakṛṣṇa regards five vital forces as the common function of all the sense-organs.[91] The Yoga also holds this view. Vyāsa regards life as the common function of all sense-organs.[92] It has five actions which are called five vital forces. Life is inferred from inhalation and exhalation during sleep.[93]

The Vaiśeṣika regards life as a particular kind of effort or volition of the self (jīvanayoniprayatna). Inhalation, exhalation and the like are its actions. They are due to the vital effort of the self. There can be no vital acts without an effort or volition of the self. Vital acts, non-voluntary actions and voluntary actions are alike due to volitions of the self.[94]

Śaṁkara considers the five vital forces to be the different modes of one common life. Inhalation, exhalation, yawning, sneezing, trembling, jumping, hunger and thirst are the functions of life.[95] Prāṇa is the air that is inhaled. Apāna is the air that is exhaled. Vyāna is the air that pervades the body. Udāna resides in the throat. It is the air that is belched out. Samāna is the air that resides in the intestines and digests food and drinks. Sadānanda speaks of them as airs.[96] They are produced by five unquintupled elements—earth, water, light, air and ether—combined with one another in which rajas predominates.[97] They are active, and, consequently, effects of rajas.[98] Mahādeva Sarasvatī and Dharmarājādhvarīndra also hold this view. The Advaita Vedānta gives a materialistic view of the nature and origin of life. The Sāṁkhya gives an idealistic view of the nature of

[89] Prāṇādyā vāyuviśeṣā eva. SPB., ii, 31.

[90] Manodharmasya kāmādeḥ prāṇakṣobhakatayā sāmānādhikaraṇyenaivaucityāt. SPB., ii, 31.

[91] Sāmānyakaraṇavṛttiḥ prāṇādyāḥ vāyavaḥ pañca. SK., 29. SKG., 29.

[92] Samastendriyavṛttiḥ prāṇādilakṣaṇā jīvanam. Tasya kriyā pañcatayī. YBh., iii, 39.

[93] YV., iii, 15, p. 209.

[94] SM., p. 471; PBh.

[95] VCM., 97, 104.

[96] Vāyavaḥ prāṇāpānavyānodānasamānāḥ. VSR., p. 18.

[97] Apañcīkṛtebhyo rajaḥpradhānebhyaḥ prāṇādayo jāyante. Subodhinī, p. 19. VSR., p. 19. ACK., pp. 65-6; VP., p. 359; Pañcadaśī, i, 22.

[98] Subodhinī, p. 19.

life. But it tends towards materialism because it regards the external and internal organs as evolutes of prakṛti or primal matter. The Vaiśeṣika gives an idealistic view of life as it traces it to a volition of the self.

The *Prapañcasāra Tantra* describes ten vital forces. Prāṇa courses upward. Apāna courses downward. Samāna assimilates food. Vyāna distributes the chyle (rasa) all over the body. Udāna accompanies life (prāṇa) and produces movements of the eyes. Nāga is the cause of belching. Kūrma is the cause of opening the eyes. Kṛkara is the cause of hunger. Devadatta is the cause of yawning. Dhanañjaya causes various sounds[99]

According to the Jaina, the self (jīva) and the not-self (ajīva) are two absolutely different substances. The former is conscious, incorporeal and immaterial, while the latter is unconscious, corporeal and material. Matter (pudgala) is not-self. Every embodied self (saṁsārī jīva) has a soul and a body. It has a gross body and a subtle body composed of infra-sensible particles of matter (karma), called kārmaṇa śarīra. Both gross body and subtle body change. When the self attains perfection, it transcends both. In discussing the relation between the states of the self (jīva) and the states of karma-matter, the Jaina makes a distinction between a substantial cause (upādāna kartā) and an external cause (nimitta kartā). Mental states are the modifications of the self, and organic states are the modifications of matter. The self is the substantial cause of psychical states, and matter is the substantial cause of organic states. And yet psychical states and organic states are external causes of each other. One psychical state is produced by an immediately preceding psychical state, and yet determined externally by an organic state. Similarly, one organic state is produced by an immediately preceding organic state, and yet determined externally by a psychical state. The mental series and the physical series are independent of, and parallel to, each other, and yet they are externally determined by each other. The relation between the mental series and the physical series is external, and yet they determine each other. Thus a mental state is the result of both these antecedent conditions, physical and mental. Similarly, a change in the body is the result of both the antecedent conditions. The Jaina emphasizes the causal

[99] Tantrik Texts, Vol. III, Calcutta, 1914, Ch. II, 10-13. Brahmavidyā Up., 66-7; Yogacūḍāmaṇi Up., 22-6.

interrelation between self and body, even though the relation between them is external; so that a change in one always involves a physical antecedent and a psychical antecedent, one being the substantial cause and the other being the external cause.[100] The self is the substantial or constituent cause of an emotion, while karma-matter is its external or indirect cause.[101] A change in dravya karma or physical karma immediately produces a change in bhāva karma or consciousness. Dravya karma is objective physical karma. Bhāva karma is its subjective counterpart in conciousness. It produces an emotion (bhāva). Dravya karma is the cause of bhāva karma, which is the cause of an emotional state (bhāva). An emotion is the effect of karmic thought, which is the effect of karmic matter. The direct and immediate cause of an emotion is bhāva karma or karmic thought. But its indirect or external cause is dravya karma or karmic matter.[102] There is a psycho-physical parallelism between mental states and organic states which are two independent series. And yet mental states are the indirect and external causes of organic states, and organic states are the indirect and external causes of mental states. The two series, though independent of, and parallel to, each other, are causally interrelated to each other. There is contiguous coexistence of the soul and karmic matter with each other. There is no direct causal action between them. The karmic particles merely by proximity cling to the soul because of their adhesive quality. The soul becomes adulterated with karmic particles even as milk is adulterated with water. But this adulteration is not due to direct causal action of karmic matter upon the soul. The soul develops an inclination towards matter because of its emotional states. This inclination is an external condition (nimitta kartā) of karmic matter. Material particles of karma so determined somehow get bound to the soul and cloud its intrinsic omniscience. Thus the Jaina steers a middle course between parallelism and interactionism.[103]

The Buddhist does not believe in a permanent self. According to Nāgasena, a person is a mind-body-complex, an aggregate of thirty two kinds of organic matter and the five constituent elements of being, outward form (rūpa), feelings (vedanā), ideas (saṁjñā), dispositions (saṁskāra), and consciousness (vijñāna)

[100] PK., 59-69; A. Chakravarty: Introduction to PK., pp. xxxvi-xxxvii.
[101] PK., 65. [102] PK., 65-70. [103] PK., 67-9.

designated by a name, even as a chariot is an aggregate of its component parts, the wheels, the framework, the ropes, the yoke, the spokes of the wheels, the axle and the like designated by the name chariot.[104] There is no permanent ego or self. The impermanent mind-body-aggregate (nāma-rūpa) is mistaken for a permanent self owing to ignorance (avidyā). Impermanent becoming is real. Permanent being is unreal. Attachment is due to false egoism. The Tathāgata is free from the delusion of self, and, therefore, devoid of attachment.[105] The body is composed of the four elements, earth, water, fire and air.[106] The Buddha does not reduce the mind to the material elements. Nor does he reduce the body to mental states. The relation of body to mind is an indeterminable question.[107] The external stimuli act upon the sense-organs and produce consciousness. Thinking generates volition. Volition produces action. In action the mind acts upon the body. Early Buddhism believes in naïve realism and interactionism. Life and consciousness are continuous. "Bhavaṅga is subconscious continuity of organic life. Consciousness springs out of the subconscious and lapses into the subconscious. Bhavaṅga is the potential state of consciousness. It is subliminal consciousness. In deep sleep the consciousness (citta) becomes one with the subconscious (bhavaṅga) or flow of organic life."[108] Body, life and consciousness are intimately related to one another. But priority is given to consciousness, since initial consciousness is the cause of the birth of a foetus in the womb.[109]

2. *The Subtle Body (sūkṣma deha, linga deha)*

The Sāṁkhya believes in the existence of the subtle body, and regards it as composed of five cognitive organs, five motor organs, manas, buddhi, and five tanmātras or subtle essences of colour, taste, odour, touch and sound. Egoism (ahaṁkāra) is included in buddhi.[110] This is Vijñānabhikṣu's interpretation of the aphorism which regards the subtle body as composed of seventeen elements. Aniruddha clearly mentions eighteen elements—intellect (buddhi), egoism (ahaṁkāra), mind (manas), ten

[104] *The Questions of King Milinda*, I, pp. 42-5.
[105] Ibid, I., S.B.E., 1890, Oxford, p. 226.
[106] Ibid, I, p. 194.
[107] AN., iii. HIP., ii, pp. 309-10.
[108] HIP., ii, pp. 313-4.
[109] Ibid, ii, p. 291.
[110] Saptadaśaikaṁ liṅgam. SPS., iii, 9. Ekādaśendriyāṇī pañca tanmātrāṇi buddhiś ceti saptadaśa. SPB., iii, 9.

sense-organs, and five tanmātras.[111] Vijñānabhikṣu makes buddhi the chief ingredient of the subtle body because it is the primary organ of the experience of pleasure and pain. Aniruddha also regards it as the principal organ of enjoyments and sufferings, and the gross body as the subordinate organ of their experience.[112] Vijñānabhikṣu regards five vital forces also as ingredients of the subtle body.[113] Life is a function of the mind (antaḥkaraṇa).

The subtle body is the ātivāhika body because the soul transmigrates with it. It pervades the gross body like the light of a lamp, though it is of minute dimension. It resides in the heart. It is the abode of manas. It is not the self, because it is composed of parts and functions for the sake of the self. The gross body is an effect of the subtle body. It is produced by the sexual union of the parents, but the subtle body is not so produced because it exists before the birth of the gross body. Though the subtle body is one, the same soul can be associated with different gross bodies in different births on account of different merits and demerits. The soul transmigrates with its subtle body when its gross body is destroyed.[114]

The subtle body is composed of parts. So it is not atomic, though it is minute in magnitude. Nor is it ubiquitous for then it would be eternal and incapable of movement. But it cannot be eternal for it is destroyed in the state of liberation. If it is eternal, the soul cannot be liberated. The soul is declared by the Vedas to transmigrate with the subtle body to the next world. So the subtle body, which is minute in magnitude, departs with the soul for its enjoyments and sufferings.[115]

The Sāṁkhya believes in the existence of an adhiṣṭhāna body which is the seat of the subtle body. It is imperceptible and composed of five subtle elements. The subtle body cannot exist independently without it.[116] When the gross body dies, the soul departs with the subtle body (liṅga deha) which is seated in the adhiṣṭhāna body. The subtle body is luminous with sattva as its chief ingredient, and so subsists in the adhiṣṭhāna body

[111] SSV., iii, 9.
[112] Sthūlaśarīrasya gauṇo bhogaḥ. SSV., iii, 8. SSVM., iii. 8; SPB., iii, 9.
[113] Liṅgadehe prāṇapañcakasyāpyantarbhāvaḥ. SPB., iii, 9.
[114] SSV., V, 103; SSVM., V, 103; iii, 8, 13; SPB., V, 103.
[115] SPS., SPB., iii, 14-16.
[116] Adhiṣṭhāna-śarīraṁ ca sūkṣmaṁ pañcabhūtātmakam. Liṅgaśarīram adhiṣṭhānaṁ vinā svātantryān na tiṣṭhati. SPB., iii, 11-12.

which is composed of five elements, even as fiery bodies like the sun are found to exist as associated with earthy substances.[117]

Caraka belives in a subtle body (ātivāhika deha) with which a soul transmigrates after death of its gross body. It is composed of the subtle elements of earth, water, light, air and ether, and manas endued with merits and demerits. It is imperceptible. But it can be perceived with a divine eye by yogins. The soul can assume another body with its aid.[118]

The Advaita Vedānta gives different accounts of the composition of the subtle body (sūkṣma deha). Śaṁkara regards it as composed of five unquintupled elements, five cognitive organs, five motor organs, five vital forces, mind (manas), intellect (buddhi), egoism (ahaṁkāra), memory (citta), nescience (avidyā), attachment (kāma), and merits and demerits (karma). It contains the potencies (vāsanā) of actions, and is the chief organ of the experience of their fruits in the form of pleasure and pain. It is the limiting adjunct (upādhi) of the empirical self until it realizes its essential nature of identity with the transcendental universal self. Dream is the manifestation of the subtle body in which objects created by subconscious impressions of waking perceptions are experienced through it. The pure self is detached (asaṅga). But the empirical self limited by the subtle body experiences pleasure and pain through it. It transmigrates with the subtle body to the next world, which continues to be its limiting adjunct till liberation is achieved. Liberation is the realization of the self's essential infinitude and absoluteness.[119] Nescience (avidyā) is unmanifest (avyakta), beginningless power of God, composed of sattva, rajas and tamas. God is infinite, eternal, universal consciousness limited by cosmic nescience. It is neither real, nor unreal, nor both, neither different, nor non-different, nor both, neither composite nor partless, nor both, but undefinable (anirvacanīya). Tamas veils the real nature of a thing, and makes it appear to be different. It projects the world of plurality. Rajas is active, and produces attachment and aversion and sufferings which are mental modes. It produces emotions and passions, and entangles the self in bondage. Sattva is transparent. The self is reflected in it and manifests the empirical world of plurality. So it also is the cause of bondage. Avidyā is composed of sattva, rajas and

[117] Liṅgaṁ ca sattvaprakāśamayam ato bhūtasaṅgatam. SPB., iii, 13.
[118] CS., CPV., iv, 2, 31-2. [119] VCM., 98-102.

tamas.[120] Kāma is attachment. Karma is of three kinds: (1) sañcita; (2) āgāmi; and (3) prārabdha. The merits and demerits existing in the empirical self, which have not yet borne fruits, are accumulated (sañcita). The merits and demerits which are acquired in this birth and will bear fruits in future birth or births are future (āgāmi). The merits and demerits which produced the present body are prenatal (prārabdha). Accumulated and future merits and demerits are destroyed by the experience of their fruits, counteracting unseen agencies, or the immediate intuition of the Ātman or Brahman. Prenatal merits and demerits are destroyed by the experience of their fruits only.[121] Sureśvara also regards the subtle body as composed of the twenty seven elements mentioned by Śaṁkara.[122] Sadānanda mentions seventeen elements of the subtle body, viz. five cognitive organs, five motor organs, five vital forces, manas and buddhi. But he includes ahaṁkāra and citta in manas and buddhi. The vital sheath, the mental sheath, and the intellectual sheath of the empirical self constitute the subtle body.[123] Dharmarājādhvarīndra mentions five unquintupled elements, five cognitive organs, five motor organs, five vital forces, manas and buddhi as the constituents of the subtle body.[124] It is the vehicle of transmigration. It is destroyed when liberation is achieved.[125]

The Upaniṣads speak of five sheaths (kośa) of the self. The gross body is the physical sheath (annamaya kośa). Five vital forces and five motor organs constitute the vital sheath (prāṇamaya kośa). Manas and five motor organs constitute the mental sheath (manomaya kośa). Buddhi and five cognitive organs constitute the intellectual sheath.[126] Mahādeva Sarasvatī gives this account of the four sheaths. Sadānanda regards the mental sheath as composed of manas and five cognitive organs.[127] This is the view of Śaṁkara. The blissful self reflected in nescience (avidyā) is called the blissful sheath (ānandamaya kośa). It is strongly manifested in deep sleep. It is slightly manifested in the waking state and dream also on the attainment of desired objects as a

[120] VCM., 113-5, 119. [121] ACK., pp. 77-8.
[122] PKV., 31-6.
[123] VSR., pp. 17, 19. Pañcadaśī, i, 23; ACK., p. 61.
[124] VP., pp. 363-4.
[125] Liṅgaśarīraṁ paralokayātrānirvāhakaṁ mokṣa-paryantaṁ sthāyi. VP., p. 363.
[126] ACK., p. 67.
[127] VSR., p. 18; VCM., 156, 169, 186.

result of the ripening of certain merits.[128] All these sheaths are not-self (anātman). The self-luminous self (ātman), pure being-consciousness-bliss is different from them. It is their witness (sākṣin). Even the blissful sheath is not-self. The self that is reflected in nescience (avidyā) is the Ātman.[129]

The Jaina believes in audārika, vaikriyika, āhāraka, taijasa and kārmaṇa bodies. (1) The audārika body is the gross body born in the womb due to the union of the parents. (2) The vaikriyika body is smaller than the audārika body, and acquired by supernatural powers by dint of austerities. (3) The āhāraka body is smaller than the vaikriyika body, and generated by auspicious karma-particles. It is pure because it is produced by excellent infra-atomic particles of karma-matter. It is non-obstructive as it does not hinder any other body, nor is it hindered by any other body. It is produced by supernatural powers due to special austerities. It is necessary for the ascertainment of the nature of the subtle objects and the observance of some restraints. (4) The taijasa body is smaller than the āhāraka body, luminous and generated by supernatural powers due to special austerities. (5) The kārmaṇa body is smaller than the taijasa body, composed of infra-atomic particles of karma-matter, and is the seed of the entire gross body. It is called karma.[130] The soul transmigrates with it. Its movement is the movement of this body.[131] It acquires audārika, vaikriyika and āhāraka bodies on certain occasions, but it retains the taijasa body and the kārmaṇa body until it attains liberation. The kārmaṇa body is the subtle body.[132]

3. *The Causal Body* (*Kāraṇa deha*)

Śaṁkara believes in the existence of the causal body made of nescience (avidyā) in which pure universal consciousness (ātman) is reflected. Avidyā is unmanifest and called avyakta. It is composed of sattva, rajas and tamas. The causal body is the cause of the subtle body and the gross body. Nescience (kāraṇa deha) supervised by the reflection of universal and eternal consciousness is transformed into these two bodies. These are the

[128] VCM., 209-10. [129] Pañcadaśī, iii, 10. VCM., 213.
[130] Sarva-śarīra-prarohaṇa-bījabhūtaṁ kārmaṇaṁ śarīraṁ karma ityucyate. SS., ii, 25.
[131] TSV., ii, 25, p. 331.
[132] U.T.S., ii, 36; SS., ii, 36-7, 41, 45-9.

modifications of avidyā, but the appearances of the Ātman or pure, transcendental, universal, eternal, undifferentiated consciousness.[133] Deep sleep is the manifestation of the causal body, in which intellect (buddhi) and all sense-organs cease to function. There are no cognitions in it and buddhi abides in avidyā, which is its cause.[134] The blissful sheath (ānandamaya kośa) constitutes the causal body which is manifested in deep sleep.[135] The Ātman is self-luminous, pure, immutable, eternally free and blissful, the witness of the three empirical conditions of waking, dream and deep sleep, and different from the five sheaths.[136] Dharmarājādhvarīndra regards it as composed of five unquintupled elements, five vital forces, five cognitive organs, five motor organs, mind (manas) and intellect (buddhi).[137] Mahādeva Sarasvatī regards it as composed of seventeen elements, viz. five cognitive organs, five motor organs, five vital forces, manas and buddhi.[138] Again, he speaks of its twenty seven constituents, viz. five unquintupled elements, egoism (ahaṁkāra), memory (citta), nescience (avidyā), desire (kāma) and merits and demerits (karma) in addition to those mentioned above.[139] The Upaniṣads speak of five sheaths of the empirical self. The gross body is the physical sheath (annamaya kośa). The five motor organs and the five vital forces constitute the vital sheath (prāṇamaya kośa). The five motor organs and manas constitute the mental sheath (manomaya kośa). The five cognitive organs and buddhi constitute the intellectcual sheath (vijñānamaya kośa).[140] Nescience (avidyā) enveloping the empirical self is the blissful sheath (ānandamaya kośa). The subtle body is composed of the vital, the mental and the intellectual sheaths.[141] It cannot exist without a gross body.[142]

4. *The Spiritual Body* (*cinmaya deha*)

Caitanya declares that a devotee surrenders himself to God at the time of initiation into spiritual praxis, who makes him full of consciousness and bliss. He develops a supernatural, spiritual body of consciousness and bliss with which he worships

[133] Cidābhāsa-vyāptam ajñānam śarīra-dvayākāreṇa pariṇamate. Pañcīkaraṇavivaraṇa, K.S.S., 1923, pp. 55-6. PKV., 39.
[134] VCM., 122-3. [135] VCM., 210. [136] VCM., 213.
[137] VP., pp. 363-4. [138] ACK., p. 61. [139] Ibid, p. 70.
[140] ACK., p. 67. [141] VCM., 156, 167, 169, 186, 209.
[142] Pañcadaśī, vi, 13.

God. Continuous practice of the recital of a name of God, a mantra, or the mystic syllable Om, concentration of attention, meditation and trance with control of breath produces a spiritual body, which is necessary for the realization of the real nature of the self (ātman) and God.[143] The causal body, the subtle body and the gross body are natural and normal to all empirical selves according to the Advaita Vedānta. But a spiritual body is supernatural (aprākṛta) and acquired by continuous spiritual practice. It is constituted by consciousness (cit) and bliss (ānanda). It is immaterial. It is called bliss-body (bhāva deha). Even the liberated souls who are intoxicated with love of God hold communion with him with supernatural spiritual bodies and form a commonwealth of spirits in a supramundane world.

[143] Caitanyacaritāmṛta, Ch. III and IV.

CHAPTER II

DEGREES OF CONSCIOUSNESS

1. *The Four Grades of Consciousness*

The *Māṇḍūkya Upaniṣad* describes four conditions of the self, which are different degrees of consciousness. The soul is four-footed, or has four conditions. The first condition is the waking state in which the soul is conscious of external objects, enjoys gross things through five cognitive organs, five motor organs, five vital principles, and mind (manas), intellect (buddhi), egoism (ahaṁkāra) and memory (citta), and is called Vaiśvānara. The second condition is the dream state in which the soul is conscious of internal objects, enjoys subtle things through the mind (manas) invested with the subconscious impressions of waking cognitions, and impelled by nescience (avidyā), attachment (kāma), and merits and demerits (karma), independently of the external sense-organs, and is called Taijasa. The third condition is deep sleep in which the soul desires no desires, and dreams no dreams. In this state the soul is centred in itself, filled with consciousness and bliss, enjoys bliss, experiences pure consciousness, and is called Prājña. In it the mental modes of waking and dream cognitions cease, the distinction of subject and object ceases and there is no trace of pain. The fourth condition is superconsciousness in which the soul is neither conscious of external objects, nor of internal objects, nor of both, nor a mass of consciousness, and transcends both consciousness and unconsciousness. It is imperceptible, uncommunicable, incomprehensible, indeterminate, unthinkable, indefinable, the essence of intuition of the self, transcendent, tranquil, good and non-dual. The soul in this highest state is called Turīya or Ātman.[1] The *Bṛhadāraṇyaka Upaniṣad* indicates in a passage that dream and deep sleep are the intermediate states between consciousness and unconsciousness, and that the soul creates objects of dream-cognitions, e.g. chariots, horses, joys, sorrows and the like[2]. The *Praśnopaniṣad* indicates in a passage that though dreams are usually mere representations of

[1] i, 2-7. SB., i, 2-7.
[2] iv, 3, 9-18.

actual waking experiences, they are sometimes absolutely novel constructions.[3] Dream is called the twilight of consciousness because it is an intermediate state between waking and deep sleep. The *Brahmopaniṣad* mentions the waking state, the dream state, deep sleep and trance (turīya). The Ātman is in the eyes in the first state; it is in the throat in the second state; it is in the heart in the third state: and it is in the head in the fourth state.[4] The *Kaivalyopaniṣad* mentions the waking state, dream and deep sleep. In the first condition the empirical self enjoys external objects produced by cosmic nescience through the external sense-organs. In the second condition it experiences pleasure and pain in an imaginary world created by its own avidyā. In the third condition it is overcome by nescience (tamas) and experiences happiness when the internal organ and the external sense-organs cease to operate.[5] The *Atharvaśikhopaniṣad* mentions four states, waking, dream, deep sleep and trance (turīya). Waking cognitions apprehend the five gross elements and their modifications. Dreams apprehend internal mental states which are due to impressions (vāsanā) of the waking cognitions of external objects. Avidyā which is the cause of unquintupled and quintupled subtle elements and their effects is apprehended in deep sleep. Trance manifests the absence of appearances (prapañca) and their effects apprehended by waking cognitions, dreams and deep sleep.[6] The *Turīyātīta Upaniṣad* mentions the state transcending the fourth (turīya) state which apprehends pure transcendental consciousness (cinmātra).[7]

The *Prapañcasāra Tantra* mentions five states, waking state, dream, deep sleep, turīya and turīyātīta. It explains the first, the second and the third states like the *Kaivalyopanisd.* In the fourth state the individual self experiences the supreme self or pure consciousness with the mind free from avidyā. In the fifth state a yogin has a pervasive experience of non-difference between his individual self and the supreme or universal self. It approaches the experience of liberation.[8]

The *Brahmabindu Upaniṣad* mentions unmanībhāva as the highest state. When the mind is completely restrained on the heart, withdrawn from objects and freed from attachment, it

[3] iv, 5. [4] Pp. 167-8. [5] 12-13; p. 143.
[6] iii, 1; Upaniṣad—Brahmayogin's commentary, Madras, 1925, pp. 16-7.
[7] 1; p. 473. (Bombay, 1948). [8] Calcutta, 1914, Ch. XIX, 46-9.

attains unmanībhāva. It is the highest state.[9] The *Nādabindu Upaniṣad* also mentions unmanībhāva. In this state the mind (manas) is dissolved in the mystic sound Aum (nāda) on which it is concentrated, and then in Brahman or pure consciousness which is represented by it. In this state the body becomes insensitive to heat and cold and the mind becomes insensitive to pleasure and pain, praise and insult, etc.[10] The *Śāṇḍilya Upaniṣad* asserts that there is dissolution of mind (cittanāśa) owing to the absence of its objects and cognitions. The mind becomes calm owing to the pacification of its agitations. It becomes free from thoughts of external objects and subjective cognitions. It is dissolved in the experience of pure, universal, transcendental consciousness (cinmātra) devoid of subject and object.[11] The *Yogaśikhopaniṣad* asserts that in unmanībhāva the mind (manas) loses all its modes (vṛtti), transcends the consciousness of virtue and vice, and is dissolved in Para Brahman. The mind is transcended in this state.[12]

According to the Tantras the ājñā cakra is the seat of the mystic sound Aum or Om. When citta is disunited from manas in consequence of repeated practice of meditation on this original sound, it becomes free from all attachment for worldly objects and becomes unmanī. This is the highest state. Another state inferior to it called samanī also is mentioned.[13]

2. *The Waking State (jāgrat)*

Mahādeva Sarasvatī defines the waking state as that in which there is the apprehension of external objects through the external sense-organs.[14] It is different from the dream state in which there is the apprehension of objects created by subconscious impressions (vāsanāmayaviṣayānubhava), but there is no perception of external objects produced by the external sense-organs because they cease to operate at the time. It is different from deep sleep in which there is the witness self's apprehension of nescience (ajñāna), but there is neither apprehension of objects created by subconscious impressions nor apprehension of external

[9] Nistaraṅgaviṣayāsaṅgaṁ saṁniruddhaṁ mano hṛdi. Yadā yātyunmanībhāvaṁ tadā tat paramaṁ padam. 4; p. 141.
[10] 38-54; pp. 285-6.
[11] Ch. I, 35-42; p. 415.
[12] Ch. VI, 61-66; p. 472.
[13] Ṣaṭcakranirūpaṇaṭīkā, 37 and 40.
[14] Indriyaiḥ viṣayānubhavāvasthā jāgradavasthā. ACK., p. 89.

objects, because the mind is dissolved in nescience at the time and the external sense-organs cease to function. In the waking state the self is limited by the causal body, the subtle body, and the gross body.[15] Dharmarājādhvarīndra also defines the waking state as that in which cognitions are produced by the external sense-organs.[16] In dream and deep sleep the sense-organs cease to function. Pure knowledge which constitutes the essence of the pure self is eternal. But sensuous knowledge in the waking condition is produced by external objects in intercourse with the external sense-organs. Sensuous cognitions are mental modes (antaḥkaraṇavṛtti) in which pure consciousness (caitanya) is reflected, and which are modified into the forms of objects.[17] The gross body is the vehicle of experience, in the waking condition, of gross objects.[18] The empirical self apprehends gross objects through the external sense-organs.[19]

3. *Dream* (*svapna*)

Dharmarājādhvarīndra defines dream as a mental mode which is an immediate apprehension of objects, which is not produced by the external sense-organs.[20] It differs from a waking cognition which is produced by an external sense-organ. It differs from deep sleep which is not a mental mode. In deep sleep the mind is dissolved in nescience (avidyā). Mahādeva Sarasvatī defines dream as the apprehension of objects created by the subconscious impressions produced by the waking perceptions in the past during light sleep when the external sense-organs cease to function and the merits and demerits capable of producing enjoyments and sufferings in the waking condition cease to operate.[21] In the dream state the empirical self is limited by the causal body and the subtle body.[22] Śaṁkara defines dreams as cognitions of objects produced by the subconscious impressions of the past waking perceptions when the external sense-organs cease to function.[23]

[15] TAS., pp. 89-90.
[16] Jāgraddaśā nāma indriya-janya-jñānāvasthā. VP., p. 387.
[17] VP., p. 387.
[18] Avasthā jāgaras tasya sthūlārthānubhavo yataḥ. VCM., 90.
[19] Ibid, 91.
[20] Indriyājanya-viṣaya-gocarāparokṣāntaḥkaraṇavṛttyavasthā svapnāvasthā. VP., p. 394.
[21] Jāgrad-bhogaprada-karmoparame sati indriyoparame jāgrad-anubhava-janya-saṁskārodbhūta-viṣayas taj-jñānāvasthā svapnāvasthā. ACK., pp. 89-90.
[22] TAS., p. 89.
[23] Karaṇeṣūpasaṁhṛteṣu jāgaritasaṁskārajaḥ pratyayaḥ svapna ityucyate. Pañcīkaraṇa, p. 2.

The subtle body is the vehicle of experience of the empirical self (jīva) in dream.[24] Śaṁkara regards dream-cognitions as recollections of waking perceptions. But Dharmarājādhvarīndra and Mahādeva Sarasvatī regard them as illusory perceptions during light sleep. This has been discussed in the first volume.

The *Mahābhārata* holds that dreams are the work of the subconscious mind (apralīna-manaḥ) which does not cease to function in light sleep; that they are creations of the mind as 'castles in the air' are built by the mind in imagination in the waking state, which gratify the person's desires; that they are modifications of sattva, rajas, or tamas of the mind (manas) impelled to act by his merits and demerits (karma); that they are produced by flatulence, bile and phlegm which are bodily humours: and that they are reproductions of waking perceptions when the external sense-organs cease to function.[25]

Caraka maintains, that a person dreams fearsome dreams when his manovahā nāḍī is filled with excessively provoked bodily humours.[26] Cakrapāṇi observes that the ten nerves ending in the heart, which is the seat of manas are called manovahā nāḍī. When a person is not fast asleep, he dreams many kinds of dreams with the mind (manas) which is the master of the external sense-organs.[22] This implies that dreams are the work of the subconscious mind during light sleep. No dreams are dreamt in deep sleep because the mind becomes unconscious in this condition. Caraka describes seven kinds of dreams, viz. seen, heard, otherwise perceived, desired, imagined, prognostic of future good or evil, and produced by provoked bodily humours such as flatulence, bile, and phlegm. Cakrapāṇi observes, that some dreams are gratifications of ungratified desires.[28] Some dreams foreshadow future events. Dreams produced by perverted bodily humours indicate the onset of a disease.[29]

4. *Deep Sleep* (*nidrā*)

The Nyāya-Vaiśeṣika does not regard sleep as a mental mode or a produced cognition. It considers sleep to be the absence of

[24] VCM., 100.
[25] Śāntiparva, ch. 216, 4-12.
[26] CS., Indriyasthāna, ch. VI, 41. Lahore, 1940.
[27] Ibid, ch. VI, 42.
[28] Ibid, ch. VI, 43.
[29] Ibid, 44-7; CPV.

cognition because of the absence of the operation of the external sense-organs and the internal sense-organ (manas). Sleep is produced when manas abides in a region which has no relation to the tactual organ even.[30] It is the abiding of manas in a part of the body devoid of any relation to the external sense-organs, which is not aided by merit born of meditation. It is different from trance (samādhi), in which manas is aided by merit born of meditation.[31]

Patañjali defines sleep as a mental mode which has for its object the cognition of the absence of waking cognitions, dreams and the like.[32] It is a kind of apprehension (anubhava) because it is remembered on waking from sleep.[33] We have recollections of sleep in such forms: 'I slept happily; my mind being cheerful produces clear and distinct knowledge'; 'I slept unhappily; my unsettled mind flits from object to object'; 'I slept heavily; my lazy mind seems to be inert'. These are the three kinds of sleep which are characterized by the predominance of purity (sattva), energy (rajas), and inertia (tamas) respectively. If there were no apprehension of sleep, there would be no recollection of it. Hence Vyāsa regards sleep as a particular mental mode which apprehends the absence of cognitions.[34] Vijñānabhikṣu also regards it as a mental mode which apprehends the absence of waking cognitions, dreams and the like. It apprehends darkness (tamas) which conceals purity (sattva) of the mind. He recognizes three kinds of sleep, viz. sāttvika, rājasika and tāmasika.[35] Some Vedāntists maintain, that tamas is manifested in sleep by the witness self (sākṣin), and not by a mental mode (vṛtti). Vijñānabhikṣu refutes this view. If tamas were manifested, he argues, by the witness self, there would be no recollection of sleep because it is immutable, and so devoid of any mode (vṛtti), and, consequently, of an impression (saṁskāra). Some Vedāntists maintain, that in sleep there is a mode of nescience (ajñāna) which is prakṛti, but that there is no mode of mind (cittavṛtti). Vijñānabhikṣu criticizes this view also. If there were a mode of prakṛti in the form of nescience in sleep, there would be a mode of nescience

[30] KR., p. 120.
[31] Yogaja-dharmānanugṛhītasya manaso nirindriya-pradeśāvasthānaṁ nidrā. SP., p. 68. MBh., p. 68.
[32] Abhāvapratyayālambanā vṛttir nidrā. YS., i, 1, 10.
[33] Sā ca samprabodhe pratyavamarśāt pratyayaviśeṣaḥ. YBh., i, 1, 10.
[34] YBh., i, 1, 10. [35] YV., i, 1, 10.

in the waking condition and dream also, and the assumption of the mind (citta) would be needless. Hence there is a mental mode (cittavṛtti) in sleep as in the waking condition and dream. Waking cognition, dream and sleep are mental modes. It may be argued, that sleep is directly manifested by the witness self (sākṣin) without a mental mode, even as pleasure is directly manifested by it without a mental mode, and that recollection may occur in the witness self. Vijñānabhikṣu urges, that the witness self is devoid of modifications, and, consequently, cannot have an impression and recollection.[36] Thus the Yoga regards sleep as a mental mode which apprehends the absence of cognitions.

The Sāṁkhya holds that intellect (buddhi) is modified into the forms of objects through the external sense-organs in the waking condition. It recognizes two degrees of sleep, viz. half sleep and deep sleep. In the former there are no mental modes in the form of objects, but there are mental modes in the form of pleasure, pain and delusion subsisting in the mind (buddhi). Otherwise there would be no recollection in such forms as 'I slept happily, unhappily or heavily'. In deep sleep there are no mental modes either in the form of cognitions of objects or in the form of feelings. It is in the nature of the absence of mental modes.[37] Vijñānabhikṣu regards deep sleep as the absence of mental modes, which is manifested by the self (puruṣa), that does not always depend upon a mental mode for its knowledge.[38] The waking condition, dream and deep sleep are known by the self which is different from them. Deep sleep, Aniruddha asserts, resembles trance (samādhi) and release (mokṣa) because there is no consciousness of external objects in them. But in deep sleep and trance the mind has potenciees of actions, while in release it is completely free from them. In the former the mind is restrained for the time being, and the seeds (bīja) of actions lie dormant in it. But in the latter the seeds of actions which are the causes of suffering are extirpated. So deep sleep and trance are not identical with release. Deep sleep is natural, while trance can be produced by the repeated practice of concentration. So deep

[36] YV., i, 1, 10.

[37] Ardhalaye viṣayākārā vṛttir na bhavati. Kintu svagatasukha-duḥkha mohākāraiva buddhi-vṛttir bhavati. Samagralaye tu buddhivṛtti-sāmānyābhāvo bhavati. Samagra-suṣuptir vṛttyabhāvarūpā. SPB., i, 148.

[38] Jñānārthaṁ puruṣasya na pariṇāmāpekṣā. SPB., i, 148.

sleep is different from trance.[39] There is distraction of the mind in the waking condition and dream. But in deep sleep there is no distraction of the mind because it is free from mental modes.[40] Aniruddha defines sleep as a mental mode or cognition which apprehends darkness.[41]

Śaṁkara regards deep sleep as the abiding of buddhi in its causal condition as nescience (avidyā) when all kinds of cognitions are destroyed.[42] In this condition the mind is dissolved in nescience (avidyā) which is its cause.[43] The Advaita Vedānta regards deep sleep as a mode of nescience (ajñāna) in which there is the manifestation of the Self (ātman) which is pure being, consciousness and bliss.[44] According to Rāmānanda Yati, in deep sleep mere nescience (ajñāna) coloured by the impressions of buddhi is the adjunct of the empirical self.[45] Buddhi is dissolved in nescience which is its cause in this condition. There is no mental mode in it. It differs from indeterminate trance (nirvikalpa samādhi) in which there is a mental mode which is modified into the form of Brahman. It differs from release (mokṣa) in which avidyā and its effects in the form of impressions are totally destroyed. But in deep sleep they persist since they operate on waking from it. It differs from embodied release in which a person abides in his essential condition in his waking state, and has mental modes which apprehend empirical objects, though he knows that they are false.[46] Mahādeva Sarasvatī defines deep sleep as the condition in which the mind abides in its essential condition as nescience (avidyā) when all determinate cognitions, false identification of the self with the gross body and the subtle body, and merits and demerits capable of producing enjoyments and sufferings in the waking condition and dream cease.[47] Raṅgojī Bhaṭṭa holds that deep sleep is manifested by the self-manifest witness self (sākṣin). It cognizes deep sleep. If it does not cognize sleep, it cannot remember on waking from sleep: 'I slept happily and did not know anything else.' This cognition is not inference since there is no mark of inference (liṅga). One's

[39] SPS., SSV., V, 116-7.
[40] Layaḥ susuptiḥ. Vikṣepaḥ svapna-jāgarite. SSVM., vi, 30.
[41] Nidrā tamo'valambi jñānam. SSV., ii, 33.
[42] Sarva-prakāra-jñānopasaṁhāre buddheḥ kāraṇātmanāvasthānaṁ suṣuptiḥ. Pañcīkaraṇa, pp. 63-4.
[43] VCM., 173.
[44] VCM., 219.
[45] VMR., p. 111.
[46] VMR., p. 130.
[47] ACK., p. 90.

deep sleep cannot be inferred from one's bright eyes, because the knowledge of invariable concomitance of deep sleep with brightness of the eyes cannot be known unless one's deep sleep is apprehended. Nor can it be inferred from another's bright eyes, because his deep sleep is not perceived by a person, and, consequently, the uniform concomitance between deep sleep and bright eyes cannot be known. Another person cannot infer his deep sleep from another's bright eyes for it will be like a blind person guiding another blind person. Hence the witness self (sākṣin) apprehends deep sleep. Waking state, dream and deep sleep are manifested by the witness self, which is different from them and self-manifest.[48] Dharmarājādhvarīndra considers deep sleep to be a mode of nescience (avidyā) which experiences nescience.[49] In this state the internal organ is dissolved in avidyā, and, consequently, has no function; but avidyā is not dissolved, and so has a function. But in the waking state and dream the internal organ operates. Mādhavācārya Vidyāraṇya holds that in deep sleep nescience (avidyā), which conceals the nature of Brahman, does not conceal the witness self (sākṣin); that it is manifested by the witness self for otherwise its existence would not be proved without the witness self to apprehend it; and that in deep sleep bliss, the Self and positive nescience are apprehended because of such recollections on waking from deep sleep as 'I slept happily and I knew nothing else'.[50] Nescience (avidyā) itself is modified into three modes which apprehend these three entities.[51] Hence Vidyāraṇya regards deep sleep as a mode of nescience, in which the mind is dissolved, and which apprehends positive nescience, bliss and self. Egoism or I-sense (ahaṁkāra) is dissolved in deep sleep, but it is produced again on waking from this state. This accounts for recollection in such a form as 'I slept happily' on waking from sleep.[52]

According to Rāmānuja, there is no complete extinction of the self-sense or I-consciousness (ahṁkāra) in deep sleep, though there is no distinct consciousness of it, and there is the absence

[48] Jāgrat-svapna-suṣuptyādi-sākṣī caitanya-vigrahaḥ. Advaita-cintāmaṇi, p. 24.

[49] Suṣuptir avidyāgocarāvidyāvrttyavasthā. VP., p. 394.

[50] Suṣuptāvanubhūta ānanda ātmā bhāvarūpājñānaṁ ceti trayam utthitena parāmṛśyate. VPS., p. 60.

[51] Avidyaivoktatrayagrāhakavṛtti-trayākāreṇa suṣuptau vivartate. VPS., p. 60.

[52] Ibid, p. 61.

of the cognitions of external objects. The mind (buddhi) is overcome by tamas in this state.[53] Nobody has such a recollection as 'I as undifferentiated consciousness devoid of the distinction of subject and object was the witness of nescience in deep sleep' on waking from it as Śaṁkara maintains. The self is not mere consciousness, but 'I' or Ego. If there is no *I*-consciousness or Ego, mere knowledge cannot be a knower.[54] *I*-consciousness persists in deep sleep and release. The self as pure subject-objectless consciousness is said to be the witness of nescience in deep sleep. But the witness is a conscious knower, an agent of immediate knowledge. It cannot be pure consciousness, which is not a knower.[55] Rāmānuja regards the self as a knower, Ego, or 'I', and thinks that *I*-consciousness, though indistinct, persists in deep sleep. Śaṁkara and Rāmānuja advocate fatigue theory of sleep.[56] The causal body or nescience (avidyā) made of sattva, rajas and tamas is the vehicle of experience of the empirical self in deep sleep when the mind is dissolved in nescience.[57]

Amṛtacandra Sūri, a Jaina thinker, criticizes the Advaita Vedānta view that deep sleep is similar to release. In release there is unique knowledge of the universe with supreme happiness, whereas in deep sleep there is neither knowledge nor happiness. In release karma-matter is completely destroyed, while in deep sleep it is not destroyed. Further, in release exertion, pride, fatigue, disease, lust, delusion, and the modifications of infra-sensible particles of karma-matter which conceal detailed knowledge are destroyed, whereas all these continue to exist in deep sleep.[58] Amṛtacandra Sūri's criticism is based on a misunderstanding of the Advaita Vedānta doctrine which distinguishes between sleep and release.

Nāgasena, a Buddhist thinker, advocates the fatigue theory of sleep. He says: "The feeling of oppression and inability in the body, of weakness, slackness, inertness that is the beginning of sleep."[59]

[53] Tamoguṇābhibhavāt parāgarthānubhavābhāvācca ahamarthasya vivikta-sphuṭa-pratibhāsābhāve'pyāprabodhāt ahamityākāreṇātmanaḥ sphuraṇāt suṣuptāvapi nāhaṁbhāva-vigamaḥ. RBS., i, 1, 1.

[54] Ahamartha eva pratyagātmā, na jnaptimatram. Ahaṁbhāva-vigame tu jnapter api na pratyaktva-siddhiḥ. Ibid, i, 1, 1.

[55] Sākṣitvaṁ sākṣāt jñātṛtvam eva, na hyajānataḥ sākṣitvam. Ibid, i, 1, 1.

[56] Śramādinimittatvāt svāpasya. SBS., iii, 2, 10. RBS., iii, 2, 10.

[57] VCM., 122-3.

[58] TSār., viii, 50-1.

[59] *The Questions of King Milinda*, II, p. 161.

Caraka maintains, that a person sleeps when his mind is tired, and, consequently, his sense-organs withdraw from their objects owing to fatigue.[60] Sleep is due to the excess of inertia (tamas), phlegm, fatigue of body and mind, disease and influence of the night.[61] Cakrapāṇi, like the Nyāyā-Vaiśeṣika, regards sleep as the retirement of manas in a region of the body free from the sense-organs.[62] Caraka advocates the fatigue theory of sleep. The *Mahābhārata* also holds that sleep is due to the fatigue of the sense-organs.[63]

5. *Theories of Sleep*

(1) The *Bṛhadāraṇyaka Upaniṣad* advocates the fatigue theory of sleep in the following passage. "As a falcon or any other bird, after having flewn in the sky, becomes tired, and folding its wings repairs to its nest, so does this person fall asleep when he desires no more desires, and dreams no dreams."[64] (2) The *Praśna Upaniṣad* holds that sleep is generated by the withdrawal of the sense-organs into the mind (manas). "As the rays of the sun are collected in the sun at the time of the sun-set, so are all the sense-organs withdrawn into the mind in deep sleep, when a person is not able to hear, nor to see, nor to smell, nor to taste, nor to touch, nor to grasp, nor to walk, nor to talk, nor to exercise generative and excretive organs. He is said to sleep."[65] (3) The same Upaniṣad also declares that sleep is produced by the mind being overpowered by light or Brahman. "When a person is overpowered by light, he dreams no dreams, and feels bliss."[66] (4) The *Chāndogya Upaniṣad* holds that sleep is caused by the movement of the soul into the arteries (nāḍī). "When a person is fast asleep, and being happy dreams no dreams, his soul moves into the veins."[67] (5) The *Bṛhadāraṇyaka Upaniṣad* holds that sleep is produced by the lodgement of the soul in purītat, a membranous sac near the heart, which sends forth seventy two

[60] Yadā tu manasi klānte karmātmānaḥ klamānvitāḥ.
Viṣayebhyo nivartante tadā svapiti mānavaḥ.
CS., Sūtrasthāna, ch. XXI, 35.

[61] Ibid, ch. XXII, 58.

[62] Svapnaś ca nirindriya-pradeśe mano'vasthānam. Ibid, Cakrapāṇivyākhyā.

[63] Indriyāṇāṃ sramāt svapnam āhuḥ.
Śāntiparva, ch. 216, 5.

[64] iv, 3, 19.

[65] iv, 2.

[66] iv, 6.

[67] viii, 6, 3.

thousand arteries called Hita to the purītat. When the soul moves through these arteries into the purītat, it is not conscious of anything, and sleeps fast in supreme happiness.[68] This theory was later developed by the Nyāya-Vaiśeṣika. (6) The same Upaniṣad also holds that sleep is produced by the lodgement of the soul in heart-ether.[69] (7) The *Chāndogya Upaniṣad* holds that sleep is caused by the mind (manas) merging in life force (prāṇa). "The mind flying in every direction, and finding rest nowhere, at last settles down on life-force."[70] (8) The same Upaniṣad also holds that in deep sleep the soul is united with Brahman. "When a person sleeps, he becomes united with the Real or Brahman, and goes to his own self."[71] The *Bṛhadāraṇyaka Upaniṣad* also holds that in deep sleep the soul is embraced by the supreme wise Self or Brahman, and is not conscious of external objects or subjective cognitions."[72]

6. *Trance (samādhi)*

Mahādevānanda Sarasvatī describes trance as a condition of the empirical self (jīva) when it becomes identical with the pure supreme Self or subject-objectless transcendental consciousness, and when all mental modes cease, and there is no false identification of the self with the gross body, the subtle body and the causal body. It is a superconscious state of complete transcendence of the threefold body or not-self (anātman) in the embodied condition.[73] Here trance is taken in the sense of indeterminate trance. In this highest state of the empirical self (jīva) it realizes its real identity with the pure universal self.[74] In the waking state the self erroneously identifies itself with the gross body, the subtle body and the causal body. In dream it wrongly identifies itself with the subtle body and the causal body. In deep sleep it identifies itself erroneously with the causal body. But in trance

[68] ii, 1, 19.

[69] Ya eṣo'ntarhṛdaya ākāsas tasmiñ chete, athaitatpuruṣaḥ svapiti nāma. ii, 1, 17.

[70] vi, 8, 2. Kaiṣītaki, iv, 19.

[71] Yatraitatpuruṣaḥ svapiti nāma satā tadā saṁpanno bhavati svam apīto bhavati. vi, 8, 1.

[72] iv, 3, 21. Ranade: *Constructive Survey of Upaniṣadic Philosophy*, pp. 122-6; M. N. Sirkar: *Vedantic Thought and Culture*, pp. 159-60.

[73] Śarīratrayavyatirekaḥ cittasya vṛttiśūnyatayātmaikārāvasthā samādhiḥ. TAS., p. 89.

[74] Tasyām avasthāyām ātmā vastutaḥ śuddhaḥ paramātmā bhavati. Ibid, p. 89.

the self completely transcends the threefold body and realizes itself as pure transcendental self-luminous consciousness.[75] In dream there is no consciousness of the gross body. In deep sleep there is no consciousness of the subtle body. In trance there is no consciousness of the causal body. It is the supreme super-conscious state of complete transcendence of the empirical life.[76] It is different from deep sleep in which the mind abides in its causal state as nescience (avidyā). But in indeterminate trance there is no mental mode. In it the mind abides in its real nature as pure consciousness or self (śuddha ātmā). Trance resembles deep sleep in that in both there is the absence of determinate cognitions.[77] Embodied release (jīvanmukti) is the complete realization of identity of the empirical or individual self (jīva) with the transcendental or universal self (ātman, paramātman) due to the complete destruction of nescience (avidyā) or false identification of the Self (ātman) with not-self (anātman).

Rāmatīrtha Yati distinguishes between deep sleep and indeterminate trance (nirvikalpa samādhi). In deep sleep the mind is dissolved in nescience (avidyā) and abides in its causal state. But in indeterminate trance a mental mode is transformed into the form of the supreme reality or pure universal consciousness (Ātman, Brahman).[78] Thus indeterminate trance is different from deep sleep. Indeterminate trance is different from release (mukti). In release there is complete destruction of nescience (avidyā) and its effects in the form of impressions (saṁskāra). But there is relapse from indeterminate trance into empirical consciousness —from identity consciousness to dualistic and pluralistic consciousness.[79] This proves that avidyā persists in indeterminate trance, which generates the consciousness of duality and plurality when there is falling off from it. Indeterminate trance is different from embodied release (jīvanmukti). In the former there is the consciousness of identity so long as it persists; but when it is replaced by empirical consciousness identity consciousness vanishes. But

[75] Samādhau śuddhasya prakāśacidrūpeṇa bhānam. Ibid, p. 89.

[76] Svapne sthūlaśarīrābhānam, suṣuptau sūkṣmaśarīrābhānam, samādhau kāraṇaśarīrābhānañca. Ibid, p. 89.

[77] Suṣuptiḥ buddheḥ kāraṇātmanāvasthānam. Samādhā vantaḥ-karaṇasya svarūpeṇa sattvāt. Ibid, p. 91.

[78] Iha tu buddhivṛtter advitīya-vastvākārākāritāyā avasthānāṅgīkārāt suṣupter bhedopapatteḥ. VMR., p. 130.

[79] Nāpi muktau ativyāptis tatrāvidyā-tatkāryasaṁskārāṇām atyantam ucchedāt. VMR., p. 130.

in the latter the identity consciousness persists in the midst of the empirical consciousness of phenomenal appearances.[80] Thus indeterminate trance is different from deep sleep, release and embodied release.

Sadānanda distinguishes between determinate trance (savikalpa samādhi) and indeterminate trance (nirvikalpa samādhi). In the former a mental mode is transformed into the one supreme reality or pure transcendental consciousness, though the consciousness of the distinction of the knower, the known and knowledge persists.[81] But in the latter a mental mode is transformed into the form of the one supreme reality or pure transcendental consciousness (Brahman), in which there is no consciousness of the distinction of the knower, the known and knowledge, and there is complete identification of the empirical self with the transcendental self (Brahman).[82]

Nṛsiṁha Sarasvatī recognizes two kinds of determinate trance and two kinds of indeterminate trance. In the first kind of determinate trance a mental mode abides in the one supreme reality (Brahman), being interpenetrated by the word 'I am Brahman'. In the second kind of determinate trance a mental mode abides without any break in the one supreme reality (Brahman), being interpenetrated by the words 'I am Brahman', in which there is the consciousness of the distinction among the knower, the known and knowledge. In the apprehension of determinate trance the one supreme reality (Brahman) is manifested to consciousness in the midst of the consciousness of the distinction of the knower, the known and knowledge. There is identity consciousness in the midst of dualistic consciousness in determinate trance. In the first kind of indeterminate trance a mental mode aided by the subconscious impressions of the apprehensions of determinate trance practised for a long time is identified with Brahman, in which there is no consciousness of the distinction among the knower, the known and knowledge. In the second kind of indeterminate trance the one pure Being-Consciousness-Bliss is manifested to consciousness without a mental mode transformed into its form, in which there is no consciousness of the distinction

[80] VMR., p. 130.

[81] Tatra savikalpo nāma jñatṛ-jñānādivikalpa-layānapekṣayādvitīya-vastuni tadākārākāritāyāś cittavṛtter avasthānam. VSR., p. 45.

[82] Nirvikalpas tu jñātṛ-jñānādi-vikalpa-layāpeksayādvitīya-vastuni tadākārā-kāritāyāś cittavṛtter atitarām ekībhāvenāvasthānam. VSR., p. 46

of the knower, the known and knowledge, and there are no subconscious impressions of the apprehensions of determinate trance, which are destroyed by the repeated practice of indeterminate trance. This is the highest stage of superconsciousness.[83]

7. *Swoon (mūrcchā)*

Mahādeva Sarasvatī, a Śaṁkarite, regards swoon as the condition in which there is the cessation of determinate cognitions brought about by the intense pain caused by the severe blow of a club or the like. It is not a waking cognition or dream because there are no cognitions in it. Nor is it death as there is recovery from swoon. Nor is it deep sleep, though there are no determinate cognitions in it, since the two states have different manifestations. Swoon is manifested by a fearful face, movements of the limbs and the like, while deep sleep is manifested by a cheerful face, a motionless body and the like.[84] Śaṁkara asserts, that swoon is not a waking state because there is no perception of external objects through the external sense-organs. Just as an archer, it may be argued, with his attention focussed on a target, does not perceive other objects, though he is in the waking state, so a person in swoon does not perceive other objects, though he is in the waking state, for his attention is focussed on the perception of pain produced by a severe blow. This argument, Śaṁkara urges, is wrong because a person is unconscious in swoon, while a person is conscious in the waking state. The archer afterwards remembers that he perceived the arrow for such a duration. But the person in swoon afterwards remembers that he was unconscious of anything for such a period, when he recovers from swoon and is restored to normal consciousness. Further, a person in the waking state keeps his body in the normal position when his mind is fixed on one object, while a person in swoon falls prostrate on the ground. So swoon is not the waking state. Nor is it dream as it is a state of unconsciousness. Nor is it deep sleep, though it is a state of unconsciousness like it in a living condition, because it differs in its expression and cause. In swoon the body trembles, there is irregular breathing, the face becomes fearful and the eyes are expanded, while in deep sleep the body

[83] Subodhinī on VSR., pp. 45-7.
[84] ACK., p. 191; TAS., p. 192.

does not tremble, there is regular breathing, the face becomes cheerful and the eyes are closed. A sleeping person is awakened by mere pressure of his hand, but a fainting person is not restored to consciousness even by the blow of a club. Swoon and deep sleep are produced by different causes. Swoon is generated by the blow of a club or the like, while deep sleep is brought about by fatigue and the like. A fainting person is never said to be asleep. So swoon is a distinct state, though it has similarity with deep sleep. It is half-way between life and death. It may lead to death. When the merits and demerits, which keep alive the body for the experience of their fruits in the form of enjoyments and sufferings, are not yet completely exhausted, the external and internal organs are restored to their normal functions. But when they are completely exhausted, the body is deprived of its life and heat. Swoon is not death, since the body retains its heat and is not deprived of its life-activities.[85]

Rāmānuja maintains that swoon is neither waking condition nor dream, since it is devoid of cognitions. It differs from deep sleep because it is produced by a severe blow or the like, while sleep is brought about by fatigue. It differs from death in which there is complete cessation of the functions of life, whereas in swoon slight activities of life go on. In death there is complete extinction of vital functioins. In swoon there are slight life-activities. In deep sleep there are greater activities of life[86] Hence swoon is a distinct condition of the self.

According to Caraka, there is slight unconsciousness (moha) in intoxication (mada). There is greater unconsciousness in swoon (mūrccā). There is complete unconsciousness in apoplexy (saṁnyāsa). When the perverted bodily humours attack the heart, the seat of consciousness, a person's consciousness is confounded.[87]

8. *Death (maraṇa)*

Mahādeva Sarasvatī regards death as the condition of the empirical self (jīva) in which all the internal and external organs cease to operate until it is associated with another body owing to the cessation of the general and particular sense of the body

[85] SBS., iii, 2, 10; Bhāmatī, iii, 2, 10.
[86] RBS., iii, 2, 10; Śrutiprakāśikā.
[87] CS., Sūtrasthāna, ch. xxiv, 27-9; CPV.

due to the destruction of the merits and demerits which produced enjoyments and sufferings of the body in the present life. In deep sleep the general sense of the body persists, since there is waking from sleep. A person devoid of it cannot wake from sleep. There is a general sense of the body such as 'I am a person' as well as a particular sense of it such as 'I am a Brāhmaṇa' in the waking condition and dream. But in death there is neither the general sense nor the particular sense of the body owing to the destruction of the merits and demerits, which were acquired in the previous birth and brought about the present birth.[88] Rāmānuja regards death as the complete cessation of all relations of the self to the body and vital forces.[89] He regards swoon as the condition in which the self exists as related to the subtle body and life.[90]

Dharmarājādhvarīndra distinguishes between death and deep sleep. In deep sleep the subtle body remains in the form of impressions (saṁskāra) in that very place. But in death it goes with the empirical self (jīva) to the next world. This is the difference between deep sleep and death. Or, the internal organ (antaḥkaraṇa) has the power of knowledge (jñānaśakti) and the power of action (kriyāśakti). In deep sleep the internal organ with the power of knowledge is destroyed, but the same organ with the power of action is not destroyed. So inhalation, exhalation and other vital functions continue in this condition.[91]

[88] ACK., p. 91; TAS., pp. 92-3.
[89] Maraṇaṁ sarva-deha-prāṇa-sambandh-oparatiḥ. RBS., iii, 2, 10.
[90] Sūkṣma-prāṇa-deha-sambandhāvasthitir mūrcchā. RBS., iii, 2, 10.
[91] VP., p. 368.

Chapter III

THE MODES OF CONSCIOUSNESS

1. *The Upaniṣads*

The *Bṛhadāraṇyaka Upaniṣad* mentions the following mental modes: (1) desire; (2) decision or determination; (3) doubt; (4) belief; (5) disbelief; (6) retention; (7) non-retention; (8) shame; (9) cognition; and (10) fear[1] Of these doubt, belief, disbelief, retention, non-retention, and cognition are different kinds of cognition; shame and fear are emotions; and desire and determination are conation. The *Aitareya Upaniṣad* advocates intellectualism when it declares: "Sensation, perception, ideation, conception, understanding, insight, opinion, imagination, feeling, memory, determination, volition, will-to-live, desire, and self-control—all these are different names of intellection."[2] It is remarkable that the different levels of intellectual experience such as sensation, perception, ideation and conception are recognized and distinguished from one another; that cognition, feeling and volition are distinguished from one another; and that all these are regarded as different names of intellection.[3] The *Aitareya Upaniṣad* advocates intellectualism and recognizes the primacy of intellect or cognition. The *Chāndogya Upaniṣad* also emphatically declares the primacy of cognition. "Intellect is better than will for only when a person thinks he wills. Intellect is the sole support of all these."[4] The *Maitrāyaṇī Upaniṣad* regards desire, determination, doubt, belief, disbelief, retention, non-retention, shame, cognition, and fear—all these as the mind itself.[5] All these are modes of the mind in its cognitive aspect. The *Bṛhadāraṇyaka Upaniṣad* recognizes three primal desires: (1)

[1] Kāmaḥ saṁkalpo vicikitsā śraddhā' śraddhā dhṛtir adhṛtir hrīr dhīr bhīr ityetat sarvaṁ manaḥ. i, 5, 3. Maitrāyaṇī, vi, 30.

[2] Saṁjñānam ājñānaṁ vijñānaṁ prajñānaṁ medhā dṛṣṭir dhṛtir matir manīṣā jūtiḥ smṛtiḥ saṁkalpaḥ kratur asuḥ kāmo vaśa iti sarvāṇyaivetāni prajñānasya nāmadheyāni bhavanti. i, 5, 2.

[3] *A Constructive Survey of Upaniṣadic Philosophy*, 1926, pp. 118-9.

[4] Cittaṁ vāva saṁkalpād bhuyo yadā vai cetayate' tha saṁkalpayate. Cittaṁ hyeṣām ekāyanam. vii, 5, 1-2.

[5] Kāmaḥ saṁkalpo vicikitsā śraddhā'-śraddhā dhṛtir adhṛtir hrīr dhīr bhīr ityetat sarvaṁ mana eva. vi, 30.

desire for sons (puttraiṣaṇā) or sex-desire; (2) desire for wealth (vittaiṣaṇā); and (3) desire for happiness in heaven (lokaiṣaṇā).[6] It declares that desire is the cause of volition, and that volition is the cause of voluntary action.[7] It destinguishes between conduct and character, and asserts that a good character is formed by habitual good conduct, and that a bad character is formed by habitual bad conduct.[8] Hence a person is ultimately what he desires.[9] His character is determined by his habitual voluntary actions. His actions are determined by his volitions. His volitions are determined by his desires. Thus his desires determine his character. The *Maitrāyaṇī Upaniṣad* distinguishes pleasure, pain and delusion from one another, and regards the self as the experiencer (bhoktā) of them.[10] The *Chāndogya Upaniṣad* declares that pleasure is derived from the attainment of the Infinite, and that pain is due to the attainment of a finite object.[11] Here pleasure (sukha) means bliss. The *Kaṭhopaniṣad* regards the self conjoined with manas and the sense-organs as the experiencer of feelings (bhoktā).[12] Thus the self is the knower, the enjoyer and the agent. Cognition, feeling and conation are recognized by the Upaniṣads.[13] The *Bhagavad Gītā* speaks of cognition (jñāna) pleasure (sukha), pain (duḥkha), desire (icchā), aversion (dveṣa), and volition (pravṛtti).[14] The distinction of cognition, feeling and conation is clearly recognized. The mind (manas) is made of purity (sattva), energy (rajas) and inertia (tamas). These guṇas are effects of prakṛti. Sattva produces knowledge and pleasure. Rajas is in the nature of attachment (rāga), and produces pain, volition and action. Tamas produces ignorance and delusion.[15]

2. *The Nyāya-Vaiśeṣika*

Kaṇāda mentions cognition, pleasure, pain, desire, aversion, volition, merit and demerit as special qualities of the self. Of these

[6] iii, 5, 1; iv, 4, 22.
[7] Sa yathākāmo bhavati tatkratur bhavati yatkratur bhavati tat karma kurute. Ibid, iv, 4, 5.
[8] Sādhukārī sādhur bhavati pāpakāri pāpo bhavati. Puṇyaḥ puṇyena karmaṇā bhavati pāpaḥ pāpena. Ibid, iv, 4, 5.
[9] Kāmamaya evāyaṁ puruṣaḥ. Ibid, iv, 4, 5.
[10] vi, 10.
[11] vii, 23, 1.
[12] Ātmendriyamanoyuktaṁ bhoketyāhur manīṣiṇaḥ. i, 3, 4.
[13] Kaṭha, i, 3, 4-5; ii, 2, 11-2; Tait. Up., iii, 7; Bṛ. Up., iv, 3, 32; iv, 4, 5. Puruṣaś cetā sa eva bhoktā. Mait. Up., vi, 10.
[14] xiii, 6, 17-8, 20; xiv, 12, 22; xviii, 36-8.
[15] BG., xiv, 5-9, 12, 16-7.

the first six are perceptible through the mind (manas).[16] Merit and demerit are imperceptible. Cognition is prior to feeling; feeling is prior to desire; desire is prior to volition. Cognition is the cause of feeling; feeling is the cause of desire; desire is the cause of volition. Volition is the cause of action. Good actions produce merits. Bad actions produce demerits. Pleasure and pain are positive opposite feelings. Desire, aversion and volition constitute conation. Pleasure produces desire. Pain produces aversion. Desire and aversion are opposite conative tendencies. Desire produces positive volition (pravṛtti). Aversion produces negative volition (nivṛtti). Positive volition produces action to appropriate the good. Negative volition produces action to reject the evil. A moral action produces merit (dharma). An immoral action produces demerit (adharma). Thus the Nyāya-Vaiśeṣika advocates the tripartite classification of mental modes. It recognizes the different grades of intellectual experience, viz., indeterminate perception resembling sensation, determinate perception, subconscious impression (saṁskāra), memory, imagination, reasoning and intuition. Impressions are imperceptible. They produce recollections. Emotions are due to intellectual confusion (moha). Actions are due to attachment (rāga), aversion (dveṣa) and delusion (moha). Thus the Nyāya-Vaiśeṣika tends towards intellectualism.

2. *The Sāṁkhya*

The Sāṁkhya holds that essence (sattva), energy (rajas) and inertia (tamas) produce pleasure, pain and delusion (moha) respectively; and that sattva produces knowledge and that rajas produces volition and action.[17] Thus a distinction is made among cognition, feeling and volition. Perception, memory, reasoning, and intuition are different kinds of cognition. Perception is either indeterminate or determinate. Pleasure, pain and delusion are feelings. Volitions are expressed in actions. The sense organs give indeterminate perception. The mind (manas) doubts. The self-sense (ahaṁkāra) apperceives. The intellect (buddhi) has determinate knowledge and decision to act. The three internal organs are essentially one. They act on past, present and future objects,

[16] VS., i, 1, 6; NS., i, 1, 10.
[17] SK., 12; SKG., 12: SK., 13; SPB., i, 127.

while the external sense organs act on present objects.[18] Knowledge constitutes the essence of the self. But feeling, volition and action belong to buddhi, which are attributed to the self. Pleasure and pain exist in the self as reflections of mental modes.[19] Attachment, aversion and consequent volitions and actions are due to false knowledge, Feelings and volitions are attributed to the self owing to non-discrimination between puruṣa and prakṛti—self and not-self. The mind-body-complex, an evolute of prakṛti constituted by sattva, rajas and tamas, is erroneously thought to be the self which is eternally pure, free, enlightened and devoid of guṇas.[20] Empirical knowledge is a mental mode. But transcendental knowledge is the intrinsic nature of the self.

4. *The Yoga*

The mind (citta) is made of essence (sattva), energy (rajas), and inertia (tamas). The mental modes are of five kinds, viz. valid knowledge, error, imagination, deep sleep and recollection. Perception, inference and testimony are valid knowledge. Thus the different degrees of intellectual experience are recognized. They are perception, memory, imagination, reasoning and intuition. Intuition is the result of discrimination (viveka), concentration of mind and trance. Pleasure, pain and delusion are the effects of sattva, rajas and tamas respectively. They are positive feelings. Desire, aversion and volition (yatna) are recognized. They are conative satates. Desire springs from pleasure; and aversion springs from pain. Merits and demerits are the potencies of actions (karmāśaya). Merits are the predisposing cause of pleasure. Demerits are the predisposing cause of pain. Mental modes produce subconscious impressions (saṁskāra), which, again, produce mental modes such as recollections. The wheel of mental modes and subconscious impressions revolves day and night.[21] Mental modes are tinged with afflictions (kleśa) or free from them. Ignorance (avidyā), egoism (asmitā), attachment (rāga), aversion (dveṣa) and fear of death (abhiniveśa) are afflictions. They are the springs of action. The afflictions spring from the potencies of actions, which produce emotions and passions such as lust,

[18] SK., 23-5, 27, 33.
[19] Pratibimbarūpeṇa puruṣe'pi sukha-duḥkhe staḥ. SPB., i, 1.
[20] SPB., i, 55-8.
[21] Vṛtti-saṁskāra-cakram aniśam āvartate. YBh., i, 5.

greed, infatuation, anger and the like. The stream of mind flows towards good when it tends towards discrimination (viveka) of the self from the not-self. It flows towards evil when it tends towards non-discrimination (aviveka). There are five conditions of the mind. (1) It is distracted (kṣipta) when it flits from object to object owing to the predominance of rajas. (2) It is deluded (mūḍha) when it is lazy, drowsy or infatuated. (3) It is occasionally steady (vikṣipta) when it is fixed on an object for some time in the midst of its unsettled condition. (4) It is concentrated (ekāgra) when it is focussed on one object. (5) It is restrained (niruddha) when all mental modes are arrested leaving only subconscious impressions behind.[22] All kinds of cognition, feeling and conation are modes of the mind (buddhi) which is a modification of prakṛti. The self erroneously identifies itself with them, and regards them as its qualities owing to ignorance (avidyā) or non-discrimination (aviveka), when it acquires an intuition of itself due to discrimination, it ceases to be influenced by avidyā.[23] The Yoga recognizes consciousness, subconsciousness, unconsciousness and superconsciousness.

5. *The Vedānta*

Śaṁkara distinguishes between the empirical self (jīva) and the transcendental self (ātman), and regards the former as the individual self and the latter as the infinite and universal self. The ātman is pure subject—objectless transcendental consciousness (cit). The empirical self is the Ātman limited by mind (manas), intellect (buddhi), egoism (ahaṁkāra) and the sense-organs. It is the knower (jñātā), the enjoyer (bhoktā) and the active agent (kartā). The distinction of cognition, feeling and volition is recognized. The internal organ (antaḥkaraṇa) is made of sattva, rajas and tamas. Sattva produces knowledge and pleasure. Rajas produces pain, attachment, aversion, passions, volition and action. Tamas produces nescience (ajñāna) and delusion. Sattva produces merit. Rajas produces demerit.[24] Perception, memory, imagination, reasoning and intuition are the different kinds of cognition.

[22] Kṣiptaṁ, mūḍhaṁ, vikṣiptam, ekāgraṁ, niruddham iti cittabhūmayaḥ. YBh., i, 1.

[23] YBh., i, 1, 2, 5, 11, 12, 13, 24, 50; ii, 3, 7, 8, 12, 14, 23-5.

[24] VCM., 106, 113-4, 118-21; Pañcadaśī, ii, 14-5; VSR., pp. 17-8; SBS., i, 1, 17, 31; i, 2, 12; i, 3, 7, 15; i, 4, 1.

Pleasure, pain and neutral feeling are the different kinds of feeling. Bliss is the highest happiness. Desire, aversion, resolution and volition are the conative states. Actions are mental, vocal and organic. They produce merits and demerits. They are imperceptible like subconscious impressions (saṁskāra). The superconscious, the conscious, the subconscious and the unconscious are recognized as the different degrees of consciousness. All these are mental modes which do not belong to the pure self (ātman) which is pure homogeneous consciousness. It can be experienced by integral knowledge (samyagjñāna) on the complete destruction of nescience.[25]

6. *The Jaina*

The Jaina advocates the tripartite classification of the modes of consciousness. All plants experience merely feeling. All animals experience feeling and conative impulse. All persons experience feeling, conation and cognition. In order of development feeling comes first, then conation, and then cognition. The embodied self has knowledge and perception of external objects, desires pleasure and dreads pain, acts for the attainment of good or the avoidance of evil, and experiences pleasure or pain. It is a knower, an experiencer (bhoktā) and an agent (kartā). A liberated soul has infinite knowledge (jñāna), infinite perception (darśana), infinite happiness (sukha) and infinite power (vīrya).[26] Thus the distinction of cognition, feeling and conation is clearly recognized. There are five kinds of cognition: sensuous knowledge, testimony, clairvoyant knowledge, telepathic knowledge of other minds, and omniscience. Perception, memory, recognition, reasoning and intuition are the different kinds of cognition. Pleasure, pain and indifference are the three kinds of feeling. Attachment, aversion and delusion are affective-conative states. Emotions, passions, instncts and volitions are recognized.[27]

7. *The Buddhist*

There is no permanent self. There is only a series of mental modes. The distinction of cognition, feeling and volition

[25] SBS., ii, 2, 11, 13; ii, 3, 16, 18, 41, 42, 51; iii, 1, 10, 11; iii, 2, 6-9, 24.
[26] DS., DSV., 4-5, 9; PK., 38-40, 125, 129-33.
[27] TS., i, 9, 11-13, 23, 29; viii, 9. HIP., ii, pp. 249-52.

is recognized. Cognition is prior to feeling; feeling is prior to craving or conation. Perception, memory, reasoning and intuition are the different kinds of cognition. Pleasure, pain and indifference are the different kinds of feeling. Emotions, passions and instincts are recognized. Thinking produces volition. Volition produces action. Actions are mental, bodily and verbal. Composite mental states and synthetic mental activity are recognized.[28]

8. *The Kinds of Sensations*

According to the Jaina, there are five kinds of sensations, tactual, gustatory, olfactory, visual and auditory. Lightness, heaviness, softness, hardness, roughness, smoothness, cold and heat are tactual sensations. Temperature, pressure and motor sensations are included in them. Pungent, bitter, sweet, sour and saline are gustatory sensations. Agreeable odour and disagreeable odour are olfactory sensations. Black, blue, yellow, white and pink are visual sensations. Human, natural, musical and non-musical sounds are auditory sensations. Musical sounds of drums (tata), musical sounds of stringed instruments (vitata), musical sounds of bells (ghana), sounds of conches (suṣira), etc., are mentioned.[29] The Buddhist recognizes five kinds of sensations, viz., visual, auditory, olfactory, gustatory and tactual. Colour and form are the two objects of visual sensations. Blue, red, yellow and white are colour sensations. Form is arrangement of parts. There are eight kinds of forms, viz. round, circular, high, low, long, short, pointed and blunt. Mist, shade, sun-light, moon-light, darkness, cloud, steam and dust have colours which are subordinate. There are eight kinds of sounds, viz. sounds uttered by beings with the aid of the elements, and sounds produced by the elements without the aid of beings, each being either pleasant or unpleasant. There are four kinds of odours, viz. strong, weak, good and bad. There are eleven kinds of touch, viz. four kinds of contact with earth, water, fire and air, cold, smooth, rough, light, heavy, hunger and thirst. Hunger and thirst are due to contact with the tactual organ within the body. There are six kinds of taste, viz. sweet, sour, saline, pungent, astringent and bitter.[30] The

[28] HIP., ii, pp. 313-7; BPs., pp. 47, 49-50, 84-91; CP., pp. 1-16.
[29] HIP., ii, p. 250. [30] AKV., i, 10.

Nyāyā-Vaiśeṣika recognizes five kinds of sensations, visual, gustatory, olfactory, tactual and auditory. White, blue, yellow, red, green, brown and motley colours are visual sensations. These colours are either bright or non-bright. Sweet, bitter, pungent, astringent, sour, saline and variegated tastes are gustatory sensations. Agreeable odour and disagreeable odour are olfactory sensations. Hot, cold, neither hot nor cold, hard and soft are tactual sensations. Temperature, pressure and motor sensations are included in them. Sound is an auditory sensation. Sounds are uttered human sounds (varṇa) and unuttered natural sounds (dhvani). Language consists of uttered sounds. The sound of a drum is a natural sound. Sounds are loud or faint. They are of different degrees of intensity. A distinction is made between a manifest (udbhūta) or sensible sensation and an unmanifest (anudbhūta) or infra-sensible sensation.[31]

Caraka refers to different theories of taste. Bhadrakāpya recognizes one kind of taste which is an object of gustatory perception. Śākunteya recognizes two kinds of taste whose properties are cutting and curbing. The former removes all bad humours from the body, while the latter only checks them. Maudgalya recognizes three kinds of taste whose properties are cutting, curbing and both. Kauśika admits four kinds of taste, viz. agreeable and wholesome, agreeable and unwholesome, disagreeable and wholesome, and disagreeable and unwholesome. Bhardvāja admits five kinds of taste appertaining to earth, water, fire, air and ether (ākāśa). Vāryovida admits six kinds of taste, viz. heavy, light, cold, hot, oily and dry. Nimi recognizes seven kinds of taste, viz. sweet, sour, saline, pungent, bitter, astringent and caustic (kṣāra). Dhāmārgava recognizes eight kinds of taste, viz. sweet, sour, saline, pungent, bitter, astringent, caustic and unmanifest (avyakta). Kāṅkāyana holds that tastes are infinite in number in consequence of the infinite variety of their substrates, virtues, effects and methods of correction. Punarvasu holds that there are only six kinds of taste, viz. sweet, sour, saline, pungent, bitter and astringent. The agreeable and disagreeable nature of tastes arises not from anything in the nature of tastes themselves but from the likes and dislikes of persons, so that what is agreeable to one may be disagreeable to another. The

[31] TK., p. 4; TSC., pp. 21-2, 28; TBh., pp. 24, 26; BhP., 100-4, 164; SM., pp. 410-3; VSU., vii, 1, 4; SP., pp. 20, 27-8; KR., pp. 52-8.

wholesome and unwholesome nature of tastes is due to their powers. It does not constitute the essential nature of tastes. The substances, in which tastes reside, are heavy, light, cold, hot, oily and dry, which are not tastes. Punarvasu does not regard caustic (kṣāra) as a taste because it is capable of being seen, touched and smelt. It is a combination of many objects which are perceived through different sense-organs, while taste is perceived through the olfactory organ only. Unmanifestness is the perception of a common taste devoid of its special qualities such as sweet, sour and the like. The substances in which tastes reside are innumerable. But tastes are not innumerable. Hence there are six tastes.[32] Caraka recognizes sixty three 'tastes' under the influence of substances, place and time.[33]

Caraka describes and explains perception, recollection, inference, supernormal mental processes and intuition. Perception is distinct knowledge produced by the intercourse of the sense-organs with their objects, the relation of the sense-organs to manas, and the relation of manas to the self. It is the knowledge of the real nature of an object at the time. Cakrapāṇi mentions six kinds of the sense-object-intercourse: (1) union, (2) inherence, (3) united inherence, (4) united inherent inherence, (5) inherent inherence, and (6) subject-predicate relation. There is external perception of sensibl objects. There is internal perception of pleasure, pain and the like.

Perception is different from doubt, illusion and other kinds of wrong knowledge, recollection and inference.[34] Non-perception is due to great proximity, great distance, barrier, weakness of the sense-organs, inattention, non-discrimination from a group of similar objects, being overpowered, and great minuteness. Collyrium in the eye is not perceived owing to its great proximity. A bird soaring high in the sky is not perceived owing to its great distance. A jar hidden behind a wall is not perceived owing to a barrier. Whiteness of a cloth is not perceived by the eyes affected by jaundice. The speech of a person near by is not heard by one whose attention is focussed on one's beloved woman's face. An orange which is in intercourse with the visual organ is not perceived because it is in a heap of similar fruits from which it cannot be discriminated. A meteor in the day time is not

[32] CS., i, 26; 8-9; CPV.
[33] Ibid, 14-23.
[34] Ibid., i, 11, 20; CPV.

perceived owing to its being overpowered by the rays of the sun. Too minute worms are not perceived even at a distance of five or six feet.[35]

Recollection is due to the perception of a cause, (2) the perception of a form, (3) similarity, (4) contrast, (5) attention, (6) habit, (7) true knowledge of reality, and (8) the perception of a part. An effect is recalled on the perception of its cause. The perception of a wild cow (gavaya) in a forest reminds one of a cow. One's father is remembered on the perception of his son similar to him. An ugly person is recalled on the perception of a beautiful person. A person fixing his mind on an object to be remembered recalls it. An object frequently perceived is easily recalled on account of habit. A person who has acquired the true knowledge of reality (tattvajñāna) remembers all things by virtue of it. When a part is perceived, the whole is recalled. When a part of a verse learned repeatedly is heard, the whole verse is recalled.[36]

Inference is preceded by perception. It cognizes the past, the present and the future. It depends upon the knowledge of the invariable concomitance between a probans and a probandum. It depends upon the perception of a probans and the recollection of the uniform relation between it and a probandum. A past cause is inferred from its effect. A future effect is inferred from its cause. A present object (e.g., odour) is inferred from its invariable correlate (e.g., colour).[37]

Intuition is derived from trance by a person who has spiritual knowledge, who performs righteous deeds, whose mind abounds in purity (sattva) untainted by energy (rajas) and inertia (tamas), and is free from fear, attachment, aversion, greed, delusion and pride.[38] The knowledge of the mental processes of other persons, clairvoyance, clairaudience, perception of supersensible objects, knowledge of past, remote and future objects, recollection of the real nature of all objects, perception of imperceptible objects at will, and non-perception of perceptible objects at will are due to supernatural powers born of meditation or concentration of the mind full of purity (sattva) but free from energy (rajas) and inertia (tamas) on the self.[39]

[35] Ibid, i, 11, 8; CPV.
[36] Ibid, iv, 1, 148-9; CPV.
[37] Ibid, i, 11, 21-2.
[38] Ibid, i, 11, 29.
[39] Ibid, iv, 1, 140-1.

CHAPTER IV

PLEASURE AND PAIN

1. *The Nature of Pleasure*

Kaṇāda (300 B.C.) says: "Pleasure and pain are different from each other, since they arise from the cognitions of a desirable object and an undesirable object, and are hostile to each other".[1] Praśastapāda (400 A.D.) defines pleasure as an agreeable feeling.[2] In the presence of desirable objects such as garlands of flowers, sandal-paste, women and the like pleasure arises from the conjunction of the mind (manas) with the self, the intercourse of the sense-organs with the objects, the perception of desirable objects, merit and the like. It is in the nature of agreeableness and produces an experience of it. It is the cause of attraction towards its objects. It gives rise to organic expressions like brightness of the eyes, etc. Śrīdhara (1000 A.D.) brings out the significance of Praśastapāda's definition. Pleasure is an agreeable feeling and in the nature of favour (anugraha), gratification or satisfaction. It brings about an experience of agreeable feeling, inclines the self in its favour and produces its satisfaction. There is no pleasure apart from the self. It is a quality (guṇa) of the self and characterized by self-satisfaction. There is no pleasure which is not felt by the self. It is a subjective feeling. In pleasure the self is agreeably affected by a desirable object. Śrīdhara enumerates the following conditions of the sensory feeling of pleasure: (1) the proximity of desirable objects such as garlands, perfumery, beloved women and the like; (2) the intercourse of the objects with the appropriate sense-organs; (3) the conjunction of the self with the mind (manas); (4) the perception of the desirable objects (iṣṭopalabdhi); (5) merit (dharma); and (6) health of the organism (svasthatā).[3]

These conditions are very significant. The sensory feeling of pleasure is excited by external perceptible objects which are desirable (iṣṭa). Their mere presence does not excite pleasure. They

[1] Iṣṭāniṣṭakāraṇaviśeṣād virodhācca mithaḥ sukha-duḥkhayor arthāntara bhāvaḥ. VS., x, 1, 1.

[2] Anugrahalakṣaṇaṁ sukham. PBh., p. 259 NTD., p. 77.

[3] PBh., p. 259; NK., pp. 259-60. NVTT., i, 1, 4; pp. 81-2; ATV., p. 130.

must stimulate the sense-organs and the mind (manas), and produce the perceptions of the objects. Attention is a condition of feeling. If the mind is pre-occupied with some other objects, pleasure is not produced by desirable objects even when they are present.[4] Pleasure arises from the perception of desirable objects as conducive to the agent's good. The self does not feel pleasure when the mind is inattentive. Merit is another condition of pleasure. It is a non-empirical condition. Merit or virtue (dharma) is the peculiar trait of character acquired by the self by virtue of its past moral deeds. It is the subjective, moral, or predisposing condition of pleasure, whereas external desirable objects are its exciting conditions. Westernal psychology does not recognize merit as a subjective condition of pleasure. It also depends on the physological condition of the body. It arises from the health of the organism (svasthatā). Śrīdhara recognizes the relation of feeling to the organism, but he does not advocate the physiological theory of feeling. Pleasure produces certain expressions in the organism, e.g. brightness of the eyes (nayanaprasāda), beaming of the face (mukhaprasāda) and the like.[5]

The *Mahābhārata* defines health as the equilibrium of the bodily humours or organic equilibrium. It defines health of the mind as the equilibrium of purity or essence (sattva), energy (rajas) and inertia (tamas).[6] The *Chāndogya Upaniṣad* says that the self feels pleasure and pain only when it is invested with a body. Neither pleasure nor pain can touch it in a disembodied condition.[7] The *Mahābhārata* regards the body as the vehicle of pleasure and pain.[8] The Nyāya also considers it to be the instrument of pleasure and pain (bhogāyatana).[9]

Gautama (200 B.C.) does not deny the existence of pleasure as a positive feeling because the predominantly painful empirical life is interspersed with pleasure[10]. Vātsyāyana (400 A.D.) says: "Attachment for favourable objects and aversion to unfavourable objects are produced by false knowledge".[11] This implies that

[4] Viṣayāntaravyāsaktasya sukhānutpādāt viyuktasya sukhābhāvāt. NK., p. 260.
[5] NK., p. 260.
[6] Śāntiparva, ch. xvi, 11, 13.
[7] Aśarīraṁ vāva santaṁ na priyāpriye spṛśataḥ. viii, 12, 1.
[8] Śāntiparva, ch. 174, 21-2.
[9] NS., NBh., i, 1, 11.
[10] NS., iv, 1, 56.
[11] Mithyājñānād anukūleṣu rāgaḥ, pratikūleṣu dveṣaḥ. NBh., i, 1, 2.

pleasure is an agreeable feeling. Vācaspati Miśra (900 A.D.) defines pleasure as a favourable or agreeable feeling.[12] Udayana (1050 A.D.) also describes pleasure as a feeling characterized by favourableness.[13] It is an object of immediate experience, says Vardhamāna (1250 A.D.), by the self in which both coinhere, which are produced at the same time.[14] Pleasure and its experience cannot coexist in the self because of the atomic nature of manas. Pleasure is quickly followed by its experience. Jayasiṁhasūri (1400 A.D.) defines pleasure as joy.[15] Keśavamiśra (1300 A.D.) defines pleasure as felicity which is experienced by all as an agreeable feeling.[16] It is an object of mental perception. Annaṁbhaṭṭa (1700 A.D.) also defines pleasure as an agreeable feeling which is experienced in such a form as 'I am happy'.[17] The same object produces pleasure in one person, and pain in another. It is not pleasant or painful to all. So pleasure and pain should be defined in terms of the individual experience of each person. Pleasure is the fruit of merit.[18] It is desired for its own sake; it does not depend upon the desire for some other object. It is the ultimate end of all our prudential actions. It is not a means to some other end.[19] Viśvanātha (1700 A.D.) states it unequivocally.

The *Bhagavad Gītā* says: "Sattva illumines owing to its transparence and gives rise to cognition. It is free from pain due to disease and thus gives rise to pleasure. Therefore it binds the self to cognition and pleasure."[20] Sattva, rajas and tamas are the constituents of the mind. They are purity or essence, energy and inertia. Sattva is the cause of cognition and pleasure which are its modifications. When sattva predominates over rajas and tamas and removes the veil, as it were, from the mental mode, it catches a reflection of the self owing to its transparence and is transformed into cognition and pleasure. Pleasure is not a quality of cognition. Both are modes of the mind (antaḥkaraṇa). Empirical pleasure is a concomitant of empirical cognition, both

[12] Sukham anukūlavedanīyam. NVTT., iv, 1, 55, p. 441.
[13] Anukūlavedanīyaṁ sukhalakṣaṇam. NVTP., i, 1, 4; p. 521.
[14] NNP., i, 1, 4; p. 521.
[15] Āhlādarūpaṁ sukham. NTD., p. 251.
[16] Prītiḥ sukham. Tacca sarvātmanām anukūlavedanīyam. TBh., p. 27.
[17] TSD., p. 91.
[18] NBh., i, 1, 20, 22; NM., p. 577; T.A., p. 11; TK., p. 17.
[19] Sukhaṁ tu jagatām eva kāmyaṁ dharmeṇa jāyate. BhP., 145, SM., p. 467.
[20] xiv, 6. Cp. xiv, 9, 11, 17.

of which are not the qualities of the pure self, but modes of the mind.[21] This is Śaṁkara's interpretation. God is the abode of absolute bliss (aikāntika sukha). Sentient pleasures due to the intercourse of the sense-organs with their objects are produced and transient and give rise to pain. But a person, whose soul is united with Brahman and devoid of attachment for empirical pleasures, enjoys imperishable bliss (akṣaya sukha) in his self. When his mind is completely restrained by the practice of meditation and absorbed in Brahman, infinite Being-Consciousness-Bliss, he acquires a beatific vision of the Self, delights in it, and shares in the supreme bliss of Brahman, which is supersensible and comprehended by the intellect or reason.[22]

According to the Sāṁkhya and the Yoga, sattva, rajas and tamas produce pleasure, pain and dejection respectively. They are the constituents of the mind (antaḥkaraṇa). Pleasure is delight or felicity.[23] It is a mode of the mind, and not a quality of the self which is detached (niḥsaṅga). Pleasure, pain and the like are unconscious modes of buddhi which is an evolute of prakṛti. They are not qualities of the self which is entirely different from prakṛti and its modes. The conscious self is reflected on the unconscious mental modes of pleasure, etc., and erroneously thinks them to be its qualities. This is the view of Vācaspati Miśra.[24] Though pleasure and pain are unconscious modes of the mind, the conscious self appropriates them because of its reflection on them and their reflection on it owing to non-discrimination.[25] This is the view of Vijñānabhikṣu (1600 A.D.). The self experiences pleasure and pain which are the fruits of merits and demerits, and the modes of buddhi owing to non-discrimination.[26] Sattva is the predominant element of buddhi. When desire which involves suffering is renounced, great happiness

[21] Jñānam iti sukhasāhacaryāt antaḥkaraṇasya dharmo, nātmanaḥ. SBG., xiv, 6.

[22] Sukhham ātyantikaṁ yat tadbuddhigrāhyam atīndriyam. BG., vi, 21. BG., xiv, 27; v, 21, 22; vi, 20.

[23] Prītiḥ sukham. SSV., i, 127. SPS., SPB., i, 127; STK., 12 Sukhānuśayī rāgah. YBh., i, 11. YS., ii, 7.

[24] Buddhitattvasya sukhādayo'pi pariṇāmabhedā acetanāḥ, puruṣas tu sukhādyananuṣaṅgī cetanaḥ, so'yaṁ buddhitattvavartinā jñānasukhādinā tatpratibimbitas tacchāyāpattyā jñānasukhādimān iva bhavati. STK., 5, pp. 86-7.

[25] Sukhaduḥkhaguṇānām cittadharmatve'pi ātmani pratibimbarūpeṇāvasthitiḥ avivekāt. SPB., vi, 11.

[26] SPS., SPB., i, 105.

emerges owing to the pre-eminence of sattva. Desirelessness is supreme happiness.[27]

Patañjali says: "Birth, length of life and experience are filled with pleasure and pain because of merit and demerit."[28] Pleasure and pain, Vyāsa (400 A.D.) asserts, are modifications of buddhi and attributed to the transcendental self (puruṣa) owing to non-discrimination. It erroneously thinks them to be its qualities.[29] False knowledge (avidyā) is the cause of the self's experience of pleasure and pain (bhoga).[30] The conjunction of the conscious self (draṣṭṛ) and the unconscious not-self (dṛśya) is the cause of empirical life. Attachment is directed towards pleasure.[31] It depends upon the recollection of pleasure which was caused by an object on a previous occasion.[32] Desire for an object the like of which caused pleasure in the past depends upon the recollection of pleasure. Attachment for recalled pleasure depends upon the recollection of it. Experienced pleasure does not depend upon the recollection of it. When an object of pleasure is perceived or remembered, attachment for it depends upon the recollection of past pleasures.[33] Pleasure and pain, merit and demerit are mental modes due to false knowledge (avidyā) which also is a quality of the mind. They do not affect the self which is eternally pure and devoid of merit and demerit, pleasure and pain.[34]

Śaṁkara (788—820 A.D.) defines pleasure as delight or agreeable feeling which is a modification of sattva of the mind. It is a quality of the mind, and not of the self.[35] It is an object of knowledge. Madhusūdana maintains, that pleasure and pain are modes of the mind (antaḥkaraṇavṛtti); that they appear to be qualities of the self because its consciousness is reflected on the mental modes; and that the self is essentially self-luminous consciousness and bliss and devoid of empirical cognition, pleasure

[27] SPB., iv, 11.
[28] Te hlādaparitāpaphalāḥ puṇyāpuṇyahetutvāt, YS., ii, 14.
[29] YBh., ii, 18;
[30] YS., YBh., ii, 24; ii, 17;
[31] Sukhānuśayī rāgaḥ. YS., ii 9.
[32] YBh., ii, 7; TV., ii, 7.
[33] Smaryamāṇe sukhe rāgaḥ sukhānusmṛtipūrvakaḥ, anubhūyamāne tu sukhe nānusmṛtim apekṣate, tatsādhane tu smaryamāṇe dṛśyamāne vā sukhānusmṛtipūrva eva rāgaḥ. TV., ii, 7.
[34] Puruṣas tvavidyāśūnyatvāt śuddhaḥ pāpapuṇyavivarjitaḥ. Cittadharmairjanmamaraṇasukhaduḥkhādibhir aparāmṛṣṭaḥ. YV., iv, 25.
[35] Sukham āhlādah. SBG., x,4. Ibid vi, 32. Sukham anukulaṁ prasannam sattvātmakaṁ kṣetram. SBG., xiii, 6.

and pain.[36] Ānandagiri maintains, that external objects produce pleasure when they are favourable to the self, and that they produce pain when they are unfavourable to it. The same object, e.g. heat or cold, produces pleasure and pain under different circumstances.[37] Rāmānuja (1017—1137 A.D.) defines pleasure as an agreeable feeling due to attachment for a desirable object, which is an accidental quality of the self in relation to buddhi.[38] Puruṣottamajī Mahārāja defines pleasure as a quality of the mind (antaḥkaraṇa) directly experienced as a favourable feeling.[39]

The Jaina regards feelings as modifications of the soul-substance. They are due to the infra-atomic particles of matter called karma, which encrust the soul. They are due to vedanīya karma. They are the effects of the environment upon the self in an embodied condition. Brahmadeva defines pleasure as feeling of joy due to the intercourse of the sense-organs with desired objects. Pūjyapāda defines it as delight which is a modification of the self. Kundakundasvāmī regards pleasure as an object of desire which is the fruit of good action (śubha karma) and a modification of the soul.[40] It naturally seeks objects that cause pleasure. The Jaina thinkers recognize the affective value of sensations. "The feeling aspect is premoninant in the case of smell and taste whereas it is indirectly associated with auditory and visual sensations."[41]

Caraka traces pleasure and pain to the harmony and disharmony of the elements and humours of the body, viz. flatulence, bile and phlegm, and to the equipoise or disequilibrium of purity (sattva), energy (rajas) and inertia (tamas) of the mind respectively.[42] The body endowed with the sense-organs and the mind both are the abodes of pleasure and pain.[43] The body is the source of physical pleasure and pain. The mind is the source of mental pleasure and pain. The proper adjustment of the mind and the sense-organs to their objects is the cause of pleasure. The

[36] MBG., ii, 14; ii, 56.

[37] ĀBG., ii, 14.

[38] RBG., ii, 56; xiii, 6.

[39] Aṇubhāṣyaprakāśa (B.S.S.), 1907, p. 1121.

[40] Prītiparitāparūpaḥ pariṇāmaḥ sukhaduḥkham. SS., v, 20. TAS., v, 27; DSV., 9; PKS., TDTD., 122.

[41] A. Chakravarty: Introduction: PKS., p. xlii.

[42] Vikāro dhātu-vaiṣamyaṁ sāmyaṁ prakṛtir ucyate.
Sukha-saṁjñakam ārogyaṁ vikāro duḥkham eva ca.
C.S., i, 9, 4; CPV..

[43] Vedanānām adhiṣṭhānaṁ manaḥ dehaś ca sendriyaḥ. Ibid, iv, 1, 136.

improper adjustment of the internal and external organs to their objects is the cause of pain. Improper adjustment consists in the over-functioning (atiyoga), under-functioning (hīnayoga), or non-functioning (ayoga) of the organs in relation to their objects. Neither the sense-organs nor their objects are the causes of pleasure and pain. But the four kinds of adjustments of them to their objects are the causes of pleasure and pain. Merits and demerits are the subjective causes of pleasure and pain respectively.[44]

Caraka maintains that there is a reciprocal relation between feeling and desire. Pleasure is the cause of desire. Pain is the cause of aversion. Desire also is a cause of pleasure. Aversion also is a cause of pain. When a desire is fulfilled, it gives rise to pleasure. When a desire is not fulfilled, it gives rise to pain. Both desire and aversion are different kinds of desire (tṛṣṇā).[45] Pleasure and pain are mental modes. The self which is free from all modes of mind (manas) appears to experience them owing to its association and false identification with manas. When the mind is concentrated on the self and acquires a pure vision of it, pleasure and pain are no longer experienced.[46] Pleasure, pain and deluson (moha) are the effects of the excess of purity (sattva), energy (rajas) and inertia (tamas) over the other two constituents of the mind. They are not modifications of the self which is immutable, but of the mind.[47] Thus Caraka follows the Sāṁkhya to this extent. He adds the physiological theory of pleasure and pain to the Sāṁkhya view. Voluntary actions (pravṛtti) always seek sentient pleasure and lead to pain in our empirical life. Renunciation of voluntary actions (nivṛtti) leads to the cessation of desires, and, consequently, to happiness. Here Caraka agrees with the Nyāya and the Sāṁkhya.[48] Sentient pleasure is not real happiness which springs from desirelessness. So Caraka distinguishes between sentient pleasure and supersensuous happiness.

2. *Kinds of Pleasure*

Praśastapāda mentions four kinds of pleasure: (1) sensuous pleasure; (2) retrospective pleasure; (3) prospective pleasure; and (4) happiness. Sensuous pleasure arises from the perception of

[44] Ibid, iv, 1, 129-32.
[45] Icchā-dveṣātmikā tṛṣṇā sukha-duḥkāt pravartate.
Tṛṣṇā ca sukha-duḥkhānāṁ kāraṇaṁ punar ucyate. Ibid, iv, 1, 134.
[46] Ibid, iv, 1, 138-9. [47] CPV., CS., iv, 4, 34, 37.
[48] Pravṛttir duḥkham, nivṛttiḥ sukham. Ibid, iv, 5, 8.

desirable objects in intercourse with the sense-organs. Retrospective pleasure arises from the recollection of past objects of enjoyment.[49] It is a pleasure of reminiscence. Prospective pleasure arises from the anticipation of future objects of enjoyment.[50] Besides these pleasures arising from the perception of present objects, the recollection of past objects, and the expectation of future objects of enjoyment, there is another superior kind of pleasure, which is felt by the wise independently of desire for enjoyment, recollection of past objects, or anticipation of future objects, and which arises from their wisdom, tranquillity, contentment and a peculiar merit.[51] Wisdom is the true knowledge of the self. Tranquillity is perfect self-control. Contentment is the absence of desire for more than bare necessities for the preservation of life. The peculiar merit is the highest excellence of virtue which makes the self completely independent of objects of enjoyment. These four virtues are the causes of this superior kind of pleasure of the wise called happiness.[52] It is rational and abiding while sensuous pleasure is physical and temporary. Happiness arises from the conquest of desires whereas pleasure springs from the gratification of desires. Praśastapāda preferred rational happiness to bodily pleasure like Epicurus. But he considered it to be higher than sensuous pleasure for its intrinsic excellence like John Stuart Mill.

Śivāditya (1000 A.D.) mentions two kinds of pleasure: (1) worldly pleasures; and (2) heavenly pleasure.[53] The former is empirical pleasure which is invariably followed by pain whereas the latter is transcendental bliss which is unalloyed joy.[54] The former is produced by our own efforts, and depends upon objects like garlands, perfumery, etc. whereas the latter is produced by mere desire and does not require any effort. Heavenly bliss is at the command of mere will, and not followed by pain. Worldly pleasure is produced by objects generated by human efforts. Heavenly bliss is produced by objects created by a mere fiat of will.[55] Jayanta Bhaṭṭa (1000 A.D.) describes heaven as the

[49] Atīteṣu viṣayeṣu smṛtijam. PBh., p. 259.
[50] Anāgatesu saṅkalpajam. PBh., p. 259.
[51] Yat tu viduṣāṁ tad vidyā-śama-sontoṣa-dharmaviśeṣa-nimittam. PBh., p. 259.
[52] NK., p. 260.
[53] Sukhaṁ sāṁsārikaṁ svargaś ca. SP., p. 26.
[54] MB., p. 26.
[55] SP., p. 69; MB., p. 69.

highest bliss.[56] Śaṅkaramiśra (1500 A.D.) describes heaven as the happiness, which is not intercepted by pain, which does not perish, which is unbroken and continuous, and which is generated by mere will.[57] Jayanārāyaṇa (1700 A.D.) contrasts heavenly happiness with worldly pleasure. The former is rational happiness which is absolutely free from pain; it is not pleasure of the body which is a cause of pain. The latter is physical pleasure which is followed by pain.[58] The *Mahābhārata* describes heavenly happiness as enduring and free from pain, and worldly pleasure as temporary and attended with pain. Worldly pleasure and pain are followed by each other in a cycle. Pain arises from ungratified desire. Pleasure arises from the removal of pain. Pleasure and pain are followed by each other in a cycle. They are not eternal but temporary. Empirical life is interspersed with pleasure and pain. Sentient pleasure (kāmasukha) due to the gratification of an isolated desire is not even a fraction of heavenly happiness (divyasukha) due to the cessation of all desires.[59] Praśastapāda describes the highest bliss in an embodied condition as due to the intuition of the Supreme Self, which springs from the extirpation of attachment and aversion and the consequent exhaustion of merits and demerits and the non-production of them in future. The happiness of contentment due to the conquest of desires and the right knowledge of the six categories of reality precedes this highest transcendental bliss, which precedes the absolute freedom (mokṣa) of the self devoid of all empirical contents. Mokṣa is the absolute extinction of pleasure and pain and the existence of the self in its intrinsic state. It transcends the state of heavenly happiness which is continuous unalloyed joy in a disembodied condition but subject to termination. It is followed by an embodied condition of the self and recurrence of bodily pleasure and pain.[60] Heavenly happiness is a hypothetical condition of the self. But transcendental bliss due to the eradication of attachment and aversion and the intuition of the Absolute Self is experienced by saints in the embodied state.

Udayana (1050 A.D.) mentions four kinds of empirical pleasure: (1) habitual pleasure; (2) pleasure of self-conceit;

[56] Svargo hi niratiśayā prītiḥ. NM., p. 505.
[57] KR., p. 123.
[58] Śāstrārthasaṅgraha, p. 377.
[59] Śāntiparva, ch. 190, 14; ch. 174, 19-21, 48.
[60] PBh., pp. 281-2; NK., pp. 282-3.

(3) sentient pleasure; and (4) anticipatory pleasure. Habitual (ābhyāsika) pleasure is derived from the habitual exercise of the limbs, for example, in hunting. Pleasure of self-conceit (ābhimānika) is the pleasure of pride derived from the use of articles of luxury, (e.g. sandal paste). Sentient (vaiṣayika) pleasure is derived from tht enjoyment of sensible objects, e.g. fragrant smell, sweet taste, musical sound, etc. Anticipatory (mānorathika) pleasure is derived from the anticipation of a future object of enjoyment, e.g. the son's birth day festivities. These pleasures are experienced as different from one another. An anticipatory pleasure is not identical with a sentient pleasure. A hungry person anticipates the pleasure of enjoying sweets in future until they are actually present to his sense-organs. But as soon as they are present he actually enjoys them and feels sentient pleasure. He never confuses anticipatory pleasure with sentient pleasure. They are produced by different causes and are different in kinds.[61] Śaṅkaramiśra (1500 A.D.) also describes these four kinds of pleasure. Physical (vaiṣayika) pleasure is produced by desired objects in intercourse with the sense-organs. Mental (mānorathika) pleasure is anticipatory pleasure. Pleasure of self-conceit (ābhimānika) is due to the false attribution of attributes of the not-self to the self. Habitual (ābhyāsika) pleasure is a bodily pleasure due to the habitual exercise of the limbs.[62] Śrīkṛṣṇa Dhūrjaṭi Dīkṣita also mentions these four kinds of pleasure, but describes their nature differently. Physical (vaiṣayika) pleasure is produced by the perception of external objects. Mental (mānorathika) pleasure is produced by the recollection or anticipation of past or future objects. Pleasure of self-conceit (ābhimānika) is due to the pride of wealth, the pride of power, the pride of learning, etc. Habitual (ābhyāsika) pleasure is produced by the repeated practice of a certain act, e.g. bowing to the sun. It is ease or facility due to habit.[63]

Mukunda Sharmā mentions two kinds of pleasure, physical and mental. The intercourse of external objects with the sense-organs is the efficient cause of physical pleasure. Cognition is the efficient cause of mental pleasure. The conjunction of the self with the mind (manas) is the non-inherent cause, and the self is

[61] NVTP., i, 1, 4; pp. 526-7.
[62] KR., p. 122.
[63] Siddhāntacandrodaya quoted in Nyāyakośa (1928), p. 1025.

the inherent cause of both kinds of pleasure. Pleasures are transient and exist for two moments. They depend upon merit which brings about the intercourse of the objects with the sense-organs or the contact of the self with the mind (manas).[64]

The Jaina recognizes three kinds of pleasure: physical, mental and spiritual. Spiritual pleasure is the feeling of freedom of the soul from the burden of karma-particles which encrust the soul. It is independent of the senses.[65] Affective consciousness or feeling is of three kinds: pleasure (śubha bhāva), pain (aśubha bhāva) and pure feeling (śuddha bhāva). Pure feeling is the innate bliss of the self, which is infinite, eternal and independent of the senses. It is the spiritual experience of the pure self. It is the enjoyment of the self by itself. It is supersensible spiritual bliss due to the experience of the innate purity of the self. It is not due to vedanïya karma.[66]

The *Bhagavad Gītā* mentions three kinds of pleasure: (1) tāmasa; (2) rājasa; and (3) sāttvika. The pleasure arising from sleep, laziness and inadvertence, which produces delusion at the beginning and at the end, is tāmasa. This is the lowest kind of pleasure. The pleasure which is produced by the intercourse of the sense-organs with their objects, which is experienced like nectar at the beginning and like poison at the end, is rājasa. It is sentient pleasure which produces a painful consequence. It is higher than tāmasa pleasure which infatuates the mind with delusion. The pleasure which springs from cheerfulness due to the intuition of the self, which is experienced like poison at the beginning, and like nectar at the end, is sāttvika. It is non-empirical, non-sentient, transcendental bliss due to the vision of the self or union with Brahman. It is the highest pleasure different in kind from sentient pleasure which arises from the gratification of a desire. It is supreme delight in the self and due to the complete renunciation or transformation of desires. Transparence or cheerfulness of mind springs from complete self-control, control of the sense-organas, manas and buddhi. When it is attained all sufferings are destroyed.[67]

According to the Advāita Vedānta, pleasure is not a quality

[64] TSC., p. 77.
[65] C. R. Jain: *Jaina Psychology*, p. 48.
[66] Saṁsāraviṣayātītaṁ siddhānāṁ avyayaṁ sukhaṁ. TSar., viii. 45. DSV., 9.
[67] BG., xviii, 37-9; ii, 55, 64, 65.

of the self but a mode of the mind. Śaṁkara says: "Pleasure is an object of knowledge, and, consequently, cannot be a quality of the knowing self. It is a modification of the internal organ or of its sattva."[68] Pleasure is a function of sattva, a constituent of buddhi.[69] It appears to be a quality of the self owing to nescience (avidyā). Rāmakṛṣṇādhari observes, that pleasure is in the nature of an effect, being a mode of the sattva of the internal organ (antaḥkaraṇa); that as a mental mode receives a reflection of a particle of consciousness of the transcendental self (caitanya) it is transformed into an empirical cognition; and that as it receives a reflection of a particle of bliss of the transcendental self it is transformed into an empirical pleasure. He further observes, that empirical pleasure is produced by external objects, e.g. garlands, perfumery, etc., in intercourse with the sense-organs: and that it is subject to quantitative variation. There are different degrees of empirical pleasure. A king's pleasure is greater than ours in quantity; the pleasure of a sovereign of the world is greater than that of a king; the pleasure of the Lord of heaven is greater than that of the sovereign of the world.[70] The different degrees of empirical pleasure depend upon different degrees of contact with external objects of enjoyment.

Dharmarājādhvarīndra recognizes two kinds of pleasure: (1) relative or empirical pleasure (sātiśaya sukha); and (2) absolute or transcendental bliss (niratiśaya sukha). The former is sentient pleasure due to the peripheral stimulation of the sense-organs by external objects and subject to increase and decrease. The latter is the highest bliss which constitutes the essence of the transcendental self and is due to the complete destruction of avidyā.[71] Avidyā is the false knowledge of the not-self or the mind-body-complex as the self. It is the erroneous identification of the empirical self with the pure self or transcendental self. The empirical self is the pure self limited by the adjuncts of manas, buddhi and ahaṁkāra. It is the psychological me, the object self. The transcendental self is pure consciousness beyond the distinction of subject and object. Transcendental or absolute bliss is not subject to increase or decrease. It is infinite (akhaṇḍānanda) bliss. It may be asked: If empirical pleasure is due to reflection of a particle of bliss of the transcendental self on a mental mode owing

[68] SBG., xiv, 6.
[69] ACK., pp. 67, 383.
[70] Śikhāmaṇi on VP., p. 407.
[71] VP., pp. 406-7.

to its proximity, why should there not be reflection of the highest bliss of the transcendental self on a mental mode so that it may be transformed into the highest bliss? Amaradāsa replies, that in empirical life the highest bliss of the transcendental self is covered by cosmic nescience (mūlāvidyā) like its highest intuition. When the empirical self (jīva) realizes its identity with the transcendental self (ātman) or Absolute (Brahman) and attains liberation, it realizes the transcendental bliss.[72] Empirical pleasure is non-eternal while transcendental bliss is eternal. Gaṅgeśa criticizes the Advaita Vedānta view.[73]

The Yoga distinguishes between sentient pleasure and rational happiness. The former is due to the gratification of desires, while the latter is due to the eradication of desires. The former is due to the impurity of attachment, while the latter is due to the washing off of all impurities of the mind. When the mind is purified, its intrinsic purity (sattva) emerges, which generates happiness. It makes the mind unperturbed and concentrated. The concentration of mind leads to the conquest of the sense-organs. It makes the mind fit for receiving an intuition of the pure self. When desires are extirpated, the mind is filled with contentment which generates rational happiness which is objectless. The Yoga distinguishes between empirical pleasure and heavenly happiness. The former is due to desires and external objects, while the latter is objectless and desireless and produced by objects created by a mere fiat of will.[74] Heavenly happiness is not unalloyed bliss but mingled with a little pain because the mind (citta) composed of sattva, rajas and tamas is not yet destroyed. Sattva produces pleasure, and rajas produces pain. But, according to the Nyāya-Vaiśeṣika and the Mīmāṁsaka, heavenly happiness is unalloyed bliss.[75]

According to the Mīmāṁsakas, there are two kinds of pleasure: (1) empirical (sāṁsārika) pleasure; and (2) transcendental (pāramārthika) pleasure. The first kind depends upon empirical objects and conditions and is produced by efforts. The second

[72] Maṇiprabhā, p. 408.
[73] TC., ii, Muktivāda, pp. 46-7. (B. I.).
[74] Santoṣād anuttamaḥ sukhalābhaḥ. YS., ii, 42. Tṛṣṇākṣayo hi santoṣaḥ. Nirviṣayaṁ śāntisukham. Kāmasukhaṁ kāmebhyo laukikaviṣayebhyaḥ sukhaṁ divyaṁ saṁkalpamātrotthaviṣayajam. YV., ii, 42.
[75] Yadyapi svargādau sukham adhikaṁ tathāpyalpam api duḥkham bhavati. YV., ii, 14, p. 110.

kind is non-empirical heavenly bliss.[76] Empirical pleasure is associated with pain. Pleasure and pain are real qualities of the self and inhere in it. They are not phenomenal and due to limiting adjuncts as the Advaita Vedānta maintains. They are objects of mental perception. Heavenly happiness is enduring, unmixed with pain, and generated by mere volition. Persons bound to embodied life never experience the so-called transcendental bliss said to be the essential nature of the pure self. The Mīmāṁsaka rejects the Advaita Vedānta view.[77] This is the view of the Prābhākara Mīmāṁsaka and the Bhāṭṭa Mīmāṁsaka.

3. *Pleasure is a positive feeling*

Uddyotakara (600 A.D.) states that sometimes relief from pain is experienced as pleasure. A porter feels the negation of pain where the burden carried by him is taken off. He does not feel positive pleasure. But the experience of the negation of pain appears to be the experience of pleasure. Pleasure is attributed to the negation of pain. The sense of relief from pain appears by contrast to be pleasure, though really it is not a feeling of pleasure. In common parlance very often the removal of pain is said to be pleasure. When persons are cured of fever they are said to be happy. Thus pleasure is a positive feeling; it does not consist in mere privation of pain.[78] Śrīdhara criticizes the view that pleasure is a negative feeling or the absence of pain. It contradicts our experience of pleasure as a positive feeling of felicity. It cannot account for two kinds of actions arising from desire and aversion and leading to the acceptance of good and the rejection of evil. These two kinds of actions are fundamentally different in nature, and depend upon two distinct kinds of feeling, pleasure and pain, which are equally positive in nature.[79] Kaṇāda emphatically asserts, that pleasure and pain are different from each other because they are produced by different causes, e.g. desired and hated objects, because they cannot coexist owing to their contradiction with each other, and because they have different organic expressions, e.g. beaming face and gloomy face. Hence pleasure cannot be mere privation of pain. Pleasure and pain are equally positive feelings.[80]

[76] TC., Vol. ii, Muktivāda, pp. 46-7 (B.I).
[77] PP., pp. 149, 153, 156-7, 159-60, 184. SD., pp. 519-22.
[78] NV., i, 1, 22.
[79] NK., p. 260.
[80] VS., x, 1. 1: VSU., x, 1, 1.

Pleasure is, says Vatsyāyana, always attended with pain, and, consequently, treated as pain.[81] Pleasure is called pain in a metaphorical sense.[82] In common parlance the negation of pain is often called pleasure.[83] But Gautama does not deny the existence of pleasure as a positive feeling, since the predominantly painful empirical life is interspersed with pleasure.[84] In the midst of pain persons feel pleasure at intervals, which cannot be denied as a positive feeling.[85] Pain is a necessary element in pleasure. Pleasure cannot be attained without experiencing pain.[86] Aniruddha, a Sāṁkhaya thinker, regards pleasure as a positive feeling which is an object of mental perception, and denies that it is a mere negation of pain, though it always involves pain.[87] Śālikānātha Miśra, a Prābhākara Mīmāṁsaka, regards pleasure as a positive feeling, and not as a mere negation of pain, because the latter is in the nature of the non-apprehension of pain which is nothing but the apprehension of the self divested of pain, and because the apprehension of pleasure is distinct from that of the self.[88] Veṅkaṭanātha, a Rāmānujist, criticizes the view that pleasure is a mere negation of pain thus. If pleasure were a mere negation of pain, then pain would be a mere negation of pleasure. If in deep sleep there is no pain even in the absence of pleasure, then there is no pleasure in it even in the absence of pain. If there is the absence of pleasure as well as the absence of pain, then pleasure must be real like pain. When the pain of carrying a burden is removed, it is figuratively said to be pleasure. But the positive enjoyment of pleasure cannot be said to be a mere negation of pain.[89] Amṛtacandra Sūri, a Jaina thinker, regards the negation of pain as a kind of pleasure.[90] But he does not identify pleasure with the absence of pain. He recognizes physical pleasure, mental pleasure and spiritual pleasure besides the negative pleasure.[91]

[81] Tayā'nuviddhaṁ duḥkhayogāt duḥkham. NBh., i, 1, 21.
[82] NSV., i, 1, 21.
[83] Dṛṣṭo hi duḥkhābhāve sukhaśabdaprayogo bahulaṁ loka iti. NBh., i, 1, 22.
[84] Na sukhasyāntarālaniṣpatteḥ. NS., iv, 1, 56.
[85] Na khalu sukhasya pratyākhyānam. Niṣpadyate khalu bādhanāntarāleṣu sukhaṁ pratyātmavedanīyaṁ śarīriṇām. NBh., iv, 1, 56.
[86] NBh., iv, 1, 58.
[87] Mānasapratyakṣeṇa bhāvarūpaṁ sukham avasīyate. SSV., v, 27.
[88] Na ca duḥkhābhāvamātraṁ sukham. Duḥkhābhāvasya duḥkhānupalambharūpatvāt. PP., p. 149.
[89] TMK., pp. 662-3; SAS., p. 663.
[90] TSar., viii, 48.
[91] TSar., viii, 47.

4. *Pleasure and Pain are two irreducible feelings*

Kaṇāda regards pleasure and pain as two distinct feelings opposed to each other. In the first place, pleasure is produced by desired (iṣṭa) objects whereas pain is produced by undesired (aniṣṭa) objects. The causes being different, the effects must differ. In the second place, pleasure and pain are opposite feelings. Pleasure is an agreeable feeling, while pain is a disagreeable feeling. They cannot coexist in the self at the same time because they are contradictory to each other. In the third place, pleasure is expressed in the beaming of the face, brightness of the eyes, etc., whereas pain is expressed in paleness of the face, depression, etc. Pleasure is the cause of attraction, while pain is the cause of repulsion. Pleasure and pain have different mental effects and different organic expressions. They are experienced by all as distinct and contradictory feelings. Hence their existence as fundamental feelings cannot be denied.[92] Pleasure is not a negation of pain; pain is not a negation of pleasure. Both are positive feelings. Gautama calls pleasure and the means of pleasure pain in a figurative sense because pleasure is always attended with pain, and not because pleasure is intrinsically pain.[93] He does not deny the existence of pleasure as a positive feeling, which is experienced by all. Pleasure and pain are the fruitions of merits and demerits.[94] This is a postulate of the orthodox systems of Indian philosophy that merits are the subjective cause of the experience of pleasure, and that demerits are the subjective cause of the experience of pain. Buddhism and Jainism also believe in this postulate. Only Cārvākas deny this.

5. *Inseparable Relation of Pleasure and Pain to each other*

Vātsyāyana asserts that pleasure is inseparably related to pain. Uddyotakara gives four interpretations of the inseparable relation of pleasure to pain. (1) Wherever there is pleasure there is pain; wherever there is pain there is pleasure. (2) What is a means to pleasure is a means to pain. (3) What is a substrate of pleasure is a substrate of pain. (4) The agent who perceives pleasure

[92] VS., VSU., VSV., x, 1, 1.

[93] NS., NBh., iv, 1, 55-6. Na vai sarvalokasākṣikaṁ sukhaṁ śakyaṁ pratyākhyātum. NBh., iv, 1, 54.

[94] Sukhaduḥkhasaṁvedanaṁ phalam. NBh., i, 1, 20. TA., p. 11; TK., p. 17.

perceives pain.[95] Empirical life, Vātsyāyana observes, abounds in pain due to contact with undesirable objects such as birth, disease, old age, death and the loss of desirable objects. Birth is not intrinsically pain in a primary sense, but it is pain since it is invariably attended with pain. It is not pain because of the absence of pleasure.[96] It is pain in a derivative sense. Pain is a necessary element in pleasure; it is unattainable without pain. Pleasure arises from the gratification of a desire (kāma). But the desire for an object (e.g. wealth) can never be completely satisfied. It is increased by gratification. When one desire is fulfilled, another springs up and clamours for satisfaction. But it cannot be satisfied; it encounters insuperable obstacles. One desire is thwarted by another desire. Thus a desire leads to mental agony. A person erroneously regards pleasure as the supreme end of life, pursues it with undivided attention and inevitably comes to grief. Pleasure brings pain in its trail as an inseparable correlate.[97] Pleasure and pain are produced and transient; they exist for two moments only. They are always related to each other. Pleasure is always experienced as related to antecedent or consequent pain. Pain is always experienced as related to antecedent or consequent pleasure. There is an inseparable relation between them, though they are different from each other. Pleasure alone cannot be pursued and pain alone cannot be shunned.[98]

Vijñānabhikṣu gives a pessimistic view of worldly life. Empirical life abounds in pain which outweighs pleasure. All pleasures are pain because they are intercepted by pain.[99] Sentient pleasure inevitably brings on consequential pain.[100] Pleasure is produced by sattva which overcomes rajas. But as it is not completely suppressed by sattva it produces a little pain. So pleasure is alloyed with a little pain. It is not entirely free from pain. There is a modification of rajas in the form of subtle pain in the experience of pleasure because of the incessant activities of sattva, rajas and tamas which are in constant conflict with one another

[95] Sukhaṁ duḥkhānuṣaktam. NBh., i, 1, 2. NV., i, 1, 2.

[96] Duḥkhānuṣaṅgāt duḥkhaṁ janmeti, na sukhasyābhāvāt. Na duḥkhaṁ janma svarūpataḥ, kintu duḥkhopacārāt. NBh., iv, 1, 58.

[97] NBh., iv, 1, 53, 57-8.

[98] Yadyapi sukhduḥkhe bhinne tathāpi parasparānuṣakte. NVTT., i, 1, 3: p. 62. Nyāyasāra, Samvat 1962, Benares, p. 108.

[99] Duḥkhasaṁbhinnatvāt sarvaṁ sukhādyapi duḥkham eva. YV., ii, 15, p. 114.

[100] Viṣayasukhasya pariṇāmaduḥkhatvam. YV., ii, 15, p. 112.

in the restless mind. Ordinary persons cannot discern this subtle pain in pleasure. But a discriminating yogin can discern it, and shuns pleasure as pain. Sentient pleasure is not the supreme good. The absolute extinction of pleasure and pain is the highest good.[101]

Aniruddha shares the pessimism of Vijñānabhikṣu. According to him pain is an indispensable element of pleasure. The pursuit of pleasure entails pain and its termination brings about pain. Even the most intense and the highest pleasure is exhausted. Hence the attainment of pleasure is not the highest goal of life; but the absolute extinction of pain is the supreme end.[102]

6. *The Nature of Pain*

Kaṇāda defines pain as a feeling produced by an undesired object (aniṣṭakāraṇa)[103] Praśastapāda defines it as a disagreeable feeling characterized by the sense of unfavourableness.[104] Pain is the opposite of pleasure. But it is not a negative feeling. It is not a mere privation of pleasure. When it is produced, it brings about its experience as an unfavourable (pratikūla) feeling and repels the self from it.[105]

Praśastapāda mentions the following conditions of the sensory feeling of pain: (1) the proximity of undesirable objects such as poison and the like; (2) the intercourse of the objects with the sense-organs; (3) the conjunction of the self with manas; (4) the perception of the undesirable object (aniṣṭopalabdhi); and (5) demerit. Śrīdhara regards organic[106] equilibrium (svasthatā) as a condition of pleasure. This implies that organic disquilibrium is a condition of pain. Dr. S. K. Maitra says: "Prospect of some good to be realized by the object (iṣṭopalabdhi) is a necessary condition of pleasure." He regards "apprehension of evil" (aniṣṭopalabdhi) as a necessary condition of pain.[107] But Praśtapada analyses the sensory feelings of pleasure and pain here in which there is no distinct element of thought. Sensory pleasure arises from the perception of desirable objects; and sensory plain arises from that of undesirable objects. Perception does not rise

[101] YV., ii, 15, p. 112.
[102] SSV., vi, 5, 6, 8.
[103] VS., x, 1, 1.1
[104] Upaghātalakṣaṇaṁ duḥkham. PBh., p. 260.
[105] NK., pp. 260-1.
[106] PBh., p. 260.
[107] *The Ethics of the Hindus* (1925), pp. 194-5.

to the level of thought at this stage. There is rudimentary thought in the prospective and retrospective pleasure and pain.

Pain gives rise to the experience of it as a disagreeable feeling. It is the cause of repulsion, intolerance or aversion towards its object. It produces certain expressions in the organism, e.g. depression (dainya) or gloomy appearance (vicchāyatā).[108]

Gautama (200 B.C.) defines pain as the feeling of being thwarted.[109] Vātsyāyana explains being thwarted as suffering or agony.[110] Vātsyāyana and Udayana describe pain as a feeling characterized by disagreeableness.[111] Varadarāja, Annaṁbhaṭṭa and others also define pain as a disagreeable feeling or suffering.[112] It springs from demerit as its specific cause. It is an object of aversion. Every one feels natural aversion towards pain because he knows that it is pain. On the other hand, every one feels aversion towards the cause of pain because he knows that it is conducive to harm. Pain is shunned for its own sake as pleasure is pursued for its own sake. Aversion towards pain is natural and unconditional. Aversion towards the cause of pain depends upon aversion towards pain caused by it.[113]

Pain is a real quality, says the Prābhākara, of the self. It is not a phenomenal quality due to the limiting adjunct of avidyā. It inheres in the self and is apprehended by mental perception.[114] The experience of pleasure and pain, the Bhāṭṭa Mīmāṁsaka asserts, constitutes embodied life. It is predominantly painful, though it is relieved by a little pleasure.[115] Pain in future life is very great due to the commission of prohibited acts and the omission of prescribed acts. Empirical pain is produced by sensible objects. It is the invariable attendant of embodied life.[116]

The *Bhagavad Gītā* regards pain as the consequence of rajas.[117] When the self transcends the guṇas—sattva, rajas and tamas—completely, and is not affected by them, it is freed from the pain of

[108] PBh., p. 260; NK., pp. 260-1.
[109] Bādhanālakṣaṇaṁ duḥkham. NS., i, 1, 21.
[110] Bādhanā pīḍā tāpa iti. NBh., i, 1, 21.
[111] Pratikūlavedanīyatvaṁ duḥkhasya. NVTP., i, 1, 4; p. 521. Duḥkhaṁ pratikūlavedanīyam. NBh., i, 1, 2.
[112] TR., pp. 128-9; TSC., p. 77; NKL., pp. 7-8; TSD., p. 91.
[113] BhP., SM., 145. NBh., iv, 1, 58.
[114] PP., pp. 149, 151, 159-60.
[115] Bahuduḥkhapariṣvaktaṁ yannāma svalpakaṁ sukham. ŚD., p. 520.
[116] ŚD., pp. 519-22.
[117] Rajasas tu phalaṁ duḥkham. xiv, 16.

birth, old age and death, and becomes immortal.[118] The Sāṁkhya also regards pain as an effect of rajas.[119] Pain is a feeling opposite to pleasure. It is not a negation of pleasure. Pleasure and pain both are positive feelings. They are not negations of each other. They are experienced as positive feelings.[120] They are mental modes as their causes, merits and demerits, are. The self is detached (niḥsaṅga) and free from them. They are not qualities of the self as the Nyāya-Vaiśeṣika and the Mīmāṁsaka maintain. The self experiences pleasure and pain, which are modes of buddhi and effects of merits and demerits, because of its erroneous identification with them. Non-discrimination is the cause of its enjoyments and sufferings.[121] The Yoga also regards pain as a disagreeable feeling which makes the self endeavour to get rid of it. It is the agitation of the mind due to the thwarting of a desire.[122] It is the cause of aversion. Pleasure and pain, the effects of sattva and rajas, are mental modes, and do not belong to the self which is eternally neutral.[123]

Śaṁkara defines pain as suffering or unfavourable or disagreeable feeling, which is a mode of the mind (antaḥkaraṇa) and an object of knowledge.[124] Madhusūdana regards it as a modification of rajas of the mind.[125] Rāmānuja defines pain as an unfavourable feeling due to the attainment of an undesirable object and the loss of a desirable object, which is an accidental quality of the self in relation to buddhi.[126] Śaṁkara regards pleasure and pain as qualities of egoism (ahaṁkāra) or the empirical self (jīva), and not of the pure self (Ātman) which is eternal bliss. He regards empirical pleasure and pain as modifications of the mind (manas).[127]

The Jaina regards pain as a modification of the soul-substance, which is in the nature of suffering (paritāpa) due to

[118] BG., xiv, 20.
[119] SK., 12; STK., 13. Aprītiḥ duḥkham. SSV., i, 127.
[120] Netaretarābhāvāḥ sukhādayo'pi tu bhāvāḥ. Bhāvarūpatā caiṣām anubhavasiddhā. STK., 12.
[121] SPS., SSV., V, 25; SPB., i, 105; vi, 11.
[122] Yenābhihatāḥ prāṇinaḥ tadupaghātāya prayatante tad duḥkham. Daurmanasyam icchābhighātāt cittasya kṣobhaḥ. YBh., i, 31. TV., iv, 24.
[123] Sa nityodāsīnaḥ puruṣaḥ. TV., iv, 24. YBh., ii, 18.
[124] Duhkhaṁ santāpaḥ. SBG., x, 4. Duḥkhaṁ pratikūlātmakaṁ jñeyatvāt kṣetram. Ibid, xiii, 6.
[125] MBG., ii, 56.
[126] RBG., II, 56; X, 4; XIII, 6.
[127] Sukhaṁ duḥkhaṁ ca taddharmaḥ sadānandasya nātmanaḥ. VCM., 107; 113.

bad action or karma-particles which encrust the soul. It is due to the intercourse of undesired objects with the sense-organs, and an object of aversion.[128]

The Buddhist regards all as pain. A person consists of five aggregates: (1) a body (rūpa), (2) feeling (vedanā), (3) perception (saṁjñā), (4) disposition (saṁskāra), and (5) self-consciousness (vijñāna). The body, the sense-organs, the sensible objects, and sensations constitute the rūpaskandha. The five aggregates are full of pain. Life is excruciating pain. "Birth is attended with pain; decay is painful; disease is painful; death is painful. Union with the unpleasant is painful; painful is separation from the pleasant; any craving that is unsatisfied, that too is painful. In brief, the five aggregates which spring from attachment are painful."[129] Sentient pleasure is transitory and attended with pain. It ought to be eschewed. There is no pleasure like peace. Nirvāṇa is the supreme pleasure. The peace of dispassion or desirelessness ought be pursued.[130]

7. *The Kinds of Pain*

Praśastapāda mentions three kinds of pain: (1) the sensory feeling of pain; (2) retrospective pain; and (3) prospective pain. Sensory pain arises from the perception of undesirable objects in intercourse with the sense-organs. Retrospective (smṛtija) pain is the pain of reminiscence. It arises from the recollection of undesired objects such as snakes, tigers and thieves perceived on some previous occasion. Prospective (saṅkalpaja) pain arises from the anticipation of future undesired objects.[131] Mukunda Śarmā mentions two kinds of pain, physical and mental. Physical pain is sensory pain. Mental pain is due to the cognitions of undesirable objects. It comprises retrospective pain and prospective pain. The intercourse of external objects with the sense-organs brought about by demerit is the efficient cause of physical pain. The conjunction of the self with the mind is the non-inherent cause, and the self is the inherent cause of both kinds of pain. A cognition is the efficient cause of mental pain.[132] Mahādeva Paṇḍita also

[128] DS., 9; DSV., 9; TDTV., 122; SS., V, 20; Tsār., V, 27.
[129] *Foundation of the Kingdom of Righteousness, 5.*
[130] DP., XV, 202-4; XIV, 181, 186. HIP., II, pp. 282, 314.
[131] PBh., p. 260; KR., p. 123.
[132] TSC., p. 77; Nyāyasāra, p. 109.

mentions physical and mental pain. The Nyāya and the Vaiśeṣika recognize ādhyātmika, ādhibhautika and ādhidaivika pain also mentioned by the Sāṁkhya.[133]

According to the Sāṁkhya there are three kinds of pain, ādhyātmika, ādhibhautika and ādhidaivika. (1) Adhyātmika pain is physical and mental. Physical pain is due to the disturbance of the flatulent, bilious and phlegmatic humorous of the body. Mental pain is due to desire, anger, greed, delusion, fear, envy, dejection and non-perception of particular features of objects. Physical pain is produced by intra-organic disorders. Mental pain is produced by mental agitations, emotions and passions. Desire is yearning for the attainment of good. Anger is aversion to evil. Greed is desire to appropriate wealth in spite of possessing it. Delusion is non-discrimination of what ought to be pursued and what ought to be shunned. Fear is fright due to the perception of harmful objects. Envy is intolerance of others' excess of prosperity. Dejection is depression due to separation from cherished objects. Non-perception of particular features of objects is in the nature of doubtful or indefinite knowledge.[134] Ādhyātmika pain depends upon factors which are not external objects. Pain depending upon external conditions is of two kinds: ādhibhautika and ādhidaivika. (2) Ādhibhautika pain is caused by men, beasts, birds, reptiles and inanimate objects. (3) Ādhidaivika pain is caused by imperceptible agents, e.g. ghosts, demons and the like.[135] Physical pain due to bodily disease can be remedied by the use of medicines prescribed by expert physicians. Mental pain can be remedied by the company of a beautiful wife, eating dainty food, drinkihg delicious drinks, wearing good clothes, ornaments, using perfumery and the like. Pain caused by physical agents can be remedied by the practice of moral precepts, residence in secure places, etc. Pain caused by supernatural agents can be remedied by incantations, gems, medicines, etc. But the threefold pain can be completely eradicated by the discriminative knowledge (viveka) of the transcendental self and its isolation from prakṛti and its evolutes, e.g. the body, the sense organs, manas, buddhi and ahaṁkāra.[136]

[133] NTD., p. 273; KR., p. 123.
[134] STK., p. 13.
[135] SSV., i, 1; p. 2-4; STK., pp. 13-4.
[136] STK., pp. 19-20, 27: SSV., SSVM., i, 1; HIP., ii, p. 73; KR., p. 123; NTD., p. 273; MBG., ii, 56.

Patañjali mentions three kinds of pain: pariṇāma-duḥkha, tāpa-duḥkha and saṁskāra-duḥkha. Sentient pleasures lead to painful consequences. Thirst for them is not quenched by their enjoyment. Repeated gratification intensifies the desire for sensuous pleasures and strengthens the capacity of the sense-organs for enjoyments. So frequent enjoyment is not a means to the attainment of pleasure.[137] Consequential pain is pariṇāmaduḥkha which afflicts a yogin even when he enjoys sentient pleasure. The pursuit of sentient pleasure entails bodily, verbal and mental actions which cause pleasure or pain to others and produce merit or demerit. These conative dispositions (karmāśaya) are produced by aversion, greed and delusion and bring about mental agony called tāpaduḥkha. Attachment for sentient pleasures involves aversion to the persons who thwart the desire for attainment of them. Aversion or anger is painful. It produces mental agony.[138] The apprehensions of pleasure and pain produce affective dispositions (saṁskāra). They produce recollections of pleasure and pain. They generate attachment and aversion. They bring about actions. They produce merits and demerits. When they ripen they produce pleasure and pain. Pleasure involves pain. The affective dispositions which produce pain are called saṁskāraduḥkha.[139] The mind by its very nature suffers from pain. Sattva (essence), rajas (energy) and tamas (inertia) which are the constituents of the mind (citta) produce pleasure, pain and delusion. They are always in conflict with one another, and tend to overpower one another. The mind is constantly active and restless, and always undergoes modifications which are attended with pain. All is painful to a discriminating person.[140] False knowledge (avidyā) is the root cause of all these kinds of pain, which can be exterminated by right discriminative knowledge of the self as distinct from prakṛti and its evolutes, the mind-body-complex. The three kinds of pain described by the Yoga are subtler than those described by the Sāṁkhya.[141] Both were

[137] Yato bhogābhyāsam anu vivardhante rāgāḥ, kauśalāni cendriyāṇām iti, tasmād anupāyaḥ sukhasya bhogābhyāsa iti. YBh., ii, 15.
[138] Tāpaduḥkhatā dveśajaḥ karmāśayaḥ. YBh., ii, 15.
[139] Sukhaduḥkhasaṁskārāśayāt tatsmaraṇam, tasmācca rāgadveṣau, tābhyāṁ karmāṇi, karmebhyo vipākaḥ. TV., ii, 15. YV., ii, 15, p. 113.
[140] Guṇavṛttivirodhācca duḥkham eva sarvaṁ vivekinaḥ. YBh., ii, 15; HIP., ii, pp. 144-5.
[141] Tadasya mahato duḥkhasamudāyasya prabhavabījam avidyā, tasyāśca samyagdarśanam abhāvahetuḥ. YBh., ii, 15.

profoundly influenced by Buddhism. The Yoga recognizes ādhyātmika, ādhibhautika and ādhidaivika pain mentioned by the Sāṁkhya.[142]

The Jaina recognizes two kinds of pain: physical and mental. He denies the existence of spiritual pain.

8. *Neutral Feeling*

The Nyāya-Vaiśeṣika does not recognize neutral feeling or feeling of indifference (upekṣā). It regards it as a mere cognition devoid of a feeling-tone. It is the cognition that an object is neither a cause of pleasure nor a cause of pain. For instance, grass is neither a cause of pleasure nor a cause of pain; so the cognition of it is that of a neutral object; it is a mere cognition devoid of a hedonic tone. Vātsyāyana speaks of the cognitions of acceptability, avoidability and neutrality of an object. An object that causes pleasure generates the cognition of its acceptability. An object that causes pain generates the cognition of its avoidability. An object that causes neither pleasure nor pain produces the cognition of its neutrality. Hence Vātsyāyana does not recognize neutral feeling as a distinct kind of feeling. He recognizes pleasure and pain only as feelings.[143]

Vidyāraṇya, a follower of Śaṁkara, mentions pleasure, pain, and neutral feeling or feeling of indifference. The empirical self (jīva) is happy, unhappy and neutral. Pleasure and pain are the effects of its merits and demerits. But neutrality is natural to the self. Neutral feeling lies midway between the two feelings. It is the phenomenal appearance of the intrinsic bliss of the self.[144]

The Sāṁkhya-Yoga regards the pure self (puruṣa) as neutral or indifferent in itself, unperturbed by feelings and emotions which are mental modes. When it acquires an intuion of itself as entirely different from prakṛti and its modifications—the mind-body-complex—it realizes its intrinsic neutrality. But the Sāṁkhya-Yoga does not regard neutrality as a feeling. It regards

[142] YBh., i, 31.

[143] Yadā jñānaṁ tādā hānopādanopekṣābuddhayaḥ phalam. NBh., i, 1, 3.

[144] Udāsīnaḥ sukhī duḥkhītyavasthātrayam etyasau. Sukhaduḥkhāntarāleṣu bhavet tūṣṇīm avasthitiḥ. Audāsīnvaṁ svabhāvataḥ. Audāsīnye nijānandabhānam. Pañcadaśī, xi. 93-95.

pleasure, pain and dejection as the effects of sattva, rajas and tamas. It regards delusion (moha) or ignorance also as an effect of tamas. But delusion is not neutral feeling. Neutrality (mādhyasthya) is an essential attribute of the pure self, which is due to its absence of attachment for prakṛti and its evolutes. Love and hatred are conquered by indifference.[145] Veṅkaṭanātha recognizes three kinds of feeling: pleasure, pain and neutral feeling.[146]

The Buddhist recognizes neutral feeling as a distinct kind of feeling. He recognizes pleasure, pain and neutral feeling (upekṣā) as three kinds of feeling (vedanā).[147] "Pleasure arises from the experience of a desired object. Pain arises from the experience of an undesired object. Neutral feeling arises from the experience of an object which is neither desired nor undesired. Pleasure and pain are opposed to each other. Neutral feeling is the absence of pleasure and pain."[148] It is different from equanimity (tatra-majhatthatā) which is an emotion.

9. *No Mixed feeling of Pleasure and Pain*

There cannot be a mixture of pleasure and pain yielding a compound feeling. They cannot be experienced simultaneously owing to the atomic nature of manas according to the Nyāya-Vaiśeṣika. There is no quality common to pleasure and pain. They are radically opposed to each other and cannot coexist in the self. So there can be no mixed feeling of pleasure and pain. The direct experience of pleasure or pain by the self in which it inheres is called bhoga. The body is the vehicle of enjoyment and suffering (bhogāyatana) which the self acquired through merits and demerits.[149] They are the specific causes of pleasure and pain. Śaṁkaramiśra maintains, that they are directly experienced as soon as they are produced; and that they are not objects of experience immediately following them.[150] Merit and

[45] SK., 12, 19; SPS., i, 163; SSV., iii, 65; TV., i, 33; YV., p. 93.

[46] Sukhaduḥkhodāsīnarūpāvasthātrayasiddhiḥ. SAS., p. 663. NSA., p. 130.

[47] AK., AKV., I, 9-13.

[48] HIP., i, p. 314. S.N., iii, 101.

[9] SP., p. 53; MB., p. 53; VSU., X, 1, 1.

[0] Svotpattyavyavahitottarakālīnasākṣātkārāviṣayaḥ tayorutpannamātra-vedyatvābhyupagamāt. KR., p. 37.

demerit not only produce pleasure and pain, but they also produce their experience.

10. *Are Pleasure and its Means Pain?*

Gautama calls birth pain because of its association with pain due to hindrance.[151] Vātsyāyana calls pleasure and its means, e.g. the body, the sense-organs and cognitions as pain.[152] Varadarāja (1150 A.D.) calls the body, the six sense-organs, the six objects, the six cognitions, pleasure and pain twenty-one kinds of pain. Bhāsarvajña (900 A.D.), Keśavamiśra (1300 A.D.), Jayasiṁhasūri (1400 A.D.) and Viśvanātha (1700 A.D.) also mention these kinds of pain. The body is pain for it is the organ of its experience. The sense-organs, the objects and the cognitions are the means to pain and so called pain. Pleasure is pain since it is invariably associated with pain.[153] Pain is unconditional pain in itself.[154] It is in the nature of being thwarted, hindered or opposed, suffering, or agony. It is chiefly and intrinsically pain.[155] The body, the sense-organs, the objects, and the cognitions are pain in a figurative sense, since they are the causes of pain. Sentient pleasure only, observes Jayasiṁhasūri, is pain for it is invariably accompanied with pain. Aniruddha also mentions these twenty-one kinds of pain[156]

Śaṁkara and Vātsyāyana evidently follow the Buddha when they regard birth, death, old age and sickness as pain because they are causes of pain They are not in the nature of pain. They are called pain in a derivative sense.[157] According to Patañjali sentient pleasures should be considered to be in the nature of pain because they result in painful consequences.[158] The yogins are afflicted with pain even when they enjoy sentient pleasure because it will lead to consequential pain.[159] They consider all

[151] Vividhabādhanāyogād duḥkham eva janmotpattiḥ. NS., iv, 1, 55.

[152] Sukhe tatsādhaneṣu ca śarīrendriyābuddhiṣu duḥkhasaṁjñā vyavatiṣṭhate. NBh., iv, 1, 55.

[153] Sukham api duḥkhānuṣaṅgād duḥkham. NSār., p. 35. TBh., p. 30. NSV., i, 1, 20.

[154] Duḥkhaṁ svata eva nirupādhikam. TR., p. 128.

[155] Duḥkhantu bādhāpīḍāsantāpātmakaṁ mukhyatayaiveti. NSār., p. 35.

[156] NTD., p. 251-2. SSV., ii, 1.

[157] Janmādayo duḥkhaṁ na punaḥ svarūpeṇaiva duḥkham iti. SBG., XIII. 8. NBh., iv, I, 58.

[158] YS., ii, 15.

[159] Pariṇāmaduḥkhatā nāma pratikūlā sukhāvasthāyām api yoginam eva kliśnāti. YBh., ii, 15. YBh., ii 14.

empirical life as pain since it abounds in pain. Prakṛti and its modifications—the external objects, the body, the sense-organs, manas, buddhi, ahaṁkāra and pleasure are pain.[160]

11. *Feeling and Cognition*

Uddyotakara distinguishes between feeling and cognition. They are entirely different in nature, and consequently cannot be identified with each other. Pleasure and pain are apprehended (grāhya) while cognition is in the nature of apprehension (grahaṇa). There is a difference between apprehension and objects of apprehension. An action (kriyā) and its object (karma) can never be one and the same. Hence pleasure and pain which are immediately apprehended by cognitions cannot be regarded as identical with them.[161] Śaṅkaramiśra maintains, that feeling can never be identified with cognition. We apprehend cognition and pleasure, he argues, as distinct from each other in such forms as 'I know' and 'I am happy or unhappy'. Here the apprehensions are different and their objects are different. To argue that pleasure is identical with cognition because pleasure is produced by the complement of conditions which produce cognition (jñānasāmagrī) is wrong, because, for the same reason, desire also may be said to be identical with cognition, since it is produced by the aggregate of conditions which produce cognition. In fact, cognition is the cause of feeling, and feeling is the cause of desire. Cause and effect cannot be identical with each other. Cognition is a prior condition of feeling and cannot be identified with it.[162]

Śaṅkaramiśra, Jayanārāyaṇa and Candrakānta Tarkālaṅkāra argue, that feeling is neither cognition in general nor a particular cognition. When there is an intercourse of an object with a sense-organ, there is the perception of it, but there is no experience of pleasure or pain. Pleasure is not produced by the sense-object-intercourse only, but by the knowledge of the object as good (iṣṭopalabdhi). Pain is not produced by the sense-object-intercourse only, but by the knowledge of the object as evil (aniṣṭopalabdhi). But perception is produced by the sense-object-intercourse only. When the existence of a fire on a hill is inferred

[160] Duḥkhabahulatvāt saṁsāra eva duḥkham. Prakṛtitatkāryasukhādikam sarvaṁ duḥkham eva vivekinaḥ. YV., ii, 15; pp. 110, 116.

[161] Sukhaduḥkhe grāhye grahaṇaṁ jñānm iti. NV., iv, 2, 34.

[162] KR., pp. 122-3.

from a smoke perceived on it, no pleasure or pain is experienced. So feeling is neither perception nor inference. Pleasure, pain, perception, inference and recollection are different from one another, because they are produced by different causes. Pleasure is produced by merit, knowledge of an object as good, etc.; pain, by demerit, knowledge of an object as evil, etc.; perception, by the sense-object-intercourse; inference, by the knowledge of a mark (liṅga); and recollection, by an impression (saṁskāra). So feeling is different from perception, inference and recollection. Pleasure or pain is directly experienced. But recollection is not direct apprehension. Hence feeling is different from recollection.[163]

The Buddhists regard pleasure and pain as modes of cognition. They are intellectualists. They consider desire, aversion and volition also as modes of cognition. Pleasure and pain are produced by the same causes as produce cognition.[164] Jayanta Bhaṭṭa (1000 A.D.) criticizes the Buddhist view. (1) It contradicts our experience. The difference between pleasure and cognition is actually perceived. Pleasure is experienced as felicity, whereas cognition is perceived as the knowledge of an object. Feeling is never experienced as the knowledge of an object.[165] The cognition of pleasure and the cognition of pain differ from each other as cognitions like doubt and illusion. Doubt apprehends an uncertain object. Illusion apprehends a non-existent object. They are cognitions of objects. Likewise, the cognitions of pleasure and pain are cognitions of objects. Pleasure and pain are internal or psychical objects. But they are never experienced as cognitions of objects. (2) The Buddhists contend, that pleasure and pain are self-manifest or self-aware; that they are both apprehending cognitions and apprehended objects; and that therefore they are modes of cognition.[166] Jayanta Bhaṭṭa urges, that even a cognition is not self-aware, far less pleasure or pain; that a cognition is cognized by another cognition; and that pleasure or pain is cognized by a cognition no sooner than it is produced.[167] So there is a difference between

[163] VSU., VSV., VSB., X, 1, 6.

[164] Sukhādīnāṁ jñānasvabhāvatvāt. Sukhādi vijñānābhinnahetujam. NM., p. 74.

[165] Jñānam eva viṣayagrahaṇarūpaṁ prakāśate na sukhaṁ duḥkhaṁ vā. NM., p. 74.

[166] Svaprakāśatvāt sukhāder na grāhyaikasvabhāvatvam. Grāhyagrahaṇasvabhāvatvāj jñānam eva tat. NM., p. 75.

[167] Utpannam eva sapadi sukhaṁ gṛhyate jñānena. NM., p. 75.

a produced pleasure and an unproduced pleasure. The former is cognized by a cognition, while the latter is not. The Buddhists, on the other hand, cannot explain why a self-manifest pleasure produced in one psychical series (santāna) does not manifest itself to another psychical series in which it is not produced. (3) Jayanta Bhaṭṭa asks whether one and the same cognition is modified into pleasure and pain or whether some cognitions are modified into pleasure, and others, into pain. On the first alternative, two contradictory feelings of pleasure and pain would be experienced at the same moment. On the second alternative, some cognitions are pleasures and other cognitions are pain, even as one cognition is the cognition of a jar and another cognition is the cognition of a cloth. Cognition which is by nature transparent is coloured by an object and becomes the cognition of the object. So the cognition of pleasure is cognition coloured by pleasure. It is not in the nature of pleasure. But pleasure is never experienced as the cognition of an object. Hence pleasure and pain are not cognitions.[168] (4) The Buddhists argue, that pleasure and pain are identical with cognitions because they are produced by the same causes. Jayanta urges, that though the self is the inherent cause, and conjunction of the self with manas is the non-inherent cause of pleasure and cognition both, yet the genus of pleasure (sukhatva) is the efficient cause of pleasure while the genus of cognition (jñānatva) is the efficient cause of cognition. Merit is the specific cause of pleasure. Demerit is the specific cause of pain. The stimulation of the sense-organs by objects, the knowledge of a mark, and impressions are the efficient causes of perception, inference and recollection.[169] Feeling is different from cognition because their efficient causes are different. (5) Further, all pleasure and pain are preceded by cognitions; sentient pleasure and pain are preceded by the recollection or anticipation of objects. But all cognitions are not preceded by cognitions. The first cognition of a fœtus in the womb or the first cognition after intoxication or swoon is not preceded by a cognition. So feelings are not identical with cognitions.[170]

Vācaspati Miśra (1000 A.D.) criticizes the Buddhist doctrine thus. (1) It is wrong to argue that feeling is identical with

[168] Tasmān na bodharūpāḥ sukhādayaḥ. NM., p. 75.
[169] Nimittakāraṇabhedād bhinnāni jñānasukhādīni kāryāṇi. NM., p. 76.
[170] NM., pp. 74-6.

cognition because both are produced by the same causes. The stimulation of the skin by sandal paste is said to produce the tactual perception of it as well as pleasure. But it does not produce pleasure in a person shivering from cold, though it produces the tactual perception of cold in him. Therefore, the same causes do not produce cognition and feeling both. (2) Cognition refers to an object (arthapravaṇa) while feeling does not refer to it. Feelings are affections or passive states of the self. It is agreeably affected by pleasure, and disagreeably affected by pain. Cognitions cognize objects, but feelings do not cognize them. (3) Cognitions are evaluated; their validity or invalidity is estimated. But feelings are neither valid nor invalid. They are devoid of epistemic value. So feelings are different from cognitions. (4) In dream pleasure and pain are said to be generated by mere cognitions. This argument is not sound. Pleasure and pain are not produced in dream. The false recollection of pleasure derived from the company of a beloved woman is produced by the false recollection of her in dream. Or, merit and demerit produce the cognitions of pleasure and pain in dream, but not the feelings of pleasure and pain. (5) Pleasure or pain may be said to be produced by the immediate apprehension (viṣayasākṣātkāra) of an object. But this assumption is wrong. God and seers have the immediate apprehension of all objects; but they are devoid of pleasure and pain. God is bodiless. Seers can apprehend all objects without the aid of the sense-organs by dint of yogic powers. Pleasure and pain depend upon the body and the intercourse of the sense-organs with objects. Hence feeling is different from cognition.[171]

Udayana (1050 A.D.) urges, that sometimes the same object (e.g. a song) produces similar cognitions in two persons; but that it produces pleasure in the one who has love for music and pain in the other who has antipathy for it. Pleasure and pain depend upon emotional dispositions or sentiments. Therefore, feeling is not identical with cognition. Udayana further urges, that the nature of a cognition is determined by the nature of its object; but that the nature of feeling is not determined by an object, but by its intrinsic nature of agreeableness or disagreeableness. Hence cognition and feeling are different in their nature.[172]

[171] NVTT., i, 1, 4; p. 80-1.
[172] NVTP., i, 1, 4; pp. 519-21.

Rāmānuja maintains, that pleasure and pain are modes of buddhi, an evolute of prakṛti, and not qualities of the self. They are due to the relation of the self to buddhi and merits and demerits which are modes of buddhi. They are not essential qualities of the self, but its accidental qualities due to its contact with buddhi which is not self.[173] Pleasure and pain are nothing but cognitions of favourable and unfavourable objects which are their causes.[174] They are the different conditions of attributive cognition.[175] There is no evidence to prove that feelings are different from cognitions. They are in the nature of cognition.[176] Śrīnivāsa and Veṅkaṭanātha Deśika, followers of Rāmānuja, also hold this view. It is open to the criticisms stated above.

12. *The Relation of Feeling to Cognition, Conation, Attention, Desire and Volition*

Praśastapāda and Śrīdhara indicate the relation of feeling with cognition and conation. The feeling of pleasure arises from the perception of a desired object (iṣṭopalabdhi), and the feeling of pain, from that of an undesired object (aniṣṭopalabdhi). Thus cognition is prior to feeling and gives rise to it. The feeling of pleasure produces attraction towards its object. The feeling of pain produces repulsion towards its object. Thus feeling is prior to conation or mental activity and gives rise to it. First, cognition; then feeling; and at last conation: these constitute the order of experience. Cognition gives rise to feeling; and feeling brings about conation.[177] Jayanta Bhaṭṭa observes that all feelings are preceded by cognitions, but that all cognitions are not preceded by cognitions. The first cognition of a fœtus and the first cognition after intoxication and swoon are not preceded by cognitions.[178] Udayana (1050 A.D.) also maintains, that in the waking state the sense-object-intercourse does not produce pleasure or pain directly, but through the medium of the perception of the

[173] NSA., pp. 129-30. [174] TMK., p. 659.

[175] Buddhirevopādhibhedāt sukhaduḥkhecchādveṣaprayatnarūpa. YMD., 27. Dharmabhūtajñānāvasthāviśeṣā eva. Ibid, p. 27.

[176] Sukhaduḥkhe jñānarūpe. NSA., p. 119.

[177] PBh., 259; NK., p. 260.

[178] Sarvaṁ sukhādi jñānapūrvakam eva. Na hi garbhādau madamūrcchādyanantaraṁ vā jñānam upajāyamānaṁ jñānāntarapūrvakam. NM., p. 76.

object.[179] Likewise, retrospective pleasure is produced by recollection, and prospective pleasure is produced by anticipation. Thus cognitions are prior to feelings. But feeling also facilitates cognition. Pleasure furthers the cognition of an object that produces it. It tends to know its object in detail and preserve it.[180]

Feeling produces conation. Pleasure produces attraction or desire to continue the stream of pleasure and enjoy the object again and again.[181] Desire is conation or mental activity. But feeling depends upon attention which is a kind of conation. When a person's attention, Śrīdhara observes, is preoccupied with something else, he fails to experience pleasure or pain because he cannot perceive a desired or undesired object.[182] Feeling produces desire. Desire for the attainment of a desired object depends upon pleasure. Desire for the rejection of an undesired object, or aversion to it, depends upon pain. The perception of a desired object produces pleasure, which generates a desire to appropriate it. The perception of a harmful object produces pain, which generates a desire to avoid or reject it.[183] Thus desire depends upon feeling which is prior to it.

But feeling also sometimes depends upon desire. An object produces intense pleasure when there is a strong desire for it. It gives more pleasure at the commencement of the feeling than later when desire is not so strong. Desire, therefore, is a cause of pleasure. The same object, which produces pleasure in a person when he has a desire for it, gives him pain when he has no desire for it. When an object is perceived with little or no desire for it, it does not produce pleasure in us, nor does its removal cause us pain. Thus pleasure and pain depend upon desire.[184]

Volition produces voluntary actions for the attainment of a desired object or the rejection of an undesired object. The former are preceded by desire while the latter are preceded by aversion. Desire depends upon pleasure. Aversion depends upon pain. Thus feeling is prior to volition. Pleasure produces volition through desire. Pain produces volition through aversion.

[179] Jāgarāvasthāyāṁ tāvad anubhavajananadvārā sukhotpattāvindriyārthasannikarṣa upayujyate. NVTP., i, 1, 4; p. 522.

[180] Prasādaḥ sukhaviṣayagrahaṇapāṭavam. NVTP., i, 1, 4; p. 532.

[181] Abhiṣvaṅgaḥ punaḥ punaḥ sukhapravāhasyāvicchedecchā. Ibid, p. 532.

[182] NK., p. 260.

[183] PBh., pp., 261-2.

[184] YVS., VI, 44, 2-4; VI, 120, 18-20. B.L. Ātreya: *Yogavāsiṣṭa and Modern Thought*, Benares, 1934, p. 83.

13. *The Memory of Feelings*

Vātsyāyana (400 A.D.) asserts, that a person desires an object and makes an effort to appropriate it which gave him pleasure in the past; and that he has aversion to an object and makes an effort to reject it which gave him pain in the past. Desire and aversion depend upon the recollection of pleasure and pain experienced in the past. When a desired object is attained, pleasure is experienced; when an undesried object is attained, pain is experienced. Praśastapāda also regards the recollection of pleasure caused by an object on a previous occasion as a condition of desire, and the recollection of pain caused by an object in the past as a condition of aversion.[185] Thus feelings leave their impressions (saṁskāra), which produce recollections of them when they are revived. Vyāsa (400 A.D.) asserts, that there are recollections of all mental modes which are tinged with pleasure, pain or delusion.[186] So he admits that there are the recollections of pleasure and pain. Vātsyāyana asserts that they remind us of their causes. The law of contiguity operates here. Viśvanātha states that pleasure and pain remind us not only of their causes but also of each other. The law of contrast operates here.[187]

12. *The Relation of Feeling to the Organism*

The *Mahābhārata* states that pleasure (sukha) and health (ārogya) are the effects of sattva or purity.[188] It is suggested here that pleasure and health of the organism go together. A similar suggestion is found in the *Bhagavad Gītā* also. "Sattva, being transparent, causes manifestation and health, and binds the self to pleasure and cognition."[189] There is a vague suggestion here that pleasure and organic equilibrium go together. Pleasure is a modification of sattva which is free from pain due to disorder of the organism. Thus pleasure is an accompaniment of health, but not a mere by-product of organic functions. Rāmānuja hints at this point in his commentary.[190] Pleasure is an invariable accompaniment of organic equilibrium. Śrīdhara distinctly mentions that health of the organism (svasthatā) is one

[185] PBh., pp. 261-2; NK., pp. 261-2.
[186] Sarvā vṛttayaḥ sukhaduḥkhamohātmikāḥ. YBh., i, 11.
[187] NBh., NSV., iii, 2, 44.
[188] Śāntiparva, ch. 313, 17.
[189] xiv, 6.
[190] Anāmayam arogatāhetuḥ. RBG., xiv, 6.

of the conditions of pleasure. This implies that disease or organic disequilibrium is a condition of pain.[191] We find a similar doctrine in the Jaina psychology. "Physical pleasure is the agreeable effect of the state of well-being of the organism. Physical pain is the reverse of this. Both pleasure and pain would be impossible if the soul were rid of the body."[192] The self has an instinctive tendency to continue the beneficial activity which gives rise to pleasure, and to discontinue the harmful activity which gives rise to pain.

13. *The Physiological theory of Pleasure and Pain*

Caraka seems to advocate distinctly the physiological theory of pleasure and pain. Disharmony of the bodily humours, e.g. the flatulent humour, the bilious humour and the phlegmatic humour, is called disease; and their harmony is called health. The harmony of the bodily humours or health is called pleasure; and their disharmony is called pain. Pleasure is organic equilibrium; pain is organic disequilibrium.[193]

14. *The Buddhist doctrine of Feeling*

Buddhaghoṣa recognizes three kinds of feeling: (1) pleasure, (2) pain; and (3) neutral feeling (upekkhā). Pleasure is agreeable. Pain is disagreeable. Neutral feeling is neither pleasure nor pain. It is not pleasure owing to the absence of pleasure. Nor is it pain owing to the absence of pain. It is a feeling opposed to pleasure and pain. It is not the mere absence of pleasure or pain. It is a positive feeling or experience of what is contrary to both the desirable and the undesirable. Its function is neutral. Its manifestation is not evident. Vasubandhu and Yaśomitra also recognize these three kinds of feeling.[194]

Pleasure has the characteristic of experiencing a desirable object. Its function is to further or intensify associated states. It is manifested as bodily enjoyment. It is associated with profitable bodily consciousness which is produced by it. Pain has

[191] NK., p. 260. [192] *Jaina Psychology*, p. 52.
[193] Vikaro dhātuvaiṣamyam sāmyam prakṛtirucyatt.
Sukhasaṁjñakam ārogyam vikāro duḥkham eva ca. CS., i, 9, 3.
[194] *The Path of Purification* E.T. of Visuddhimagga of Buddhaghoṣa, Colombo, Ceylon, 1956, iv, 162; xiv, 200; iv, 193; xiv, 99; xv, 28; xvi, 1; Mettasutta, 59; AK., AKV., I, 9-13.

the characteristic of experiencing an undesirable object. Its function is to hinder or wither associated states. It is manifested as bodily suffering. It is associated with unprofitable bodily consciousness which is produced by it. Feeling of indifference has the characteristic of being felt as neutral. Its function is not to intensify or weaken associated states much.[195] Its manifestation is not evident. Feeling (vedanā) is so called because it is felt. Whatever has the characteristic of being felt should be collectively regarded as feeling aggregate (vedanāskandha).[196] Its function is to exploit the stimulus of the environment. Pleasure leads to acceptance of its object. Pain leads to rejection of its object. Neutral feeling leads to no reaction. The proximate cause of feeling is contact or sense-object-intercourse. There are six kinds of feeling produced by the contact of the eye, the ear, the nose, the tongue, the body and the mind with their objects.[197] Pain is gross compared with pleasure and neutral feeling because it is disturbing and overpowering. Pleasure and neutral feeling are subtle compared with pain because they are satisfying and quiet respectively. Both pleasure and pain are gross compared with neutral feeling because they involve intervention and cause disturbance. The neutral feeling is subtle compared with pleasure and pain because it is peaceful and quiet.[198] A feeling that has an inferior physical basis is gross, while one that has a superior physical basis is subtle. A gross feeling is inferior, while a subtle feeling is superior.[199] Buddhaghoṣa distinguishes between bodily pleasure and bodily pain, mental joy and mental grief, and neutral feeling (upekkhā) and equanimity (majjhatthatā). Neutral feeling belongs to the sphere of sense. It is neither pleasure nor pain, but a positive feeling of indifference. But equanimity is the neutral attitude of the mind at the occurrence of bodily pleasure, bodily pain, mental joy and mental grief.[200] It promotes neutrality towards beings and is manifested as the quietening of attraction (rati) and aversion (arati).[201]

There are many kinds of suffering (duḥkha): intrinsic suffering (dukkha-dukkha), suffering in change (vipariṇāma-dukkha), suffering due to formation (sankhāra-dukkha), and then concealed

[195] Ibid, xiv, 127-8.
[196] Ibid, xiv, 125.
[197] Ibid, xvii, 51, 227; vii, 14.
[198] Ibid, xiv, 200.
[199] Ibid, xiv, 208.
[200] Ibid, xiv, 102, 127.
[201] Ibid, ix, 96.

suffering, exposed suffering, indirect suffering and direct suffering. Bodily pain and mental pain are called intrinsic suffering because of their essential nature of painfulness. Bodily pleasure and mental pleasure are called suffering in change because they produce pain when they change. Neutral feeling and the three remaining formations of the three planes are called suffering due to formations because they are oppressed by rise and fall. Some bodily and mental afflictions are not evident and can be known by questioning. They are concealed suffering. The bodily and mental afflictions which are evident and can be known without questioning are exposed suffering. Birth and the like are called indirect suffering, because they are the basis of one kind of suffering or another. Birth is the basis of many sufferings. Ageing is the basis of bodily and mental suffering. Death is suffering. Bodily affliction and mental affliction are intrinsic suffering. Intrinsic suffering is called direct suffering.[202] The Buddhists hold that pleasure is the fruit of good deeds, and that pain is the fruit of evil deeds done in the past. Being experienced and enjoyed is the characteristic of feeling (vedanā).[203]

[202] Ibid, xvi, 34-5, 43-6, 50.
[203] *The Questions of King Milinda*, I, p. 93.

CHAPTER V

SPRINGS OF ACTION: DESIRE, AVERSION AND EMOTIONS

1. *The Nyāya Account*

Gautama maintains that faults (doṣa) are the ultimate springs of action because they urge the self to act. They are the moving forces from which actions spring.[1] There are three faults, viz. attachment, aversion and delusion.[2] They are the efficient causes of action, and prompt the self to act. Vātsyāyana asserts, that attachment and aversion urge the knowing self to do actions, which are either moral or immoral.[3] Attachment is the desire to appropriate an object that afforded pleasure in the past. Aversion is the desire to avoid an object that caused pain on a previous occasion. Delusion is the false knowledge (mithyājñāna) of the body, the sense-organs and the like as the self which is distinct from them. Attachment and aversion are due to delusion.[4] Attachment is characterized by attraction or love; aversion, by anger or intolerance; and delusion, by false knowledge.[5] Volitions due to attachment for agreeable objects and aversion for disagreeable objects spring from delusion or false knowledge. Delusion is destroyed by right knowledge. Attachment and aversion are destroyed by the destruction of false knowledge.[6]

The springs of action may be classified under three main heads, viz. attachment, aversion and delusion. Vātsyāyana mentions five springs of action under attachment (rāga): (1) sexual craving (kāma); (2) jealousy (matsara); (3) desire for acquisition (spṛhā); (4) will-to-live (tṛṣṇā); and (5) greed (lobha). Uddyotakara explains their nature in the following manner. (1) Sexual craving or lust (kāma) is desire for sex-union.[7] It is the yearning felt by men for union with women. It is commonly said: "Unless

[1] Pravartanālakṣaṇā doṣāḥ. NS., i, 1, 18.
[2] Tat trairāśyaṁ rāgadveṣamohārthāntarabhāvāt. NS., iv, 1, 3.
[3] Jñātāraṁ hi rāgādayaḥ pravartayanti puṇye pāpe vā. NBh., i, 1, 18.
[4] Yatra mithyājñānaṁ tatra rāgadveṣau. NBh., i, 1, 18.
[5] NBh., iv, 1, 3. [6] NBh., iv, 1, 2, 6.
[7] Kamaḥ strīgato' bhilāṣaḥ. NV., iv, 1, 3.

a man feels sex-impulse he does not adorn himself." Here it is suggested that there is the sex-urge at the root of the æsthetic impulse. (2) Jealousy (matsara) is solicitude for the preservation of one's wealth. It is unwillingness to part with one's inexhaustible wealth which is not diminished by enjoying or giving.[8] If a person shows solicitude for the preservation of the water of a public well, and desires to deprive others of the benefit of its inexhaustible water, he betrays this kind of jealousy. It is extreme selfishness. (3) Spṛhā is desire to appropriate others' wealth by lawful means.[9] (4) Tṛṣṇā is the will-to-live or hankering for continuation of life after death. It is hankering after rebirth.[10] (5) Greed (lobha) is desire for misappropriating others' wealth by unlawful means.[11] Jayanta Bhaṭṭa and Vācaspati Miśra explain the nature of the springs of action under desire after Uddyotakara.[12] Viśvanātha explains matsara as the desire to prevent others from possessing the things which are necessary for them even without any self-interest. He explains tṛṣṇā as the desire of a person that his wealth may never suffer any diminution. Its another form is miserliness (kārpaṇya) or unwillingness to part with one's wealth even for urgent and legitimate purposes. Viśvanātha adds fraudulence (māyā) and boastfulness (dambha) to Vātsyāyana's list. (6) Māyā is the desire to deceive others. It corresponds to upadhā described by Praśastapāda. (7) Dambha is the desire to display one's superiority by hypocrisy and sanctimoniousness.[13]

Vātsyāyana mentions five springs of action under aversion (dveṣa): (1) anger (krodha); (2) envy (īrṣyā); (3) jealousy (asūyā); (4) malevolence (droha); and (5) resentment (amarṣa).[14] Uddyotakara explains the nature of these springs of action in the following manner: (1) Anger is an emotion which produces disorders in the body, the seat of the sense organs. It is expressed in redness of the eyes and other organic expressions.[15] It is the cause of organic expressions, and not their effect. (2) Envy is the desire to prevent others from possessing the common objects which

[8] Akṣīyamāṇavastvaparityāgecchā matsaraḥ. NV., iv, 1, 3.
[9] Asvavastvādānecchā spṛhā. NV., iv, 1, 3.
[10] Punarbhavaprārthanā tṛṣṇā. NV., iv, 1, 3.
[11] Pramāṇaviruddhaparadravyāpahārecchā lobhaḥ. NV., iv, 1, 3.
[12] NM., pp. 500-1; NVTT., p. 414.
[13] NSV., iv, 1, 3.
[14] NBh., iv, 1, 3.
[15] Śarīrendriyādhiṣṭhāna vaikṛtya hetuḥ krodhaḥ. NV., iv, 1, 3. NSV., iv, 1, 3.

have not been taken by anybody.[16] (3) Jealousy is intolerance of the good qualities of another person.[17] A person has jealousy when he cannot tolerate the good qualities of another person. (4) Malevolence is the desire of a person to do harm to another person, though he is powerless to do any harm.[18] (5) Resentment is intolerance of any harm done to a person.[19] These are different forms of aversion. Jayanta Bhaṭṭa explains the nature of the springs of action under aversion after Uddyotakara. He defines the nature of anger as inflaming or blazing up (prajvalana) after Praśastapāda, which is the cause of organic expressions in the eyes, the eye-brows and the like.[20] He defines resentment as the desire to retaliate on the wrong-doer, which is not manifested in organic expressions.[12] Viśvanātha explains resentment as aversion of a person for his malefactor due to his sense of powerlessness to take revenge on him.[22] He adds cruelty (hiṁsā) and self-reproach (abhimāna) to Vātsyāyana's list of five springs of action under aversion. (6) Cruelty is the expression of malevolence.[23] Others regard it as malevolence. (7) Self-reproach is aversion for oneself due to inability to do harm to a malefactor.[24]

Vātsyāyana mentions four springs of action under delusion (moha): (1) error (mithyājñāna); (2) doubt (vicikitsā); (3) pride (māna); and negligence (pramāda).[25] Uddyotakara explains the nature of these springs of action in the following manner: (1) Error is false knowledge or misapprehension of one object as what it is not.[26] (2) Doubt is the indefinite cognition which takes the form 'What may this be?' (3) Pride or self-conceit is the false sense of superiority by attributing non-existent qualities to oneself or by exaggerating the importance of one's existent qualities.[27] It is the feeling of self-importance which is expressed in such a form as 'Oh! How great I am'. It is vanity. (4) Negligence

[16] Sādhāraṇe vastuni parābhiniveśapratiṣedhecchā īrṣyā. NV., iv, 1, 3.
[17] Paraguṇākṣamatā asūyā. NV., iv, 1, 3.
[18] Aśaktasya paraṁ pratyapacikīrṣā drohaḥ. NV., iv, 1, 3.
[19] Apakārāsahiṣṇutā amarṣaḥ. NV., iv, 1, 3.
[20] Akṣibhruvādivikārahetuḥ prajvalanātmakaḥ krodhaḥ. NM., p. 501.
[21] Adarśitamukhādivikāraḥ paraṁ prati manyur amarṣaḥ. NM., p. 501.
[22] Kṛtāparādhe asamarthasya dveṣaḥ. NSV., iv, 1, 3.
[23] Hiṁsā tu drohajanyā. NSV., iv, 1, 3.
[24] Abhimānaḥ apakāriṇyakiñcitkarasyātmani dveṣaḥ. NSV., iv, 1, 3.
[25] NBh., iv, 1, 3.
[26] Viparyayajñānaṁ mithyājñānam atasmiṁstaditipratyayaḥ. NV., iv, 1, 3. NM., p. 501.
[27] Vidyamānāvidyamānaguṇādhyāropeṇātmotkarṣapratyayo mānaḥ. NV., iv, 1, 3. NM., p. 501.

consists in not performing one's duties though one is capable of performing them.[28] Jayanta Bhaṭṭa explains the nature of these springs of action after Uddyotakara. Viśvanātha defines doubt as the knowledge of contradictory qualities in the same object.[29] He adds (5) hypothetical reasoning (tarka), (6) fear (bhaya), and (7) grief (śoka) to Vātsyāyana's list of four springs of action under delusion. (5) Hypothetical reasoning consists in the attribution of a generic quality on the attribution of specific quality.[30] (6) Fear is the knowledge of one's inability to avert a calamity when it is about to befall one.[31] Here an emotion is identified with its cause. (7) Grief is the knowledge of one's inability to regain the cherished objects which are lost.[32] Here also an emotion is identified with its cause. Viśvanātha includes the false attribution of inferiority to a person possessed of superior qualities also in self-conceit (māna).[33] Fear and grief are regarded by him as forms of false knowledge. All emotions are due to delusion (moha) or false knowledge (mithyājñāna). They are intellectual disorders. Thus the Nyāya advocates an intellectualist theory of emotions.

2. *The Vaiśeṣika Account*

Praśastapāda mentions eight kinds of desire: (1) desire for sex-union (kāma); (2) desire for eating food (abhilāṣā); (3) attachment (rāga); (4) desire to realize a remote end (saṅkalpa); (5) compassion (kāruṇya); (6) dispassion (vairāgya); (7) desire to deceive others (upadhā); and (8) a desire concealed in the mind (bhāva). (1) Lust is the desire for sex-gratification.[34] It is a desire arising from an organic appetite. (2) Abhilāṣā is the desire for taking food and drink.[35] It is a desire arising from hunger and thirst which are organic appetites. (3) Attachment (rāga) is the desire to enjoy objects of pleasure again and again.[36] These are egoistic desires. It is a "secondary passion" of an enduring nature

[28] Śaktasya kartavyākaraṇaṁ pramādaḥ. NV., iv, 1, 3. NM., p. 501.
[29] Ekadharmikaviruddhabhāvābhāvajñānaṁ saṁśayaḥ. NSV., iv, 1, 3.
[30] Vyāpyāropād vyāpakaprasañjanaṁ tarkaḥ. NSV., iv, 1. 3.
[31] Bhayaṃ aniṣṭahetūpanipāte tatparityāgānarhatājñānam. NSV., iv, 1, 3.
[32] Śokaḥ-iṣṭaviyoge tallābhānarhatājñānam. NSV., iv, 1, 3.
[33] Guṇavati nirguṇatvadhīrupasmayo'pi māne'ntarbhavati. NSV., iv, 1. 3.
[34] Maithunecchā kāmaḥ. PBh., p. 261.
[35] Abhyavahārecchā' bhilāṣaḥ. PBh., p. 261.
[36] Punaḥ punar viṣayānurañjanecchā rāgaḥ. PBh., p. 261.

in Martineau's language. (4) Resolve (saṅkalpa) is the desire to realize a remote end and attain an object which is not yet attained.[37] (5) Compassion (kāruṇya) is the desire to remove the miseries of others without any self-interest.[38] It is a purely altruistic desire prompted by pure sympathy. (6) Dispassion (vairāgya) is the desire to renounce objects of enjoyment due to the knowledge of their faults.[39] It is desirelessness or the negation of desires for enjoyments. (7) Upadhā is the desire to deceive others.[40] It is an egoistic desire. (8) Bhāva is a concealed desire.[41] It is not manifested in organic expressions.

Śaṁkara Miśra mentions eleven kinds of desire including the eight desires mentioned by Praśastapāda. He adds spṛhā, lobha and tṛṣṇā to these desires. (9) Spṛhā is the desire to appropriate objects which belong to others by lawful means.[42] (10) Greed (lobha) is the desire to misappropriate others' property by unlawful means.[43] (11) Miserliness (tṛṣṇā) is unwillingness to part with one's possessions even in urgent matters of imperative necessity.[44] Mahādeva Paṇḍita rightly calls it miserliness (kārpaṇya). He also mentions these eleven kinds of desire. He defines thirst (tṛṣṇā) as the yearning of the mind which springs out of greed.[45] Śaṁkara Miśra borrows his additional springs of action under desire from the Nyāya classification. Praśastapāda enumerates different kinds of desires according to the different actions desired, e.g. desire to do, desire to steal, desire to go, etc.[46]

Praśastāpāda mentions five kinds of aversion: (1) anger (krodha); (2) malevolence (droha); (3) impotent rage (manyu); (4) intolerance (akṣamā); and (5) anger of humiliation (amarṣa). Śrīdhara explains these different kinds of aversion. (1) Anger (krodha) is the aversion which is momentary and produces disturbances in the body, the sense-organs and the like.[47] It is a strong emotion which produces organic disturbances in the body

[37] Anāsannakriyecchā saṅkalpaḥ. PBh., p. 261.
[38] Svārtham anapekṣya paraduḥkhaprahāṇecchā kāruṇyam. PBh., p. 261.
[39] Doṣadarśanād viṣayatyāgecchā vairāgyam. PBh., p. 261.
[40] Paravañcanecchā upadhā. PBh., p. 261.
[41] Antarnigūḍhecchā bhāvah. PBh., p. 261. KR.. p.124.
[42] Paradravyādānecchā spṛhā. KR., p. 124.
[43] Anyāyena paradravyādānecchā lobhah. KR., p. 124.
[44] Avaśyakartavyepi svadravyāparityāgecchā tṛṣṇā KR., p. 124. Cf. NM. pp. 500-1.
[45] Nyāyasāra, p. 112.
[46] PBh., p. 261; NK., p. 262.
[47] Śarīrendriyādivikārahetuḥ kṣaṇamātrabhāvī dveṣaḥ krodhaḥ. NK., p. 262.

and the sense-organs. (2) Malevolence (droha) is the aversion which is not manifested in organic expressions, which is harboured in the mind for a long time, and which ultimately finds expression in doing mischief to the enemy.[48] It is not an emotion but a sentiment or emotional disposition which is the permanent effect of the experience of many emotions. (3) Imponent rage (manyu) is the aversion which is concealed in the mind by an injured person who is powerless to do mischief to the enemy in return.[49] It is not an emotion but a sentiment or emotional disposition. (4) Intolerance (akṣamā) is aversion to the superior qualities of others.[50] (5) Anger of humiliation (amarṣa) is the aversion which arises from the discomfiture of one's good qualities.[51] Śaṁkara Miśra borrows this interpretation from Śrīdhāra. He explains amarṣa as aversion for the superior qualities of others due to the apprehension of the discomfiture of one's own good qualities.[52] He adds two more kinds of aversion to the list of Praśastapāda. (6) Envy (īrṣyā) is aversion for a person who has done great mischief to one.[53] (7) Vindictiveness (abhyasūyā) is the aversion of a powerless person intolerant of the mischief done to him, which is concealed and harboured in the mind for a long period of time, but which does not find expression in doing harm to the enemy in return.[54] It is a sentiment.

3. *The Yoga Account*

Patañjali describes false knowledge (avidyā), egoism (asmitā), attachment (rāga), aversion (dveṣa) and instinctive fear of death (abhiniveśa) as five kinds of afflictions (kleśa). (1) False knowledge consists in knowing the non-eternal as eternal, the impure as pure, the painful as pleasant, and the not-self as the self. The impermanent earth is known as permanent. The impure body composed of flesh, blood and bone is known as pure. Empirical pleasure which is fraught with pain is known as pleasure. The

[48] Alakṣitāvikāraś cirānubaddhāpakārāvasāno dveṣo drohaḥ. NK., pp. 262-3.

[49] Apakṛtasya pratyapakārāsamarthasyāntarnigūḍho dveṣo manyuḥ. NK., p. 263.

[50] Paraguṇadveṣo' kṣamā. NK., p. 263.

[51] Svaguṇaparibhavasamuttho dveṣo' marṣah. NK., p. 263.

[52] Svaguṇaparibhavaśaṁkinaḥ paraguṇavidveṣo'marṣaḥ. KR., pp. 125-6.

[53] Paramapyapakurvati vidveṣa īrṣyā. KR., p. 126.

[54] Apakārāsahiṣṇor asamarthasya parāpa-kārāparyavasāyī nigūḍhaś cirakālāvasthāyī dveṣo' bhyasūyā. KR., p. 126. Nyāyasāra, p. 113.

external objects, conscious and unconscious, which are objects of enjoyment, the body, which is the vehicle of enjoyment, and the mind, which is the internal organ of enjoyment, are known as the self. Avidyā is positive false knowledge. It is neither valid knowledge nor the absence of valid knowledge. (2) Egoism is the false identification of unconscious mind (buddhi) with conscious self (puruṣa). The self is the conscious knower; buddhi is an unconscious object of knowledge. The self is the experiencer (bhoktṛ), while buddhi is the experienced object (bhogya). They are entirely heterogeneous in their nature. Experience (bhoga) is due to the false identification of the two with each other or non-discrimination between them. Discrimination of them from each other brings about liberation. (3) Attachment is the desire to appropriate an object that caused pleasure in the past. It is due to the recollection of pleasure experienced on a previous occasion. (4) Aversion is anger towards an object that caused pain in the past. It is due to the recollection of pain experienced on a previous occasion. (5) Fear of death is instinctive. It is due to the predispositions (saṁskāra) of the experience of intense pain of death in many past births. It is not due to perception, inference or testimony. It is common to the wise and the ignorant. The instinctive urge to cling to life is its expression. The primitive will-to-live is the strongest desire due to avidyā or misapprehension of the mind-body-complex as the self. All afflictions (kleśa) are due to false knowledge (avidyā) and can be destroyed by right knowledge. The Yoga, like Spinoza, regards emotions as intellectual disorders which can be cured by true knowledge.[55]

4. *The Account of the Upaniṣads*

The Bṛhadāraṇyaka Upaniṣad speaks of three primal desires: (1) desire for sons (puttraiṣaṇā); (2) desire for wealth (vittaiṣaṇā); and (3) desire for enjoyment in heaven (lokaiṣaṇā). The first is the sex-desire. The second is the will-to-power. The third is the will-to-live corresponding to the fear of death (abhiniveśa) mentioned by Patañjali. It comprises the will-to-pleasure here and hereafter. All these are different forms of the fundamental desire for sentient pleasure.[56]

[55] YS., YBh., YV., TV., ChV., ii, 3, 5-9. HIP., ii, pp. 141-3.
[56] Etaṁ vai tam ātmānaṁ viditvā brāhmaṇāḥ puttraiṣaṇāyāśca vittaiṣaṇāyāśca lokaiṣaṇāyāśca vyutthāyātha bhikṣācaryaṁ caranti. Bṛ. Up., iii, 5, 1.

5. *The Advaita Vedānta Account*

Śaṁkara mentions two kinds of desire: (1) desire for the not-self (anātma-vāsanā) and (2) desire for the self (ātma-vāsanā). The former is subdivided into three kinds: (1) bodily desires (deha-vāsanā); (2) social desires (lokavāsanā); and (3) intellectual desires (śāstravāsana). All desires for the satisfaction of organic needs—hunger, thirst, sex-desire and the like—constitute bodily desires. The desires for power, fame, wealth, enjoyment and the like constitute social desires. The desire for erudition in the scriptures is the intellectual desrie. All these are desires for the not-self. But the desire for the immediate apprehension of the Self (Ātman) or the Absolute is absolutely different from the desires mentioned above. When all desires for external objects (bāhyavāsanā) are exterminated and the mind is fixed on the inner Self, the intuition of it dawns. The desire for the Self (paramātmavāsanā) or Brahman is hidden behind the net of desires for the not-self (anātmavāsanā). When they are destroyed by steadfast devotion to the Self, the desire for the self shines forth.[57] Śaṁkara identifies the pure Self (Ātman) with Brahman or the Absolute. He regards the empirical self (jīva) as the universal pure consciousness (Ātman) limited by egoism (ahaṁkāra). When the desire for the Self or the ultimate Reality (sadvāsanā) is manifested, the egoistic desires (ahaṁvāsanā) are eclipsed.[58]

Śaṁkara reduces the desire for sons, the desire for wealth, and the desire for happiness on earth and in heaven to one primal desire for non-eternal empirical pleasure.[59] All desires for means are the desire for the end, which springs from avidyā and is the cause of aitions. Avidyā is the false sense of duality or plurality. It gives rise to desire which generates actions. Our empirical life of bondage is due to nescience, desire and actions.[60] One is released from bondage by acquiring an intuition of the Self.[61]

6. *The Buddhist Account*

Thirst (tṛṣṇā) or craving is the cause of the suffering. It is threefold: (1) thirst for sensual pleasures (kāma-tṛṣṇā), (2) thirst

[57] VCM., 271-7. [58] VCM., 319.

[59] Sarvā hi sādhanecchā phalecchaiva. Yā hyeva puttraiṣaṇā sā vittaiṣaṇā, yā vittaiṣaṇā sā lokaiṣaṇā; ata ekaiva eṣanā. SB., Bṛ. Up., iii, 5, 1.

[60] Avidyā-kāma-karma-lakṣaṇaṁ saṁsāra-bījam. SB., Kena Up., iv, 9.

[61] Ātmānam avagamya mṛtyumukhāt avidyā-kāma-karma-lakṣaṇāt pramucyate. SB., Kaṭh. Up., i, 3, 15.

for being or will-to-live (bhava-tṛṣṇā), and (3) thirst for wealth and power (vibhava-tṛṣṇā). The craving for sensual delight, the craving for a future life, and the craving for success in the present life are the fundamental springs of action.[62] Attachment (rāga), aversion (doṣa) and delusion (moha) are the primary emotions which are the springs of actions. Greed, lust and passion are the different kinds of attachment. Anger, hate and malevolence are the different kinds of aversion. Delusion is ignorance.[63] The *Dhammapada* mentions the desire for sons, the desire for wealth, and the desire for happiness on earth and in heaven described by the Upaniṣads.[64] The will-to-live is the primordial desire which is due to avidyā. Ignorance is the knowledge of the impermanent mind-body-complex and objects of enjoyment as permanent. Impermanent change is real, whereas the permanent being is unreal. But the eternal Brahman or Ātman, according to the Advaita Vedānta, is real, whereas the non-eternal mind-body-complex and the world are unreal; avidyā is the knowledge of the impermanent mind-body-complex as the permanent Self. Buddhism is the antithesis of the Advaita Vedānta.

7. *The Jaina Account*

The Jaina regards attachment (rāga), aversion (dveṣa) and delusion (moha) as the basic springs of action, which are the causes of bondage. They produce infraatomic karma-particles which encrust the soul. Emotions (akaṣāya) are mirth or laughter (hāsya), indulgence in sentient pleasure (rati), non-indulgence in it (arati) or languor, sorrow (śoka), fear (bhaya), disgust (jugupsā), sex-feeling of a woman (strīveda), sex-feeling of a man (puṁveda), and a eunuch's sex-feeling (napuṁveda). Passions (kaṣāya) are anger (krodha), pride (māna), deceit (māyā), and greed (lobha) in different degrees of intensity.[65] There are four instincts (saṁjñā): (1) the instinct for food (āhārasaṁjñā) including the preying instinct and the like; (2) the instinct of fear (bhayasaṁjñā) based on the instinct of self-preservation; (3) the sexual instinct

[62] MN., i. 5, 4. cp. Jung also holds that the will-to-live, the sex instinct and the will-to-power are the primal urges of human nature. HIP., ii, pp. 282—3. *Foundation of Kingdom of Righteousness*, 7.
[63] AN., i, 134; HIP., ii, p. 317; DP., i, 20; xviii, 17; xxiv, 23-5.
[64] DP., vi, 9; xxiv. 12; xxvi, 28.
[65] PK., 142, 146; TDTV., 149; SS., viii, 8; TSV., viii, 9; TAS., v, 28-9.

(maithuna) or the mating instinct; and (4) the instinct of acquisition (parigraha) including the instinct for collection and the instinct for possession.[66] "There are feelings corresponding to these instinctive appetites which may colour the consciousness of a Jīva."[67] This view faintly resembles McDougall's view that primary emotions are the conscious correlates of instinctive acts. Instincts aer modified, controlled and even eradicated by severe discipline. Suicide defies the instinct of life; celebacy conquers the sexual urge; saints eradicate the instincts of acquisition, collection and possession; omniscient persons overcome even hunger and thirst.[68]

8. *Caraka's Account*

Caraka describes three fundamental desires (eṣaṇā): (1) desire for the preservation of life (prāṇaiṣaṇā); (2) desire for wealth (dhanaiṣaṇā); and (3) desire for a blessed after-life (paralokaiṣaṇā). Since all achievements depend on life, one should try to preserve his life, health, and remedy disease. Then one should preserve his wealth because without it one is tempted to commit sins, and cannot enjoy long life. Then one should seek a blessed life in the other world.[69] Desire for life is the instinct for self-preservation, the will-to-live, life-energy. It corresponds to bhava-tṛṣṇā of the Buddhist, and abhiniveśa of Patañjali. Desire for wealth comprises the instinct of acquisition, the instinct of collection and the instinct of possession described by William James.[70] Desire for after-life is based on the will-to-live. It is the instinct for continuation of life. It may be said to be the instinct for self-transcendence or the instinctive craving for the Beyond. These three primary desires are the springs of all our actions. These are the three fundamental motives. The biological instinct of self-preservation, the worldly desire for the acquisition of wealth, and the other-worldly desire for self-transcendence sum up all springs of actions.[71]

Caraka speaks of the new-born child's smile, fear, crying,

[66] PK., 140; TDTV., 140.
[67] A. Chakravarty: Introduction to PK. (E.T.), p. xlii.
[68] *Jaina Psychology*, p. 21.
[69] CS., i, 11, 2-4.
[70] *Principles of Psychology*, Vol. II.
[71] DHIP., Vol. II, p. 415.

sucking the breast and the like, which he has not yet learnt from experience.[72] These are unlearned and instinctive acts. The Nyāya explains them by the impressions (saṁskāra) of these experiences in the previous births. It proves the pre-existence of the soul from the expressions of joy, fear, sorrow, etc., exhibited by the new-born child.[73]

Caraka maintains, that envy (irṣyā), grief (śoka), fear (bhaya), anger (krodha), pride (māna), hatred (dveṣa) and the like are affections of the mind (manovikāra) due to the perversion of the intellect (prajñāparādha).[74] He speaks of fear, grief, anger, greed, delusion (moha), envy, pride and false knowledge (mithyādarśana) as false correlation (mithyāyoga) of the mind to its states.[75] He, like Vātsyāyana, traces all emotions and passions to the perversion of the intellect (prajñāparādha). Confusion of the intellect is at the root of all emotions. For instance, sorrow is due to (1) comprehension of non-eternal things as eternal due to confusion of the intellect (buddhivibhraṁśa), (2) lack of self-control or power of withdrawing the mind from immoral actions (dhṛtivibhraṁśa), (3) lapse of memory or forgetfulness of the nature of right knowledge (smṛtivibhraṁśa), and (4) unhygienic conduct. All emotions are due to prajñāparādha which is defined as confusion of the intellect, lack of self-control and lapse of memory (dhī-dhṛti-smṛti-vibhraṁśa) which provoke all bodily humours and produce maladies, and also as error of judgment (viṣama-vijñāna) and as wrong action (viṣama-pravartanā) proceeding from erroneous judgment. Prajñāparādha may be taken in the wider sense of error of judgment or intellectual perversion.[76] Fear, attachment, aversion, greed, delusion, and pride should be controlled by a virtuous person by the right knowledge of their causes.[77]

[72] CS., i, 11, 20.
[73] NS., NBh., iii, 1, 19-24.
[74] CS., i, 7, 38.
[75] CS., i., 11, 36.
[76] DHIP., Vol. II, pp. 415-7.
[77] CS., i, 11, 19.

Chapter VII

EMOTIONS

1. *The Vedāntist analysis of Emotions*

(1) *Attachment* (*rāga*).—The *Bhagavad Gītā* regards attachment as an effect of rajas (energy) of mind, which generates clinging (āsaṅga) and yearning (tṛṣṇā). Madhusūdana defines attachment as a mental mode in the nature of attraction which compels the mind to attend to objects of enjoyment. The mind is tinged with the nature of the objects of attachment, and is focussed on them owing to the false identification of the self with them. The essential characteristic of attachment is constant attention to its objects. Madhusūdana defines attachment also as love or affection which is in the nature of being always engrossed in its objects.[1] Keśava Kāśmīrī also defines attachment as attraction (āsakti) for objects of desire. It is in the nature of intense delight in the objects of enjoyment which have already been attained, attended with a desire that they be never destroyed. Attachment is intense delight in cherished possessions accompanied by a desire for perpetual enjoyment of them. Sadānanda also defines attachment as attraction and affection of the mind for objects of desire. Nīlkaṇṭha and Viśvanātha define attachment as delight in objects of enjoyment.[2]

Ānandagiri regards attachment (rāga) as a kind of yearning (tṛṣṇā) which is in the nature of attraction for the objects of pleasure, with which the mind is tinged and in which it is engrossed, and which were enjoyed in the past. Thus he identifies attachment with yearning. Baladeva also identifies attachment with yearning.[3]

Viśvanātha regards attachment (rāga) as sexual attraction (anurâga) which is evoked at the sight of a woman. Rāmānuja

[1] Rago viṣayeṣu rañjanātmakaś cittavṛttiviśeso' tyantābhiniveśarupaḥ. MBG., ii, 56. Rāgaḥ sadā tadabhiniviṣtarūpo' bhiṣvaṅgaḥ. *Ibid*, xvii, 5.

[2] Rāgo visayeṣu prītiḥ. NBG.. iv, 10. VNBG., iv, 10; TPBG., ii, 56; BPBG., xvii, 5.

[3] Anubhūtābhiniveśe viṣayeṣu rañjanātmakas tṛṣṇābhedaviśeṣaḥ. ĀBG., ii, 56. Rāgas tṛṣṇā. BBG., ii. 59.

also regards attachment as attraction of man and woman for each other.[4]

Vedāntadeśika Veṅkaṭanātha regards attachment as attraction for any object other than God. Hanumān regards attachment as attraction for a desired object perceived by any sense-organ. Śrīdharasvāmī regards attachment as attraction for any favourable object that gives pleasure to the self. Repulsion is the opposite of attraction, which is excited by an object of aversion or an unfavourable object which gives pain to the self.[5]

Rāmānuja and Varavaramuni define attachment as intense desire for pleasant objects which have not yet been attained.[6] Śrīdharasvāmī, Viśvanātha, Dhanapati Sūri and Rāmakaṇṭha define attachment as desire for objects of enjoyment.[7]

Attachment can be destroyed by the true knowledge of the self. Attachment for sensible objects of enjoyment cannot cease until the self is intuited.[8]

(2) *Clinging* (*āsaṅga*).—Saṁkara defines āsaṅga as clinging to a desired object which has been attained. Clinging is characterized by delight of the mind.[9] Śrīdharasvāmī also defines āsaṅga as extreme delight in a desired object which has already been attained.[10] Madhusūdana and Sadānanda define āsaṅga as desire to preserve an object attained even when its destruction is imminent. Rāmakaṇṭha defines āsaṅga as deep engrossment of the mind in an object of pleasure. It springs from the contemplation of such an object. Saṅga is engrossment of the mind in the objects which are the causes of love, hatred and other taints.[11] Rāmānuja defines āsaṅga as a yearning for union with beloved persons, e.g., sons, friends and the like. Keśava Kāśmīrī defines it as embracing an object attained owing to an excess of delight in it. It is a desire for the continued enjoyment of an object even after its attainment. Dhanapati Sūri also defines āsaṅga as hugging (saṁśleṣa) an object, which has already been attained,

[4] VNBG., ii, 56 ; iii, 34 ; RBG., xiv, 7.
[5] RBTC., iv. 10 ; HBG., iii, 34 ; SBG., SrBG., NBG., iii, 34.
[6] Anāgateṣu spṛhā rāgaḥ. RBG.. ii, 56. VMBG., ii, 56 ; iv, 10.
[7] Rāgaḥ sukhaviṣayo' bhilāṣaḥ. RKBG., ii, 58. *Ibid*, iii, 17 ; xvii, 5 : xiv. 7. SrBG., VNBG., ii, 59.
[8] ATBG., iv, 10 ; VMBG., ii, 60.
[9] Āsaṅgaḥ prāpte viṣaye manasaḥ prītilakṣaṇaḥ saṁśleṣaḥ. SBG., xiv, 7.
[10] Prāpte'rthe prītir viśeṣeṇāsaktiḥ. SrBG., xiv, 7.
[11] Saṅgas tadekalīnatvam. RKBG., xiv, 7. *Ibid*. ii, 64 ; iii, 9. MBG., BPBG., xiv, 7.

characterized by an agreeable feeling.[12] Rāmakaṇṭha defines clinging (saṅga) as attraction (āsakti) for an object, which is in the nature of not-self, with which the self wrongly identifies itself, and in which the mind is deeply engrossed. It is engrossment of the mind in a pleasant object due to egoism. The self wrongly thinks: 'I am pleased with it'; 'It is mine'. Śaṁkara regards saṅga as delight in an object which is the cause of attachment. Nīlakaṇṭha defines it as the feeling of 'mineness' (mamatā) in sons and other objects of love. Veṅkaṭanātha also defines it as hugging sons, wealth and other objects of love. Rāmānuja regards desire as a ripening of clinging. Desire springs out of intense clinging.[13]

(3) *Thirst or yearning* (*tṛṣṇā*).—Śaṁkara defines tṛṣṇā as a yearning for the attainment of an object, which has not yet been attained.[14] Śrīdharasvāmī, Madhusūdana, Dhanapatisūri, Keśava and Śaṅkarānanda give the same definition of yearning. Rāmānuja defines tṛṣṇā as a yearning for the attainment of all pleasant objects, e.g., sounds, colours, odours, etc.[15] Rāmakaṇṭha defines tṛṣṇā as a yearning for the enjoyment of an object of pleasure.[16] Nīlakaṇṭha regards tṛṣṇā as a state of tension between the present state of dissatisfaction and the future state of satisfaction with a pleasant object which is not yet attained, but which is attainable.[17] Ānandagiri regards tṛṣṇā as excessive clinging while he regards clinging as delight in an object of attachment. Thirst or yearning is an intense state of clinging to an object of enjoyment.[18] Hanumān and Veṅkaṭanātha reiterate Śaṁkara's definition of tṛṣṇā. Vedāntadeśika Veṅkaṭanātha distinguishes between yearning (tṛṣṇā) and clinging (saṅga). Yearning is produced by the objects which are in intercourse with the five sense-organs. But clinging is produced by the recollection or imagination of the objects (e.g. sons, friends, etc.) with which one wrongly identifies oneself.[19]

[12] MBG., RBG., TPBG., BDBG., xiv, 7.
[13] RKBG., xiv, 6; xv, 5; SBG., ii, 62; BrGBG., xv, 5. Kāmaḥ saṅgasya vipākadaśā. RBG., ii, 62.
[14] Tṛṣṇā aprāptābhilāṣaḥ. SBG., HBG., BrGBG., xiv, 7.
[15] RBG., xiv, 7. RBTC., SrBG., MBG., BDBG.. TPBG., xiv, 7.
[16] Tṛṣṇā viṣayarasapipāsā. RKBG., xiv, 7.
[17] Tṛṣṇā prāpyamāṇeṣvartheṣvatṛptiḥ. NBG., xiv, 7.
[18] Tṛṣṇā udriktāsaktiḥ. ĀBG., ii. 62.
[19] Tṛṣṇā sāṁsparśika-samasta-viṣayā. Saṅgastu ābhimānika-viṣayaḥ. RBTC., xiv, 7.

(4) *Desire* (*kāma*).—Śaṁkara defines desire as a yearning for objects which are not perceived at present. It is a craving for objects which are not yet attained. He distinguishes desire from attachment which is attraction for objects which have been attained. Śrīdharasvāmī and Varavaramuni also distinguish between desire and attachment in a similar manner. Desire is a craving for objects which have not yet been attained, while attachment is a yearning for the attainment of more of the objects which have already been attained, but which are again desired.[20]

Śaṁkara identifies kāma with desire (icchā). Desire is directed towards an object of pleasure, which is perceived or remembered. Madhusūdana defines desire as a craving for an object of pleasure. Rāmakaṇṭha regards kāma as desire for external objects. Ānandagiri regards desire as yearning (tṛṣṇā) for the attainment of an object. Baladeva also identifies desire with yearning.[21] Rāmakaṇṭha regards desire as resolution (saṁkalpa) which is in the nature of yearning for the enjoyment of an object, which is a means to momentary pleasure that ultimately ends in pain. He regards desire also as attachment which pursues pleasure. He sometimes identifies desire with attachment and yearning.[22] In fact, attachment produces clinging; clinging generates thirst or yearning; thirst gives rise to desire. They are closely connected with one another.

Viśvanātha regards desire as a form of ignorance (ajñāna). Rāmānuja also regards it as a craving for the enjoyment of an object due to delusion. Śrīdharasvāmin regards desire as a cause of pleasure, and of sorrow and mental agony which spring from pleasure.[23]

(5) *Satisfaction* (*santoṣa*).—Rāmakaṇṭha maintains that when desires for objects are gratified, satisfaction is felt on the attainment of their objects. Desire produces the pleasure of satisfaction. When desires are not fulfilled owing to the non-attainment of their objects, the pain of dissatisfaction is felt. Thus desire is prior to pleasure or pain.[24]

(6) *Lust* (*kāma*).—Buddhaghoṣa regards kāma as enjoyment

[20] Kāmas tṛṣṇā asannikṛṣṭa-viṣayeṣu, rāgo rañjanā prāpteṣu visayesu. SBG., vii, 11. SrBG., VMBG., vii, 11.

[21] Kāmas tṛṣṇā. BBG., ii. 62. SBG., ii, 55, 70; v, 23; xviii, 53; MBG., xvi, 18; RKBG., iii, 44, 48; iv, 10; ĀBG., v, 23.

[22] Tṛṣṇābhilāṣo rāgaḥ. RKBG., xiv, 12. *Ibid.* xvi, 10, 12; iii, 37.

[23] VNBG., RBG., SrBG., iii, 39.

[24] RKBG., x, 4.

of sentient pleasure in a general sense. He regards kāma as sexual pleasure in a narrow sense, and calls it lust (kāmachanda). Madhusūdana regards lust as craving for the union of man and woman for each other. Rāmānuja also regards it as yearning for sexual union, which is an instinctive desire due to the false identification of the self with the body. He calls it rāga. Viśvanātha regards rāga as craving for union with a member of the other sex.[25] The Jaina divides lust into three kinds: (1) lust of man for woman; (2) lust of woman for man; and (3) lust of a eunuch. These are specific kinds of lust.

(7) *Detachment* (*asakti*).—Śaṁkara regards detachment as the extirpation of the primal desires for sons, wealth, and happiness on earth and in heaven. It is the extermination of the instinctive desires for pleasure, sex and power. Rāmakaṇṭha regards detachment as non-engrossment of the mind in the objects, which yield even the most transient pleasure. It is also non-engrossment of the mind in the objects of enjoyment, which are permitted by the śāstras. It is the absence of attachment or indifference due to one's being always contented with the experience of the supreme bliss of the Ātman or Brahman.[26]

Detachment is dispassion. Śaṁkara regards dispassion as internal and external renunciation of objects of enjoyment. External renunciation is renunciation in action. Internal renunciation is renunciation in mind. Renunciation is extirpation of attachment for egoism and external objects of enjoyment. Dispassion is aversion to enjoyment of sentient pleasures either in this world or in the next. It consists not only in resisting the allurements of the senses, but also in cultivating a positive contempt for all kinds of objects of enjoyment whether they are perceived or not. Dispassion is detachment or thirstlessness for objects of enjoyment, perceptible or imperceptible. Attachmentt is attraction for forbidden objects which yield sentient pleasure. Detachment is the absence of attachment. Madhusūdana regards dispassion as a mental mode which counteracts attachment for all perceptible and imperceptible objects. The mind preoccupied with objects of enjoyment should be diverted from them to Self (ātman) by the

[25] POP., iv, 24. Kāmaḥ strī-puṁsayoḥ paraspara-vyatikarābhilāṣaḥ. MBG., v, 24. *Ibid*, xvi, 12. Rāgo yoṣit-puruṣayor anyonya-spṛhā. RBG., xiv, 7. VNBG., iii, 34.

[26] Asaṅgaḥ puttra-vitta-lokaiṣ-aṇādibhyo vyutthānam. SBG., xv, 3. RKBG., iii, 19; xiii, 9; xvi, 2.

practice of dispassion. The gratification of desires is a function of the internal organ,[27] which is not-self. The mind distracted by enjoyment should be pacified by the practice of right knowledge, dispassion and discrimination between manas and self. This is Śaṁkara's suggestion. Gross attachment is destroyed, Ānandagiri asserts, by discarding subjection of the sense-organs to their objects which yield sentient pleasure through discrimination (viveka). Subtle attachment is destroyed by integral knowledge (samyagjñāna) of Brahman. Nescience (ajñāna) or ignorance of the Ātman is the root cause of attachment, which is destroyed by the destruction of nescience. Attachment is destroyed by the immediate experience of the Ātman which is the abode of supreme bliss. Dispassion can be increased, Rāmānuja avers, by constant contemplation of the faults of the objects of pleasure, which are different from the self that is the proper object of meditation. Rāmakaṇṭha regards dispassion as the absence of attachment, or freedom from love and hatred. Patañjali regards detachment as the absence of attachment for all natural and supernatural objects of enjoyment.. Puruṣottamajī regards renunciation (tyāga) as detachment. Veṅkaṭanātha regards it as giving up attachment for all kinds of agreeable objects. It is a saintly quality.[28]

(8) *Desirelessness.*—Rāmakaṇṭha regards a person as desireless (nirāśīḥ), who is devoid of desires for non-eternal enjoyments, which constitute a bondage because it is a cause of transmigration. The absence of freedom is desire and bondage. One who is free from desire for sentient enjoyment and bondage is desireless. Śaṁkara, Ānandagiri and Vallabha regard desirelessness as the renunciation of desires for fruits of actions. Rāmānuja and Hanumān also are of the same view. Nīlkaṇṭha traces the absence of desire for fruits of actions to the knowledge that one is impelled by God in performing them. Veṅkaṭanātha ascribes it to the conviction that the actions are performed as the worship of God. Vallabha regards desirelessness as aversion for happiness in heaven. Rāmānuja regards desirelessness also as freedom from desires for all objects which are different from the self.

[27] VCM., 373; SBG., xiii, 8; Dṛṣṭādṛṣṭa-viṣayeṣu vaitṛṣṇyam, SBG., xviii, 52. MBG., xviii, 52.

[28] SB., Māṇḍūkya Kārikā, iii, 43-44; SBG., xiii, 9. ĀBG., NBG., RBG.. ii, 59; RKBG., xiii, 8-9; xviii, 49, 53; xiii, 8. RBG., xviii, 52. YS. i 15; ATBG., BrGBG., xvi, 2.

Nīlakaṇṭha regards desirelessness also as the absence of desire for supernatural powers born of meditation, or as undivided devotion to meditation. Śaṁkara, Ānandagiri, Veṅkaṭanātha and Puruṣottamajī regards desirelessness as the renunciation of all desires, thirsts or longings. Puruṣottamajī includes the absence of desire for liberation in desirelessness.[29]

(9) *Love or Affection* (*abhiṣvaṅga*).—Śaṁkara defines affection as a kind of attachment (sakti). He regards it as the feeling of identity of oneself with some other entities, e.g., sons, wife, house, servants and the like. Love is sympathetic identification of others' emotions of happiness and misery with one's own emotions. Madhusūdana regards love as intense delight in, and sympathetic identification with, near and dear ones, who are regarded as parts of 'I'. Varavaramuni regards love as intense delight in wife, sons, house and the like as the means of bodily comforts and selfish enjoyments. Rāmakaṇṭha defines love as identification of oneself with objects which are not-self and causes of sentient pleasure. Hanumān regards love as the sense of 'I' in another person. Nīlkaṇṭha defines love as false identification of oneself with another person.[30] Vedāntadeśika Veṅkaṭanātha regards love as excessive attachment. Ānandatīrtha defines attachment as affection, and regards love as a very mature state of affection. Rāmakaṇṭha defines love (abhisneha) as deep attachment for objects of desire. He regards anabhisneha as the absence of love.[31]

Veṅkatanātha regards love (abhisneha) as a mental mode in which tamas predominates, and in which one attributes another person's prosperity and adversity to oneself, and feels joy and sorrow at his joy and sorrow. He regards anabhisneha as the absence of such love for dear persons, and even for one's body and life. Nīlakaṇṭha regards love as feeling happy or miserable, boastful or humiliated, when another beloved person feels happy or miserable, boastful or humiliated. He includes love for wife, body, life and wealth in abhisneha. Anabhisneha is the absence of such love. Śaṁkara regards anabhisneha as the absence of love for even the body and life. Hanumān gives the same definition

[29] RKBG., ii, 50; SBG., ĀBG., TDBG., NBG., BrGBG., iii. 30; iv, 21; vi, 10; ATBG., iv, 21; vi. 10.

[30] Abhiṣvaṅgo nāma saktiviśeṣa eva anyasyātmabhāvanālakṣaṇaḥ. SBG., xiii, 9. MBG., VMBG., HBG., NBG., xiii, 10.

[31] Abhiṣvaṅgaḥ atisaktiḥ. RBTC.. xiii, 10. Sneha evātipakvo' bhiṣvaṅgaḥ. Mādhva Bhāṣya on BG., xiii, 10. RKBG., ii, 59.

of anabhisneha. Rāmānuja regards it as indifference or absence of love for dear ones everywhere. Ānandagiri regards anabhisneha as the absence of love for all objects of enjoyment. Vedāntadeśika Veṅkaṭanātha regards anabhisneha as the absence of love and endearment for dear persons and the absence of joy at the union with dear persons, and the absence of sorrow at the separation from them. Vallabha regards anabhisneha as dispassion for all objects of enjoyment on earth and in heaven. Puruṣottamajī regards anabhisneha as the absence of love and hatred. One who welcomes and praises his friend because he is favourable to him, and who rebukes and shuns his enemy because he is hostile to him, forgets that God is the indwelling Spirit in all persons who belong to him. Hence a devotee of God is devoid of love and hatred.[32]

(10) *Non-affection* (*anabhiṣvaṅga*).—Śaṁkara regards non-affection as the absence of affection or feeling of identity of oneself with an entity other than the self. Rāmakaṇṭha regards non-affection as renunciation of false identification of oneself with all objects, which are in the nature of not-self, and which produce sentient pleasure. Madhusūdana regards non-affection as extirpation of this false sense of egoism or identification of self with not-self. Rāmānuja regards non-affection as the absence of love for sons, wife, house and the like except as the means for the performance of religious rites. Varavaramuni also gives the same definition of non-affection. He defines it also as indifference or the absence of affection for all objects of love. Baladeva and Viśvanātha define non-affection as the absence of love under all conditions, in all circumstances. It is unconditional negation of love. But Baladeva asserts that a trace of affection exists in non-affection owing to the presence of compassion for all. Vāmana regards renunciation (tyāga) as renunciation of love or affection (sneha) and of all objects of enjoyment.[33] It is a saintly quality.

(11) *Joy* (*harṣa*).—Buddhaghoṣa defines joy as an emotion which is manifested as mental enjoyment which has the

[32] BrGBG., NBG., SBG., HBG., RBG., ĀBG.. RBTC., TDBG., ATBG. ii, 57.

[33] Dṛṣṭasukhahetusu sutakalatrabhavanādiṣu anabhiṣvaṅgaḥ sarvasva-graha-parityāgaḥ. RKBG., xiii, 9. SBG., MBG., RBG., xiii, 9; VMBG., xiii, 9; ii, 57. RBG.,VNBG., BBG., ii, 57; AVBG., xvi, 2.

characteristic of experiencing a desirable object. Its function is to exploit the desirable aspect of an object in one way or another.[34] Śaṁkara regards joy as exaltation (utkarṣa) of the mind, which arises from union with a beloved person, or attainment of a desired object.[35] Ānandagiri defines joy as a kind of elation (ullāsaviśeṣa) of the mind, or a mental mode which manifests bliss (ānanda) due to union with a beloved person. It is not bodily pleasure, but mental happiness. Śrīdharasvāmī regards joy as energy (utsāha) of the mind due to the attainment of a cherished object or the union with a beloved person. Veṅkaṭanātha also defines joy as energy of the mind due to the same cause. It is in the nature of elation, elevation, or encouragement of the mind. Joy is satisfaction (santoṣa) consequent on the fulfilment of a desire according to Varavaramuni. Keśava Kāśmīrī defines joy as a particular kind of felicity (prītiviśeṣa) which is evoked by the attainment of a desired object. Rāmakaṇṭha regards joy as the experience of felicity which arises from the fulfilment of a desire for a covetable object, or the success of a voluntary action consequent on the realization of the desired end. Joy arises from the advent of prosperity, the accomplishment of success of an endeavour, the conquest of an adversary, and the like. Intense joy is expressed in brightness of the face, horripilation, shedding tears, etc.[36]

(12) *Anger (krodha)*.—The *Bhagavad Gītā* says: "Desire springs from attachment; anger arises from desire. Both attachment and anger are products of energy (rajas) of mind. Anger is a door to hell because it leads to the destruction of the self".[37] Śaṁkara defines anger as aversion for hostile objects, which are perceived or remembered and painful to the self.[38] Rāmakaṇṭha regards anger as an emotion which is characterized by aversion.[39] Madhusūdana also regards anger as aversion for a hated object (aniṣṭavidveṣa). He defines anger as a mental mode characterized

[34] POP., xiv, 128.

[35] Iṣṭaprāptau harṣaḥ. SBG., xviii, 27. Ibid, xii, 15.

[36] ĀBG., i, 12; xvii, 8; SrBG., xii, 15; xvii, 8; RKBG., xviii, 26-27; BrGBG., SBG., TPBG., xii, 15; VMBG., i, 12; SBG., RBG., ATBG., VMBG., xviii, 27.

[37] BG., ii, 62; iii, 37; xvi, 21.

[38] Krodhaḥ ātmanaḥ pratikūleṣu dṛśya-māneṣu śrūyamāṇeṣu smaryamāṇeṣu vā dveṣaḥ. SBG., v, 23.

[39] Krodhaḥ dveṣalakṣaṇaḥ. RKBG., xvi, 21. MBG., xvi, 18.

by inflaming. Nīlakaṇṭha and Baladeva also give the same definitions of it.[40]

Anger arises from the obstruction of a desire by an agent, conscious or unconscious.[41] This is Śaṁkara's view. But Baladeva asserts that anger arises from the obstruction of a desire by a conscious agent. Viśvanātha Cakravartī regards desire as an effect of rajas, and anger as an effect of tamas, and maintains that anger is due to thwarted desire. Rāmānuja defines anger as a perversion of the mind caused by another conscious agent who is the cause of separation from cherished objects or persons and encounter with hostile objects or persons. Anger is evoked by a person who is the cause of the non-attainment of the object of a desire.[42]

Ānandagiri defines anger as a mental mode, which arises from subjection or oppression by another person, and which gives rise to a desire to inflict injury on oneself and the wrong-doer. In intense anger a person inflicts injury upon himself. But generally, as Rāmānuja observes, anger is a perversion of the mind which is expressed in the persecution of the wrong-doer. Madhusūdana also remarks that anger is a desire to inflict injury on the malefactor.[43] Rāmakaṇṭha defines anger as excitement of the mind and the sense-organs due to aversion. Aversion is a desire to destroy the object or chastise the being that thwarts a desire.[44] Rāmakaṇṭhha observes that both anger and fear may arise from the obstruction of a desire; that anger is wrath towards an object of pain or a cause of the obstruction of a desire, which can be counteracted; but that fear is evoked by an object which is the cause of the obstruction of pleasure or of the emergence of pain, which cannot be counteracted.[45] Varavaramuni defines anger as a perversion of the mind due to separation from a dear object or person caused by another agent,—which causes pain to the

[40] Krodho' bhijvalanātmā. MBG., ii, 62. *Ibid*, ii, 56. Krodhaḥ cittajvalaḥ. BBG., ii, 62. NBG., ii, 62.

[41] Kāmāt kutaś cit pratihatāt krodho' bhijāyate. SBG., ii, 62. BBG., iii, 37.

[42] VNBG., iii, 37; RBG., ii, 56, 62.

[43] Krodhaḥ paravaśikṛtyātmānaṁ svaparāpakārapravṛttihetur buddhivṛttiviśeṣaḥ. ĀBG., ii, 56. Krodhaḥ parapīḍāphala-cittavikāraḥ. RBG., xvi, 4. MBG., VMBG., xvi, 4

[44] Krodhaḥ dveṣanimittakaḥ cittendriyakṣobhaḥ. RKBG., xviii, 53. Tadupaghāta-pravṛttihetur dveṣaḥ. *Ibid*, iii, 37.

[45] Bhayaṁ sukhapratīghātahetor aśakyapratīkārāt santrāsaḥ. Krodhaḥ śakyapratīkāraṁ prati roṣaḥ. RKBG., ii, 58. *Ibid*, iv, 10.

latter. Anger is a mental perversion which is the cause of inflicting injury upon the offender.[46] Vedāntādeśika Veṅkaṭanāth regards anger as a desire to destroy all objects or persons that thwart love or attachment for an object.[47]

Vallabha defines anger as intolerance of the non-attainment of an object of desire. Sadānanda regards anger as a mental mode in the nature of flaming up (abhijvalana) which is a cause of one's own pain and another's pain. It is a cause of great suffering. Keśava Kāśmīrin regards anger as internal flaming up which causes pain to oneself and another person. It is a mental perversion which arises from the thwarting of a desire for an object. It arises from the contemplation of the defects of a hostile object which is perceived, and produces aversion for it. It is a cause of inflicting injury on another person. Śaṅkarānanda regards anger as a mental agitation (cittakṣobha) which is a cause of doing harm to another person, and which produces great evil. Dhanapatisūri maintains that anger is evoked by the perception of persons, who thwart one's desire for an object, or who abuse, oppress, or persecute one, and that anger is intolerance of the thwarting of a desire. Rāghavendra regards anger as a perversion of a mind which causes infliction of injury on another person. Śaṅkarānanda regards anger as ripening of aversion, which produces mental excitement. It deflects even a cultured person from the path of virtue, enrages even an old person, and excites and causes pain to a person who regrets for his irascible temper. Anger is expressed in the trembling of the body, perspiration, the biting of the lips, red eyes, red face and the like.[48]

Suśruta regards anger as a particular perversion of the defects (doṣa) which bring about disharmony of the bodily humours—flatulence, bile and phlegm. Sexologists maintain that anger is a particular mental mode which arises from obstruction to the sex-impulse. It arises from violent obstruction to any kind of desire either for sex-gratification, or for wealth, or for performing religious rites, or for liberation. It is favourable to inflicting injury on the malefactor. This is the view of political thinkers. The Śābdikas maintain that anger is a particular

[46] Priyaviśleṣādihetuparaduḥkhāpādakasvamanovikaraḥ krodhaḥ. VMBG., ii, 56. *Ibid*, xvi, 4.
[47] Tadvirodhiṣu nirasanecchā krodhaḥ. (Tat = rāgaviṣaya). RBTC., iv, 10.
[48] BPBG., TPBG., TBBG., RGBG., BDBG., iv, ii; xii, 15. v, 23, 26; xvi, 4.

mental mode which is favourable to chastisement of the offender.[49] The Sāṁkhya maintains that a person encountering opposition, obstruction or defeat from some person gets angry. Anger is a modification of rajas due to the non-fulfilment of a desire.

(13) *Resentment* (*amarṣa*).—Śaṁkara defines 'amarṣa' as intolerance due to the thwarting of one's efforts in attaining the objects which are desired. He takes it in the sense of resentment in which Uddyotakara takes it. Resentment is akin to anger which arises from obstructed desire. Vallabha also takes it in the sense of anger due to failure in attaining objects of desire. Nīlakaṇṭha also regards 'amarṣa' as intolerance of the non-attainment of a desired object.[50].

(14) *Non-anger* (*akrodha*).—Śaṁkara defines non-anger as the suppression of anger aroused in a person who is chastised or injured by other persons. Nīlkaṇṭha and Veṅkaṭanātha also give the same definitions of non-anger. Madhusūdana regards non-anger as the immediate suppression of anger in a person who has been abused or chastised by others. Śrīdharasvāmī defines non-anger as non-evocation of anger in the mind of a person even when he is chastised by another person. Rāmānuja regards non-anger as a person's freedom from mental perversion which is generated by oppression by another person. Puruṣottamajī regards non-anger as the absence of mental agitation (kṣobha) in a person, even when he is chastised by another person without any cause. Vedāntadeśika Veṅkaṭanātha distinguishes between non-anger and forgiveness. Non-anger is the absence of anger even when its exciting cause is present (e.g., persecution). If a person is devoid of any mental perversion towards persons who have not done him any harm, he has mere indifference, but not forgiveness.[51] Rāmakaṇṭha defines non-anger as the absence of any mental agitation called anger which is the cause of violence and destroys moral judgment. Anger is said to be a door to hell. It can be conquered, Veṅkaṭanātha observes, by discrimination only which prevents the

[49] Nītisāra. Laghumañjuṣā. Nyāyakośa, 1928, p. 244.

[50] Amarṣo' bhilaṣita-pratighāte asahiṣṇutā. SBG., xii, 15. NV., iv, 13. TDBG., NBG., xii, 15.

[51] Niraparādheṣu nirvikāratā hyaudāsīnyamātram. Na tu kṣamā. RBTC., xvi, 2.

evocation of anger by destroying its roots in the shape of potencies of nescience (avidyā).[52]

(15) *Grief* (*śoka*).—Buddhaghoṣa defines sorrow as a burning in the mind due to the loss of relatives and the like. Although it is the same as grief in meaning, it is characterized by inner consuming which is manifested as continual suffering. It is intrinsic suffering which consumes the mind. Grief is mental pain which is characterized by mental oppression. Its function is to distress the mind. It is manifested as mental affliction. It is intrinsic suffering and produces bodily suffering. It is expressed in tearing the hair, weeping, striking the breast, twisting and writhing, undergoing many kinds of suffering, and committing suicide. Sorrow is due to separation from objects of sense desires. If desires and lust elude a person, he is affflicted with sorrow.[53]

Śaṁkara regards grief as mental agony (santāpa) due to the advent of a calamity or the loss of a cherished object or a beloved person.[54] Madhusūdana defines grief as bewilderment of the mind (cittavaikalya) due to the death of beloved persons who are identified with the self. Grief is evoked by the loss of wealth or the death of wife, sons, relatives, cattle and the like. It is aroused by the frustration of one's endeavours for the realization of an end.[55] Ānandagiri defines grief as mental agony due to the absence of desirable objects which are sought, or the presence of undesirable objects which are shunned. Keśava Kāśmīrī defines grief as dejection (viṣāda) due to bereavement. Rāmakaṇṭha regards grief as dejection due to the non-attainment of the object of a desire or the failure of a voluntary enterprise. It is the effect of brooding on the loss of a cherished object. Grief is a mental perversion due to non-discrimination between self and not-self,—which overwhelms the heart and causes utter bewilderment of the mind. Grief combined with mental bewilderment is

[52] SBG., NBG., BrGBG., MBG., RBG., ATBG., RKBG., xvi, 2; BG., BrGBG., xvi, 21.
Akrodhaḥ tāḍitasyāpi citte krodhānutpattiḥ. SrBG., xvi, 2.
[53] POP., xvi, 48, 51; xvii, 276.
[54] Aniṣṭaprāptau iṣṭaviyoge ca śokaḥ. SBG., xviii, 27. *Ibid*, xii, 17.
[55] NBG., RBG., VMBG., xii, 17; RKBG., xviii, 27; ATBG., BrGBG., RBTC., xviii, 35; VMBG., xviii, 27, ii, 8; MBG., i, 27.

the cause of intense delusion. Grief and delusion eclipse discriminative knowledge, and are the seeds of embodied life.[56]

Grief is expressed in paleness of the face, dryness of the mouth, burning of the skin, fatigue of the external sense-organs and the internal organs, pain in the limbs, and the like.[57]

(16) *Dejection (viṣāda).*—Śaṁkara defines dejection as depression of spirit (avasāda) which is expressed in gloomy appearance. Madhusūdana and Ānandagiri observe that dejection brings about languor (glāni) of the cognitive and motor sense-organs, and that depression means depression of the sense-organs. Rāghavendra defines dejection as depression of the mind, which is produced by grief owing to delusion, and which brings about the cessation of the operation of all sense-organs. The *Bhagavad Gītā* describes the organic expressins of dejection. Arjuna, in deep dejection, describes the expressions of his emotion thus: "My limbs fail, my mouth has become dry, my body trembles, and the hairs of my body stand on end. The bow slips from my hand, and my skin burns all over. I am not able to stand, and my mind whirls." Śrīdharasvāmin regards dejection as pain due to the loss of a cherished object. Ānandagiri defines it as mental agony (upatāpa) due to an enterprise which causes the death of relatives. Keśava Kāśmīrī defines dejection as gloom (kheda). Rāmakaṇṭha defines dejection as the absence of enterprise. Vedāntadeśika Veṅkaṭanātha mentions useless expenditure of wealth as a cause of dejection.[58]

(17) *Fear (bhaya).*—Pāṇiṇisūtra (i, 4, 25) implies that fear arises from the possibility of danger to oneself from another object or creature. Buddhaghoṣa mentions the knowledge of danger as the cause of fear, which is overcome by true knowledge. A person dedicated to the Enlightened One does not experience fear.[59] Śaṁkara describes fear as terror (trāsa). Rāmānuja defines fear as a painful emotion which arises from the perception of a cause

[56] ĀBG., i, 29; ii, i; TPBG., xviii, 15; RKBG., xviii, 27, 35, 54; MBG., SrBG., ii, 3; SBG., ii, 11.

[57] B.G., i, 28-29; ii, 8; RKBG., ii, 8; SBG., xii, 17; xviii, 27; ĀBG., xviii, 35, 54; MBG., i, 29; xviii, 15, 26.

[58] B.G., i, 29-30; SBG., ĀBG., MBG., TPBG., xviii, 35; TDBG., i, 28; SrBG., ii, 14; ĀBG., i, 27.
Viṣādaḥ anutsāhaḥ. RKBG., RBTC., xviii, 35.

[59] POP., xxi, 37; iii, 124.

of the loss of a cherished object or the advent of an evil.[60] Varavaramuni defines fear as a painful emotion which is evoked by the perception of a cause of a future pain. Rāmānuja and Vedāntadeśika Veṅkaṭanātha attribute fear to the apprehension of danger which will destroy one's good in future.[61] Ānandagiri observes that fear is experienced by a person to whom harm has been done. Unless a person has suffered injury, he cannot apprehend evil and feel an emotion of fear. Madhusūdana and Veṅkaṭanātha regard fear as a mental mode which is in the nature of depression (dainya), and which is evoked in a person who cannot counteract the cause of the destruction of an object of attachment.[62] Fear is an asthenic emotion. Rāmakaṇṭha defines fear as dread which is excited by the apprehension of the loss of a desired object. Or, fear is dread which is evoked by an object which is the cause of obstruction of pleasure, which cannot be counteracted. Or, fear is dread which arises from encountering causes of suffering which can be counteracted with great difficulty.[63] Fear arises from the perception of a thief, a tiger, a serpent, or any other dangerous object. It is expressed by trembling, horripilation, weakness of the limbs, and burning of the skin. It produces some disorder in the eyes. Śrīdharasvāmī traces anxiety to fear. Anxiety is mental agitation which is generated by fear. Fear can be counteracted by true knowledge. It ultimately arises from the extermination of one's self, which is wrongly identified with the mind-body-complex or not-self. When the self is known as different from it, it completely destroys fear.[64]

(18) *Anxiety* (*udvega*).—Nīlakaṇṭha defines anxiety as bewilderment caused by fear.[65] Madhusūdana and Veṅkaṭanātha define anxiety as a mental mode, which is in the nature of bewilderment (vyākulatā), and which is evoked by a situation that threatens one's life and security. For instance, when a person

[60] SBG., xii, 15. Priyaviśleṣāpriyāgamana-hetudarśananimittaṁ duḥkhaṁ bhayam. RBG., ii, 56.
[61] Āgāmiṣṭavirodhyaniṣṭāgamotprekṣā bhayam. RBTC., iv, 10. RBG., x, 4.
[62] ĀBG., ii, 56. Dainyātmakaś cittavṛttiviśeṣo bhayam. MBG., BrGBG., ii, 56.
[63] Bhayaṁ sukhapratīghātahetor aśakyapratīkārāt santrāsaḥ. RKBG., ii, 58. Bhayaṁ duḥkhahetor duṣkara-pratikārāt trāsaḥ. *Ibid*, x, 4. *Ibid*, xviii, 35.
[64] Udvego bhayādinimittaś, cittakṣobhaḥ. SrBG., xii, 15. ĀBG., i, 29; ii, 56; xii, 15, TPBG., NBG., BDBG., xii, 15; ATBG., iv, 10; NBG., iv, 10.
[65] Udvegaḥ tatkṛtaiva vyākulatā. NBG., xii, 15. Tat=bhaya.

finds himself in a lonely forest alone without any means of subsistence, he experiences mental confusion called anxiety. Keśava Kāśmīrī and Sadānanda also regard anxiety as mental perplexity. Śrīdharasvāmī and Daivajña Paṇḍita Sūrya define anxiety as mental agitation (cittakṣobha) due to fear and the like emotions. Dhanapatisūri defines anxiety as solicitude which is evoked when a person is attacked or threatened by wicked persons. Rāghavendra defines anxiety as a kind of trembling of the mind (manaḥkampa). Vallabha defines anxiety as brooding (cintā) which is caused by encountering a hostile agent. Śaṅkarānanda regards anxiety as an emotion which is evoked in a person when he is confronted with an evil which is a cause of death. Vedāntadeśika Veṅkaṭanātha avers that anxiety is evoked by the abusive language of a malevolent person even though he does not inflict injury on one.[66]

(19) *Security* (*abhaya*).—Rāmakaṇṭha describes security as the absence of fear due to encounter with causes of pain which cannot be counteracted. It is the emotion of self-confidence. Rāmānuja regards security as due to the destruction of the cause of fear.[67] Varavaramuni attributes fearlessness to the execution of the commands of God who is the ruler of the whole universe. Puruṣottamajī also ascribes fearlessness to taking refuge in God,—which destroys even the fear of death.[68]

(20) *Greed* (*lobha*).—Buddhaghoṣa describes greed as an emotion, which is characterized by grasping an object, and which is excited by thinking of enjoyment of objects that lead to bondage. Its function is sticking, and it is manifested as not parting with one's wealth. It is a defilement, and generates fraud, deceit, pride, discontent, vanity and evil desires. Avarice is akin to greed, which is characterized by concealing one's own success that has been achieved. Its function is not to bear sharing one's wealth with others, and it is manifested as shrinking or as meanness. It is a mental perversion, which is evoked by one's own success.[69]

The *Bhagavad Gītā* regards rajas (energy) of the mind as the cause of greed. Śaṁkara defines greed as habitual disinclination

[66] NBG., MBG., BrGBG., TPBG., BPBG., SrBG., BDBG., TBBG., TDBG., RBTC., xii, 15.
[67] Abhayaṁ bhayābhāvo viśvastacittatā. RKBG., x, 4. SBG., x, 4.
[68] RBG., ATBG., x, 4; VMBG., xviii, 30. [69] POP., xiv, 173.

to part with one's wealth. Vallabha defines greed as miserliness.[70] Nīlakaṇṭha defines greed as a hankering for more of what has been acquired. Puruṣottamajī regards greed as desire to acquire more of what has been acquired owing to worldly attachment for objects of enjoyment and constant flitting of the mind from object to object, which are expressed in constant endeavours to acquire them.[71] Hanumān defines greed as acceptance of wealth, which is prohibited by the scriptures and unwillingness to part with one's wealth which ought to be expended according to the injunctions of the scriptures. Dhanapatisūri and Śrīdharasvāmī define greed as ever-recurrent desire for the acquisition of wealth in spite of one's possessing abundant wealth. Sadānanda also defines it as constantly increasing desire for the acquisition and accumulation of wealth, which is never gratified even by the amassing of a large fortune. Madhusūdana defines greed as desire to appropriate others' property and inability to part with one's own wealth even for religious purposes when its expenditure is obligatory. Rāmakaṇṭha regards greed as continually increasing yearning for objects of enjoyment, or as continuance of a desire for objects even after they are attained, or as inordinate desire for the misappropriation of others' wealth. Rāmānuja defines greed as unwillingness to part with one's possessions even without a purpose, and identifies it with miserliness. Śaṅkarānanda also defines greed as intolerance of parting with one's wealth, and regards it as miserliness.[72]

(21) *Longing* (*spṛhā*).—Śaṁkara defines longing as yearning (tṛṣṇā) for all common objects. Madhusūdana defines it as desire to appropriate objects belonging to others, good or bad, by any means, fair or foul. Śrīdharasvāmī defines it as desire to appropriate objects, good or bad, as soon as they are perceived here and there. Rajas or energy of the mind is the cause of spṛhā.[73] Sadānanda defines spṛhā as a desire for all kinds of objects, precious or trifling, belonging to others, and misappropriating them by any means, fair or foul, when they are perceived. He identifies spṛhā with greed (lobha). Keśava Kāśmīrī defines spṛhā

[70] Lobhaḥ svakīyadravyasyātyāgaśilatā. SBG., xiv, 12. Lobhaḥ kārpaṇyam. TDBG., xiv, 12.
[71] Lobhaḥ prāptādhike gardhaḥ. NBG., xiv, 12. ATBG., xiv, 12.
[72] HBG., BDBG., SrBG., BPBG., MBG., RKBG., RBG., TDBG., xiv, 12.
[73] BG., SBG., MBG., SrBG., xiv, 12.

as a thirst or craving for objects which are common property.[74] But Śaṅkarānanda and Rāghavendra take spṛhā in the sense of desire for an object which is not yet attained. Vallabha defines spṛhā as desire for an object which is not fit for being acquired by a person. Nīlakaṇṭha defines spṛhā as desire for the appropriation of another's wealth perceived by a person.[75]

(22) *Absence of Longing* (*niḥspṛhatā*).—Śaṁkara observes that one who is free from all longings for perceptible and imperceptible objects of enjoyment, is fit for concentration on the Ātman at the time. Rāmānuja and Hanumān also regard the renunciation of all hankerings as a precondition for concentration on the self. Puruṣottamajī regards the absence of all hankerings for objects of enjoyment as a necessary condition for meditation on God only. Hanumān regards a person, who has no longing for his body and life even, as a neutral, desireless spectator. He follows Śaṁkara in his view. Veṅkaṭanātha describes desirelessness as favourable to trance (samādhi). When the manas is rigidly controlled and rendered free from mental modes and divested of rajas and tamas, it becomes free from all desires for objects of enjoyment, and concentrated on the Self (ātman) only, and is modified into it. Though it can assume the forms of all objects owing to its translucence because of execessive predominance of sattva, it does not assume those forms because the mental modes are arrested. It attains the state of trance. Vallabha observes that a person becomes devoted to superconscious trance (asamprajñāta samādhi), when his manas is concentrated on the Inner Self (pratyagātman), and becomes free of longing for supernatural powers born of meditation. Rāmakaṇṭha regards one as devoid of longing, who has renounced all desires for happiness here and hereafter, which are non-eternal, because he has experienced his Ātman, which is always complete everywhere. One becomes free from longing when he renounces all desires and recognizes one's self as the non-dual pure conciousness which is eternally contented. Madhusūdana regards a person as devoid of longing, who has renounced desires for external objects of enjoyment, (e.g. house), internal objects of pleasure (e.g., building castles in the air), and subconscious

[74] Spṛhā sarva-sāmānya-vastu-viṣayā tṛṣṇā. TPBG., xiv, 12.
[75] BPBG., TPBG., TBBG., RGBG., ATBG., NBG., xiv, 12.

impressions (vāsanā) of desires, who has no desire even for the preservation of life, and who is devoid of the sense of 'I' and 'mine'. Complete desirelessness or higher dispassion presupposes the arrest of all mental modes, and is an internal means of accomplishing superconscious trance. The freedom from desires for perceptible and imperceptible objects of enjoyment is the result of deliberation on their faults. Desirelessness depends upon egolessness.[76]

(23) *Hope* (*āśā*).—Śaṁkara defines hope as craving for a desired object which is attainable, but which is not yet known or attained. Ānandagiri defines vain hope as yearning for an object, the means to which is unattainable or unknown. Vedāntadeśika Veṅkaṭanātha observes that hope is directed towards the realization of a preconceived end, while deliberation is concerned with merits and demerits of the intended course of action. Hopes are said to be countless because their objects are innumerable.[77] Śaṁkara regards expectation (pratīkṣā) as waiting for a known desired object, which is attainable.[78] Madhusūdana defines vain hope as desire for an object, the means to which is either unknown or unattainable. It is a fetter because it is a cause of bondage.

(24) *Non-greed* (*aloluptva*).—Śaṁkara defines non-greed as the unaffected condition of the sense-organs in the presence of their objects. It is the absence of any desire for enjoyment even when its objects are present.[79] Madhusūdana, Nīlakaṇṭha, Veṅkaṭanātha and Hanumān give the same definitions of non-greed. Śrīdharasvāmī defines non-greed as the absence of greed. Rāmānuja defines non-greed as the absence of desire for all objects of enjoyment. Vedāntadeśika Veṅkaṭanātha defines non-greed as the absence of immoral desires for the gratification of the sense-organs. Ānandatīrtha defines non-greed as the absence of attachment (rāga), and identifies it with detachment or dispassion. Puruṣottamajī defines non-greed as the absence of constant flitting

[76] SBG., RBG., HBG., ATBG., BrGBG., TDBG., vi, 18; RKBG., xviii, 49; ii, 73; MBG., ii, 71; vi, 18.

[77] Āśā anirjñāta-prāpyeṣṭārtha-prārthanā. SB., Kaṭha Up., i, 1, 8. ĀBG., xvi, 12. Cintā kartavya-viṣayā, āśā tu phalaviṣayā. RBTC., xvi, 12.

[78] Nirjñāta-prāpyārtha-pratīkṣanaṁ pratīkṣā. SB., Kaṭha Up., i, 1, 8.

[79] Aloluptvam indriyaṇām visayasannidhau avikriyā. SBG., xvi, 2. MBG., NBG., BrGBG., HBG., xvi, 2.

of the mind from object to object in quest of sentient pleasure.[80] Non-greed is regarded as a divine virtue.

(25) *Egoism (ahaṁkāra)*.—Rāmakaṇṭha regards egoism as false knowledge of not-self as self.[81] It generates pride in learning, wealth, beauty, noble birth and the like. Madhusūdana regards egoism as false conceit that 'I am the best person'. Ānandagiri regards conceit (māna) as egoism. Śaṁkara regards egoism as considering oneself as endowed with excellent qualities, some of which are wrongly attributed to oneself. It is false knowledge (avidyā) which is the root of all taints and immoral actions. Rāmakaṇṭha regards egoism as identification of the mind (manas), the body and the sense-organs with the self, which is the principal taint of the empirical self.[82]

(26) *Pride (mada)*.—Rāmakaṇṭha defines pride as inflation of mind (cittodreka). Madhusūdana maintains that pride consists in false attribution of great excellence to oneself, though one is devoid of any excellence. Ānandagiri regards pride as arrogance which is the cause of despisement of others.[83] Śaṁkara regards mada as intoxication with the enjoyment of sensible objects due to over-estimation of its value to oneself. Ānandagiri distinguishes between pride (mada) and conceit (abhimāna). Pride or inflation of mind is the cause of despisement of great persons. Conciet is the false attribution of excellent qualities to oneself.[84] Keśava Kāśmīrī defines mada as joy due to the enjoyment of objects forbidden by the moral code. Madhusūdana also regards it as eagerness to enjoy forbidden objects. Sadānanda defines it as an emotion which produces attachment for enjoyment of sentient pleasures. Nīlakaṇṭha regards mada as intoxication due to pride. He regards pride (garva) as conceit due to wealth. Hanumān identifies pride (mada) with boast (darpa). Madhusūdana regards mada as arrogance, which is due to false attribution of excellence to oneself, though one is really devoid of any excellence, which is the cause of despising great persons. Śrīdhara-

[80] Aloluptvaṁ viṣayeṣu nisspṛhatvam. RBG., xvi, 2. SrBG., RBTC., ATBG., Mādhva Bhāṣya on BG., xvi, 2; BG., xvi, 2.

[81] Ahaṁkāraḥ anātmanyātmapratipattinibandhanaṁ mithyājñānam. RKBG., iii, 40.

[82] MBG., xvi, 5; ĀBG., xv, 5; SBG., xvi, 18; RKBG., xviii, 53.

[83] Utseko mado mahadavadhīraṇe hetuḥ. ĀBG., xvi, 4. RKBG., MBG., xvi, 10.

[84] Utseko mado mahadavadhīraṇe hetuḥ, ātmanyutkṛṣṭatvādhyāropo'bhimānaḥ. ĀBG., xvi, 4. SBG., xviii, 35.

svāmī defines boast (darpa) as inflation of the mind due to wealth, learning and the like. Hence pride (mada) and boast (darpa) are different modes of the puffing up of the mind (citta).[85] Veṅkaṭanātha regards pride (garva) as delusion due to conceit because of wealth, learning, rich relatives and the like. He regards arrogance (mada) as false attribution of non-respectability to one's preceptors and and other superiors. This shows that mada, garva and darpa are different modes of inflation of the mind.[86]

(27) *Inordinate self-conceit* (*atimāna*).—Ānandagiri and Śrīdharasvāmī regard conceit (māna) as egoism (ahaṁkāra). Madhusūdana regards self-conceit as demonstration of one's respectability, though one is not really worthy of being respected. Śaṁkara regards inordinate self-conceit (atimāna) as attributing excess of respectability to oneself. Ānandagiri and Śrīdharasvāmī also regard excessive self-conceit as false attribution of supreme excellence to oneself. Śaṁkara regards humility (nātimānitā) as the absence of inordinate self-conceit. Rāmakaṇṭha regards conceit as false identification of the self with the body and the sense-organs which are non-eternal, and erroneously regarding enjoyments, which depend upon the not-self, as 'mine'. When conceit (māna) becomes stable at all times, it becomes inordinate (atimāna). Humility (nātimanitā) is the absence of excessive self-conceit. Buddhaghoṣa regards vanity of conceit (mana-mada) as conceit that is evoked by one's conceiving 'I am superior'.[87]

(28) *Self-praise* (*ātmasambhāvanā*).—Śaṁkara regards self-praise as trumpeting one's own glory as being endowed with all excellent qualities, and not being praised by virtuous persons. Rāmakaṇṭha regards self-praise as a form of egoism, false self-conceit, or wrong consideration of oneself as endowed with excellent qualities. Self-praise is not praise by another person who can rightly distnguish between excellences and blemishes. Rāmānuja regards self-praise as self-glorification. Vedāntadeśika Veṅkaṭanātha observes that a virtuous person feels shy when he is praised by others, and that self-praise is a vice. Nīlakaṇṭha

[85] MBG., xvi, 10. Darpo dhana-vidyādinimittaṁ cittasyautsukyam. SrBG., xvi, 4. TPBG., MBG., BPBG., xviii, 35; NBG., xvi, 17; HBG., xvi, 10.

[86] BrGBG., xvi, 17.

[87] ĀBG., SrBG., MBG., SBG., RKBG., xvi, 3; xv, 5; MBG., xiii, 7; xvi, 10; POP., viii, 247, n. 71.

regards self-praise as regarding oneself as great. Puruṣottamajī regards self-praise as self-glorification which consists in showing off one's real or imaginary qualities to others, as distinguished from being praised by devout persons.[88]

(29) *Haughtiness* (*stambha*).—Śaṁkara regards a person as haughty, who does not show respect to respectable persons. Rāmānuja regards a person as haughty, who thinks himself to be perfect. Hanumān and Vedāntadeśika Veṅkaṭanātha regard a person as haughty, who does not bow even to his preceptor and gods. Veṅkaṭanātha regards haughtiness as immodesty. Nīlakaṇṭha regards haughtiness as the absence of showing respect to superior persons. Puruṣottamajī regards haughtiness as the absence of modesty or humility. Rāmakaṇṭha also regards haughtiness as immodesty or lack of humility to superior persons endowed with excellent qualities, who are generally regarded as worthy of veneration. A haughty person does not bow to a superior person owing to engrossment in false conceit (abhimāna) because he considers himself to be full of all excellent qualities. He never submits to any one or thinks himself to be inferior to any one. Haughtiness is insolence, arrogance, immodesty. It implies pride (mada) and conceit (māna) which are in the nature of egoism.[89]

(30) *Boast* (*darpa*).—Śaṁkara regards boast (darpa) as an emotion which succeeds excessive joy and brings about transgression of duty.[90] The Smṛti says: "An elated person feels proud, and a proud person transgresses his duty." Rāmānuja regards boast as joy due the experience of desired objects, which deludes the self in the determination of duties.[91] Pride is the cause of delusion or non-discrimination of duties. It generates confusion of intellect, warps moral judgment, and leads to transgression of duty. So there is not much difference between Śaṁkara's definition and that of Rāmānuja. Madhusūdana regards darpa as intoxication (mada) due to intense joy and bringing about violation of the Moral Law. Rāmakaṇṭha regards it as inflation of mind owing to the acquisition of a little supernatural power born of meditation. He also regards it as a perversion of the mind in the form of joy, delusion and the like due to

[88] SBG., RKBG., RBG., RBTC., NBG., ATBG., xvi, 17.
[89] SBG., RBG., RBTC., BrGBG., NBG., ATBG., RKBG., xvi, 17.
[90] Darpo nāma harṣāntarabhāvī dharmātikramahetuḥ. SBG., xviii, 53.
[91] Kṛtyākṛtyāvivekakaro viṣayānubhavanimitto harṣaḥ. RBG., xvi, 4.

self-praise. He considers it to be a kind of self-conceit (abhimāna). Madhusūdana regards darpa as a particular kind of pride which springs from the possession of wealth and having wealthy kinsmen and relatives, and which produces despisement of great persons. Śrīdharasvāmī defines darpa as puffing up of the mind due to the possession of wealth, learning and the like. Keśava Kāśmīrī defines darpa as despisement of another person due to the false consideration of one's superiority and respectability. He defines it also as haughtiness (auddhatya) due to one's wealth, learning and other excellences. It is the cause of despising other great persons. Śaṅkarānanda defines darpa as inflation of the mind (cittodreka) due to one's wealth, learning, beauty, noble family, meritorious actions and the like, which is the cause of despising great persons. Sadānanda also defines arrogance as puffing up of the mind (utseka) due to the possession of great wealth and the like. Dhanapatisūri and Madhusūdana define darpa as inflation (utseka) or pride (mada) due to the possession of great wealth, rich relatives and the like, which is the cause of one's despising great persons. Rāghavendra shows another aspect of arrogance. It ignores a cause of fear owing to pride, though it is present.[92]

(31) *Non-egoism or pridelessness* (*anahaṁkāra*).—Ānandagiri identifies egoism (ahaṁkara) with pride (garva), and non-egoism with pridelessness. Śaṁkara regards egolessness as the absence of egoism. Veṅkaṭanātha and Nīlakaṇṭha consider non-egoism to be the absence of pride or arrogance.[93] Rāmānuja regards non-egoism as the absence of false identification of the self with the body which is not-self.[94] It is also the absence of false identification of the 'not-mine' with the 'mine'. Varavaramuni regards non-egoism as the cause of the absence of longing (spṛhā) for objects of enjoyment, and treats egolessness as the absence of desire for exerting one's own freedom of the will because of the realization that the Divine Will impels the human will. Non-egoism implies non-possession or the absence of the sense of 'mine' (mamatā) in all objects which are different from the self. Rāmakaṇṭha includes in egolessness the absence of the sense of

[92] MBG., SrBG., RKBG., TPBG., BPBG., BDBG., RGBG., xvi, 4; RKBG., xviii, 53.
[93] ĀBG., SBG., BrGBG., NBG., xiii, 9.
[94] Anahaṁkāraḥ anātmani dehe ātmābhimānarahitatvam. RBG., xiii, 9.

'I' and 'mine' due to the destruction of the sense of freedom of the will and of the sense of ownership and possession.[95] Śaṁkara and Hanumān regard a person as devoid of egotism (nirahaṁkāra), who is devoid of self-praise due to the possession of learning and the like. Jayatīrtha defines ahaṁkāra as false conceit of being a doer (kartā) or free agent, and regards one as egoless, who is devoid of this false conceit.[96]

(32) *Absence of the sense of 'mine'* (*nirmamatā*).—Śaṁkara regards a person as nirmama, who is devoid of the sense of 'mine' in the objects which are obtained without any voluntary effort even for the preservation of one's life. Hanumān regards a person as nirmama, who is devoid of the sense of 'mine' even in his body. Puruṣottamajī regards a person as nirmama, who has conquered the sense of 'mine' in his mind-body-complex. Rāmānuja regards one as nirmama, who is devoid of the sense of 'mine' in the body which is not-self. Jayatīrtha regards one as nirmama, who is devoid of the false conceit of ownership or 'mine'.[97]

(33) *Envy* (*amarṣa, mātsarya*).—Ānandagiri regards envy (amarṣa) as intolerance of another person's prosperity or exaltation. Śrīdharasvāmī defines envy as intolerance of another person's gain. Puruṣottamajī also regards amarṣa as envy at another's exaltation. Madhusūdana defines envy as intolerance of another person's superior qualities. Keśava Kāśmīrī regards envy as intolerance of another person's prosperity and happiness. Sadānanda regards amarṣa as intolerance of the loss of one's cherished objects. Śaṅkarānanda regards amarṣa as impatience or lack of endurance of inevitable pangs of suffering during illness. Rāmānuja regards matsara as intolerance of natural evils such as storm, sun, rainfall and the like, which can be conquered by the conviction that they are due to one's potencies of actions acquired in previous births. Veṅkaṭanātha supports his view. Puruṣottamajī also regards the firm conviction that the attainment or non-attainment of a desired object or success or failure of our voluntary efforts depends upon the will of God as an antidote to intolerance. Śaṁkara, Nīlakaṇṭha and Veṅkaṭanātha regard

[95] VMBG., xviii, 49; RBG., vi, 10; RKBG., xviii, 53.
[96] SBG., HBG., JTBG., ii, 71.
[97] SBG., HBG., ATBG., RBG., JTBG., ii, 71.

amarṣa as intolerance (asahiṣṇutā). But Hanumān regards it as anger (krodha).[98]

Śaṁkara takes 'matsara' in the sense of enmity (vaira), and a person devoid of enmity as 'vimatsara'. Śrīdharasvāmī gives the same meanings of the two terms. Ānandagiri takes 'matsara' in the sense of desire for one's own exaltation (utkarṣa), which is preceded by intolerance of others' exaltation. He takes 'matsara' in the sense of envy. Madhusūdana also regards 'matsara' as envy which is aroused by another's gain, or intolerance of another's exaltation, or as enmity. He regards one as vimatsara, if one is devoid of any feeling of enmity. One who is devoid of envy is devoid of enmity.[99] Nīlakaṇṭha takes 'matsara' in the sense of envy or agony at the sight of another's gain. An envious person suffers mental agony (santāpa) at another's exaltation. Hanumān regards a person as vimatsara, who is devoid of anger (krodha) or resentment. Puruṣottamajī regards one devoid of mental agitation when reviled by a wicked person as vimatsara. Veṅkaṭanātha regards one as vimatsara, who endures heat, cold, sun, rain, etc., which are causes of pleasure and pain, because of the strong belief that they are due to one's potencies of actions in the previous births. Matsara is intolerance of natural evils which befall us. Freedom from matsara is ungrudging endurance of natural evils which cause us inevitable sufferings.[100]

Buddhaghoṣa describes envy as being jealous of another's success. It is excited by the perception of another's success, and manifested as averseness from that. Its function is to be dissatisfied with that. It is a fetter which ought to be broken.[101]

(34) *Intolerance of excellence* (*abhyasūyā*).—Hanumān identifies asūyā with envy (īrṣyā). Veṅkaṭanatha, Śrīdharasvāmī and Madhusūdana define asūya as fault-finding (doṣadṛṣṭi). Ānandagiri and Vedāntadeśika Veṅkaṭanātha define asūya as detection of non-existing faults in excellent qualities.[102]

[98] Amarṣa asahiṣṇutā parakīya-prakarṣasya. ĀBG., xii, 15. Amarṣaḥ parasya labhe asahanam. SrBG., xii, 15. Amarṣaḥ parotkarṣāsahiṣṇutā. ATBG., xii, 15. SBG., NBG., HBG., BrGBG., MBG., BPBG., AT G., AT G., xii, 15. SBG., NBG., HBG., BrGBG., MBG., BPBG., ATBG., TBBG., xii, 15; RBG., iv, 22.

[99] Vimatsaro nirvaira-buddhiḥ. SBG., iv, 22. Parotkarṣāmarṣa-pūrvikā svasyotkarṣa-vāñchā (matsaraḥ). ĀBG., iv, 22. SrBG., iv, 22.

[100] NBG., HBG., ATBG., BrGBG., iv, 22. [101] POP., xiv, 172.

[102] Guṇeṣu doṣāviṣkaraṇam asūyā. ĀBG., RBTC., iii, 31. HBG., iii, 32; BrGBG., MBG., xviii, 71; SrBG., iii, 31.

Śaṁkara defines abhyasūyā as intolerance of the excellent qualities of persons who are in the path of morality and religin. Rāmānuja and Varavaramuni define asūyā as detection of imaginary blemishes in an instructor or in his thesis, or as finding out faults in the meanings of the scriptures which are full of excellent qualities. Hanumān regards abhyasūyā as discovering unreal merits and defects in God who is the inner guide of a person, and in divine incarnations such as Rāma and Kṛṣṇa.[103] Śrīdharasvāmī regards abhyasūya as false attribution of vices to the excellent qualities of persons treading the path of rectitude and piety. Fraudulence and other vices are attributed to compassion and other virtues of preceptors and the like who perform the religious rites prescribed by the Vedas. Veṅkaṭanātha defines abhysūyā as false attribution of ignorance, fraud and other vices to the preceptor's wise instructions.[104] Puruṣottamajī takes abhyasūa in a general sense, and defines it as false ascription of faults to persons devoid of faults.[105] Anasūya is the absence of fault-finding.

(35) *Non-censoriousness* (*apaiśuna*).—Saṃkara defines censoriousness as exposing another person's faults or vulnerable points to others. Śrīdharasvāmī regards slander as backbiting or exposing the faults of another person to others behind his back, and defines non-slander as the absence of backbiting.[106] Hanumān defines non-slander as concealing the faults of another person. It is not only the absence of backbiting, but also hiding others' faults. Rāmānuja regards non-slander as non-assertion of anything which is injurious to another person. Puruṣottamajī defines non-slander as the absence of calumniating another person, which is motivated by the knowledge that God is the in-dwelling Spirit in all persons. Rāmakaṇṭha defines censoriousness as exposure of others' faults, and regards non-censoriousness as non-exposure of others' faults or absence of fault-finding spirit.[107]

(36) *Hate* (*dveṣa*).—Śaṃkara defines hate as the repulsion of

[103] SBG., xvi, 18; RBG., VMBG., iii, 31; xviii, 71.

[104] Abhyasūyā sanmārgavartiṇām guṇeṣu doṣāropaḥ. SrBG., xvi, 18. BrGBG., xvi, 18.

[105] Abhyasūyakāḥ doṣarahiteṣu doṣāropakāḥ. ATBG., xvi, 18.

[106] Paiśunaṁ parokṣe paradoṣa-prakāśanaṁ tadvarjanam apaiśunam. SrBG., xvi, 2. SBG., NBG., JTBG., RKBG., xvi, 2.

[107] Apaiśunaṁ para-randhra-pracchādanam. HBG., xvi, 2. RBG., ATBG., RKBG., xvi, 2.

the mind to an undesirable object which is attained. It is repulsion towards an object the like of which caused pain to a person on a previous occasion. It arises from the recollection of past pain. It is a quality of the mind (antaḥkaraṇa), and not a quality of the self. It is an object of cognition. Śaṁkara's analysis of hate is like that of Praśastapāda.[108] Nīlakaṇṭha regards hate as an emotion opposed to love or attachment, which seeks the removal of pain or a cause of pain. Madhusūdana identifies hate with anger which is a mental mode contrary to longing (spṛhā) for the appropriation of a desired object. Hate is a desire for the avoidance or removal of an undesirable object. Sadānanda also identifies hate with anger and loathing. Dhanapatisūri defines hate as a desire for the avoidance of an object perceived, which caused pain to a person in the past. Keśava Kāśmīrī regards hate as an emotion which is expressed in an action to remove a hostile object. Veṅkaṭanātha regards hate as a mental mode which is in the nature of mental agony (santāpa) which is evoked by the sight of a person who is the cause of one's separation from a beloved person or loss of a cherished object.[109]

Śaṁkara maintains like the Naiyāyika that love and hate are actuated by delusion. A person under delusion identifies his self with the body, feels love and hate, attraction and repulsion, performs good and bad actions, and earns merits and demerits. But a person, who is not under delusion and knows the self to be distinct from the body, does not feel love and hate, does not feel inclined to perform good and bad actions, and does not acquire merits and demerits. A person under delusion is subject to birth and death. A person who has acquired true knowledge of the self attains liberation. Thus both Śaṁkara and the Naiyāyika give an intellectual analysis of love and hate. Both regard destruction of delusion (moha) or nescience (avidyā) as the cause of liberation. The *Bhagavad Gītā* regards tamas or inertia of the mind as the cause of delusion. Śaṁkara explains delusion as non-discrimination (aviveka). He regards ajñāna as non-discrimination or wrong cognition as to what is duty and what is not.[110]

[108] SBG., xii, 17; xiii, 6; PBh., p. 261.
[109] NBG., MBG., BPBG., BDBG., TPBG., xiii, 6; BrGBG., ii, 56.
[110] SBG., xiii, 2; xiv, 13; xvi, 4.

(37) *Absence of Hatred* (*adveṣa*).—The *Bhagavad Gītā* asserts that a devotee of God is devoid of hatred for any creature.[111] Śaṁkara observes that he does not hate even a person who has caused him suffering because he realizes that all creatures are identical with his Ātman. Veṅkaṭanātha also remarks that a devotee does not feel any hatred for hostile persons. Śrīdharasvāmī asserts that a devotee is devoid of hatred for superior persons, friendly towards equal persons, and compassionate to inferior persons. Rāmakaṇṭha ascribes a devotee's absence of hatred for all creatures to his realization that they are not avoidable because they are identical with the one Ātman or Brahman, and that manas untainted by the taint of hatred is favourable to such identity-consciousness. Puruṣottamajī traces the absence of a devotee's hatred for all creatures to his knowledge that they are the means of the sport of God in the world drama.[112]

(38) *Non-enmity* (*avaira*).—The *Bhagavad Gitā* asserts that a devotee of God is devoid of enmity towards all creatures.[113] Ānandagiri defines enmity as doing harm to a person out of hatred[114]. A person devoid of enmity does no harm to any creature, even to one who has done great harm to him. Rāmakaṇṭha regards such a person as devoid of hatred (dveṣa). Rāmānuja regards such a person as devoid of enmity towards all creatures due to the absence of any cause of enmity towards them, and because of the knowledge that they depend upon God who is their Inner Guide, and that one's pain is due to one's own sin, and that happines in all beings is due to union with God, and that misery in them is due to separation from God. Vendāntadeśika Veṅkaṭanātha also observes, that a devotee's absence of enmity towards any creature is due to the absence of its cause, and not to the injunction of the śāstras; that he is deeply attached to God and consequently averse to all other things, and indifferent to trifling joys and sorrows of the world, and does not feel any hostility towards the causes of sufferings; that he does not feel any hatred for his wrong-doer, because he knows that his own sin is the cause of his suffering caused by another

[111] Adveṣṭā sarvabhūtānāṁ. BG., xii, 13.
[112] Uttameṣu dveṣaśūnvaḥ sameṣu maitraḥ hīneṣu kṛpāluḥ. SrBG., xii, 13. SBG., BrGBG., RKBG., ATBG., xii, 13.
[113] Nirvairaḥ sarvabhūteṣu. BG., xi, 55.
[114] Dveṣapūrvakāniṣṭācaraṇaṁ vairam. ĀBG., xi, 55.

person, and that the latter is impelled by God in his act of malevolence.[115]

(39) *Mastery* (*īśvarabhāva*).—Śaṁkara regards mastery as demonstration of a master's power (prabhuśakti) over the ruled persons. Rāmakaṇṭha defines mastery as assertion of one's superiority to others and intolerance of one's subordination to them. Rāmānuja defines mastery as the feeling of power to control the destiny of oneself and others. Vedāntadeśika Veṅkaṭanātha regards mastery as the false sense of determining others' actions, and asserts that favouring the virtuous and cultured and punishing the vicious and wicked are included in mastery. Veṅkaṭanātha regards mastery as the power of influencing, controlling and subjecting other people. Puruṣottamajī defines mastery as the false sense of one's omnipotence, or as efficiency in exercising power over other people and subjecting them. Hanumān regards mastery as the feeling that one is supreme in all respects. Nīlakaṇṭha regards mastery as the power of subjecting and punishing the vicious. Śrīdharasvāmī defines mastery as the power of subjection. Madhusūdana defines mastery as exhibition of the power of ruling over the ruled for the protection of the subjects.[116]

(40) *Spiritedness (tejas)*.—Śaṁkara defines tejas as boldness. Nīlakaṇṭha also defines it as boldness as distinguished from fierceness. Madhusūdana defines spiritedness as boldness or capacity of not being overpowered by such foolish persons as women and children. Rāmānuja and Varavaramuni define spiritedness as invincibility or power of not being overpowered, defeated or humiliated by others, or as insubordination to other wicked persons. Rāmakaṇṭha defines tejas as innate spiritedness which is the cause of one's incapability of being vanquished by others. Puruṣottamajī regards spiritedness as boldness due to the grace of God. Hanumān defines tejas as valour (pratāpa).[117]

(41) *Modesty or absence of Egotism (amānitva)*.—Śaṁkara regards modesty as the absence of self-glorification which is a manifestation of vanity (māna), that consists in trumpeting forth

[115] SBG., RKBG., RBG., RBTC., xi, 55.

[116] Īśvarabhāvaḥ prabhutvaṁ parādhīnatvāsahiṣṇutvam. RKBG., xviii, 43. SBG., RBG., RBTG., ATBG., NBG., xviii, 43; HBG., ATBG., xvi, 15. Īśvarabhāvo loka-niyamana-śaktiḥ BrGBG., xviii, 43.

[117] Tejaḥ parānabhibhavanīyatva-kāraṇaṁ svābhāvikam ojaḥ. RKBG., xvi, 3. SBG., NBG., MBG., RBG., VMBG., ATBG., HBG., xvi, 3.

one's merits. Ānandagiri regards vanity as false attribution of excellence to oneself, and modesty as the absence of vanity. Śrīdharasvāmī regards modesty as the absence of self-glorification or trumpeting forth one's own excellent qualities. Hanumān regards vanity as self-praise, and modesty as the absence of self-praise. Veṅkaṭanātha, Puruṣottamajī and Nīlakaṇṭha regard modesty as the absence of praising one's real or imaginary excellent qualities. Rāmānuja regards modesty as the absence of despisement of superior persons. Vedāntadeśika Veṅkaṭanātha regards modesty as the absence of vanity (māna), which is the pride of learning, wealth, property, rich relatives and the like,—that is a cause of despising superior persons. Rāmakaṇṭha regards modesty as pure resolution (saṁkalpa), which is in the nature of knowledge, because it is a cause of the manifestation of the discriminative knowledge of the Ātman. Varavaramuni regards humility as self-surrender to another superior person or being. Puruṣottamajī regards humility to God as due to the knowledge that He is the supreme Being.[118]

Śaṁkara regards humility (vinaya) as discipline or restraint of the sense-organs and the internal organs (upaśama). Ānandagiri interprets discipline as the absence of egotism or haughtiness. Rāmakaṇṭha regards humility as self-restraint in accomplishing the ends enjoined by the śāstras.[119]

(42) *Self-abasement (nirveda)*.—Ānandagiri considers the knowledge of the faults of birth and death (saṁsāra) as the cause of self-abasement. Hanumān and Nīlakaṇṭha regard it as dispassion. Madhusūdana also defines it as the absence of attachment and yearning for objects of enjoyment (vaitṛṣṇya). Varavaramuni defines self-abasement as the feeling of frustration. Vedāntadeśika Veṅkaṭanātha defines it as self-despisement (svāvajñā). Delusion counteracts the production of self-abasement. Vallabha regards nirveda as detachment for fruits of actions. Veṅkaṭanātha regards it as suspreme dispassion (para vairāgya). Puruṣottamajī regards it as liberation. Ānandagiri observes that when the discriminative knowledge of the Ātman

[118] Amānitvaṁ svaguṇa-ślāghā-rāhityam. SrBG., xiii, 7. SBG., ĀBG., HBG., BrGBG., ATBG., NBG., RBG., RBTC., RKBG., xiii, 7; ATBG., VMBG., xviii, 65.

[119] Vinaya upaśamaḥ. SBG., v, 18. Upaśamo nirahaṁkāratvam anauddhatyam. ĀBG., v, 18. RKBG., v, 18.

dawns, all objects which are in the nature of the not-self are experienced to be fruitless. Hence detachment for them is generated when the Self gets discriminative knowledge of itself. Nīlakaṇṭha remarks that nirveda or detachment generates endurance of pleasure and pain, heat and cold, and the like.

Rāmakaṇṭha means by nirveda anxiety (udvega), and by anirveda freedom from anxiety. Rāmānuja means by nirveda sorrow, and by anirveda joy. Veṇkaṭanātha regards nirveda as repentance (anutāpa) which arises from the knowledge that yoga has not been accomplished in the course of such a long period of time. He regards anirveda as the absence of repentance, or patience (dhairya) due to the conviction that yoga must be accomplished in this birth or a future birth, and that there is no necessity for hurry about it. Śrīdharasvāmī regards nirveda as relaxation of earnest efforts for the accomplishment of yoga owing to the feeling of pain.[120]

(43) *Emotions are due to false knowledge.*—Śaṁkara maintains that negligence in the quest for one's real nature produces delusion (moha). Delusion produces egoism (ahaṁkāra). Egoism produces bondage. Bondage produces suffering. Forgetfulness of the real nature of the Self produces intellectual disorders (dhīdoṣa) in a person who pursues pleasures of the senses. Intellectual disorders are the causes of emotions. Delusion is destroyed by discriminative knowledge (viveka) which is due to the distinct knowledge of the Self (Ātman) or Brahman.

All persons, Rāmakaṇṭha asserts, have their right knowledge eclipsed by their individual nescience, and cannot discriminate between reality and unreality, and are, consequently, infected by mental perversions like joy, sorrow and the like. But the yogins who have an intuitive experience of Ātman or Brahman in all beings are not affected by emotions. Thus emotions are intellectual disorders.[121]

(44) *Delusion (moha).*—Śaṁkara defines delusion as non-discrimination (aviveka), or absence of right knowledge of moral actions and immoral actions, or bewilderment (vicittabhāva) due to nescience (ajñāna), which is the cause of all evils in worldly

[120] SBG., ĀBG., HBG., MBG., VMBC., RBTC., NBG., ATBG., TDBG., BrGBG., ii, 52; NBG., BrGBG., SrBG., RKBG., vi, 23.
[121] RKBG., xviii, 54; VCM., 322-24, 346.

a neutral feeling leading to neither acceptance nor rejection of an object.[127]

(45) *Non-delusion* (*asaṁmoha*).—Śrīdharasvāmī defines non-delusion as the absence of perplexity, and distinguishes it from intelligence (buddhi) or skill in discriminating between the essential and the inessential, and knowledge (jñāna) which relates to the nature of the self. Śaṁkara regards non-delusion as clear moral insight into one's duty in a concrete situation without confusion, whereas intelligence is the capacity for comprehending the nature of subtle things, and knowledge regarding the self and other entities. Madhusūdana defines non-delusion as discrimination between right and wrong without perplexity under complex circumstances at the very moment. Rāmakaṇṭha regards non-delusion as certain discriminative knowledge of the ontological reality, as contradistinguished from indeterminate knowledge (manas) and determinate knowledge (buddhi) which are tainted by error and delusion, and observes that only aspirants for liberation are capable of acquiring non-delusion.[128] Śaṁkara, Rāmānuja, Vedāntadeśika Veṅkaṭanātha, Hanumān, Veṅkaṭanātha, Vallabha and Nīlakaṇṭha regard non-delusion as moral discrimination between right and wrong. Puruṣottamajī defines moha as the absence of discrimination, and sammoha as complete non-discrimination. Ānandatīrtha and Jayatīrtha regard delusion as desire to commit sins, and non-delusion as the absence of an immoral desire.

Rāmānuja regards delusion as error or illusion, and non-delusion as the sublation of it by valid knowledge. Vedāntadeśika Veṅkaṭanātha regards delusion (sammoha) as illusion or knowing dissimilar objects as similar, and non-delusion (asammoha) as valid knowledge that contradicts the illusion. Silver perceived in the past and recalled at present is attributed to a nacre which is perceived, and generates the illusion of silver, which is sublated by the valid perception of the nacre as nacre. Rāmānuja regards intelligence (buddhi) as the capacity of the manas for ascertaining the real nature of things, and knowledge (jñāna) as certain knowledge of the distinction between a conscious self (cit)

[127] NBh., iv, 1, 3; SDS., p. 326.

[128] Asaṁmoho vyākulatvābhāvaḥ. SrBG., x, 4. Asaṁmohaḥ pratyutpanneṣu boddhavyeṣu kartavyeṣu cāvyākulatayā vivekena pravṛttiḥ. MBG., x, 4. SBG., RKBG., x, 4.

and unconscious matter (acit). Vāmana regards the ignorance of a rope as nescience (moha), the illusion of a serpent as delusion (sammoha), and the sublation of the illusion as non-delusion (asammoha); the ignorance of the Self as nescience, the illusion of duality as delusion, and the sublation of the illusion of duality as non-delusion.[129] Rāmakaṇṭha defines delusion as nescience which is in the nature of the absence of discrimination between the self and the not-self. Varavaramuni regards delusion as the illusion which springs from nescience. Non-delusion is discriminative knowledge of the self as distinguished from the not-self.[130]

(46) *Forgiveness* (*kṣamā*).—Śaṁkara defines forgiveness as the unaffected condition of the mind of a person even when he is reviled or chastised. He defines non-anger (akrodha) as the suppressison of anger which arises from one's being abused or chastised by others. He distinguishes between forgiveness and non-anger. When no change or perversion is produced in the mind of a person when he is abused or persecuted, he has forgiveness. But when a change or perversion is produced in the mind, but it is suppressed by the person, he has non-anger. In forgiveness the mind is not at all subject to anger, while in non-anger the mind is subject to anger, but it is quickly suppressed. Ānandagiri defines forgiveness as the unaffected condition of the mind (avikṛtacittatā) in the midst of praise or dispraise. It is the unperturbed condition of the mind even under sufficient provocation. It is abstention from inflicting injury on the malefactor who has done harm to a person. Śrīdharasvāmī regards forgiveness as suppression of anger by a person even when he is vanquished, abused, or despised. He identifies it with non-anger. Sometimes he identifies it with tolerance.[131] Rāmānuja defines forgiveness as the absence of any agitation of mind, though a cause of mental agitation is present. Rāmakaṇṭha defines it as tolerance of others' malevolence in spite of one's complete power of retaliating on them, or as the power of being unaffected in mind, body and actions by the

[129] SBG., RBG., RBTC., HBG., BrGBG., TDBG., NBG., ATBG., Mādhva Bhāṣya, JTBG., ii, 63; AVBG., x, 4.

[130] Saṁmohaḥ ātmānātmādi-vastu-vivekavirahātmakam ajñānam. RKBG., ii, 65. Ajñāna-saṁmohaḥ ajñāna-mūlako bhramaḥ. VMBG., xviii, 71.

[131] SBG., x, 4; xii, 13; xiii, 17; xvi, 2 & 3; ĀBG., x, 34; xviii, 42; xiii, 7; SrBG., xvi, 3; x, 4.

injury done by others, or as the power of being unperturbed in presence of the causes of anger and other perversions of mind. Madhusūdana also gives the same definition of forgiveness. Ānandagiri defines it as non-infliction of injury on a malefactor without anger. Puruṣottamajī defines it as non-production of anger in a person who has been injured by a malefactor, though he is capable of taking revenge upon him. Hanumān defines it as imperturbability of the mind even in presence of causes of anger. Forgiveness is mental, verbal and bodily.[132]

(47) *Compassion* (*dayā, karuṇā*).—Buddhaghoṣa describes compassion as an altruistic emotion which is characterized as promoting alleviation of suffering. Its function is intolerance of others' suffering. It is manifested as non-cruelty. Its proximate cause is the perception of helplessness in others overwhelmed by suffering. It succeeds when it makes cruelty subside, and it fails when it brings about sorrow. Madhusūdana, after Śaṁkara, defines compassion as commiseration for beings afflicted by sufferings. Śrīdharasvāmī regards it as kindness to distressed creatures. But Rāmakaṇṭha regards it as kindness to all distressed creatures with a desire to deliver them from their distress. Compassion comprises sympathy for the pain of others and active desire and effort for removing it. Mādhavācārya defines compassion as the desire to relieve the miseries of others without any selfish motive. Rāmānuja defines it as inability to bear the sufferings of all creatures. It is spontaneous commiseration for miseries of the whole sentient creation.[133] Rāmānuja and Varavaramuni regard compassion as intolerance of the sufferings of all creatures. Vedāntadeśika Veṅkaṭanātha observes that intolerance of others' sufferings is the cause of the desire to remove them. Puruṣottamajī observes that compassion for persons devoid of devotion to God is expressed in giving instructions to them for reminding them of Him. A compassionate person cannot bear the sight of the sufferings of others. Hanumān defines compassion as the sense that the distressed beings ought to

[132] RBG., x, 4; xvi, 3; RKBG., x, 4; xii, 14; xiii, 7; xvi, 3; MBG., xiii, 7; Mādhva Bhāṣya, xvi, 3; HBG., xvi, 2; ATBG., xvi, 3, RBTC., xii, 13.

[133] POP., ix, 94; SBG., xii, 13; xvi, 2; SDS., p. 225; RBG., MBG., SrBG., xvi, 2. Dayā sarvaprāṇiṣu kleśāpanneṣu tadujjihīrṣayā karuṇā. RKBG., xvi, 2. YS., i, 33; HIP., ii, pp. 336-37; TS., SS., vii, 9-12; HIP., ii, p. 254.

be delivered from their distress.[134] Vedāntadeśika Veṅkaṭanātha describes compassion as unconditional (nirupādhika). A compassionate person, Nīlakaṇṭha observes, does not desire to persecute a distressed person who has done him harm. But, on the contrary, he desires to deliver him from his misery. Kṛṣṇa Candra Smṛtitīrtha regards compassion as an altruistic emotion which is expressed in a desire to remove the miseries of others. Vāmana regards compassion as a tender emotion which is expressed in treating others as one's own self in thoughts, words and actions. The *Bhagavad Gītā* describes compassion as a saintly quality.[135]

Patañjali enjoins the cultivation of friendship (maitrī) for all creatures, gladness (muditā) for the virtuous, compassion (karuṇā) for the distressed, and indifference (upekṣā) to the vicious. This Yoga conception of meditation (bhāvanā) on the altruistic emotions corresponds to the Buddhist conception of sublime meditations (brahmavihāra). According to the Jaina also, the moral aspirants should meditate on friendship (maitrī) or good will for all living beings, delight (pramoda) at the sight of virtuous persons, compassion (kāruṇya) for distressed creatures, and neutrality (mādhyasthya) to vicious persons.

(48) *Benevolence* (*dāna*).—It consists in renouncing one's right to one's wealth in favour of another person without any mental reservation. Charity is sacrifice of one's wealth for the benefit of beggars. It is the cause of non-rejection of their prayer. Charity is making a gift of one's wealth to another person. It is of two kinds: (1) Charity is motivated by compassion for beggars, and aims at alleviating their misery, and not at a specific act of charity. (2) charity is given to a particular person, at a particular time, in a particular place, under particular circumstances. Benevolence is expressed in charity which consists in making gifts of one's wealth earned by lawful means, and in distributing articles of food to beggars to the best of one's ability. Charity, again, is of three kinds: (1) sāttvika; (2) rājasa; and (3) tāmasa. That charity is impelled by sattva, which is made to a fit person,

[134] Dayā bhūteṣu sarveṣu duḥkhāsahiṣṇutvam (tannirākaraṇecchā). RBG., RBTC., VMBG., xvi, 2. Dayā bhūteṣu rakṣitavya-buddhiḥ. HBG., xvi, 2. ATBG., xvi, 2.

[135] RBTC., NBG., xii, 13. Caṇḍti, Suprabhā, v, 66; AVBG., xvi, 2; BG., xvi, 2.

at proper time, in a proper place, as a duty without any desire for fruits. The recipient of gift is not one who did good to the donor. That little charity is impelled by rajas, which is made to a person who did good to the donor, as a requital for his good or with a desire to enjoy its fruits. That charity is impelled by tamas, which is made to an unfit person, at improper time, in an improper place, out of disregard or hatred for the recipient. Rāmakaṇṭha observes that knowledge and mental entities are transmitted to the recipient without ceasing to belong to the donor, though physical articles of wealth are given away by the donor to the recipient. Abhinavagupta regards charity as giving away money, food or other articles acquired by lawful and moral means to proper persons. The *Bhagavad Gītā* describes charity as a saintly quality.[136]

(49) *Tenderness (mārdava).*—Śaṁkara defines tenderness as the absence of cruelty. Nīlakaṇṭha, Śrīdharasvāmī, Madhusūdana and Hanumān define tenderness as soft-heartedness or non-cruelty. Rāmakaṇṭha regards tenderness as excessive tender-heartedness due to the constant thought of all creatures as identical in their essence with the supreme Self (ātman), that is the essence of one's own self. Puruṣottamajī defines tenderness as the capacity for sympathising with the sufferings of others. Rāmānuja, Veṅkaṭanātha and Varavaramuni regard tenderness as the absence of rudeness and fitness for keeping the company of saintly persons. Tenderness is a saintly quality (daivī sampat).[137]

(50) *Harshness (pāruṣya).*—Śaṁkara, Nīlakaṇṭha and Ānandagiri regard harshness as saying harsh words to others. But Śrīdharasvāmī and Hanumān regard it as cruelty. Rāmakaṇṭha regards pāruṣya as harshness in thoughts, words and deeds.[138] Rāmānuja defines harshness as one's nature which causes anxiety to good persons. Puruṣottamajī regards harshness as rudeness or inability to realize the sufferings of others. A rude person cannot identify himself with distressed persons and feel sympathy for

[136] MBG., xviii, 43; xvi, 1; SBG., RBG., HBG., xvi, 1; RKBG., x, 5; AGBG., xvi, 1; BG., xvi, 1.

[137] Mārdavaṁ mṛdutā, akrauryam. SBG., xvi, 2. SrBG., MBG., HBG., RKBG., NBG., xvi, 2. Mārdavam akāṭhinyaṁ sādhujana-saṁsleṣārhatā. RBG., VMBG., BrGBG., xvi, 2. Mārdavaṁ para-duḥkhābhijñatvam. ATBG., xvi, 2.

[138] Pāruṣyaṁ vāk-citta-ceṣṭānāṁ rukṣatā. RKBG., xvi, 4. SBG., ABG., SrBG., xvi, 4.

their distress. He is callous to others' misery. Madhusūdana regards harshness as the habit of speaking harsh words to one's face. Śaṁkara gives the following example of rudeness in speech. A rude person calls a blind person possessed of beautiful eyes, an ugly person handsome, and a poor person very rich. The *Bhagavad Gitā* describes harshness as a demoniac quality (āsurī sampat).[139]

(51) *Cruelty (krūratā)*.—Rāmakaṇṭha regards cruelty as killing or hurting others with calculated violence. It is an expression of anger, which is a mental perversion, that generates infliction of injury on another person or killing him because it destroys the power of discriminating between right and wrong.[140]

(52) *Non-violence (ahiṁsā)*.—Śaṁkara regards non-violence as non-injury to living beings. Ānandagiri, Madhusūdana, Vāmana and Rāmānuja regard it as non-violence in thoughts, words and deeds. Non-violence in mere deeds is not true non-violence. The mind must be purged of all thoughts of non-violence. Rāmakaṇṭha defines non-injury (adroha) as the absence of desire to kill animals. He defines violence (droha) as desire to kill animals. He defines ahiṁsā as abstention from the act of killing animals, which is prohibited by the scriputures, and motivated by lust, anger and greed, and from causing others to commit the act, and from approving of others' commission of the act. Rāmānuja defines adroha as non-obstruction to the free actions of others. He takes it not only in the sense of non-malevolence, but also in the sense of non-interference with others' freedom. Vedāntadeśika Veṅkaṭanātha defines ahiṁsa as abstention from causing pain to oneself and others. It is non-violence to oneself and others. Śaṁkara defines non-injury (adroha) as the absence of desire to kill others or non-injury in thought. Ānandatīrtha and Puruṣottama define gentleness (saumyatva) as mildness or absence of cruelty. Non-violence is a saintly quality.[141]

(53) *Gladness (muditā)*.—Buddhaghoṣa describes gladness as gladdening which is produced by others' success. Its proximate cause is the perception of others' success. Its function consists in

[139] Paruṣyaṁ kārkaśyaṁ paraduḥkhāna-bhijñatā. ATBG., xvi, 4. MBG., xvi, 4; BG., xvi, 4.

[140] RKBG., xvi, 19; xvi, 2, 4.

[141] Madhva Bhāṣya, ATBG., xvii, 16; BG., xvi, 2; SBG., SrBG., xvi, 2; xiii, 7; ĀBG., MBG., RBG., xiii, 7; RKBG., AVBG., xvi, 2; RBTC., xvi, 2; SBG., xvi, 3.

being devoid of envy. It is manifested as the elimination of aversion. It succeeds when it makes aversion subside, and it fails when it produces merriment. Patañjali and Vyāsa assert that we should cultivate gladness at the righteous persons, which is a means of tranquillising the mind, and that we acquire a strength of gladness by repeatedly practising it on such persons.[142]

(54) *Cheerfulness (saumanasya)*.—Śaṁkara describes 'saumanasya' as mental equilibrium or cheerfulness which is inferred from brightness of the face and the like, and ascribes it to the abiding of the self in its essential nature. Rāmakaṇṭha describes it as the highest bliss. Ānandagiri regards cheerfulness as unaffectedness of the self by any emotions and passions, and attributes it to the self's abiding in its intrinsic blissful nature. Madhusūdana regards cheerfulness as desire to do good to all and not harbouring thoughts of doing harm to others. Ānandagiri also regards cheerfulness as good will for all and not thinking of doing harm to others. Rāmānuja defines cheerfulness (saumyatva) as favourable attitude of the mind towards others' prosperity and happiness. Nīlakaṇṭha regards cheerfulness as desire for the good of all. Veṅkaṭanātha defines cheerfulness as the absence of perplexity due to anxiety for objects of enjoyment. Hanumān repeats Śaṁkara's definition.[143]

(55) *Purity of Mind (manaḥprasāda)*.—Śaṁkara takes purity of mind as the self's abiding in its true nature (svāsthya), or as transparence of the mind (manas). Ānandagiri explains it as its unagitated condition and freedom from anxiety. Rāmānuja explains it as freedom of the mind from anger and other emotions. Varavaramuni regards purity of mind as its untaintedness or freedom from the taint of anger and the like, or as its freedom from afflctions (kleśa), actions (karma), fruition (vipāka), and potencies (āśaya). Madhusūdana explains it as freedom of the mind from uneasiness owing to anxiety for worldly objects, or as its transparence which renders it fit for acquiring immediate experience of the supreme Self. Transparence of the mind is the manifestation of the supreme bliss due to the destruction of all

[142] POP., ix, 95; YS., YBh., i, 33; iii, 23.

[143] Saumanasyaṁ sarvebhyo hitaiṣitvam ahitācintanaṁ ca. ĀBG., xvii, 16. Saumyatyaṁ manasaḥ pareṣām abhyudaya-prāvaṇyam. RBG., xvii, 16. SBG., ĀBG., MBG., xiv, 24; xvii, 16; RBG., NBG., BrGBG., RKBG., HBG., xvii, 16.

its taints such love, hate, anger and the like. It is due to the suppression of all mental modes in regard to external objects. Nīlakaṇṭha regards purity of mind as translucence of the mind brought about by washing off the impurities of doubt and resolve, assimilation and discrimination, which depend upon desire and aversion which are extirpated. When desire and aversion are destroyed owing to the destruction of nescience, there is no longer any differentiation of desired and hated objects. When the mind is purged of love and hatred, desire and aversion, it becomes translucent and fit for acquiring an immediate experience of Brahman. Nīlakaṇṭha regards purity of mind also as detachment consequent on the conquest of the mind. Śrīdharasvāmī regards it as tranquillity (śānti). Puruṣottamajī regards it as its translucence due to constant meditation on the true and the good and its natural tendency not to wander to objects of enjoyment. Jayatīrtha regards it as natural proneness of the mind not to enjoy pleasurable objects owing to the destruction of all sufferings and mediate knowledge of Brahman. Rāmakaṇṭha regards purity of mind as its natural freedom from the taints of love, hatred and the like. Mental purity is a saintly quality.[144]

(56) *Purification of the Mind (sattvasaṁśuddhi)*.—Śaṁkara regards sattvasaṁśuddhi as behaving with others with a pure mind free from deceit, hypocrisy and falsehood. Rāmānuja means by it a mind untainted by rajas and tamas. Vedāntadeśika Veṇkaṭanātha defines purification of the mind as purging it of all taints such as desire, attachment, envy, deceit and the like by overcoming rajas and tamas. Hanumān regards purification of the mind as non-deceit. Śaṁkara regards inner purity as purity of mind (manas) and intellect (buddhi) due to the absence of attachment, aversion, hypocrisy and the like. Rāmakaṇṭha regards mental purification as washing off impurities of the knowledge of difference, and making the internal organ fit for acquiring the knowledge of identity. Mental purification is a saintly quality.[145]

[144] SBG., ĀBG., RBG., MBG., ATBG., Sr BG., NBG., VMBG., JTBG., ii, 64; xvii, 16; VCM., 236, 335; VMBG., i, 27. Prasādaḥ sarvānarthanivṛttyā paramānandāvirbhāvaḥ. ĀBG., xviii, 54. RKBG., xvii, 16; BG., xvi, 1.

[145] SBG., RBG., RBTG., HBG., xvi, 1; SBG., xvi, 3. RKBG., xvi, 1. BG., xvi, 1.

(57) *Purity of Motive or Intention (bhāvasaṁśuddhi)*.—Śaṁkara regards purity of motive as freedom of the mind from hypocrisy, falsehood and fraudulence (māyā) in one's social conduct. Nīlakaṇṭha, Hanumān and Veṇkaṭanātha regard purity of motive as the absence of hypocrisy in one's behaviour with others. Puruṣottamajī regards it as the absence of hypocrisy in showing one's affections towards others. Ānandagiri regards it as untaintedness of the mind by love, hatred and other passions.[146] Rāmānuja defines purity of motive as freedom of the mind from anxiety for objects which are different from the self. Vedāntadeśika Veṅkaṭanātha regards purity of motive as inner purity of the mind accompanied by the purity of overt actions. For example, sex-restraint not only means abstention from bodily self-indulgence, but also refraining from secretly lusting after a woman in thought. It is total abstention from sex-indulgence in thought, word and deed. Varavaramuni and Rāmakaṇṭha regard purity of motive as purifying the mind by increasing sattva and overcoming rajas and tamas. It is excellent purity of the mind brought about by the repeated practice of washing off impurities. Straightness (ārjava) is the absence of hypocrisy, which is the cause of the success of particular mental, verbal and bodily actions, because one has adopted the path of the realization of Brahman, that is by nature straight. Straightness (ārjava) is sincerity or harmony of thoughts with words and actions. It is an essential factor of purity of the mind. Vāmana regards straightness as equality towards one's son, friend, wife, enemy, and oneself without any distinction. It is a saintly quality.[147]

(58) *Natural Purity of the Self*.—Śaṁkara asserts that the self is blissful when it abides in its intrinsic nature without any modifications. Ānandagiri also observes that its blissful state consists in its immutability and absence of lapse from existing in its essential nature. Madhusūdana and Śrīdharasvāmī also are of the same view.

Rāmakaṇṭha observes that the natural purity of the self is due to its identification with Brahman because of the destruction

[146] Bhāva-saṁśuddhiḥ hṛdayasya rāgādi-mala-vikalatā. ĀBG., xvii, 16. SBG., xvi, 1; NBG., HBG., BrGBG., ATBG., xvii, 16.

[147] RBG., RBTC., VMBG., xvii, 16; RKBG., xvii, 16; xvi, 1; xiii, 7; AVBG., xvi, 1; BG., xvi, 1.

of the consciousness of duality as the result of the immediate experience of the empirical world as full of one's eternal Self (ātman). The self is beyond good and evil which are empirical and relative to the intellect (buddhi). When merits and demerits of the mind (citta) are completely worn out, then only can the self realize its intrinsic transcendent purity. When it transcends the intellectual, relative, empirical, dualistic consciousness and reaches the level of pure identity—consciousness, it realizes its essential purity.[148]

(59) *Firmness (dhṛti).*—The *Bhagavad Gītā* defines dhṛti as the power by which the activities of manas, life and sense-organs are sustained.[149] Śaṁkara regards dhṛti as the absence of depression in all conditions. Ānandagiri defines it as a mental mode which stimulates the body and the sense-organs even in great adversity. Rāmakaṇṭha defines dhṛti as self-consciousness (ahaṁpratyaya) which is the cause of the preservation of life. It is the absence of depression in spite of the presence of a cause of depression. It is characterized by the absence of falling off of vital power.[150] Śrīdharasvāmī regards dhṛti as steadiness of mind in spite of its being depressed by sorrow and the like. Śaṁkara regards it as buoyancy of mind by virtue of which it quickly recovers from depression. It is a mental mode which prevents the body and the sense-organs which are fatigued from lapsing into inactivity. It counteracts their depression due to fatigue, and restores them to the normal condition. Madhusūdana regards dhṛti as non-depression of the aggregate of the body and the sense-organs even in great adversity. It is the power of preserving the normal condition of the mind-body-complex in spite of the causes that generate fatigue.[151]

Tāmasī dhṛti is the concentration of mind by which a person clings to sleep, fear, grief, dejection and pride owing to the predominance of inertia (tamas). It is the mental power which sustains the activities of mind, life and sense-organs impelled by

[148] Svasthaḥ svātmani sthitaḥ prasannaḥ avikriyaḥ. SBG., xiv, 24. Prasannatvaṁ svāsthyād apracyutir avikriyatvam. ĀBG., xiv, 24. SrBG., xiv, 24; RKBG., xviii, 54; BG., SBG., ii, 50.

[149] Dhṛtyā yayā dhārayate manaḥprāṇendriyakriyāḥ. BG., xviii, 33.

[150] SBG., ĀBG., xviii, 43; RKBG., xiii, 6: xvi, 3.

[151] Mahatyām api vipadi dehendriya-saṁghātasyānavasādaḥ. MBG., xviii, 43. Dhṛtir duḥkhādibhir avasāde cittaśya sthirīkaraṇam. SrBG., xvi, 3. SBG., xvi, 3.

these motives. It is the worst kind of dhṛti, and should be discarded.[152]

Rājasī dhṛti is the concentration of mind by which it is fixed on virtue, wealth and happiness as the ends to be realized by voluntary actions in which a person desires their fruits. It is the power that sustains the activities of mind, life and sense-organs for the attainment of earthly ends,—but not for the attainment of liberation.[153]

Sāttvikī dhṛti is the unswerving concentration of mind, which sustains its activities and those of vital forces and sense-organs, and which enables the mind to be fixed on Brahman. It regulates the activities of the mind-body-complex for union with Brahman. It is constancy of mind in regard to absorption in the supreme Self. It springs from pure sattva which is the cause of the true knowledge of the reality or Ātman, which leads to liberation.[154]

Dhṛti is equanimity of mind in the midst of pleasure and pain. It is mental equilibrium undisturbed by joy, fear and anger. A wise person unperturbed by good and evil rests in his self which is full of tranquillity and enjoys the highest bliss. The tranquillity of his mind (cittaprasāda) is like the unflickering flame of a lamp, and is expressed in his undisturbed sleep. A person having mental equilibrium rests in his self (svastha), and is indifferent to pleasure and pain.[155] Śaṁkara observes that a person with mental equilibrium abides in his self, and is in a state of bliss (prasanna). Ānandagiri explains this bliss as complete isolation of the self from which it does not swerve at all,—an absolutely unaffected condition of the self which rests content with the fullness of its perfection. Vāmana regards equanimity as perfect equipoise of the mind in prosperity and adversity, joy and sorrow, or as the unswerving knowledge that 'I am the immortal self', or as release from the bondage of empirical life and duties prescribed by the Vedas and accomplishment of the knowledge of identity of the empirical self (jīva) with the transcendental Self or Ātman.[156]

[152] BG., xviii, 35; SBG., RKBG., xviii, 35.
[153] SBG., RKBG., xviii, 34.
[154] SBG., ĀBG., RKBG., xviii, 33.
[155] MBh., Śāntiparva, ch. 162, 19-20; ch. 245, 10-11. BG., xiii, 9.
[156] SBG., xiv, 24. Prasannatvaṁ svāsthyād apracyutir avikriyatvam. ĀBG., xiv, 24 AVBG., xiv, 3.

It is a saintly quality.

(60) *Forbearance* (*kṣamā*).—Madhusūdana defines forbearance as imperturbability of the mind by joy, sorrow and the like.[157] Vāmana regards forbearance as the arrest of mental agitation (cittakṣobha) when a person is chastised by another person by his thoughts, words or deeds, and as equality (samatva) towards friends and foes. Kṛṣṇa Candra Smṛtitīrtha regards forbearance as the power of enduring the injury inflicted by another person. Puruṣottamaji defines forbearance as tolerance of all moral transgressions. The *Bhagavad Gītā* describes forbearance as a saintly quality.[158]

Forbearance and equality imply higher wisdom (dhīratva). Pleasure and pain, joy and sorrow, heat and cold cannot unruffle the equanimity of a wise person. They cannot generate any agitation in his mind. The death of near and dear ones cannot produce delusion and grief in him, because he has realized that death is transmigration of the immutable self to another body for wearing off the load of merits and demerits, and that it is not extinction of the self. He is neither elated nor depressed by praise or blame, friendship or enmity, affluence or indigence.[158] It is a saintly quality.

(61) *Contentment* (*tuṣṭi*).—Śaṁkara defines contentment as the sense of sufficiency in all acquisitions. Ānandagiri defines it as satisfaction on the fulfilment of a desire. Madhusūdana regards it as the extirpation of all desires. Patañjali asserts that supreme bliss arises from contentment which is due to the annihilation of all desires.[159] Rāmakaṇṭha maintains that the mind is contented when it is not, in the least, affected by the taint of dejection at all times under all circumstances.[160] He also defines it as good will for all creatures. Varvaramuni regards contentment as considering all beings as identical with oneself and cherishing good will for them. Self-contentment (ātmatuṣṭi) is the highest bliss, which is the essence of one's Self and experienced at the time of self-realization. It springs from the extirpation of all desires for

[157] Kṣamā harṣa-viṣādayor avikṛta-cittatā. MBG., x, 34.

[158] Kṣamā sarvātikramaṇa-sahanarūpā. ATBG., x, 34. BG., xvi, 3; Caṇḍī, Suprabhā, v, 38, AVBG., xvi, 3; BG., ii, 13, 15; xiv, 24; BG., xvi, 3.

[159] SBG., x, 5. Tṛṣṇākṣayaḥ santoṣaḥ. MBG., x, 9. YS., ii, 42. ĀBG., iii, 17.

[160] Tuṣṭiḥ sarvathā sarvadā viṣāda-doṣānākrānta-cittatvam. RKBG., xvi, 3.

external objects. It is the experience of the bliss of the Self (ātman). The *Bhagavad Gītā* asserts that a person has contentment, if he is pleased with any article he gets without any effort of volition. Rāmakaṇṭha regards contentment as delight in all beings, which aims at liberation, bliss being the common essence of all beings.[161]

(62) *Equanimity* (*samatā*).—Buddhaghoṣa describes equanimity as being characterized by promoting neutrality towards all beings. Its function is to realize equality of all beings. It is manifested as the cessation of acceptance and avoidance. It succeeds when it makes love and hatred subside, and it fails when it produces worldliminded indifference of ignorance.[162] The *Bhagavad Gītā* describes it as indifference or neutrality to joy and sorrow on the attainment of good and evil. A person with equanimity does not feel joy when he attains good; nor does he feel sorrow when he meets evil. Rāmānuja regards equanimity as equality of attitude to oneself, friends and foes, good and evil. Śrīdharasvāmī regards it as equipoise of mind undisturbed by love and hate, joy and sorrow, etc. Rāmakaṇṭha describes it as the unperturbed state of the mind when it is free from perversions like joy, grief and the like.

Equanimity is indifference (audāsīnya) or neutrality (mādhyasthya). It is the state of not being perturbed by love, hate, joy, grief and other modes of sattva, rajas and tamas. It is impartiality to friends and foes.[163] It is indifference to all objects which are in the nature of not-self because of one's being contented with the immediate experience of the Ātman which is different from them. They are the modifications of essence (sattva), energy (rajas) and inertia (tamas), whereas the Ātman is different from them.[164] Indifference is the renunciation of desire or expectation of fruits of actions. It is the absence of desire for sentient pleasure. It is independence of all objects which are different from the self. It is the absence of desire for

[161] VMBG., x, 5; RKBG., iii, 17; x, 5; SBG., SrBG., iii, 17; BG., xii, 19.
[162] POP., ix, 96.
[163] BG., ii, 57; xiii, 9; xiv, 24; RBG., vi, 51. Samatā samacittatā, rāgadveṣarāhityam, harṣaviṣādarāhityam. SBG., SrBG., x, 5; RKBG., xiii, 9; HBG., ii, 15.
[164] Guṇātiriktātmāvalokana-tṛptatvāt anyatrānātmavastuni udāsīnaḥ. TDBG., xiv, 23. BrGBG., RBG., BG., xiv, 23; SBG., RBTC., xii, 16.

the attainment of pleasure or for the removal of pain or its cause..[165]

(63) *Equality* (*samatva*).—Śaṁkara defines equality as neutrality to pleasure and pain, and impartiality to all as equal to oneself because of their real essence as Brahman or Ātman. Rāmānuja defines equality as regarding all creatures that are different from Brahman as equally devoid of any value. Śrīdharasvāmī defines equality as considering all creatures as manifestations of God because of the absence of agitation due to attachment and aversion. Rāmakaṇṭha defines equality of mind as its unbiased attitude towards all or its unperturbability by joy and sorrow.

Śaṁkara regards equality as imperturbability of the mind. Ānandagiri regards it as freedom of the mind from love and hatred, and eradication of the false conceit of one's sense of 'mineness'. Vallabha regards equality as the absence of elation and depression in joy and sorrow which are the modes of sattva and rajas respectively.

Śaṁkara regards transcendence of sattva, rajas and tamas (nistraiguṇya) as desirelessness. Hanumān regards it as the extirpation of love, hatred and other emotions and passions. Rāmānuja regards it as the abiding of the mind always in sattva devoid of rajas and tamas. Puruṣottamajī regards equality (samatā) as feeling all objects and beings everywhere as equal manifestations of God.[166]

(64) *Tranquillity* (*śānti*).—Śaṁkara regards love, hate and delusion as taints (kaṣāya), and maintains that when the mind (manas) becomes free from all taints, it becomes tranquil. Tranquillity is its calmness characterized by the complete cessation of its determinations and agitations. It is the withdrawal of manas from worldly enjoyments, and due to perfect control of it. Śrīdharasvāmī regards tranquillity as the cessation of all activities of manas in the Ātman. Rāmānuja regards tranquillity as cultivation of the habit of restraining the sense-organs from their natural tendency to enjoy their objects. Varavaramuni regards tranquillity as the immediate experience of the highest bliss, which constitutes the essence of the self, due to perfect control of

[165] RBTC., BrGBG., RBG., NBG., xii, 16.

[166] SBG., RBG., ii, 45, xviii, 54; SrBG., RKBG., xviii, 54; HBG., ii, 45; ATBG., x, 5.

the internal and external sense-organs. Puruṣottamajī regards tranquillity as stability of the mind. Rāmakaṇṭha asserts that tranquillity is characterized by the absolute cessation of all determinations and agitations of the mind. He regards supreme tranquillity as due to the immediate experience of one's Self (ātman) consequent on the destruction of all mental confusions and determinations.[167] Hanumān considers tranquillity to be characterized by the cessation of avidyā or false knowledge of difference. Nīlakaṇṭha identifies tranquillity with liberation which is due to the destruction of egoism.[168]

A person who does not meditate on the Self (Ātman), and whose manas cannot rest in it, cannot enjoy the bliss of beatitude. A restless mind which hankers after objects of sentient enjoyment cannot enjoy the supreme eternal bliss. A restless mind cannot enjoy the bliss of the self. A person who cannot concentrate his mind on the immediate experience of the self, cannot arrest its activities and enjoy tranquillity. A person whose mind is not yet free from activities is not calm, and an agitated mind cannot enjoy the bliss of tranquillity.[169]

The *Bhagavad Gītā* regards egolessness and desirelessness as the causes of peace of mind. It is due to the mental renunciation of desires for objects of pleasure. Desirelessness springs from the recognition of the eternally fulfilled, non-dual, pure consciousness as the Self.[170] Peace springs from egolessness. Egoism consists in the identification of the body, mind, and vital forces with the self. 'Mineness' (mamakāra) consists in thinking the objects of pleasures of the body and the sense-organs as 'mine'. The sense of ownership (parigraha) is consideration of one's body, wife, sons, wealth and the like as one's own possessions. Rāmakaṇṭha regards peace as perfect calmness due to the cessation of all agitations and determinations of the mind consequent on devotion to the real nature of the self which is eternal and changeless.[171]

[167] Śāntaḥ ātmānubhavaikarasaḥ. VMBG., xviii, 53. Ibid, xvi, 2; xviii, 35. SBG., SrBG., RBG., xvi, 2. SB., Śvet. Up., vi, 21; SB., Māṇḍūkya Kārikā, iv, 90; SB., Kaṭha Up., iii, 2, 13; i, 3, 9; ATBG., xvi, 2; RKBG., v, 28; iv, 39.

[168] HBG., NBG., ii, 71.

[169] SBG., HBG., RBG., SrBG., VNBG., ii, 66.

[170] BG., ii, 72. Nityatṛptādvaya-cinmātra-pratilabdhātmapratyayātmatvāt niḥspṛhaḥ. RKBG., ii, 73.

[171] RKBG., ii, 73; xviii, 53, 54.

(65) *Endurance (titikṣā)*.—Śaṁkara, Ānandagiri and Śrīdharasvāmī regard endurance as the power of enduring extreme heat and cold, pleasure and pain, and the like. A patient person should not be affected by joy and sorrow evoked by external situations. Hanumān and Veṅkaṭanātha regard endurance as the power of enduring physical hardships. Rāmānuja asserts that pleasure and pain due to the contact of a sense-organ with an object are produced and destroyed, and that hence they should be endured with patience. Ānandatīrtha avers that sensations of heat and cold and feelings of pleasure and pain do not constitute the essential nature of the self, because they depend upon the relation of experiencer (viṣayī) and experienced object (viṣaya) between the self and them. Jayatīrtha asserts that this subject-object-relation depends upon false identification of the self with the body. This false sense of identity should be discarded and heat and cold should be endured. Nīlakaṇṭha asserts that they are only mental modes which are false appearances which persist in waking condition only, and that they should, for that reason, be endured.[172]

(66) *Friendship (maitrī)*.—Śaṁkara defines friendship as love for, and attitude towards a friend. Madhusūdana and Śrīdharasvāmī observe that friendship is felt for equal persons while hatelessness is felt for superior persons, and compassion is felt for inferior distressed persons. Madhusūdana describes friendship as love or affection (snigdhatā). Veṅkaṭanātha observes that hatelessness is felt for hostile persons, that friendship is felt for favourable persons who are desirous of knowing the nature of reality, and that compassion is felt for the distressed persons who are not desirous of knowing the nature of reality. Nīlakaṇṭha remarks that friendship implies love as distinguished from indifference. Vedāntadeśika Veṅkaṭanātha includes in friendship a desire to do good to a friend. It implies sympathetic identification with joys and sorrows of a friend and active desire to alleviate his suffering and enhance his happiness. Rāmānuja inculcates the cultivation of friendship for all persons, favouorable and hostile. Rāmakaṇṭha also regards one as a friend (maitra), who feels friendship or good will for all beings. Rāmakaṇṭha observes that a true devotee of God has no hatred (dveṣa)

[172] SBG., ABG., SrBG., HBG., BrGBG., RBG., Mādhya Bhāṣya, JTBG., NBG., ii, 14.

or enmity (vaira) for all creatures, because they are one's own Self (ātman) and not worthy of rejection.[173]

(67) *Wonder* (*vismaya*).—Śaṁkara asserts that wonder is evoked by the perception or recollection of an extraordinary object (adbhuta). Ānandagiri defines wonder as the emotion of surprise, astonishment, or amazement. Hanumān defines wonder as curiosity. Madhusūdana defines wonder as ordinary surprise (laukika-citta-camatkāra) or transcendental amazement of the mind (alaukika-citta-camatkāra). The former is excited by the perception or recollection of a very uncommon and unprecedented object. The latter is evoked by the perception or recollection of an extraordinary superhuman or divine manifestation. When Arjuna saw the cosmic form of God, his permanent emotional disposition of wonder was excited by the sight of God who was the supporting cause (ālambana-vibhāva), and of His cosmic manifestation which was the exciting cause (uddīpana-vibhāva); his wonder was nourished and strengthened by his firmness, ascertainment, joy and other accessory states, and expressed in horripilation (sāttvikabhāva) and obeisance to the divine cosmic form with folded hands (anubhāva). Arjuna's emotion was a superhuman wonder. But wonder excited by the sight of an undivine uncommon object is ordinary (laukika). Vallabha and Varavaramuni regard this wonder as the permanent emotional disposition which is evoked by the perception or recollection of a marvellous object which was never perceived before, and turned into a wonderful sentiment (adbhutarasa), which is in the nature of supreme bliss. Puruṣottamajī observes that in Arjuna's wonder there is a feeling of contrast between himself as an insignificant creature and God as an infinite, eternal, omnipotent creator. Wonder generates joy.[174]

(68) *Shame* (*hrī*).—Śrīdharasvāmī and Madhusūdana define shame as fear of social disapproval before committing an immoral action.[175] It restrains a person from committing a sin. Rāmakaṇṭha regards shame as disgust for immoral thoughts, words and deeds due to the apprehension that honest persons will

[173] Uttameṣu dveṣaśūnyaḥ sameṣu maitraḥ hīnesu kṛpāluḥ. SrBG., xii, 13. RBG., SBG., MBG., BrGBG., NBG., RBTC., RKBG., xii, 13.

[174] Āścaryabuddhir vismayaḥ. ĀBG., xi, 14. Vismayaḥ kutūhalam. HBG., xviii, 77. MBG., TDBG., VMBG., ATBG., xi, 14. SBG., ATBG., BrGBG., xviii, 77.

[175] Hrīr akārya-pravṛttau lokalajjā. SrBG., MBG., xvi, 2.

condemn one if one commits them. Varvaramuni regards shame as moral disapprobation of a wrong action.[176] Rāmānuja regards shame as disapproval of an immoral action, and recoiling from it. Vedāntadeśika Veṅkaṭanātha observes that virtuous persons feel shame or moral disapprobation not only at their own immoral actions but also at those of others. Wrong actions produce moral disapproval or shame (hrī) in the conscience or moral reason of a virtuous person, by virtue of which he recoils from them. Puruṣottamajī regards shame as moral disapprobation of common immoral actions relating to secular life, and also of the non-performance of religious duties such as service to God in this worldly life of separation from Him. Ānandagiri regards shame as a mental mode which is in the nature of censure or disapproval, which prevents the commission of an immoral action. Vāmana regards shame as recoiling from an immoral deed. It impels a person to perform a moral action and dissuades him from committing an immoral action. The moral sense of shame is acquired from a virtuous life, and blunted by a vicious life. Kṛṣṇa Candra Smṛtitīrtha regards shame as the apprehension of others' knowledge of a wrong action committed by a person. The *Bhagavad Gītā* describes shame or moral sense as a saintly quality.[177]

(69) *Remorse* (*anutāpa*).—The *Dhammapada* avers that a moral action ought to be performed because it does not produce remorse, and that an immoral action ought not to be committed because it produces remorse. Buddhaghoṣa gives the following account of remorse. When a vile action has been committed by a person, it excites remorse in him. Its characteristic is regret, and its function is to sorrow about what has been done. The omission of what should have been done also produces remorse. Its proximate cause is what has and what has not been done. It is manifested as remorse. Kumārila mentions a doctrine that an act is moral if it produces approbation in conscience, and that an act is immoral if it produces remorse (hṛdayakrośa) in it. He criticizes the view and maintains that, an act is moral if the Vedas prescribe it, and that an act is immoral if they prohibit it. But

[176] RKBG., VMBG., xvi, 2.

[177] Lajjā akārya nivṛtti-hetuḥ garhā-nimitta-manovṛttiḥ. ĀBG., xvi, 2. Jugupsā hrīr akarmasu. Bhāgavata, xi, 19, 40; AVBG., xvi, 2; Caṇḍī, Suprabhā, v, 44; BG., xvi, 2.

he does not deny the fact that a moral action produces moral approbation in conscience, and that an immoral action produces moral disapprobation and remorse in it. Remorse is a moral sentiment or emotion.[178]

(70) *Transcendence of the Sense of Duality* (*nirdvandvatā*).—Śaṁkara regards the causes of pleasure and pain as the two opposite extremes of contrariety. He regards a person who has conquered the sense of conflict between them as transcending the sense of duality. Ānandagiri regards transcendence of duality as endurance of heat and cold and other dualities, which depends upon the constant excess of purity (sattva) in the mind. Śrīdharasvāmī takes it in the sense of desirelessness due to the conquest of the sense of duality. Veṅkaṭanātha regards a person whose mind has excess of pure sattva, and is devoid of love and hatred, which are modes of rajas and tamas, as beyond the sense of duality. Vallabha regards a person who endures three kinds of pain, physical, mental and supernatural, and who has abundance of sattva in his mind, which alone functions, as beyond the sense of duality. Puruṣottamajī regards a person, who does not experience that he is or has pleasure and pain, as beyond the sense of duality. Rāmānuja regards a person whose mind has excess of purity (sattva) devoid of energy (rajas) and inertia (tamas), and who has conquered all conflicts of the empirical world as beyond the sense of duality. Rāmakaṇṭha regards a person, who has conquered attachment and aversion which are fetters to bondage, as beyond the sense of duality. He also regards a person, who is not affected by joy, sorrow, clinging, old age and death, as transcending duality. Duality is due to false identification of the self with the mind-body-complex, an aggregate of sattva, rajas and tamas, which is in the nature of not-self. Vedāntadeśika Veṅkaṭanātha regards a person who has destroyed merits and demerits and attained supramoral perfection as beyond the sense of duality. Ānandatīrtha and Jayatīrtha regard a person who feels success and failure as equal as beyond the sense of duality. Veṅkaṭanātha regards a person who has transcended the conflict between heat and cold, hunger and thirst, and the like, who does not feel the distinction between them in trance, and who experiences the distinction during lapse from trance into

[178] POP., xiv, 174; SV., 2, 246; IIP., p. 293; DP., xxii, 9.

empirical consciousness, but who knows the distinction to be a false appearance, as transcending the sense of duality. Nīlakaṇṭha regards a person who has transcended the conflict between pleasure and pain, praise and insult, friend and foe, heat and cold, and the like, and who feels the sense of equality in all objects and persons everywhere as beyond the sense of duality. Rāmānuja regards a person who endures indispensable pain due to heat and cold and the like until he has completely executed the means to release as transcending the sense of duality. The sense of duality (dvandva) springs from false identification of the self with the body (moha). When demerits are destroyed by merits and sattva, rajas and tamas cease to have their sway on the mind owing to devotion to God, a person becomes free from the sense of duality.[179]

(71) *Transcendence of sattva, rajas and tamas (nistraiguṇya).* —Śaṁkara takes nistraiguṇya as desirelessness. Ānandagiri interprets it as supermoral purity due to the destruction of merits, demerits and their mixtures which are the effects of the three primordial psychical impulses. Nīlakaṇṭha regards aversion for transmigration to heaven, world and hell which are the effects of sattva, rajas and tamas as nistraiguṇya. Complete destruction of desire for happiness on earth and in heaven is necessary for liberation. Rāmānuja asserts that the destruction of the three guṇas leads to the extirpation of ignorance and desire, and generates desirelessness. Vedāntadeśika Veṅkaṭanātha regards aversion for liberation and ignorance of the right means to liberation as effects of tamas, and proneness to desire as an effect of rajas and tamas. Hence he inculcates their suppression by generating excess of sattva in the mind. Puruṣottamajī regards a person who has devotion to God and meditates on Him, and who is devoid of sattva, rajas and tamas as nistraiguṇya. Vallabha also regards a person who has taken refuge with God and conquered the guṇas as nistraiguṇya. Hanumān regards a person who has extirpated love and hatred which are effects of rajas and tamas as nistraiguṇya. Veṅkaṭanātha regards a person, who has acquired excess of pure sattva in his mind, suppressed rajas and tamas completely, and conquered all desires for happiness, as nistraiguṇya. One who is not affected by sattva, rajas and tamas, but

[179] SBG., ABG., Br GBG., TDBG., ATBG., RBG., NBG., RBTC., ii, 45; Mādhva Bhāṣya, JTBG., RBG., BrGBG., iv, 22; vii, 28; RKBG., ii, 46; v, 3.

who is simply the indifferent spectator of their actions, who is impartial to all, and who abides in the essential nature of the self, transcends the guṇas. Equality, impartiality, imperturbability, tranquillity and inactivity are the characteristics of such a person who transcends the three primordial impulses. Rāmānuja regards a person devoid of love and hatred, desire and aversion as transcending the guṇas (guṇātīta). Vallabha regards a person, who is contented with the immediate experience of the Ātman which is different from the guṇas, and who is indifferent to all objects which are not-self, as guṇātīta. Rāmakaṇṭha regards a person, who is not affected by the causes of positive actions and negative actions leading to pleasure and liberation because of his being established in his eternal and immutable nature, and whose manas is not veiled by rajas and tamas, as guṇātīta.[180]

(72) *Indifference* (*udāsīnatā*).—The *Bhagavad Gītā* asserts that an indifferent person is not affected by sattva, rajas and tamas which are the constituents of manas. Śaṁkara regards indifference as impartiality to friends and foes, and considers it to be an essential characteristic of an ascetic. Vedāntadeśika Veṅkaṭanātha regards a person, who is neutral to all, and who has renounced desires for fruits of actions, as indifferent. Śrīdharasvāmī regards a person who is impartial and dispassionate as indifferent. Veṅkaṭanātha regards a person, who is devoid of the sense that he is the doer of actions (kartā), but who knows himself to be the mere witness (sākṣin) of the actions of sattva, rajas and tamas, as indifferent. Buddhi is constituted by the three guṇas, which compel it to act. The self is the mere inactive witness of its actions. In its essential nature it is not affected by the actions of buddhi, or of its constituent guṇas or primordial psychical impulses. Vallabha observes that a devotee is efficient in the worship of God, but indifferent to worldly affairs. Nīlakaṇṭha regards indifference as equality of mental reaction to praise and censure.[181]

(73) *Independence* (*anapekṣatā*).—Śaṁkara regards a person as independent, who does not depend upon the relations of the body, the sense-organs and their objects. Ānandagiri and Rāmānuja regard independence as desirelessness or absence of desire

[180] SBC., ĀBG., NBG., RBG., RBTC., ATBG., TDBG., BrGBG., ii, 45; SBG., xiv, 23; BG., xiv, 24-26; RBG., TBBG., xiv, 23; RKBG., xiv, 25.
[181] BG., xiv, 23; SBG., RBTC., SrBG., BrGBG., TDBG., NBG., ii, 16.

for all objects which are different from the self. Nīlakaṇṭha regards independence as absence of desire for the attainment of pleasure and the removal of pain or its means. Śrīdharasvāmī regards a person as independent, who is devoid of longing even for the objects which are obtained without any voluntary effort. Vallabha regards a person as independent, who does not want anything but service to God, and who does not care a straw for liberation in the shape of the sight of God, similarity with Him, proximity to Him, or His sovereignty. Puruṣottamajī regards a person as independent, who does not depend upon any object other than his mind for prayer and service to God. Vedāntadeśika Veṅkaṭanātha distinguishes between independence and neutrality. The former is renunciation of desire for fruits of actions, while the latter is indifference.[182]

2. *Sattva, Rajas and Tamas are the roots of Emotions*

The *Mahābhārata* traces all emotions to essence or purity (sattva), energy (rajas) and inertia (tamas) of the manas. Sattva produces pleasure; rajas, pain; and tamas, delusion or false knowledge. Sattva gives rise to cheerfulness, joy and equanimity. Lust, anger, greed, fear, fatigue, dejection, grief, vanity, conceit and infatuation arise from rajas and tamas. Excessive joy, delight, bliss, pleasure and mental equilibrium arise from sattva. Discontent, mental agony, grief, greed and intolerance are due to rajas. Non-discrimination, delusion and languor are due to tamas. Physical and mental pleasure are due to sattva; physical and mental pain, to rajas. Whatever is perceived with a pleasant feeling-tone is an effect of sattva. Tranquillity and purity of the mind also are its effects. Whatever is perceived with an unpleasant feeling-tone is an effect of rajas. Whatever is perceived with a neutral feeling-tone and cannot be definitely ascertained is an effect of tamas. Concentration of the mind (citta) on the self in its essential state, dispassion, forgiveness, nobility and the like are modes of sattva. Egoism, mendacity, lust, anger, and enterprise for the attainment of objects of desire, pride, vanity and hatred are modes of rajas. Delusion, indolence, oversight and the like are the modes of tamas.[183]

[182] SBG., ABG., RBG., NBG., SrBG., TDBG., RBTC., ATBG., xii, 16.
[183] Śāntiparva, ch. 212, 21-23; ch. 219, 26-31; ch. 246, 21-26; ch. 313, 24.

The *Bhagavad Gītā* regards pleasure and joy as modes of sattva; pain, sorrow, attachment, thirst, clinging, longing, greed. lust and the like as modes of rajas; and delusion, indolence, oversight and the like as modes of tamas.

Śaṁkara treats all emotions, lust, anger, greed, delusion, fear, dejection, grief, joy, sorrow and the like as the modes of Māyā which is the root cause of the phenomenal world. Vidyāraṇya regards dispassion, forgiveness, nobility and the like as the modes of sattva; lust, anger, greed and the like as the modes of rajas; and indolence, delusion, drowsiness and the like as the modes of tamas.[184]

3. *Control of Emotions*

The mind is purified, Śaṁkara asserts, by removing its impurities such as love, hate and the like by reflecting on counter excellences.[185] Love and hate cannot be dispelled by concentrating attention on their objects. The more their objects are attended to, the more they gain in strength and intensity. They can be dispelled only in an indirect manner by reflecting on the opposite ideas. Then they die of inanition. Śaṁkara shows acute psychological insight here.

The *Mahābhārata* describes the origin, interrelation and control of emotions. Anger springs from greed, is increased by others' faults, and suppressed by forgiveness. Lust springs from desire (saṁkalpa), is increased by indulgence, and suppressed by abstinence from sex-gratification due to wisdom. Greed always springs from false knowledge (ajñāna), and is suppressed by true knowledge of the transitoriness of all objects of enjoyment. Delusion (moha) springs from false knowledge, and leads a person to commit sinful acts through habit. It quickly disappears when it arises in a wise person's mind because it cannot stand the light of reason. Pride (mada) springs from the possession of noble lineage, learning, wealth and the like, and is quickly suppressed when it is known. Jealousy (īrṣyā) springs from sex-desire (kāma) and joy, and is suppressed by wisdom (prajñā). Deep resentment (asūyā) is felt by a person who is powerless to

[184] BG., xiv, 6-9, 12-13, 16-17, 39.
SB., Śvet. Up., i, p. 47. Pañcadaśī, 14-15.

[185] Pratipakṣabhāvanayā rāgādimalānām apanayanaṁ śaucam. SBG., xiii, 7.

retaliate on a powerful enemy who has inflicted injury upon him, and is suppressed by compassion (kāruṇya). Grief (śoka) springs from the loss of an object of love, and is quickly suppressed by the knowledge of its antidote.

Lust and anger are suppressed when desire and aversion are suppressed. Anger springs from delusion or intellectual confusion (jñānasaṁmoha), and generates a desire (kāma). Desire produces greed and infatuation (moha), which generate pride (māna) and arrogance (darpa). They give rise to egoism (ahaṁkāra) which leads to action. Egoism is the main spring of of all actions.

Anger, joy and dejection spring from one another. Attachment and aversion are due to ignorance of the transitoriness of their objects. Anger is suppressed by forgiveness. Love and hatred are suppressed by the true knowledge of the transitoriness of their objects. Lust is suppressed by abstinence from sex-desire. Fear is suppressed by vigilance (apramāda). Desire, aversion and yearning are suppressed by firmness (dhairya). Greed and delusion are suppressed by contentment. Conjecture (vitarka) is suppressed by definite knowledge (niścaya). A person who has controlled his sense-organs is not subject to lust, anger, greed, vanity, haughtiness, self-glorification, wrath, envy, and disparagement of others.

Greed gives rise to anger, lust or yearning, delusion, deceit, vanity, desire to kill, intolerance, shamelessness, desire to appropriate others' property, jealous preservation of one's wealth, excessive thirst, pride of birth, learning, beauty and wealth, ill-will for creatures, desire to do harm to them, distrust of all, crookedness to all, envy, disparagement of others, self-glorification, cunning and the like.

Delusion or false knowledge (ajñāna) is at the root of all emotions and passions. Attachment, antipathy, infatuation, joy, grief, egoism, lust, anger, pride, desire, aversion, agony, envy—all these are determined by delusion or false knowledge. Thus all emotions and passions are due to some intellectual confusion.[186]

Śaṁkara regards self-control (ātma-vinigraha) as restriction of the activities of the mind-body-sense-organs which are naturally directed towards objects of enjoyment to the path of self-realization.

[186] Śāntiparva, ch. 163; ch. 162, 11; ch. 213, 3-4; ch. 212, 20; ch. 8; ch. 273, 5-6, 8, 10, 11; ch. 160, 18; ch. 158, 4-7, 10, 14; ch. 159, 7.

It is not merely negative, but also positive in its nature. It consists in cultivating firmness in the pursuit of self-realization. Madhusūdana regards self-control as restraining the natural tendencies of the mind (manas), the body and the sense-organs towards worldly enjoyments which are unfavourable to the attainment of liberation, and harnessing their services to the pursuit of it. Veṅkaṭanātha also is of the same view. Śaṁkara lays stress on the restraint of the mind as the essence of self-control, which is withdrawal of the mind from all objects. Puruṣottamajī regards endurance of physical hardships such as hunger and thirst, heat and cold, etc. as the physical basis of self-control. Rāmānuja regards self-control as restraint of the body and the sense-organs, which are causes and effects and injurious to the self, and withdrawal of the mind from the objects which are different from the real nature of the self. Hanumān regards self-control as restraint of the natural activities of the body and the sense-organs, and control of the mind. Veṅkaṭanātha regards self-control as pre-eminently restraint of the mind. Puruṣottamajī regards mind-control as withdrawal of the mind from all objects of sentient pleasure. Nīlakaṇṭha regards self-control as restriction of the activities of the body and the sense-organs. Control of the mind, the body and the external sense-organs by the self (ātman), which is their master, is the essence of self-control. False identification of the self with the mind-body-complex is the root of self-gratification or abandonment to sentient pleasure. Rāmakaṇṭha regards self-control as the self's restraining the manas from immoral actions.[187]

4. *Patañjali's analysis of Emotions and their interrelation*

Patañjali maintains that all vicious (kliṣṭa) actions are prompted by delusion (avidyā), egoism (asmitā), attachment (rāga), aversion (dveṣa), and will-to-live (abhiniveśa). Of these afflictions (kleśa) delusion is the most fundamental. It is the root of egoism, attachment, aversion, and will-to-live, the last four of which develop from egoism. They are of the same stuff as delusion.[188] In Sāṁkhya-Yoga philosophy thoughts and feelings

[187] SBG., xiii, 8; xvii, 16; MBG., BrGBG., NBG., ATBG., HBG., RBG., xiii, 8; xvii, 16; RKBG., xvii, 16.
[188] YS., ii, 3-4.

are not intrinsically different from one another because they are made of sattva, rajas and tamas which constitute the mind. So it may regard attachment and aversion as modifications of delusion. Vātsyāyana also recognizes delusion as the root of attachment and aversion. But he cannot regard them as developed from delusion because he regards feelings and conations as different from cognitions. He can at best regard attachment and aversion as determined by delusion or false knowledge. Jayanta, therefore, recognizes delusion, attachment and aversion as independent springs of action, though attachment and aversion are determined by delusion.

Patañjali defines delusion as false knowledge of non-eternal things as eternal, impure things as pure, pain as pleasure, and not-self as self. Egoism (asmitā) is non-discrimination of the self from the mind (buddhi) and false identification of them with each other. Attachment (rāga) is desire of a person for an object which afforded him pleasure on a previous occasion, and which is recalled by him at present. Aversion (dveṣa) is antipathy of a person for an object which caused him pain in the past, and which is recalled by him at present. Fear of death (abhiniveśa) implies will-to-live.[189]

Patañjali regards greed (lobha), anger (krodha) and delusion (moha) as the fundamental springs of action. They are at the root of cruelty, mendacity, theft, adultery and the like. Animal slaughter may be actuated by greed for its flesh or skin, or by anger due to injury received from the animal, or by the false notion that animal slaughter will secure the person merit. A person may indulge these passions in three ways: (1) by his own overt action; (2) by causing another person to commit the action; and (3) by approving of another's action. A person may slaughter an animal with his own hand, or get an animal slaughtered by another person, or by approving of another person's slaughtering an animal.[190]

Patañjali recognizes three degrees of passions: (1) mild (mṛdu), moderate (madhya), and violent (adhimātra). Vyāsa divides each of these, again, into three subclasses: the least mild (mṛdumṛdu), moderately mild (madhyamamṛdu), and intensely

[189] YS., ii, 5-9.
[190] YS., ii, 34; YBh., ii, 34.

mild (tīvramṛdu); mildly moderate (mṛdumadhya), moderately moderate (madhyamamadhya), and intensely moderate (tīvramadhya); mildly violent (mṛdutīvra), moderately violent (madhyamatīvra), and intensely violent (adhimātratīvra).[191]

Patañjali speaks of controlling passions by focussing attention on the thoughts of opposite excellences (pratipakṣa-bhāvanā). Passions cannot be controlled by concentrating attetntion on them. They cannot be simply willed away or thought out of their existence. The more you fix your attention on them, the more they gather in strength. They can be controlled by thinking of their evil consequences, or counteracted by meditating on the opposite virtues. Meditation on God, the perfect embodiment of Truth, Good, Beauty, and the Holy purges the mind of evil passions and taints, and purifies and ennobles it.[192]

Envy is eradicated by cultivating good will or friendship (maitrī) for all happy persons. Malevolence is extirpated by cultivating compassion (karuṇā) for all distressed persons and animals. Intolerance is destroyed by cultivating gladness or cheerfulness (muditā) at the sight of all virtuous persons. Anger is removed by cultivating indifference (upekṣā) for all vicious persons. The repeated practice of experiencing these noble emotions brings about excess of sattva in the mind (buddhi) and decrease of rajas and tamas, and makes it stable and immobile.[193] The highest bliss can be derived from contentment (santoṣa), which is in the nature of extirpation of desires for sentient pleasure, or the absence of all worldly objects of bodily enjoyment except those which are attained without any exertion of the will, and which are indispensably necessary for bare subsistence.[194]

5. *The Jaina analysis of Emotions*

The Jaina divides emotions into two main classes: (1) sakaṣāya emotions; and (2) akaṣāya emotions. The former are gross emotions which have a tendency to stain the purity of the soul. The latter have no such tendency to corrupt the soul.

[191] YS., YBh., ii, 34.
[192] YS., YBh., ii, 33-34, 45.
[193] YS., YBh., i, 33.
[194] YS., YBh., ii, 32, 42.
DSV., 70; Gommatasāra, Karmakāṇḍa, 786.

The sakaṣāya emotions are the following: (1) Anger (krodha) which springs from thwarted desire. When a person is thwarted, obstructed, or opposed in the attainment or enjoyment of an object of desire, he is thrown into a state of anger. (2) Pride (māna) or conceit which consists in self-glorification due to the possession of cherished objects. (3) Deceit (māyā) by means of which an object of desire is sought to be attained. (4) Greed (lobha) or craving for an object which is not yet attained. These gross emotions are called passions. There are many passions which are formed out of the four primary passions. They are but modifications of the soul-substance or different forms of its agitation.

The akaṣāya emotions are the following: (1) Mirth or laughter (hāsya); (2) Attraction (rati); (3) Repulsion (arati); (4) Sorrow (śoka); (5) Fear (bhaya); (6) Disgust (jugupsā); (7) Sex-feeling of women (strīveda); (8) Sex-feeling of men (puruṣaveda); (9) Sex-feeling of eunuchs (napuṁsakaveda).[195]

The sakaṣaya emotions are of four degrees of intensity. They are irresistible, over-powering, strong and mild. The most intense and durable passions are called anantānubandhi. The passions in this state are permanent as lines engraved on a stone. The next degree of their intensity is called pratyākhyāna. The passions in this state are less durable and last like lines on earth. The next degree of their intensity is called apratyākhyāna. The passions in this state are less durable and last like lines on dust. The least degree of their intensity is called saṁjvalana. The passions in this state are the least durable. They are momentary, and quickly disappear like lines on water. These examples beautifully describe the different degrees of intensity and duration of passions.[196]

Anger, pride, deceit and greed are gross emotions or passions which stain the purity of the soul. They are but violent forms of desire which is a craving for possession or enjoyment of an object. They produce a disturbance in the soul, throw it into a state of agitation, and interfere more or less with calmness of thought. This emotional agtiation of thought is called impure thought.[197]

[195] DSV., 70; Gommatasāra, Karmakāṇḍa, 786.
[196] DS., (E.T.), p. 38 n; Gommatasāra, Jīvakāṇḍa, 22.
[197] PKS., 145.

. Passions are impediments to self-knowledge and self-realization. Only those persons who have extirpated all passions which have a tendency to taint the soul can be on the path of righteuosness. Those who are agitated by passions can never realize the self. Attachment and aversion are the internal causes of bondage, and determine its duration and intensity.[198]

[1] Commentary on PKS., 113. DS., (E.T.), 68.

BOOK II

THE PSYCHOLOGY OF THE ALAṆKĀRA

CHAPTER VIII

THE NATURE OF ÆSTHETIC EMOTION (RASA)

1. *The Nature of Æsthetic emotion* (*Rasa*)

Viśvanātha (1400 A.D.) defines the rasa as an æsthetic emotion which is experienced by persons of taste as identical with the emotion of the person represented on the stage by an actor, or depicted in a drama and the like, owing to the predominance of sattva (purity) in them, rajas (energy) and tamas (inertia) being suppressed. It is experienced as an emotion, entire and indivisible (akhaṇḍa), self-luminous (svaprakāśa), made up of cognition and bliss (ānanda-cinmaya), free from the cognitions of other objects (vedyāntara-sparśaśūnya), akin to the realization of the Absolute (brahmāsvāda-sahodara), and of the essence of transcendental wonder (lokottara-camatkāra-prāṇa).[1]

(1) An æsthetic emotion is experienced as an indistinguishable mass of feelings, emotions and sentiments. When it is experienced by a person, he cannot distinguish the psychical elements involved in this unique and indivisible psychosis.

(2) An æsthetic emotion is not purely an affective state. It is a cognitive-affective experience since it is composed of cognition and joy.

(3) An æsthetic experience is self-luminous or self-aware. It is experienced by itself, and not by any other mental mode.[2] It contains an element of cognition which is self-conscious. So the æsthetic experience is self-aware.

(4) An æsthetic emotion is free from the touch of cognitions of other objects. When a person experiences an æsthetic emotion,

[1] Sattvodrekād akhaṇḍa-svaprakāśānanda-cinmayaḥ.
Vedyāntarasparśaśūnyo brahmāsvāda-sahodaraḥ.
Lokottara-camatkārapräṇaḥ kaiścit pramātṛbhiḥ.
Svākāravad-abhinnatvenāyam āsvādyate rasaḥ.
Rajastamobhyām aspṛṣṭam manaḥ sattvam ihocyate.
SDP., p. 71.

[2] Rasaḥ svayam eva svādyate, svābhinna-svāda-viṣayaḥ. SDPV., p. 59.

he becomes unconscious of all other objects, and is lost in his own æsthetic enjoyment.

(5) An æsthetic enjoyment is similar to the realization of Brahman.[3] A person of taste experiences an æsthetic enjoyment even as a yogin experiences Brahman. Like the direct and immediate experience of Brahman the æsthetic experience is the direct and immediate experience of the rasa free from cognitions of all other objects. In both kinds of experience there is immediacy. Just as in the intuitive realization of Brahman the subject is lost in Brahman, so in the æsthetic enjoyment of the rasa the subject is lost in the enjoyment. In both there is an ecstasy of joy in which the distinction of subject and object is lost.

(6) Transcendental wonder constitutes the essence of an æsthetic enjoyment. It is different from the ordinary sentiment of wonder (vismaya). It is extraordinary or transcendental in character (alaukika), because it is felt by an appreciative spectator (sāmājika) who identifies himself with the person whose emotion is represented by the actor on the stage. Wonder is of the nature of expansion of the mind (citta-vistāra). It always constitutes the core of an æsthetic enjoyment. Only it is not ordinary surprise but extraordinary wonder.[4] This extraordinary wonder (camatkāra) has been compared to the 'wonder-spirit' of the modern critics, which is described by Viśvanātha as a kind of expansion of the mind called surprise. It implies that the marvellous always underlies the æsthetic enjoyment (rasa).[5]

(7) An æsthetic emotion is experienced when rajas and tamas of the mind are suppressed, and its sattva predominates over them. Sattva manifests experience, whereas rajas produces restlessness and tamas induces unconsciousness.

(8) An æsthetic experience is distinctive in character. It is different from conation (kṛti) and cognition (jñapti). It is a certain function of the mind called relish (svādana) or enjoyment.[6] The rasa is of the nature of enjoyment or actual æsthetic

[3] SDP., p. 71.

[4] Rase sāraś camatkāraḥ sarvatrāpyanubhūyate.
Taccamatkārasāratve sarvatrāpyadbhuto rasaḥ.
SDP., p. 73.

[5] S. K. De: *The Theory of Rasa in Sanskrit Poetics*, Sir Ashutosh Silver Jubilee Volumes, Vol. III, Calcutta, 1925, p. 234.

[6] Vilakṣaṇa evāyaṁ kṛtijñapti-bhedebhyaḥ svādanākhyaḥ kaścid vyāpāraḥ. SDP., p. 75.

experience. It is nothing but this æsthetic enjoyment which is an emotional experience.[7]

Dhanañjaya (1000 A.D.) maintains, that æsthetic enjoyment or relish (svāda) is essentially joyful in nature, which springs from the bliss of the self owing to the appreciation of the meaning of poetry or drama.[8] Dhanika explains it in the following manner. The permanent emotional dispositions are excited in the mind of the spectator by the skilful acting of the actor. The spectator identifies himself with the person who is represented by the actor and whose emotion is simulated by him, and feels the same emotion. He forgets, for the time being, the distinction between himself and others, and experiences intense joy of the self which is evoked in him.[9]

Śārṅgadeva (1300 A.D.) maintains, that æsthetic enjoyment (rasa) is produced in the connoisseur of poetry or drama by the determinant and exciting causes (vibhāva) and expressions of ordinary emotions (anubhāva), and accessory emotions (vyabhicāribhāva) existing in the actors who try to simulate them by their histrionic skill. It excites the permanent emotional dispositions (sthāyibhāva) of love (rati), mirth (hāsa) and the like in the connoisseur. It is an extraordinary emotion free from the consciousness of self and not-self, friend or foe, etc., and devoid of all distinctions of conditions, space, time and the like, and rests in perfect peace of the self since it is free from all obstacles. It is different from a flash of intuition (prātibha), perception, recollection and other kinds of knowledge, and from the intuitive experience of Brahman (brahma-samvit), since it is associated with permanent emotional dispositions of love, mirth and the like. It is in the nature of joy, self-aware, and called relish or æsthetic enjoyment.[10]

Viśvanātha observes, that there can be no æsthetic enjoyment without subconscious impressions (vāsanā) or emotional dispositions of love, anger and the like. Vāsanā is a particular

[7] Rasasya āsvādānatiriktatvam uktam. SDP., p. 74.

[8] Svādaḥ kāvyārtha-sambhedād ātmānanda-samudbhavaḥ. DR., p. 174. SDP., p. 74.

[9] Pratyastamita-svapara-vibhāge sati pravalatara-svānandodbhūtiḥ svādaḥ. DRA., p. 175.

[10] Brahma-saṁvid-visadṛśī nānā-ratyādi-saṁgamāt.
Sukharūpā svasaṁvedyā saṁvid āsvādanābhidhā.
SR., ii, p. 813.

kind of psychical disposition or emotional complex.[11] These emotional dispositions are either innate or acquired, and necessary conditions of æsthetic enjoyment. Philosophers are incapable of æsthetic enjoyment since they are devoid of innate emotional dispositions. Some affectionate persons also are incapable of æsthetic enjoyment because they are devoid of acquired emotional dispositions (vāsanā). Dharmadatta has truly said: "Only appreciative persons of taste endowed with emotional dispositions can experience æsthetic emotions. Those who are devoid of these dispositions are as good as a piece of wood, a wall, and a stone in the theatre hall." They are dead to all æsthetic enjoyment, and nothing can evoke æsthetic emotions in them. Emotional dispositions are indispensable preconditions of æsthetic enjoyment.[12]

Only persons of æsthetic taste are the experiencers of æsthetic emotions (rasa). Just as the adepts in meditation on God can experience the ecstatic bliss of the realization of Him, so only persons of taste endowed with accumulated merits can experience the ecstatic joy of æsthetic enjoyment.[13] Persons devoid of taste are incapable of æsthetic enjoyment.

Viśvanātha observes, that an æsthetic emotion (rasa) springs from the bliss of the self (ātmānanda) when it realizes the meaning of poetry and enjoys it; and that it is not distinct from this æsthetic enjoyment. It can never be made known to others because it can never exist apart from its being experienced by a person of taste.[14] It is incapable of being proved since its existence is inseparable from its experience. The only proof of its existence is its experience by persons of æsthetic taste.[15] Æsthetic enjoyment by appreciative cultured persons is its own proof, and it cannot be proved by any other kind of knowledge. It is *sui generis* and self-evident.

The proof of an æsthetic emotion (rasa) is carvaṇā or æsthetic enjoyment. It is not different from carvaṇā, and is its own proof. 'Carvaṇā', 'svāda' and 'āsvāda' are synonymous terms, which mean actual enjoyment of an æsthetic emotion. An æsthetic

[11] Na jāyate tadā svādo vinā ratyādi-vāsanām. SDP., p. 81. Vāsanā saṁskāra-viśeṣaḥ. SDPJ., p. 81.
[12] SDP., p. 82.
[13] Puṇyavantaḥ pramiṇvanti yogivad rasasantatim. SDP., p. 74.
[14] Nāyaṁ jñāpyaḥ svasattāyāṁ pratītyavyabhicārataḥ. SDP., p. 88.
[15] Sacetasām anubhavaḥ prāmāṇaṁ tatra kevalam. SDP., p. 77.

emotion is identical with its actual enjoyment (āsvāda). It is not a capacity for experiencing an æsthetic emotion, nor a latent impression (vāsanā) or emotional disposition. It is a concrete actualized emotional disposition felt by a person of taste as a concrete emotion. It is not a mental structure, but a mental function.[16]

Viśvanātha observes, that the various conditions which produce an æsthetic emotion in a person of taste can do so only through an activity (vyāpāra) which is known as sympathetic identification (sādhāraṇīkṛti).[17] The appreciative spectator experiences the emotions which were actually experienced long ago by those who are represented on the stage by actors owing to the peculiar power of the activity of the various conditions of the æsthetic experience,—which is called sympathy. It enables him to identify himself with the represented persons, and experience the same emotions in himself. Sympathetic identification generated by various conditions of æsthetic experience in the appreciative spectator of the dramatic performance enables him to experience the very same emotions of the persons represented, transformed into an extraordinary (alaukika) æsthetic emotion (rasa), the essence of which is a thrill of joy and wonder. If the conditions of æsthetic enjoyment fail to produce this sympathetic rapport in the cultured spectator, they can never evoke an æsthetic emotion in him. There must be an illusory sense of identity (sādhāraṇīkṛti), a feeling of 'at-one-ment', projection and identification, on account of which the experiencer (pramātṛ) feels an æsthetic emotion in himself as identical with the emotion of the person represented on the stage. The permanent emotional dispositions or sentiments of love, energy and the like are evoked in the appreciative spectator owing to this illusory sense of identity, and are experienced by him as æsthetic emotions (rasa).[18]

In æsthetic enjoyment there is a peculiar sense of make-belief on account of which the emotion felt by the cultured spectator is experienced as his own and yet not quite his own, and as another's and yet not quite another's.[19] In this condition of the

[16] Pramāṇaṁ carvaṇaivātra svābhinne viduṣāṁ matam. SDP., p. 92.
[17] Vyāparo' sti vibhāvādeḥ nāmnā sādhāraṇīkṛtiḥ. SDP., p. 82.
[18] Sādhāraṇyena ratyādir api tadvat pratīyate. SDP., p. 83.
[19] Parasya na parasyeti mameti na mameti ca. SDP., p. 83.

mind there is not a complete identification, but an illusory sense of identification which is vaguely felt as illusory at the time. This is the characteristic of 'make-belief'.

An æsthetic emotion (rasa) is not in the nature of an effect (kārya). Though æsthetic enjoyment (carvaṇā) is identical with an æsthetic emotion (rasa), sometimes it appears and sometimes it disappears; it is not always experienced but occasionally. On account of this occasional appearance and disappearance of the æsthetic emotion the nature of an effect is attributed to it, though it is not really an effect in its true nature.[19a]

(1) An æsthetic emotion (rasa) is an extraordinary (alaukika) emotion since it is proved by its own enjoyment (carvaṇā), and incompassable by the ordinary processes of knowledge. It is self-luminous, self-manifest, self-evident. (2) It is a unique experience generated by various conditions, in which the rasa only is brought to consciousness and there is no other consciousness of anything else. (3) Joy is the essence of an æsthetic emotion, which springs from the bliss of the self (ātmānanda). A common emotion may be pleasant or painful; but an æsthetic emotion is joyful in character. (4) An æsthetic emotion is disinterested, while a common emotion is interested, and serves a purpose of the individual. (5) An æsthetic emotion is impersonal, while a common emotion is immediately personal. (6) An æsthetic emotion is generic and common to all other trained spectators, and devoid of any personal significance. (7) An æsthetic emotion contains an element of transcendental wonder (citta-camatkāra) which is in the nature of expansion of the mind awakened by the marvellous. (8) An æsthetic emotion presupposes the existence of innate or acquired emotional dispositions (vāsanā), an innate capacity for æsthetic enjoyment, and sympathetic rapport with the actors and the persons represented by them. (9) It is a unique and underived experience, though it is evoked by a variety of conditions. It is inseparable from its enjoyment, which is its proof. (10) It is akin to the intuitive experience of Brahman, in which the subject is lost in the object and there is no consciousness of any other objects. In an æsthetic enjoyment an appreciative spectator is lost in the enjoyment of the object, and has no consciousness of any other objects. It is

[19a] SDP., p. 89.

inferior to the intuitive experience of Brahman, and derives its joyful essence from the bliss of the Ātman, or Brahman.[20]

When a permanent emotional disposition (sthāyibhāva), being aroused by the determinant and exciting causes (vibhāva), accessory states (sañcāribhāva), and expressions of emotions (anubhāva), vibrates over the heart-strings of the appreciative spectator, it is experienced as an æsthetic emotion (rasa). Keith calls it a dramatic sentiment. But we shall call it an æsthetic emotion, since in modern western psychology a permanent subconscious emotional disposition is called a sentiment. But an æsthetic experience of a drama enacted on the stage is in the nature of an actual conscious emotion called æsthetic enjoyment. Sully designates an æsthetic emotion an æsthetic sentiment because it is evoked by the ideal of beauty. He similarly designates an intellectual emotion an intellectual sentiment, and a moral emotion a moral sentiment because they are evoked by the ideals of truth and good respectively. But Sully's designations are not in conformity with the modern usage. A sentiment is a permanent emotional disposition which is subconscious, whereas an emotion is an actual mental process which is conscious. The former is a mental structure, whereas the latter is a mental functon. But we shall sometimes call individual æsthetic emotions sentiments to avoid cumbrous expressions.

Dhanañjaya maintains, that different æsthetic emotions have different effects on consciousness. The erotic emotion and the ludicrous emotion bring about blooming (vikāśa) of consciousness. The heroic emotion and the emotion of wonder generate expansion (vistāra) of consciousness. The emotions of horror and fear produce agitation (kṣobha) of consciousness. The emotions of fury and pathos bring about obstruction (vikṣepa) of consciousness. Here mental vikāsa is compared to that of a flower's bloom, and vistāra to the spreading of the branches of a tree on all sides, while kṣobha is compared to the agitation of an ocean, vikṣepa to obstructions lying in the path of a strong wind.[21] This is the reason why the æsthetic emotion of laughter arises from the erotic emotion, the æsthetic emotion of pathos, from that of

[20] A. B. Keith: *The Sanskrit Drama*, 1924, p. 318; S. K. De: *The Theory of Rasa in Sanskrit Poetics*, Vol. III, Calcutta, 1925, p. 233.
[21] Kāvyasāhityamīmāṁsā quoted in *The Heyapakṣa of Yoga*, Bombay, 1931, p 199.

fury, the æsthetic emotion of wonder, from that of heroism, and the æsthetic emotion of terror, from that of horror. They are not related to each other as cause and effect, but they have similar effects on consciousness, though they are produced by different causes.[22]

2. *The Origin of an Æsthetic Emotion (Rasa)*

Bharatamuni asserts, that an æsthetic emotion is evoked by the combination of the determinant causes (vibhāva), the expressions (anubhāva), and the accessory states including transitory emotions (vyabhicāribhāva).[23] The Rhetoricists put different interpretations on this text.

(1) Bhaṭṭa Lollota maintains, that a permanent emotional disposition or sentiment (stāhyibhāva) is strengthened and roused to consciousness by the combination of the determinant cause and the expressions of an actor on the stage, and turned into an æsthetic emotion.[24] The permanent emotional dispositions are evoked by the determinant cause and the expressions in co-operation with each other, and produce an æsthetic emotion. The determinant cause evokes a permanent emotional disposition, and produces an æsthetic emotion out of it. The expressions (anubhāva) and the determinant cause (vibhāva) are not co-existent with a permanent emotional disposition as an actual conscious mental process, but are so with a permanent, subconscious, emotional disposition (vāsanā) or sentiment. Daṇḍin says, "The permanent sentiment of love (rati) is transformed into the erotic æsthetic emotion (śṛṅgāra-rasa)." "The permanent sentiment of anger is converted into the æsthetic furious emotion."[25] Abhinava Gupta gives this account of Bhaṭṭa Lalloṭa's view.[26] Mammaṭa Bhaṭṭa (1100 A.D.) gives the following account of Bhaṭṭa Lolloṭa's view. A permanent emotional disposition (e.g., love) is evoked by the determinant cause and the exciting cause, and made fit for being experienced by the expressions of an actor, which are the effects of such an emotion, strengthened by the accessary emotions and states, and attributed to him who represents and

[22] DRA., p. 175. *The Dramatic Sentiments*, p. 25.
[23] Vibhāvānubhāva-vyabhicāri-saṁyogād rasaniṣpattiḥ. NTS., p. 272.
[24] Tena sthāyyeva vibhāvānubhāvādibhir upacito rasaḥ. NSAG., p. 272.
[25] Kāvyādarśa, ii, 281, 283.
[26] NSAG, p. 272.

imitates another person (e.g., Rāma), and experienced by a spectator as belonging to the actor.[27]

(2) Śaṅkuka maintains that, an æsthetic emotion is an imitation of the person represented by an actor; that the determinant causes are the causes; that the expressions are the effects; and that the accessary states are the psychical correlates of the emotion of an actor, which is an imitation of the permanent emotional disposition or sentiment of the person (e.g., Rāma) represented by him. The sentiment of the person represented by the actor is inferred from the marks (liṅga) mentioned above. The determinant causes are known from the drama; the expressions are known from training; the accessary emotions or states are known from one's own expressions of similar emotions or states. But the permanent emotional disposition or sentiment of the person represented by the actor is not said but acted by him. The power of conveying a meaning to the spectator by acting is different from that of speaking words. Hence a permanent emotional disposition or sentiment of the person represented by an actor is imitated by him, and converted into an æsthetic emotion; so that the latter partakes of the nature of the former, and is produced by it.[28] The æsthetic experience is different from valid knowledge, illusion, doubt and knowledge of similarity. Abhinava Gupta gives this account of Śaṅkuka's view. Mammaṭa Bhaṭṭa gives the following account of it. The permanent emotional disposition of a person (e.g., Rāma) is inferred from the artificial determinant causes, the expressions and the accessory states manifested by an actor, which are the marks of inference. But though it is inferred, its æsthetic enjoyment is different from any other inference. The permanent emotional disposition of a spectator is roused to consciousness and transformed into an æsthetic emotion and relished by him. It is atributed to the actor, though it does not exist in him.[29]

(3) Bhaṭṭanāyaka maintains, that an æsthetic emotion is not experienced, nor produced, nor manifested. If it were produced in a spectator, he would experience grief when the æsthetic pathetic emotion (karuṇa rasa) was produced in him. But, in

[27] MKP., pp. 66-67.

[28] Tena ratir anukriyamāṇā śṛṅgāra iti tadātmakatvaṁ tatprabhavatvaṁ ca yuktam. NSAG., p. 273. Anukaraṅarūpatvādeva nāmāntareṇa vyapadiṣṭo rasaḥ. Ibid, p. 272.

[29] MKP., p. 69.

fact, he has no such experience. Such an experience is not possible. It is neither perception, nor recollection, nor inference, nor testimony. Nor can an æsthetic emotion be produced for the same reasons. Nor can it be manifested, for if it were dormant at first and then manifested, there would be different degrees of its manifestation. But all spectators feel the same pathetic æsthetic emotion when an actress acts the exile of Sītā. Hence an æsthetic emotion is different from apprehension, recollection, inference, testimony and the like; it is brought about by the activity of the determinant causes, etc., called bhāvakatva, with which a spectator identifies himself, and which produce a make-belief and an illusion (moha), and enjoyed by a relish (bhoga) similar to the intuitive realization of Brahman, which is characterized by rest in the experience of its own essential nature of the Self as pure consciousness and bliss owing to the predominance of sattva interpenetrated by rajas and tamas,—which is transformed into melting (druti), expansion (vistāra) and unfoldment (vikāsa) of the mind. Abhinava Gupta gives this account of Bhaṭṭanāyaka's view.[30] Mammaṭa Bhaṭṭa gives a similar account of his view. An æsthetic emotion is neither apprehended nor produced nor manifested by anything in the self or outside it. But a permanent emotional disposition or sentiment (sthāyibhāva) is roused to consciousness (bhāvyamāna) through the activity (vyāpāra) called revival (bhāvakatva) by the determinant causes, etc., with which a spectator identifies himself, and transformed into an æsthetic emotion which is enjoyed by æsthetic enjoyment, that is an immediate, self-manifest and blissful experience owing to the predominance of sattva which overcomes rajas and tamas.[31]

(4) Abhinava Gupta (1200 A.D.) maintains, that an æsthetic erotic sentiment (śṛṅgāra rasa) is similar to the intuitive experience of Brahman, which creates an extraordinary wonder (alaukika-camatkārakārī), which is devoid of the consciousness of any other object of knowledge (vedyāntara-samparka-śūnya), and which is common to all appreciative spectators of the same drama enacted on the stage, who have the same subconscious permanent

[30] NSAG., p. 277.

[31] Vibhāvādi-sādhāraṇīkaraṇātmanā bhāvakatva-vyāpāreṇa bhāvyamānaḥ sthāyī sattvodreka-prakāśānandamaya-saṁvid-viśrānti-satattvena bhogena bhujyate iti bhaṭṭanāyakaḥ. MKP., p. 70.

emotional disposition or sentiment of love (rati); and that an æsthetic erotic sentiment is the spectators' sentiment of love, which is revived conjointly by the same determinant causes, exciting causes and expressions and actings of the actor who represents some person (e.g., Rāma) and imitates his emotion (e.g. love for Sītā), and which is suggested (vyāñjita) and relished (carvyamāṇa) by them. Their sentiment is revived and manifested, enters their hearts, permeates their whole organisms, eclipses all their other experiences, and is experienced as an æsthetic emotion (rasa), which is an extraordinary experience, neither indeterminate nor determinate and yet like both. An æsthetic emotion is not an effect of the knowledge of the determinant causes and the like, for in that case it would exist even after the destruction of their knowledge. But the destruction of the knowledge of the determinant causes and the like and the destruction of the æsthetic emotion are experienced together, and an æsthetic emotion is said to exist so long as its determinant causes, etc., exist. Nor is an æsthetic emotion caused to be known (jñāpya), even as an already existing jar is caused to be known by light, because an æsthetic emotion does not exist already. Nor is it made known by the knowledge of the determinant causes, etc., because it is apprehended by self-awareness (svasaṁvedana). But it is suggested by the determinant causes, etc., and relished by a spectator.[32] An æsthetic experience is different from perception and other means of valid knowledge, and the intuitive experience of Brahman, which apprehends Brahman only and no other object. An æsthetic emotion is apprehended by transcendental (alaukika) self-aware experience. It is not indeterminate perception, because it is produced by the knowledge of the determinant causes and the like. Nor is it determinate perception, because it being relished and consisting of transcendental bliss is apprehended by self-aware experience (svasaṁvedana). It is neither indeterminate nor determinate experience, and yet like them both, which shows that it transcends ordinary experience, and that it does not involve contradiction.[33]

(5) Kavikarṇapūra Goswāmī regards the permanent emotional disposition or sentiment as the inherent cause, the determinant

[32] Sa ca na kāryaḥ nāpi jñāpyaḥ, api tu vibhāvādibhir vyañjitaś carvaṇīyaḥ. MKP., p. 74.
[33] MKP., pp. 71-76.

cause and the exciting cause as the efficient causes, a particular modification of the sentiment as the non-inherent cause of the manifestation of the æsthetic emotion, but not of the æsthetic emotion itself.[34]

[4] Commentary, ALK., sl., 32, p. 121.

Chapter IX

SENTIMENTS (STHĀYIBHĀVA)

1. *The Nature of Sthāyibhāvas*

Śiṅga Bhūpāla (1400 A.D.) defines permanent emotional dispositions or sentiments (sthāyibhāva) thus: "Those emotions are called permanent emotions (sthāyibhāva) which cannot be suppressed by other similar and dissimilar emotions. They are permanent emotions, which transform other emotions into themselves, even as the ocean transforms the waves into itself."[1] Bharata has described eight kinds of permanent emotions: (1) love (rati), (2) mirth (hāsa), (3) energy (utsāha), (4) wonder (vismaya), (5) anger (krodha), (6) grief (śoka), (7) disgust (jugupsā), and (8) fear (bhaya).

Jagannātha (1700 A.D.) gives the following distinction between permanent emotions (sthāyibhāva) and transitory emotions (vyabhicāribhāva). Both these kinds of emotions are mental modes and consequently momentary. Both these are present in the mind as emotional dispositions (vāsanā). Sthāyibhāvas are not permanent as emotional dispositions. When an emotion is manifested very frequently, it is known as a dominant emotion (sthāyibhāva). But when an emotion is not frequently manifested but appears occasionally like flashes of lightning, it is called an accessory emotion (vyabhicāribhāva).

Jagannātha says that permanent emotions are said to be permanent, because they are not obscured by favourable or hostile emotions. Jagannātha criticizes this view, and maintains, that permanent emotions exist for a long time in the mind, and are related to their determinant causes. They are permanent because they endure as long as the corresponding æsthetic emotions endure, and are not hidden by emotions either favourable or hostile to them. The transitory emotions, on the other hand, do not endure as long as the æsthetic emotions endure, but appear and disappear in the course of the æsthetic experience. Thus they are different from the permanent emotions.[2]

[1] RS., p. 145, cp. DR., 1865, p. 160.
[2] RG., pp. 53-54.

Some maintain, that the eight emotions, viz., love (rati), mirth (hāsa), grief (śoka), anger (krodha), energy (utsāha), fear (bhaya), disgust (jugupsā), and wonder (vismaya) are permanent emotions. Jagannātha criticizes this view, and maintains, that when one of the so-called permanent emotions becomes intense, some other permanent emotion subsides or decreases in intensity and serves as its transitory or accessory emotion. Thus even a permanent emotion becomes an accessory or subsidiary emotion, when it feeds and develops another prominent permanent emotion. Therefore Jagannātha recognizes the following distinctive marks of permanent and transitory emotions: (1) In the first place, an emotion which attains a great degree of intensity is a permanent emotion, while an emotion which does not attain great intensity is a transitory or subsidiary emotion. (2) In the second place, an emotion which is produced by many determinant causes is a permanent emotion, while an emotion which is produced by a few determinant causes is a transitory emotion.[3] Thus anger is an intermediate subsidiary emotion in the heroic sentiment which is based on the emotion of energy, which increases in intensity. Energy is an intermediate subsidiary emotion in the furious sentiment which is based on the emotion of anger which increases in intensity. When an intermediate subsidiary emotion is excited by many determinant causes in order to intensify the principal emotion, we have rasālaṅkāra.[4]

Śārṅgadeva (1300 A.D.) maintains, that love, mirth and the like are permanent emotions, when they are produced by many determinant and excitant causes, but that they are transitory emotions, when they are generated by a few determinant and excitant causes.[5] Kallinātha observes, that love, mirth and the like are permanent emotions when they are produced by many determinant and excitant causes, because they are preserved in the structure of the mind as strong predispositions.[6] But when they are generated by a few determinant and excitant causes, they are transitory emotions, because their predispositions are overcome by contrary ones.[7]

[3] RG., p. 54.
[4] RG., p. 55. SR., Vol. ii, pp. 830-31.
[5] SR., Vol. ii, p. 840.
[6] Dṛḍha-saṁskāra-vattayā sthirā bhavanti. Kalānidhi, SR., p. 840.
[7] Abhibhūta-saṁskāra-vattayā vyabhicāriṇo bhavanti. Ibid, p. 840.

Mirth is a transitory emotion in the erotic sentiment; love, in the quietistic sentiment; anger, in the heroic sentiment; fear, in the pathetic sentiment; disgust, in the furious sentiment; energy and wonder, in all æsthetic sentiments; desirelessness (śama) exists in all æsthetic sentiments, but it does not exist in them as a transitory emotion on account of its persistence.[8] It may be argued, that even the so-called permanent emotoins are momentary by their very nature when they are actually felt as concrete emotions, and that they endure for three moments. But Śārṅgadeva remarks, that it is true that they are momentary as concrete emotions, but that still they are permanent as emotional dispositions or sentiments. They are preserved in the structure of the mind as psychical predispositions (saṁskāra). In that case, it may be objected, self-abasement and other transitory emotions also may be regarded as permanent emotions, since they also exist in the mind as emotional dispositions (saṁskāra). Śārṅgadeva disputes this contention, and urges that this is not possible because the dispositions of the transitory emotions are overpowered by the strong dispositions of the permanent emotions. Hence self-abasement and other transitory emotions cannot attain permanence. The emotions which are strong even as dispositions are permanent, and the emotions which are weak even as dispositions are transitory. The emotional dispositions which can be easily realized as concrete actual emotions are permanent emotions. The emotions which quickly disappear even as dispositions are transitory.[9]

Hemacandra (1200 A.D.) regards the sthāyibhāvas as innate in character. He says: "Every creature that is born is found to be endowed with these permanent emotional dispositions (sthāyibhāva). For instance, every one has aversion to pain and desire for pleasure; every one has an instinctive tendency to seek pleasure and avoid pain. Everybody is endowed with the instinct of mating, sex-emotion, or love (rati). He thinks himself to be superior to others, and laughs at them (hāsa). He apprehends the loss of his superiority, and feels sorrow (śoka). He feels anger (krodha) at any injury done to him. Then he firmly resolves (utsāha) to remove the cause of his injury. He gets

[8] Śamaḥ sarva-raseṣvasti sthairyatve' vyabhicāryasau. SR., Vol. ii, p. 840.
[9] SR., pp. 831-32; kalānidhi.

afraid (bhaya) of his ruin. He feels disgust (jugupsā) at any improper thing done. He feels wonder (vismaya) at the sight of any strange conduct of others. When he desires to renounce anything, he obtains tranquillity of mind (śama) owing to passionlessness. There is not a single animal devoid of these emotional dispositions. Only in some creatures, some one of these emotional dispositions is more predominant, while in others it is less predominant. In some it is excited by proper objects, while in others it is excited by improper objects. In other words, in some it is moral, while in others it is immoral."[10]

Viśvanātha defines sthāyibhāvas as those permanent emotional dispositions which cannot be obscured by favourable or hostile emotions, and which are the basis of æsthetic emotions.[11] They have been called by others permanent moods or dominant emotions. P. V. Pathak rightly calls them emotional dispositions. "We can compare the different sthāyibhāvas," he says, "to permanent emotional dispositions. The structure of our mind consists of systems of dispositions. Along with cognitive and conative 'constellations', the structure contains emotional ones too. We might call them sentiments. The several bhāvas do not *happen,* for they are always there in the structure of the human mind. Their particular manifestations are seen, but they remain in the background and 'perfume' the whole mind and its functioning."[12]

2. *Rati (love)*

The *Nāṭyaśāstra* takes 'rati' in a wide sense, and defines it as in the nature of an intense delight which arises from the attainment of the object desired.[13] It is excited by the perception of dear ones, appropriate seasons, garlands, perfumery, ornaments, fine buildings, absence of hostility and the like. Śāradātanaya (1200 A.D.) defines rati as desire characterized by a feeling of pleasure for objects agreeable to the mind. It is in the nature

[10] Na hi etat citta-vṛtti-vāsanā-sūnyaḥ prāṇī bhavati. Kevalaṁ kasyacit kācit adhikā bhavati cittavṛttiḥ, kācit ūnā. KS., p. 125.

[11] Aviruddhā viruddhā vā yaṁ tirodhātum akṣamāḥ.
Āsvādāṅkura-kando' sau bhāvaḥ sthāyīti sammataḥ.
SDP., p. 212.

[12] *The Heyapakṣa of Yoga,* pp. 194-95.

[13] Ratir nāma pramodātmikā. Iṣṭārtha-viṣaya-prāptyā ratiḥ samupajāyate. NTS., p. 350.

of desire.[14] Viśvanātha defines rati as the inclination of the mind towards agreeable objects.[15] It is called attachment (anurāga) or love (prema). Vidyābhūṣaṇa also defines rati as attachment (pravaṇatā) of the mind to dear objects.

Hemacandra defines rati as sex-love of a young couple deeply attached to each other and desirous of union. The same emotion of love is excited in each other under fitting circumstances. It is in the nature of mutual confidence and union, and generates joy. Dhanañjaya defines rati as intense delight (pramoda) excited by a young couple deeply attached to each other. Vidyānātha (1400 A.D.) also defines rati as desire for sex-union which gives intense pleasure to each of the young couple attached to each other. Kumārsvāmī (1500 A.D.) remarks, that this sex-love is a mental function which is in the nature of intense joy.[16]

Śiṅga Bhūpāla (1400 A.D.) defines rati as the permanent emotional disposition of love felt by a young man and young woman for each other. Firstly, rati is a permanent emotional disposition or sentiment entertained by a young couple for each other. It is manifested as an actual emotion occasionally when it is excited by fitting circumstances. Secondly, it is based on the sex-instinct which is present in an intense degree in young persons. Thirdly, it is mutual desire for union with each other. Real love is reciprocal, not one-sided. It is a reciprocoal emotion which is felt by a young couple for each other. Love felt by a young man for a young woman who does not feel the same emotion for him is not real love.[17]

Love is excited by nature (nisarga), undivided attention (abhiyoga), connection (saṁsarga), sense of ownership (abhimāna), similarity (upamā), spiritual intimations (adhyātma), and objects (viṣaya) such as sound, touch, form, taste and odour. Pārvatī conceived love for Śiva owing to nature (nisarga) because it was independent of perceptible causes such as beauty and the like, and was in the nature of a predisposition of the previous birth

[14] Mano' nukūleṣu artheṣu sukha-saṁvedanātmikā icchā ratiḥ. BPK., p. 34.

[15] Ratir mano' nukūle' rthe manasaḥ pravaṇāyitam. SDP., p. 213. SKM., p. 38.

[16] Pramodātmā manovṛtti-viśeṣaḥ. PR., RP., p. 229. DR., p. 178.

[17] Yūnor anyonya-viṣayā sthāyinīcchā ratir bhavet. RS., p. 145.

(janmāntara-vāsanārūpa). Abhiyoga is concentration of mind on the object of love. Constantly thinking of a person excites love for him. Sometimes love is excited by association (saṁsarga) with an object of love. Rāma conceived love for Sītā owing to her connection with the great Janaka. Sometimes love is excited by the sense of ownership. Mādhava's love for Mālatī was due to his exclusive affection for her independently of any desire for other beautiful objects. Sometimes love is excited by the perception of an object similar to the beauty of the beloved person. Though the love of Daśaratha for his beloved wife was hidden by the excitement of hunting, it was excited by the sight of beautiful feathers of a peacock resembling the hairs of his wife. Sometimes love is excited by spiritual intimations which bear clear testimony to its existence. Duṣyanta's mental agony clearly testified to his love for Śakuntalā, though he forgot her under the influence of a curse. These spiritual intimations may be called vaticinations of the heart. Sometimes love is excited by the perception of a sound. A milk-maid conceived love for Kṛṣṇa on hearing the sweet notes of his flute, though she had never seen him before. Similarly, love is excited by the touch of the beloved person, the sight of his or her beauty, sweet taste of the lips, odour of his or her body, etc. Śāntanu's love for Satyavatī was excited by the perception of the odour of her body.[18]

Śiṅga Bhūpāla describes six stages of love, viz. (1) premā, (2) māna, (3) praṇaya, (4) sneha, (5) rāga, and (6) anurāga, even as a tree passes through six stages such as sprouts, twigs, buds, flowers, fruits, and enjoyment of fruits.[19] (1) Premā (love) is the union of a young couple by ties of affection devoid of difference. It links them together by the silken ties of love, and abolishes all difference between them.[20] (2) Māna (sulk) is crookedness of emotion (bhāvakauṭilya) which is experienced as an independent emotion, and unites the young couple with the ties of love. It arises out of love as an independent emotion owing to suspicion of foul play, and is manifested in disparagement (avajñā) of the beloved person. (3) Praṇaya (intense love) unites the young

[18] Ibid, pp. 145-49.
[19] Ibid, verse 109, p. 149.
[20] Premā bhedarahitaṁ bhāvabandhanam. Ibid, p. 149.

couple by generating mutual confidence (bhāvavisrambha) through all possible physical and mental accessories brought about by sulks. It is the return of mutual confidence of the young couple when the cloud of suspicion is blown away, and love wells up in the hearts of the lovers with greater intensity. (4) Sneha (melting of the heart) is the result of deep mutual confidence. When the mutual confidence of the young couple reaches its culmination by feasting the eyes on the beauty of each other, their hearts melt into deep affection. Sneha is of three kinds: (*i*) prauḍha, (*ii*) madhyama, and (*iii*) manda. (*i*) The love which afflicts the heart of one of the young couple, who does not know the mental state of the other owing to his sojourn in a foreign country is called prauḍha sneha. For instance, the love of an anxious wife for her husband in a foreign country, whose feelings for her she does not know exactly is prauḍha sneha. (*ii*) The love of one, which tolerates the beloved person's affection for another, is called madhyama sneha. (*iii*) The love of a person, which neither adores nor ignores the beloved, and which is diverted to another person if the former feels sulky towards him, is called manda sneha. (5) Rāga is the excess of love (sneha-prakarṣa) by which even intense sorrow is turned into joy. It is of three kinds: (*i*) kusumbharāga, (*ii*) nīlīrāga, and māñjiṣṭharāga. (*i*) Kusumbharāga is the excess of love (rāga) which colours the mind in a moment and disappears in a moment, though it appears in all its intensity. (*ii*) Nīlīrāga is the excess of love (rāga) which is neither increased nor destroyed, when it once tinges the mind. (*iii*) Māñjiṣṭharāga is the excess of love (rāga) which tinges the mind in no time, but is not destroyed even after a long time, and which is manifested in all its intensity. (6) Anurāga is the excess of love (rāga) which attains the state of self-consciousness, and is expressed in the ecstasy of physical union. It floods the soul with its warmth and fervour, and continues so long as the thrill of physical union continues. It is the climax of love expressed in the ecstasy of physical union. The basis of love, even in its most intense form, is the sex-instinct.

Rati is sex-love which is based on the sex-instinct. Others regard delight (prīti) as a variety of love (rati). Siṅga Bhūpāla criticizes this view, and urges that delight which is not connected with the sex-instinct (asamprayoga-viṣayā) does not differ from joy (harṣa); that it is a variety of joy, and not a variety of sex-love.[21]

Rāmacandra and Guṇacandra define love (rati) as attachment of a young couple to each other. It is manifested in their mutual confidence and union based on the sex-instinct. It is sex-attraction and sex-love, and different from love for gods, friends and beautiful objects, which is in the nature of delight (prīti). The latter is characterized by mere desire or attraction. Though it follows from sex-love, it is devoid of sex-attraction.[22] This is a very significant passage. The essence of secondary love, e.g. love for gods or devotion, love for friends or friendship, and love for beautiful objects or æsthetic emotion of the beautiful is desire. They come into being after sex-love, emerge from it, and are purged of their sexual character. When sex-love is sublimated, it is transformed into pure love in various forms. These secondary forms of love are transitory emotions, whereas sex-love (rati) is a permanent emotional disposition or a primary emotion.

Keśavamiśra quotes the following verse[23] in his *Alaṅkāraśekhara*, which may be translated thus. We have awe for our king, reverence for our preceptor or spiritual guide, sages, and gods, and affection for our sons. These are various forms of love (rati). The erotic sentiment (śṛṅgāra) is based on that kind of rati which is based on the sex-instinct. Thus rati comprises sex-love, affection and reverence.

Vāmana refers to a doctrine that regards friendship, reverence, and affection or tender emotion as varieties of rati. Friendship (sneha) is the love of equals for each other. Reverence (bhakti) is the love of the inferior for the superior. Affection (vātsalya) is the love of the superior for the inferior. Vāmana refers to another doctrine which recognizes seven kinds of rati. Friendship (sneha) is the love of equals for each other. It is also called prema. When it is untainted by any desire (niṣkāma), it is called maitrī, which is Platonic love. Reverence (bhakti) is the love of the inferior for the superior. Affection (vātsalya) is the

[21] Ibid, pp. 145-55.

[22] Eṣā ca kāmāvasthānuvartinyā abhilāṣa-mātra-sārāyā vyabhicāriṇyā devatādiṣu bandhuṣu manohara-vastuṣu ca prītirūpāyāśca rater vilakṣaṇaiva. NDP., p. 176.

[23] Ratir bhavati devādau munau puttre nṛpe gurau.
Śṛṅgāras tu bhavet saiva yā kāntāviṣayā ratiḥ. P. 72.

love of the superior for the inferior. Ābandha is the love of animate creatures for inanimate objects.[24]

This concept of *rati* (love) roughly corresponds to the Freudian concept of *Libido*. Dr. Glover, an orthodox Freudian, explains its meaning thus: "It corresponds roughly with the popular use of the word 'love' and includes in its scope not only love between the sexes, but every relationship in which the word 'love' is appropriate, e.g. self-love, love of parents and of children, friendship and even love for inanimate objects and abstract ideas. Psychoanalysis has shown that all these forms of 'loving' are fundamentally manifestations of the sexual instinct."[25]

Śārṅgadeva defines rati as love of a young couple for each other, which gives rise to consummate joy enduring from the beginning to the end and being sustained by the sex-instinct or lust.[26] In rati there is the feeling of complete identification (aikya) of the young couple with each other. They melt into one in love which finds its expression in sport. This love of man and woman for each other, which is based on the sex-instinct and sustained by it, is a permanent emotional disposition (sthāyibhāva). But love for God and the like is a transitory emotion. Jagannātha also regards sex-love (rati) of a young couple for each other as a permanent emotional disposition, but love for a deity, the preceptor, the sons and the like as a transitory emotion.[27] Kavikarṇapūra (1500 A.D.) distinguishes between love and delight. Love (rati) is based on the sex-instinct, but delight (prīti) is not based on it.[28] Rati is colouring the mind with joy and inclines it towards the enjoyment of pleasure.[29] Prīti is of four kinds: (1) Prīti, (2) maitrī, (3) sauhārdda, and (4) bhāva. (1) The delight of a man in his wife's female friends or that of a woman in her husband's male friends is called prīti. The delight of Kṛṣṇa and his friend, Arjuna's wife, Draupadī in each other was prīti. (2) The delight of two male friends or that of two female friends in each

[24] BB., Bombay, 1901, pp. 116-17.

[25] *Social Aspects of Psycho-analysis* quoted by McDougall in *Outline of Abnormal Psychology*, p. 162.

[26] Strīpuṁsayor uttamayor yūnoḥ pūrṇasukhodayā. Prārambhāt phalaparyantavyāpini smarasaṁbhṛtā. SR., Vol. ii, p. 819.

[27] RG., p. 55.

[28] Samprayoga-viṣayā ratiḥ. Asamprayoga-viṣayā prītiḥ. ALK., pp. 124-25.

[29] Ratiś cetorañjakatā sukha-bhogānukūlyakṛt. Ibid, p. 124.

other is called maitrī (friendship). (3) The delight of a man and a woman in each other devoid of any mental perversion and always appearing to be the same is called sauhārdda (ideal love)[30] It is mutual delight. (4) The delight of a person in gods and the like is called bhāva. The nature and varieties of love (rati) will be discussed again later.

A young man and a young woman, who excite love in each other, are its principal determinant cause (ālambana vibhāva). Garlands, proper seasons, hills, town, buildings, rivers, the moon, breeze, gardens, tanks, sandal paste, perfumery, humming of bees and the like are its exciting causes (uddīpana-vibhāva). Love is excited by poetry, music and the like also.[31]

Contraction of the eye-brows, side-long glances, sweet words, smiling face and the like are the expressions (anubhāva) of love (rati). Inhibition of actions, goose-flesh, perspiration, trembling, and faltering voice are its involuntary organic expressions[32]

All transitory emotions except disgust, indolence, fierceness and death-like condition are the accessory states (vyabhicāri-bhāva) of love (rati).[33]

3. *Mirth* (*hāsa*).

Śāradātanaya defines hāsa as the blooming of the mind which is a particular kind of delight.[34] Viśvanātha defines mirth as the blooming of the mind (cetovikāsa) which is excited by unnatural voice and the like. Hemacandra gives the same definition. Jagannātha defines mirth as a mental mode called unfolding (vikāsa) arising from the perception of distorted speech, appearance and the like. Vidyābhūṣaṇa defines mirth as the blooming of the mind produced by the perception of unnatural appearance, voice, dress and the like. Kumārasvāmī (1500 A.D.) defines mirth as a change of the mind (manovikāra), which is produced by the perception of one's own or another's unnatural or strange dress, language, appearance, stammering, hump on the back, etc. Acyutarāya defines mirth as the blooming of the

[30] Nirvikārā sadaikābhā sā (prītiḥ) sauharddam. ALK., p. 67.
[31] KS., AC., p. 107; SDP., p. 216; BPK., p. 59.
[32] SDP., p. 216; RS., p. 145; NTS., p. 350; BPK., p. 59.
[33] NTS., p. 307; BPK., p. 59; KS., pp. 68-69; SDP., p. 146.
[34] Prīter viśeṣaś cittasya vikāso hāsa ucyate. BPK., p. 34.

mind, which is produced by the perception of curious objects.[35] Rāmacandra and Guṇacandra define mirth as the blooming of the mind which is permeated by a thrill of delight.[36]

Mirth or the comic emotion is characterized by the blooming of the mind because it frees the mind from depression and relaxes it. *Kāvyamīmāṁsā* (900 A.D.) compares the blooming of the mind to the unfolding of a flower, which has already been referred to. We can understand it in the light of McDougall's analysis of laughter. He says, "Laughter is essentially relaxation from all effort. . . . . We seek the ludicrous, the grotesque, the absurd, the ridiculous, not because they are in themselves pleasing, but because they make us laugh, and laughter does us good, makes us feel better and brighter, frees us from depression, prevents our thinking of depressing things".[37]

The *Nāṭyaśāstra* describes mimicry of other's actions, fun, incoherent talk, obtrusiveness, foolishness, etc., as the exciting causes of mirth. Śāradātanaya mentions ugly appearance and dress, strange conduct, actions and words, shamelessness, fickleness, unnatural eating, sight of disfigured limbs, disguise, narration of faults, etc., as the exciting causes of mirth, which is generally found in women and low persons. Śiṅga Bhūpāla defines mirth (hāsa) as a change (vikāra) of the mind, which arises from awkward speech, appearance, dress and actions, and imitation of others' speech, appearance, dress or actions owing to fickleness. Incoherent raving is awkward speech. Awkward appearance is illustrated by extremely dwarfish appearance, possession of long, projecting teeth, etc. Misplacement of ornaments in different parts of the body is awkward dress. Awkward gait, etc., are awkward actions. Hemacandra mentions awkward appearance and dress, inappropriate to the place, time and age, and of peculiar colours, dancing in a peculiar manner, mimicry of others' gait, talking in an unusual manner, decorating the body in an unnatural way, etc., as the determinant causes (vibhāva) of mirth. He recognizes also sympathetic induction of laughter.[38]

McDougall also speaks of "awkward, defective, or bizarre

[35] KS., AC., pp. 113-14, SKM., p. 38; SDP., p. 213; PR., RA., p. 230; SSār., p. 106; NDP., p. 176.
[36] Rañjanonmādānuviddhaś cittasya vikāso hāsaḥ. NDP., p. 176.
[37] *Outline of Psychology*, p. 166.
[38] NTS., p. 351; BPK., p. 59; RS., p. 155; KS., AC., pp. 113-14.

modes of attire, of address, of speech, of gait, of eating" as ludicrous things. The ludicrous, he observes, always involves "some maladjustment, something inappropriate".[39]

Hemcandra mentions throbbing of the nose, the lips and the cheeks, blooming and contraction of the eyes, redness of the face, holding the sides, perspiration, etc., as the expressions (anubhāva) of mirth (hāsa). Viśvanātha mentions contraction of the eyes, smiling of the face, etc., as the expressions of mirth. Śiṅga Bhūpāla mentions throbbing of the nose, the lips, the cheeks, etc., as the expressions of mirth.[40]

The more cultured a person is, the more restrained are the expressions of his emotions. Bharatamuni gives the following description of six kinds of laughter. (1) In smita the cheeks brighten up a little, the glances of the eyes become graceful, and the teeth are not visible. In hasita the face and the eyes brighten up, and the teeth are slightly visible. In vihasita the eyes contract, the cheeks dimple, the voice becomes sweet, and the face becomes red. In upahasita the nose is expanded, the eyes squint, and the head and the shoulders are bent. In apahasita the eyes are filled with tears, and the head and the shoulders swing upwards on inappropriate occasions. In atihasita the eyes are expanded and suffused with tears, a loud cry is set up, and the sides are held with hands. The most cultured persons have slight smile (smita) and smile (hasita). The persons of mediate culture have gentle laughter (vihasita) and laughter of ridicule (upahasita). The low uncultured persons have vulgar laughter (apahasita) and violent laughter (atihasita). The first two are superior types, the second two, middling types, and the last two, inferior types. Bharatamuni mentions two kinds of comic emotion, viz., (1) self-centred and (2) centred in others.[41]

Darwin gives an elaborate account of the expression of laughter, a brief summary of which is given here resembling the account given above. "We hear of 'laughter holding both his sides' (cp. pārśvagrahaṇa). From the shaking of the body, the head nods to and fro. The upper and lower orbicular muscles of the eyes are more or less contracted. In laughing and broad

[39] *Outline of Psychology*, p. 166.
[40] KS., AC., pp. 113-14; SDP., p. 240; RS., p. 155.
[41] PR., RP., p. 230; KS., AC., pp. 114-15; SDP., pp. 240-41; NTS., pp. 314-16; BPK., p. 60.

smiling the cheeks and upper lips are much raised, the nose appears to be shortened, and the skin on the bridge becomes finely wrinkled in transverse lines, with other oblique longitudinal lines on the sides. The upper front teeth are commonly exposed. A bright and sparkling eye is as characteristic of a pleased or amused state of mind, as is the retraction of the corners of the mouth and upper lip with the wrinkles thus produced. Under extreme laughter the eyes are too much suffused with tears to sparkle. During excessive laughter the whole body is often thrown backward and shakes, or is almost convulsed; the respiration is much disturbed; the head and face become gorged with blood with the veins distended; and the orbicular muscles are spasmodically contracted. Tears are freely shed."[42]

Dissimulation, indolence, apprehension, shyness, inconstancy, sleeping, dreaming, awaking, envy, etc., are the accessory states (vyabhicāribhāva) of mirth. Dissimulation is the inhibition of the expressions of emotions. Shame also is an accessory state of mirth.[43]

Bharatamuni mentions throbbing of the lips, nose and cheeks, expansion, contraction and closing of the eyes, perspiration, redness of the face, holding the sides, etc., as the organic expressions of mirth. Śāradātanaya mentions inactivity, perspiration, trembling, horripilation, shedding tears, change of colour, and change of voice as the spontaneous organic expressions of mirth.[44]

4. *Grief (śoka)*

Viśvanātha defines grief (śoka) as affliction of the mind (cetovaiklavya) owing to the loss of cherished objects (iṣṭanāśa) and the befalling of a calamity (aniṣṭāpti). It is in the nature of mental agony (antaḥsantāpa) due to separation from, or death of dear ones such as sons and the like. Jagannātha also defines grief as affliction (vaiklavya) of the mind due to separation from sons, etc., or their death. Hemacandra describes grief as an emotion which is characterized as widowedness or deprivation (vaidhurya). In grief the mind feels widowed or deprived of its cherished possessions. It is a feeling of deprivation. It is a permanent emotional disposition characterized by widowedness of

[42] EEMA., pp. 207-14.
[43] KS., AC., p. 114; SDP., p. 240; NTS., p. 313.
[44] NTS., p. 313; BPK., p. 60.

the mind.[45] Vidyānātha (1400 A.D.) defines grief as the excess of sorrow (duḥkhātibhūmi) owing to bereavement or death of near and dear ones. Vidyābhuṣaṇa also defines grief as excessive distress of the mind (cittakleśātiśaya) due to bereavement and the like. Śāradātanaya defines grief as affliction of all the sense-organs (sarvendriya-parikleśa). In grief not only the mind is overwhelmed, but also the sense-organs and the motor organs are afflicted. This definition beautifully describes the paralysing effect of grief on the mind and the sense-organs. Kumārasvāmī observes that grief arises also from the attainment of undesired objects. Śiṅga Bhūpala defines grief as affliction of the mind (cittakleśa) which arises from the loss of wealth, poverty, distress of friends, etc. Acyutarāya describes grief as a mental mode produced by the loss of cherished objects. Grief is defined as affliction of the mind due to the loss of cherished objects or befalling of a calamity. Rāmacandra and Guṇacandra define grief as mental pain permeated by self-abasement. A person stricken with grief indulges in disparaging himself.[46]

Bharatamuni mentions separation from dear ones or their death, loss of wealth, death, captivity, accidents or any other misfortune, affliction owing to a curse, etc., as the determinant causes (vibhāva) of grief. Śāradātanaya mentions loss of cherished objects, curse, distress, sudden calamity, death of beloved persons, loss of wealth, exile from one's country, accidental loss, poverty, sickness, etc., as the determinant causes of grief. Hemacandra mentions the loss of desired objects (iṣṭaviyoga) and befalling of a calamity (aniṣṭasamprayoga) as the determinant causes of grief. Thus we are overcome with grief when we are deprived of our cherished objects, bereaved of beloved persons, or overtaken by a calamity.[46a]

In western psychology also we find a similar account of the psychology of grief. Bain says, "Our own loss by the withdrawal of those we love and our share in the evil that befalls them—are the two sides wherein we are vulnerable through our affections. (Cp. Iṣṭajanaviyoga and aniṣṭasamprayoga). With respect to the

[45] Citta-vaidhurya-lakṣaṇaḥ śokaḥ sthāyibhāvaḥ. KS., AC., p. 116; RG., p. 39.
Iṣṭanāśādibhiś cetovaiklayaṁ śokaśabdabhāk. SDP., p. 213.
[46] Nirvedānuviddhaṁ duḥkhaṁ śokaḥ. NDP., p. 176.
[46a] NTS., p. 352; BPK., p. 62; KS., p. 116.

deprivation (cp. vaidhurya) of what we have become attached to —the pain is deep and intense according to the power of the attachment and the pleasure it affords."[47] Stout also speaks of "loss and misfortune" as the appropriate objects of grief.[48] Ladd also says, "To snatch from the hand of the child some bauble that gives it pleasure will often elicit a grieved cry. . . . Animals and very young children sometimes evince remarkable signs of this emotion on missing companions that have died or been removed."[49] McDougall says, "A man whose life-long ambition is thwarted will suffer the pangs of grief."[50] Thus grief is due to deprivation, bereavement, or any other calamity.

Bharatamuni mentions self-abasement, languor, anxiety, agitation, delusion, fatigue, fainting, fear, dejection, sickness, mental agony, inactivity, insanity, epilepsy, terror, indolence, death-like condition, immobility, tremor, change of colour, weeping, loss of voice, etc., as the accessory states (vyabhicāribhāva) of the permanent emotional disposition of grief. Hemacandra mentions all these and other painful feelings as the accessory states of grief.[51]

Bharatamuni mentions shedding tears, repentance, lamentation, pallor, change of voice, drooping limbs, prostration on the ground, loud cry, sighing, inactivity, insanity, fainting, death-like condition and the like as the expressions of grief. Śāradātanaya adds dryness of the mouth, loss of memory, beating oneself, rolling on the ground, throwing of arms, trembling, sobbing, hard breathing, chastising the body, dejection, self-abasement, anxiety, eagerness, misery, perplexity, mental agony, epilepsy and indolence to Bharatamuni's list. He observes, that in women and low persons grief produces a determination to die. In persons of moderate culture also grief produces a death-like condition and a desire to die. In cultured persons even intense grief is pacified by discrimination (viveka). Hemacandra mentions emaciation of the body also as an expression of grief. Viśvanātha mentions raving also as an expression (anubhāva) of it.[52]

Śāradātanaya describes three kinds of crying. (1) Vilāpa is

[47] *The Emotions and the Will*, p. 146.
[48] *Groundwork of Psychology*, p. 191.
[49] *Psychology Descriptive and Explanatory*, p. 539.
[50] *The Energies of Men*, 1939, p. 237.
[51] NTS., p. 318; KS., AC., p. 116.
[52] NTS., p. 351; SDP., p. 244; BPK., pp. 62-63; KS., AC., ,p. 116.

crying along with the relating of the qualities of the dead person. (2) Paridevita is crying with sobs. (3) Ākranda is crying loudly in a paroxysm of grief. Vilāpa is found in persons of the lowest culture. Paridevita is found in persons of moderate culture.

Śāradātanaya describes three kinds of weeping. (1) In weeping due to jealousy there are quivering of the lips, shedding tears with sighing, shaking of the head, trembling, lowering of the eye-brows, and eyeing crookedly. (2) In weeping due to joy there are brightening of the cheeks, shedding cold tears, horripilation, and choking of voice. (3) In weeping due to grief there are raving, prostration on the ground, profusely shedding tears, rolling on the ground, and lamenting slowly. Weeping is generally found in women, and sometimes in the lowest persons.[53]

Darwin also gives a similar account of the expressions of grief. "Persons suffering from excessive grief seek relief by violent and almost frantic movements; but when their suffering is somewhat mitigated, yet prolonged, they no longer wish for action, but remain motionless and passive (cp. stambha). Their circulation becomes languid, the face pale; the muscles flaccid; the eye-lids droop; the head hangs on the contracted chest; the lips, cheeks, and lower jaw all sink downwards (cp. gātrasraṁsana). The breathing becomes slow and feeble, and is often interrupted by sighs."[54] Lange's description of the expressions of grief also resembles the account given by the Sanskrit Rhetoricists. "The chief feature," he says, "in the physiognomy of grief is perhaps its paralysing effect on the voluntary movements (cp. stambha). . . . His voice is weak and without resonance (cp. svarabheda). . . . The neck is bent, the head hangs, the relaxation of the cheek-and-jaw-muscles makes the face look long and narrow, the jaw may even hang open (cp. gātrasraṁsana). . . . The vascular muscles are more strongly contracted than usual, so that the tissues and organs of the body become anæmic. The immediate consequence of this bloodlessness is pallor (cp. vaivarṇya) and shrunkenness, and the pale colour and collapsed features are the peculiarities which give to the victim of grief his characteristic physiognomy, and often give an impression of emaciation (cp. tānava). Another regular consequence of the bloodlessness of the

[53] BPK., pp. 72-73.
[54] EEMA., pp. 181-82.

skin is a feeling of cold, and shivering (cp. kampa). . . . Such is the diminution of the various secretions. The mouth grows dry, the tongue sticky, and a bitter taste ensues which is only a consequence of the tongue's dryness (cp. mukhaśoṣana). There is one of the most regular manifestations of grief, and that is the weeping with its profuse secretion of tears (cp. aśrupāta)."[55] The western psychologists account for the different expressions of grief.

5. *Anger (krodha)*

Jagannātha defines anger as a mental mode called 'inflaming' due to grave offence to oneself, or to one's preceptor, relatives, etc., in the form of chastisement and the like.[56] Vidyābhūṣaṇa also describes anger as 'blazing up' of the mind due to hostility and the like.[57] Vidyānātha defines anger as 'inflaming' of the mind (manaḥ-prajvalana) due to some injury done to a person. Kumārasvāmī describes anger as the state of the mind in which it is 'inflamed' (prajvalitā manovṛtti) owing to contempt, persecution and other such misconduct of the enemy or the like. Siṅga Bhūpala defines anger as 'blazing up' of the mind (cittajvalana) due to others' disparagement, persecution and the like. It is an emotion which consumes the mind. Rāmacandra and Guṇacandra define anger as being possessed by intense heat (paritāpāveśa) of the mind, which is the cause of hatred and desire to do harm. It is the cause of chastising the wrong-doer. Mental heat or agony consumes the mind, and does not cool down until the angry person wreaks vengeance upon him.[58]

Viśvanātha defines anger as an emotion of fierceness which is roused by hostile objects.[59] Rāmacandra Tarkavāgīśa explains it as excess of the desire to do harm. Hemacandra also defines anger as the emotion of being roused to fierceness (taikṣṇyaprabodha). Vāmana also gives the same definition of anger, and explains it as intensity of the desire to do harm. Fierceness (taikṣṇya) is the desire to do harm (apacikīrṣā). Anger is a

[55] Quoted by William James in his "*Principles of Psychology*, Vol. II, pp. 443-44.

[56] Guru-bandhu-vadhādi-paramāparādha-janmā prajvalanākhyaḥ krodhaḥ. RG., p. 39.

[57] Prātikūlyādinā cittajvalanaṁ krodhaḥ. SKM., p. 38.

[58] PR., RP., p. 231; RS., p. 158; NDP., p. 176.

[59] Pratikūleṣu taikṣṇyasyāvabodhaḥ krodhaḥ. SDP., p. 213.

mental mode which is the cause of great intensity of this desire. This fierceness is the tendency to crush, destroy, or break down opposition. Acyutarāya defines fierceness as the desire to destroy (dhvaṁsecchutā). He gives a psychological explanation of the phenomenon, and asserts, that the emotion of anger arises from the thwarting of a desire.[60] Śāradātanaya observes, that anger is the cause of fierceness.[61] Thus the emotion of anger is exicted by opposition, aggression, or hostility.

Jagannātha distinguishes between anger (krodha) and revenge (amarṣa). Both are produced by offence of another person. Jagannātha regards the difference between them as one of degree. Anger is the cause of destroying the offender. Revenge, on the other hand, is evoked by lesser offence, and is the cause of not speaking harsh words, but of keeping silence. Anger is a permanent emotional disposition, while revenge is a transitory emotion. Anger is manifested in an eager desire to crush or destroy the malefactor, while revenge is harboured within the mind, and not expressed in immediate action to punish the malefactor, but in keeping silence.[61a]

Śāradātanaya describes three kinds of anger: krodha, kopa and roṣa. Krodha is rage which is found mostly in furious persons. Kopa is mild anger which is found in modest persons. Roṣa is anger arising from love between husband and wife. Krodha is a stormy passion which persists in the infuriated person until it realizes its end. Kopa is quickly controlled and prevented from realising its end. But if it is excited repeatedly, then it is increased in intensity. Roṣa is generally pacified when it is controlled.[62] Siṅga Bhūpāla also describes these three varieties of anger. Krodha is fury found in cruel persons, which terminates in killing the opponent. It is the most intense anger. Kopa is mild anger found in heroes, which makes the person affected by it even welcome his opponent. Roṣa is anger arising from love between husband and wife. When love is crossed by any conduct of the husband or the wife, anger (roṣa) is evoked

[60] Vicchedād abhilāṣasya vṛttiḥ krodhaḥ. SSār., p. 106. KS., p. 126; BB., Poona, 1933, p. 112.

[61] Tejaso janakaḥ krodhaḥ. BPK., p. 35.

[61a] Krodhaḥ para-vināśādihetuḥ. Kṣudrāparādha-janmā tu paruṣa-vacanāsaṁbhāṣanādihetuḥ. Amarṣākhyo vyabhicārīti vivekaḥ. RG., p. 39.

[62] BPK., p. 72.

in the person until he or she is convinced of her or his sincere love for the other. It is expressed in crooked glances, quivering of the lips, redness of the corner of the eyes, sighing, wrinkling of the eyebrows and the like. Enemies and servants are the objects of fury (krodha). Friends and superiors are the objects of mild anger (kopa). The beloved person is the object of anger (roṣa) due to jealousy.[63]

Bharatamuni mentions insult, abuse, false allegations, threatening, acts of hostility and the like as the determinant causes (vibhāva) of anger. Śaradātanaya mentions also disparagement, harsh words, persecution, resolve to take one's wife, encroachment on one's property, sudden seizure of houses, fields, wives, etc., jealousy, abusing one's country, birth, family, conduct, learning, heroism, etc., disobeying one's orders, etc. as the determinant causes of anger. Hemacandra adds stealing one's wife, ridicule, mischief, a servant's abuse, etc., as the determinant causes of anger.[64]

A similar account of the emotion of anger is found in western psychology also. Stout says, "Any kind of opposition, any thwarting of psychic activity may cause anger." "Any condition which thwarts conation may give rise to an outburst of destructive violence." "In general, anger tends to be aroused when there is obstruction of impulse which is independently aggressive." "Anger is essentially a general impulse to crush and destroy." Shand says, "Anger desires to injure or pain its object."[65] Mellone and Drummond say, "The emotion of anger is characterized by a tendency to break down opposition. The characteristic attitude of anger is active resistance and aggression."[66] McDougall relates the emotion of anger to the instinct of pugnacity. He says, "The condition of its excitement is any opposition to the free exercise of any impulse, any obstruction to the activity to which the creature is impelled by any one of the other instincts. And its impulse is to break down any such obstruction and to destroy whatever offers this opposition."[67]

[63] RS., p. 158.
[64] NTS., p. 353; BPK., p. 62; KS., AC., p. 116.
[65] *A Manual of Psychology*, 1910, pp. 321-322. Ibid, 1932, p. 372; *Groundwork of Psychology*, p. 204.
[66] *The Elements of Psychology*, 6th edition, p. 252.
[67] *Introduction to Social Psychology*, pp. 59-60.

Anger is expressed by blood-shot eyes, frowning, grinding of teeth, throbbing of the cheeks, biting of the lips, clenching the fists, thumping them, beating, throwing on the ground, oppression, seizing, throwing of weapons, drawing or shedding blood, cutting, etc. These are mentioned by Hemacandra. Bharatamuni mentions also dilation of the nostrils and upturned eyes as the expressions of anger. Viśvanātha mentions also fierce looks and threatening as its expressions. Śāradātanaya mentions also compression of the lips, frequent throbbing of the cheeks, horripilation, perspiration and trembling as the expressions of anger. Rāmacandra Tarkavāgīśa adds redness of the face also to the list of organic expressions.[68] Siṅga Bhūpāla describes the following expressions of anger. Anger towards an enemy is expressed by frequent biting of the lips, frowning, grinding of teeth, closing and pressing the fists, trembling of the body, looking at one's arms, readiness to take up arms, roaring and the like. Anger towards a servant is expressed by threatening, shaking of the head, chiding in various ways, frequently looking at him, etc. Anger towards a friend is expressed by tears coming out of the corners of the eyes, silently pondering, inactivity, sighing frequently, speechlessness, downcast face, casting glances crookedly, etc. Anger towards superiors is expressed by blaming oneself, downcast face, not replying to their queries, faltering voice, perspiration, etc.[69] Śāradātanaya mentions the following expressions of anger. Anger towards an enemy is expressed by crooked frowning, licking the corner of the mouth with the tongue, severely looking at the weapons, restless movements, etc., also. Anger towards a servant is expressed by eyeing him frequently, flourishing the fingers and threatening, etc., also. Anger towards a friend is expressed by shyness, hanging down the head, breathing quickly, lying down in a secret place also. Anger towards the beloved woman is expressed by glances with red eyes, throbbing of the lips, slight contraction of the eye-brows, and slight distortion of a part of the body. Anger towards superiors is expressed by hanging down of the head, bathing in perspiration, stammering voice, and silence also.

Śāradātanaya describes eight stages of anger. In the first

[68] KS., AC., p. 116; NTS., p. 353; p. 321; SDP., p. 147.
[69] RS., pp. 158-59.

stage, a person censures the qualities of the opponent with whom he is angry. In the second stage, he speaks harsh words. In the third stage, he ponders on the means of killing him. In the fourth stage, he feels a desire to kill him. In the fifth stage, he takes a weapon. In the sixth stage, he vehemently attacks and kills him brushing aside all obstacles. In the seventh stage, he drinks the blood of the dead opponent and disembowels him. In the eighth stage, if the angry person is hindered by obstacles from realizing his end, he voluntarily courts death. This is the description of savage fury uncontrolled by reason.[70]

Bharatamuni mentions right knowledge, determination, energy, excitement, revenge, instability, fierceness, pride, perspiration, trembling, horripilation, stammering, etc., as the accessory states (vyabhicāribhāva) of anger. He mentions also arrogance, envy, intoxication and cruelty as the accessory states. Śāradātanaya mentions also fainting, jealousy, recollection, patience, and dissimulation or inhibition of the manifestations of emotions as the accessory states. Hemacandra mentions the same states as accessory.[71]

Darwin's elaborate description of the expressions of anger contains all the expressions given above with their scientific explanation and biological significance. He says, "Under moderate anger the action of the heart is a litle increased, the colour heightened, and the eyes became bright. The respiration is likewise a little hurried. The mouth is commonly compressed, and there is almost always a frown on the brow. Instead of the frantic gestures of extreme rage, an indignant man unconsciously throws himself into an attitude ready for attacking his enemy.... The fists are commonly clenched."[72] Again, Darwin says, "Rage exhibits itself in the most diversified manner. The heart and circulation are always affected; the face reddens, with the veins on the forehead and neck distended. The respiration is likewise affected; the chest heaves, and the dilated nostrils quiver. The body is commonly held erect ready for instant action. The mouth is generally closed with firmness, showing fixed determination, and the teeth clenched or ground together. Such gestures

[70] RS., pp. 158-59; BPK., pp. 71-72.
[71] NTS., p. 322; BPK., p. 62; KS., AC., p. 116.
[72] EEMA., p. 255.

as the raising of the arms, with the fists clenched, as if to strike the effender, are common. The excited brain gives strength to the muscles, and at the same time energy to the will."[73]

6. *Fear* (*bhaya*)

Siṅga Bhūpāla and Śārdātanaya define fear as extreme restlessness of the mind. Viśvanātha defines fear as bewilderment of the mind, which is evoked by the power of dreadful objects. Hemacandra, Rāmacandra and Guṇacandra also define fear as bewilderment.[74] Vāmana gives the same definition of fear, and explains bewilderment as intense aversion for impending grief excited by the power of anger of an infurited person.[75] Vidyābhūṣaṇa defines fear as great instability of the mind (cittācāpalya) produced by the perception of dreadful objects. Vidyānātha asserts, that fear is the cause of the instability of the mind, and that the emotion of fear arises from the apprehension of evil on seeing dreadful objects or on hearing dreadful sounds Acyutarāya regards the perception of hostile objects (pratikūlopalambha) as the cause of fear.[76] Jagannātha defines fear as bewilderment due to the apprehension of great evil on the perception of dreadful objects like a tiger and the like.[77] A. B. Keith says, "The apprehension of danger, accompanied with a painful emotion unhinging in extreme cases—is called fear (bhaya)".[78]

Jagannātha distinguishes between fear (bhaya) and terror (trāsa). Fear is a permanent emotional disposition, while terror is a transitory emotion. When there is the apprehension of a great danger, fear is evoked. But when there is no such apprehension, terror is excited. Others maintain that terror is evoked by a sudden natural calamity, whereas fear is aroused by one's own misconduct.[79]

[73] Ibid, p. 248.

[74] Bhayaṁ cittasya calanam. BPK., p. 35. Raudraśaktyā tu janitaṁ cittavaiklavyadaṁ bhayam. SDP., p. 213. Vaiklavyaṁ bhayam. KS., AC., p. 126. Cittasya atīva cāñcalyam. RS., p. 165. NDP., p. 176.

[75] Vaiklavyaṁ bhāvi-duḥkhe utkaṭo dveṣaḥ. BB., p. 112.

[76] SKM., p. 38; PR., RP., p. 233; SSār., p. 107.

[77] Vyāghra-darśanādi-janmā paramānarthaviṣayako vaiklavyākhyaḥ sa bhayam. RG., p. 39.

[78] *The Dramatic Sentiments*, Calcutta, 1881, p. 17.

[79] Autpātika-prabhavas trāsaḥ, svāparādhotthaṁ bhayam. RG., p. 39.

Bharatamuni mentions the perception of ferocious beasts, elephants, darkness of the night, inclement weather, serpents, sounds of animals, hooting of owls, unoccupied houses, dense forests, mountains, caves, roaming at night, offending the preceptor or the king, etc., as the determinant causes (vibhāva) of fear. Hemacandra mentions the sight of demons, or the hearing of their unnatural sounds, and the sight or hearing of the persecution of one's relatives also as the causes of fear. Śāradātanaya mentions the sight of animals of hideous appearances, the hearing of terrible sounds, going to deserted places, and entering the battle-field also as the causes of bear. Śiṅga Bhūpāla mentions the sight or hearing of dreadful objects as the cause of fear, and remarks, that it is generally found in low and mediocre persons. In cultured persons fear is excited by supernatural objects. In low and mediocre persons fear is excited even by slight causes, which appears as a natural (sahaja) emotion to them. They are easily susceptible to fear. But cultured persons do not give expression to fear. In them fear is so much restrained that even when it is excited in them by the excess of supernatural causes, it appears as artificial. Śiṅga Bhūpāla mentions the dreadful objects which evoke fear as of three kinds: (1) dreadful in appearance, e.g. ghosts, demons, etc; (2) dreadful in actions, e.g. tigers, wolves, etc.; (3) dreadful on account of greatness, e.g. gods, men with supernatural powers, etc.[80]

Bharatamuni mentions hideous noise, sight of ghosts, panic, ominous cry of jackals and owls, staying in an empty house or forest, sight of death or captivity of dear ones, or hearing of it, or discussion about it, offending one's superior or the king, etc., as the exciting causes of the permanent emotional disposition of fear on which the terrible sentiment is based.[81]

Stout says, "A loud noise for which we are unprepared startles us with a momentary alarm. Many people cannot help being scared by a reverberating peal of thunder, though they know that it is harmless. . . . The sudden approach of an object, the abrupt occurrence of an intense sensation, stimulate to action: there is a demand for practical adjustment to the obstructive experience. At the same time its very suddenness or intensity disconcerts and

[80] NTS., p. 354; KS., AC., p. 118; BPK., p. 63; RS., pp. 165, 168.
[81] NTS., E.T., BI., vi, 68-69.

startles, so that efficient reaction is not possible. This is more conspicuously so, where the impression is not only sudden but unfamiliar. Mere unfamiliarity or strangeness, apart from suddenness or exceptional intensity, suffices to cause fear even in a violent form."[82] McDougall says, "The instinct of fear or flight is one of the strongest and the most widely distributed instincts throughout the animal kingdom. In man and in most of animals this instinct is capable of being excited by any sudden loud noise, independently of all experience of danger or harm associated with such noises. . . . In most animals this instinct may be excited by a variety of objects and sense impressions prior to all experience of hurt and danger. In some of the more timid creatures every unfamiliar sound or sight is capable of exciting it. . . . In most young children unmistakable fear is provoked by any sudden loud noise. . . . In some intense fear is excited on the first introduction at close quarters to a dog or cat. . . . In other persons, again, fear is excited by the noise of the high wind, and though they may be in a solidly built house that has weathered a hundred storms, they will walk restlessly to and fro throughout every stormy night. . . . The excitement of fear is not necessarily, or indeed usually, the effect of an intelligent appreciation or anticipation of danger."[83]

Bharatmuni mentions inactivity, perspiration, choking voice, horripilation, trembling, loss of voice, pallor, apprehension, fainting, trembling, dejection, excitement, restlessness, perplexity, terror, epilepsy, death-like condition and the like as the accessory states of the emotion of fear. Hemacandra mentions also terror (trāsa) and misery as the accessory states of fear.[84]

Bharatmuni gives the following account of the organic expressions of fear. Trembling of the hands and the feet, shaking of the whole body, palpitation of the heart, perspiration, terror, inactivity, dryness of the mouth, lapping with the tongue, change of colour, loss of voice, searching for a shelter, running away, uttering a loud cry, etc., are the expressions of fear. Hemacandra mentions also dryness of the lips, seeing with wandering eyes, pallor of the face, and stammering utterance as the expressions

[82] *A Manual of Psychology*, London, 1938, p. 373.
[83] *An Introduction to Social Psychology*, London, 1946, pp. 30, 44, 45, 46.
[84] NTS., p. 327; E.T., vi, 68; KS., AC., p. 118.

of fear. Viśvanātha mentions horripilation, looking in all directions, insensibility also as the expressions of fear. Śiṅga Bhūpāla mentions hiding one's limbs and looking with the face turned backward also as the expressions of fear.[85]

It should be noted here that these organic expressions of the emotion of fear also reinforce and strengthen it. They do not exhaust the emotion of fear, but reinvigorate it. Thus, at first, there is an incipient emotion of fear; then there are the organic expressions of it; and, at last, there is the intensified emotion of fear strengthened by the organic expressions.

McDougall says, "The dilated pupil, the starting eye, the dry mouth, the arrested digestion, the pallor of the skin, the rapid pulse and breathing, the voiding of urine, all these are symptoms of fear—together they constitute the unmistakable expression of fear."[86] "Fear, once aroused, haunts the mind. It is thus the great inhibitor of action, both present action and future action."[87] Darwin's description of the expression of fear is similar to the Sanskrit Rhetoricists' account. In fear, "the heart beats quickly and violently, so that it palpitates or knocks against the ribs; . . . . the skin instantly becomes pale. . . . Perspiration immediately exudes from it. . . . The hairs on the skin stand erect; and the superficial muscles shiver. In connection with the disturbed action of the heart, the breathing is hurried. The salivary glands act imperfectly; the mouth becomes dry, and is often opened and shut. . . . One of the best-marked symptoms is the trembling of all the muscles of the body; and this is often seen in the lips. From this cause, and from the dryness of the mouth, the voice becomes husky or indistinct, or may altogether fail!"[88] Ribot gives a summary of Lange's account of the physiology of fear. "The characteristic marks of fear are a convulsive tremor, in extreme cases, suppression of all movements; voice hoarse and broken, or complete dumbness, arrest of the salivary secretion; the mouth dry, the tongue adhering to the palate; cold sweats, 'goose-flesh', bristling of the hair, arrest of respiration,

[85] NTS., pp. 354-55; E.T., vi, 68, 72; KS., AC., p. 118; SDP., p. 252; RS., p. 165.
[86] *An Outline of Psychology*, London, 1931, p. 322.
[87] *An Introduction to Social Psychology*, p. 47.
[88] EEMA., pp. 306-08.

oppression, constriction of the throat, shiverings, spasm of the heart; pallor and peripheral anæmia."[89]

7. *Disgust (jugupsā)*

Śāradātanaya defines disgust as the shrinking of the mind characterized by hatred.[90] Hemcandra also defines disgust as an emotion characterized as the shrinking of the mind, which is evoked by the perception of loathsome objects, e.g., worms, insects, wounds, vomiting, etc., which are its determinant causes (vibhāva). Kumārasvāmī also defines disgust as the shrinking of the mind (manaḥsaṁkoca) produced by the perception of loathsome objects, e.g. blood., vomiting etc. Vidyābhūṣaṇa also defines disgust as the enfolding or contraction of the mind (cittamudraṇa) produced by the perception of loathsome objects. Vāmana asserts, that disgust is evoked by the perception of immensity of faults which excite hatred.[91] Viśvanātha defines disgust as hatred (garhā) which is excited by the percpetion of loathsome qualities of objects. Bharatamuni mentions the sight or hearing of loathsome objects, or the description of such things as the causes of disgust.[92] Śiṅga Bhūpāla defines disgust as contraction of the mind (manasaḥ saṁkocanam) which is excited by the sight or hearing of loathsome objects. Jagannātha defines disgust as a mental mode called hesitancy produced by the sight of ugly objects.[93] It is the recoiling of the mind from a repulsive, ugly, disagreeable, or loathsome object. Rāmacandra and Guṇacandra define disgust as an emotion which is excited by the knowledge of ugliness or loathsomeness of objects.[94] Not only loathsome objects should be perceived, but must be known to be loathsome, in order to evoke the emotion of disgust.

Śāradātanaya divides disgust into two kinds: kṣobha and udvega. The former is the shrinking of the mind, while the latter is the shrinking of the body. The former is excited by the sight

[89] *The Psychology of the Emotions*, p. 208.
[90] Nindātmā cittasaṅkoco jugupsā. BPK., p. 35. Saṁkoco jugupsā. KS., AC., p. 126.
[91] PR., RP., p. 234; SKM., p. 38; BB., p. 112.
[92] Doṣekṣaṇādibhir garhā jugupsā viṣayodbhavā. SDP., p. 213. NTS., p. 355.
[93] Kadarya-vastu-vilokana-janmā vicikitsākhyaś cittavṛttiviśeṣo jugupsā. RG., p. 40.
[94] Kutsitatvādhyavasāyo jugupsā. NDP., p. 176.

of blood and the like. The latter is physical in nature. A person with mental shrinking gets afraid, fades, feels aversion, faints again and again, regains his senses, weeps, walks away, becomes dejected, abuses, shows mercy, roams, is struck with terror, sits silently, and hides himself. A person with bodily shrinking covers his face with cloth, covers his nose, contracts his eyes, turns his face aside, advances with quick steps, and spits frequently.[95]

Bharatmuni gives the following account of the expressions of disgust. It is expressed by the shrinking of the whole body, spitting, vomiting, narrowing the mouth and the eyes, covering the nose, bending down the head, walking imperceptibly, etc. Śiṅga Bhūpāla mentions also turning aside the face, shaking the whole body, hurried movement, spitting frequently, and speaking ill of the loathsome objects. Hemacandra mentions also palpitation of the heart, and turning the nose aside as the expressions of disgust.[96]

A similar account of the expressions of disgust is found in western psychology. Darwin says, "With respect to the face, moderate disgust is exhibited in various ways: by the mouth being widely opened, by spitting, by blowing out of the protruded lips, by a sound as of clearing the throat. . . . Extreme disgust is expressed by movements round the mouth identical with those preparatory to the act of vomiting. The mouth is opened widely, with the upper lip strongly retracted, which wrinkles the sides of the nose, and with the lower lip protruded and everted as much as possible. This latter movement causes the contraction of the muscles which draw downwards the corners of the month."[97] McDougall relates the emotion of disgust to the instinct of repulsion. He says, "The impulse of repulsion seems to be excited by the contact of slimy and slippery substances with the skin, and to express itself as a shrinking of the whole body (cp. sarvāṅga-saṁkocana). The common shrinking from slimy creatures with a 'creepy' shudder seems to be the expression of this impulse."[98]

Bharatamuni mentions epilepsy, anxiety, insanity, despair, intoxication, fear, agitation, sickness, and death-like condition as

[95] BPK., p. 67.
[96] NTS., pp. 355-56; E.T., vi, 72, 74; (Bib. Ind.). RS., p. 164, verse 147; KS., AC., p. 119.
[97] EEMA., p. 269.
[98] *Introduction to Social Psychology*, p. 56.

the accessory states of the odious sentiment. Śāradātanaya mentions also aversion, languor, fainting, anger, sleep, delusion, and ascertainment of duty as the accessory states of disgust. Hemacandra mentions fierceness also as an accessory state (vyabhicāri-bhāva) of disgust.[99]

8. *Wonder* (*vismaya*)

Śāradātanaya defines wonder as astonishment of the mind.[100] Viśvanātha defines wonder as expansion of the mind at the sight of various objects which transcend the bounds of experience.[101] Expansion is unfoldment (vikāsa).[102] Vidyānātha also defines wonder as expansion of the mind which arises from the perception of unprecedent objects which were never perceived before.[103] Vāmana quotes a definition of wonder as expansion of the mind which arises from the perception of greatness or sublimity of objects.[104] Kumārasvāmī agrees with Viśvanātha in explaining the nature of the objects which excite the emotion of wonder. They must be extraordinary and beyond the limits of our common experience. Acyutarāya ascribes the emotion of wonder to the perception of strange objects (citravastu). Vidyābhūṣaṇa also defines wonder as expansion of the mind due to the perception of supernatural objects.[105] Śiṅga Bhūpāla defines wonder as expansion of the mind due to the perception of objects which transcend our ordinary experience (lokottara). Jagannātha defines wonder as unfoldment of the mind produced by the sight of extraordinary objects. It is a shock of excitement due to the perception of something which was never perceived before.[106] Rāmacandra and Guṇacandra regard wonder as an emotion that is evoked by the knowledge of superiority or excellence.[107]

[99] NTS., p. 329; E.T., vi, 72; vii, 115; BPK., p. 63; KS., AC., p. 119.

[100] Vismayaś cittavaicitryam. BPK., p. 35.

[101] Vividheṣu padārtheṣu lokasīmātivartiṣu Visphāraś cetaso yastu sa vismaya udāhṛtaḥ. SDP., p. 213.

[102] Cittavistārātmā vismayaḥ. KS., AC., p. 120.

[103] Apūvrārtha-saṁdarśanāc cittavistāro vismayaḥ. PR., p. 235.

[104] Vismayaś cittavistāro vastu-māhātmya-darśanāt. BB., p. 112; Kāvyapradīpa, p. 98.

[105] RP., p. 235; SSār., p. 107.

[106] Alaukika-vastu-darśanādi-janmā vikāsākhyo vismayaḥ. RG., p. 39. RS., p. 157; Keith: *The Dramatic Sentiments*, p. 17.

[107] Utkṛṣṭatvāvasāyo vismayaḥ. NDP., p. 176.

Sarveśvarācārya defines wonder as amazement produced by the perception of supernatural objects.[108]

Bharatamuni mentions disguise, acts of magic, superhuman deeds, wonderful hand-writing, handiwork, learning, skill, etc., as the determinant causes (vibhāva) of wonder. Śāradātanaya mentions also the sight of aerial chariots, pleasure gardens, assembly houses, etc., the co-existence of hostile objects in harmony, the occurrence of impossible events, and attainment of desired objects at a time and in a place not imagined before as the causes of wonder. Hemacandra mentions also the sight of supernatural objects, the attainment of desired objects, sudden change of appearance, dexterity in throwing spears, and the sight of magnificent temples as the causes of wonder. Kumārasvāmī mentions the sudden attainment of desired objects, the perception of supernatural objects and the like as the determinant causes of the emotion of wonder.[109] Thus the Sanskrit Rhetoricists maintain, that the unusual, the sudden, the unfamiliar, the extraordinary, the sublime, and the supernatural excite the emotion of wonder.

Bharatmuni quotes, "Wonder is excited by superhuman deeds and arises from joy."[110] The Ālaṅkārikas define the emotion of wonder as expansion of the mind because it generates pleasurable elation and heightens activity of the mind. It may be understood in the light of Sully's analysis of the emotion of wonder. According to him, at first, there is "a mental shock or disturbance, due to a sudden presentation of something for which attention is not prepared." Then there is a self-preservative reaction in the form of intense attention. "This intensified attention is the source of agreeable feelings, first of heightened activity, then of relief, of self-adjustment, and of intellectual mastery. . . . The realization of something new and extraordinary is in itself exhilarating, and, under favourable circumstances, we find wonder manifesting itself as distinctly pleasurable elation involving an energetic and prolonged reaction of attention."[111]

McDougall relates the emotion of wonder to the instinct of curiosity. He says, "The native excitant of the instinct would

[108] Atilokaiḥ padārthaiḥ syād vismayātmā raso'dbhutaḥ. STS., p. 58.
[109] NTS., p. 356; ET., vi, 74; BPK., p. 61; KS., AC., pp. 119-20; RP., p. 235.
[110] Karmātiśaya-nirvṛtto vismayo harṣasambhavaḥ. NTS., p. 355.
[111] *Outlines of Psychology*, p. 362.

seem to be any object similar to, yet perceptibly different from, familiar objects habitually noticed. It is therefore not easy to distinguish in general terms between the excitants of curiosity and those of fear; for one of the most general excitants of fear is whatever is strange or unfamiliar. The difference seems to be mainly one of degree, a smaller element of the strange or unusual exciting curiosity while a larger and more pronounced degree of it excites fear."[112] Thus, according to McDougall also, the strange, unusual, or unfamiliar excite the instinct of curiosity, which is felt as the emotion of wonder. Bain says, "Wonder contains surprise, attended with a new and distinct effect, the effect of contemplating something that rises far above common experience, which elevates us with the feeling of superiority."[113] (Cp. Viśvanātha). Sully says, "If instead of being merely unexpected at the moment, the object is strange and unfamiliar, the feeling of surprise passes into the more prolonged state of wonder or astonishment."[114]

Bharatamuni mentions expansion of the eyes, gazing with winkless eyes, knitting of the eye-brows, horripilation, shaking of the head, applause and the like as the expressions of the emotion of wonder. He mentions also tremor, choking of voice, and perspiration as the expressions of wonder. Hemacandra mentions also shedding tears, exclamation, and waving the fingers and the cloth as the expressions (anubhāva) of wonder.[114a]

Darwin's description of the expression of wonder is similar to the account given above. He says, "The eyes and mouth being widely open is an expression universally recognized as one of surprise or astonishment. . . . Every sudden emotion, including astonishment, quickens the action of the heart, and with it the respiration."[115] Ribot gives a summary of Darwin's account of the expression of the emotion of wonder. "The eyes and mouth are wide open, the eye-brows raised, the sudden shock is followed by immobility, the pulsations of the heart, and the respiratory movements are accelerated, etc."[116]

[112] *Introduction to Social Psychology*, pp. 57-58.
[113] *The Emotions and the Will*, 1899, p. 86.
[114] *Outlines of Psychology*, p. 362.
[114a] NTS., pp. 356, 330; KS., AC., pp. 119-20.
[115] EEMA., pp. 294, 298.
[116] *The Psychology of the Emotions*, p. 369.

Bharatamuni mentions excitement, quickness, joy, instability of the mind, contentment, insensibility, insanity, fainting, inactivity, shedding tears, perspiration, choked voice, horripilation, etc., as the accessory states (vyabhicāribhāva) of wonder. Inactivity, shedding tears, perspiration, choked voice, and horripilation are the organic expressions of the emotion of wonder; and they also intensify and heighten it. Śāradātanaya asserts, that the accessory states of wonder are the same as those of the sentiment of love. Hemacandra mentions joy, flurry, inactivity, etc., as the accessory states of wonder.[117]

9. *Energy* (*utsāha*)

Bharatamuni describes energy as the nature of an excellent person.[118] Śāradātanaya defines energy as quick action of the mind in all actions undertaken by a person.[119] Hemacandra defines energy as firm zeal.[120] Viśvanātha also defines energy as firm zeal in works undertaken. Vidyānātha defines energy as firm endeavour (stheyān prayatnaḥ). Kumārasvāmī explains firmness (sthairya) as eagerness (autsukya), and describes energy as eager endeavour in the performance of actions whcih require superhuman power. Acyutarāya defines energy as a function of the mind called superiority which arises from power.[121] Jagannātha also defines energy as a mental mode called superiority (aunnatya) which is evoked by the recollection of another's prowess, charity and the like.[122] Vidyābhūṣaṇa defines energy as quick, firm resolve of the mind.[123] Vāmana also defines energy as quick action of the mind or firm zeal (saṁrambha) in works undertaken. Siṅga Bhūpāla defines energy as a quick function of the mind (satvarā mānasī vṛttiḥ) which arises from strength, patience, help of a patron, etc. Energy is of two kinds, natural (sahaja) and acquired (āhārya). Natural energy may be due to strength, patience, or help of a patron. Acquired energy also may

[117] NTS., pp. 330-31, 379; BPK., p. 61. KS., AC., pp. 119-20.
[118] Utsāho nāma—uttamaprakṛtiḥ. NTS., p. 353.
[119] Utsāhaḥ sarvakṛtyeṣu satvarā mānasī kriyā. BPK., p. 35.
[120] Saṁrambhaḥ stheyān utsāhaḥ. KS., AC., p. 126.
[121] Utsāhaḥ śaktisambhūtā vṛttir aunnatya-nāmikā. SSār., p. 107. SDP., p. 213; PR., RP., p. 232.
[122] Para-parākrama-dānādi-smṛti-janmā aunnatyākhya utsāhaḥ. RG., p. 39.
[123] Stheyasī satvaraā ca cittāsaktir utśāhaḥ. SKM., p. 38.

be due to strength, patience or patronage. Energy is the emotion of power in the language of Bain. Rāmacandra and Guṇacandra define energy as enterprize in piety, charity, fight and other acts, which is the absence of indolence (anālasya).[124]

Bharatamuni mentions absence of dejection, power, patience, heroism, etc., as the determinant causes (vibhāva) of the emotion of energy. Śāradātanaya mentions also excessive purity (sattva) of the mind, renunciation, absence of wonder, right knowledge, ascertainment of duty in realizing certain ends, military strength, influence, possession of an invincible army, renown, glory, modesty, diplomacy, masterfulness, power of good counsel, and power of men and money, etc., as the causes of energy. Hemacandra mentions also the hero's political wisdom, self-restraint, determinate knowledge of the situation without delusion, power of defeating the enemy, renown of invincibility, prowess, skill in the application of stratagems, and reviling as the determinant causes of the emotion of power.[125]

Bharatamuni mentions patience, charity, skilful diplomacy, etc., as the consequents (anubhāva) of the emotion of energy. Śāradātanaya mentions also firmness, heroism, influence, rebuke, proper employment of treaty and other political devices, grave and dignified language, etc., as the consequents of energy. Hemacandra mentions also valour, gravity, and diplomacy as the consequents of energy. Siṅga Bhūpāla mentions also waiting and making a speech as the consequents of energy.[126]

Bharatamuni regards patience, ascertainment of duty, pride, fierceness, excitement, revenge, recollection, horripilation, etc., as the accessory states (vyabhicāribhāva) of the sentiment of energy. Śāradātanaya regards awakening, exhilaration, joy, eagerness, conjecture and envy also as the accessory states of energy.[127]

[124] BB., p. 112; RS., p. 156; NDP., p. 176.
[125] NTS., p. 353; BPK., pp. 60-61; KS., AC., Viveka, p. 117.
[126] NTS., p. 353; BPK., p. 61; KS., AC., p. 117; RS., p. 156.
[127] NTS., p. 324; BPK., p. 61. KS., AC., p. 117.

Chapter X

ACCESSORY STATES: TRANSITORY EMOTIONS (VYABHICĀRIBHĀVA)

1. *The Nature of Accessory States or Transitory Emotions (vyabhicāribhāva)*

Śāradātanaya beautifully describes the nature of accessory states. The vyabhicāribhāvas are so called because they promote and develop the permanent emotional dispositions (sthāyibhāva). The former appear and disappear in the latter in the same way as waves appear and disappear in the ocean. Just as waves appearing and disappearing in the ocean contribute to its excellence and are transformed into it, so the accessory states appearing and disappearing in the permanent emotional dispositions promote and intensify them, and are themselves developed by the latter, and with their aid are transformed into an æsthetic emotion (rasa).[1] Hemacandra asserts, that vyabhicāribhāvas are so called because they are subordinate to the permanent emotional dispositions, surrender their specific virtues to them, and help them in various ways.[2] Viśvanātha gives the following literal meaning of vyabhicāribhāvas. They are accessory states which particularly help, promote and strengthen the permanent emotional dispositions (sthāyibhāva) in which they emerge and disappear. They are the feeders of the permanent emotional dispositions or sentiments.[3] The latter have been compared to the thread of a garland which runs through the beads. They always persist in the structure of the mind in the midst of transitory emotions (vyabhicāribhāva) which come and go. The permanent emotional dispositions or sentiments (sthāyibhāva) are not obscured by transitory emotions. But the former are strengthened

[1] Sthāyinyunmagna-nirmagnās tathaiva vyabhicāriṇaḥ.
Puṣṇanti sthāyinaṁ svāṁ śca tatra yānti rasātmatām.
BPK., pp. 25-26; DR., p. 139.

[2] Vividhān ābhimukhyena sthāyidharmopajīvanena svadharmārpaṇena ca caranti iti vyabhicāriṇaḥ. KS., AC., p. 128.

[3] Viśeṣād ābhimukhyena caranto vyabhicāriṇaḥ.
Sthāyinyunmagna-nirmagnāḥ.
SDP., p. 181.

by the latter. The transitory emotions have been compared to the bubbles of the ocean, which appear for a short time and then disappear in the sentiments.[4] Śiṅga Bhūpāla also describes the relation of transitory emotions to permanent emotional dispositions in a similar manner. The former are called vyabhicāribhāvas because they promote and develop the latter to a great extent. The transitory emotions are also called sañcāribhāvas because they quicken the movement of emotions; in other words, they intensify the permanent emotional dispositions. The former appear and disappear in the latter, even as waves appear and disappear in the ocean. The former intensify the latter, and are transformed into them.[5]

Hemacandra describes the transitory emotions (sañcāribhāvas) in the following manner: (1) Dhṛti is contentment (santoṣa). (2) Smṛti is recollection (smaraṇa). (3) Mati is ascertainment of the real nature of an object (arthaniścaya). (4) Vrīḍā (shame) is contraction of the mind (cittasaṁkoca). (5) Jāḍya (inactivity) is non-ascertainment of one's duty (arthāpratipatti). (6) Viṣāda (dejection) is oppression or pain of the mind (manaḥpīḍā). (7) Mada is the combination of exhilaration and intoxication. (8) Vyādhi (sickness) is the agony of the mind (manastāpa). (9) Nidrā (sleep) is the closing of the mind (manaḥsaṁmīlana). (10) Supta is the deep condition of sleep or dreamless sleep. (11) Autsukya (eagerness) is intolerance of time (kālākṣamatva). (12) Avahittha (dissimulation) is the suppression or concealment of the expressions of emotions (ākāragupti). (13) Śaṅkā is the apprehension of harm (aniṣṭotprekṣā). (14) Cāpala (instability) is inconstancy of the mind (ceto'navasthāna). (15) Ālasya (apathy) is indifference to the pursuit of the ends of life—happiness, wealth, virtue and liberation (puruṣārtheṣu anādara). (16) Harṣa (joy) is elation or cheerfulness of the mind (cetaḥprasāda). (17) Garva (pride) is disparagement of others (parāvajñā). (18) Augrya is fierceness (caṇḍatva). (19) Prabodha (wakefulness) is sleeplessness (vinidratva). (20) Glāni (languor) is loss of strength (balāpacaya). (21) Dainya (misery) is loss of energy or vitality (anaujasya). (22) Śrama (fatigue) is exhaustion (kheda). (23) Unmāda (insanity) is derangement of the mind

[4] BB., p. 113.
[5] Viśeṣeṇa ābhimukhyena caranti sthāyinaṁ prati. Sañcārayanti bhāvasya gatiṁ sañcāriṇo' pi te. RS., p. 98.

(cittaviplava). (24) Moha (fainting) is stupor (mūḍhatva). (25) Cintā (anxiety) is anxious pondering (dhyāna). (26) Amarṣa (revenge) is the desire to retaliate (praticikīrṣā) on the wrong-doer. (27) Trāsa (fright) is mental shock (cittacamatkāra). The mind is not prepared to perceive an object, and is shocked by it in fright. So there is an emotion of wonder (camatkāra) in it due to mental shock. (28) Apasmāra (epilepsy) is possession by a demon (āveśa) or epileptic fit. (29) Nirveda (self-abasement) is self-disparagement (svāvamānana). (30) Āvega (flurry) is excitement (saṁbhrama). (31) Vitarka (guess) is conjecture (saṁbhāvanā). (32) Asūyā (envy) is intolerance (akṣamā). (33) Mṛti (death) is death-like condition (mriyamānatā).[6]

2. *Self-abasement (nirveda)*

Viśvanātha defines self-abasement as self-disparagement (svāvamānana) arising from the knowledge of the reality, adversity, jealousy and other causes.[7] The knowledge of the reality is the knowledge that God alone is real, and that the world is not ultimately real. Vāmana ascribes self-disparagement to discrimination between the eternal and the non-eternal, the self and the not-self, and the feeling of miserableness (dainya). Nirveda is self-abasement or the sense of worthlessness of the self endowed with the organism. Hemacandra defines nirveda as self-disparagement due to disease, reproach, chastisement, poverty, bereavement, true knowledge of the reality, etc. Vidyānātha defines nirveda as the consciousness of the fruitlessness or transitoriness of all things (niṣphalatvabuddhi). Śāradātanaya defines nirveda as vacantness of the mind (śūnyacittatva). It is so called because it arises from the loss of wealth. It is produced by poverty, mental agony, suffering, bereavement, envy at others' prosperity, true knowledge of the reality, etc. Siṅga Bhūpāla defines nirveda as the consciousness of fruitlessness (niṣphalatvamati), or the sense of transitoriness of all things, which arises from the knowledge of the reality, poverty, danger, separation from the beloved person, jealousy, etc.; or the feeling of self-disparagement (svātmāvamānana). Vidyābhūṣaṇa defines nirveda as the feeling of one's worthlessness. Rāmacandra and Guṇacandra define nirveda as dispassion

[6] KS., AC., p. 127.
[7] Tattvajñānāpadīrṣyāder nirvedaḥ svāvamānanam. SDP., p. 183.

(vairasya) due to distress, poverty, sickness, insult, envy, error, scolding, chastising, loss of cherished objects, sight of the superhuman powers of others. Dispassion is repugnance to the world.[8] Jagannātha defines nirveda as aversion to all objects of enjoyment due to discrimination of the eternal and the non-eternal.[9] It is produced in low persons by reviling, insult, disease, beating, poverty, loss of cherished objects, envy at another's prosperity, etc. Nirveda is produced in excellent persons by disrespect and the like.

Jagannātha regards it as a permanent emotional disposition (sthāyibhāva). But he regards the indifference to worldly objects produced by domestic quarrel or the like as a transitory emotion.[10] Rāmacandra and Guṇacandra do not regard nirveda as a permanent emotional disposition, since it is not invariably present in any of the æsthetic emotions (rasa), and it appears occasionally. Mammaṭa regards self-abasement as a permanent emotional disposition which generates the æsthetic emotion of tranquillity (śāntarasa). Rāmacandra and Guṇacandra urge that Mammaṭa contradicts himself when he describes nirveda as the permanent emotional disposition corresponding to the æsthetic emotion of tranquillity in one place, and describes it as the transitory emotion (vyabhicāribhāva) which promotes the same æsthetic emotion of tranquillity in another place.[10]

Bharatamuni mentions poverty, sickness, insult, abuse, reproach, bereavement, knowledge of truth, etc., as the causes of self-disparagement. Sarveśvarācārya defines nirveda as self-disparagement, which is produced by the knowledge of truth, befalling of a calamity, jealousy, etc., and which is known to all. This definition is the same as that of Dhanañjaya and Viśvanātha. Rūpa Goswāmī mentions great distress, separation from the beloved, commission of sins, omission of duties, and jealousy as the causes of self-disparagement. Jīva Goswāmī defines nirveda as self-disparagement. Viśvanātha Cakravartī defines it as self-condemnation (ātmadhikkāra).[11] Śārṅgadeva mentions censure,

[8] BB., p. 113; KS., AC., ii, 48, p. 139; PR., p. 243; BPK., pp. 15, 28; RS., pp. 98-99; SKM., p. 40; NDP., p. 177.

[9] Nityānitya-vastu-vicāra-janmā viṣaya-virāgākhyo nirvedaḥ. RG., p. 39.

[10] Ayaṁ ca raseṣu aniyatatvāt kādācitkatvāt vyabhicārī, na sthāyī. NDP., p. 177. RG., p. 39.

[11] NTS., p. 356; STS., p. 49; DR., p. 140; SDP., p. 183; UNM., pp. 572-74; LR., p. 572; ANC., p. 572. Mahārti-viprayogerṣyāsadvivekādikalpitaṁ svāvamānanaṁ nirvedaḥ. BRS., p. 439.

abuse, sickness, anger, beating, poverty, loss of cherished objects, and intolerance of another's prosperity as the determinant causes (vibhāva) of self-abasement in low persons. He regards insult and the knowledge of truth as the determinant causes of self-abasement in excellent persons.[12]

Self-disparagement is expressed by weeping, crying, sighing, breathing hard, attainment of real knowledge (sampradhāraṇa), change of colour, choking of voice, etc. It gives rise to anguish, anxiety, brooding, depression, misery, indifference to all things, depression of the face and the eyes, etc. It is expressed by weeping, sobbing and the like by women and low persons. It leads to the dawn of knowledge of the reality and renunciation in yogins and adepts.[13]

3. *Languor* (*glāni*)

Rāmacandra and Guṇacandra define languor as powerlessness (aśakti) due to disease, old age, physical exertion, vomiting, evacuation of the bowels, hunger, thirst, and various kinds of physical and mental pain. Languor is the loss of strength owing to various kinds of physical exertion such as physical exercise, travelling, sexual intercourse, physical pain such as disturbance of sleep and the like. Hemacandra defines languor as the loss of strength (balāpacaya) due to disease, mental agony, fasting, hunger, thirst, travelling, disturbance of sleep, excessive drinking, penance, old age, prolonged exercise of art, etc. Viśvanātha defines languor as the loss of vitality due to sexual intercourse, mental agony, hunger, thirst and the like. Jagannātha defines languor as a kind of painful feeling due to the loss of strength which is produced by mental anguish and physical disease. Some define languor as the loss of strength produced by sickness and the like. Jagannātha criticizes this view. An emotion (bhāva) is in the nature of a mental mode (cittavṛtti), and cannot, therefore, consist in the loss of strength. Languor is sometimes defined as the loss of strength produced by mental agony and physical disease. But Jagannātha urges that this definition really implies

[12] SR., ii, p. 841.
[13] NTS., p. 356; KS., AC., ii, 48, p. 139; DR., p. 140; BPK., p. 15; SDP., p. 183; SR., ii, p. 841; NDP., p. 177.

that languor is the feeling of pain (duḥkha) produced by the loss of strength.[14] Rūpa Goswāmī, like Viśvanātha, defines languor as loss of vitality (niṣprāṇatā) due to the loss of vital power which nourishes and strengthens the body, mental agony, misery, fatigue, etc. Jīva Goswāmī defines languor as the loss of strength due to fatigue, mental anguish, animal enjoyment and the like. Sarveśvarācārya defines languor as powerlessness of the body due to hunger, thirst, sexual intercourse, etc.[15] Bharatamuni mentions vomiting, purgation, disease, austerities, observance (niyama), fasting, mental agony, excessive exhilaration, drinking of liquor, excessive physical exercise, travelling, hunger, thirst, disturbance of sleep, and the like as the determinant causes of languor.[16]

Bharatamuni mentions faint voice, sunken cheeks, lustreless eyes, pale face, slow gait, trembling, loss of energy, emaciation of body, pallor, change of voice and the like as the expressions of languor. Śāradātanaya mentions also perspiration and laboured breathing as the expressions of langour. Hemacandra mentions also relaxed body and walking like a distressed person as the expressions of languor. Dhanañjaya mentions also exhaustion of the limbs and vocal organs, actions showing weakness, and loss of vitality. Śiṅga Būpāla mentions whirling of the eyes as an expression of languor. Rāmacandra and Guṇacandra mention exhaustion of the body as an expression of languor.[17] Darwin says, "Trembling is excited by exhaustion after excessive fatigue."[18]

4. *Apprehension* (*śaṅkā*)

Bharatamuni says, "Apprehension is in the nature of suspense, and aroused in women and persons of the inferior type."[19] It arises from theft, plunder, offending the king, committing sins, etc. Śāradātanaya also defines apprehension as an emotion in the nature of suspense (sandeharūpa) which is generally found in women and inferior persons. Śaṅkā is so called because it mars

[14] Ratyāyāsa-manastāpa-kṣut-pipāsādi-sambhavā glānir niṣprāṇatā. SDP., p. 209, Ādhivyādhi-janya-bala-hāni-prabhavo duḥkhaviśeṣo glāniḥ. RG., p. 99. Ibid, pp. 99-100. NDP., p. 177; KS., AC., ii, 39, p. 136.

[15] Glānir niṣprāṇatā. BRS., pp. 448-49. Glānir nirbalatā. LR., p. 580. Glāniḥ śarīra-vaivaśyam. STS., p. 49.

[16] NTS., p. 357.

[17] NTS., p. 357; BPK., p. 15; KS., AC., p. 136; DR., p. 141; RS., 102; SDP., p. 209; STS., p. 50; NDP., p. 177.

[18] EEMA., pp. 64-65.

[19] Śaṅkā nāma sandehātmikā strīnīcaprabhavā. NTS., p. 357.

the enjoyment of pleasure.[20] Apprehension of evil prevents a person from enjoying present pleasures. It is produced by the causes mentioned by Bharatamuni. Hemacandra defines apprehension as expectation of evil due to one's own or others' theft, adultery, hostility and the like.[21] Dhanañjaya defines apprehension as expectation of evil due to one's own misconduct or others' cruelty. Viśvanātha also defines apprehension as expectation of evil arising from one's own faults or others' cruelty.[22] Śiṅga Bhūpāla defines apprehension as expectation of one's own evil (svāniṣṭotprekṣaṇa) due to theft, committing an offence, etc. Apprehension is of two kinds. It arises either from one's own conduct or from others' conduct. Rāmacandra and Guṇacandra define apprehension as oscillation of the mind, which consists in its unsettled state due to agitation and doubt.[23] It arises from one's own or others' wrong actions. Jagannātha defines apprehension as a mental mode in such a form as 'What evil will befall me'. Sarveśvarācārya defines apprehension as the loss of understanding (pratibhā-kṣaya) due to the befalling of a calamity, which arises from one's own misconduct or others' cruelty. Rūpa Goswāmi defines apprehension as expectation of one's own harm due to one's own theft or others' cruelty. Jīva Goswāmi defines apprehension as expectation of one's own harm, which gives rise to fear. Fear is an effect of apprehension, and consists in great restlessness of the mind.[24]

Jīva Goswāmi distinguishes between apprehension and fear. Apprehension is anticipation of harm to oneself, which is the cause of fear. Fear is excessive instability of the mind due to offence, sight of dreadful objects, etc. Viśvanātha Cakravartī observes, that both apprehension and fear are evoked by misconduct. But they are distinct from each other. First, they differ in intensity. When fear is very intense, it is a permanent emotion called bhaya. But when it is not intense, it is a transitory emotion called apprehension. When it is intensified and

[20] Śaṁ sukhaṁ kutsayati yā sā. BPK., p. 28.
[21] Caurya-pāradāryāder viruddhācaraṇād aniṣṭotprekṣā śaṅkā. KS., AC., ii, 32, p. 133.
[22] Parakrauryātmadoṣādyaiḥ śaṅkā' narthasya tarkaṇam. SDP., p. 200. DR., p. 134.
[23] Dolanaṁ kṣobha-sandehābhyām anavasthitatvaṁ cetasaḥ. NDP., p. 178. RS., p. 108.
[24] Svāniṣṭotprekṣaṇaṁ śaṅkā. Bhayaṁ tasyāḥ kāryam. Bhayaṁ cittāticāñcalyam. LR., p. 590. RG., p. 99; UNM., pp. 590-92; STS., p. 50.

deepened by its distinguishing characters, it becomes the permanent emotion of fear which is the basis of the æsthetic emotion of terror. Secondly, there is a causal relation between apprehension and fear. Apprehension is the cause of fear, but fear is not the cause of apprehension.[25]

Apprehension is expressed by frequently casting sidelong glances, covering the face, dryness of the mouth, licking with the tongue, pallor of the face, loss of voice, slightly trembling limbs, dry lips, dry throat, downcast face, darkness of the face, fatigue, etc. Śāradātanaya mentions also shedding tears, and looking at all sides, and trembling of the thigh as expressions of apprehension. Apprehension springing from oneself, he asserts, is expressed by looking piteously; and apprehension springing from others is expressed by movements of the limbs, changes in the pupils, eye-brows and looks. Siṅga Bhūpāla mentions also languid speech as an expression of apprehension. Apprehension of evil due to one's own misconduct is indicated by signs such as changes in the eyelashes, eye-brows, pupils and vision. Hemacandra, Viśvanātha, Jagannātha and Dhanañjaya mention these expressions of apprehension. Sarveśvarācārya mentions fright and anguish as consequents of apprehension. Jagannātha observes that trembling is due to fear which is generated by apprehension.[26]

5. *Envy (asūyā)*

Bharatamuni mentions finding fault with others, intolerance of others' wealth, prosperity, intellectual powers, learning, luxury and the like as the determinant causes of envy. Findng fault with others is an effect of envy, rather than its cause. Bharatamuni mentions it as a consequent of envy also. Dhanañjaya defines envy as intolerance of the prosperity of others (parotkarṣākṣamā) due to pride, wickedness and ill-will. Hemacandra defines envy as intolerance (akṣamā) of others' prosperity, wealth, learning and other superior qualities. Śāradātanaya mentions others' good fortune, wealth, intellectual attainments, luxury, prosperity and the like as the determinant causes of envy. Viśvanātha defines envy as intolerance of others' superior qualities and prosperity

[25] LR., pp. 591-92.
[26] NTS., p. 358; BPK., p. 16; RS., p. 108. KS., AC., ii, 32, p. 133; SDP., p. 300; RG., p. 99; DR., p. 142; STS., p. 50.

because of arrogance.[27] Śiṅga Bhūpala defines envy as finding fault even with the excellent qualities of others due to intolerance of their prosperity, wealth, learning, heroism and the like. Rāmacandra and Guṇacandra define envy as intolerance of the superior qualities of others because of hatred, guilt and pride, and impatience of others' prosperity, power, learning, beauty, etc. Śārṅgadeva mentions hatred of another person's wealth, power, learning, talents, good fortune, etc., as the determintnt causes of envy. Vidyānātha defines envy as intolerance of another person's superiority due to pride, malice and anger. Jagannātha defines envy as a mental mode, which arises from the sight of another's superiority, and which gives rise to speaking ill of others.[28] Rūpa Goswāmī defines envy as aversion or hatred for another person's prosperity or good fortune.[29] Jīva Goswāmī also gives the same definition of envy. Sarveśvarācārya defines envy as intolerance of another person's exaltation because of pride, wickedness and anger.[30] This definition resembles Dhanañjaya's definition.

Envy is expressed by denouncing others in an assembly of men, decrying their virtues, eyeing jealously, remaining with a downcast face, frowning, disparagement, abuse, etc. Bharatamuni mentions these expressions of envy. Śāradātanaya mentions not casting glances, despising others, and change in facial expression also as the expressions of envy. Rāmacandra and Guṇacandra mention also finding fault with others' superior qualities and good actions, denial of others' good qualities, contempt, ill-will and anger as the manifestations of envy. Śārṅgadeva mentions ignoring another person's merits, turning the eyes away from him, and casting them down, and revenge as the consequents of envy. Hemacandra mentions eyeing, jealous speech, and anger also as the consequents of envy. Dhanañjaya and Viśvanātha mention signs of anger and ill-will also as the expression of envy. Sarveśvarācārya mentions threatening also as an expression of envy.[31]

Darwin thinks that envy, "a complex state of mind", is not

[27] Asūya' nyaguṇarddhīnām auddhatyād asahiṣṇutā. SDP., p. 205. Akṣamārūpāsūyā. KS., AC., p. 142. NTS., p. 358; DR., p. 147; BPK., p. 16.

[28] Parotkarṣa-darśanādijanyaḥ paranindādi-kāraṇībhūtaś cittavṛttiviśeṣo' sūyā. RG., p. 115. RS., p. 134; NDP., p. 178; SR., ii, p. 843.

[29] Dveṣaḥ parodaye' sūyā. BRS., p. 512. LR., p. 636.

[30] Garva-daurjanya-manyubhyaḥ parotkarṣākṣamāsūyā. STS., p. 50.

[31] NTS., p. 358; BPK., p. 16; NDP., p. 178; SR., ii, p. 843; KS., AC., ii, 51; p. 142; DR., p. 147; SDP., p. 205; STS., p. 50; RS., p. 134.

revealed by "any fixed expression, sufficiently distinct to be described or delineated."[32] He says, "A man may have his mind filled with the blackest hatred or suspicion, or be corroded with envy or jealousy; but as these feelings do not at once lead to action, and as they commonly last for some time, they are not shown by any outward sign, excepting that a man in this state assuredly does not appear cheerful or good-tempered. If indeed these feelings break out into overt acts, rage takes their place, and will be plainly exhibited."[33]

6. *Exhilaration* (*mada*)

Dhanañjaya defines exhilaration as excess of joy (harṣotkarṣa) due to drinking wine. Śiṅga Bhūpāla defines exhilaration as the blending of exhilaration with confusion of the intellect due to drinking wine.[34] Hemacandra, Viśvanātha and Vidyānātha define exhilaration as the fusion of joy with stupefaction or confusion of the intellect due to drinking wine.[35] Acyutarāya defines exhilaration as the mental condition which arises from excessive joy or drinking wine. Bharatamuni regards the drinking of wine as the cause of exhilaration. Śāradātanaya mentions drinking wine, wealth, learning, birth in a noble family, embracing a beautiful wife, etc., as the determinant causes of exhilaration. He regards exhilaration as excess of joy due to intoxication, pride, or gratification of the sex-instinct and the æsthetic impulse. Rāmacandra and Guṇacandra follow Bharatamuni, and ascribe exhilaration to drinking wine. Jagannātha defines exhilaration as a mental mode called excessive elation produced by drinking wine, etc.[36] Rūpa Goswāmī defines exhilaration as excessive elation, which destroys the power of judgment for the time being, and which is produced by the drinking of wine or excess of perversion of the mind due to sex-love.[17] Viśvanātha Cakravartī defines exhilaration

[32] EEMA., p. 274.
[33] Ibid, p. 78.
[34] Madas tu ānanda-sammoha-sambhedo madirākṛtaḥ. RS., p. 104. DR., p. 104.
[35] Madyapānād ānanda-sammohayoḥ. saṁgamo madaḥ. KS., AC., p. 131. Sammohānanda-sambhedo mado madyopayogajaḥ. SDP., p. 187. PR., RP., p. 245.
[36] Madyādyupayogajanmā ullāsākhyaḥ cittavṛtti-viśeṣo madaḥ. RG., p. 102.
[37] Vivekahara ullāso madaḥ sa dvividho mataḥ. Madhupānabhavo' naṅga-vikriyā-bharajo' pi ca. BRS., p. 453.

as intoxication which destroys the power of discrimination, and which is produced by drinking wine. Jīva Goswāmī follows Rūpa Goswāmī in defining exhilaration as excessive elation which destroys the power of discrimination between right and wrong. Sarveśvarācārya defines exhilaration as excess of joy (harṣotkarṣa) due to the attainment of an object of desire, sex-gratification, drinking wine, etc.[38]

Bharatamuni describes three kinds of intoxication, viz. light, medium and excessive. Light intoxication is expressed by smiling face, sweet singing, joyful body, slightly faltering words, slightly unsteady gait, and relates to persons of the superior type. Medium intoxication is expressed by drunken and rolling eyes, drooping arms, or arms restlessly thrown about, unsteady gait, and relates to persons of the middling type. Excessive intoxication is expressed by loss of memory, inability to walk, cough, hiccough, spitting, vomiting, protruding the tongue, and relates to persons of the inferior type. Śāradātanaya describes the expressions of intoxication thus: intoxication due to drinking wine is of three kinds: light, medium and excessive. Light intoxication is expressed by the face beaming with joy and spotted with visible little drops of sweat, indistinct words, broken and unconnected speech, devious footsteps, and seeing one and catching another with hands. Medium intoxication is expressed by walking slowly with faltering steps, interrupted footsteps, throwing relaxed arms about, looking at the sky, uninterrupted and continuous raving, lapse of memory at every step, speaking to the sky, trying to be supported by the sky, and other such actions. Excessive intoxication is expressed by loss of memory, loss of consciousness, inability to proceed at every step, grave voice, laboured breathing, and other such actions. Further, light intoxication due to drinking wine is expressed by revolving the pupils of the eyes, seeing with tired corners of the eyes, and brightness of the corners of the eyes. Medium intoxication is expressed by contraction of the eye-lids, restless pupils, and trembling eye-lashes. Excessive intoxication is expressed by disorder in winks of the eyes, sunken pupils, and looking downwards. Some intoxicated persons sleep; others sing; others laugh; others weep; others speak harsh words very often. The best persons sleep; the mediocre persons dance

[38] Mado madhupānotthā mattatā vivekaśūnyā. ANC., p. 585. Mado vivekaharollāsaḥ. LR., p. 585. STS., p. 50.

and sing; the worst persons weep and laugh. Intoxication due to learning, nobility of birth, and wealth is expressed by not replying to one's queries, insulting words, showing disrespect even to friends, and other such actions. Intoxication due to embracing a beautiful wife is expressed by joy, vanity, disrespect to others, redness of the eyes, using perfumery, decorating the body, and the like. Dhanañjaya mentions faltering limbs, faltering speech, faltering gait, laughter, crying, and sleep as expressions of exhilaration due to intoxication. Rāmacandra and Guṇacandra mention horripilation, sweet redness of the face, uttering slightly confused sounds, graceful gait, tottering, and whirling also as the expressions of intoxication. Viśvanātha asserts, that in intoxication the cultured persons lie down; that the mediocre persons laugh and sing; and that the inferior persons talk rudely and weep. Hemacandra and Śiṅga Bhūpāla mention expressions of light, moderate and excessive intoxication, which are mentioned by the Rhetoricists whose views are given above.[39]

7. *Fatigue* (*śrama*)

Bharatamuni mentions a long journey on foot, physical exercise, etc., as the determinant causes of fatigue. Śāradātanaya mentions physical exercise, travelling, dancing, sex-gratification, etc., as the causes of fatigue. Śrama is so called because it exhausts and hurts the limbs. Hemacandra defines fatigue as the depression of the body as well as the mind due to physical exercise, travelling, etc.[40] Dhanañjaya defines fatigue as lassitude (kheda) due to long journey, sex-gratification, etc. Viśvanātha gives the same definition of fatigue. Śiṅga Bhūpāla defines fatigue as mental depression (manaskheda) due to long journey, dancing, sex-enjoyment, etc. Rāmacandra and Guṇacandra define fatigue as weariness (sāda) or exhaustion (śoṣa) of the limbs due to physical exercise, sexual intercourse, etc. Sarveśvarācārya defines fatigue as mental depression (kheda) due to the exhaustion of all limbs.[41] Jīva Goswāmī defines fatigue as the feeling of distress (kleśa) or pain. Rūpa Goswāmī mentions long

[39] NTS., pp. 359-60; BPK., pp. 16-18; NDP., p. 178; DR., p. 150; SDP., p. 187; RS., pp. 104-05; KS., AC., p. 131.

[40] Manaḥ-śarīra-khedaḥ śramaḥ. KS., AC., p. 136. NTS., p. 360; BPK., p. 18.

[41] Khedaḥ sarvāṅga-viśrāntaḥ śramaḥ. STS., p. 50.

travelling, dancing, sexual union, etc., as the causes of fatigue. Jagannātha defines fatigue as a kind of depression (khedaviśeṣa) which is produced by excessive physical exertion such as long travelling, physical exercise, etc. He distinguishes fatigue from languor (glāni). Languor arises from the loss of strength (balahāni), whereas fatigue arises from the activity of the body even when there is strength of it.[42]

Fatigue is expressed by cramp, gentle rubbing of the body, deep breathing, walking slowly, yawning, belching, contraction of the mouth and the eyes, etc. Bharatamuni mentions these expressions of fatigue. Śāradātanaya mentions shampooing the legs and indistinct sounds also as the expressions of fatigue. Dhanañjaya mentions perspiration also as its expression. Rāmacandra and Guṇacandra mention shampooing the limbs and panting also as the expressions of fatigue. Viśvanātha mentions sleep, and Jagannātha mentions stretching the limbs as the expressions of fatigue. The expressions mentioned by Hemacandra and Śiṅga Bhūpāla are included in the lists of Bharatamuni and Śāradātanaya.[43]

In western psychology Woodworth is inclined to think that fatigue is an emotion. He says: "Fatigue from muscular activity is an organic state consisting largely in the accumulation in the muscles and in the blood of the waste products of muscular action, especially carbon dioxide and lactic acid. These substances, carried about by the blood, lower the activity of the organs through which they circulate. There may be local fatigue sensations in the exercised muscles and joints, and also a general diffuse weariness. There is clearly a set towards certain overt behaviour, namely, towards rest. The organic state is preparatory for rest, in the sense that it predisposes the organism for rest and unfits it for activity."[44]

8. *Indolence (ālasya)*

Bharatamuni mentions lassitude, nature, sickness, pregnancy, satiety, etc., as the determinant causes of indolence, and observes,

[42] DR., p. 143; RS., p. 104; SDP., p. 186; NDP., pp. 178-79; UNM., pp. 583-86; LR., p. 583; RG., p. 103.

[43] NTS., p. 360; BPK., p. 18; DR., p. 143; NDP., pp. 178-79; SDP., p. 186; RG., p. 103; KS., AC., p. 136; RS., 104.

[44] *Psychology*, 1930, p. 300.

that it relates to women and men of the inferior type. Śāradātanaya defines indolence as want of vigour of the limbs of the body.[45] Hemacandra defines indolence as indifference to objects of desire due to physical exertion, satiety, sickness, pregnancy, nature, etc.[46] Dhanañjaya and Viśvanātha define indolence as aversion for movement due to fatigue, pregnancy, etc.[47] Vidyānātha defines indolence as the loss of the power of exertion in performing duties. Acyutarāya defines indolence as mental lethargy or aversion for work. Śiṅga Bhūpāla defines indolence as inclination to work with a great difficulty arising from nature, fatigue, contentment, pregnancy, dependence, etc.[48] Rāmacandra and Guṇcandra define indolence as aversion for work (karmānutsāha) due to fatigue, contentment, nature, sickness, pregnancy, etc. Śārṅgadeva mentions excessive contentment, natural tendency, pregnancy, disease, fatigue, etc., as the causes of indolence. Sarveśvarācārya defines indolence as lethargy which generates depression of all limbs of the body due to prosperity, exertion, pregnancy, etc. Rūpa Goswāmī defines indolence as disinclination to work due to satiety, fatigue, etc., in spite of the presence of physical strength.[49] Viśvanātha Cakravartī defines indolence as the absence of desire to perform an action which ought to be done in spite of the presence of the power to do so. If indolence refers to an object of attachment, it leads to the destruction of attachment.[50] Jagannātha defines indolence as disinclination of the mind to work due to excessive contentment, pregnancy, sickness, fatigue, etc.[51]

Jagannātha distinguishes indolence from languor and inactivity. In languor there is the absence of strength, whereas in indolence there is no lack of strength, though in both there is the absence of work. Thus indolence (ālasya) is different from languor (glāni). In indolence the power of discrimination between what is duty and what is not, is present. But in inactivity (jaḍatā) the power of discrimination is not present. Further, there is no

[45] Aṅgānām anullāsaḥ ālasyam. BPK., p. 31. NTS., p. 361.
[46] Puruṣārtheṣvanādara ālasyam. KS., AC., p. 134.
[47] Ālasyaṁ śrama-garbhādyair jāḍyam. SDP., p. 196. DR., p. 154.
[48] Kṛcchrāt kriyānunmukhatvam. RS., p. 120.
[49] Sāmarthyasyāpi sadbhāve kriyānunmukhatā. BRS., p. 483.
[50] PR., p. 246; SSār., p. 132; NDP., p. 185; SR., ii, p. 845; BRS., p. 483; ANC., p. 607; STS., p. 52.
[51] Atitṛpti-garbha-vyādhi-śramādi-janyā cetasaḥ kriyānunmukhatā ālasyam. RG., p. 114.

stupor (moha) in indolence, but inactivity is either preceded or succeeded by stupor. Thus indolence is different from inactivity.[52]

Bharatamuni mentions aversion for all works, sitting, lying down, drowsiness, sleep, etc., as the expressions of indolence. Hemacandra mentions the same expressions of indolence. Śāradātanaya mentions giddiness of the head, yawning, rubbing the eyes, and inactivity of the body and the mind also as the expressions of indolence. Śiṅga Bhūpāla mentions also stretching out the limbs and fondness for clinging to bed or seat as the expressions of indolence.[53]

The *Bhagavad Gītā* regards indolence as the effect of tamas or inertia of mind. Śrīdharasvāmī defines it as lack of energy. Ānandagiri defines it as obstruction of energy owing to lack of initiative. Madhusūdana defines it as incapacity for an effort of volition and action. It counteracts the act of volition which is the effect of rajas. Rāmānuja defines it as lack of energy in actions or want of exertion.[54]

9. *Misery* (*dainya*)

Bharatamuni mentions distress, mental anguish, etc., as the determinant causes of misery. Dhanañjaya and Viśvanātha define misery as loss of mental vigour owing to poverty, misfortune and the like.[55] Dhanika defines misery as powerlessness or depression of the mind due to poverty, vomiting, etc. Hemacandra defines misery as loss of mental vigour or spiritlessness (anaujasya) due to distress, mental anguish and the like.[56] Vidyānātha defines misery as the opposite of haughtiness (anauddhatya), or wretchedness owing to the loss of energy arising from indigence. Acyutarāya defines misery as a mental mode which is produced by sorrow and the like. Śiṅga Bhūpāla defines misery as mindlessness (naiścittya) due to distress, mental agony, etc.

[52] Atra nāsāmarthyam. Nāpi kāryakāryavivekaśūnyatvam. Tena kāryākaraṇarūpasyānubhāvasya tulyatve'pi glāner jaḍatāyāścāsya bhedaḥ. RG., p. 114.

[53] NTS., p. 361; KS., AC., p. 134; BPK., p. 18; RS., p. 120; SDP., p. 196; DR., p. 154; NDP., p. 185.

[54] BG., xiv, 8; SrBG., ĀBG., MBG., RBG., xiv, 8.

[55] Daugartyādyair anaujasyaṁ dainyam. SDP., p. 185; DR., p. 145; DRA., p. 145.

[56] Daurgatya-manastāpādibhyo' naujasyaṁ dainyam. KS., AC., p. 136.

Śāradātanaya mentions eagerness, anxiety, mental agony, poverty, etc., as the causes of misery. Rāmacandra and Guṇacandra define misery as impotence or powerlessness of the mind (manaḥklaivya), which is produced by distress, poverty, vomiting, etc. Śārṅgadeva mentions anxiety, eagerness, mental anguish, distress, etc., as the causes of misery. Sarveśvarācārya defines misery as the loss of power in all limbs (anaujasya) due to misfortune and the like. Jagannātha defines misery as a mental mode produced by sorrow, poverty, offence, etc.[57] It is said to consist in the loss of mental vigour (anaujasya) due to uneasiness, mental anguish, poverty and the like.[58] Rūpa Goswāmī defines misery as the loss of mental vigour or spiritlessness due to sorrow, terror, offence, etc.[59] Jīva Goswāmī explains spiritlessness as thinking oneself to be much inferior to others.[60] Viśvanātha Cakravartī also defines misery as the feeling of inferiority due to sorrow, terror, and one's own or another's misconduct.[61]

Bharatamuni mentions the loss of self-command, giddiness of the head, heaviness of the body, absent-mindedness, giving up the cleansing of the body, etc., as the expressions of misery. Hemacandra mentions also covering the head as an expression of it. Śāradātanaya mentions trembling of the head, uncleanness of the dress, and splitting of the head also as the expressions of misery. Dhanañjaya and Dhanika mention black and dirty appearance and dress also as an expression of it. Śiṅga Bhūpāla mentions inactivity of the limbs also as an expression. Sarveśvarācārya mentions aversion for work also as an expression. Jagannātha regards speaking of one's own inferiority also as an expression. Rūpa Goswāmī descrbies begging, impotence of intelligence, dirtiness, anxiety, and inactivity of the body as the consequents of misery. The expressions mentioned by Rāmacandra and Guṇacandra and Viśvanātha are included in those mentioned above.[62]

[57] PR., p. 246; SSār., p. 132; RS., p. 101; BPK., p. 18; NDP., p. 183; SR., ii, p. 843; STS., p. 51.

[58] Duḥkha-dāridryāparādhādijanitaḥ cittavṛttiviśeṣo dainyam. RG., p. 100.

[59] Duḥkha-trāsāparādhādyair anaurjityantu dīnatā. BRS., p. 446.

[60] Anaurjityam ātmani atinikṛṣṭatāmananam. BRS., DSM., p. 446.

[61] UNM., pp. 578-79; ANC., p. 578.

[62] NTS., p. 361; KS., AC., p. 136; BPK., p. 18; DR., DRA., p. 145; RS., p. 101; STS., p. 51; RG., p. 100; BRS., p. 446; NDP., p. 183; SDP., p. 185.

10. *Anxiety* (*cintā*)

Bharatamuni regards the loss of wealth, theft of cherished possessions, poverty and the like as the determinant causes of anxiety. Śāradātanaya also mentions these as the causes of anxiety, and describes it as brooding with regard to objects of desire, or in the nature of conjecture as to the present or future condition of oneself or of dear ones, which is different from recollection.[63] Dhanañjaya defines anxiety as brooding due to the non-attainment of objects of desire.[64] Hemacandra defines anxiety as pondering due to poverty, theft of cherished possessions, loss of wealth, etc., which is different from recollection and conjecture. Śiṅga Bhūpāla defines anxiety as in the nature of brooding (dhyāna) due to the non-attainment of desired objects, loss of wealth, etc. Viśvanātha defines anxiety as brooding due to the non-attainment of good.[65] Rāmacandra and Guṇacandra define anxiety as mental agony (mānasī pīḍā) due to the non-attainment of good and the attainment of evil. Jagannātha defines anxiety as brooding due to the non-attainment of good and befalling of a calamity[66] Śārṅgadeva observes, that conjecture (vitarka) is either coexistent with anxiety, or precedes it, or succeeds it. Sarveśvarācārya defines anxiety as continuous brooding (dhyānaikatānatā) due to the loss of good and the apprehension of an impending evil. Rūpa Goswāmī defines anxiety as brooding due to the attainment of good or evil. Viśvanātha Cakravartī defines anxiety as brooding for the attainment of good or the avoidance of an impending evil.[67]

Bharatamuni mentions sighing, deep breathing, mental agony, meditation, reflecting with downcast eyes, emaciation of the body, etc., as the expressions of anxiety. Śāradātanaya mentions also vacantness of the mind, sobbing, and looking at the sky as the expressions of anxiety. Śiṅga Bhūpāla mentions also hanging down of the head; Hemacandra mentions also distress; Viśvanātha mentions also uneasiness, desolateness or feeling of

[63] Vitarkātmā bhavec cintā smṛter anyā pratīyate. BPK., p. 18; Ibid, p. 28; NTS., p. 361.

[64] Dhyānaṁ cintehitānāpteḥ. DR., p. 146.

[65] Dhyānaṁ cintā hitānāpteḥ. SDP., p. 210; KS., AC., p. 138; RS., p. 128.

[66] Iṣṭāprāptyaniṣṭaprāptyādijanitā dhyānāparaparyāyā cintā. RG., p. 101. NDP., p. 179.

[67] SR., ii, p. 844; STS., p. 50; BRS., p. 498; ANC., p. 621.

emptiness of the mind, and vacant look; Rāmacandra and Guṇacandra mention also fixed gaze and inactivity of the sense-organs; Jagannātha mentions also paleness, writing on the ground, discontentment, recollection and uncleanness of the body as the expressions and consequents of anxiety. Sarveśvarācārya mentions distress of the mind (cittavaiklavya) and mental anguish as the consequents of anxiety.[68]

11. *Stupor* (*moha*)

Bharatamuni mentions accidental injury, adversity, severe blow, sickness, fear, agitation, recollection of past enmity, etc., as the determinant causes of stupor. Śāradātanaya defines stupor as vacantness of the mind (cittasya sūnyatvam), in which it becomes blank, empty of contents, or unconscious, and which arises from brooding on past enmity, exhilaration, due to intoxication, accidental injury, envy, fear, severe blow, agitation, and obstacle to remedy these. In stupor the mind swoons into unconsciousness. Hemacandra defines stupor as stupefaction of the mind due to beating, hostility, fear, calamity, recollection of past enmity, threatening, etc. Moha is also the condition of the mind prior to stupor or unconsciousness. Dhanañjaya defines stupor as unconsciousness (vicittatā) due to the contemplation of objects of fear, sorrow, agitation, etc. Viśvanātha defines stupor as unconsciousness due to fear, sorrow, excitement, brooding on misfortune, etc.[69] Vidyānātha defines stupor as fainting (mūrchana) due to fear, sorrow, and anxious brooding. In stupor the mind becomes unconscious of the real nature of objects according to Acyutarāya. Vāmana defines stupor as unconsciousness (vicittatā) in which cognitions are not produced.[70] Sarveśvarācārya defines stupor as unconsciousness (vicittatā) due to fear, pain, possession by a spirit, brooding on past enmity, etc. Rūpa Goswāmī defines stupor as unconsciousness (hṛnmūḍhatā) of the mind due to excessive joy, separation from beloved persons, fear, dejection, etc. Jīva Goswāmī defines stupor as lapse of

[68] NTS., p. 361; BPK., pp. 18-19; RS., p. 128; KS., AC., p. 138; DR., p. 146; SDP., p. 210; NDP., p. 179; RG., p. 101; STS., p. 50.

[69] Moho vicittatā bhīti-duḥkhāvegānucintanaiḥ. SDP., p. 190. NTS., p. 362; BPK., p. 19; KS., AC., p. 137; DR., p. 153.

[70] Vicittatā cittena jñānājananam. BB., KPK., p. 113. PR., p. 248; SSār., p. 133.

consciousness.[71] Śiṅga Bhūpāla defines stupor as stupefaction of the mind (cittasya mūḍhatā) due to danger, fear, death of dear persons, etc. Śārṅgadeva mentions oppression by spirits, bodily suffering, loss of cherished objects, blow at a vital part of the body, fear due to the sight of a terrible being, a thief, or the like, and brooding on past enmity which cannot be avenged as the determinant causes of perplexity. Śārṅgadeva does not regard moha as lapse of consciousness. He defines it as a mental mode which is in the nature of non-ascertainment of duty. For example, when a person perceives the cause of fear but cannot find out its remedy, he is at a loss to know what he ought to do. Such mental perplexity is called moha.[72] Jagannātha also defines moha as a mental mode which consists in the non-ascertainment of the real nature of things due to fear, separation from beloved persons, and the like. Others regard moha as a kind of brooding called blankness of the mind in which many conflicting states simultaneously perplex the mind.[73] Rāmacandra and Guṇacandra define moha as unconsciousness (acaitanya). But they do not regard it as complete lapse of consciousness, but as the absence of knowledge whether one should perform an action or refrain from it. Moha is not complete unconsciousness but a faint degree of consciousness devoid of the power of discrimination. It arises from a severe blow to a vital part of the body, intense pain, attack of a thief, a serpent, a tiger, or the like, persecution of the king, revolution in a country, natural calamity, e.g. an outbreak of fire, flood, perception of an enemy, etc.[74]

12. *Recollection* (*smṛti*)

Bharatamuni defines recollection as the recall of emotions produced by pleasure and pain.[75] Śāradātanaya defines recollection as the reproduction of the objects which gave pleasure or pain in the past, at a particular time, in a particular place, and which have been forgotten for a long time.[76] He also defines it as a

[71] Moho hṛnmūḍhatā harṣād viśleṣād bhayataḥ viṣādādeḥ. BRS., p. 477. UNM., pp. 602-04. Moho līnacittatā. LR., p. 602. STS., p. 50.

[72] Kāryāniścayinī cittavṛttir mohaḥ. SR., ii, p. 854; RS., p. 117.

[73] Vastutattvānavadhāriṇī cittavṛttir mohaḥ. RG., p. 98.

[74] NDP., p. 181.

[75] Smṛtir nāma sukha-duḥkha-kṛtānāṁ bhāvānām anusmaraṇam. NTS., p. 362.

[76] Sukha-duḥkhānuṣaṅgiṇām ciravismṛtavastūnāṁ smaraṇaṁ smṛtiḥ. BPK., p. 19. Ibid, p. 31.

particular kind of cognition of an object which was perceived in the past. It is the recall, reproduction, or reinstatement of objects perceived on a previous occasion. It is a representative cognition due to the revival of a subconscious impression.[77] Śiṅga Bhūpāla defines recollection as the apprehension of the objects perceived in the past.[78] Dhanañjaya and Viśvanātha define recollection as the cognition of an object as perceived in the past.[79] Jagannātha defines recollection as a cognition which is produced by a subconscious impression.[80] It is not produced by the stimulation of the sense-organs by external objects. But it is produced by the subconscious impression of a past perception. Śārṅgadeva defines recollection as recalling the objects which yielded pleasure or pain on a previous occasion, and have been forgotten for a long time.[81] His definition resembles that of Śāradātanaya.

Bharatamuni mentions health of the organism (svāsthya), the perception of similar objects (samānadarśana), reflection (cintā), habit or repetition (abhyāsa), an example, a bad night, disturbed sleep, etc., as the determinant causes of recollection. Rāmacandra and Guṇacandra mention also a subconscious impression (saṁskāra), attention (praṇidhāna), and vividness of previous perception (darśanapāṭava) as the causes of recollection. They mention repetition of similar experience as a cause of recollection. Jagannātha mentions a kind of reflection (cintāviśeṣa), which revives a subconscious impression, as the determinant cause of recollection. Hemacandra mentions the visual, tactual, and auditory perception of similar objects, repetition and concentration of the mind (praṇidhāna) as the causes of recollection. Śiṅga Bhūpāla mentions health of the organism (svāsthya), reflection (cintā), firm repetition (dṛḍhābhyāsa) of similar experiences, perception of similar objects (sadṛśālokana), etc., as the causes of recollection.[82]

The health of the organism is a great aid to memory because it deepens the impression. The perception of an object similar to one perceived in the past revives the impression (saṁskāra) of

[77] Smṛtiḥ saṁskārasahitā sattvasthā buddhiḥ BPK., p. 29.
[78] Smṛtiḥ pūrvānubhūtārthapratītiḥ. RS., p. 126.
[79] Smṛtiḥ purvānubhūtārtha-viṣaya-jñānam. SDP., p. 201. DR., p. 149.
[80] Saṁskārajanyaṁ jñānaṁ smṛtiḥ. RG., p. 95.
[81] SR., ii, p. 845.
[82] NTS., p. 362; NDP., p. 180; RG., p. 96; KS., AC., p. 129; RS., p. 126. SDP., p. 201; UNM., pp. 618-19; LR., p. 618; SR., ii, pp. 844-45; BRS., p. 495. IPC., Ch. xx.

it and recalls it to the mind. Repetition of similar experience is an indispensable condition of organic memory or rote memory. Reflection is a condition of active memory because it is necessary to control the forces of association. The law of similarity operates in recollection.

Recollection is expressed by shaking the head, raising the eye-brows, turning the face upward, looking at the sky, gazing, lowering the eye-brows, etc.[83]

13. *Contentment* (*dhṛti*)

Bharatamuni mentions heroism, learning, knowledge of the scriptures, purity of conduct, devotion to the superiors, acquisition of wealth sufficient for the fulfilment of desires, enjoying sports, etc., as the determinant causes of contentment. Śāradātanaya mentions these causes of contentment, and adds the attainment of the objects of desire also as its cause. Hemacandra mentions austerites; Dhanañjaya mentions the attainment of power; Rāmacandra and Guṇacandra mention devotion to gods, and special powers; Rūpa Goswāmī mentions the absence of sorrow and the attainment of the best person as an object of love; Śārṅgadeva mentions discrimination, devotion to the preceptor, attainment of an object in excess of one's desire, and play; Siṅga Bhūpāla mentions the fulfilment of desires for many objects, modesty, knowledge (jñāna), and wisdom (vijñāna) also as the causes of contentment. Rāmacandra and Guṇacandra explain knowledge as discrimination between reality and unreality or intensive and extensive knowledge of the scriptures. They observe, that contentment contributes to development of the body (dehapuṣṭi). It is significant to note that contentment of the mind exerts a congenial influence upon the body. Śārṅgadeva includes play among the causes of contentment, because it is an instrument of self-fulfilment.[84]

Siṅga Bhūpāla defines contentment as desirelessness (naiḥspṛhya) of the mind. Viśvanātha defines contentment as the fulfilment of desires due to the acquisition of knowledge, the attainment

[83] NTS., pp. 362-63; KS., AC., p. 129; NDP., p. 180; SR., ii, p. 844.

[84] NTS., p. 363; BPK., pp. 19-20; KS., AC., p. 129; DR., p. 143; NTD, p. 180; UNM., pp. 626-28; SR., ii, p. 844.

of a desired object, and the like.[85] Vidyānātha defines contentment as the feeling of fulfilledness or self-satisfaction (naiḥspṛhya). In this state of fullness (purṇatā) there is perfect mental equipoise. Vāmana quotes a definition of contentment as the complete fulfilment of desires (spṛhāparyāptatā) due to the attainment of their objects, and the consequent cessation of desires (icchānivṛtti).[86] Śāradātanaya defines contentment as a condition of the mind in which joy and grief are felt as equal. Joy does not thrill the mind; nor does grief depress it. It is a state of perfect equipoise due to intellectual clarity of vision. Joy and grief affect the mind only when it suffers from intellectual confusion. Jagannātha defines contentment as a mental mode, which removes the distress of the mind due to greed, grief, fear, and the like, and which is produced by right knowledge, learning of the scriptures, etc.[87] Rūpa Goswāmī defines contentment as the feeling of self-fulfilledness due to true knowledge, the absence of pain, and the attainment of the supreme end of life.[88] Jīva Goswāmī defines contentment as the feeling of fullness which consists in steadiness, stability, or tranquillity of the mind.[89] Viśvanātha Cakravartī regards contentment as a cause of stability (sthairya) of the mind. Jīva Goswāmī explains Rūpa Goswāmī's definition thus: contentment is the tranquillity of the mind due to the direct apprehension of God, the absence of pain because of being related to God, and the attainment of love for God (prema), which is the supreme end of life.[90] Sarveśvarācārya defines dhṛti as the experience of great enjoyment due to knowledge, power, contentment, and the like. There is the attainment of great joy which is desired in this state.[91]

Bharatamuni mentions unperturbed enjoyment of the objects attained and not repenting for those objects which are lost, stolen, destroyed, or not yet attained. Śāradātanaya mentions being unaffected by good or evil, performance of duties appropriate to the occasion, and not repenting for things past, lost, or unattained.

[85] Jñānābhiṣṭāgamādyaistu sampūrṇaspṛhatā dhṛtiḥ. SDP., p. 206. RS., p. 128.

[86] PR., p. 249; Kṛṣṇānandī on SKM., Bombay, 1897, p. 39; BB., p. 114.

[87] Lobha-śoka-bhayādi-janitopaplavanivāraṇa-kāraṇībhūtaś cittavṛttiviśeṣo dhṛtiḥ. RG., p. 99; BPK., p. 29.

[88] Dhṛtiḥ syāt pūrṇatā jñāna-duḥkhābhāvottamāptibhiḥ. BRS., p. 503.

[89] Dhṛtiḥ pūrṇatā manaso' cāñcalyam. LR., p. 626. ANC., p. 626.

[90] DSM., p. 503.

[91] STS., pp. 50-51.

Hemacandra and Dhanañjaya mention unperturbed enjoyment of things (avyagrabhoga) as the expression of contentment. Viśvanātha mentions excessive joy, smile, flash of insight, words expressing contentment, etc., as the expressions of contentment.[92]

14. *Shame (vrīḍā)*

Bharatamuni defines shame as an emotion which arises from the performance of an action which ought not to be done.[93] It is produced by the transgression of the commands of superiors, or disregarding them, non-fulfilment of vows, repentance and the like. A person who has committed an improper or immoral action and repents for it, feels shame. If his commission of a sin is perceived by other virtuous persons, then also he feels shame. Dhanañjaya and Viśvanātha define shame as the opposite of insolence (dhārṣṭyābhāva) due to one's misconduct. Vāmana explains the negation of insolence as contraction of the mind. Some define it as enfolding of the mind (cetonimīlana). Śiṅga Bhūpāla defines shame as the opposite of great arrogance (atidhṛṣṭatā) which arises from committing an immoral action, non-performance of remedy for one's misconduct, company of a stranger, praise, censure, etc. Here shame includes shyness. Vidyānātha defines vrīḍā as contraction of the mind due to love, excessive praise, and the like. He takes vrīḍā in the sense of modesty. Śāradātanaya defines shame as contraction of the mind (cetaḥsaṁkoca) due to one's misconduct. Śārṅgadeva defines shame as repentance (anutāpa) after committing an action which is condemned by the virtuous. It is produced by disregarding the commands of the preceptor, or transgressing them, breaking one's promise, repentance after making gifts, etc. Sarveśvarācārya takes vrīḍā in the sense of shame or moral disapprobation of an immoral action (e.g. adultery), and shyness which is a cause of a young lady's excellence. Rāmacandra and Guṇcandra define vrīḍā as the opposite of immodesty, or shyness, which arises from repentance for one's misconduct. Their definition resembles those of Dhanañjaya and Viśvanātha. Hemacandra defines shame as contraction of the mind (cetaḥsaṁkoca) due to one's immoral

[92] NTS., p. 363; BPK., p. 20; KS., AC., p. 129; DR., p. 143; SDP., p. 206.

[93] Vrīḍā nāma akārya-karaṇātmikā. NTS., p. 363. Ibid, pp. 363-64.

actions. Jagannātha defines shame as a mental mode which is produced in men by committing immoral actions, and in women by looking at the faces of men. Rūpa Goswāmī defines vrīḍā as shyness due to the company of strangers, and praise, and shame due to dispraise and one's misconduct, and characterizes the emotion as the opposite of immodesty (adhṛṣṭatā).[94]

Bharatamuni mentions covering the face, pondering with the downcast face, scribbling on the ground, biting the nails, rolling the cloth round the fingers, etc., as the expressions of shame. Śāradātanaya mentions also hanging down the head, scratching with the nails, indistinct voice, slinking away at a distance, not going out anywhere, and restlessness everywhere. Śiṅga Bhūpāla and Śārṅgadeva mention talking secretly; Dhanañjaya, Rāmacandra and Guṇacandra mention hiding the limbs; Śārṅgadhara mentions also touching the cloth or the finger-ring; Dhanañjaya and Jagannātha mention also change of colour; and Hemacandra mentions also touching the ears as the expressions of shame.[95]

Darwin says, "Under a keen sense of shame there is a strong desire for concealment. We turn away the whole body, more especially the face, which we endeavour in some manner to hide. An ashamed person invariably casts down his eyes or looks askant. In most cases the face, ears, and neck are the sole parts which redden. Blushes commence more commonly on the cheeks, afterwards spreading to the ears and neck. Persons who feel shame for moral delinquency, are apt to avert, bend down, or hide their faces."[96]

15. *Inconstancy* (*capalatā*)

Bharatamuni regards love, hatred, envy, impatience, malice, hostility, etc., as the determinant causes of inconstancy. Śāradātanaya also regards love, hatred, envy, jealousy, hostility, etc., as the causes of unsteadiness. He defines unsteadiness as longing for objects which ought not to be desired, or which are evil in their nature. In this state the mind wanders to improper objects

[94] DR., p. 152; SDP., p. 204; BB., p. 114; RS., p. 123; PR., p. 249; BPK., p. 19; SR., ii, p. 845; STS., p. 52; NDP., p. 183; KS., AC., p. 130; RG., p. 97; BRS., p. 487; UNM., pp. 611-13.

[95] NTS., pp. 363-64; BPK., p. 19; RS., p. 123; SR., ii, p. 845; DR., p. 152; NDP., p. 183; RG., p. 98; KS., AC., p. 130.

[96] EEMA., pp. 339-40, 329, 348.

to which it should not pay attention.[97] Dhanañjaya, Viśvanātha and Vidyānātha define inconstancy as instability of the mind due to love, hatred, jealousy and the like. Vāmana accepts this definition, and explains instability as indiscretion or unthinking action (avimṛṣyakāritā).[98] Śiṅga Bhūpāla defines inconstancy as lightness of the mind (cittalāghava) due to love, hatred and the like. Rāmacandra and Guṇacandra define inconstancy as rashness (sāhasa) or indiscretion (avimṛṣyakāritā) due to love, hatred, mental perplexity, etc. Hemacandra defines inconstancy as instability of the mind (ceto'navasthāna) due to love, hatred, envy, malice, etc. It is indiscretion or unthinking action. Sarveśvarācārya defines inconstancy as instability of the mind due to ficklemindness like that of a monkey (markaṭa-cittatā). Jagannātha defines inconstancy as a mental mode which is produced by intolerance, hostility, envy, love, hatred, jealousy, and the like. Śārṅgadeva mentions love, hatred, envy, jealousy, revenge, and hostility as the determinant causes of inconstancy or instability of the mind. Rūpa Goswāmī defines inconstancy as fickleness of the mind (cittalāghava) due to love, hatred and the like. Jīva Goswāmīi also defines inconstancy as fickleness of the mind. Viśvanātha Cakravartī explains it as the absence of gravity.[99]

Bharatamuni mentions harsh words, rebuke, beating, killing, oppression, and the like; Śāradātanaya mentions unthinking action, threatening, punishment, harshness, and insult also; Śiṅga Bhūpāla mentions embracing, supporting, turning out one without any consideration, and commanding also; Dhanañjaya and Viśvanātha mention wanton actions at one's pleasure; Rāmacandra and Guṇacandra mention unrestrained actions; Śārṅgadeva mentions indiscreet actions as the expressions of inconstancy.[100]

16. *Joy* (*harṣa*)

Bharatamuni mentions the fulfilment of desires, union with beloved persons, contentment of the mind, the favour of gods, the

[97] Ayogye cāpadārthe ca duḥspṛhā cāpalaṁ bhavet.
Palāyate cāpadārthe manas taccāpalaṁ bhavet.
BPK., p. 31. Ibid, p. 20; NTS., p. 364.

[98] Mātsarya-dveṣa-rāgādeś cāpalyaṁ tvanavasthitiḥ.
DR., p. 160; SDP., p. 207. PR., p. 250; BB., p. 114.

[99] Cāpalaṁ cittalāghavam. LR., p. 639. RS., p. 135; NDP., p. 179; KS., AC., p. 134; STS., p. 53, RG., p. 116; SR., ii; BRS., p. 513; ANC., p. 639; UNM., pp. 639-41.

[100] NTS., p. 364; BPK., p. 20; RS., p. 135; DR., p. 160; SDP., p. 207; NDP., p. 179; SR., ii.

king and the spiritual guide, receiving good food, clothing and money, and enjoying them as the determinant causes of joy. Śāradātanaya defines joy as cheerfulness of the mind, which is evoked by approaching an object of desire, attainment of a desired object, enjoyment of beautiful objects, gratification of friends, and attainment of inconceivable objects of desire. The elation of the mind thrills the sense-oragns with joy, and imparts joy to others.[101] Hemacandra defines joy as cheerfulness of the mind (cetaḥprasāda) due to the causes mentioned by Bharatamuni. He mentions the joy of a friend also as a cause of one's joy. Dhanañjaya defines joy as attachment (prasakti) due to festive occasions and the like. Dhanika defines it as cheerfulness of the mind (cetaḥprasāda) due to the birth of a son, the advent of the beloved person and the like. Viśvanātha defines joy as cheerfulness of the mind due to the attainment of a cherished object.[102] Rāmacandra and Guṇacandra define joy as attachment (prasakti) or blooming of the mind (cetovikāsa) due to the attainment of good, the avoidance of evil, and other like causes. It also arises from sharing in the enjoyments and festivities of the son and the like. Acyutarāya defines joy as a particular kind of pleasure (sukhaviśeṣa) due to the fulfilment of desires. Jagannātha also defines joy as a particular kind of pleasure (sukhaviśeṣa) due to the attainment of an object of desire. It is excess of elation of the mind due to the acquisition of a rare, splendid treasure and the like.[103] Śiṅga Bhūpāla defines joy as cheerfulness of the mind (manaḥprasāda) due to the attainment of the fit objects of desire, union with friends, favour of the spiritual guide, the king and gods. Śārṅgadeva also gives the same definition of joy. Sarveśvarācārya defines joy as excess of delight (pramoda) due to the attainment of desired objects, festivities and the like. Its expressions pervade all limbs of the organism. Rūpa Goswāmī and Jīva Goswāmī define joy as cheerfulness of the mind (cetaḥprasannatā) due to the attainment of cherished objects at the proper time.[104]

Bharatamuni mentions beaming of the face, brightness of the

[101] Harṣo manaḥprasādaḥ. BPK., p. 20. Ibid, p. 30. NTS., p. 364.

[102] Harṣa iṣṭāvāpteḥ manaḥprasādaḥ. SDP., p. 204. KS., AC., p. 134; DR., DRA., p. 145.

[103] Iṣṭaprāptyādijanmā sukhaviśeṣo harṣah. RG., p. 95; NDP., p. 182; SSār., p. 134.

[104] RS., p. 130; SR., ii. p. 846; STS., p. 54; BRS., p. 505; UNM., pp. 629-30; LR., p. 629.

eyes, speaking sweet words, embracing, shedding tears, horripilation, perspiration, etc., as the organic expressions of joy. Śāradātanaya mentions also patting with caressing, renunciation, and making gifts as expressions of joy. Dhanañjaya and Viśvanātha mention choked voice also as an expression of joy. Śiṅga Bhūpāla mentions also pressing the palms as an expression of joy. Hemacandra reiterates Bharatamuni's list of expressions of joy. Sarveśvarācārya observes, that joy affects all organs of the body.[105]

Darwin says, "Joy quickens the circulation, and this stimulates the brain, which again reacts on the whole body. Under a transport of joy there is a strong tendency to various purposeless movements, and to the utterance of various sounds. We see this in our young children, in their loud laughter, clapping of hands, and jumping for joy. . . . When peals of laughter are uttered, with rapid and violent spasmodic expirations, tears stream down the face. From the excitement of pleasure, the circulation becomes more rapid; the eyes are bright, and the colour of the face rises. A man in this state holds his body erect, his head upright, and his eyes open. There is no drooping of the features, and no contraction of the eye-brows. On the contrary, the frontal muscle tends to contract slightly; and this smooths the brow, removes every trace of a frown, arches the eye-brows a little, and raises the eye-lids. The whole expression of a man in good spirits is exactly the opposite of that of one suffering from sorrow. In joy the face expands, in grief it lengthens."[106] McDougall says, "Expressions of pleasant feeling are the various bodily consequences which flow from the augmentation of energy brought by the feeling: the bright eye, the glowing face, the expanded chest, the straightened back, the quick elastic step and the loud hearty cheerful voice."[107]

17. *Agitation (āvega)*

Agitation (āvega) is so called because it is the flurry of the mind due to the occurrence of an event in an improper place and at an improper time, which is unexpected, and which agitates the mind. This is the view of Śāradātanaya. He regards the

[105] NTS., p. 365; BPK., p. 20; DR., p. 145; SDP., p. 204; RS., p. 130. KS., AC., p. 134; STS., p. 54.

[106] EEMA., pp. 74, 75, 167, 219.

[107] *The Energies of Men*, p. 142.

hearing of good or evil, being overtaken by a calamity, a sudden disaster, like a storm, a heavy downpour, an outbreak of fire, running amuck of an elephant, shooting of meteors, being struck by a lightning, the eclipse of the sun or the moon, the sight of a comet, earth-quake, etc., as the determinant causes of agitation. Bharatamuni mentions a natural calamity, like a storm, a heavy downpour, an outbreak of fire, running amuck of an elephant, hearing of good or evil, a disaster, an attack, etc., as the determinant causes of agitation. Hemacandra mentions these causes of agitation, and defines it as flurry or haste (sambhrama). Viśvanātha defines agitation as haste due to excitement.[108] Vidyānātha defines agitation as hurry of the mind (cittasambhrama) due to the advent of good or evil. Vāmana quotes a definition of agitation as hurry of the mind due to excess of evil. Śiṅga Bhūpāla defines agitation as flurry of the mind due to a natural calamity (e.g. a volcanic eruption, the appearance of a comet, etc.), a storm, a downpour, an outbreak of fire, the sight of an infuriated elephant, hearing of good or evil, and danger from an enemy. Rāmacandra and Guṇacandra define agitation as flurry (sambhrama) or excitement (saṁkṣobha) due to the sudden and unexpected advent of good or evil. It arises from good such as sight or hearing of the sudden appearance of a god, the advent of the spiritual guide, the superiors, or the beloved person, unexpected prosperity, etc. It arises from evils such as physical calamities like an outbreak of fire, earthquake, a storm, a heavy downpour, the sight of an infuriated elephant, a serpent, a thief, etc. Jagannātha defines agitation as a mental mode called flurry (sambhrama) which is brought about by excess of evil.[109] Sarveśvarācārya defines agitation as flurry (sambhrama) which suddenly arises in the mind from the advent of good or evil. Rūpa Goswāmī defines agitation as hurry of the mind due to the sight or hearing of the advent of good or evil. Viśvanātha Cakravartī defines agitation as flurry of the mind devoid of the power of ascertaining duty.[110]

Bharatamuni mentions looseness of all limbs, distraction of

[108] Āvegaḥ sambhramaḥ. SDP., p. 184. BPK., pp. 20, 31; NTS., p. 366; KS., AC., p. 140.

[109] Anarthātiśayajanitā cittasya sambhramākhyā vṛttir āvegaḥ. RG., p. 113; PR., p. 251; BB., p. 114; RS., p. 111; NDP., p. 179; STS., p. 51.

[110] Āvegaś cittasambhramaḥ itikartavyatāmūḍhaḥ. ANC., p. 594. BRS., p. 463; UNM., pp. 595-99.

the mind, change of colour of the face, surprise and the like as the expressions of agitation. Agitation due to hearing a good news is expressed by getting up, embracing, giving away clothes and ornaments, shedding tears, horripilation and the like. Agitation due to hearing of an unpleasant news is expressed by falling on the ground, rolling about on a rough surface, running away, lamenting, crying and the like. Agitation is expressed by superior and mediocre persons by firmness, and by inferior persons by running away. Śiṅga Bhūpāla mentions drooping of all limbs, turning one's face, running away, pallor of the face, wonder, dejection, etc., as expressions of agitation. Rāmcandra and Guṇacandra regard joy, wonder, etc., as the mental consequences of agitation due to the advent of good. They regard praising, flattering, speaking words expressing hope, etc., as its verbal expressions. Apprehension, dejection, fear, etc., are the mental consequences of agitation due to the advent of evil. Lamentation, crying, incoherent talk, etc., are its verbal expressions. Drooping of all limbs, pallor of the face, contraction of the body, running away, irritation of the eyes, withdrawing hastily, looking back, falling on the ground, trembling, perspiration, immobility, etc., are its bodily expressions. These organic expressions are accompanied by firmness in the superior persons, and by restlessness in the inferior persons. Bharatamuni mentions turning aside, rubbing the eyes, covering the body with cloth, walking quickly, etc., as the expressions of agitation due to a storm; contraction of the whole body, running away, searching for a safe refuge, etc., as the expressions of agitation due to a heavy downpour; irritation of the eyes by smoke, contraction of the body, shaking the body, escaping, avoiding, etc., as the expressions of agitation due to an outbreak of fire; running away quickly, walking quickly, immobility, trembling, looking back, etc., as the bodily expressions, and fear and surprise as the mental consequences of agitation due to running amuck of an infuriated elephant; suddenly running away, taking up the armour and weapons, getting upon a chariot, riding a horse or an elephant, etc., as the expressions of agitation due to a sudden attack of an enemy. Hemacandra mentions surprise as a mental consequence of agitation, and covering the face, searching for a secure shelter, the eyes being blinded by smoke, running away quickly, lamentation, horripilation, taking up arms, etc., as the bodily expressions of agitation. Śāradātanaya mentions fear, surprise, dejection and repentance as the mental consequents of agitation due to the sudden advent of an evil. Sarveśvarācārya mentions joy as a mental consequent of agitation due to the advent of good, and sorrow as a mental consequent of agitation due to the advent of evil.[111]

Woodworth says, "We can think of excitement as a state which occurs in actually running a race or playing a game or taking an examination, or in being ready for such an activity and also in fear and anger. Anger is excitement with the addition of its own peculiar quality; and fear of the energetic sort is excitement plus its own peculiar quality. These peculiar qualities have to do with overt activity for which the organism is set; for attack in anger, for escape in fear."[112]

18. *Perplexity* (*jaḍatā*).

Bharatamuni defines perplexity as non-ascertainment of one's duty in a complex situation.[113] It is the condition of the mind when a person is at a loss to know what he should do. It is the loss of the power of comprehension of one's duty. It involves confusion of the intellect and impotence of the will. In this condition a person cannot ascertain what is good and what is evil, what is pleasure and what is pain, owing to delusion, and silently submits to the will of another person. Thus there is no susceptibility to feelings and emotions also in this condition. Dhanañjaya and Viśvanātha define perplexity as inability to ascertain one's duty on seeing or hearing of good or evil.[114] Śāradātanaya defines perplexity as non-comprehension of one's duty at all times, in all actions, which arises from seeing or hearing of good or evil, and mental agony. In this state there is no discrimination between good and evil, pleasure and pain. Śiṅga Bhūpāla defines perplexity as non-comprehension of one's duty (apratipatti) on hearing of good or evil, separation from beloved persons, etc. Śārṅgadeva defines mental perplexity as inability

[111] NTS., p. 365; RS., p. 111; NDP., p. 179; KS., AC., p. 140; BPK., pp. 20-21; STS., p. 51.

[112] *Psychology*, 1930, p. 298.

[113] Jaḍatā nāma sarva-kāryāpratipattiḥ. NTS., p. 366.

[114] Apratipattir jaḍatā syādiṣṭāniṣṭadarśana-śrutibhiḥ. DR., p. 144; SDP., p. 188.

to ascertain one's duty under particular circumstances. In this state a person sees things with his eyes, and hears things with his ears, and perceives a situation, but cannot decide on the course of action he ought to adopt. It is produced by the sight or hearing of good or evil, and disease. It either precedes or succeeds fainting (moha).[115] Rāmacandra and Guṇacandra define mental perplexity as inability to ascertain one's duty (kāryājñāna) because of the perception of good or evil, sickness, etc. In this condition a person perceives the circumstances, but cannot determine his duty owing to dullness of his mind; his mind is irresolute as to the course of action to be adopted by him. Rūpa Goswāmī defines perplexity as non-ascertainment of one's duty (apratipatti) due to the perception of good or evil, separation from the beloved person and the like, which precedes or succeeds fainting (moha). Jīva Goswāmī and Viśvanātha Cakravartī define perplexity as the loss of the power of determining one's duty.[116] Jagannātha defines perplexity as a mode of the mind in which it cannot ascertain its duty, which is produced by anxiety, eager expectation, fear, separation, and the sight or hearing of good or evil. It arises before or after stupefaction.[117]

Jagannātha distinguishes between perplexity (jaḍatā) and stupor (moha). In the former visual perception, auditory perception, tactual perception, etc., are produced by the proper sense-organs, but there is no comprehension of one's duty, whereas in the latter these perceptions are not produced at all.[118] Rāmacandra and Guṇacandra also distinguish between perplexity and stupor. In the former there is the full blaze of distinct consciousness, though there is no power of determining one's duty under circumstances which are definitely known, whereas in the latter there is no consciousness at all.

Rāmacandra and Guṇacandra distinguish between perplexity and epilepsy (apasmāra). In both there is loss of the power of determining one's duty. But in the former there is distinct consciousness of objects, whereas in the latter there is confusion

[115] Kāryāviveko jaḍatā paśyataḥ śṛṇvato'pi vā. SR., ii, p. 847.

[116] Jāḍyam apratipattiḥ. LR., ANC., p. 608; UNM., pp. 608-10. BRS., p. 484; NDP., pp. 184-85.

[117] Cintotkaṇṭhā - bhaya - viraheṣṭāniṣṭa - darśanaśravaṇādi - janyāvaśya-kartavyārtha-pratisandhāna-vikalā cittavṛttir jaḍatā. RG., p. 113.

[118] Ibid, p. 114.

(vaikalya) of the mind with unconsciousness or a faint degree of consciousness.[119]

Vāmana distinguishes between perplexity and indolence. In the former there is the desire to work, but there is no capacity to work owing to perplexity of mind, whereas in indolence (ālasya) there is aversion to work.[120]

Perplexity is inability to act due to anxiety, suspense, fear and the like. Sarveśvarācārya defines perplexity as inability to act due to the non-comprehension of one's duty.[121] It arises from the sight of the beloved person, and the like. Hemacandra defines perplexity as non-comprehension of the meaning of a situation, which brings about inactivity.[122] It is due to the sight or hearing of an extremely agreeable or disagreeable object, separation from a beloved person, fear, anxiety, suspense and the like. These intense emotions unhinge the mind, suspend the power of moral judgment, and incapacitate the will to act.[122a]

Śārṅgadeva defines jaḍatā as mental perplexity or non-comprehension of one's duty, and regards non-discrimination between good and evil as its mental consequent. Bharatamuni regards being guided by others as a mental consequent of perplexity. Śāradātanaya regards lack of discrimination between pleasure and pain, non-discrimination between good and evil, and being controlled by others as the mental consequents of perplexity. Śiṅga Bhūpāla, Rāmacandra and Guṇacandra also regard dependence on others (pāravaśya) as a mental consequent of perplexity. When a person is in the state of mental perplexity and cannot decide on a definite course of action, he is easily guided by others. His will becomes susceptible to the suggestions of others in whom he has faith, and his uncritical acceptance of their suggestoins removes the state of indecision and arrest of the will. Mental perplexity is the cause of indecision which blocks the will.[123]

Bharatamuni mentions not talking to anybody, not speaking distinctly, silence, gazing with winkless eyes, etc., as the organic expressions of mental perplexity. Śāradātanaya mentions

[119] NDP., p. 185.
[120] Kriyāsvapāṭavaṁ jāḍyam, ālasye tu kriyādveṣaḥ. BB., p. 114.
[121] Pratipatterabhāvena stabdhatā jaḍatā matā. STS., p. 52.
[122] Apratipattir jāḍyam. KS., AC., p. 130.
[122a] Jīvānanda's commentary, SDP., p. 188.
[123] SR., ii, p. 847; NTS., p. 366; BPK., p. 21; NDP., pp. 184-85; RS., p. 121.

lack-lustre eyes; Śiṅga Bhūpāla mentions inability to hear also as organic expressions of mental perplexity. Dhanañjaya, Viśvanātha, Hemacandra, Rāmacandra and Guṇacandra, and Śārṅgadeva also mention these organic expressions.[124]

19. *Pride* (*garva*)

Bharatamuni regards the attainment of superiority in influence, noble birth, personal beauty, youth, learning, power, wealth and the like as the determinant causes of pride. Śāradātanaya defines pride as the sense of one's own superiority to others.[125] Dhanañjaya defines garva as pride (mada) due to one's superiority in birth, beauty, strength, wealth, etc. Hemacandra defines pride as disparagement of others (parāvajñā) due to superiority of learning, strength, birth, influence, age, beauty, wealth and the like. Vidyānātha defines pride as the feeling of one's own superiority or self-conceit which gives rise to the despisement of others. Śiṅga Bhūpāla defines pride as disparagement of others due to superiority in wealth, beauty, age, rank, learning, strength, etc. Rāmacandra and Guṇacandra define pride as the feeling of one's own superiority (ātmanyādhikyadhīḥ) attended with disparagement of others due to superiority in birth, attainments, intelligence, age, power and the like. Viśvanātha defines pride as intoxication due to superiority in influence, beauty, learning, noble birth, etc.[126] Rūpa Goswāmī defines pride as contempt of others (anyahelana), which arises from good fortune, beauty, youth, excellent qualities, attainment of desired objects, and the like. Jīva Goswāmī and Viśvanātha Cakravartī give the same definition of pride. Jagannātha defines pride as contempt of others due to the knowledge of one's superiority in beauty, wealth, learning and the like.[127]

Śārveśvarācārya observes, that pride intoxicates all persons. Śārṅgadeva observes, that inferior persons generally feel pride very often owing to superiority in family dignity, beauty, strength,

[124] NTS., p. 366; BPK., p. 21; RS., p. 121; DR., p. 144; SDP., p. 188; NDP., pp. 184-85; KS., AC., p. 130.

[125] Ātmano garīyastvabhāvo garvaḥ. BPK., p. 31; NTS., p. 366.

[126] Garvo madaḥ prabhāva-śrī-vidyā-satkulādijaḥ. SDP., p. 194. DR., p. 148; KS., AC., p. 135; PR., p. 252; RS., p. 106; NDP., p. 184.

[127] Rūpa-dhana-vidyādi-prayuktātmotkarṣa-jñānādhīna-parāvahelanaṁ garvaḥ. RG., p. 104. BRS., p. 455; UNM., pp. 585-88; LR., p. 585; ANC., p. 585.

power, learning, wealth and age. The superior persons feel pride at moments only; pride passes through their minds like flashes of lightning. Women feel pride very often.[128]

Bharatamuni mentions envy, delusion, disregard of others, and disobedience to others as the mental consequents of pride. Śāradātanaya mentions revenge, and Viśvanātha mentions hauteur also as the mental consequents of pride. Bharatamuni mentions not responding to others' queries, not talking to others, looking at one's arms, shoulders and other limbs with conceit, contemptuous laughter, harshness of words, insulting words, and departing from the place, etc., as the expressions of pride. Śāradātanaya mentions looking at the sky, looking down upon even those persons who are under protection, ridicule, reviling without any cause, and distortion of the limbs also as the expressions of pride. Śiṅga Bhūpāla mentions turning one's back even while speaking, flat denial, and not looking at the person who addresses also as the expressions of pride. Hemacandra mentions unnatural gestures with eyes and limbs also as the expressions of pride. Viśvanātha mentions the display of the limbs with vanity also as the expression of pride.[129]

Darwin similarly says, "A proud man exhibits his sense of superiority over others by holding head and body erect. He is haughty, or high, and makes himself appear as large as possible; so that metaphorically he is said to be swollen or puffed up with pride. The arrogant man looks down on others, and with lowered eyelids hardly condescends to see them; or he may show his contempt by slight movements of the nostrils or lips."[130]

20. *Dejection* (*viṣāda*)

Bharatamuni mentions inability to finish the work undertaken, accidental calamity and the like as the determinant causes of dejection. Śāradātanaya mentions persecution of the king, loss of property by theft, hindrances, etc., as the causes of dejection (viṣāda), which is so called because in this emotion the mind is wearied in various ways.[131] Dhanañjaya defines dejection as the

[128] STS., p. 52; SR., ii, p. 849.

[129] NTS., p. 366; BPK., p. 22; SDP., p. 194; RS., p. 107; KS., AC., p. 135.

[130] EEMA., pp. 275-76.

[131] Manaso vividhaḥ sādaḥ viṣādaḥ. BPK., p. 28. Ibid, pp. 21-22; NTS., p. 367.

loss of energy owing to the non-completion of the work undertaken by a person.[132] Vāmana accepts this definition of dejection, and explains the loss of energy as the lack of vigour (utsāhanāśa). Viśvanātha also defines dejection as the loss of energy (sattvasaṁkṣaya) due to the absence of the means for the attainment of ends.[133] Sarveśvarācārya also reiterates the definition of Dhanañjaya. Hemacandra also defines dejection as menttal agony due to the failure of the work begun because of the absence or loss of means for its completion.[134] Vidyānātha defines dejection as the depression of spirit (cetaso bhaṅgaḥ) arising from the thought of the loss of means, unsuccessful attempt, the sense of guilt, hindrance, calamity, etc. Śiṅga Bhūpāla defines dejection as repentance (anutāpa) owing to the non-completion of the work undertaken, the non-attainment of the objects of desire, danger and knowledge of one's guilt. Rūpa Goswāmī defines dejection as repentance due to the non-attainment of desired objects, frustration of a work commenced, befalling of a calamity, and misconduct.[135] Jīva Goswāmī and Viśvanātha Cakravartī also define dejection as repentance. Jagannātha defines dejection as repentance which is evoked by offending the king or the spiritual guide, and frustration of desires.[136] Rāmacandra and Guṇacandra define dejection as drooping of spirits (tānti) accompanied by the loss of energy owing to the non-attainment of good, which is the unobstructed accomplishment of a work commenced, or the attainment of its reverse. Śārṅgadeva mentions the non-completion of a work undertaken even in the presence of means, befalling of a great calamity, offending the king, committing theft, etc., as the determinant causes of dejection.[137]

Bharatamuni mentions the following organic expressions of dejection. It is expressed in the superior and mediocre persons by searching for a helper, devising means, loss of vigour, distraction of the mind, sighing, etc., and in the inferior persons by

[132] Prārabdha-kāryāsiddheḥ viṣādaḥ sattvasaṁkṣayaḥ. DR., p. 159.

[133] Upāyābhāvajanmā tu viṣādaḥ sattvasaṁkṣayaḥ. SDP., 206; STS., p. 53; BB., p. 114.

[134] Upāyābhāva-nāśābhyāṁ prārabdhasya kāryasya bhaṅgān manaḥpīḍā viṣādaḥ. KS., AC., p. 131.

[135] Iṣṭānavāpti-prārabdhakāryāsiddhi-vipattitaḥ aparādhād api anutāpo viṣaṇṇatā. BRS., p. 443. PR., p. 253; RS., p. 100; LR., ANC., p. 574; UNM., pp. 574-77.

[136] Iṣṭāsiddhi-rājagurvādyaparādhādi-janyo' nutāpo viṣādaḥ. RG., p. 112.

[137] NDP., p. 182; SR., ii, p. 846.

running away, licking the corners of the mouth, looking down, dryness of the mouth, sighing, pondering, sleep, etc. Śāradātanaya mentions searching for a helper, thinking of the means, etc., as the expressions of dejection in the superior persons; absent-mindedness, loss of energy in the presence of obstacles, and lying down as the expressions of dejection in the mediocre persons; and brooding, sighing, fainting, etc., as the expressions of dejection in the inferior persons. Śiṅga Bhūpāla mentions mental confusion (vaicittya) as a consequent of dejection in the persons of the middling type; change of colour, and crying also as expressions of dejection in the inferior persons. Rāmacandra and Guṇacandra mention thinking of the means of escape from the cause, searching for a helper, depression of spirit, etc., as the expressions of dejection in the superior and mediocre persons. Śārṅgadeva reiterates Bharatamuni's list of expressions of dejection, and observes, that the expressions in these persons are endowed with energy. Sarveśvarācārya mentions laboured breathing, sighing, and searching for a helper as the organic expressions of dejection, and mental anguish as its psychical consequent. Viśvanātha mentions the same expressions of dejection. Hemacandra borrows the list of expressions of dejection from Bharatamuni.[138]

Darwin similarly says, "As soon as the sufferer is fully conscious that nothing can be done, despair takes the place of frantic grief. The sufferer sits motionless, or gently rocks to and fro; the circulation becomes languid; respiration is almost forgotten, and deep sighs are drawn. All this reacts on the brain and prostration soon follows with collapsed muscles and dulled eyes." "It is remarkable how small a depression of the corners of the mouth gives to the countenance an expression of low spirits or dejection, so that an extremely slight contraction of these muscles would be sufficient to betray this state of mind."[139]

21. *Impatience* (*autsukya*)

Bharatamuni mentions separation from the beloved persons, recollection of them, sight of a garden, etc., as the determinant

[138] NTS., p. 367; BPK., p. 22; RS., p. 100; NDP., p. 182; SR., ii, p. 846; STS., p. 53; SDP., p. 206; KS., AC., p. 131.
[139] EEMA., pp. 80, 200.

causes of impatience. Dhanañjaya defines impatience as intolerance of the passage of time owing to desire for a beautiful object of enjoyment, love and flurry. Śāradātanaya defines impatience as intolerance of the passing of time (kālātipātāsahatva) due to separation from dear ones and recollection of them. Hemacandra defines impatience as intolerance of delay owing to the perception of an object of desire or its recollection.[140] Śiṅga Bhūpāla defines impatience as intolerance of the passage of time (kālākṣamatva) owing to separation from an object of desire or love, the perception of a desired object, the desire to see a beautiful object or the like. Rāmacandra and Guṇacandra define eagerness as looking forward to the object of desire or love (iṣṭābhimukhya) which arises from its recollection, the desire to see a beautiful object, love, greed, etc. Śārṅgadeva regards separation from the beloved person and reminiscences of him or her as the determinant causes of impatience. Rūpa Goswāmī defines impatience as intolerance of the passage of time, which arises from the longing for the sight of an object of desire or love, or for its attainment.[141] Jīva Goswāmī defines eagerness as impatience of the passage of time owing to a longing for an object.[142] Sarveśvarācārya defines eagerness as impatience of the passage of time owing to love, regard, longing for union with a beloved person, and desire for the attainment of a cherished object.[143] Viśvanātha defines eagerness as intolerance of the lapse of time owing to the non-attainment of the object of desire or love. It is impatience of delay in attaining the object of desire or love.[144] Jagannātha defines eagerness as the intense desire: 'Let this object of desire or love be mine at once'. It is evoked by separation from the beloved person, and increased by the reminiscences of him or her.[145]

Bharatamuni mentions deep sighs, brooding with downcast eyes, drowsiness, sleep, desire to sleep, heaviness of the body, etc., as the expressions of impatience. Hemacandra mentions hurry, casting eyes in all directions, emaciation of the body also as the

[140] Iṣṭānusmaraṇa-darśanāder vilambāsahatvam autsukyam. KS., AC., p. 133; NTS., p. 367; DR., p. 159; BPK., pp. 21, 29; BB., p. 114.

[141] Kālākṣamatvam autsukyam iṣṭekṣāptispṛhādibhiḥ. BRS., p. 506. UNM., pp. 631-32; RS., p. 132; NDP., p. 184; SR., ii, p. 847.

[142] Autsukyaṁ spṛhayā kālayāpanākṣamatvam. LR., p. 631.

[143] Kālākṣamatvam autsukyam. Hṛdyavastu-suhṛd-yoga-ratyāsthādestadudbhavaḥ. STS., p. 53.

[144] Iṣṭānavāpter autsukyaṁ kālakṣepāsahiṣṇutā. SDP., p. 198.

[145] Adhunaivāsya lābho mamāstvitīcchā autsukyam. RG., p. 112.

expressions of eagerness. Śāradātanaya mentions quick breathing; Dhanañjaya mentions perspiration; Śiṅga Bhūpāla mentions lying in bed, rising from bed and deep breathing; Rāmacandra and Guṇacandra mention restlessness of the body, speech and vision, and incoherent talk also as expressions of impatience.

Hemacandra mentions feeling of emptiness of the mind; Viśvanātha mentions mental agony; Śāradātanaya mentions anxiety; Dhanañjaya mentions delusion; Śiṅga Bhūpāla mentions restlessness; Jagannātha mentions flurry; Rāmacandra and Guṇacandra mention restlessness of the mind and anguish; and Sarveśvarācarya mentions terror, mental anguish and delusion as the mental consequents of impatience.[146]

22. *Fierceness* (*ugratā*)

Bharatamuni mentions theft, robbery, offence to the king, abuse and the like as the determinant causes of fierceness. Śāradātanaya mentions injury to one's son, friend, wife and the like as the cause of fierceness, and defines it as a mental mode which results in punishing others without sufficient provocation. Dhanañjaya defines fierceness as cruelty (caṇḍatva) which arises from offence, harsh words, and cruelty of a wicked person. Cruelty is intolerance of the causes of fierceness with pride. Hemacandra defines fierceness as wrathfulness (caṇḍatva) which arises from theft, malevolence, abusive language and the like. Viśvanātha defines fierceness as wrathfulness (caṇḍatva) which arises from the prowess and offence of the enemy. Acyutarāya defines fierceness as the desire to destroy the enemy (dhvaṁsecchā) due to his abuse or insult. Śiṅga Bhūpāla defines fierceness as wrathfulness which arises from the enemy's offence, insult, abusive language and the like. Śārṅgadeva regards fierceness as of the nature of mercilessness (nirdayātmaka). Rāmacandra and Guṇacandra define fierceness as pitilessness (nairghṛṇya) which arises from misconduct of the wicked, the ferocious, the mendacious, the fraudulent, in the form of abusive language, theft and the like. Sarveśvarācārya defines fierceness as wrathfulness (caṇḍatā) which is evoked by the slandering and abusive language of the wicked. Rūpa Goswāmī defines fierceness as wrathfulness

[146] NTS., p. 367; KS., AC., p. 134; BPK., p. 21; DR., p. 159; RS., p. 132; NDP., p. 184; SDP., p. 198; BB., pp. 114-15; STS., p. 53.

(caṇḍatva) which is excited by misconduct, abusive language and the like. Jīva Goswāmī defines fierceness as wrathfulness (caṇḍatā). Viśvanātha Cakravartī defines wrathfulness as behaviour hostile to sensuous pleasure due to harsh language and other kinds of misconduct. Jagannātha defines fierceness as a mental mode in such a form as 'what shall I do to him?', which arises from another's abuse, insult and the like. It is said: 'Fierceness is of the nature of cruelty which is aroused by oppression of the king, ascription of faults which do not really exist, pursuit of a thief, etc.[147]

Jagannātha distinguishes between fierceness (ugratā) and anger (krodha). Anger is a permanent emotional disposition or sentiment, whereas fierceness is a transitory emotion.[148] Jagannātha distinguishes between revenge (amarṣa) and fierceness. Revenge is harboured in the mind, and does not burst forth in fierceness of outward conduct. Sometimes there is no fierceness in revenge.[149]

Bharatamuni mentions rebuke, taking one captive, persecution, killing, etc., as the expressions of fierceness. Hemacandra repeats these expressions of the emotion. Śāradātanaya mentions very cruel actions such as chastisement, persecution, killing, etc., as the expressions of fierceness. Dhanañjaya and Viśvanātha mention perspiration, shaking of the head, threatening, beating, etc., as the expressions of fierceness. Śiṅga Bhūpāla mentions redness of the face and the eyes also as an expression of the emotion.[150]

23. *Revenge (amarṣa)*

Revenge is excited, Bharatamuni avers, in a person who is abused or insulted by those who are superior in learning, wealth, prowess or strength. Śāradātanaya also gives the same definition, but adds the qualification that the person in whom revenge is

[147] NTS., p. 370; BPK., pp. 23. 29; DR., p. 145; BB., p. 115; KS., AC., p. 135; SDP., p. 189; SSār., p. 136; RS., p. 132; SR., ii, p. 843; NDP., p. 182; STS., p. 52; BRS.. p. 508; UNM., pp. 632-34; LR., p. 633; ANC., p. 633; RG., p. 109.

[148] Nāpi asau krodhaḥ. Tasya· sthāyitvena asyāḥ saṁcāriṇītvenaiva bhedāt. RG., p. 110.

[149] Ibid, p. 110.

[150] NTS., p. 370; KS., AC., p. 135; BPK., p. 23; DR., p. 145; SDP., p. 189; RS., p. 132.

evoked should be abused or insulted in a public place. Hemacandra defines revenge as the desire to retaliate on a person who is superior in learning, wealth or strength, and who abuses or insults one.[151] Dhanañjaya defines revenge as revengefulness (abhiniviṣṭatā) due to reproach, insult, etc. Viśvanātha defines revenge as determination to retaliate on the malefactor, which is excited by reproach, abuse, insult and the like.[152] Dhanañjaya and Viśvanātha both define revenge as abhiniviṣṭatā which is explained as deep-rooted anger.[153] Vidyānātha defines revenge as blazing up of the mind (cetaḥprajvalana) or being enraged at the offender, and identifies revenge with intense anger, rage or wrath. Rāmacandra and Guṇacandra define revenge as desire for retaliation (pratikārecchā) which is evoked by rebuke, insult, etc. Sarveśvarācārya defines revenge as good persons' being engrossed in the faults of others, which arises from reproach, negligence or wrath.[154] Rūpa Goswāmī defines revenge as intolerance of reproach, insult and the like.[155] Jīva Goswāmī defines revenge as intolerance of rebuke or insult by another. Śārṅgadeva defines revenge as the desire for retaliation (pratikārasprhātmaka), which arises from rebuke or contempt of persons who are superior in learning, wealth, strength or power. Jagannātha defines revenge as a mental mode which is excited by another person's contempt due to envy or some other cause.[156]

Jagannātha distinguishes between revenge and anger in the following manner. First, anger is a permanent emotional disposition (sthāyibhāva), whereas revenge is a transitory emotion (vyabhicāribhāva) which promotes, nourishes and strengthens a permanent emotional disposition. Secondly, the objects of anger and revenge are different. Thirdly, their expressions also are different in that in anger there is the desire to crush or destroy the enemy, whereas in revenge there is disinclination to speak, and in that anger is ready to burst out into an outward expression, whereas revenge is concealed within the mind. Rāmacandra

[151] Pratikriyecchā amarṣaḥ. BPK., p. 22. Praticikīṣārupo' marṣaḥ. KS., AC., p. 138. NTS., p. 369.

[152] Nindākṣepāpamānāder amarṣo' bhiniviṣṭatā. SDP., 196. DR., p. 148.

[153] Abhiniviṣṭatā sthiraḥ krodhaḥ. BB., p. 115.

[154] Amarṣaḥ sadbhiḥ doṣeṣvabhiniveśanam. STS., p. 52. PR., p. 256; NDP., p. 180.

[155] Adhikṣepāpamānādeḥ amarṣo' sahiṣṇutā. BRS., p. 509.

[156] Parakṛtāvajñādi-nānāparādhajanyaḥ cittavṛttiviśeṣaḥ amarṣaḥ. RG., p. 108. LR., p. 634; SR., ii, p. 846.

and Guṇacandra distinguish between revenge and anger in the following manner. Revenge is the desire to do harm to a person who has done harm, whereas anger is the desire to do harm to a person, though he has done no harm.[157]

Bharatamuni mentions shaking the head, brooding with downcast eyes, meditation, searching for the means, courage, determination, etc., as the consequents (anubhāva) of revenge. Hemacandra and Śiṅga Bhūpāla repeat these expressions of the emotion. Viśvanātha mentions redness of the eyes, shaking the head, knitting the eye-brows, and threatening as the expressions of revenge. Dhanañjaya mentions threatening and beating; Jagannātha mentions silence and harsh language, Śārṅgadeva mentions aimless brooding and energy of the mind; Rāmacandra and Guṇacandra mention trembling; Sarveśvarācārya mentions revolving the eyes and taking the enemy captive as the expressions of revenge.[158]

24. *Terror (trāsa)*

Terror (*trāsa*) is the excess of fear (bhaya). The former is a transitory emotion (vyabhicāribhāva), while the latter is a permanent emotional disposition (sthāyibhāva). Bharatamuni mentions flashes of lightning, the shooting of meteors, the roar of thunder, earthquake, threatening clouds, howling of ferocious beasts, etc., as the determinant causes of terror. Śāradātanaya mentions landslides, shooting of meteors, being struck by lightning, encountering ferocious animals, demons, etc., as the determinant causes of terror. Dhanañjaya defines terror as agitation of the mind (manaḥkṣobha) excited by the roar of a thunder and the like causes. Vidyānātha defines terror as agitation of the mind (cittakṣobha) owing to sudden fright. Viśvanātha mentions a whirlwind, a flash of lightning, the shooting of meteors, etc., as the determinant causes of terror. Sarveśvarācārya defines terror as the trembling of the mind (manasaḥ kampaḥ), which is evoked by the sight of an elephant, dense clouds, a collision, or the hearing of the roar of a thunder. Rūpa Goswāmī (1500 A.D.) defines terror as agitation of the mind, which is excited by the sight of

[157] RG., p. 108; NDP., p. 180.
[158] NTS., pp. 369-70; KS., AC., p. 138; RS., p. 133; SDP., p. 196; DR., p. 148; RG., p. 108; SR., ii, p. 846; NDP., p. 180; STS., p. 52.

a flash of lightning, or the hearing of the terrible cries of ferocious beasts.[159] Jīva Goswāmī (1600 A.D.) defines terror as the trembling of the mind which is suddenly roused by the sight or hearing of terrible objects, and which causes violent shaking of the body.[160] Viśvanātha Cakravartī also repeats this definition.

Hemacandra defines terror as in the nature of wonder or astonishment of the mind, which is suddenly evoked by the perception of a whirlwind, the roar of a thunder, earthquake, a volcanic eruption, a hailstorm, the shooting of meteors, the flash of lightning, a demon, a huge animal, a terrible cry, etc.[161] Rāmacandra and Guṇacandra define terror as wonder, which suddenly throws the mind into agitation and alarm, and which is evoked by the perception of terrible objects, the roar of a thunder, terrific sounds, fierce beasts, dead bodies, etc.[162] Jagannātha defines terror as the mental mode of an alarmed person, which is excited by the sight of a dreadful beast, the hearing of the roar of a thunder and the like causes.[163] Nāgeśa Bhaṭṭa quotes a definition of terror as the agitation of the mind, which is evoked by the perception of natural calamities, and which causes trembling, etc.[164] Mañjunātha explains the emotion of terror as sudden agitation of the mind, which unhinges and unsettles it.[165] Śiṅga Bhūpāla defines terror as restlessness of the mind (cittacāñcalya), which is evoked by the sight of a flash of lightning, a ghost, or a serpent, or by the hearing of the roar of a lion or any other ferocious beast. Śārṅgadeva defines terror as sudden wonder of the mind, which is roused by a natural calamity, the sight of a dreadful being, or the hearing of a terrible sound, and which violently shakes the body.[166]

Hemacandra distinguishes between terror and fear thus. Terror is sudden wonder and alarm aroused by natural calamities and the like causes, in which the mind is so shocked and startled that it loses its balance and power of discrimination. But in fear

[159] Trāsaḥ kṣobho hṛdi taḍidghorasattvogranisvanaiḥ. BRS., p. 461.
[160] Gātrotkampī manaḥkampaḥ sahasā trāsa ucyate. LR., p. 592. ANC., p. 592.
[161] Cetaścamatkṛtirūpas trāsaḥ. KS., AC., p. 138.
[162] Cakitodvegakāri camatkāraḥ. NDP., p. 183.
[163] Bhīror ghora-sattva-darśana-sphūrjathuśravaṇādi-janmā cittavṛtti-viśeṣaḥ trāsaḥ. RG., p. 105.
[164] Autpātikair manaḥkṣepas trāsaḥ kampādikārakaḥ. GMP., p. 105.
[165] Manaḥkṣepaś cittavṛttiviśeṣaḥ. GMPS., p. 105.
[166] Gātrotkampī camatkāraḥ sahasā trāsa ucyate. SR., ii, p. 851. RS., pp. 109-10.

the mind is not so overpowered, and does not lose its balance altogether, but thinks of before and after.[167] Śārṅgadeva also distinguishes between terror and fear in a similar manner. Terror is suddenly evoked by the perception of dreadful objects, while fear arises from thinking of before and after—reflection on a dreadful situation and its bearing on one's welfare. In terror there is no deliberation, while in fear there is deliberation on cause and effect, a distinct anticipation of danger.[168] Rūpa Goswāmī quotes the same verse, and distinguishes between terror and fear in the same manner. Jīva Goswāmī also holds the same view.

Rāmacandra and Guṇacandra distinguish between terror and fear thus. In terror the mind is startled and thrown into sudden agitation by the perception of dreadful objects, whereas in fear there is the loss of energy owing to the apprehension of evil.[169]

Viśvanātha Cakravartī distinguishes terror (trāsa) from apprehension (śaṅkā) and fear (bhaya) thus. Terror is the sudden flutter of the mind produced by the perception of a flash of lightning or the like. Apprehension is slight fear arising from thinking of before and after or distinct anticipation of evil. Terror is sudden emergence of intense fear at the stage of perception, while apprehension is fear at the stage of imagination and thought. Apprehension becomes fear when it is intensified and heightened.[170]

Bharatamuni mentions the contraction of the body, trembling, violent shaking, motionlessness, horripilation, stammering utterance, etc., as the organic expressions of terror. Hemacandra adds unconsciousness and gazing with winkless eyes to the list given above. Śāradātanaya mentions perspiration and fainting; Śiṅga Bhūpāla mentions frequent winks of the eyes and being supported by objects by one's side; Śārṅgadeva mentions the closing of the eyes and the drooping of the limbs; Sarveśvarācārya mentions falling on the ground also as the organic expressions of terror. Śiṅga

[167] Cetaścamatkārarūpas trāso bhayāt pūrvāparavicāravato bhinna eva. KS., AC., p. 138.

[168] Gātrotkampī camatkāraḥ sahasā trāsa ucyate.
Pūrvāparavicārotthaṁ bhayaṁ trāsāt pṛthag bhavet.
SR., ii, p. 851. BRS., p. 463; LR., p. 592.

[169] Anartha-sambhāvanātaḥ sattva-bhraṁśo bhayam ityanayor bhedaḥ. NDP., p. 183.

[170] Traso' kasmād vidyudādibhir manasaḥ kampaḥ, purvāpara-vicārotthā śaṅkā saivātisāndrā bahūla bhayam iti trāsa-śaṅkā-bhayānāṁ bhedaḥ. ANC., p. 592.

Bhūpāla and Jagannātha mention delusion (vibhrānti) as a mental consequent of terror.[171]

Darwin's account of terror is similar to that of the Sanskrit Rhetoricists given above. He says, "The word 'fear' seems to be derived from what is sudden and dangerous; and that of terror from the trembling of the vocal organs and body. I use the word 'terror' for extreme fear. Fear is often preceded by astonishment, is so far akin to it, that both lead to the senses of sight and hearing being instantly aroused. In both cases the eyes and mouth are widely opened, and the eye-brows raised. The frightened man at first stands like a statue motionless and breathless, or crouches down as if instinctively to escape observation." "The heart beats quickly and violently. The skin instantly becomes pale, as during incipient faintness. The skin is much affected under the sense of great fear as in the marvellous, in which perspiration immediately exudes from it.... The hairs also on the skin stand erect; and the superficial muscles shiver. In connection with the disturbed action of the heart, the breathing is hurried. The salivary glands act imperfectly; the mouth becomes dry, and is often opened and shut. . . . One of the best-marked symptoms is the trembling of all the muscles of the body; and this is often seen in the lips. The voice becomes husky or indistinct, or may altogether fail."[172] "Fear is expressed by trembling, the erection of the hair, cold perspiration, pallor, widely open eyes, the relaxation of most of the muscles, and by the whole body cowering downwards or held motionless."[173]

"As fear increases into an agony of terror, the heart beats wildly, or may fail to act, and faintness ensues; there is a death-like pallor; the breathing is laboured; the wings of the nostrils are widely dilated; the eye-balls are fixed on the object of terror; or they may roll restlessly from side to side; the pupils are enormously dilated. All the muscles of the body may become rigid, or may be thrown into convulsive movements."[174] "Terror causes the body to tremble. The skin becomes pale, sweat breaks out, and the hair bristles. The breathnig is hurried. The heart bears quickly, wildly, and violently. The surface seems bloodless

[171] NTS., p. 373; KS., AC., p. 138; BPK., p. 24; RS., p. 110; SR., ii, p. 851; RG., p. 105; STS., p. 52.
[172] EEMA., pp. 306, 307, 308.
[173] Ibid, p. 384.
[174] Ibid, p. 309.

and the strength of the muscles soon fails. Utter prostration soon follows, and even fainting."[175]

25. *Deliberation* (*vitarka*)

Bharatamuni mentions doubt, conflicting judgments, and conflict of opinions as the determinant causes of deliberation.[176] Śāradātanaya defines deliberation as a particular cognition relating to objects perceived in the past. It is deliberation as to the real nature of an object perceived on the basis of the recollection of objects perceived in the past.[177] It arises from doubt, non-ascertainment of the real nature of objects perceived at a distance, conflicting judgments, and recollection of forgotten objects. Dhanañjaya defines conjecture (vitarka) as deliberation (vicāra) arising from doubt. Viśvanātha defines conjecture as deliberation to come to a decision, which arises from doubt.[178] Hemacandra borrows Bharatamuni's definition, and characterizes vitarka as deliberation as to the real nature of an object. It arises from doubt, desire to know the special features of an object (vimārśa), and apprehension of the absence of one of the two alternatives by contradictory evidence (vipratipatti).[179] Śiṅga Bhūpāla defines vitarka as conjecture (ūha) which arises from doubt (saṁśaya), conflicting judgments (vimarśa-pratyaya), etc. It is in the nature of deliberation to come to a decision whether an object is real or unreal. Rāmacandra and Guṇacandra define conjecture (tarka) as deliberation as to whether one of the alternatives in a doubtful perception is true (ekasambhāvana), which arises from doubt or conflicting judgments. Sarveśvarācārya defines conjecture as deliberation about the real nature of an object of doubtful perception.[180] Rūpa Goswāmī defines conjecture as deliberation which arises from reasoning and doubt.[181] Jīva Goswāmī explains reasoning (vimarśa) as consideration of the mark of inference for

[175] Ibid, p. 76.

[176] Vitarko nāma sandeha-vimarśavipratipattyādibhir utpadyate. NTS., p. 374.

[177] Vitarkaḥ anubhūte' rthe dhīviśeṣaḥ. BPK., p. 31. Ibid, p. 25.

[178] Tarko vicāraḥ sandehāt. SDP., p. 210. DR., p. 157.

[179] Sandeha-vimarśa-vipratipattyādibhyaḥ saṁbhāvanā-pratyayo vitarkaḥ. KS., AC., p. 142. KSV., p. 142.

[180] Vitarkas tu vicāraḥ syād atisandigdhavastuni. STS., p. 51. RS., p. 127; NDP., p. 183-84.

[181] Vimarśāt saṁśayādeśca vitarkastūha ucyate. BRS., p. 496. UNM., LR., ANC., p. 620.

investigating the cause of an event. Jagannātha defines vitarka as conjecture, which arises from doubt, and which is favourable to determinate knowledge.[182]

Jagannātha distinguishes between conjecture and anxiety (cintā). Anxiety is in the nature of suspense, and does not necessarily lead to determinate knowledge (niścaya), though it involves brooding such as 'what will happen?', 'how will it happen?', and so on. But conjecture leads to determinate knowledge.[183]

Bharatamuni mentions various discussions, settling the question, concealment of the counsel, etc., as the expressions of conjecture or deliberation. Hemacandra mentions the shaking of the head, the knitting of the eye-brows, various attempts to know the real nature of an object, accepting one alternative and rejecting the other, etc., as the expressions of conjecture. Sarveśvarācārya mentions turning the head aside; Nāgeśa Bhaṭṭa mentions pulling off; Dhanañjaya, Viśvanātha and Sarveśvarācārya mention the tossing of the head and the fingers also as the expressions of conjecture.[184]

26. *Ascertainment* (*mati*)

Ascertainment (mati) arises, Bharatamuni asserts, from reflection on many scriptures or branches of learning, removal of doubt (ūhāpoha) and the like causes. Śāradātanaya defines ascertainment as in the nature of reflection by which the self comes to ascertain the real and the unreal, right and wrong, which arises from the knowledge of many scriptures.[185] Dhanañjaya defines ascertainment as comprehension of the reality (tattvadhī) due to the removal of erroneous notions, instructions, knowledge of the scriptures, etc. Hemacandra defines ascertainment as the determination of the nature of an object, which arises from the removal of doubt by reflection on the scriptures, etc.[186] Viśvanātha defines

[182] Sandehādyanantaraṁ jāyamāna ūho vitarkaḥ. RG., p. 111. Sa ca niścayānukūlaḥ. GMP., p. 111.

[183] Na cāsau cintā, cintāyāḥ niyamena niścayaṁ prati aprayojakatvāt. GMP., p. 111.

[184] NTS., p. 375; KS., AC., p. 142; STS., p. 51; GMP., p. 111; DR., p. 157; SDP., p. 210.

[185] Sadasanniścayakarī mananātmā matir bhavet. BPK., p. 31. Ibid, p. 22. NTS., p. 371.

[186] Śāstra-cintanohāpohādibhyo' rthaniścayo matiḥ. KS., AC., p. 130. DR., p. 153; PR., p. 258.

ascertainment as the determination of one's duty in accordance with the codes of morality, etc.[187] Śiṅga Bhūpāla defines ascertainment as the determination of the real nature of an object (artha-nirdhāraṇa) after deciphering the meaning of many scriptures. Rūpa Goswāmī defines ascertainment as the determination of the real nature of an object after reflecting on the meanings of the scriptures.[188] Jīva Goswāmī and Viśvanātha Cakravartī define ascertainment as the determination of truth or duty after deliberation.[189] Sarveśvarācārya defines mati as the valid comprehension of an object, or the right determination of one's duty, in accordance with the scriptures and the codes of morality approved by the virtuous.[190] Jagannātha defines mati as ascertainment of truth or duty after deliberation on the meanings of the injunctions of the scriptures.[191]

Śārṅgadeva defines ascertainment as a flash of insight into a new thing (apūrva-pratibhāna) which arises from the discussion of the scriptures, and the application of the method of agreement in presence and agreement in absence (anvaya-vyatireka). A. B. Keith says, "The ascertainment of a question by a process of didactic ratiocination is called Mati."[192] Rāmacandra and Guṇacandra (1200 A.D.) define mati as a flash of insight (pratibhā) or wisdom (prajñā) by means of which one can come to new decisions and interpretations about controversial and doubtful matters. It arises from meditation on the prohibitions and injunctions of the scriptures and calculation of probabilities, and dispels errors, doubts and illusions.[193]

Ascertainment (mati) is expressed by instructing disciples, and dispelling doubt as to the meaning of certain texts which admit of many interpretations. This is Bharatamuni's list of expressions of ascertainment, which is repeated by Hemacandra. Śāradātanaya mentions also contentment of the mind, and behaving like a learned person; Śiṅga Bhūpāla mentions also the knitting of the

[187] Nīti-mārgānusṛtyāder artha-nirdhāraṇaṁ matiḥ. SDP., p. 202.
[188] Sāstrādīnāṁ vicārottham artha-nirdhāraṇaṁ matiḥ. BRS., p. 500.
[189] Matir vicārottham artha-nirdhāraṇam. LR., ANC., p. 624.
[190] Matis tattvagatā buddhir aduṣṭā śiṣṭa-sammatā.
Sāpi niṣpadyate loke śāstrādes tattva-sampadaḥ.
STS., p. 50.
[191] Śāstrādi-vicāra-janyam arthanirdhāraṇaṁ matiḥ. RG., p. 104.
[192] *The Dramatic Sentiments*, Calcutta, 1881, p. 22. SR., ii, p. 848.
[193] Pratibhānaṁ matiḥ. Nava-navollekhaśālinī prajñā pratibhānam. NDP., pp. 179-80.

eye-brows, performance of duty, and cessation of deliberation; Viśvanātha mentions smile, contentment, satisfaction, and sense, of dignity; Nāgeśa Bhaṭṭa mentions the performance of duty without any apprehension and the removal of doubt; and Sarveśvarācārya mentions the removal of error or doubt, the excess of excellence, and definite knowledge of the real and the unreal, right and wrong as the consequents and expressions of ascertainment.[194]

27. *Dissimulation* (*avahittha*)

Bharatamuni defines dissimulation as the concealment of appearance due to shame, fear, defeat, the sense of superiority, hypocrisy, etc.[195] It is the suppression of the manifestations of emotions. In dissimulation, Dhanañjaya observes, organic expressions of emotions are not manifested outward because they are inhibited owing to shyness. Śāradātanaya defines dissimulation as the suppression of the organic signs and expressions of emotions, and ascribes it to fear, shame, the sense of dignity, and hypocrisy.[196] Hemacandra gives the literal meaning of avahittha: it is so called because the mental modes are not manifested in outward expressions in this state. It consists in the inhibition of the knitting of the eye-brows, redness of the face and other organic manifestations of emotions owing to modesty, hyprocrisy, fear, the sense of dignity, etc.[197] Rāmacandra and Guṇcandra define dissimulation as the suppression of the expressions of emotions (vikriyārodha) due to immodesty, fear, shyness, the sense of dignity, insincerity, and the like cause. Immodesty is the common factor in all the determinant causes of dissimulation. A modest person cannot suppress the organic manifestations of emotions even under the influence of the sense of dignity, insincerity, etc. The expressions of emotions which are suppressed in dissimulation are change in the eye-brows, redness of the face etc. Avahittha literally means non-manifestation of emotions or mental modes (cittavṛtti). Śārṅgadeva defines dissimulation as the

[194] NTS., p. 371; KS., AC., p. 130; BPK., p. 22; RS., p. 128; SDP., p. 202; GMP., p. 104; STS., p. 50.

[195] Avahitthaṁ nāma ākārapracchādanātmakam. NTS., p. 370.

[196] Avahittham iṅgitākāra-gūhanam. BPK., p. 31. Ibid, p. 22.

[197] Na bahiḥsthaṁ cittaṁ yena. Bhrūvikāra-mukharāgādīnām ācchādanakāriṇī cittavṛttir avahittham avahitthā vā. Ibid, p. 133.

emotion (bhāva) which seeks to conceal the expressions of an emotion due to fear, shyness, immodesty, hypocrisy, and the sense of dignity. Sarveśvarācārya defines dissimulation as control of the mind or an emotion and its organic manifestations owing to shyness and the like causes at the proper time.[198] Rūpa Goswāmī defines dissimulation as the concealment of the organic expressions of emotions due to a certain emotion.[199] Jīva Goswāmī explains Rūpa Goswāmī's definition thus, Dissimulation consists in the desire to conceal the organic expressions of an emotion which a person desires to conceal under the influence of some other emotion by manifesting some other artificial emotion which he does not actually feel. He quotes a definition of dissimulation as an artificial emotion which seeks to conceal the organic expressions of a genuine emotion.[200] He defines dissimulation as the concealment of the organic expressions.[201] Rūpa Goswāmī ascribes dissimulation to hypocrisy, shyness, over-courteousness, shame, fear, and the sense of dignity.[202] Jagannātha defines dissimulation as a particular emotion which is produced for the concealment of the organic expressions of joy and other emotions owing to shyness and the like.[203] It is due to fear, shyness, insolence, hypocrisy, and the sense of dignity. Śiṅga Bhūpāla defines dissimulation as the concealment of the organic expressions of an emotion (ākāragupti) owing to hypocrisy, the sense of superiority, diplomacy, modesty, fear, benevolence, shamelessness, and defeat or the feeling of inferiority. Viśvanātha defines dissimulation as the inhibition of the organic expressions of joy and other emotions owing to fear, shyness, the sense of dignity and the like.[204]

Dissimulation is expressed, Bharatamuni asserts, by talking of other things, looking downward, break in conversation, feigned patience, etc. Hemacandra repeats Bharatamuni's list of organic expressions of dissimulation. Śāradātanaya mentions vacant smile, sudden break in conversation, false patience,

[198] Kāle manaḥ-saṁvaraṇam avahitthaṁ vidur budhāḥ.
Lajjādi-vikriyā-hetus tatsamutpattikarmaṇaḥ. STS., p. 53.
NDP., p. 184; SR., ii, p. 847.

[199] Avahitthākāraguptir bhaved bhāvena kena cit. BRS., p. 489.

[200] Anubhāva-pidhānārtho' vahitthaṁ bhāva ucyate. DSM.

[201] Avahitthā ākāra-guptiḥ. LR., p. 614.

[202] UNM., pp. 614-18.

[203] Vrīḍādibhir nimittair harṣādyanubhāvānām gopanāya janito bhāvaviśeṣo' vahittham. RG., p. 109. GMP., p. 109.

[204] Bhaya-gaurava-lajjāder harṣādyākāraguptir avahitthā. SDP., p. 197. RS., p. 124.

looking at distant objects, feeling agony within and showing pride without as the mental consequents and organic expressions of dissimulation.[205] Śiṅga Bhūpāla mentions talking of irrelevant things, and looking in other directions also as the expressions. Viśvanātha mentions engaging in other actions, abruptly introducing another subject in the course of conversation, and looking away as the expressions of dissimulation. Sarveśvarācārya mentions turning the face aside, irrelevent talk, and feigned bewilderment as the consequents and expressions of dissimulation.[206]

Darwin says: "The free expression by outward signs of an emotion intensifies it. On the other hand, the repression, as far as this is possible, of all outward signs softens our emotions. He who gives way to violent gestures will increase his rage; he who does not combat the signs of fear will experience fear in a greater degree. . . . These results follow partly from the intimate relation which exists between almost all the emotions and their outward manifestations; and partly from the direct influence of exertion on the heart, and consequently on the brain."[207]

28. *Sickness (vyādhi)*

Bharatamuni takes vyādhi in the sense of a physical disease due to the excess of the flatulence, the bile, or the phlegm of the body, or due to their combination.[208] Śāradātanaya also takes vyādhi in the sense of a physical disease due to change of climate, change of season, and provocation of the bodily humours.[209] Śārṅgadeva also defines vyādhi as a physical disease due to the provocation of one, two, or three humours of the body, flatulent, bilious and phlegmatic, and also to lust (kāma). Viśvanātha also defines sickness as a physical disease, fever or the like, due to the provocation of the bodily humours.[210] Sarveśvarācārya also defines sickness as a physical disease due to the bodily humours or their combination.[211] Śiṅga Bhūpāla defines sickness as fever due to

[205] Antarvyathā-bahir-garva-bhāvanetyavahitthajā. BPK., p. 22.
[206] RS., p. 124; SDP., p. 197; STS., p. 53.
[207] EEMA., pp. 388-89.
[208] Vyādhir nāma vāta-pitta-kaphasannipāta-prabhavaḥ. NTS., p. 371.
[209] Vyādhiḥ deśa-kālādi-doṣa-vaiṣamyasambhavaḥ. BPK., p. 23.
[210] Vyādhir jvarādir vātādyaiḥ. SDP., p. 202. SR., ii. p. 848. Vyādhayaḥ sannipātādyāḥ. STS., p. 51. RS., p. 117.

the provocation of the bodily humours (doṣodreka), separation from the beloved, etc. Thus, he recognizes both the physical and the mental causes of bodily diseases.

Hemacandra defines sickness as mental agony owing to separation from the beloved, yearning for the beloved, and the like. It is called sickness because it is a cause of bodily disease. It is a condition of the mind which generates ailments of the body.[212] Vāmana quotes a definition of vyādhi as mental agony owing to separation from the beloved, which produces a disease in the body.[213] In this definition the mental cause of a physical disease is recognized. Rūpa Goswāmī defines vyādhi as a mental state or emotion (bhāva) which is generated by bodily diseases, fever and the like, which are due to the provocation of the bodily humours, separation from the beloved, and other mental causes.[214] Jīva Goswāmī and Viśvanātha Cakravartī define vyādhi as perversion of the mind, which resembles bodily diseases such as fever and the like.[215] Jagannātha defines vyādhi as mental anguish due to physical diseases, pangs of separation and the like.[216] It is due to mental causes as well as physical causes such as provocation of the bodily humours either severally or collectively.

Rāmacandra and Guṇacandra define vyādhi as suffering of the body and the mind (aṅga-manaḥ-kleśa) owing to the provocation of the bodily humours severally or collectively.[217] They recognize only the organic conditions as the causes of sickness which is both physical suffering and mental agony.

Bharatamuni mentions fever and the like as particular diseases. Fever is of two kinds, e.g. fever attended with heat, and fever attended with cold. The former is expressed by throwing out the hands, feet and other limbs, desire to lie down on the ground, anointing the body with sandal paste, desire for cold, groaning, dryness of the mouth, crying out, etc. The latter is expressed by trembling, violent shaking of the whole body,

[212] Virahābhilāṣādibhyo manastāpo vyādhihetutvād vyādhiḥ. KS., AC., p. 132.
[213] Virahāder manastāpo vyādhir duḥsthāṅgatādikṛt. BB., p. 115.
[214] Doṣodreka-viyogādyair vyādhayo ye jvarādayaḥ.
Iha tatprabhavo bhāvo vyādhir ityabhidhīyate.
BRS., p. 476.
[215] Vyādhir jvarādi-pratirūpo vikāraḥ. LR., ANC., p. 601.
[216] Roga-virahādi-prabhavo manastāpo vyādhiḥ. RG., p. 105.
[217] NDP., p. 180.

shrinking, desire for heat, bristling of the hair, deflection of the chin, turning aside the nose, dryness of the mouth, groaning, etc. The other diseases are expressed by narrowing down the mouth, inactivity of the body, drooping of the eyes, breathing quickly, roaring, crying out, trembling, etc. Hemacandra mentions dryness of the mouth, looseness of the limbs, and throwing out the limbs as the expressions of sickness or mental agony. Śiṅga Bhūpāla mentions immobility of the body, looseness of the limbs, uttering indistinct sounds, dryness of the mouth, drooping of the eyes, throwing out the limbs, breathing quickly, etc., as the expressions of sickness. The expressions mentioned by Viśvanātha and Jagannātha are included in those stated above.[218]

29. *Epilepsy* (*apasmāra*)

Bharatamuni mentions being possessed by a supernatural deity, a yakṣa, a nāga, a rākṣasa, a piśāca, or supernatural evil spirits, a constant recollection of such beings, eating food left after some one's partaking of it, staying in a deserted house, eating food and sleeping at improper times, derangement of the bodily humours and the like as the determinant causes of epilepsy. Śāradātanaya mentions being possessed by supernatural evil spirits, constant brooding on them, going to lonely cremation or burial grounds, violating the rules of seasons, provocation of the bodily humours, impurity, etc., as the causes of epilepsy. He regards epilepsy as perversion of memory or false recollection of objects or complete loss of memory. Apasmāra is so called because it recollects objects perceived in the past as something different from what they were. Śāradātanaya regards apasmāra as lapse of memory, but he ascribes it to natural or supernatural causes. Dhanañjaya defines apasmāra as unconsciousness due to being possessed by supernatural spirits, sorrow and other causes. Viśvanātha defines apasmāra as confusion of the mind due to the influence of the planets and the like causes. P. V. Kane calls apasmāra dementedness.[219] Hemacandra defines apasmāra as a mental mode which is in the nature of being possessed by a

[218] NTS., p. 371; KS., AC., p. 132; RS., p. 117; SDP., p. 202; RG., p. 105.

[219] Manaḥkṣepastvapasmāro grahādyāveśanādijaḥ. SDP., p. 193. NTS., p. 368; BPK., pp. 23, 31; DR., p. 152. *Mirror of Composition*, p. 101.

supernatural spirit, and ascribes it to the causes mentioned by Bharatamuni.[220] Vidyānātha defines apasmāra as epileptic giddiness due to sorrow, infatuation and the like causes. He recognizes the mental causes of epilepsy. Vidyābhūṣaṇa defines apasmāra as the lapse of consciousness (cittavilupti) due to the provocation of the bodily humours caused by sorrow. He ascribes apasmāra directly to a physiological condition, but indirectly to a mental cause. Śiṅga Bhūpāla defines epilepsy (apasmṛti) as commotion of the mind (cittakṣobha) due to the provocation of the bodily humours, possession by supernatural evil spirits and the like causes. The *Bālabodhinī* defines apasmāra as lapse of memory due to a mental disease or intense sorrow.[221] The literal meaning of apasmāra is lapse of memory, which is confusion of the mind owing to physical diseases, hatred, terror, separation from dear ones, etc. Rāmacandra and Guṇcandra define apasmāra as confusion (vaikalya) of the mind due to being possessed by ghosts, provocation of the bodily humours, going to an impure, uninhabited place, contact with impure objects, etc. Mental confusion consists in the lack of discrimination between right and wrong.[222] Rāmacandra and Guṇacandra recognize only the physiological and supernatural causes of epilepsy, which is due to the provocation of the bodily humuors or to the influence of ghosts and the like causes. They do not recognize the mental causes of epilepsy. But they clearly recognize apasmāra as a mental condition which consists in non-discrimination between what is one's duty and what is not. Sarveśvarācārya defines apasmāra as being possessed by ghosts, demons and other supernatural evil spirits due to the performance of black magic. He recognizes only supernatural causes of apasmāra, and defines it as becoming a medium of supernatural evil spirits. Rūpa Goswāmī defines apasmāra as mental confusion due to the provocation of the bodily humours because of mental suffering.[223] Jīva Goswāmī quotes Rūpa Goswāmī's definition of apasmāra, but adds separation from the beloved as a cause of it. Jagannātha defines apasmāra as a kind of disease due to the intensity of the pangs

[220] Āveśarūpo' pasmāraḥ. KS., AC., p. 139.

[221] Ādheścātyantaduḥkhāder apasmāras tathāvidhaḥ. BB., p. 115, PR., p. 255; SKM., p. 40; RS., p. 116.

[222] Vaikalyaṁ kṛtyākṛtyāvivecakatvaṁ so' pasmāraḥ. NDP., p. 178.

[223] Duḥkhottha-dhātu-vaiṣamyādudbhūtaś citta-viplavaḥ apasmāraḥ. BRS., p. 475. STS., p. 53.

of separation from the beloved persons, and of grief, fear, disgust and other emotions, and due to the influence of supernatural beings.[224] He recognizes the influence of intense emotions as well as that of supernatural agents on apasmāra. He believes in the psychical as well as the supernatural causes of epilepsy.

Apasmāra is expressed by trembling, laboured breathing, violent shaking, running, falling down, perspiration, immobility, foaming in the mouth, licking the lips, rising in an unconscious condition, etc. Bharatamuni gives this list of expressions of epilepsy. Hemacandra mentions also throbbing, falling on the ground, loud cry, and panting also as the expressions of epilepsy. Śāradātanaya mentions terrible eyes, and terrible sound from the throat; Śiṅga Bhūpāla mentions biting the lips, striking the arms, profuse secretion of saliva, and changes in the eyes; Rūpa Goswāmī mentions throwing of the arms, very loud raving, and deep revolving of the pupils also as the expressions of epilepsy. The expressions mentioned by Rāmacandra and Guṇacandra, Nāgeśa Bhaṭṭa, Viśvanātha, and Sarveśvarācārya are included in those mentioned above.[225]

30. *Mental Derangement* (*unmāda*)

Bharatamuni mentions death of beloved persons, loss of wealth, accidental hurt, derangement of the bodily humours, derangement of the mind (cittavikāra), etc., as the determinant causes of insanity. Hemacandra defines insanity as mental derangement due to bereavement, loss of wealth, calamity, provocation of the bodily humours, influence of planets and the like causes.[226] Śāradātanaya defines insanity as derangement of the mind in which it is thrown off its balance. It is produced in the superior persons by the loss of cherished objects or the death of beloved persons; it is produced in mediocre persons by the frustration of desires; it is produced in the inferior persons by the loss of wealth.[227] Visvanātha defines insanity as bewilderment of the

[224] Viyoga-śoka-bhaya-jugupsādīnām atiśayād grahāveśādeś cotpanno vyādhi-viśeṣo' pasmāraḥ. RG., p. 116. LR., p. 601.

[225] NTS., p. 368; KS., AC., p. 139; BPK., p. 23; RS., p. 116; UNM., p. 601. NDP., p. 178; GMP., p. 116; SDP., p. 193; STS., p. 53.

[226] Iṣṭaviyoga-dhananāśābhighāta-vātasannipāta-grahādibhyaś cittaviplava unmādaḥ. KS., AC., p. 137. NTS., p. 372.

[227] Udañcati mano yasmād unmādaś cittaviplavaḥ.- BPK., p. 29. Ibid, p. 24.

mind due to lust, grief, fear and the like.[228] Vidyābhūṣaṇa defines insanity as delusion of the mind (hṛdbhrānti), which is excessive confusion of the mind (citta-saṁkṣobha) due to anxiety, joy, grief, etc. Vidyānātha defines insanity as non-discrimination between the animate and the inanimate creatures, and treating them alike.[229] Dhanañjaya defines insanity as thoughtless and incoherent action (aprekṣākāritā), due to the provocation of the bodily humours, the influence of planets, etc. Śiṅga Bhūpāla defines insanity as derangement of the mind (citta-vibhrānti) owing to bereavement and loss of cherished objects. The *Bālabodhinī* quotes a definition of insanity as mental derangement (cittavibhrama) due to the provocation of the bodily humours, and the influence of the planets and supernatural agents.[230] This definition recognizes the physiological cause and the supernatural cause of insanity. The same work quotes another definition of insanity as bewilderment of the mind due to anxiety, joy, grief, etc.[231] This definition recognizes the influence of emotions on insanity. Vāmana observes, that bewilderment of the mind (cittaviplava) is the same thing as mental derangement (citta-vibhrama). Rāmacandra and Guṇacandra define insanity as derangement of the mind (manovipluti) owing to the provocation of the bodily humours and the influence of supernatural agents. They do not recognize the influence of emotions on insanity.[232]

Sarveśvarācārya defines insanity as doing actions which cannot be forecast by others beforehand because of the absence of valid knowledge, knowing things as different from what they really are, grief and other overmastering emotions which completely upset the mind.[233] Actions of insane persons are actuated by motives, which emerge at the moment, and which are not systematically connected with their other mental states, and cannot, therefore, be forecast by others beforehand. They lose the systematic unity of their minds, and suffer from illusions,

[228] Citta-sammoha unmādaḥ kāma-śoka-bhayādibhiḥ. SDP., p. 199.

[229] STK., p. 40; Kṛṣṇānandī on STK., p. 39; PR., p. 259.

[230] Sannipāta-grahādibhya unmādaś citta-vibhramaḥ. BB., p. 116. DR, p. 158; RS., p. 115.

[231] Utkaṇṭhā-harṣa-śokāder unmādaś citta-viplavaḥ. BB., p. 116.

[232] NDP., pp. 182-83.

[233] Anirūpitakāritvam unmādaḥ jñānābhāvānyatātparya-śokādibhyaḥ jāyate. STS., p. 51.

hallucinations and delusions. Their minds are unhinged and upset by intense grief and other overpowering emotions.

Rūpa Goswāmī defines insanity as mental derangement due to excessive joy, intense pangs of separation from the beloved person, and the like.[234] Jīva Goswāmī repeats Rūpa Goswāmī's definition. Viśvanātha Cakravartī defines insanity as delusion of the mind (cittavibhrama).

In the superior persons, Śārṅgadeva observes, insanity is caused by separation from the beloved person. In the inferior persons it is caused by the loss of wealth. In all persons it is caused by the provocation of all bodily humours in combination. Insanity is a kind of disease (vyādhi), but it has been separately mentioned because it is brought about by separation from the beloved person and adds to its charm. Similarly, epilepsy is a kind of disease, but it is separately mentioned because it adds to the charm of the æsthetic sentiments of horror and terror.[235]

Jagannātha defines insanity as knowing things as different from what they really are because of separation from the beloved person, great calamity, excessive joy and the like causes. Insanity involves illusions, hallucinations and delusions, and is caused by overmastering emotions and passions which upset the mind completely. Normal illusions of silver in a nacre, a serpent in a rope, etc., are not due to intense and overpowering emotions.[236] Jagannātha regards insanity as a disease and includes it in vyādhi. But he separately mentions it in order to point out its separate characteristics as contrasted with other diseases. Nāgeśa Bhaṭṭa makes this observation.

Rāmacandra and Guṇacandra distinguish between epilepsy and insanity in that the former is confusion (vaikalya) of the mind, while the latter is derangement of the mind, and in that the former is an accessory emotion in the sentiments of horror and terror, while the latter is an accessory state in the erotic sentiment of separation (vipralambha) in the superior persons and in the pathetic sentiment in the inferior persons.[237]

[234] Unmādaḥ hṛdbhramaḥ prauḍhānandāpad-virahādijaḥ. BRS., p. 472. UNM., pp. 599-600; L.R., ANC., p. 599.

[235] SR., ii, pp. 848-49.

[236] Vipralambha-mahāpattiparamānandādi-janmā tu anyasmin anyāvabhāsaḥ. RG., p. 110. GMP., p. 110.

[237] NDP., p. 183.

Insanity is expressed by unmotived laughing, weeping, crying, reading, singing, dancing, sitting, standing, lying down, running, raving, smearing the body with dust and ashes, wearing rags, soiled cloth, etc., using earthen pots, etc., as ornaments, imitation of others, and many other senseless acts. This list of expressions is mentioned by Bharatamuni. Hemacandra reiterates his list. Śāradātanaya mentions decorating the body with grass, sitting at the edge of the bed, restlessness, and other incoherent acts also as the expressions of insanity. Rāmacandra and Guṇacandra mention also abusing, and scattering dust and ashes as the expressions of insanity. The expressions mentioned by Dhanañjaya, Viśvanātha, Rūpa Goswāmī and Sarveśvarācārya are included in those stated above.[238]

31. *Dream* (*svapna*)

Bharatamuni mentions interruption of sleep, enjoying objects of the sense organs, infatuation, spreading the bed and dragging the bed on the ground, etc., as the determinant causes of dream. Illusory perceptions of the objects of the senses which are not altogether inoperative during light sleep are dream-illusions. Subjective perceptions of unreal objects during sleep brought about by infatuation when the senses are entirely inactive are dream-hallucinations. Viśvanātha defines dream as the apprehension of objects during sleep, which gives rise to anger, excitement, fear, languor, joy, grief and other emotions.[239] Dreams excite emotions which are their psychical consequents. Acyutarāya defines dream as slightly germinating consciousness.[240] In dream there is not complete lapse of consciousness, but there is an undercurrent of subconsciousness. Rūpa Goswāmī defines dream as the apprehension of many objects caused by sleep.[241] Dream is expressed by deep breathing, languidness of the body, closing the eyes, inactivity of all the sense-organs, dreaming, etc.[242]

[238] NTS., p. 372; KS., AC., p. 137; BPK., p. 24; NDP., p. 183; DR., p. 158; SDP., p. 199; BRS., p. 472; STS., p. 51.

[239] Svapno nidrām upetasya viṣayānubhavas tu yaḥ. Kopāvega-bhaya-glāni-sukha-duḥkhādi-kārakaḥ. SDP., p. 192. NTS., pp. 368-69.

[240] Kiṁcit aṅkuritaṁ cittam. SSār., p. 135.

[241] Suptir nidrā-vibhāvā syān nānārthānubhavātmikā. BRS., p. 518.

[242] NTS., pp. 368-69.

32. *Sleep (nidrā)*

Sleep is caused by weakness, fatigue, exertion, intoxication, indolence, deep thinking, overeating, natural tendency to sleep, keeping awake throughout the night, etc. Bharatamuni mentions these determinant causes of sleep. Dhanañjaya defines sleep as the closing or enfoldment of the mind (manaḥ-sammīlana) due to anxiety, indolence, exhaustion, etc. Hemacandra defines sleep as the involution of the mind (manaḥsammīlana) due to exhaustion, exertion, intoxication, indolence, anxiety, excessive eating, natural tendency to sleep, etc. Śāradātanaya mentions fatigue, languor, weakness, indolence, intoxication, anxiety, overeating, fasting, pain, grief, etc., as the determinant causes of sleep. He gives the etymological meaning of nidrā which is so called because it makes all the sense-organs cease their operations at once. Viśvanātha defines sleep as the lapse of consciousness owing to fatigue, exertion, intoxication, etc.[243] Siṅga Bhūpāla defines sleep as the enfoldment of the mind (mononimīlana) because of intoxication, nature, physical exertion, absence of anxiety, fatigue, etc. It is interesting to note that when the mind becomes free from anxiety, it easily sinks into sound sleep. Rāmacandra and Guṇacandra define sleep as the cessation of the activity of the sense-organs (indriyāvyāpṛti) due to fatigue, indolence, weakness, keeping awake late at night, excessive eating, intoxication, fatigue, exhaustion, anxiety, drowsiness, etc. In sleep the external sense-organs cease to function, but the internal organ of mind continues to function. The inactivity of the sense-organs means cessation of the apprehension of objects by them. Śārṅgadeva defines sleep as the first stage of the withdrawal of the sense-organs from their respective objects.[244] It is produced by over-eating, natural tendency, anxiety, indolence, intoxication, exhaustion, etc. Sarveśvarācārya defines sleep as the involution of the mind due to excruciating pain, intense grief, mental confusion, mental agony, etc.[245] Rūpa Goswāmī defines sleep as the enfolding of the mind owing to anxiety, indolence, natural

[243] Cetaḥsammīlanaṁ nidrā śrama-klama-madādijam. SDP., p. 197. NTS., p. 367; DR., p. 151; KS., AC., p. 132; BPK., pp. 22, 29.

[244] Nidrā indriyāṇām prathamā nivṛttiḥ svasvagocarā. SR., ii, p. 851. RS., p. 136; NDP., p. 181.

[245] Sammīlanaṁ hi cittasya nidreti parigīyate. Duḥkhātireka-vaiklavya-manaḥ-khedādibhir bhavet. STS., p. 53.

tendency, physical exertion, etc.[246] Viśvanātha Cakravartī defines sleep as the involution or closing of the mind.[247] Jagannātha also defines sleep as the enfoldment of the mind due to fatigue and the like causes.[248]

The *Bālabodhinī* quotes a definition of sleep as the cessation of the functions of the external sense-organs and the mind owing to fatigue, etc.[249] It distinguishes between dream and dreamless sleep in that in the former the mind functions, while in the latter it ceases to function.

Sleep is expressed by gravity of the face, rolling of the body, revolving the eyes, yawning, dullness, deep breathing, languidness of the body, closing the eyes, inactivity, rubbing the body, etc. Bharatamuni mentions these expressions. Hemacandra repeats Bharatamuni's list of expressions. Rāmacandra and Guṇacandra mention also brightness of the face, stretching out the limbs, and shaking the head; Śārṅgadeva mentions restlessness of the body, sighing, and relaxation of the muscles also; Śāradātanaya mentions also rubbing the eyes; Sarveśvarācārya mentions also acts of comfort as the expressions of sleep.[250]

The *Bhagavad Gītā* regards sleep as an effect of tamas (inertia) of the mind. Śrīdharasvāmī defines sleep as exhaustion of the mind or its involution.[251] He advocates the fatigue theory of sleep. Rāmānuja also advocates this theory, and defines sleep as the cessation of the functions of all sense-organs owing to their fatigue. There are two degrees of sleep, dream and dreamless sleep. Dream is the cessation of the functions of all external sense-organs. Dreamless sleep (suṣupti) is the cessation of the functions of the external senses and the mind as well. Madhusūdana observes that sleep is a mental mode caused by the predominance of tamas, which counteracts the effects of sattva and rajas both, viz., cognition and volition. Rāmakaṇṭha regards sleep as unconsciousness owing to the cessation of the powers of all sense-organs. Nīlakaṇṭha advocates the fatigue theory of sleep.[252]

[246] Cintālasya-nisarga-klamādibhiś citta-mīlanaṁ nidrā. BRS., p. 515.
[247] Nidrā citta-nimīlanam. ANC., p. 642.
[248] Śramādi-prayojyaṁ cetaḥsammīlanaṁ nidrā. RG., p. 104.
[249] Nidrā vyāpāra-vaimukhyam indriyāṇāṁ śramādibhiḥ. BB., p. 115.
[250] NTS., pp. 367-68; KS., AC., p. 132; NDP., p. 181; SR., ii, p. 851; BPK., p. 23; STS., p. 53.
[1] Cittasyāvasādo layaḥ. SrBG., xiv, 8.
[2] BG., RBG., MBG., xiv, 8; RKBG., xiv, 8; xviii, 39; NBG., ii, 60.

33. *Deep Sleep* (*supta*)

Dhanañjaya maintains that deep sleep (supta) arises from sleep (nidrā). Hemacandra defines profound sleep as depth of sleep which arises from sleep.[253] Vidyānātha defines profound sleep as abundance of sleep (nidrā-samudreka). Śāradātanaya distinguishes between sleep and deep sleep in that the former gives rise to the latter. Śiṅga Bhūpāla defines deep sleep as nothing but abundance of sleep.[254] Śārṅgadeva regards supta as in the nature of deep sleep which is produced by sleep, and suggests that the mind is not inoperative in this condition. Rāmacandra and Guṇacandra define deep sleep as excess of sleep (nidrāprakarṣa) in which the action of the mind (manas) still persists in the form of vague attention, though it is slightly obstructed. Supta is not dreamless slumber, but profound sleep which is disturbed by dreams. In this state the external sense-organs cease to function, but the mind does not become inoperative. It is not a state of unconsciousness. Dim consciousness still lingers with the minimum degree of attention. Rāmacandra and Guṇacandra define deep sleep as excess of sleep and yet practically identifies it with sleep. They regard deep sleep as an intermediate condition between dream and dreamless sleep. Jīva Goswāmī and Viśvanātha Cakravartī regard supti as dream.[255] Jagannātha defines supta as cognitions which arise from sleep, and identifies it with dream because dream-cognitions are apprehended during light sleep.[256]

Deep sleep is expressed by closing the eyes, deep breathing, inactivity of the sense-organs, insensibility to touch, absence of actions, etc. Śāradātanaya gives this list of expressions. Rāmacandra and Guṇacandra mention the expreience of cognitions of objects still lingering in the mind expressed by talking during deep sleep and complete withdrawal of the external sense-organs from their objects as the expressions of deep sleep. Śārṅgadeva mentions talking during dream, motionlessness of the body, and

[253] Nidrodbhavaṁ suptam. KS., p. 132. Nidrāyā eva gāḍhāvasthā suptam. KS., AC., p. 132. DR., p. 150.

[254] Suptiḥ nidrāsamutthā. BPK., p. 23. Udreka eva nidrāyaḥ suptiḥ syāt. RS., p. 137. PR., p. 255.

[255] Suptiḥ svapnaḥ. LR., ANC., p. 643. SR., ii, p. 847; NDP., pp. 181-82.

[256] Nidrā-vibhāvottha-jñānaṁ suptam. RG., p. 106.

complete insensibility of the external sense-organs also as the expressions of deep sleep.[257]

34. *Awaking* (*vivodha*)

Viśvanātha defines awaking as the return of consciousness, which is produced by the causes of the removal of sleep.[258] Acyutarāya defines awaking as the emergence of sensuous consciousness or self-consciousness after sleep. Śiṅga Bhūpāla defines awaking as the regaining of consciousness after sleep, which is produced by a dream, a touch, a loud sound, a full dose of sleep, etc. Śāradātanaya mentions loud sounds, touches, terrible dreams, interruption of sleep, a heavy meal, etc., as the determinant causes of awaking. Prabodha (awaking) is so called because in this condition the self perceives all objects or becomes alive to them. Bharatamuni mentions interruption of sleep as a consequence of a heavy meal, bad dreams, the hearing of loud sounds, touching sharp objects, etc. Hemacandra defines awaking as the obsence of sleep (vinidratva) or its removal due to a sound, a touch, a dream, talking in dream, interruption of sleep, a heavy meal, etc. Rāmacandra and Guṇacandra define awaking as emergence of consciousness after sleep due to a loud sound, a touch, a dream, a heavy meal, etc. Sarveśvarācārya defines awaking as the removal of sleep (nidrābhāva) due to contentment, sound sleep, etc. Rūpa Goswāmī defines awaking as the return of consciousness after sleep is destroyed. Sleep is, in its essential nature, nescience (avidyā) or delusion (moha).[259] Viśvanātha Cakravartī defines awaking as the cessation of sleep. Jagannātha defines awaking as emergence of consciousness after the cessation of sleep, which is brought about by full enjoyment of sleep, a dream, a loud sound, a sharp touch, etc.[260] Awaking is an accessory state.

Awaking is expressed by yawning, rubbing the eyes, leaving the bed, rubbing the body, etc. Bharatamuni mentions these expressions of awaking. Hemacandra and Śāradātanaya mention

[257] BPK., p. 23; NDP., pp. 181-82; SR., ii, p. 847.

[258] Nidrāpagama-hetubhyo vivodhaś cetanāgamaḥ. SDP., p. 191.

[259] Avidyā-moha-nidrāder dhvaṁsād bodhaḥ prabuddhatā. BRS., p. 519; SSār., p. 136; RS., p. 138; BPK., pp. 23, 29; NTS., p. 369; KS., AC., p. 135; NDP., p. 185; STS., p. 54.

[260] Prabodho nidrā-nivṛttiḥ. ANC., p. 645. Nidrā-nāśottaraṁ jāyamāno bodho vivodhaḥ. RG., p. 107. GMP., p. 107.

throwing the hands, cracking the joints of the fingers, turning the neck and the body from side to side also; Śiṅga Bhūpāla mentions scratching the head also; Viśvanātha mentions stretching out the limbs, closing the eyes, looking at the limbs also; Sarveśvarācārya mentions the trembling of the head and opening the eyes also as the expressions of awaking. On awaking the eyes are slightly opened and then closed because they are dazzled by light, and then they are opened.[261]

35. *Death-like condition* (*maraṇa*)

Bharatamuni mentions intestinal disorder, pain of the liver, imbalance of the bodily humours, a boil on the cheek, fever, cholera and other diseases; or, accidental hurts, e.g., the bite of a serpent, the drinking of poison, the cutting by a weapon, the attack of a ferocious beast, being run over by an elephant, a horse, a chariot, or any other vehicle as the determinant causes of death-like condition. Hemacandra defines death-like condition as a state prior to death, which is generated by sickness or accidental hurt.[262] Fever and the like are diseases. Accidental hurts are a serpent's bite, a cut by a weapon, an attack of an infuriated elephant, and the like. Maraṇa (death-like condition) is the condition of the body and the mind just before death, because after death there can be no consciousness. Jagannātha defines death-like condition as a state just prior to death, which is in the nature of swoon or unconsciousness brought about by physical diseases and the like.[263] It does not mean the extinction of life or death, because it is a bhāva which is a mental mode. Death is not a mental mode. All bhāvas are rendered possible by the conjunction of life with the body, since they persist along with their expressions in an embodied mind. Life is a necessary condition of all mental modes (bhāva). The *Bālabodhinī* quotes a definition of death-like condition as a state prior to death owing to diseases and the like causes.[264] It also quotes a definition of death-like condition as the beginning of the exit of life from

[261] NTS., p. 369; KS., AC., p. 135; BPK., p. 23; RS., p. 138; SDP., p. 191; STS., p. 54; NDP., p. 185; SDPJ., p. 191.

[262] Mṛteḥ prāgavasthā mṛtiḥ. KS., AC., p. 143. NTS., p. 372.

[263] Rogādi-janyā mūrchhārūpā maraṇa-prāgavasthā maraṇam. RG., p. 110. GMP., p. 110.

[264] Rogādyaiḥ prāgavasthā maraṇasya mṛtir matā. BB., p. 116.

the body, which generates fainting or unconsciousness, stupefaction of the sense-organs, convulsion of the limbs, etc. Others identify death-like condition with swoon (mūrchā). Acyutarāya defines maraṇa as the death-like condition of the mind due to separation from the beloved person. Śāradātanaya mentions sickness (e.g. fever, etc.) or a sudden calamity (e.g. being struck by lightning, being struck by weapons, etc.) as the cause of the death-like condition.[265]

Rāmacandra and Guṇacandra define maraṇa as the desire to die (mṛtyusaṁkalpa) due to diseases or accidents. It is the determination (adhyavasāya) to die arising from the knowledge that the evil is incurable. It springs from utter despair due to helplessness. Maraṇa, in the sense of death or the extinction of vital force, cannot be represented on the stage.[266]

Śiṅga Bhūpāla defines death as separation of the embodied soul from the vital force called dhanañjaya, due either to a disease or to a severe blow. Viśvanātha defines maraṇa as death or extinction of life in the body due to its being pierced in its vital parts by an arrow, etc.[267] Rūpa Goswāmī defines mṛti (death) as the extinction of life due to dejection, sickness, terror, a severe blow, physical exertion, etc.[268] Very often it is regarded as a mental mode prior to death, and death is regarded as its expression. Jīva Goswāmī defines death as the departure of life from the body.[269] Death is defined as the commencement of the exit of life from the body. Jīvānanda regards grief, mental anguish, etc., also as the causes of death. Sarveśvarācārya defines death as the disintegration of the body into the five constituent elements, e.g. earth, water, air, light and ether, due to separation from the beloved persons, physical diseases, and accidents.[270]

The death-like condition is expressed by languor of the body, looseness of the limbs, inactivity, closing the eyes, hiccough, chocked breathing, uttering faint and indistinct sounds, not looking at kinsmen and relatives, etc., when it is due to physical diseases. These expressions are mentioned by Bharatamuni.

[265] BB., p. 116; SSār., p. 137; BPK., p. 24.
[266] NDP., p. 181.
[267] Śarādyair maraṇaṁ jīvatyāgaḥ. SDP., p. 194. RS., p. 118.
[268] Viṣāda-vyādhi-saṁtrāsa-saṁprahāra-klamādibhiḥ prāṇatyago mṛtiḥ. BRS., p. 481. Ibid, p. 482.
[269] Mṛtiḥ prāṇatyāgaḥ. LR., p. 605.
[270] Jīvasyodgamanārambho maraṇam. KPD., quoted in SDPJ., p. 195. STS., pp. 52-53.

Śāradātanaya mentions pallor of the body, pain, and disordered actions of the relaxed limbs also; Śiṅga Bhūpāla mentions inactivity of the sense-organs also; Hemacandra mentions paralysis of the limbs also; the *Bālabodhinī* mentions fainting and convulsion of the limbs also as the expressions of the death-like condition due to sickness. Rāmacandra and Guṇacandra state the incapacity of the sense-organs to apprehend their objects, unsteady bodily actions, gloomy appearance, suddenly falling on the ground, trembling, shaking, emaciation, foaming, paralysis of the shoulders and the hands, unexpected movements of the body, and dullness of the mind also as the expressions and consequents of the death-like condition. The death-like condition due to accidental cut by a weapon is expressed by sudden fall on the ground, trembling, throbbing, etc. These expressions are mentioned by Bharatamuni. He states emaciation of the body, trembling, heat of the skin, hiccough, foaming, paralysis of the shoulder, motionlessness and death as the expressions of the death-like condition due to a snake-bite or drinking poison. Hemacandra mentions the paralysis of the limbs also as its expression.[271]

36. *Are there other Accessory Emotions?*

Śiṅga Bhūpāla observes, that hypocrisy (dambha), affection (sneha), jealousy (īrṣyā), regret (udvega) and other emotions are not specifically mentioned, because they are included in the thirty three transitory emotions mentioned above. For instance, hypocrisy which is characterized by deception of others is included in insincerity (jihmatā) or dissimulation (avahittha) which consists in suppression of emotions. Affection (sneha) which is characterized by melting of the heart (cittadravatā) is included in joy. Jealousy (īrṣyā) which consists in intolerance of the gift of one's own property, or in scrupulous regard for one's honour, is included in intolerance (amarṣa). Jealousy in regard to others' property, i.e. intolerance of others' enjoying the gift of others' property, is included in envy (asūyā). Regret is sometimes included in self-abasement (nirveda), and sometimes in dejection (viṣāda). The *Bhāvaprakāśikā* says: "If there are other emotions because

[271] NTS., pp. 372-73; BPK., p. 24; RS., p. 118; KS., AC., p. 143; BB., p. 116; NDP., p. 181.

of their specific nature as mental modes, they are all included in transitory emotions."[272]

The same transitory emotions are excitants (vibhāva) of some emotions, and consequents (anubhāva) of other emotions. They are generally causes (kāraṇa) of some emotions, and effects (kārya) of other emotions.[273] For example, mental agony (santāpa) is the excitant cause of misery (dainya) and the consequent of languor (glāni). Agony generates misery. Languor generates agony. Dealing a severe blow is the excitant cause of insensibility (pralaya) and fainting (moha), and it is the consequent of fierceness (augrya). Dejection (viṣāda) is the excitant cause of inactivity (stambha) and it is the consequent of flurry due to a physical calamity. Physical disease (vyādhi) gives rise to languor (glāni), inactivity (stambha), insensibility (pralaya), etc.[274]

The transitory emotions function in two ways. They are either independent or dependent. When they stand by themselves, and do not feed other emotions, they are independent (svatantra). But when they feed, promote and develop other emotions, they are dependent on them (paratantra). Thus, self-abasement (nirveda) may feed the emotion of anger and depend upon it. Or, it may be independent of other emotions. Similarly, dejection (viṣāda) may feed the erotic sentiment (śṛṅgārarasa) and depend upon it. Or, it may be experienced alone as an independent emotion.[275]

37. *Emergence, Subsidence, Blend and Friction of Emotions*

The transitory emotions have four conditions, viz. (1) emergence, (2) subsidence, (3) blend, and (4) friction.[276]

(1) The distinct emergence or manifestation of an emotion due to the causal operation of its complement of conditions is called its rise or origin (udaya). It refers to the emergence of a

[272] RS., p. 139.

[273] Vibhāvā anubhāvāś ca te bhavanti parasparam.
Kārya-kāraṇa-bhāvas tu jñeyaḥ prāyeṇa lokataḥ.
Ibid, p. 139.

[274] Ibid, pp. 139-40.

[275] Vyabhicāriṇaḥ paraposakatāṁ prāptāḥ paratantrāḥ. Tadabhāve svatantrāḥ bhāvāḥ. RS., p. 140.

[276] Bhāvasya śāntir udayaḥ sandhiḥ śabalatā matā. SDP., p. 275. RS., p. 143; KPK., p. 103; ANC., p. 646.

single emotion. When a woman casts her eyes filled with tears on her female friend being rejected by her lover at whose feet she threw herself, but could not win his grace, dejection emerges in her mind.

(2) When two similar or dissimilar emotions arising from the same or different causes are blended with each other, they give rise to a blend (sandhi) of emotions.[277] The blend of emotions is the simultaneous emergence of two emotions, which do not overpower each other, but which are capable of overpowering each other, in the mind of the same person. It is an unsettled state of the mind because of mutual repression of them. Two similar emotions may be blended with each other. Inactivity due to the sight of an agreeable object may be blended with inactivity due to the sight of a disagreeable object. Here two similar transitory emotions due to different causes are blended with each other. When a lover performs an extremely difficult task, his beloved lady simultaneously experiences a blend of joy and dejection. Similarly, there may be a blend of anxiety and intolerance, and flurry and joy. The two emotions which are blended with each other may be produced by the same cause or by different causes. When a maiden hears of a proposal for her marriage, she experiences a blend of shyness and joy. The exquisite beauty of a young woman, which pleases a young man's eyes and captivates his heart, but which is beyond his reach and unattainable, gives rise to a blend of joy and mental agony in his mind. Here two dissimilar emotions are blended with each other.[277a]

(3) When many emotions are evoked in the mind in quick succession and conflict with and inhibit one another, there is a compound emotion in which the constituent emotions do not lose their identity.[278] An emotion which inhibits another emotion is opposed to it. An emotion which is inhibited by another emotion is not fully manifested to consciousness because the opposite causes interfere with its complete manifestation. When many conflicting emotions are evoked in quick succession—the former being repressed by the latter—there is a combination of

[277] Sarūpayor bhinnayor vā sandhiḥ bhāvayor yūtiḥ. ANC., p. 647. RS., p. 143.

[277a] UNM., pp. 647-50; SDPJ., pp. 275, 56; KPK., p. 105.

[278] Śabalatvaṁ tu bhāvānāṁ saṁmardaḥ syāt parasparam. RS., p. 144.

conflicting emotions.[279] Thus, pride, dejection, envy, anxiety, recollection, revenge, self-abasement, and ascertainment of duty may be evoked in quick succession in a person's mind, and inhibit one another for the exclusive possession of it. Similarly, conjecture, anxiety, ascertainment of duty, recollection, apprehension, misery, contentment and impatience may be evoked in a person's mind in quick succession. Such states of the mind in which it experiences many emotions in quick succession—the former being inhibited by the latter—are called compound emotions (bhāvaśābalya).[280]

(4) When an emotion arises and reaches its culmination, and then subsides and disappears, this disappearance of the emotion is called bhāvaśānti.[281] The intense sulks of Kamalā which could not be destroyed by the convincing arguments of her confidantes, and which could not be shaken by the persuasive talks of messengers, were dispelled by a slight blowing of Kṛṣṇa's flute. This is an example of the disappearance of the emotion of jealousy.

38. *Bhāva and Rasa, Bhāvābhāsa and Rasābhāsa*

The subsidiary emotions appearing as principal emotions, love for a god, a sage, the spiritual guide, the king, etc., and a permanent emotional disposition or sentiment just awakened and immediately subsiding are called bhāvas. They are not nourished by the determinant cause, the expressions of the actors, accessory emotions and the like, and are not, for that reason, developed into æsthetic emotions (rasa).[282] This is Viśvanātha's view. Udbhaṭa also maintains, that a bhāva is an incipient æsthetic emotion, but that it is not a fully developed rasa. A rasa is an æsthetic emotion in a fully developed form, while a permanent emotional disposition or sentiment (sthāyī bhāva) exists as a latent impression (vāsanā) in the mind of a person. When a

[279] Śābalyaṁ bhāvānām uttarottarasaṁmardaḥ. ANC., p. 650. SDPJ., pp. 275, 56.

[280] RS., pp. 144-45; SDP., pp. 275-78; UNM., LR., ANC., pp. 646-50; KPK., pp. 105-06.

[281] Ātyārudhasya bhāvasya vilayaḥ śāntir ucyate. RS., p. 144. Śāntir bhāvasya layaḥ. ANC., p. 651. UNM., p. 651.

[282] Sañcāriṇaḥ pradhānāni devādiviṣayā ratiḥ.
Udbuddhamātraḥ sthāyī ca bhāva ityabhidhīyate.
SDP., p. 265.

18

permanent emotional disposition is roused to consciousness and nourished and strengthened with the help of its accessories, it assumes the form of an æsthetic emotion (rasa). If it is not sufficiently strengthened and heightened so as to attain the status of an æsthetic emotion, it remains all the while as an incipient æsthetic emotion (bhāva).[283]

There is no æsthetic emotion (rasa) without an emotion (bhāva); and there is no emotion which cannot be developed into an æsthetic emotion with the aid of favourable conditions. An æsthetic emotion and an emotion are closely connected with each other.[284] An accessory emotion becomes predominant in a particular æsthetic emotion, even as in a delicious drink one of its ingredients (e.g. black pepper, sugar, etc.) becomes manifest at a particular time. Different accessory emotions become manifest in different æsthetic emotions.[285]

Insanity and other accessory emotions and states are not permanent emotional dispositions (sthāyī bhāva), though they attain apparent permanency somewhere owing to the operation of some causes, because the hero of a drama does not act principally in those conditions. When a bhāva and a rasa are excited by inappropriate and immoral objects, they are called a semblance of bhāva and a semblance of rasa.[286] An æsthetic emotion (rasa), an incipient æsthetic emotion (bhāva), their semblances, the emergence and disappearance of an emotion, the blend of two emotions, and the compound of many conflicting emotions —all these may be considered as æsthetic emotions (rasa) when they are relished and enjoyed by appreciative connoisseurs.[287]

39. *The Relation of Transitory Emotions to one another*

Rāmacandra and Guṇacandra maintain, that some transitory emotions are related to each other as cause and effect. For

[283] Kāvyālaṅkārasārasaṁgraha, Bombay Sanskrit Series, 1925, p. 96.

[284] Na bhāvahīno'sti raso, na bhāvo rasavarjitaḥ.
Parasparakṛtā siddhir anayoḥ rasabhāvayoḥ.
SDP., p. 265.

[285] Udrekaḥ kasyacit kvāpi tathā sañcariṇo rase. Ibid, p. 268.

[286] Anaucitya-pravṛttatve ābhāso rasa-bhāvayoḥ. Ibid, p. 269. KPK., p. 101.

[287] Rasabhāvau tadābhāsau bhāvasya praśamodayau. Sandhiḥ śabalatā ceti sarve'pi rasanād rasāḥ. Ibid, p. 264.

instance, sickness is the cause of self-abasement (nirveda); anxiety and awaking are the causes of recollection; fatigue gives rise to indolence. Even improper transitory emotions give rise to laughter.[288]

[288] Vyabhicāriṇām utpādyotpādakabhāvaḥ. NDP., p. 186.

Chapter XI

SĀTTVIKABHĀVA

1. *The Nature of Sāttvikabhāvas*

The sāttvikabhāvas are the spontaneous organic manifestations of emotions, which spring from sattva only. Sattva is an innate virtue of the mind which manifests emotions abiding in the self.[1] They are different from the other organic expressions because they spring from sattva only.[2] Viśvanātha gives this definition of sāttvikabhāvas. Śiṅga Bhūpāla defines sattva as that quality of the mind, which inclines the mind towards joy and grief of others, and evokes similar emotions in it, which are characterized by pleasure and pain. He defines sāttvikabhāvas as those states which arise from the sattva of the mind excited by emotions. Śāradātanaya also holds this view.[3] Bharatamuni regards sattva as a virtue of the mind, which enables it to concentrate itself on an object, and which is manifested in horripilation, shedding tears, change of colour, etc. An actor imitates the spontaneous organic expressions of the emotions of the person whom he represents on the stage, and his imitations of them also are called sāttvikabhāvas. They are eight in number: (1) inactivity (stambha), (2) perspiration (sveda), (3) bristling of the hairs of the body (romāñca), (4) change of voice (svarabheda), (5) trembling (vepathu), (6) change of colour (vaivarṇya), (7) shedding tears (aśru), and (8) insensibility (pralaya).[4]

Śāradātanaya describes how sāttvikabhāvas help and promote one another. (1) In immobility (stambha), trembling, goose-flesh, perspiration, faltering voice, and shedding tears also appear either simultaneously or successively. In some cases of immobility, goose-flesh, change of voice, perspiration and trembling appear together owing to the intensity of the exciting causes. Sometimes when there is immobility, change of voice and

[1] Vikārāḥ sattva-sambhūtāḥ sāttvikāḥ parikīrtitāḥ. SDP., p. 179.
[2] Sattvamātrodbhavatvāt te bhinnā apyanubhāvataḥ. Ibid, p. 179.
[3] RS., pp. 179. BPK., p. 14.
[4] NTS., pp. 374-75.

shedding tears appear. (2) In goose-flesh (romāñca), trembling and immobility appear frequently. (3) In trembling (vepathu), perspiration, goose-flesh, and shedding tears appear naturally. (4) In change of colour (vaivarṇya), shedding tears always occurs, but trembling and immobility appear sometimes.[5]

First, Śāradātanaya observes, that the sāttvikabhāvas excited by the determinant causes develop and intensify the emotions.[6] Here he distinctly points out that these organic expressions are not only expressions of emotions, but that they also strengthen and intensify the emotions. Thus, the determinant causes (vibhāva) evoke initial emotions; then these emotions are manifested in organic expressions; and then these organic expressions, again, react upon the emotions and reinvigorate them. Thus, emotions are prior to organic expressions. The Sanskrit Rhetoricists are advocates of the common-sense theory of the relation of emotions to organic expressions. They recognize the importance of organic expressions in the structure of emotions, but they do not identify emotions with organic expressions. Secondly, the very term 'anubhāva' distinctly shows that organic expressions (anubhāva) occur after (anu) the emotions. Thirdly, the Rhetoricists observe, that sometimes the different emotions have the same expression. Tears are the expressions of fear, anger, joy and grief; there are cold tears of joy and hot tears of grief. Change of colour is the expression of anger, fear, excessive joy, dejection and grief. Trembling is the expression of fear, joy, anger, etc. Change of voice is the expression of anger, joy and fear. Horripilation is the expression of anger, fear, joy and wonder. Perspiration is the expression of anger, fear, joy, shame, pleasure and languor. Immobility is the expression of anger, fear, wonder, pride, joy and dejection. Insensibility is the expression of pain, excessive joy and grief. These facts prove that organic expressions do not constitute an emotion, because the same organic expression cannot constitute different emotions. Fourthly, the Ālaṅkārikas point out that the organic expressions correlative to particular emotions appear without any emotions. For instance, tears are excited not only by emotions but also by cold, yawning, winkless gaze for a long time, disease, smoke,

[5] BPK., p. 32.
[6] Pralaya-stambha-kampāśru-sveda-romodgamādayaḥ puṣyantyanubhavotkarṣam vibhāvair api dīpitāḥ. Ibid, p. 32.

application of collyrium, etc. Trembling follows not only from emotions, but also from disease, infirmity, exertion, cold, etc. Change of voice is produced not only by emotions, but also by disease, intoxication, fever, etc. Horripilation arises not only from emotions, but also from disease, cold, etc. Change of colour is the effect of not only emotions, but also of being scorched by the sun, sickness, cold, fatigue, etc. Perspiration is the effect not only of emotions, but also of fatigue, physical exercise, heat, fever, etc. Insensibility is the effect not only of emotions, but also of intoxication, sleep, disease, severe blow, etc.[7] Hence emotions are not constituted by their organic expressions.

Rūpa Goswāmī and Jīva Goswāmī describe four degrees of intensity of the sāttvikabhāvas. (1) When a sāttvikabhāva is manifested a little, either singly or in combination with another, so that it can be suppressed, it is said to be in a smoking condition (dhūmāyita). (2) When two or three sāttvikabhāvas are manifested very distinctly, so that they can be suppressed with a great difficulty, they are said to be in a kindled condition (jvalita). (3) When three, four or five intense sāttvikabhāvas are simultaneously manifested very distinctly, so that they cannot be suppressed, they are said to be in a blazing condition (dīpita). (4) When five, six or all the sāttvikabhāvas are simultaneously manifested distinctly, and attain the highest degree of intensity, they are said to be in a vehemently blazing condition (uddīpita).[8]

2. *Eight kinds of Sāttvikabhāvas*

(1) *Stambha.*—It is defined by Viśvanātha as immobility or inhibition of all bodily actions due to fear, joy, sickness, etc.[9] Śāradātanaya defines it as the inhibition of actions (ceṣṭāvighāta). In stambha a person remains conscious, but he does not act or move, his limbs remain motionless, and his mind remains blank.[10] It is due to intoxication, anger, fear, wonder, pride, joy, dejection, etc., in the inferior and mediocre persons. Vidyānātha defines stambha as the inhibition of all actions due to obstructed consciousness, which is expressed in inertness and immobility. It is

[7] BPK., pp. 14-15.
[8] UNM., LR., pp. 565-70.
[9] Stambhaś ceṣṭāpratīghāto bhaya-harṣāmayādibhiḥ. SDP., p. 180.
[10] Sacetano'pi niśceṣṭo niṣprakampo jaḍākṛtiḥ.
Stabdhagātraś ca śūnyaś ca stambhavan iti kathyate.
BPK., p. 14. Ibid, p. 31.

due to deep affection, fear, despair, wonder, etc. Bharatamuni describes stambha as unconsciousness, immobility, inertness, and stiffness of the body, which is due to joy, fear, grief, wonder, dejection, wrath, etc.[11] Śiṅga Bhūpāla defines stambha as unconsciousness, blanknessness of the mind, and immobility, which is due to joy, fear, anger, dejection and wonder.[12] Rāmacandra and Guṇacandra define stambha as the inactivity of the hands, the legs and the other limbs in spite of the efforts of the self to move them. Here there is the activity of the self (antaḥparispanda) in the shape of effort or volition, but there is no activity of the limbs.[13] Immobility is the expression of wonder, fear, disease, intoxication, etc. Rūpa Goswāmī mentions joy, fear, wonder, dejection and revenge as the emotions which produce immobility. Śārṅgadeva mentions joy, love, fear, pain, dejection, wonder, anger and confusion as the causes of immobility.[14]

(2) *Sveda.*—It is perspiration or oozing out of droplets of sweat from the pores of the skin owing to fatigue and the like causes.[15] Rāmacandra and Guṇacandra mention fatigue, fear, shame, disease, absorbing heat, grief, summer, physical exercise, etc., as the causes of sweat. Śiṅga Bhūpāla mentions joy, anger, fear, physical exertion and fatigue as the causes of perspiration. Śārṅgadeva states mental anguish, joy, shyness, anger, fear, disease, fatigue, fainting, oppression, blow, being scorched by the sun, physical exercise, etc., as the causes of sweat. Śāradātanaya asserts that perspiration is due to anger, fear, joy, shyness, languor, pleasure, etc. Bharatamuni regards sweat as the expression of anger, fear, joy, shame, pain, fatigue, disease, heat, blow, physical exercise, languor, oppression, etc. Viśvanātha defines perspiration as oozing out of sweat from the skin of the body owing to sexual union, heat, physical exertion, etc. Kumārasvāmī regards sweat as the expression of joy, shame, fear, anger, etc.[16]

(3) *Romāñca.*—Śāradātanaya describes it as horripilation or

[11] Harṣa-bhaya-śoka-vismaya-viṣāda-roṣādisambhavaḥ stambhaḥ. NTS., p. 375. Ibid, p. 376. PR., RA., p. 139.

[12] Saṁjñāvirahitatvaṁ ca śūnyatā niṣprakampatā. RS., p. 89.

[13] Yatne' pyaṅgākriyā stambho harṣādeḥ. NDP., p. 186.

[14] UNM., pp. 546-48; SR., ii, p. 854.

[15] Svedo romajalasrāvaḥ śramādeḥ. NDP., p. 187.

[16] NDP., p. 187; RS., p. 90; SR., ii, p. 854; BPK., p. 14; NTS., p. 375; SDP., p. 180; PR., RA., p. 241.

bristling of the hairs of the body (romanirgama) owing to anger, fear, joy, etc. Rāmacandra and Guṇacandra ascribe gooseflesh to wonder, energy, joy, anger, touch, cold, sickness, rubbing of the body, etc. It is expressed by softness of the body, expansion of the eyes, whistling through the teeth, etc. Viśvanātha and Rūpa Goswāmī regard gooseflesh as the expression of joy, wonder, fear, etc. Vidyānātha and Kumārasvāmī regard horripilation as the expression of excessive joy, courage, fear, wonder, etc.[17] Bharatamuni describes gooseflesh as the expression of touch, fear, cold, joy, anger, and sickness.[18]

(4) *Svarabheda.*—Bharatamuni defines it as change of voice due to fear, joy, anger, old age, fierceness, sickness and intoxication.[19] Śāradātanaya defines svarabheda as change of the voice that is natural to a person due to anger, joy, fear, exhilaration because of drinking wine, etc. It is faltering voice, broken voice, choked voice, unnatural voice. Rāmacandra and Guṇacandra define svarabheda as change of natural voice, either its increase or decrease, which is the expression of joy, fear, anger, love, harshness, intoxication, old age, etc. It is expressed by shyness, laughter, self-abasement, etc. Kumārasvāmī regards change of voice as the expression of joy, grief, fear, sickness, etc. Śiṅga Bhūpāla considers joy, grief, etc., to be the causes of change of voice. Śārṅgadeva repeats the causes of change of voice mentioned by Bharatamuni. Viśvanātha defines change of voice as modification of natural voice due to intoxication, excessive joy, sickness, etc. Rūpa Goswāmī mentions dejection, wonder, revenge, joy and fear as the causes of change of voice.[20]

(5) *Kampa.*—Viśvanātha defines it as trembling of the body owing to deep love, hatred, physical exertion, etc.[21] Rāmacandra and Guṇacandra define kampa as throbbing, trembling, or slight movement of the body owing to fear, joy, anger, cold, disease, touching the beloved person, etc.[22] It is expressed by perversion

[17] Harṣādbhuta-bhayādibhyo romāñco romavikriyā. SDP., p. 180. BPK., pp. 14, 31; NDP., p. 187; UNM., pp. 551-53; PR., RA., p. 240.

[18] Sparśa-bhaya-śīta-harṣāt krodhād rogāc ca romāñcaḥ. NTS., p. 376.

[19] Svarabhedo bhaya-harṣa-krodha-jarā-raukṣya-roga-mada-janitaḥ. NTS., p. 376.

[20] Mada-sammada-pīḍādyair vaisvaryaṁ gadgadaṁ viduḥ. SDP., p. 180. BPK., pp. 14, 31; NDP., p. 187; PR., RA., p. 242; RS., p. 93; ŚR., ii, p. 855; UNM., pp. 553-56.

[21] Rāga-dveṣa-śramādibhyaḥ kampo gātrasya vepathuḥ. SDP., p. 180.

[22] Bhayāder vepathur gātraspandaḥ. Spandaḥ kiñcitccalanam. NDP., p. 186.

of speech, gait, and actions of the body. Bharatamuni describes trembling as the expression of cold, fear, joy, wrath, touch, old age, and sickness.[23] It is expressed by quivering (vepana), throbbing (sphuraṇa), and shivering (kampa). Śāradātanaya defines vepathu as violent trembling of the heart (hṛdayotkampa) owing to fear, joy, wrath, etc. Śiṅga Bhūpāla defines kampa as throbbing, trembling of the limbs, and the like due to joy, terror, anger, old age, etc. Vidyānātha and Kumārasvāmī regard trembling as the expression of love, fear, anger, fever, old age, etc. Śārṅgadeva describes four kinds of trembling: tremor (vepana), throbbing (sphuraṇa), trembling (kampa), and shaking (vepathu). These differ in intensity,—the succeeding being more intense than the preceding. Trembling is due to terror, joy and revenge according to Rūpa Gosvāmī.[24]

(6) *Vaivarṇya.*—It is change of colour or complexion due to contempt and the like.[25] It is the expression of reproach, mental agony, fear, anger, sickness, cold, fatigue, strong sun, etc. It is expressed by looking in different directions, biting the nails, shame, etc. Rāmacandra and Guṇacandra hold this view. Śārṅgadeva mentions fear, anger, disease, fainting, fatigue, cold and sun as the causes of change of colour. Śāradātanaya ascribes change of colour to anger, fear, languor, etc. Śiṅga Bhūpāla defines vaivarṇya as change of colour in the face due to dejection, anger, the sun, etc. Vidyānātha mentions despair, intoxication, rage, fear, heat, cold, etc., as the causes of change of colour. Rūpa Gosvāmī attributes it to dejection, wrath and fear. Viśvanātha traces change of colour to dejection, intoxication, rage, etc. Bharatamuni mentions anger, fear, fatigue, disease, physical exertion, heat and cold as the causes of change of colour.[26]

(7) *Aśru.*—It is shedding tears. Bharatamuni mentions excessive joy, indignation, fear, grief, smoke, application of collyrium, yawning, gazing with winkless eyes, cold and disease as the causes of shedding tears. Śāradātanaya regards fear, anger, grief, etc., as the causes of shedding tears. Tears of joy on an auspicious

[23] Śīta-bhaya-harṣa-roṣa-sparśa-jarā-rogajaḥ kampaḥ. NTS., p. 375. Ibid, p. 376.

[24] BPK., pp. 15, 31 ; RS., p. 93 ; PR., RA., p. 240 ; SR., ii, p. 855 ; UNM., pp. 557-58.

[25] Chāyāvikāro vaivarṇyaṁ kṣepādeḥ. NDP., p. 187.

[26] Viṣāda-mada-roṣādyair varṇānyatvaṁ vivarṇatā. SDP., p. 180. Śīta-krodha-bhaya-śrama-roga-klama-tāpajaṁ ca vaivarṇyam. NTS., p. 376. SR., ii, p. 855 ; BPK., pp. 15, 31 ; PR., RA., p. 241 ; UNM., pp. 559-60.

occasion are cold; tears of grief on an inauspicious occasion are hot. Śiṅga Bhūpāla regards dejection, wrath, joy, smoke, etc., as the causes of shedding tears. Śārṅgadeva mentions joy, revenge, fear, grief, smoke, collyrium, yawning, gazing with winkless eyes, extreme cold and disease as the causes of shedding tears. Vidyānātha regards shedding tears as the expression of excessive joy, grief, fear, anger, etc. Viśvanātha regards shedding tears as the expression of anger, grief and excessive joy.[27] Rāmacandra and Guṇacandra mention excessive joy, revenge, fear, grief, laughter, yawning, gazing with fixed eyes, smoke, sickness, etc., as the causes of shedding tears. It is expressed by throbbing of the nose, flow of cold, spitting, faltering voice, etc. Rūpa Gosvāmī mentions joy, wrath and dejection as the causes of shedding tears. Śārṅgadeva mentions three kinds of tears: tears of joy, tears of grief, and tears of jealousy. The tears of joy attended with the recollection of sorrow are accompanied with blooming cheeks. The tears of pure and unmixed joy come out of the corners of the eyes, and are attended with bristling of hair. The tears of grief fall in a stream, and are attended with loud lamentation and restless movements of the limbs. The tears of jealousy in women are attended with sighing due to the thought of another's prosperity, quivering lips and cheeks, crooked glances, and frowning. The superior and mediocre persons do not shed tears in their own danger or distress, but they do so at the sight of others' distress. Women and inferior persons shed tears in their own distress and also at the sight of others' distress.[28]

(8) *Pralaya.*—It is the loss of consciousness. Śiṅga Bhūpāla defines it as unconsciousness due to grief, severe blow, etc.[29] Śāradātanaya defines pralaya as the complete cessation of the mental operations, verbal and bodily actions, inactivity and immobility. There is the complete loss of the power of acting in this condition.[30] Viśvanātha defines pralaya as the cessation of all cognitions and actions owing to excessive joy and grief.[31] Vidyānātha defines pralaya as the complete stupefaction of the sense-organs because of joy, grief, intoxication, sleep, beating, etc.

[27] Aśru netrodbhavaṁ vāri krodha-duḥkha-praharṣajam. SDP., p. 180. NTS., p. 376; BPK., pp. 14, 31; RS., p. 95; SR., ii, p. 855; PR., RA., p. 242.
[28] NDP., p. 187; UNM., pp. 561-62; SR., ii, p. 829.
[29] Pralayo duḥkha-ghātādyaiś ceṣṭā tatra visaṁjñatā. RS., p. 96.
[30] Vākkāyamanasāṁ prāyaḥ pralayaḥ naṣṭaceṣṭatā. BPK., p. 32.
[31] Pralyayaḥ sukha-duḥkhābhyāṁ ceṣṭā-jñāna-nirākṛtiḥ. SDP., p. 180.

Śāradātanaya regards excessive joy, excruciating pain, intense grief, etc., as the causes of unconsciousness. Śārṅgadeva regards unconsciousness as the expression of intoxication, swoon, severe blow, sleep, fainting, fatigue, etc. Rāmacandra and Guṇacandra define pralaya as fainting (mūrchana) due to anger, blow, intoxication, etc., which is expressed by languor, disease, stupefaction of the senses, perspiration, deep breathing, etc. Rūpa Gosvāmī mentions intense joy and grief as the causes of unconsciousness. Bharatamuni mentions fatigue, fainting, intoxication, sleep, injury, stupor, etc., as the causes of unconsciousness, which is expressed by inactivity, motionlessness, inaudible breathing, falling on the ground, etc.[32]

In western psychology we find similar accounts. Woodworth says, "The cat's hair rises in fear or anger, and goose flesh in the human being is the same response, produced by tiny muscles under the control of the so-called 'sympathetic' nerves............The sweat glands are similarly aroused, and in strong emotion the perspiration may stand in beads upon the skin. Even in momentary thrills of fear, surprise, embarrassment or expectancy, the sweat glands are stimulated to a slight degree by their nerves, and the result is a momentary change in the electrical condition of the skin, which is called the psychogalvanic reflex."[33] Darwin says, "Several of our strongest emotions—grief, great joy, love, and sympathy lead to the free secretion of tears............Extreme pain, rage, terror, joy, the passion of love—all have a special tendency to cause the muscles to tremble."[34] "Trembling is excited by cold to the surface, by general failure of power in old age, by exhaustion after excessive fatigue; locally from severe injuries such as burns............Of all the emotions fear notoriously is the most apt to induce trembling; but so do occasionally great anger and joy."[35] "Trembling is a frequent consequence of extreme rage. The paralysed lips then refuse to obey the will, 'and the voice sticks in the throat'; or it is rendered loud, harsh, and discordant. The hair sometimes bristles."[36] "Rage exhibits itself in the most diversified manner. The face reddens or becomes purple with the veins on

[32] PR., RA., p. 240; BPK., p. 32; SR.. ii, p. 855; NDP., p. 187; UNM., pp. 563-64; NTS., pp. 376-77.
[33] *Psychology*, 1930, pp. 294-95.
[34] EEMA., p. 226.
[35] Ibid, pp. 64-65.
[36] Ibid, p. 251.

the forehead and neck distended............On the other hand, the action of the heart is sometimes so much impeded by great rage, that the countenance becomes pallid or livid."[37] In intense pain "perspiration bathes the body, and drops trickle down the face. The circulation and respiration are much affected. Hence the nostrils are generally dilated and often quiver; or the breath may be held until the blood stagnates in the purple face. If the agony be severe and prolonged, these signs all change; utter prostration follows, with fainting or convulsions."[38] Thus, the sāttvikabhāvas mentioned by the Sanskrit Rhetoricists as the spontaneous expressions of emotions are mentioned by the western psychologists also who give their physiological explanations.

[37] Ibid, pp. 248-49.
[38] Ibid, p. 68.

Chapter XII

DIFFERENT KINDS OF ÆSTHETIC EMOTIONS OR SENTIMENTS (RASA)

1. *Vibhāva, Anubhāva, Vyabhicāribhāva and Rasa.*

Jagannātha describes the relation of the determinant causes (vibhāva), the ensuant causes (anubhāva), and the accessory emotions or states (vyabhicāribhāva) to the æsthetic emotions or sentiments (rasa). The basic determinant causes (ālambana vibhāva) and the excitant causes (uddīpana vibhāva), which excite ordinary emotions (bhāva), become the determinant causes of æsthetic emotions or sentiments (rasa), when they are represented in poetry or drama, or on the stage. The expressions of ordinary emotions, which occur after (anu) emotions (bhāva) and as such are called anubhāvas, become ensuant causes (anubhāva) of æsthetic emotions or sentiments, when they are represented in poetry or drama, or on the stage. Those emotions and states which are excited together with (saha) the æsthetic emotions or sentiments and promote and develop them are called the accessory emotions or states (vyabhicāribhāva) of the latter.[1] Śārṅgadeva defines anubhāvas as the expressions or effects of ordinary emotions, which are artificially produced by expert actors on the stage by simulating the corresponding emotions. These expressions of the actors make the spectators infer the corresponding emotions in them.[2]

It is the permanent emotional dispositions or sentiments (sthāyibhāva) that are transformed, as we have already seen, into æsthetic emotions or sentiments (rasa) with the help of the determinant causes (vibhāva), the expressions (anubhāva), and accessory or transitory emotions or states (vyabhicāribhāva), when they are relished and enjoyed by the appreciative spectators of a dramatic performance. Of all these constituents of æsthetic emotions or sentiments the permanent emotional dispositions or sentiments (sthāyibhāva) are the predominant elements, though

[1] RG., (B.S.S.), p. 57.
[2] SR., ii, pp. 819-20.

they are not, in themselves, æsthetic sentiments (rasa). They are ordinary (laukika) sentiments, while æsthetic sentiments are extraordinary (alaukika) emotions.[3] Rasas are æsthetic emotions, and not permanent emotional dispositions or sentiments. But we shall call them æsthetic sentiments after Sully in conformity with the prevailing custom and to avoid cumbrous expressions. We shall call æsthetic emotion of love erotic sentiment, æsthetic emotion of mirth comic sentiment, æsthetic emotion of grief pathetic sentiment, æsthetic emotion of anger furious sentiment, æsthetic emotion of fear terrible sentiment, æsthetic emotion of wonder marvellous sentiment, æsthetic emotion of disgust odious sentiment, and æsthetic emotion of energy heroic sentiment.

Unlike his predecessors, Śāradātanaya mentions eight kinds of excitants (uddīpanavibhāva) which are attached to the eight kinds of æsthetic sentiments (rasa): (1) lalita; (2) lalitābhāsa; (3) sthira; (4) citra; (5) khara; (6) rukṣa; (7) nindita; and (8) vikṛta. They are respectably attached to the eight kinds of æsthetic sentiments, viz., (1) erotic sentiment, (2) comic sentiment, (3) heroic sentiment, (4) marvellous sentiment, (5) furious sentiment, (6) pathetic sentiment, (7) odious sentiment, and (8) terrible sentiment. They evoke the æsthetic sentiments with the assistance of either one, two, or three other emotions.

(1) Those vibhāvas which produce delight of the mind and are perceived by the appropriate sense-organs are called lalita. They are the causes of the intensity (utkarṣa) of the erotic sentiment. (2) Those vibhāvas which being indicated, seen, heard, or recalled excite laughter are called lalitābhāsa. They manifest the intensity of mirth or the wealth of laughter. They are the causes of the intensity of the comic sentiment. (3) Those vibhāvas which being seen, heard, remembered, or thought produce firmness are called sthira. They promote the heroic sentiment. (4) Those vibhāvas which being felt in the heart always excite wonder are called citra. They promote the marvellous sentiment. (5) Those vibhāvas which are capable of producing distress in the mind are called khara. They promote and intensify the furious sentiment. (6) Those vibhāvas which being perceived at once draw tears from the eyes are called rukṣa. They excite the pathetic sentiment. (7) Those vibhāvas which repel a person and compel him

[3] Vibhāvair anubhāvaiś ca yukto vā vyabhicāribhiḥ.
Āsvādyatvāt pradhānatvāt sthāyyeva tu raso bhavet. BB., p. 98.

to close his eyes quickly are called nindita. They promote the odious sentiment. (8) Those vibhāvas which produce commotion in the mind are called vikṛta. They promote the terrible sentiment.[4]

The æsthetic sentiments (rasa) are based on particular sentiments or permanent emotional dispositions (sthāyibhāva). The erotic sentiment, the comic sentiment, the pathetic sentiment, the furious sentiment, the heroic sentiment, the terrible sentiment, the marvellous sentiment, and the odious sentiment are based on the permanent emotional dispositions of love, mirth, grief, anger, energy, fear, wonder and disgust respectively. These are the natural correlates of each other. But these permanent emotional dispositions become accessory states (vyabhicāribhāva) of those æsthetic sentiments (rasa) which are not their natural correlates, and feed, promote and intensify them. Mirth or amusement is the accessory emotion which feeds the erotic sentiment and the heroic sentiment. Anger is the accessory state of the heroic sentiment. Disgust is the accessory state of the sentiment of quietness.[5]

The determinant causes, the excitant causes, the permanent emotional dispositions or sentiments, the transitory emotions, the expressions of emotions exhibited by the actors, and the spontaneous expressions of emotions are the causes of an æsthetic sentiment. They are called bhāvas because they generate an æsthetic sentiment, which is a unique extraordinary emotion which produces transcendental wonder. An æsthetic sentiment (rasa) is not a compound emotion composed of the constituent emotions. It is one, unique, indivisible emotional experience.[6]

2. *Bhāva and Rasa*

Mammaṭa distinguishes between bhāva and rasa. The permanent emotional dispositions and the transitory emotions which are not developed into æsthetic sentiments (rasa) are called bhāvas. The permanent emotional disposition of love (rati) for gods, sages, spiritual guides, the king, sons and the like is called a bhāva, because it is not developed into the æsthetic sentiment

[4] BPK., pp. 4-5.
[5] NDP., p. 176. Ratyādayo' pyaniyate rase syur vyabhicāriṇaḥ. SDP., p. 211.
[6] SDP., pp. 84, 214.

(rasa).[7] The permanent emotional disposition of love which is fully developed into the erotic sentiment (śṛṅgārarasa) is not called a bhāva. The transitory emotions also excited by the determinant causes are called bhāvas. Vāmana elaborates this view and states that the permanent emotional dispositions of mirth, grief, anger, fear, disgust, wonder and energy also, which are not developed into æsthetic sentiments (rasa), are called bhāvas; and that the transitory emotions also which are evoked by determinant causes independently of other emotions are called bhāvas.[8] Viśvanātha also holds the same view. According to him, the transitory emotions which are manifested as independent emotions are bhāvas. Love for gods, sages, spiritual guides, etc., is a bhāva. The permanent emotional dispositions or sentiments, which are just manifested as actual emotions but are not developed by determinant and excitant causes, ensuant causes, and transitory emotions into æsthetic sentiments, are called bhāvas.[9] The transitory emotions also are sometimes predominant in a confused mass of emotional experience, even as in a drink composed of many constituents one ingredient is a predominant element. Such predominant transitory emotions also are called bhāvas.[10]

3. *The Eight Æsthetic Sentiments* (*Rasa*)

Rāmacandra and Guṇacandra give an ingeneous explanation of the order of the æsthetic sentiments generally given in the Alaṅkāra literature. The erotic sentiment is treated first because its basic permanent emotional disposition of sex-love (rati) is common to all animals and men, very familiar to all, and agreeable to all. The comic sentiment is treated next because mirth follows love. The pathetic sentiment is treated next because it is opposed to the comic sentiment. The furious sentiment is treated next because it is principally directed towards an object (artha), even as love is principally directed towards an object. The heroic sentiment is treated next because virtue (dharma) is the predominant element in it, even as happiness (kāma) and wealth (artha) follow

[7] Ratir devādi-viṣayā vyabhicārī tathañjitaḥ bhāvaḥ proktaḥ. KPK., p. 98.

[8] BB., p. 118.

[9] Sañcāriṇaḥ pradhānāni devādi-visayā ratiḥ.
Udbuddhamātraḥ sthāyi ca bhāva ityabhidhīyate. SDP., p. 265.

[10] SDP., p. 268.

from virtue. The terrible sentiment is treated next because the heroic sentiment consists in assuring the frightened of protection. The odious sentiment is treated next because the frightened persons excite disgust in persons of holy nature. The marvellous sentiment is treated next because the odious sentiment is removed by it. The quiet sentiment is treated at last because the root of virtue is tranquillity (śama). These are the nine æsthetic sentiments recognized by Rāmacandra and Guṇacandra, which colour the mind very easily and excessively fit in with human motives. They recognize the possibility of other sentiments also, *e.g.*, the sentiment of greed (laulya) which is based on the permanent emotional disposition of desire for acquisition (gardha), the sentiment of affection (sneha) which is based on the permanent emotional disposition of tenderness (ārdratā), the sentiment of passion (vyasana) which is based on the permanent emotional disposition of attachment (āsakti), the sentiment of agony (duḥkha) based on the permanent emotional disposition of repulsion (arati), the sentiment of joy (sukha) based on the permanent emotional disposition of contentment (santoṣa). Others include them in the nine sentiments mentioned above.[11]

A brief treatment of the æsthetic sentiments (rasa) is given here. The erotic sentiment (śṛṅgāra) has love (rati) for its permanent emotional disposition (sthāyibhāva), the beloved person for its determinant cause (ālambana vibhāva), garlands, sandal paste, etc., for its excitant cause (uddīpana vibhāva), casting glances, etc., for its ensuant cause (anubhāva), and shyness, etc., for its transitory emotions (vyabhicāribhāva). The comic sentiment (hāsya) has mirth or amusement (hāsa) for its permanent emotional disposition, a person with an awkward appearance, dress and the like for its determinant cause, awkward appearance, etc., for its excitant cause, blooming of the cheeks, etc., for its ensuant cause, and fatigue, etc., for its transitory states. The pathetic sentiment (karuṇa) has grief (śoka) for its permanent emotional disposition, a dead body, etc., for its determinant cause, their qualities for its exciting cause, lamentation, crying, etc., for its ensuant cause, and misery, etc., for its transitory emotions. The furious sentiment (raudra) has anger for its permanent emotional disposition, the enemy for its determinant cause, the harm done by him for its excitant cause, self-glorification for its

[11] NDP., p. 163.

ensuant cause, and pride, etc., for its transitory emotions. The heroic sentiment (vīra) has energy (utsāha) for its permanent emotional disposition, the enemy, the learned, and the distressed for its determinant cause, the harm done by the enemy, the qualities of the learned, and the misery of the distressed for its excitant cause, redress of grievance, charity, etc., for its ensuant cause, and joy, flurry, anxiety, etc., for its transitory emotions. The terrible sentiment (bhayānaka) has fear (bhaya) for its permanent emotional disposition, dreadful beings for its determinant cause, their actions for its excitant cause, running away, etc., for its ensuant cause, and mental perplexity, etc., for its transitory emotions. The odious sentiment (bībhatsa) has disgust (jugupsā) for its permanent emotional disposition, stool, urine, etc., for its determinant cause, their stinking odour, etc., for its excitant cause, spitting, etc., for its ensuant cause, and languor, etc., for its transitory emotions. The marvellous sentiment (adbhuta) has wonder (vismaya) for its permanent emotional disposition, a person who performs wonderful actions for its determinant cause, his wonderful actions for its excitant cause, being startled, etc., for its ensuant cause, and joy, etc., as its transitory emotions.[12]

4. *The Erotic Sentiment* (*Śṛṅgārarasa*)

The erotic sentiment is based on the permanent emotional disposition (sthāyibhāva) of sex-love (rati).[13] Bharatamuni avers, that the erotic sentiment is compared to whatever is pure, holy and bright in the world. It is in the nature of the excellence of a young couple, who are its basic determinant cause. The sex-love (rati), Abhinavagupta observes, which is the basis of the erotic sentiment, is not the transitory emotion of lust, but the permanent emotional disposition of love which persists till it culminates in a completely joyful experience.[14] A favourable young man and a loving young woman are the basic determinant cause (ālambana vibhāva) of the erotic sentiment. Another's wife and a loving prostitute are not its determinant cause. The moon, sandal-paste, the spring season, pleasure gardens, the humming of bees, etc., are the excitant causes (uddīpana vibhāva) of the erotic

[12] BB., pp. 98-99.
[13] Śṛṅgāro nama rati-sthāyibhava-prabhavaḥ. NTS., p. 300.
[14] NTS., pp. 300-01; NSAG., p. 302.

sentiment. Looking at the face of the beloved person, hearing of his or her qualities, contraction of the eye-brows, sidelong glances, etc., are the ensuant cause (anubhāva) of the erotic sentiment. All transitory emotions and states except fierceness, indolence, disgust and death-like condition are its accessory states (vyabhicāribhāva). It is based on the permanent sentiment of love (rati).[15]

Bharatamuni recognizes two kinds of the erotic sentiment: (1) union or enjoyment (sambhoga), and separation (vipralambha). Dhanañjay divides the erotic sentiment into three kinds: (1) ayoga, (2) viprayoga, and (3) sambhoga. (1) Ayoga is the absence of union of a young couple who are deeply attached to each other and are possessed of one heart, as it were, owing to ill-luck, distance, or dependence on others. (2) Viprayoga is separation of a young couple who have mutual confidence and deep love for each other. Viprayoga is of two kinds: (i) māna, and (ii) pravāsa. Māna is of two kinds: (i) praṇayamāna, and (ii) īrṣyāmāna. Praṇayamāna is the breach of love which terminates in anger. Īrṣyāmāna is the anger of a woman due to jealousy brought about by her husband's love for another woman. Pravāsaviprayoga is separation of a young couple deeply attached to each other owing to the young man's departure to a foreign land on business, or owing to a curse or a sudden calamity. Sambhoga is the mutual enjoyment of a young couple deeply attached to each other by seeing, touching each other, and in other ways. It is their union which is attended with intense joy.[16]

Rāmacandra and Guṇacandra define sambhoga as enjoyment in the form of seeing, touching each other, and the like by a young couple who are attached to, and have deep love, for each other. The sentiment of union can be evoked only if the young couple reciprocate their love for each other. It cannot be excited if both of them are not deeply attached to, and crave for union with, each other. If they are deeply attached to each other, their dependence on others may stand in the way of their union and generate the sentiment of privation (vipralambha). The sentiment of union and the sentiment of privation are the two states of the erotic sentiment which is in the nature of mutual confidence

[15] SDP., p. 216; RG., p. 40.
[16] NTS., p. 303; DR., pp. 181, 184-90.

and union.[17] They are not the two varieties of the sentiment of love (śṛṅgāra) inasmuch as even in the sentiment of union there may exist the sentiment of privation, and even in the sentiment of privation there may exist the sentiment of union in imagination. The erotic sentiment is, therefore, characterized by a combination of both.[18] When the element of union is predominant in it, it is called the sentiment of union, and when the element of privation is predominant in it, it is called the sentiment of privation. When the sentiment of love attains excellence owing to the interpenetration of the sentiment of union and the sentiment of privation, it produces great transcendental wonder.[19]

Jagannātha beautifully describes the nature of the erotic sentiments of union and separation. There is the sentiment of union (saṁyoga), when the lover is united with the beloved person. There is the sentiment of separation (vipralambha), when the lover is separated from the beloved person. Union does not mean coexistence of the young couple in the same place. Similarly, separation does not mean their existence in different places. The young couple may lie in the same bed, and yet are not united with each other, when, for example, jealousy separates one from the other. Likewise, even when they exist in different places, they are not necessarily separated from each other. Though they are physically separated, they may feel the intense joy of union in their hearts. Thus, union and separation are not physical in nature; they are mental modes called union or enjoyment and separation or privation; they are in the nature of consciousness in such forms as 'I am united with my beloved' and 'I am separated from my beloved.' Union (saṁyoga) is the mental union of the young couple, and separation (viyoga) is the mental separation of them. They are mental modes which do not necessarily depend upon physical union or separation. They depend upon different transitory emotions and states excited by the determinant causes, though the same permanent emotional disposition of sex-love (rati) underlies both. Their difference depends upon their different accessory emotions and states. Union is the feeling

[17] Etau dvau avasthā-viśeṣau āsthābandhātmaka-ratiprakarṣarūpasya śṛṅgārasya. NDP., p. 164.

[18] Sambhoge'pi vipralambha-sambhāvanā-sadbhāvāt vipralambhe'pi manasā sambhogānuvedhād ubhaya-saṁvalita-svabhāvaḥ śṛṅgāraḥ. NDP., p. 164.

[19] Avasthādvayamīlana-nibandhane sātiśayaś camatkāraḥ. NDP., p. 164.

of union of two persons enamoured of each other, and separation is the feeling of their separation from each other. They are mental in nature and depend upon mental conditions.[20]

The sentiment of union is of various kinds, viz., seeing each other, kissing each other, insinuation, etc. The sentiment of privation is of four kinds: (1) māna, (2) śāpa; (3) icchā, and (4) viraha. (1) Māna (sulks) is anger due to jealousy and breach of love.[21] (2) Śāpa (curse) is the metamorphosis of the lover, though he is in a proximate place. In the *Kādambarī*, Vaiśampāyana is transformed into a parrot by Mahāśvetā. (3) Icchā is the desire of a newly married young woman dependent on her parents for union with her lover. (4) Viraha is non-approach of a young woman who has already enjoyed union with her lover, but who is engaged in some other business, even in the absence of her dependence on her parents.[22]

Viśvanātha recognizes two kinds of the erotic sentiment, viz., the sentiment of privation (vipralambha) and the sentiment of union (sambhoga). The former is the intense love which is unable to secure union with the beloved person.[22a] The latter is the sentiment of union with the beloved person—mutual enjoyment of a young couple deeply attached to each other—in the shape of seeing and touching each other and the like.[23] The former is the pain of non-attainment, while the latter is the joy of union. The sentiment of privation is of four kinds: (1) pūrvarāga, (2) māna, (3) pravāsa, and (4) karuṇa.

(1) Pūrvarāga is the foretaste of love of a young couple, who have been attached to each other (saṁrūḍha-rāga), before their union. It is the dawn of love of a young couple who have fallen in love with each other on seeing or hearing of each other, but who have not yet been able to unite with each other. They may hear of each other from messengers, bards, or friends. Or they may see each other in pictures or in dreams. In this state of privation love passes through ten stages (kāmadaśā): (1) longing

[20] RG., p. 41.

[21] Irṣyā-praṇayabhaṅgābhyām vaimanasyaṁ mānaḥ. NDP., p. 164.

[22] Sambhūta-bhogayor mātādyabhāve'pi karyāntara-vyāpṛtatayā' nanusarpaṇaṁ virahaḥ. NDP., p. 165. Ibid, pp. 164-65.

[22a] Yatra tu ratiḥ prakṛṣṭā nābhīṣṭam upaiti vipralambho' sau. SDP., p. 217.

[23] Darśana-sparśanādīni niṣevate vilāsinau.
Yatrānuraktāvanyo'nyaṁ sambhogo' yam udāhṛataḥ. SDP., p. 237.

(abhilāṣa), (2) anxiety (cintā), (3) recollection (smṛti), (4) narration of the good qualities of the beloved person (guṇakathana), (5) distress (udvega), (6) raving (sampralāpa), (7) frenzy or insanity (unmāda), (8) sickness (vyādhi), (9) perplexity (jaḍatā), and (10) death-like condition (mṛti). (1) At first, there is longing for union with the beloved person. (2) Then, there is anxiously thinking out the means for securing union with the person loved. (3) Then, there is recollection of the beloved person. (4) Then, there is speaking of the virtues of the object of love. (5) Then, there is the feeling of distress owing to separation. (6) Then, there is aimless raving owing to wandering of the mind. (7) Then, there is frenzy or temporary derangement of the mind, which consists in non-discrimination between animate and inanimate beings. (8) Then, there is sickness which is expressed in deep sighs, pallor, emanciation of the body and the like. (9) Then, there is perplexity which consists in physical and mental inertness. (10) At last, there is the death-like condition.[24]

Viśvanātha mentions three kinds of pūrvarāga, which are named fancifully after (1) the indigo (nīlīrāga), (2) the safflower (kusumbharāga), and (3) the madder (mañjiṣṭhārāga). (1) The love which has dawned upon the mind, which is not increased much, and yet which does not depart, e.g., the love of Rāma and Sītā for each other, is called the indigo love (nīlīrāga).[25] The indigo is a fast colour that stands washing. (2) The love which shines but departs, is called the safflower love (kusumbharāga). The dye of safflower fades in the washing.[26] (3) The love which does not depart, and which shines much is called the madder love.[27] The first kind of love is not very intense but steadfast. The second kind of love is very intense but fickle. The third kind of love is very intense and permanent.[28]

(2) Māna (sulks) is indignation based on love. It is of two kinds: (i) sulks arising from affection (praṇayamāna), and (ii) sulks arising from jealousy (īrṣyāmāna). (i) Praṇayamāna is the causeless anger of the lovers in spite of their profound love for each other, which is simply due to crookedness or "capricious waywardness

[24] SDP., p. 219.
[25] Na cāti śobhate yan nāpaiti prema manogatam. Taṁ nīlīrāgam ākhyānti. SDP., p. 225.
[26] Kusumbharāgaṁ tat prāhur yadapaiti ca śobhate. SDP., p. 225.
[27] Mañjiṣṭhārāgam āhus taṁ yannāpaityatiśobhate. SDP., p. 225.
[28] Ballantyne: E.T., SDP., (B.I.), Calcutta, 1875, p. 115.

of affection."[29] (ii) Irṣyāmāna is the indignation of a woman caused by her husband's attachment to another woman, which is seen, heard, or inferred by her from his talks in dreams, signs of enjoyment, and his blurting out the name of his beloved woman within her hearing. It is indignation due to jealousy.[30] The wife's indignation may be pacified by her husband by employing six expedients, e.g., conciliation (sāma), division (bheda), presents (dāna), submission (nati), disregard (upekṣā), and change of humour (rasāntara) in succession. Conciliation is affectionate language; division is winning over her female friends to his side; presents are ornaments and the like bestowed on the wife on some pretext; submission is falling at her feet. When these expedients have failed, the husband should resort to disregard for her, or eject her anger by sudden terror or joy.[31]

(3) Pravāsa is melancholy due to the departure of the husband to a foreign country on urgent business, or owing to the curse of a deity, or a confusion in the midst of which one of the lovers is separated from the other. It is expressed by sobbing, sighing, weeping, falling on the ground, dirtiness of the body and clothes, wearing a single braid etc. Squalor of the person, fever, pallor, emaciation, apathy, desolateness, supportlessness, being absorbed in the thought of the lover, frenzy, swoon, and death-like condition are the stages of love in separation. Fever is due to separation. Apathy is distaste for all things. Desolateness is the absence of attachment to all things. Supportlessness is the blankness of the mind. Absorption in the thought of the lover is seeing his vision within and without. The exile of the lover due to business is of three kinds: (i) future, (ii) present and (iii) past.[32]

(4) Karuṇavipralambha is the pain of separation felt by either of the young couple on the death of the other who may be brought back to life through the intervention of a supernatural being. The pathetic sentiment (karuṇa) is based on the permanent emotional disposition of grief (śoka), whereas the sentiment of privation (vipralambha) is based on the permanent emotional disposition of love (rati), which is inspired by the hope of enjoying reunion.[33]

[29] Dvayoḥ praṇayamānaḥ syāt pramode sumahatyapi. Premnaḥ kuṭilagāmitvāt kopo yaḥ kāraṇaṁ vinā. SDP., p. 226.

[30] Patyur anyapriyāsaṅge dṛṣṭe' thānumite śrute īrṣyāmāno bhavet strīṇām. SDP., p. 227.

[31] SDP., pp. 230.

[32] SDP., pp. 231-33.

[33] SDP., pp. 236-37.

Jagannātha maintains that when a young woman enamoured of a young man is separated from him, and conscious that the beloved person is alive, the emotion of love (rati) is the dominant emotion which is intensified by the affliction of grief. This emotion is the erotic sentiment of privation (vipralambha) because love (rati) is the dominant emotion here, and grief (śoka) is a transitory or subsidiary emotion. When a young man or a young woman is separated from his or her beloved person and conscious that the lover is dead, but believes the beloved person will somehow be brought to life by the grace of God, the emotion is the erotic sentiment of privation (vipralambha), like the sentiment of privation due to separation from the beloved person for life, since the determinant cause of the emotion is not destroyed completely. This emotion is not the pathetic sentiment (karuṇa), since the dominant emotion here is not grief but love. It is not a separate sentiment called karuṇavipralambha or the sentiment of privation based on love, as Viśvanātha erroneously maintains. This is a purely erotic sentiment (śṛṅgāra) in whcih love is the dominant emotion, and which is intensified by the subsidiary emotion of grief. Thus, Jagannātha differs from Viśvanātha on the nature of karuṇavipralambha.[34]

The question is raised how privation (vipralambha) which is by nature painful can be regarded as an æsthetic sentiment (rasa). Śārṅgadeva replies that the sentiment of privation is based on love and consequently can be developed into an æsthetic sentiment.[35] Besides, the sentiment of union and the sentiment of privation cannot be divorced from each other. Even at the time of union there may be apprehension of separation in future; so that the joy of union may be blended with the pain of separation in future. And even at the time of separation which is painful in nature, there may be the joy of expectation of future union. Thus, the pain of separation may be blended with the joy of union. Hence it is easy to relish the sentiments of union and separation which heighten the charm of each other.[36]

Some describe the following stages of love: (1) delight in

[34] RG., p. 39.
[35] Nanu duḥkhātmakaḥ kasmād vipralambho raso mataḥ.
Maivaṁ ratyanusandhānaṁ vipralambhe'pi dṛśyate.
SR., ii, p. 821.
[36] Vipralambhodbhavā śaṅkā sambhoge dustyajā dhruvam.
Itaretara-citratvād rasatvaṁ sulabhaṁ tayoḥ. SR., ii, p. 821.

seeing the beloved person (nayanaprīti), (2) attachment of the mind (cittāsaṅga), (3) desire for union (saṅkalpa), (4) disturbance of sleep (nidrāccheda), (5) emaciation of the body (tanutā), (6) aversion to all objects (viṣayanivṛtti), (7) shamelessness (trapānāsa), (8) frenzy (unmāda), (9) swoon (mūrcchā), and (10) death-like condition (mṛti).[37]

Bharatamuni mentions self-despisement, languor, apprehension, envy, fatigue, anxiety, impatience, sleep, dream, awaking, sickness, insanity, epilepsy, inactivity and death-like condition as the accessory emotions and states of the erotic sentiment of privation. Śāradātanaya mentions fainting, excitement, dejection, misery, and conjecture also as its accessory states. He mentions emaciation, sighing, immobility, trembling, shedding tears, change of colour, faltering voice, etc., as its ensuant cause. Śārṅgadeva adds remorse to Bharatamuni's list of the accessory states of the erotic sentiment of privation.[38]

Sambhoga is the sentiment of union in which a young couple deeply enamoured of each other see, touch and enjoy each other in various ways. There can be no union or enjoyment (sambhoga) if both are not deeply attached to each other. It is impossible to describe the various kinds of union in kissing, embracing and the like. Hence some sober Rhetoricists recognize only one kind of erotic sentiment. Others recognize four kinds of the sentiment of union: (1) union after the dawn of love (pūrvarāga), (2) union after sulkiness (māna), (3) union after separation due to absence (pravāsa), and (4) union after death-like condition (karuṇa). The sentiment of union is deepened by previous pain of separation. Some maintain that the sentiment of union cannot be developed without the sentiment of privation.[39]

The sentiment of union is evoked by the six seasons, the moon, the sun, their rise and settings, garlands, anointments, adornments, articles of the beloved person, residence in an excellent house, breeze, gambols in water, rambles in groves, the morning, draughts of honey, the night, hearing of, or seeing the beloved, games, sports and the like.[40] A young man and a young woman deeply attached to each other are the main determinant causes

[37] SDP., p. 224.
[38] NTS., p. 306; BPK., p. 33; SR., ii, pp. 820-21.
[39] Na vinā vipralambhena sambhogaḥ puṣṭim aśnute. SDP., p. 239. Ibid, pp. 237-38.
[40] NTS., p. 303; SDP., p. 238.

of the sentiment of love (śṛṅgāra). Poetry, songs, music, dance, danger, the spring season, fine clothes and ornaments, pictures of geese, etc., also are the determinant cause of the erotic sentiment. Brightness of the eyes and the face, smile, graceful changes of the limbs, allegations, languor, indolence, fatigue, sports, picking flowers, going to a pleasure-garden, playing in water, etc., are the ensuant cause of the erotic sentiment. It is expressed by energy (utsāha) or elation of the mind which produces brightness of the face and the eyes, flattery, bodily pain and mental agony consequent on the non-attainment of objects of desire, indignation due to jealousy and break of love, joy, flattery, glances of the eyes, knitting of the eye-brows, etc. These are the expressions of the sentiment of union (sambhoga). Sidelong glances, graceful gait, sweet words, beautiful movements of the limbs, etc., also are its expressions.

All transitory emotions except indolence, fierceness and disgust are the accessory states of the erotic sentiment of union. This is Bharatamuni's view. Rāmacandra and Guṇacandra mention the pleasant emotions of contentment, etc., as the accessory states of the sentiment of union, and include the emotion of energy (utsāha) also in them. Though energy is a permanent emotional disposition or sentiment (sthāyibhāva), yet it is an accessory emotion in the erotic sentiment of union. Energy is the elation of mind which is expressed in the beaming of the eyes and the face. Śāradātanaya regards exhilaration, fatigue, inhibition of the manifestations of other emotions, joy, pride, recollection, contentment, envy, languor, apprehension, conjecture, shamelessness, horripilation, trembling and perspiration as the accessory states of the erotic sentiment of union.[41]

5. *The Comic Sentiment (Hāsyarasa)*

The comic sentiment is based on the permanent emotional disposition (sthāyibhāva) of mirth or amusement (hāsa). The person who assumes an unnatural appearance, speaks in an unnatural voice, or performs unnatural actions is the principal determinant cause (ālambana vibhāva) of the comic sentiment, and his actions are its excitant cause (uddīpana vibhāva). It is evoked

[41] Utsāho nayana-vadana-prasādakārī cittollāsaḥ. NDP., p. 166. Ibid, pp. 165-66; NTS., pp. 305-06; SDP., p. 238; BPK., p. 33.

by the imitation of others' appearance, strange dress, displaced ornaments, etc., shamelessness, fickleness, magic, abusive language, sight of a distorted body, narration of unnatural appearance, unnatural dress, etc., disfigured limbs, awkward appearance such as lameness and the like, singing through the nose, awkward actions not fitting in with nature, country; time, age, circumstances and the like, emitting sounds by pressing the armpits, imitation of others' language, dancing in an awkward manner, etc. The comic sentiment is excited by these determinant causes (vibhāva) either in oneself or in others. Throbbing of the lips, the nose, the cheeks, blooming of the eyes, partly closing the eyes, reddening of the face, holding the sides, holding the belly, clapping the hands, contraction and expansion of the eyes, perspiration, shedding tears, etc., are the ensuant cause (anubhāva) of the sentiment of laughter. Dissimulation, indolence, dozing, sleep, dream, awaking, envy, joy, energy, wonder, languor, fatigue, fainting, apprehension, shyness, flickleness, shamelessness, perspiration, shedding tears, bristling of the hairs, etc., are the accessory emotions and states of the comic sentiment.[42]

There are six kinds of laughter: vihāsa, upahāsa, smita, hāsa, apahāsa, and atihāsa. Vihasita is well-timed laughter with blushes on the face in a sweet voice. Upahasita is laughter with the shaking of the head and the shoulders. Smita is smile in which teeth are not visible. Hasita is smile in which teeth are just visible. Upahasita is ill-timed laughter with tears in the eyes and shaking of the head and the shoulders. Atihasita is immodest laughter in a loud voice with the sides pressed with the hands. The first and the second kinds of laughter are found in persons of moderate culture. The third and the fourth kinds of laughter are found in persons of the highest culture. The fifth and the sixth kinds of laughter are found in uncultured persons. The sentiment of laughter is generally found in abundance in the inferior persons of vicious character.[43]

6. *The Pathetic Sentiment* (*Karuṇarasa*)

The pathetic sentiment is based on the permanent emotional disposition (sthāyibhāva) of grief (śoka). It is evoked by the death

[42] NTS., pp. 312-13; BPK., pp. 5, 33; RS., p. 193; DR., p. 195; SR., ii, p. 825; SDP., p. 240; NDP., p. 166.
[43] NDP., p. 167.

of dear persons who were cursed or distressed, loss of wealth, persecution, captivity, banishment, loss by theft, sudden encounter with a danger, etc. It is excited by the loss of cherished objects and the attainment of undesired objects. The objects of grief are its principal determinant cause (ālambana vibhāva). Their conditions which produce mental agony are its excitant cause (uddīpana vibhāva). Shedding tears, lamentation, dryness of the mouth, pallor, drooping of the limbs, sighing, sobbing, lapse of memory, change of voice, immobility, loss of consciousness, crying, incoherent raving, accusing bad luck, striking the body, striking the chest, throwing of the limbs, etc., are the ensuant cause (anubhāva) of the pathetic sentiment. Śārṅgadeva distinguishes between vilāpa and paridevita. The former is crying attended with praising the qualities of the deceased person, while the latter is crying attended with the realization of ill-luck in oneself or in others. Self-despisement, languor, anxiety, impatience, agitation, fainting, fatigue, fear, dejection, misery, sickness, insanity, epilepsy, terror, indolence, perplexity, illusion, sleep, recollection, death-like condition, insensibility, trembling, pallor, choked voice, shedding tears, immobility, etc., are the accessory states (vyabhicāribhāva) of the pathetic sentiment.[44]

The question is raised how the pathetic sentiment can be an æsthetic sentiment which is pleasant (sukhātmaka) in nature. The pathetic sentiment excites the permanent emotional disposition of grief, and is consequently painful in nature. If it be an æsthetic sentiment, it must be of the essence of joy, and cannot give rise to tears, etc., which are the effects of grief. If it be not an æsthetic sentiment, an appreciative connoisseur will not be induced to read poetry portraying the pathetic sentiment. The following reply is given to the question. Though the pathetic sentiment awakens the painful emotional disposition of grief, it contains an element of transcendental joy (alaukikasukha) which emerges from the sentiment of grief, its determinant and excitant causes, it ensuant cause, and its transitory emotions and states. This is the reason why appreciative spectators are induced to read poetry portraying the pathetic sentiment, or to witness a drama exhibiting it. Though the pathetic sentiment appears to be a blend of joy and grief, yet the emotion of grief

[44] NTS., p. 317; NSAG., pp. 317-19; BPK., p. 6; SR., ii, pp. 827-28; DR., p. 197; RS., p. 198; NDP., p. 167; SDP., p. 244.

is transformed into the æsthetic sentiment (rasa), because the veil which obscures the bliss of the self is broken and the supreme bliss of the self is manifested in its intensity and becomes the object of a strong desire. A spectator is induced to witness a drama embodying the pathetic sentiment because of the manifestation of the supreme joy of the self, and the absence of strong aversion to the element of grief in the sentiment of pathos. The pathetic sentiment contains a predominant element of transcendental joy (alaukikasukha) owing to the manifestation of the supreme bliss of the self, and a modicum of grief owing to the revival of the permanent emotional disposition of grief. This is the reason why spectators are induced to witness a tragedy. Further, shedding tears, etc., are either the expressions of grief which is excited by the histrionic art of the actor, or the expressions of transcendental joy which is manifested in the æsthetic sentiment of pathos. Shedding tears and the like are the expressions of grief as well as joy. Devout persons shed tears on hearing of the glories of God on account of the exuberance of joy which is excited by it. Even a trace of grief is not possible in this case. Thus, the pathetic sentiment can be an æsthetic sentiment (rasa), though it awakens the painful emotional disposition of grief.[45]

Dhanika also gives the same reply. The pathetic sentiment contains an element of joy and an element of grief (sukhaduḥkhātmaka), and yet it is essentially blissful (ānandātmaka) in nature, even as the erotic sentiment of union is pre-eminently joyful in nature, though it contains the subordinate sadistic element of pain due to scratching, beating and the like. Though the ordinary (laukika) emotion of grief is painful, the extraordinary (alaukika) æsthetic sentiment of pathos is blissful in nature. If it were painful, no one would be induced to witness a tragedy on the stage. Hence the pathetic sentiment, like the other æsthetic sentiments, is blissful in nature.[46]

The pathetic sentiment is different from the erotic sentiment of privation, because the former is based on the permanent emotional disposition of grief, while the latter is based on the sentiment of love. It has already been discussed in connection with the erotic sentiment of privation.[47]

[45] BB., pp. 99-100.
[46] DRA., pp. 175-76.
[47] SDP., p. 245.

7. *The Furious Sentiment* (*Raudrarasa*)

The furious sentiment is based on the permanent emotional disposition of anger (krodha), and is the cause of fight.[48] Bharatamuni, like McDougall, relates anger to the instinct of fight. The enemy is its principal determinant cause (ālambana vibhāva), and his actions are its excitant cause (uddīpana vibhāva). The sentiment of wrath is evoked by attack by an enraged person, reviling one's country, birth, family, learning, actions, etc., false allegations, harsh words, infliction of injury on a person, his wife or dear ones, insult, envy, striking with the fists or with a weapon, cutting with a sword, piercing with a stake, falling on a person, hostile actions, robbing one of one's kingdom or entire property, fighting, eagerness for fighting, the desire to kill, killing, persecution of a servant, captivity, loathing of the enemy, etc. Beating, throwing on the ground, persecution, cutting, piercing, taking up arms, attacking with weapons, shedding blood, striking the shoulders and the arms, striking the ground, threatening, brandishing weapons, closing the fists, dealing blows with fists, tearing with the nails, grinding the teeth, compression of the lips, pressing the palms, biting the lips, making a resolve, frowning, self-glorification, reviling, angry looks, redness of the face and the eyes, trembling, throbbing of the cheeks, quivering of the lips, perspiration, breaking the limbs of the offender, etc., are the ensuant cause (anubhāva) of the furious sentiment. Excitement, revenge, restlessness, fierceness, pride, absenc of confusion, energy, perspiration, trembling, immobility, horripilation, stammering, joy, recollection, intoxication, envy, jealousy, fatigue, stupor, shamelessness, concealment of the expressions of emotions, insanity, etc., are the accessory emotions and states (vyabhicāribhāva) of the furious sentiment. It should be noted here that energy (utsāha) which is an accessory state of the furious sentiment is a transitory emotion, but that energy which is the basis of the heroic sentiment is a permanent emotional disposition. Permanent emotional dispositions also can function as accessory states of the other æsthetic sentiments (rasa) of which they are not the basic sentiments.[49]

[48] Raudro nāma krodha-sthāyibhāvā-tmakaḥ saṁgrāmahetukaḥ. NTS., p. 319.

[49] NTS., pp. 319-21; BPK., p. 33; SDP., pp. 245-46; RS., p. 197; SR., ii, p. 830-31; NDP., pp. 167-68; RG., p. 40; DR., p. 193. Sthāyino'pi cotsāhādayo rasāntaraṁ prati vyabhicāritāṁ svīkurvanti. NDP., p. 168.

Viśvanātha distinguishes the furious sentiment from the heroic sentiment of fight (yuddhavīrarasa). In the former there is redness of the face and the eyes, while in the latter they are non-existent, though both are evokd by the enemy that is their principal determinant cause. Redness of the face and the eyes is the manifestation of anger which is a mode of inertia (tamas), but not of energy (utsāha) which is a mode of essence (sattva) of the mind. Anger is the basic sentiment of the furious sentiment, while energy is the basic sentiment of the heroic sentiment of fight.[50]

8. *The Heroic Sentiment (Vīrarasa)*

The heroic sentiment is based on the permanent emotional disposition (sthāyibhāva) of energy or courage (utsāha). The enemy and the like are its principal determinant cause (ālambana vibhāva), and their actions are its excitant cause (uddīpana vibhāva). The heroic sentiment is evoked by presence of mind, political wisdom, diplomacy, military strength consisting in infantry, cavalry, elephantry, etc., power of overcoming the enemy, capacity for fighting, power of inspiring dread in the enemy, the influence of men and money, self-restraint, heroism, valour, modesty, prowess, determination of duty, purity, delusion, absence of dejection, wonder, etc. Heroes endowed with strength, prowess, energy, liberality and armed with weapons, etc., are the determinant cause of the sentiment of heroism. Firmness, patience, heroism, making gifts, diplomacy, searching for the means, etc., are the ensuant cause (anubhāva) of the heroic sentiment. Contentment, ascertainment of duty, pride, excitement, fierceness, revengefulness, recollection, conjecture, intoxication, jealousy, awaking, impatience, bristling of the hairs of the body, perspiration, etc., are the accessory emotions and states (vyabhicāribhāva) of the sentiment of heroism.[51]

The heroic sentiment (vīrarasa) is of four kinds: (1) the heroic sentiment of liberality (dānavīra), (2) the heroic sentiment of piety (dharmavīra), (3) the heroic sentiment of fight (yuddhavīra), and (4) the heroic sentiment of compassion (dayāvīra). Paraśurāma

[50] Raktāsyanetratā cātra bhedinī yuddhavīrataḥ. SDP., p. 247. SDPJ., p. 247.

[51] NTS., pp. 324-25; NSAG., pp. 324-25; BPK., pp. 5, 33; DR., p. 191; SR., ii, p. 833; SDP., p. 248; NDP., p. 168; RG., pp. 45-51.

was famous for the first kind of heroism, Yudhiṣṭhira, for the second, Rāmacandra, for the third, and Jīmutavāhana, for the fourth. Liberality consists in giving away all possessions unconditionally. Courage or energy in making gifts is the permanent emotional disposition of the heroic sentiment of liberality. It is evoked by Brāhmaṇas, the principal determinant cause, their purity, determination and the like, the excitant cause, the gift of all property, the ensuant cause, and joy, contentment, etc., the accessory cause. Talking with a smile, smiling looks, generosity in bestowing favours, approval by words, patience in the midst of danger, exultation, mediation, negotiation for peace, exciting soldiers by reviling the enemy, consideration of merits and demerits, etc., are the ensuant cause of the heroic sentiment of liberality. Firmness, joy, ascertainment of duty, pride, recollection, etc., are the accessory states of the heroic sentiment of liberality.

The heroic sentiment of fight is evoked by the enemy to be vanquished, the principal determinant cause, and his actions, the excitant cause. The desire to fight even in the absence of help, not running away from the battle-field, assuring the frightened of protection, etc., are the ensuant cause (anubhāva) of the heroic sentiment of fight. Joy, pride, excessive delight, etc., are its accessory emotions.

The heroic sentiment of compassion is evoked by distressed persons, the principal determinant cause, and their entreaties and supplications, the excitant cause. Rescuing persons in peril, even at the cost of self-interest and life, consolatory words, firmness, etc., are the ensuant cause of this sentiment. Firmness, ascertainment of duty, etc., are its accessory states.[52]

Rāmacandra and Guṇacandra distinguish the heroic sentiment of fight from the the furious sentiment (raudra), though both involve fighting. The former is based on the permanent sentiment of energy enlightened by political wisdom, while the latter is based on non-discrimination between right and wrong, egoism and absence of political wisdom.[53]

Viśvanātha distinguishes the heroic sentiment of compassion from the sentiment of quietness (śānta). The former is full of egoism, while the latter is free from all taint of egoism. There

[52] SDP., pp. 248-52; RS., pp. 195-96; NDP., p. 168.
[53] NDP., p. 168.

is neither joy nor grief, neither love nor hatred, neither desire nor anxiety, in the latter which is the highest of all æsthetic sentiments. The former is based on the permanent sentiment of energy (utsāha), while the latter is based on the permanent sentiment of tranquillity (śama) or peace due to dispassion for objects of pleasure. The sentiment of quietness is different from the heroic sentiments of liberality and piety also for the same reasons.[54]

9. *The Terrible Sentiment* (*Bhayānakarasa*)

The terrible sentiment is based on the permanent emotional disposition (sthāyibhāva) of fear (bhaya).[55] Dreadful objects are its principal determinant cause (ālambana vibhāva), and their actions which strike terror into one's hearts are its excitant cause (uddīpana vibhāva). It is evoked by the sight of beasts with dreadful sounds, the hearing of the howling of jackals, the hooting of owls, the sight of shooting meteors, going to empty houses, forests, cemetery, or cremation ground, seeing or hearing of chastisement or captivity of one's kinsmen or relatives, offence to the spiritual guide, the elders, or the king, striking with weapons, fettering, killing, strutting about in the battle-fields, etc., which are its determinant and excitant causes. Trembling of hands and legs, contraction of the body, restlessness of the eyes, drooping of the limbs, dryness of the mouth, the lips, the throat, and the palate, palpitation of the heart, changes of the body, the face, and the eyes, fainting, immobility, horripilation, perspiration, pallor of the face, change of voice, trembling of the whole body, aimless looking, etc., are the ensuant cause (anubhāva) of the sentiment of terror. Its accessory emotions and states (vyabhicāri-bhāva) are apprehension, stupor, misery, excitement, instability, perplexity, terror, epilepsy, self-abasement, anxiety, languor, intoxication, dejection, sickness, indolence, death-like condition, trembling, horripilation, perspiration, stammering voice, pallor and inactivity, which feed, nourish and intensify it. Disgust also, which is a permanent emotional disposition, is its accessory emotion according to Viśvanātha.[56]

[54] Nirahaṅkārarūpatvād dayāvīrādir eṣa no. SDP., p. 259. *Ibid*, pp. 259-61.

[55] Bhayānako nāma bhayasthāyibhāvātmakaḥ. NTS., p. 326.

[56] NTS., pp. 326-27 ; NSAG., pp. 326-27 ; DR., p. 196 ; SR., ii, pp. 834-35 ; NDP., pp. 1 1-69 ; BPK., pp. 6, 34 ; SDP., pp. 252-53 ; RS., p. 199 ; RG., p. 55.

10. *The Odious Sentiment* (*Bībhatsarasa*)

The odious sentiment is based on the permanent emotional disposition of disgust.[57] Stinking flesh, blood, marrow, etc., are its principal determinant cause (ālambana vibhāva), and the appearance of worms in them is its excitant cause (uddīpana vibhāva). The sentiment of horror is excited by the sight or hearing of loathsome, disagreeable or undesirable objects, contemptible appearance, filthy dress, detestable actions, persons afflicted with leprosy, ugly objects, stinking odours, nauseating tastes, touching loathsome objects, unpleasant sounds, obnoxious objects, blood, pus, phlegm, stool, entrails, worms, vomiting etc.

Dhanañjaya describes three kinds of the sentiment of horror, viz., udvega, kṣobhaṇa, and ghṛṇāśuddha. The first kind is excited by objects with stinking odours, worms, vomiting, etc. The second kind is excited by entrails, blood, fat, flesh, etc. The third kind is excited by the sight of buttocks, breasts, etc., owing to dispassion. Śārṅgadeva also describes three kinds of the odious sentiment, viz., impure, pure, and very pure. When it is excited by impure things like stool and the like, it is impure (aśuddha). When it is excited by pure things like blood and the like, it is pure (śuddha). When it is excited by the sense of transitoriness and worthlessness of the world, it is very pure (atyantaśuddha).

The shrinking of the whole body, turning the face aside, contraction of the eyes, narrowing the mouth, shrinking of the limbs, covering the nose and the ears, reviling, shaking the body, closing the eyes, irregular footsteps, vomiting, spitting, palpitation of the heart, etc., are the ensuant cause (anubhāva) of the odious sentiment. Stupor, agitation, sickness, epilepsy, dejection, inconstancy, perplexity, misery, languor, fatigue, insanity, fear, ascertainment of duty, eagerness, apprehension, death-like condition, trembling, perspiration, gooseflesh, change of colour, faltering voice, shedding tears, immobility, and unconsciousness are the accessory states of the odious sentiment.[58]

13. *The Marvellous Sentiment* (*Adbhutarasa*)

The marvellous sentiment is based on the permanent emotional disposition of wonder.[59] Extraordinary objects beyond

[57] Bībhatso nāma jugupsā-sthāyibhāvātmakaḥ. NTS., p. 328.
[58] NTS., NSAG., pp. 328-29; BPK., pp. 6, 34; DR., p. 192; NDP., p. 169; SDP., p. 254; SR., ii, p. 836; STS., p. 57.
[59] Adbhuto nāma vismaya-sthāyi-bhāvātmakaḥ. NTS., p. 329.

the limits of our common experience are its principal determinant cause (ālambana vibhāva), and the greatness of their qualities is its excitant cause (uddīpana vibhāva). It is evoked by the sight of heavenly beings, the attainment of rare covetable objects, going to pleasure-gardens, temples, mansions, assembly houses, the sight of disguise, magical feats, wonderful appearance, dress and conduct, exceedingly beautiful objects, captivating beauty, words, odours, tastes, touches, dance, songs, etc. All words, actions, and craftsmanship which transcend the bounds of our ordinary experience are the determinant cause (vibhāva) of the marvellous sentiment. It is excited by strange (vicitra) or extraordinary objects, events or actions, whereas the comic sentiment is evoked by unnatural or distorted (vikṛta) appearance, actions, etc. Strange superhuman or supernatural objects excite the marvellous sentiment.

Opening the eyes widely, gazing with winkless eyes, applause, cheering, moving the hands, the face, or the fingers, waving handkerchiefs, gift of wealth, cries of joy, trembling, horripilation, perspiration, shedding tears, faltering voice, etc., are the ensuant cause (anubhāva) of the marvellous sentiment. Agitation, flurry, perplexity, joy, contentment, conjecture, pride, recollection, ascertainment, anxiety, intoxication, awaking, eagerness, perspiration, horripilation, faltering voice, inactivity, shedding tears, insensibility, etc., are the accessory states of the sentiment of wonder.[60]

14. *The Quiet Sentiment* (*Śāntarasa*)

Bharatamuni is said to define the sentiment of quietness as based on the permanent emotional disposition of desirelessness, which is the cause of liberation.[61] It is evoked by the knowledge of the reality, desire for renunciation, purity of motives and actions, etc., which are its determinant cause. Sense-restraints, moral observances, concentration of the mind on different centres of the body, meditation on the self, prayer, compassion for all creatures, etc., are its ensuant cause. Self-abasement, recollection, contentment, cleanliness, horripilation, immobility, etc., are its transitory states. The quiet sentiment is the matrix (prakṛti) of

[60] NTS., NSAG., pp. 329-30; NDP., p. 169; SR., ii, pp. 836-37; BPK., pp. 6, 33; DR., p. 195; SDP., p. 255; RS., p. 197; STS., p. 58; RG., pp. 52-53.

[61] Śānto nāma śamasthāyibhāvātmako mokṣa-pravartakaḥ. NTS., p. 332.

the other sentiments which are its modificaions (vikāra). They emerge from it and merge in it. When their causes appear, they emerge out of it, and when the former are destroyed, the latter disappear in it. It is free from pleasure and pain, joy and grief, aversion and envy, and permeated by impartiality to all. It is replete with good will for all beings, free from the clamour of the sense-organs which are completely controlled, and full of bliss owing to abiding in the self. Thus, there are nine æsthetic sentiments including the quiet sentiment.[62] The scholars opine, that this portion dealing with the quiet sentiment is an interpolation of the commentator, Abhinavagupta, who recognized the sentiment of quietness, and that Bharatamuni recognized only eight æsthetic sentiments.[63]

Abhinavagupta elaborately discusses the different views on the quiet sentiment. Some opine, that there is a distinct quiet sentiment which is based on the permanent emotional disposition of tranquillity (śama), evoked by austerities, company of yogins, etc., the determinant cause, expressed by the absence of love, anger, etc., and nourished by contentment, ascertainmnt, etc., the accessory states.

Others criticize this view thus. Tranquillity (śama) and quietness (śānta) are synonymous. Austerities, study of the scriptures, etc., are not the determinant cause of the quiet sentiment, because they are not immediately followd by quietness. If the knowledge of the reality (tattvajñāna) be said to be its determinant cause, then austerities and the like are not its determinant cause. The absence of love, anger, etc., is not its expression, bcause it is not absent from its contrary instances. The cessation of all activities is not its expression, because it cannot be acted on the stage. Further, even sleep, stupor and the like are expressed by deep inhalation and exhalation, lying and other activities. Contentment and the like are not the accessory states of the quiet sentiment, because the attainment of desired objects attended with contentment cannot exist in the quiet sentiment. Mere inactivity cannot be a means of the knowledge of the reality. Even persons who have attained integral knowledge are found to be afflicted by the distress of others, not to speak of worldly persons. Hence there is no quiet sentiment.

[62] NTS., pp. 332-35.
[63] NDP., i, preface, pp. 8-9; NTS., vi, 15.

Others criticize this view and recognize the quiet sentiment as a distinct æsthetic sentiment based on the permanent emotional disposition of self-despisement (nirveda) due to the knowledge of the reality, and not due to poverty. The other sentiments are related to wealth, happiness and virtue, the ends of life. But the quiet sentiment is related to liberation, the supreme end of life. Self-despisement due to the knowledge of the reality overcomes the other permanent emotional dispositions, and is the strongest permanent sentiment. Love, anger, grief and the like admit of various kinds, but self-despisement does not. It may be urged that those who regard self-despisement due to the knowledge of the reality as the basic permanent sentiment of the quiet sentiment, regard the knowledge of the reality as its determinant cause. But how can the cause of dispassion (vairāgya) be its determinant cause? The knowledge of the reality may be said to be its determinant cause as a means to dispassion. But that would be an unwarranted stretch of a rule. Further, self-despisement or dispassion is the knowledge that all objects are worthy of being rejected. One who has acquired dispassion exerts himself to acquire the knowledge of the reality, which brings about liberation. The knowledge of the reality does not produce dispassion. It may be argued that the persons who have acquired the knowledge of the reality are always found to have strong dispassion, as Patañjali says, "Dispassion for the guṇas—sattva, rajas and tamas and their modifications—arises from discriminative knowledge of the self". This argument is invalid, because dispassion, according to Patañjali, is the highest excellence of the knowledge of the reality. Hence dispassion or self-despisement (nirveda) due to the knowledge of the reality is not the basic permanent sentiment of the æsthetic sentiment of quietness.

It may be argued, that attachment and aversion to objects, the root cause of false knowledge, according to Akṣapāda, are pacified by the knowledge of the reality, which is, therefore, the cause of dispassion that is characterized by the destruction of faults such as attachment, aversion and delusion; and that dispassion due to the knowledge of the reality is the determinant cause of the quiet sentiment, because dispassion is nirveda. This argument is wrong because self-despisement (nirveda) is a mental mode in which there is a stream of grief, whereas dispassion (vairāgya) is the destruction of joy, grief, etc. Let dispassion itself be self-despisement. Self-despisement due to the knowledge of the reality is synonymous with tranquqillity (śama). It is better not to designate it as self-despisement. It should be called tranquillity (śama). 'Tranquillity' (śama) and 'quiet sentiment' (śāntarasa) are not the same, because the former is an ordinary (laukika) emotion or sentiment, whereas the latter is an extraordinary (alaukika) æsthetic sentiment (rasa), even as mirth (hāsa) is an ordinary emotion or sentiment, whereas the comic sentiment (hāsya) is an extraordinary æsthetic sentiment. Hence self-despisement (nirveda) is not the basic permanent sentiment of the quiet sentiment.

Others opine, that delight in the self, (ātmarati) or love of the true Self, as distinguished from self-love, egoism, or love of the ego, is the basic permanent sentiment of the quiet sentiment. Bharata mentions only eight permanent sentiments, love, mirth, etc. If there is a distinct quiet sentiment, it must be based upon one of these permanent sentiments. Hence the quiet sentiment is based upon the permanent sentiment of love of the Ātman. A person knows all objects to be modifications of prakṛti, the world as worthy of rejection, and all objects as injurious, acquires discriminative knowledge of the self, eschews all objects of enjoyment, obtains excellence of the self free from entanglements of prakṛti, and achieves liberation.

This view is wrong, because, in that case, all permanent sentiments roused by extraordinary causes and transformed into æsthetic sentiments would bring about liberation, and because, then, none of the so-called permanent sentiments would be permanent. A sentiment cannot be said to be permanent in relation to a variety of emotions which differ according as their determinant causes differ. If the permanent sentiments differ in different persons, then the æsthetic sentiments based on them will be innumerable. This objection may be obviated by assuming that there is only one æsthetic sentiment because all æsthetic sentiments result in the attainment of liberation. But, in that case, the heroic sentiment and the furious sentiment would be the same, because both are directed to the destruction of the enemy. Hence love of the Ātman cannot be the basic permanent sentiment of the quiet sentiment.

Others maintain, that love, anger, and other sentiments are the basic permanent sentiments in the quiet sentiment. This view is wrong because mental modes do not occur simultaneously, and because they conflict with one another.

What, then, is the basic permanent sentiment of the quiet sentiment? The knowledge of the reality is its permanent basis, because it is the means to liberation. The knowledge of the reality is the knowledge of the self. The self itself endowed with the pure attributes of knowledge and bliss and untainted by objects is the permanent basis of the quiet sentiment. The knowledge of the self is the permanent basis of the permanent sentiments, which emerge out of it when their specific causes appear and merge in it when they are destroyed. The quiet sentiment should be distinctly mentioned because it is relished as a distinct æsthetic sentiment. The nature of the self endowed with pure knowledge and bliss cannot be apprehended by ordinary experience, because it is manifested as tainted by some other mental modes in our empirical consciousness. Tranquillity (śama) means the intrinsic nature of the self. Love and other permanent sentiments are particular taints which are attributed to the self, though they are mental modes—the mind being constitued by sattva, rajas and tamas. Æsthetic sentiments based on them also are its empirical modes or accessory states. Hence there is a distinct quiet sentiment based on the permanent sentiment of tranquillity that is characterized by the knowledge of the self.[64] Dispassion, aversion for worldly life, etc., are its determinant cause. Reflection on the scriptures dealing with liberation, and the like are its ensuant cause. Self-despisement, ascertainment, recollection, contentment, etc., are its accessory states. The quiet sentiment is experienced as supreme knowledg and bliss characterized by transcendental joy free from all pain and misery.[65]

Mammaṭa recognizes the æsthetic sentiment of quietness which is based on the permanent emotional disposition of self-despisement.[66] Bharata placed self-despisement (nirveda) first in the list of transitory emotions just after the permanent sentiments. Mammaṭa interprets this order to mean that self-despisement is both a permanent sentiment and a transitory emotion, and that

[64] Ātmasvarūpam eva tattvajñānaṁ śamaḥ. Tattvajñānalakṣaṇasya ca sthāyinaḥ samasto' yaṁ laukikālaukika-cittavṛttikalāpo vyabhicāritām abhyeti. NSAG., p. 337.

[65] NSAG., pp. 340-41. Ibid, pp. 332-41.

[66] Nirveda-sthāyibhāvo'sti śānto'pi navamo rasaḥ. KPK., p. 96.

the æsthetic sentiment of quietness is based on the permanent sentiment of self-despisement.

Hemacandra defines the quiet sentiment as an æsthetic sentiment which is based on the permanent sentiment of tranquillity (śama) characterized by desirelessness.[67] Tranquillity is the intrinsic nature of the self which is experienced when desires for external objects of enjoyment are destroyed. When the essential nature of the self is purged of all taints of love, fear and other emotions, the self is freed from all pain and becomes supreme bliss and consciousness. Self-despisement (nirveda) is not the permanent sentiment of the quiet sentiment, because it is a transitory emotion due to poverty, and not to the knowledge of the reality. An emotion which arises from poverty partakes of the nature of grief. Liberation arises from the knowledge of the reality, but not from self-despisement. Dispassion arises from self-despisement; endeavours for the knowledge of the self arise from dispassion; the knowledge of the self arises from these endeavours; and liberation arises from the knowledge of the self. Hence self-despisement is not the permanent sentiment of the sentiment of quietness.[68] But desirelessness (śama) is its permanent sentiment.

Hemacandra avers, that the quiet sentiment is not included in the odious sentiment, though it is in the nature of disgust for objects of enjoyment, because disgust is its transitory emotion, and not its permanent sentiment, and because disgust is completely destroyed when the quiet sentiment is produced.[69]

Rāmacandra and Guṇacandra also recognize the quiet sentiment and consider desirelessness (śama) to be the permanent sentiment on which it is based. They regard self-despisement as a transitory emotion because it is not an invariable element in any æsthetic sentiment (rasa), and appears occasionally.[70]

Viśvanātha recognizes the quiet sentiment and regards tranquillity (śama) as its permanent sentiment. He calls the quiet sentiment the sentiment of the best of persons.[71] Unsubstantiality of all objects on account of their transitoriness or the nature of

[67] Tṛṣṇākṣayarūpaḥ śamaḥ sthāyibhāvaś carvaṇāṁ prāptaḥ śānto rasaḥ. KŚ., AC., p. 121.

[68] KSV., p. 121.

[69] KS., AC., pp. 123-24.

[70] Ayaṁ ca raseṣvaniyatatvāt kādācitkatvācca vyabhicārī na sthāyī. NDP., p. 177.

[71] Śāntaḥ śama-sthāyibhāva uttama-prakṛtir mataḥ. SDP., p. 256.

the infinite Self is its principal determinant cause (ālambana vibhāva). A holy hermitage, places of pilgrimage, beautiful gardens, company of saints, etc., are its excitant cause (uddīpana vibhāva). Horripilation and the like are its ensuant cause (anubhāva). Self-despisement, joy, recollection, ascertainment of the nature of reality, compassion for all creatures, etc., are its accessory states (vyabhicāribhāva)[72]

Rāmacandra and Guṇacandra mention fear of rebirth as gods, men, hellish beings, and brutes, aversion for objects of enjoyment, frequent meditation on the nature of reality—self and not self, merits and demerits, and the scriptures which propound the means to liberation, control of passions like lust, anger, greed, pride, delusion and envy, cultivation of a spirit of independence, etc., as the determinant cause of the quiet sentiment. They regard forgiveness or endurance of threats, chastisement, captivity and the like, meditation on the distinction between self and not self, fixed gaze, good will, intense joy, compassion, indifference etc., as the ensuant cause of the quiet sentiment. They regard self-despisement, ascertainment, recollection, contentment, etc., as its accessory states.[73]

Śārṅgadeva recognizes the quiet sentiment and regards it, like Abhinavagupta, as the natural condition of the self in which it renounces attachment to worldly objects and exists in its inherent bliss. It is free from the taint of external objects, devoid of the sense of difference, unperverted by love and other emotions, and manifested as the supreme bliss and consciousness of the one self.[74] Śārṅgadeva regards self-despisement arising from the knowledge of the reality as the permanent sentiment of the quiet sentiment, and joy, contentment, true knowledge, recollection, ascertainment of truth and duty, intoxication due to supreme bliss as its accessory states. Some regard śama or natural aversion to worldly objects as its permanent emotional disposition. Kumārasvāmī identifies nirveda with śama by which he means desirelessness or freedom from desires due to dispassion.[75]

Some deny the possibility of the quiet sentiment on the ground that an actor does not feel the emotion of desirelessness

[72] SDP., pp. 256-57. [73] NDP., p. 170.
[74] Parānanda-ghanaikātma-nirbhāsaḥ śānta ucyate. SR., ii, p. 838. Ibid, ii, p. 839.
[75] SR., ii, p. 838. Ibid, ii, p. 839. PR., p. 236.

(śama), which is said to be its basic permanent sentiment. Jagannātha advances the following arguments against this view. First, even if the actor does not feel the emotion of desirelessness, he can simulate its expressions and excite the quiet sentiment in an appreciative connoisseur by his acting and histrionic skill. An actor does not feel an æsthetic sentiment (rasa), which is felt by an appreciative spectator only. It is wrong to argue that an actor cannot represent the emotion of desirelessness by his acting if he does not himself feel the emotion. We find that an actor can simulate the expressions of fear, anger and the like without feeling these emotions in the least by repeated practice in the histrionic art. Similarly, he can simulate the expressions of the emotion of desirelessness without feeling the emotion himself. Secondly, it may be argued that the quiet sentiment characterized by apathy towards worldly objects cannot be excited even in an appreciative spactator in the midst of dramatic performance, songs, music and the like because they are in conflict with the sentiment. This argument is invalid, because songs, music, etc., are not in conflict with the quiet sentiment inasmuch as it is actually excited in the appreciative spectators in the presence of these things. A hypothesis is made to account for actual facts. Thirdly, thinking of worldly objects in general cannot be regarded as conflicting with the quiet sentiment, because, in that case, its determinant cause, viz., transitoriness of the world, and its excitant cause, viz., company of saints. pilgrimage and the like also, would be regarded as conflicting with it. Hence the quiet sentiment can be developed on the stage and excited by poetry and drama both, and is, therefore, a distinct æsthetic sentiment. It is based on the permanent emotional disposition of self-despisement. All phenomena of the world are its determinant cause, equality towards all beings is its ensuant cause, and ascertainment and the like are its accessory states.[76]

Udbhaṭa also recognizes the quiet sentiment as a distinct æsthetic sentiment. Indurāja also recognizes it and regards desirelessness (śama) as its basic sentiment.[77]

Some deny the possibility of the quiet sentiment, because attachment and aversion, which have been deeply rooted in our nature for ages, cannot be uprooted. Others deny its possibility,

[76] RG., p. 43.
[77] Kāvyālaṅkārasārasaṅgraha, Bombay, 1925, p. 52. Laghuvṛtti, p. 50.

because it is included in the heroic sentiment, the odious sentiment and the like, and because desirelessness (śama) which consists in the cessation of all functions cannot be represented on the stage.

Dhanañjaya maintains that self-despisement is not a permanent sentiment, because it is not developed into an æsthetic sentiment (rasa). Dhanika avers, that self-abasement is not a permanent sentiment, because it does not persist in the midst of favourable or hostile emotions. Hence they deny the possibility of developing the quiet sentiment on the stage.[78]

Śāradātanaya also does not recognize the quiet sentiment as a distinct æsthetic sentiment (rasa) based on the permanent sentiment of desirelessness (śama), because desirelessness consisting in the cessation of all mental operations cannot be acted on the stage, since it has no organic expressions.[79]

15. *The Sentiment of Parental Affection (Vatsalarasa)*

Viśanātha recognizes the sentiment of parental affection as a distinct æsthetic sentiment, because it contains a distinct element of transcendental wonder.[80] It is based on the permanent sentiment of parental affection (vatsalatāsneha). The children are its principal determinant cause (ālambana vibhāva), and their learning, heroism and other qualities and actions are its excitant cause (uddīpana vibhāva). Embracing the children, touching their body, kissing their heads, gazing at them, shedding tears of joy, bristling of the hairs of the body, etc., are its ensuant cause (anubhāva). Apprehension of evil, joy, pride, etc., are its accessory states (vyabhicāribhāva).[81]

Bain says, "Tenderness is a pleasurable emotion, variously stimulated, whose effort is to draw human beings into mutual embrace."[82] Darwin says, "As affection is a pleasurable sensation, it generally causes a gentle smile and some brightening of the eyes. A strong desire to touch the beloved person is commonly felt. We long to clasp in our arms those we tenderly love.[83]

[78] DR., p. 165, DRA., p. 166.
[79] BPK., p. 26.
[80] Sputaṁ camatkāritayā vatsalañca rasaṁ viduḥ. SDP., p. 262.
[81] SDP., p. 262.
[82] *Mental and Moral Science*, 1868, p. 239.
[83] EEMA., pp. 221-22.

16. *Is the Sentiment of Devotion (Bhaktirasa) possible?*

Some maintain that there is the æsthetic sentiment of devotion distinct from that of quietness (śāntarasa). The former is based on the permanent sentiment of love (anurāga) for God, whereas the latter is based on the permanent sentiment of dispassion (vairāgya). Love and dispassion are contrary to each other. Hence the sentiment of devotion cannot be included in the quiet sentiment. God is the principal determinant cause of the devotional sentiment; horripilation, shedding tears, etc., are its ensuant cause; joy and like are its accessory states.

Jagannātha criticizes this view. Love of a young couple for each other is a permanent sentiment, but love for God is a trasitory emotion, and cannot be developed into an æsthetic sentiment. It is a bhāva and not a rasa, as has already been explained. It may be argued that man's love for woman also is a transitory emotion (bhāva) because it is of the nature of love (rati), like love for God; or that love for God is a permanent sentiment while love of man for woman is a transitory emotion, because there is no reason disproving either of the views. Jagannātha argues that such arguments will lead to utter confusion. It may be argued similarly that love for sons also is a permanent sentiment, like love of man for woman; and that disgust, grief, etc., are pure emotions. But this is absurd. Hence there is no distinct sentiment of devotion.[84] The question will be discussed again later.

Some maintain, that reverence or devotion (bhakti), affection (sneha), and greediness (laulya) are distinct æsthetic sentiments based on the permanent sentiments of faith (śraddhā) tenderness (ārdratā), and longing (abhilāśa) respectively. Śārṅgadeva citicizes this view. Reverence and affection directed towards men are varieties of love (rati). They are transitory emotions called bhāvas and cannot be developed into æsthetic sentiments, since they are not permanent sentiments (sthāyibhāva). Love for God, sages, spiritual guide, king, or sons, etc., is regarded by Mammaṭa also as a transitory emotion (bhāva) which cannot be developed into an æsthetic sentiment (rasa). Only love of man for woman and love of woman for man are premanent sentiments. Reverence and affection of man and woman for each other may be developed into æsthetic sentiments (rasa); but they are not

[84] RG., (B.S.S.), pp. 75-76.

distinct rasas, but the erotic sentiment (śṛṅgāra) is based on the permanent sentiment of love rati). Sītā's reverence (bhakti) for Rāma is a form of love (rati); and Rāma's affection (sneha) for Sītā also is a form of love (rati). Hence there are no æsthetic sentiments of devotion and affection. Greediness (laulya) is longing for inappropriate or unattainable objects, which excites laughter. Rāvaṇa's longing for Sītā excites laughter in the audience. So greedines is not a distinct æsthetic sentiment but included in the ludicrous sentiment. Śārṅgadeva recognizes nine æsthetic sentiments including the quiet sentiment.[85]

Abhinavagupta also does not recognize the æsthetic sentiments of affection, greediness, and devotion. The æsthetic sentiment of affection (sneha) is said to be based on the permanent sentiment of tenderness (ārdratā). But affection is intense attachment (abhiṣaṅga) which is reduced to love, energy, and the like emotions. Affection of a child for the parents is reduced to fear. Affection of a young couple for each other is resolved into sex-love. Affection of a father for his children is reduced to tenderness. Abhinavagupta does not recognize the sentiment of greediness (laulya) based on the permanent sentiment of attachment to objects of pleasure, because it is resolved into mirth or love. He rejects the æsthetic sentiment of devotion (bhakti), because it is reduced to love or fear.[86]

Darwin says, "Devotion is chiefly expressed by the face being directed towards the heavens, with the eye-balls upturned. A humble kneeling posture, with the hands upturned and palms joined, appears to us, from long habit, a gesture so appropriate to devotion, that it might be thought to be innate."[87] But Darwin does not regard them as innate or truly expressive actions. Wedgwood suggests that the attitude is one of slavish subjection.[88]

There are seven tones (svara): (1) ṣaḍja, (2) ṛṣabha, (3) gāndhāra, (4) madhyama, (5) pañcama, (6) dhaivata, and (7) niṣāda. Nārada maintains that these svaras have emotional values. The marvellous and the heroic sentiments are excited by ṣaḍja; the furious sentiment, by ṛṣabha; the quiet sentiment, by gāndhāra; the ludicrous sentiment, by madhyama; the erotic

[85] SR., ii, pp. 839-40.
[86] NSAG., p. 341.
[87] EEMA., pp. 227-28.
[88] Ibid, p. 228.

sentiment, by pañcama; the odious sentiment, by dhaivata; the pathetic sentiment, by niṣāda. Thus, æsthetic sentiments (rasa) are excited by seven svaras.[89]

17. *Are there Painful Æsthetic Sentiments?*

Mammaṭa regards æsthetic sentiments (rasa) as similar to the experience of Brahman which is blissful in nature. Viśvanātha also regards æsthetic enjoyment as one, indivisible, self-manifest, conscious and blissful, and similar but inferior to the immediate experience of Brahman.[90] But Rāmacandra and Guṇacandra divide æsthetic sentiments into two classes, viz., pleasant and painful.[91] The erotic sentiment, the comic sentiment, the heroic sentiment, the marvellous sentiment, and the quiet sentiment, which are evoked by beneficial determinant causes, are pleasant in nature. The pathetic sentiment, the furious sentiment, the odious sentiment, and the terrible sentiment, which are evoked by harmful determinant causes are painful in nature.[92] Some opine, that all æsthetic sentiments are pleasant in nature. Rāmacandra and Guṇacandra urge that this view contradicts our experience. The sentiments of terror, horror, pathos and fury produce distress (kleśa) in the persons experiencing them, and they produce pain in the appreciative spectators of a drama. They could not afflict them, if they were in the nature of the experience of pleasure (sukhāsvāda). But why do persons go to witness tragedies which evoke the pathetic sentiment which is painful in nature? Rāmacandra and Guṇacandra reply that even the painful sentiments evoke the marvellous sentiment (camatkāra) when the direct experience of the æsthetic sentiments has ceased, because the power of the poet and the histrionic skill of the actor produce a vivid picture of the actual realities that are represented on the stage. The spectators are deluded by the marvellous sentiment generated by the power of the poet and the actor, which produces a thrill of joy in them, into the belief that the painful æsthetic sentiments of pathos and the like also are in the nature

[89] Saṅgītamakaranda (G.O.S.), 1920, p. 2.

[90] Brahmāsvādam iva anubhāvayan. KPK., p. 74. Akhaṇḍa-svaprakāśānanda-cinmayaḥ bhramāsvāda-sahodaraḥ rasaḥ. SDP., p. 71.

[91] Sukha-duḥkhātmako rasaḥ. NDP., p. 158.

[92] Iṣṭa-vibhāvadi-prathita-svarūpa-sampattayaḥ śṛṅgāra-hāsya-vīrādbhuta-śāntāḥ sukhātmānaḥ. Aniṣṭa-vibhāvādyupanītātmānaḥ karuṇa-raudra-bībhatsa-bhayānakāḥ duḥkhātmānaḥ. NDP., p. 159.

of supreme joy (paramānanda). They go to witness tragedies in greed of the experience of this joy of the marvellous.[93]

The actors evoke æsthetic sentiments (rasa) in the minds of the appreciative spectators by their histrionic art. But do they feel the same æsthetic sentiments which they call forth in the spectators? Dhanañjaya opines, that the actors may feel the same æsthetic sentiments in their own minds, which they evoke in the minds of the spectators; but that they do not feel the ordinary (laukika) emotions of love, mirth, grief and the like, but the extraordinary (alaukika) æsthetic sentiments (rasa) corresponding to them.[94] Rāmacandra and Guṇacandra also are of the same view. It is wrong to hold, they aver, that the actors never feel the æsthetic sentiments which they try to evoke in the minds of the audience. They argue that, the actors sometimes feel the æsthetic sentiments in trying to evoke them in the audience, even as public women sometimes actually feel the emotion of love which they simulate to please others in greed of money, and as singers sometimes feel intense joy while singing to please others by their songs.[95]

18. *The Causal Relation, Conflct and Harmony of the Æsthetic Sentiments* (*Rasa*)

Rāmacandra and Guṇacandra opine, that among the æsthetic sentiments some are related to each other as cause and effect. For example, the heroic sentiment (vīra) produces the sentiment of wonder (adbhuta); the strength of a hero excites wonder in the people. The heroic sentiment generates the sentiment of love (śṛṅgāra); Arjuna's heroism excited love in Draupadī. The furious (raudra) sentiment is expressed by chastisement, imprisonment, killing, etc., which give rise to the sentiments of pathos (karuṇa) and terror (bhayānaka). Further, all sentiments excite similar sentiments in others. The sight of a person with the erotic sentiment (śṛṇgāra) excites the sentiment of love in others. The sight of a person with the comic sentiment (hāsya) excites the sentiment of laughter in others. All sentiments having for their

[93] Anenaiva sarvāṅgāhlādakena kavinaṭaśaktijanmanā camatkāreṇa vipralabdhāḥ paramānandarūpatāṁ duḥkhātmakeṣu api karuṇādiṣu sumedhasaḥ pratijānate. NDP., p. 159.

[94] DR., DRA., p. 174.

[95] NDP., p. 160.

determinant causes improper objects excite the sentiment of laughter. Rāvaṇa's immoral sentiment of love for Sītā, an improper object, excites the ludicrous sentiment in honest persons. Even the improper comic sentiment excites the sentiment of laughter.[96]

There is conflict (virodha) among some æsthetic sentiments (rasa), and harmony (avirodha) among others. Viśvanātha gives the following account of the conflict of the æsthetic sentiments. The erotic sentiment is in conflict with the pathetic sentiment, the odious sentiment, the furious sentiment, the heroic sentiment, and the terrible sentiment. The comic sentiment is in conflict with the terrible sentiment and the pathetic sentiment. The pathetic sentiment is in conflict with the comic sentiment and the erotic sentiment. The furious sentiment is in conflict with the comic sentiment, the erotic sentiment, and the terrible sentiment. The heroic sentiment is in conflict with the terrible sentiment and the quiet sentiment. The terrible or fearful sentiment is in conflict with the erotic sentiment, the heroic sentiment, the furious sentiment, the comic sentiment, and the quiet sentiment. The odious or horrible sentiment is in conflict with the erotic sentiment. The quiet sentiment is in conflict with the heroic sentiment, the erotic sentiment, the furious sentiment, the comic sentiment, and the terrible sentiment.[97]

Jagannātha makes a very significant observation. There can be no conflict among the æsthetic sentiments, since they do not exist in the mind of the hero but in the mind of the connoisseur. But there can be conflict among emotions in a person's mind. Further, there can be no conflict among the corresponding æsthetic sentiments, because they are all characterized by transcendental joy. By the so-called conflict of æsthetic sentiments we mean conflict of the corresponding permanent sentiments; and by the so-called harmony of æsthetic sentiments we mean harmony of the corresponding permanent sentiments.[98] Jagannātha gives the following account of conflict and harmony among the permanent sentiments. Love is in conflict with

[96] NDP., p. 185.
[97] SDP., p. 263.
[98] Rasa-padena tadupādhiḥ sthāyibhāvo gṛhyate, rasasya sāmājikavṛttitvena nāyakādyavṛttitvāt, advitīyānandamayatvena virodhāsambhavācca. RG., p. 58.

disgust and grief. Energy or courage is in conflict with fear. Tranquillity is in conflict with anger and love.

Kallinātha gives the following account of conflict among the æsthetic sentiments. The erotic sentiment is in conflict with the odious sentiment; the heroic sentiment, with the fearful sentiment; the furious sentiment, with the pathetic sentiment; the marvellous sentiment, with the ludicrous sentiment; the odious sentiment, with the erotic sentiment; the fearful sentiment; with the heroic sentiment; the pathetic sentiment, with the furious sentiment; the ludicrous sentiment, with the marvellous sentiment; and the quiet sentiment, with the erotic sentiment, and seven other sentiments.[99]

There is harmony, Jagannātha avers, among the following permanent sentiments. Energy or courage is in harmony with love, anger and wonder. Love is in accord with mirth and wonder.[100]

Rāmacandra and Guṇacandra observe, that there is conflict between two independent and equally strong contrary æsthetic sentiments which abide in the same hero together or in quick succession.[101] There is no conflict between two contrary æsthetic sentiments of unequal strength in the same hero, or between two contrary æsthetic sentiments of equal strength abiding in two heroes. There is no conflict between the heroic sentiment in one hero and the fearful sentiment in another hero, though they are of equal strength. There is no conflict between two contrary æsthetic sentiments, if another æsthetic sentiment in harmony with the first intervenes between them.[102]

[99] Kalānidhi on SR., ii, p. 856.
[100] RG., p. 57.
[101] Ekatra svairiṇos tulyaśaktyor yoge viruddhatā. NDP., p. 171.
[102] NDP., pp. 171-73.

Chapter XIII

EMOTIONS DERIVED FROM LOVE

1. *The Causes and Kinds of Nascent Love (Rati)*

In this chapter we shall discuss the various kinds of love, the stages of love, and the emotions derived from love as described by Rūpa Goswāmī (1600 A.D.) in *Ujjvalanīlamaṇi*. Nascent love (rati) is a permanent emotional disposition or sentiment (sthāyibhāva) which is the basis of the erotic sentiment. Sex-love between a young couple is reciprocal.[1] It is evoked by the following causes: (1) expression (abhiyoga), (2) object (viṣaya), (3) relation (sambandha), (4) the sense of ownness (abhimāna), (5) objects especially connected with the lover (tadīyaviśeṣa), (6) resemblance (upamā), and (7) nature (svabhāva). (1) Abhiyoga is the expression of one's sentiment of love (bhāvavyakti) by oneself or by another. (2) Sound, touch, odour, form, taste, etc., are called objects. The lover's voice or the sound of his flute excites the love of the beloved woman. His touch excites her love. The odour of his garland evokes her love. His beauty excites her love. (3) The exuberance of the qualities of beauty, high birth, prowess, excellence of character, etc., is called relation. (4) The knowledge that the lover is one's very own (abhimāna) excites the sentiment of love. The feeling of ownness (mamatā) is the essence of abhimāna, which is deep and pristine. It excites love without depending on beauty, high birth, prowess, and other qualities of the lover. (5) The objects which have special connection with him (tadīya viśeṣa) excite love in the loving woman. The footprints of the lover, the place frequently visited by him, his dear friends, etc., excite love in the beloved woman. (6) If one object has some resemblance to another object, the former is called resemblance (upamā) of the latter. A milkmaid of Vṛndāvana feels love for Kṛṣṇa at the sight of fresh dark clouds which resemble him in colour. She sees a rainbow in the clouds and remembers the peacock feathers on Kṛṣṇa's crest. She sees a flash of lightning

[1] UNM., p. 652; ANC., p. 652.

in the clouds and remembers Kṛṣṇa wearing a yellow cloth. (7) Spontaneity (svabhāva) is the love which does not depend upon any extraneous causes, but which emerges of itself.[2] It is of two kinds: (1) nature (nisarga), and (2) essence (svarūpa). (1) A mass of subconscious impressions produced by the repeated practice of deep meditation on the excellences of the lover during many births is called innate nature (nisarga) or congenital love.[3] It is roused to consciousness by the hearing of beauty and other excellencess of the lover. But the contribution of these determinant causes is insignificant. Congenital love spontaneously wells up from within owing to the prenatal impressions. It is not determined by the lover's beauty and other excellences or by his attitude towards the beloved woman. (2) An unproduced and self-generating entity which excites nascent love is called the essence (svarūpa).[4] The milkmaid's love for Kṛṣṇa is innate, eternal, and self-generating. The essence (svarupa) is of three kinds: (*i*) inherent in Kṛṣṇa (kṛṣṇaniṣṭha), (*ii*) inherent in the milkmaids (lalanāniṣṭha), and (*iii*) inherent in both (ubhayaniṣṭha). (*i*) The essence inherent in Kṛṣṇa is easily attainable by all persons except those who are of a devilish nature. (*ii*) The essence inherent in the milkmaids quickly excites deep love for Kṛṣṇa in those milkmaids who never saw him or heard of him before. (*iii*) The essence inherent in both Kṛṣṇa and the milkmaids excites love in both at the same time independently of any extraneous conditions. This kind of innate love inherent in both is different from the innate love inherent in the milkmaids; for the former excites nascent love in all good persons, and the latter excites love in the other milkmaids who never saw him or heard of him before, whereas the innate love inherent in both at once melts the hearts of the milkmaids and manifests the quality of melting their hearts in Kṛṣṇa.[5]

Nascent love (rati) is of three kinds: (1) ordinary (sādharaṇī), (2) becoming (samañjasā), and (3) powerful (samarthā).

[2] Bahirhetvanapeksī tu svabhāḥ. UNM., p. 671.

[3] Nisargaḥ sudṛḍhābhyāsajanyaḥ saṁskāraḥ. UNM., p. 672. LR., p. 672.

[4] Ajanyas tu svataḥsiddhaḥ svarūpaṁ bhāva iṣyate. UNM., p. 674.

[5] UNM., Sthāyibhāva, 1-2, 10, 12, 14-16, 19-20, 23-24, 26-27, pp. 652-78, LR., ANC., pp. 652-78; *Kṛṣṇa of Vṛndāvana*, Dacca, 1927, pp. 353-62. Sajjanamātra-ratidāyakatvaṁ kṛṣṇaniṣṭhaṁ svarūpam, adṛṣṭāśrutasyāpi kṛṣṇasya sphūrtimattvaṁ lalanāniṣṭhaṁ svarūpaṁ śrīkṛṣṇadarśanamātra-drautyātiśayavattvaṁ gopīkṣobhātiśayakāritvañceti dvayam ubhayaniṣṭham. ANC., p. 679.

(1) The kind of nascent love which does not attain great intensity, and which is often evoked at the sight of the lover and caused by a craving for enjoyment is called ordinary. It is manifestly caused by a craving for enjoyment because it does not attain much intensity. If the desire for enjoyment decreases, the nascent love also decreases. Hence craving for enjoyment is the cause of this kind of nascent love, and consequently it is called ordinary (sādhāraṇī).[6]

(2) The kind of intense nascent love which is evoked by hearing of the excellences of the lover, which generates a false sense of wifehood, and which sometimes manifests a craving for enjoyment, is called becoming (samañjasā).[7] In the ordinary nascent love the craving for enjoyment is always manifest as a separate entity, whereas in becoming nascent love it is manifest at times and latent in it at other times. Ordinary nascent love does not become very intense, while seemly nascent love attains great intensity.

(3) The nascent love in which the craving for enjoyment is more prominent than it is in the ordinary and the becoming nascent love, and in which there is identity of love in the lover and the beloved woman both, is called powerful (samarthā).[8] Powerful nascent love is the most intense of the three kinds of love (rati). It becomes so intense that it makes the beloved woman forget her rank, virtue, piety, patience, modesty and the like, and makes her unaffected by any other emotion.[9] The milkmaids of Vṛndāvana entertained this kind of powerful nascent love for Kṛṣṇa, and all their voluntary actions were inspired by holy love for him, and aimed at his happiness only.[10] Their love was pure because it did not aim at their own sentient pleasure.

Enjoyment is of two kinds. The first kind consists in the gratification of one's sense-organs by the beloved person. The second kind consists in the concentration of thought on gratifying the sense-organs of the beloved person. The first kind is lust

[6] Asāndratvād rater asyāḥ sambhogecchā vibhidyate. UNM., p. 682. Ibid, LR., pp. 682-83.
[7] Kvacid bhedita-sambhoga-tṛṣṇā sāndrā samañjasā. UNM., p. 683.
[8] Ratyā tādātmyam āpannā sā samartheti bhaṇyate. UNM., p. 687.
[9] Samarthā sarva-vismāri-gandhā sāndratamā matā. UNM., p. 687. ANC., p. 687.
[10] Asyāṁ kṛṣṇa-saukhyārtham eva kevalam udyamaḥ. UNM., p. 689. Kṛṣṇa-saukhyārtha-mātrodyamatvād asyā rateḥ śuddhatvam. LR., p. 689.

(kāma) because it seeks one's own pleasure. The second kind is holy love (rati) because it seeks the pleasure of the beloved person.[11] Jīva Goswāmī makes this distinction between lust (kāma) and love (rati). Kṛṣṇadāsa Kavirāja also distinguishes between them in a similar manner. They are contradictory to each other because they have contradictory characteristics. First, lust seeks the gratification of one's own sense-organs (ātmendriya-prīti), whereas love seeks the gratification of Kṛṣṇa's sense-organs (kṛṣṇendriyaprīti). Lust seeks egoistic pleasure, while love seeks altruistic happiness. Secondly, lust is momentary, while love is abiding. Thirdly, lust is blind and dark, while love is transparent and bright. The milkmaids abandon social, moral, and religious codes of conduct, do not minister to their bodily needs, relinquish their own pleasures, and serve Kṛṣṇa for the sake of his delight only. Their love for him is transcendent attachment (anurāga) which is spotless and pure (śuddha). Fourthly, the milkmaids' joy at the sight of Kṛṣṇa is infinitely greater than his joy at the sight of them. They feel extremely happy because Kṛṣṇa becomes happy when he sees them. Their happiness nourishes, strengthens and intensifies Kṛṣṇa's happiness. Fifthly, the milkmaid's love enhances the sweet graces (mādhurya) of Kṛṣṇa and is gratified thereby. The abode (āśraya) of love (prema) is filled with joy when the object (viṣaya) of love is filled with joy. The milkmaids are the abode of love; Kṛṣṇa is the object of their love. If they aim at their own joy of love, it interferes with their joy of serving Kṛṣṇa, and consequently they spurn it. Unconditional love (nirupādhi prema) always delights in the happiness of its object, and not in that of its abode. Lastly, pure devotion is desireless; it does not desire even liberation; it desires only service of Kṛṣṇa with unconditional love. Hence the milkmaids' love for Kṛṣṇa is natural and spontaneous and free from the taint of lust—untainted, radiant and pure like pure gold. Rādhā is the most excellent, the most beatutiful, the most accomplished, the most fortunate, and the most loving. The other milkmaids are the instruments of the increase of the joy (rasa) of Kṛṣṇa's love-games with Rādhā. She is the most beloved of Kṛṣṇa, the cherished object of his supreme love, without whom the other milkmaids are not the causes of his happiness.

[11] Pūrvecchā kāmaḥ svahitonmukhatvāt. Uttarecchā tu ratiḥ priyajana-hitonmukhatvāt. LR., p. 686. CCA., BK. I, Ch. IV.

2. *The Stages and Variants of Ardent Love (Prema)*

The powerful nascent love between a young couple which binds their hearts together, and which is never destroyed even in the presence of the causes of its destruction, is called ardent love (premā).[12] When nascent love (rati) becomes so intense that it cannot be affected by any other sentiment, it becomes ardent love (premā). Nascent love (rati) gradually develops into (1) ardent love (premā), (2) affection (sneha), (3) sulks (māna), (4) intimacy (praṇaya), (5) attachment (rāga), (6) transcendent attachment (anurāga), and (7) transcendental love (bhāva). These are called ardent love (premā) because they are its derivatives.

(1) Ardent love (premā) is of three kinds: (*i*) mature, (*ii*) moderate, and (*iii*) inferior. (*i*) Ardent love is mature (prauḍha) when the lover's heart is afflicted by the thought that the beloved woman will feel mental agony because of his unavoidable delay in meeting with her without knowing the state of his mind. (*ii*) Ardent love is moderate (madhyama) when the lover can cherish the thought of another beloved woman in the course of enjoying union with a beloved woman. (*iii*) Ardent love is inferior (manda) when it neither shows regard to nor disregards another beloved woman in spite of the utmost familiarity. These are the three grades of the lover's ardent love.

A beloved woman's ardent love also has three stages. (*i*) Her ardent love is mature (prauḍha) when it cannot bear separation in the least from the lover. (*ii*) Her ardent love is moderate (madhyama) when it can bear separation with a great difficulty. (*iii*) Her ardent love is inferior (manda) when it disappears at times from her heart.[13]

(2) When ardent love reaches its acme of excellence, manifests the apprehension of its object, and melts the heart, it is called affection (sneha). When such affection dawns on the mind, it is never satisfied with the sight of the lover.[14] The melting of the heart (manodrava) is of three kinds, inferior, moderate, and strong according as it is caused by contact with

[12] Sarvathā dhvaṁsarahitaṁ satyapi dhvaṁsakāraṇe.
Yadbhāvabandhanaṁ yūnoḥ sa premā parikīrtitaḥ.
UNM., p. 694.

[13] UNM., sthāyibhāva, 44, 48-50, 52, 53, 55; pp. 692-704.

[14] Āruhya paramāṁ kāṣṭhāṁ premā ciddīpadīpanaḥ.
Hṛdayaṁ drāvayanneṣa sneha ityabhidhīyate.
UNM., sthāyibhāva, 57; p. 705. Ibid, p. 707.

the lover's body, at the sight of him, and by hearing about him. In affection there are greater melting of the heart, a more intense yearning for the vision of the lover, and a deeper apprehension of him in the heart than in ardent love.

Affection is of two kinds: (1) melted-butter-like affection (ghṛtasneha), and (2) honey-like affection (madhusneha).

(1) When affection is full of mutual excessive adoration, it is called melted-butter-like affection. It is not savoury in itself, but it becomes very savoury when it is mixed with some other emotion. It is congealed through the cooling influence of mutual adoration. It is called melted-butter-like affection because it resembles melted butter, which is not savoury in itself, but which becomes savoury when it is mixed with some other ingredient, and which is congealed by cold temperature.[15]

(2) When affection is marked by an excess of the sense of 'mineness' in the object of love, i.e., the sense that 'thou art mine—mine alone', it is called honey-like affection. It is so called because it resembles honey. It is sweet in itself, contains various relishes (rasa) in a subtle form, intoxicates one with a thrill of joy, and warms the body. Honey is sweet in itself, and does not require the assistance of any other ingredient to make it sweet; it contains the juices of various kinds of flowers, intoxicates one who drinks it, warms one's body, and always remains in a liquid state.[16] The sense 'I am thine' marks melted-butter-like affection, whereas the sense 'thou art mine' marks honey-like affection.[17]

(3) When affection assumes counterfeit hostility and makes the lover experience new sweetness of the beloved person, it is called sulks (māna). New sweetness is what was never experienced before. Hostility is assumed indignation. Crookedness is assumed by the beloved woman to conceal her real affection or melting of the heart for the lover.[18]

[15] Ātyantikādaramayaḥ sneho ghṛtam itīryate.
Bhāvāntarānvito gacchan svādodrekaṁ na tu svayam.
Ibid, pp. 710-11.

[16] Madīyatvātiśayabhāk priye sneho bhaven madhu.
Svayaṁprakaṭamādhuryo nānārasasamāhṛtiḥ.
Ibid, p. 714.

[17] Tadīyatāmayo ghṛtasnehaḥ, madīyatāmayo madhusnehaḥ. ANC., p. 714.

[18] Snehastūtkṛṣṭatāvāptyā mādhuryaṁ mānayan navam.
Yo dhārayatyadākṣiṇyaṁ sa māna iti kīrtyate.
UNM., p. 716. LR., p. 716.

Sulks are of two kinds: (*i*) dignified (udātta) and (2) graceful (lalita). Melted-butter-like affection is transformed into dignified sulks; and honey-like affection is modified into graceful sulks. Dignified sulks (udātta māna) are of two kinds: (*i*) dākṣiṇya, and (*ii*) vāmyagandha. In the former melted-butter-like affection assumes incomprehensible sulkiness and gravity of appearance to conceal real emotions in the mind. In the latter melted-butter-like affection manifests a little indignation in external appearance and assumes an unfavourable attitude to conceal the melting of the heart. Both these kinds of sulks are dignified (udātta māna). When honey-like affection assumes sulkiness which is experienced independently as a modification of the heart's melting, the sulks are called graceful (lalita māna).[19]

(4) When sulks attain the state of trust, they develop into intimacy (praṇaya).[20] Trust is confidence or absence of reverence due to the feeling of identity of one's body, life, mind, intellect, clothes and the like with those of the beloved person. Trust is the essence of intimacy.[21] Trust is of two kinds: (*i*) maitra, and (*ii*) sakhya. (*i*) Maitra is non-intimate friendship or trust mingled with modesty.[22] (*ii*) Sakhya is intimate friendship or trust free from fear, which brings the beloved person under one's control.[23]

There is mutual causation of intimacy and sulks. Sometimes affection is transformed into intimacy which is modified into sulks. Sometimes affection is transformed into sulks which are modified into intimacy.[24]

Dignified sulks (udātta-māna) blended harmoniously with non-intimate friendship (maitra) are called extreme friendship (sumaitra). Graceful sulks (lalita-māna) blended harmoniously with intimate friendship (sakhya) are called extreme intimacy (susakhya).[25]

(5) When intimacy attains great excellence in which extreme pain is experienced as great pleasure, it is called passionate

[19] UNM., pp. 716-17; ANC., pp. 717-18. UNM., pp. 720-21.

[20] Māno dadhāno visrambhaṁ praṇayaḥ procyate budhaiḥ. UNM., p. 725.

[21] UNM., p. 726. Visrambho viśvāśaḥ sambhrama-rāhityaṁ tacca svaprāṇa-mono-buddhi-deha-paricchadādibhiḥ kānta-prāṇa-mano-buddhyāder aikya-bhāvana-janyam. ANC., p. 725.

[22] Maitraṁ visrambho vinayānvitaḥ. UNM., p. 726.

[23] Visrambhaḥ sādhvasonmuktaḥ sakhyaṁ svavaśatāmayaḥ. UNM., p. 728.

[24] Kārya-kāraṇatā'nyonyam ataḥ praṇaya-mānayoḥ. UNM., p. 731.

[25] UNM., p. 731.

attachment (rāga). In it the cause of pain is experienced as the cause of pleasure, and the cause of pleasure also is experienced as the cause of pain.[26] Passionate attachment is of two kinds: (1) blueness (nīlimā), and (2) redness (raktimā). Blueness is of two kinds: (i) blue passionate attachment (nīlīrāga), and (ii) green passionate attachment (śyāmārāga). (i) The passionate attachment which is not destroyed, which does not shine very much outwardly, and which veils the transitory emotions attached to itself, is called blue passionate attachment.[27] (ii) The passionate attachment which is slightly tinged with timidity, which is slightly more pronounced than blue passionate attachment, and which takes a long time to develop itself, is called green passionate attachment.[28]

Redness (raktimā) also is of two kinds: (i) safflower passionate attachment (kusumbharāga), and (ii) madder passionate attachment (mañjiṣṭhārāga). (i) The passionate attachment which colours the mind very quickly, and which shines very much by manifesting the beauty of other kinds of attachment, is called the safflower passionate attachment.[29] The dye made from safflower is not naturally fast, but it becomes so when it is mixed with some other mordant substance. Similarly safflower passionate attachment is not naturally constant, but it is found to be constant in Shyāmalā and other milkmaids because of their association with Rādhā's campanions who cherish madder passionate attachment for Kṛṣṇa. (ii) The passionate attachment which is never destroyed, which does not depend upon other kinds of passionate attachment, and which constantly shines by its intrinsic quality, is called the madder passionate attachment. Rādhā and Kṛṣṇa cherished this kind of attachment for each other.[30] The madder dye does not fade on washing it with water.

[26] Duḥkham apyadhikaṁ citte sukhatvenaiva vyajyate.
Yatas tu praṇayotkarṣāt sa rāga iti kīrtyate.
UNM., p. 736. ANC., p. 737.

[27] Vyaya-sambhāvanā-hīno bahirnātiprakāśavān.
Svalagnabhāvāvaraṇo nīlīrāgaḥ satāṁ mataḥ.
Ibid, 740.

[28] Bhīrutauṣadhisekādir ādyāt kiñcit prakāśabhāk.
Yaś cireṇaiva sādhyaḥ syāt sa shyāmārāga ucyate.
UNM., pp. 742-43.

[29] Kusumbharāgaḥ sa jñeyo yaś citte sajjati drutam.
Anyarāgaccavivyañjī śobhate ca yathocitam.
UNM., pp. 744-45, ANC., p. 746.

[30] Ahāryo' nanyasāpekṣo yaḥ kāntyā vardhate sadā.
Bhavenmāñjiṣṭharāgo'sau rādhāmādhavayor yathā.
UNM., p. 747. ANC., p. 747.

Similarly the madder passionate attachment is not affected by its transitory emotions. It is self-existent (svataḥsiddha) and independent of other emotions. It always increases in brilliance owing to its intrinsic quality. It is not limited in brilliance like the safflower passionate attachment.

(6) The passionate attachment which grows newer every moment, and which makes the beloved person, who is always experienced, appear ever newer, is called transcendent attachment (anurāga).[31] Though Rādhā saw Kṛṣṇa many a time before, she caught a vision of him on Govardhana and beheld in him exquisite beauty. It was so exquisite that her eyes were powerless to perceive even at atom of the matchless beauty that shone forth in the tiniest part of his body. This was due to her deep yearning for him, which was transcendent attachment. Mutual submissiveness (parasparavaśībhāva), distraction of love (premavaicittya), strong desire to be born among inanimate beings, and a vivid manifestation of the lover even in separation are found in transcendent attachment. Mutual submissiveness is found in ardent love (premā), etc., but it is more prominent in transcendent attachment. In ardent love, etc., submissiveness is more prominent in the lover, while in the beloved woman it is toned down by shyness, dissimulation and the like. But in transcendental attachment there is no room for dissimulation, pride, envy, etc., in her owing to her intensity of longing, and, consequently, her submissiveness also is prominent in it. Hence in transcendent attachment mutual submissiveness is fully manifested both in the lover and in the beloved woman.

Strong desire to be born among inanimate beings is found in transcendent attachment. Rādhā once expressed a strong desire to be born as a bamboo, because the bamboo wherefrom Kṛṣṇa's reed was made had performed arduous austerities in its previous births in order to be played upon by him.

The manifestation of the lover is present even in nascent love (rati). But in transcendent attachment there is a vivid manifestation of the lover in ever-increasing charms. When Kṛṣṇa left Vṛndāvana for Mathurā, the vision of Kṛṣṇa flashed forth before Rādhās mind's eye here, there and everywhere. This

[31] Sadānubhūtamapi yaḥ kuryānnavanavaṁ priyam.
Rāgo bhavannavanavaḥ so'nurāga itīryate.
UNM., p. 753. ANC., pp. 753, 757.

manifestation was so vivid that it appeared as his actual presence. The distraction of love will be discussed later.

(7) When transcendent attachment attains the state of mere self-awareness through supreme excellence, is manifested outwardly in abundant spontaneous organic expressions, and acts upon all kindred persons who are present and cherish the same sentiment, it is called transcendent love (bhāva).[32] It has three characteristics: (1) it is distinctly experienced by itself; (2) it is fully manifested in the body in the form of many spontaneous organic expressions; (3) it acts upon all persons who are present and have transcendent attachment (anurāga). (1) When a milkmaid of Vṛndāvana becomes absorbed in the experience of the relish of Kṛṣṇa's sweetness, she forgets herself as the subject of the experience and Kṛṣṇa as its object and knows her experience only. In this state her transcendental attachment in its supreme excellence is transformed into the experience of joy only. This is the first element of joy. Then Kṛṣṇa though experienced already through ardent love (prema) and the like is experienced anew through transcendental attachment in its supreme excellence. This is the second element of joy. Then transcendent attachment arising from the experience of Kṛṣṇa is experienced. This is the third element of joy. When transcendental attachment attains the state of mere self-awareness, it generates the threefold joy mentioned above.[33] (2) Transcendent attachment in the state of its supreme excellence is distinctly manifested in the body. Five, six, or all spontaneous organic expressions (sāttvikabhāva) simultaneously appear in it, which can be perceived by all. (3) Transcendent attachment in its supreme excellence acts upon all persons who are present and cherish the same sentiment for Kṛṣṇa and excites the same emotion in them according to their receptivity (yāvadāśrayavṛtti). Passionate attachment (rāga) is the basis of transcendent attachment (anurāga), which is the basis of transcendent love (bhāva). When it is manifested abundantly in the body, it rouses similar emotions in the kindred souls.

[32] Anurāgaḥ svasaṁvedyadaśāṁ prāpya prakāśitaḥ.
Yāvadāśrayavṛttiś ced bhāva ityabhidhīyate. UNM., pp. 761-62.

[33] Kṛṣṇānubhavarūpa iti prathamaṁ sukham. Tataś ca premādibhir anubhūtacaro'pi kṛṣṇaḥ samprati anurāgotkarṣeṇa anubhūyate iti dvitīyaṁ sukham. Tataś ca kṛṣṇānubhavato'yam anuragotkarṣo' nubhūyate iti tṛtīyaṁ sukham. ANC., p. 762.

Transcendental love (bhāva) was confined to the milkmaids of Vṛndāvana only who were not married to Kṛṣṇa. This was unattainable by his wives at Dwārakā because it is selfless, desireless, devoid of desire for enjoyment, self-forgetful, and defiant of social codes of morality and religious ceremonialism. Transcendental love (bhāva) contains nascent love (rati), affection (sneha), sulks (māna), intimacy (praṇaya), passionate attachment (rāga), and transcendent attachment (anurāga). Transcendental love is the supreme excellence of passionate attachment.[34]

Transcendentatl love (bhāva) has two distinctive characteristics. (1) It is full of indescribable matchless sweetness which is more intense than the nectar of heaven: unequalled and unsurpassed sweetness, which is not acquired from any object, constitutes its essence. (2) Transcendental love transforms the mind into itself. It transforms not only the minds of the persons who cherish it, but also their sense-organs; so that their activities produce joy in Kṛṣṇa's mind and bring him under their control.[35]

Transcendent love (bhāva) is of two kinds: (i) exalted (rūḍha), and (ii) superexalted (adhirūḍha). (i) Transcendent love is called exalted (rūḍha) when five, six, or all spontaneous organic expressions (sāttvikabhāva) are simultaneously manifested in it.[36] It is manifested by some or all of the following secondary states: (1) unbearableness of separation even for an instant (nimeṣāsahatā), (2) agitation of the hearts of the persons in proximity (āsannajanatā-hṛḍvilodana), (3) instantaneousness of an aeon (kalpakṣaṇatva), (4) languishing because of the fear that Kṛṣṇa is suffering pain though he is really enjoying pleasure (khinnatvaṁ tatsaukhye' pyārtiśaṅkayā), (5) forgetting all things including one's self despite the absence of stupor and the like (mohādyabhāvepyātmādi-sarva-vismaraṇam), and (6) feeling an instant as an aeon (kṣaṇasya kalpatā).[37] (1) When after a long stretch of time the milkmaids of Vṛndāvana enjoyed the sight of Kṛṣṇa in the battlefield of Kurukṣetra, they became intolerant of the winks of their eyes, which interrupted their vision. They mentally embraced him in their hearts, though he is inaccessible to the

[34] Premnaḥ sarvotkarṣa-paramāvadhirūpāvasthāpyeṣa bhāvo mahābhava-paraparyāyaḥ. ANC., p. 766. Ibid, pp. 763-64; UNM., p. 765.
[35] Varāmṛta-svarūpa-śrīḥ svaṁ svarūpaṁ mano nayet. UNM., p. 766. ANC., p. 766.
[36] Uddīptāḥ sāttvikā yatra sa rūḍha iti bhaṇyate. UNM., p. 767.
[37] UNM., p. 768.

yogins constantly united with the supreme Self (paramātman). Kṛṣṇa is the God of love incarnate who is beyond the reach of the mystics but accessible to selfless, single-minded transcendent love (bhāva). (2) Then the hearts of the milkmaids heaved so much with the tide of transcendent love that the hearts of the warriors were stirred to their very depths, the hearts of the Kuru family were melted, and Kṛṣṇa's wives went into raptures. (3) Even an aeon appeared to the milkmaids to be an instant while they enjoyed the ecstasy of transcendent love for Kṛṣṇa. The moon-lit night of the love-dance (rāsa) with Kṛṣṇa appeared to them to be an instant. (4) They languished for sorrow fearing that touch with their bodies gave Kṛṣṇa pain while he really enjoyed pleasure. (5) When their hearts were replete with transcendent love and their souls were completely merged in him, they forgot their selves, bodies, and all things. They forgot this world for they relinquished modesty and fear of social opprobrium; and they forgot the next world because they transcended virtue. They were completely merged in Kṛṣṇa, even as yogis are completely absorbed in Brahman in indeterminate trance shaking off their names and forms. (6) When united with Kṛṣṇa the nights of ecstasy of enjoyment appeared to them to be instants. But when separated from him even an instant appeared to them to be an aeon.[38]

(ii) When transcendental love acquires a more ineffable state of perfection than its exalted form, it is called superexalted (adhirūḍha). When many spontaneous organic expressions (sāttvika-bhāva) of the secondary states of exalted transcendent love appear simultaneously and reach an indescribable state of excellence, the transcendent love is called superexalted.[39] If all the pleasures and pains of the phenomenal worlds and the non-phenomental realms were heaped separately, they would not compare even with the semblance of a drop of the sea of pleasures and pains which spring from superexalted transcendent love of Rādhā. The pleasures and pains that surge from such supreme love are incomprehensible to ordinary mortals. In such super-exalted transcendent love the pleasure of union and the pain of separation coexist in their immeasurableness and end in infinite

[38] UNM., pp. 769-79; ANC., p. 778. *Kṛṣṇa of Vṛndāvana*, pp. 388-91.
[39] Rūḍhoktebhyo' nubhāvebhyaḥ kāmapyāptā viśiṣṭatām.
Yatrānubhāvā dṛśyante so' dhirūḍho nigadyate. UNM., p. 780.

bliss. But in phenomenal heaven and hell pleasure and pain do not coexist simultaneously and are not immeasurable.[40]

Superexalted transcendent love is of two kinds: (i) exhilarator (modana), and (ii) inebriator (mādana).

(I) When many or all spontaneous organic expressions (sāttvikabhāva) of superexalted transcendent love are simultaneously manifested both in Rādhā's body and in Kṛṣṇa's body, it is called the exhilarator (modana).[41] Faltering voice, immobility, horripilation, perspiration, shedding tears, and trembling are found in both. When Rādhā saw Kṛṣṇa in the camp at Kurukṣetra their superexalted transcendent love in the form of the exhilarator was profusely manifested in its sāttvika states in both. At the sight of her Bhadrā's voice was chocked with emotion. Kālindī began to shed tears, Satyabhāmā began to reel, and Rukminī turned pale. After some time when Rādhā's exhilarator subsided a little, Kṛṣṇa's wives regained self-control, bowed to Rādhā and went to their abodes. But Rādhā was so overpowered with her emotion that she could not enquire about them. The exhilarator is possible only in Rādhā and her intimate confidantes, and not to be found elsewhere; it is the sport of God's power of bliss (hlādinīśakti).[42] It is not possible in Candrāvalī and others. Rādhikā and her intimate companions cherished honey-like affection (madhusneha) for Kṛṣṇa; and the exhilarator (modana) is its excellent mode. Candrāvalī and others cherished melted-butter-like affection (ghṛtasnaha) for him, and consequently could not have the exhilarator. The milkmaids' extra-nuptial transcendent love (bhāva) for Kṛṣṇa was superior to that of his wives for him. The transcendent love of Rādhā and her intimate companions was superior to that of the other milkmaids. The transcendent love of Rādhā for Kṛṣṇa was superior to that of her intimate confidantes because it was a supreme mode of God's exhilarating energy.[43] Rādhā's transcendental love for Kṛṣṇa was greater than his love for her.

[40] Adhirūḍha-mahābhāve tu saṁvoga-vivoga-lakṣaṇa-sukhaduḥkhayor nistulayor dvayoreva yaugapadyād eva nistulasukharūpatvam. ANC., p. 782. *Kṛṣṇa of Vṛndāvana*, pp. 392-97.

[41] Modanaḥ sa dvayor yatra sāttvikoddīptasauṣṭhavam. UNM., p. 781.

[42] Rādhikāyutha evāsau modano na tu sarvataḥ.
Yaḥ śrīmān hlādinīśakteḥ suvilāsaḥ priyo varaḥ. UNM., p. 784.

[43] Yaḥ (modanaḥ) hlādinīśakteḥ parama-vṛtti-rūpas tāvad bhagavadbhāvamātram. LR., p. 784. UNM., p. 786.

The exhilarator during separation becomes the infatuator (mohana). In this state the spontaneous organic expressions are manifested in superabundance under the overpowering influence of separation.[44] Five, six, or more sāttvikabhāvas are profusely manifested in it at the same time. Rādhā was the abode of the infatuator, in whom it appeared very frequently when she was separated from Kṛṣṇa after his departure from Vṛndāvana to Mathurā. The infatuator (mohana) is expressed in external organic manifestations which are heightened by its accessory state of stupor (moha).[45] When Uddhava came to Rādhā from Mathurā with a message from Kṛṣṇa, her teeth chattered from shiver, her speech was stuck in her throat, her tears flooded the ground, the hair of her body bristled and her complexion turned white. These were the organic expressions of her infatuator (mohana) under the overpowering influence of separation. The infatuator is marked by the following secondary states: (i) Kṛṣṇa's fainting away even while he was in the embrace of his wives; (ii) Rādhā's desiring Kṛṣṇa's happiness though she were to undergo unbearable sufferings for it; (iii) the agitation of the universe (brahmāṇḍakṣobhakāritva), (iv) weeping of birds and animals, (v) a yearning for union with Kṛṣṇa as the elements of the body after death, and (vi) holy madness of love (divyonmāda). (i) When Kṛṣṇa's hair bristled with joy in the embrace of Rukminī at Dwārakā, Rādhā flashed in his mind, and he remembered his sports with her and fainted away. (ii) Though Rādhā was extremely afflicted by separation from Kṛṣṇa and would be transported with joy on his return from Mathurā, she sent him a message to live there for ever if that afforded him happiness. (iii) Nāndīmukhī went to Dwārakā and related to Kṛṣṇa how the whole universe was agitated when Rādhā fell into the state of the infatuator (mohana) on being separated from him. Men on earth began to cry aloud; the serpents in the nether regions grew restless; the gods in heaven perspired profusely; and Lakshmī and other goddesses in Vaikuṇṭha burst into tears. All the denizens of the phenomenal and non-phenomenal realms were intensely afflicted with pain despite their enjoying supreme joy. The infatuator being the essence of God's

[44] Modano'yaṁ praviśleṣadaśāyāṁ mohano bhavet.
Yasmin virahavaivaśyāt sūddīptā eva sāttvikāḥ. UNM., p. 787.

[45] Prāyo vṛndāvaneśvaryāṁ mohano'yam udañcati.
Samyag vilakṣaṇaṁ yasya kāryaṁ sañcāri mohataḥ. UNM., p. 789.

absorbing love, and the withdrawal of it from all other objects due to the fixation of her mind and sense-organs on one object. Her mind was completely absorbed in Kṛṣṇa as the mind of a yogin is absorbed in Brahman in trance (samādhi). Her mind was not deranged, and her sense-organs were not impaired like those of a yogin in trance. Holy madness is said to be similar to hallucination because both are characterized by monoideism wherein the mind is dominated by one idea, and because in both an image is so vivid that it appears to be a percept.[48]

Holy madness is of two kinds: (1) incoherent behaviour (udghūrṇā), and (2) incoherent raving (citrajalpa). (1) The former is expressed in Rādhā's various strange behaviour in expectation of Kṛṣṇa's arrival as if he were present at Vṛndāvana, although, in reality, he was far away, under the overpowering influence of separation.[49] (2) The latter consists in talking to the dearest friend of Kṛṣṇa about him, which evinced her various emotions due to her concealed anger, and which betrayed her intense anxiety for him. Incoherent raving is of ten kinds: (*i*) prajalpa, (*ii*) parijalpa, (*iii*) vijalpa, (*iv*) ujjalpa, (*v*) saṁjalpa, (*vi*) avajalpa, (*vii*) abhijalpa, (*viii*) ājalpa, (*ix*) pratijalja, and (*x*) sujalpa.

(*i*) Prajalpa consists in talking about Kṛṣṇa's inefficiency by assuming an attitude of disregard for him and through a speech expressive of envy, jealousy, and pride. (*ii*) Parijalpa consists in talking about Kṛṣṇa's cruelty, fraudulence, fickleness and hinting at her wisdom and proficiency. (*iii*) Vijalpa consists in insinuating against Kṛṣṇa by assuming an attitude of concealed sulks and speaking words clearly expressive of envy. (*iv*) Ujjalpa consists in reviling Kṛṣṇa with envy and talking about his fraudulence through words full of jealousy and pride. (*v*) Saṁjalpa consists in talking about Kṛṣṇa's ingratitude and the like by showing an incomprehensible attitude of reviling with irony. (*vi*) Avajalpa consists in talking with jealousy about Kṛṣṇa's being unworthy of being an object of attachment because of his cruelty, lustfulness, and shrewdness. (*vii*) Abhijalpa consists in talking about Kṛṣṇa's being fit for being shunned, because he causes distress even to those who are without any support in life through words

[48] Rādhāgovinda Nath: *Gauḍīya Vaiṣṇava Darśana*, Part iv, ch. xiii. (Bengali), Calcutta, 1959.
[49] Vilakṣaṇam udghūrṇā nānāvaivaśyaceṣṭitam. UNM., p. 797.

full of repentance. (*viii*) Ājalpa consists in talking about Kṛṣṇa's crookedness and causing sufferings to others, and in insinuating others' causing pleasure to others, out of self-despisement. (*ix*) Pratijalpa consists in talking about Kṛṣṇa's being unfit to be approached because of his being always in the company of women, and in showing proper respect to his messenger. (*x*) Sujalpa consists in asking a messenger of Kṛṣṇa about his welfare with gravity, humility, fickleness, and anxiety due to simplicity.[50]

(2) When superexalted transcendent love, which is the essence of God's exhiliriting energy, exalts all kinds of love to their highest pitch of excellence, which is the highest kind of love, and which always abides in Rādhā alone, is called the inebriator (mādana).[51] It is the supreme mode of exhilarating energy. When the exhilarator (modana) attains the state of the highest excellence, it becomes the inebriator (mādana). It manifests nascent love (rati), ardent love (prema), affection (sneha), the sulks (māna), intimacy (praṇaya), passionate attachment (rāga) transcendent attachment (anurāga), and transcendental love (bhāva). Rādhā is the only abode of this kind of supreme love. The inebriator (mādana) excels all kinds of love including the infatuator (mohana). It manifests all the permanent sentiments of love to their utmost extent. It manifests all the sāttvikabhāvas to the utmost. Although in the infatuator (mohana) all the sāttvikabhāvas are manifested simultaneously, yet in the inebriator they are manifested simultaneously in their supreme excellence. The infatuator is experienced in separation, while the inebriator is experienced in the enjoyment of union, and replete with maddening rapture. The inebriator is the quintessence of exhilarating energy—which is its essential property. It always exists in Rādhā alone—which is its accidental property. During union with Kṛṣṇa the inebriator is manifested in her, although it always abides in her in a latent state; during separation it remains concealed in her.

The inebriator (mādana) has the following secondary states: (*i*) strong jealousy for unconscious objects which are not worthy

[50] UNM., sthāyibhāva, 140-45, 147, 149, 151-53.
[51] Sarvabhāvodgamollāsī mādano'yaṁ parāt paraḥ.
Rājate hlādinīsāro rādhāyam eva yaḥ sadā. UNM., p. 823.

of it, and (*ii*) eulogizing objects which were in contact with Kṛṣṇa's body in spite of enjoying him constantly. All kinds of enjoyment of union are experienced simultaneously in the inebriator at the sight of Kṛṣṇa or at the recollection of him. The inebriator is unique, ineffable, incomprehensible and inscrutable: it is as incomprehensible as the non-phenomenal Eros, Kṛṣṇa, all-attracting Love incarnate.[52] It is called the inebriator because it inebriates Rādhā like heavenly nectar with the ecstasy of maddening joy. It differs from the exhilarator (modana) in that the former maddens the whole being with rapturous joy, while the latter affords extreme joy without maddening.[53]

Ordinary nascent love (sādhāraṇī rati) is manifested in one or two sāttvika states which can be suppressed (dhūmāyita). Becoming love (samañjasā rati) and powerful love (samarthā rati) are manifested in two or three sāttvika states simultaneously which can be suppressed with great difficulty (jvalita). Powerful love and ardent love (prema) are manifested in the sāttvika states mentioned above in their excellence. Affection (sneha), the sulks (māna), intimacy (praṇaya), passionate attachment (rāga) and transcendent attachment (anurāga) are manifested in four or five sāttvika states simultaneously which cannot be suppressed (dīpta). Exalted transcendent love (rūḍhabhāva) is manifested in five, six, or all sāttvika states simultaneously in their splendour (uddīpta). Superexalted transcendent love (adhirūḍhabhāva) is manifested in the sāttvika states mentioned above in their splendour and supreme excellence (sūddīpta). The exhilarator (modana), the infatuator (mohana), and the inebriator (mādana) are manifested in this way.[54]

Ordinary nascent love (sādhāraṇī rati) occurs frequently, although it assumes superior, mediocre, and inferior forms in different times, places, and abodes. Ordinary nascent love culminates in ardent love (prema); becoming nascent love (samañjasā rati) culminates in transcendent attachment (anurāga); powerful nascent love (samarthā rati) culminates in transcendent love (bhāva). Kṛṣṇa's wives cherished the seven permanent

[52] Mādanasya gatiḥ susṭhu madanasyeva durgamā.
UNM., p. 830.

[53] ANC., p. 829; *Kṛṣṇa of Vṛndāvana*, pp. 407-09; *Gauḍīya Vaiṣṇava Darśana*, Vol. IV, Ch. XIV.

[54] UNM., ANC., p. 832.

sentiments for Kṛṣṇa—nascent love, ardent love, affection, the sulks, intimacy, passionate attachment, and transcendent attachment. Some playmates of Kṛṣṇa also cherished these seven kinds of love for him. But Subala and some intimate playmates cherished transcendent love (bhāva) also for him.[55]

[55] UNM., pp. 833-34.

BOOK III

THE PSYCHOLOGY OF SEX

Chapter XIV

THE EVOLUTION OF SEX-CONSCIOUSNESS

1. *The Age-Cycle in relation to the Evolution of Sex-consciousness*

The adolescent girl who is married, devoted to her husband, and endowed with modesty, sincerity and other qualities, is changed at the advent of her youth by the dawn of sex-love. She shrinks from caresses, is mild in her indignation, and extremely shy. She is called an artless girl (mugdhā).[1] She is averse to amorous dalliance, submissive to her female friends, extremely shy in wooings, and yet secretly engaged in agreeable acts of sex-exploration, incapable of speaking sweet or harsh words, always disinclined to the sulks, and only looks at her offending lover with tearful eyes.[2]

At the first blush of youth the girl changes in her appearance. Her waist becomes thin, and her loins become bulky; her belly is depressed, and her breasts are developed; the line of hair on her body becomes straight; her glances fall into a sidelong habit; her face beams and her eyes become bright; the pupils of her eyes become a little restless; and she feels a desire to look at her admirer. These are the characteristics of the advent of youth in a girl.

There is a marked change in her demeanour. She sets her footsteps slowly and lazily on the ground; she seldom goes out of her inner apartments; she no longer laughs without restraint, but practises some bashful restraint every moment. She speaks little, and that little, touched by some deep covert significance; she looks at her female friend with a frown, who entertains her

[1] Prathamāvatīrṇa-yauvana-madana-vikārā.
Kathitā mṛduś ca māne samadhika-lajjāvatī mugdhā. SDP., p. 117.
[2] UNM., p. 149.

with conversation about her sweetheart. She shrinks from caresses of her lover, and casts down her eyes, when he looks at her. She does not speak, when he speaks to her; she remains away from the bed, turning her back upon him; and when she is forcibly embraced by him, she trembles. When her female friends, who conduct her to the bed-chamber, are about to retire, she also tries to go out. She is extremely shy and gentle in her indignation. At her husband's first offence she does not know how to convey a sarcasm with amorous movements of the limbs; she only weeps and tears roll down her cheeks.[3]

In the full bloom of youth the woman becomes an adept in caressings, waxes in youth and passion, becomes a little bold in speech, and moderate in modesty. The woman in such a state is called youthful (madhyā).[4] Her passion and bashfulness are equal; she is capable of sex-union till she faints; she is sometimes gentle and sometimes rough in her indignation.[5]

Her passion becomes more pronounced, and her youth overflows through the whole body. Her hands become soft and tender; her bust becomes full and well-rounded; she becomes as bright as gold; she has restless eyes with the flash of sidelong glances; her voice becomes sweet. Love gets possession of her whole being; she utters indistinct sounds expressive of love. She shakes off her maiden coyness, and becomes proficient in caressings. She becomes a little bold in speech and moderately modest. Her shyness and passion become equal. When her lover casts his wistful eyes on her, she conceals her smile a little and looks down; and when he looks in some other direction, she casts her eyes on him.[6]

When the woman grows mature in youth, she becomes blind with passion; her youth deepens into maturity; she becomes an expert in all kinds of caressings; she bears a lofty deportment; she has little modesty; and she rules her lover while locked in his embrace. The woman in this state is called mature (pragalbhā).[7] She is in the full bloom of youth, blind with

[3] SDP., pp. 117—20; *The Mirror of Composition*, p. 68.
[4] Madhyā vicitrasuratā prarūḍha-smara-yauvanā.
Īṣat-pragalbha-vacanā madhyama-vrīḍitā matā. SDP., p. 120.
[5] UNM., p. 159.
[6] SDP., p. 121; UNM., p. 160.
[7] Smarāndhā gāḍhatāruṇyā samasta-rata-kovidā.
Bhāvonnatā daravrīḍā pragalbhākrāntanāyakā.
SDP., p. 122.

passion, eager for sex-union, proficient in manifesting various emotions of love, aggressive in amorous dalliance, very harsh in her indignation, and very bold in her speech and acts.[8]

Her waist is very thin; her buttocks are bulky; and her footsteps are somewhat slow. Her breasts are very high; her eyes are long; her eye-brows are curved; and her speech is full of covert significance. These are the features of the mature woman in her full-grown youth. She is blind with passion and proficient in every kind of dalliance. She is lofty in demeanour, and shakes off her shyness to a great extent. She no longer remains submissive to her lover in his wooings and amorous dalliance, but rules him and commands him to satisfy her longings in all possible ways.[9]

The youthful and mature women are further subdivided into patient (dhīrā), impatient (adhīrā), and partly patient and partly impatient (dhīrādhīrā). These are the six kinds of women. The patient woman possesses self-command; the impatient woman does not possess self-command. The partly patient and partly impatient woman partly possesses and partly does not possess self-command. The youthful patient woman (madhyā dhīrā) burns her offending lover with mere taunts, when she gets angry. The partly patient and partly impatient youthful woman (madhyā dhīrādhīrā) burns him with taunts and tears, when she gets angry. The impatient youthful woman (madhyā adhīrā) assails him with harsh words, when she gets angry. The patient mature woman (pragalbhā dhīrā) suppresses the expressions of anger, remains unconcerned in amorous dalliance, while outwardly showing respect to her lover, when she gets angry. The partly patient and partly impatient mature woman (pragalbhā dhīrādhīrā) distresses her lover with ironical speeches, when she gets angry. The impatient mature woman (pragalbhā adhīrā) scolds and beats her lover, when she gets angry. Each of these varieties of women is either high (jyeṣṭha) or low (kaniṣṭha) in the affections of her lover.[10]

[8] UNM., pp. 171-72.
[9] SDP., pp. 122-25.
[10] SDP., pp. 126-30; UNM., pp. 165, 167-68, 180, 183-84.

2. *The Behaviour of an Artless Enamoured Girl and the Behaviour of Enamoured Women in general.*

When looked at by her lover, an artless enamoured girl shows bashfulness, and never looks straight at him in return; she looks at him furtively, or when he is walking about, or sideways. Even when she is asked questions many times by her lover, she generally gives him brief answers slowly in a faltering voice with a downcast face. She always listens attentively to talks about him carried on by others,—turning her eyes elsewhere and pretending indifference. Such is the behaviour of an artless girl enamoured of her lover.

An enamoured woman wishes her lover to remain always by her side; she does not come within his sight without being adorned. Sometimes on the pretext of covering or fastening her hair, she plainly displays her armpit, her breasts, or her navel to him. She gratifies his attendants by sweet words and affectionate behaviour. She reposes her confidence in his friends, and treats them with great respect. She dilates on his virtues among his female friends, and makes presents of her own wealth to them. She sleeps when he sleeps; she rejoices in his joys, and grieves in his grief; she fully shares in his joys and griefs. Remaining within his sight, she always feasts her eyes on her lover from a distance. She speaks to her friends in his presence infatuated with love. She laughs without any cause on seeing any trifling thing which does not provoke laughter in others. Likewise she scratches her ear, loosens or fastens her hair, yawns, stretches out her limbs, or embraces and kisses a child without any apparent cause. She paints an ornamental mark on the forehead of her female friend. She scribbles on the ground with the tip of her toe, casts side-long glances, bites her nether lip, and speaks to her lover with a downcast face. She does not leave the place where her lover is to be seen, and comes to his room on some pretext of business. She wears a piece of cloth or an ornament presented by her lover, and frequently gazes at it. She always rejoices in his company, and pines and withers in separation from him. She holds his character in high esteem, and loves whatever is dear to him. She begs of him things of a little value as keepsakes. She sleeps with her face towards her lover and does not turn her back upon him while sleeping. In his presence, she betrays signs of deep love such as trembling, stammering, gooseflesh, change of colour, etc. The enamoured girl speaks sweet, truthful and affectionate words to her lover. Among these acts, the more bashful acts belong to the young wife; those with moderate bashfulness belong to the youthful wife; those with little or no modesty belong to women who are others' wives, maturely bold women, and courtesans.[11]

3. *The Natural Graces of Youth*

The natural graces (alaṅkāra) of the woman, which are the spontaneous expressions of her youth, and which spring from their sattva, are twenty eight in number. Among them, (1) stir (bhāva) or the first stirring of love, (2) flutter (hāva) or its stronger expression, and (3) amorous flutter (helā) distinctly indicative of love are produced by bodily movements. (4) Love-adornment (śobhā), (5) brilliancy (kānti), (6) radiance (dīpti), (7) sweetness (mādhurya), (8) boldness (prāgalbhya), (9) meekness (audārya), and (10) constancy—these seven arise naturally without any effort. (11) Playful imitation (līlā), (12) splendour (vilāsa), (13) simplicity in dress (vicchitti), (14) slight (vivvoka), (15) hysterical delight (kilakiñcita), (16) ardent longing (moṭṭāyita), (17) affected repulse (kuṭṭamita), (18) confusion (vibhrama), (19) voluptuous gracefulness (lalita), (20) arrogance (mada), (21) the suppression of the manifestations of love through bashfulness (vikṛta), (22) pining (tapana), (23) simplicity verging on silliness (maugdhya), (24) distractedness (vikṣepa), (25) imperious curiosity (kutūhala), (26) giggling (hasita), (27) fright (cakita), and (28) sportiveness (keli)—these eighteen arise naturally.

The first ten natural graces of women described above belong to men also. They are (1) stir (bhāva), flutter (hāva), (3) amorous flutter (helā), (4) love-adornment (śobhā), (5) brilliancy (kānti), (6) radiance (dīpti), (7) sweet grace (mādhurya), (8) boldness (pragalbhatā), (9) meekness (audārya), and (10) constancy (dhairya). But they especially enhance the charm of women.[12]

The natural graces of the young woman are described below:

(1) Stir (bhāva).—The first change in the mind of a girl yet unaffected is called stir. It is a change, barely awaking (udbud-

[11] SDP., pp. 170-72. Kāmasūtra.
[12] SDP., pp. 150-51; UNM., pp. 496-97.

dhamātra) in her mind, which has been calm and unaltered from birth onward.. This is the sign of the first dawn of youth in her, which is beautifully described in the following verse. "There is the same spring time; there is the same south wind; and this is the same maiden;—yet her mind is found not to be the same". The environment is the same; but her mind reacts to it in a different way owing to the first stirring of youth. This shows that she is entering on a new phase of life. The unperturbed state of the mind despite the presence of a cause of its perturbation is called sattva. The first perturbation of the sattva of the mind at the advent of youth is called stir, which resembles the germination of a seed.[13]

(2) Flutter (hāva).—The stir (bhāva), the alteration of which is slightly visible through organic expressions such as changes in the eyes, the eye-brows and the like, so as to reveal the desire for union with the lover (sambhogecchāprakāśaka), is called flutter. It is a stronger expression of the natural emotion than the stir (bhāva) which is prior to the desire for union. Stir makes the eyes slightly restless; but flutter makes the eyes, eye-brows, etc., expand and move more restlessly, and the neck tilt a little.[14]

(3) Amorous flutter (helā).—The stir (bhāva), the alteration of which is perceived very distinctly, is called amorous flutter (helā). The flutter (hāva) which is distinctly indicative of amorous emotions, is called amorous flutter. It is expressed in the loosening of the garment, heaving of the breasts, sidelong glances, beaming of the cheeks and the face, perspiration, etc. In the full bloom of youth the inner stirrings of the woman are distinctly manifested in the agitation of all her limbs, so that her female friends are in doubt whether she is any longer the artless girl (mugdhā) as before or has entered on the next stage of a woman's life (madhyā).[15]

(4) Love-adornment (śobhā).—The adornment of the body or the grace of the limbs, which springs from beauty, youth, loveliness, toilette, etc., is called love-adornment. Dishevelled hair, red rolling eyes, etc., are its organic expressions.

[13] Nirvikārātmake citte bhāvaḥ prathama-vikriyā. SDP., p. 152. UNM., pp. 498-99.
[14] SDP., p. 152; UNM., p. 500.
[15] SDP., p. 153; UNM., pp. 501-02.

(5) Brilliancy (kānti).—The love-adornment (śobhā) heightened by the unfolding of love, which adds to the personal attractions of the loving woman, is called brilliancy. It is loveliness of the body which is enhanced by the accession of sex-love.

(6) Radiance (dīpti).—The brilliancy (kānti) which is exceedingly heightened by age, enjoyment, place, time, and excellences, is called radiance. Here age implies blooming youth, place such as a secluded flowery bower, and time, as a moon-lit night.

(7) Sweetness (mādhurya).—The loveliness of the playful movements of the body in all states, is called sweetness.

(8) Boldness (prāgalbhya).—Freedom from fear or shyness in amourous dalliance is called boldness. The bold women make their lovers their slaves, by embracing them when embraced, by kissing them when kissed, and biting them when bitten. They fully reciprocate the wooings of their lovers.[16]

(9) Meekness (audārya).—Humility in all circumstances is called meekness. The woman does not show the least sign of haughteur, even when she is offended.

(10) Constancy (dhairya).—The steadfast condition of the mind, free from vanity is called constancy. The calmness of the heart even in the height of anguish is called constancy. The woman, in this condition, has unwavering attachment to her lover even in the midst of trying circumstances.

(11) Playful imitation (līlā).—The woman's imitation of her lover in respect of gestures, dress, ornaments, and loving expressions, is called playful imitation.

(12) Splendour (vilāsa).—The peculiar charm in gait, standing, sitting, etc., in the woman, and her displaying the beauty of her face, the grace of her looks, and other personal charms to the best advantage at the sight of her lover or on hearing of his advent, are called splendour. It is due to her union with her lover.

(13) Simplicity in dress (vicchitti).—A simple dress and meagre adornment of the woman, which heighten her personal charms, are called meagreness of adornments.

(14) Slight (vivvoka).—The woman's indifference to a present from her lover owing to excessive pride or piquancy is called slight.[17]

[16] SDP., pp. 154-56; UNM., pp. 502-06.
[17] SDP., pp. 157-61; UNM., pp. 506-11, 521.

(15) Hysterical delight (kilakiñcita).—The blending of smile, crying with tears dried up, laughter, fear, anger, fatigue, etc.,—all arising from intense joy of the woman due to her union with her dearest lover, is called hysterical delight. It is the mingling of pride, longing, joy, sorrow, envy, fear and anger out of intense joy of union with the lover. There is the simultaneous manifestation of these conflicting emotions in the form of smiles and cries.[18]

(16) Ardent longing (moṭṭāyita).—When the mind of a woman is completely absorbed in her lover who is talked of by others, and she involuntarily scratches her ear and performs other such actions, it is called ardent longing. The manifestation of ardent longing due to the absorption of a woman's mind in the thought of her lover on recollection of him or on receipt of a news about him is called moṭṭāyita.[19]

(17) Affected repulse (kuṭṭumita).—The lover suddenly taking his beloved woman by the hair, the breasts, or the nether lip, her pretended prohibition in the shape of shaking the head or the hands, through flurry, despite her inner joy, is called affected repulse. There is outward manifestation of her affected anger (bahiḥkrodha) with real joy in her heart (hṛtprīti).[20]

(18) Confusion (vibhrama).—When the woman puts on ornaments in wrong places through flurry because of intense love or joy on hearing of the advent of her lover, it is called confusion. It is putting on a necklace, a garland, and other ornaments and adornments in wrong places through exuberance of love and flurry at the time of meeting the lover in a love-tryst.

(19) Voluptuous gracefulness (lalita).—When the woman adorns her limbs in an elegant manner, it is called gracefulness. That which manifests the disposition and gracefulness of the limbs and the charm of the sidelong glances is called gracefulness.

(20) Arrogance (mada).—A change in the woman brought about by the pride of prosperity, youth, etc., is called arrogance.

(21) Bashfulness (vikṛta).—When the woman does not speak through shyness on an occasion when she ought to speak, it is called bashfulness. When her inner desire is not expressed in

[18]Garvābhilāṣa-rudita-smitāsūyā-bhaya-krudhām.
Saṅkarīkaraṇaṁ harṣād ucyate kilakiñcitam.
UNM., p. 516; SDP., pp. 161-62.

[19] SDP., p. 162; UNM., p. 518.

[20] SDP., p. 163; UNM., p. 519.

words owing to shyness, sulks, jealousy, etc., but indicated by some indirect hints, it is called bashfulness.

(22) Pining (tapana).—The woman's actions arising from her being possessed by lust or love (smarāveśa) owing to separation from her lover are called pining. She heaves deep sighs, rolls on the ground, casts longing eyes on his way, weeps for a long time, flings her weak arms hither and thither, longs to sleep but cannot, and yearns to be reunited with her lover even in dreams.

(23) Silliness (maugdhya).—When the woman asks questions in the presence of her lover, as if through ignorance, about what she knows very well, it is called silliness by those who know things rightly.

(24) Distraction (vikṣepa).—The woman's incomplete arrangement of ornaments, looking in vain in all directions, and slowly blabbing secrets out,—when she is near her lover,—constitute distraction.

(25) Curiosity (kutūhala).—The woman's excessive curiosity to see a beautiful object is called curiosity.

(26) Giggling (hasita).—The woman's unmotived laughter which is the spontaneous expression of the bloom of her youth is called giggling.

(27) Fright (cakita).—The woman's flurry through fear before her lover from some cause or other is called fright. It is great restlessness through excessive fear without a sufficient cause before the lover.

(28) Sportiveness (keli).—The woman's playing while walking out with her lover is called sportiveness.[21]

4. *Eight Classes of Heroines in a Drama*

Eight classes of heroines are described by the Sanskrit Rhetoricists: (1) svādhīnabhartṛkā, (2) khaṇḍitā, (3) abhisārikā, (4) kalahāntaritā, (5) vipralabdhā, (6) proṣitabhartṛkā, (7) vāsakasajjā, and (8) virahotkaṇṭhitā.

(1) Svādhīnabhartṛkā.—The woman, who is attracted by various amorous movements of the lover's limbs, and whose lover being attracted by her proficiency in amorous dalliance does not leave her company, is called svādhīnabhartṛkā. Her lover is under

[21] SDP., pp. 164-70; UNM., pp. 513, 523-24, 527-28; *Kṛṣṇa of Vṛndāvana,* pp. 558-61.

her control, and does not leave her proximity. She wanders about and plays in a forest, in the water, and picks flowers in his company.

(2) Khaṇḍitā.—The woman, who burns with jealousy when her lover comes to her, bearing the marks of his union with some other beloved woman (e.g. her cowife), is called khaṇḍitā. When the lover does not come at the appointed time at night to a woman, but spends the night with some other beloved woman, and comes to her the next morning bearing the marks of union with the other, she is called khaṇḍitā. She feels indignation, heaves deep sighs, and keeps silent.

(3) Abhisārikā.—The woman who, being under the influence of intense sex-love, herself approaches her lover, or is made to approach him by her female friends, is called abhisārikā. She veils her face, conceals her limbs in her clothes, does not allow her ornaments to rattle or tinkle owing to shyness, and is attended by one dear confidante. She is clad in white clothes in a moon-lit night, and clad in black clothes in a dark night, while approaching her lover.

(4) Kalahāntaritā.—The woman who repels her flattering lover because of anger and repents for it, is called kalahāntaritā. Her repentance is expressed in mental agony, languor, deep sighs, raving, etc.

(5) Vipralabdhā.—The woman who feels extremely humiliated because her lover does not come to her even after making an intimation to her that he would come, is called vipralabdhā. She feels self-despisement, anxiety, distress, etc.; and her distress is expressed in deep sighs, shedding tears, fainting, etc.

(6) Proṣitabhartṛkā.—The woman who is afflicted with anguish due to love because her lover has gone to a distant land on various kinds of business, is called proṣitabhartṛkā. Her anguish is expressed in talking about her lover, misery, emaciation of her body, wakefulness, dirtiness, restlessness, inactivity, anxiety, etc.

(7) Vāsakasajjā.—The woman who is adorned by her confidantes after they have decorated her bed-chamber on knowing that her lover will come to her, is called vāsakasajjā. The woman who adorns her body, decorates her bed-chamber, and anxiously awaits her lover's arrival on being definitely assured of it by him,

is called vāsakasajjā. She makes resolutions about her amorous dalliance with him, watches his road, talks with her confidantes about him, and frequently looks at his female messenger.

(8) Virahotkaṇṭhitā.—The woman who is afflicted with sorrow because her lover cannot come to her by chance, although he was resolved on coming,—is called virahotkaṇṭhitā. If the unoffending lover does not come even long after the appointed time, his beloved woman becomes very anxious owing to separation, and is called virahotakaṇṭhitā.[22]

[22] SDP., pp. 137-39, 141-44; UNM., pp. 192, 195-204.

BOOK IV

THE PSYCHOLOGY OF RELIGION

Chapter XV

RELIGIOUS EMOTIONS

1. *Faith* (*śraddhā*)

Saṁkara defines faith as belief in God, which is deeply tinged with an emotion, which leads to the accomplishment of all means to realize the supreme end, and which produces transparence and tranquillity of the mind. Baladeva defines faith as firm belief in God. Viśvanātha Cakravartī defines faith as belief in the existence of God as proved by the scriptures. Thus, it includes belief in the validity of the intuitions of the seers to whom God revealed the scriptures. Rāmakaṇṭha defines faith as the seed of all fruitions of spiritual disciplines. The highest fulfilment is the realization of Brahman. Varavaramuni defines faith as determinate knowledge of the existence of God as the Supreme Person (puruṣottama), who creates, maintains and dissolves the world, who is worshipped by the rites prescribed by the Vedas, who is the giver of all fruits of actions, and whose existence is proved by the Upaniṣads,— which is attended with firm faith.[1]

Śraddhā is of three kinds: (1) sāttvikī, (2) rājasī, and (3) tāmasī. (1) Sāttvikī śraddhā is the faith of a person in whose mind sattva (purity) is the predominant element. It is expressed in the worship of gods in accordance with the methods prescribed by the śāstras. (2) Rājasī śraddhā is the faith of a person in whose mind rajas (energy) is the predominant element. It is expressed in the worship of Yakṣas and demons (rakṣas) in accordance with the methods prescribed by false śāstras. (3) Tāmasī śraddhā is the faith of a person in whose mind tamas (inertia) is the predominant element. It is expressed in the worship of

[1] Śraddhā yatpūrvakaḥ sarva-puruṣārtha-sādhana-prayogaḥ cittaprasādaḥ āstikyabuddhiḥ. SB., Muṇḍ. Up., ii, 7; SBG., vi, 37. Samasta-siddhi-bīja-bhūtā śraddhā. RKBG., xii, 20. BBG., VNBG., iv, 39; VMBG., xviii, 42; ix, 23.

ghosts and evil spirits in accordance with the methods prescribed against the śāstras.[2]

Śāṇḍilya distinguishes between faith and devotion. Devotion (bhakti) is not identical with faith for the following reasons. First, faith is more general than devotion; faith is common to all actions, while devotion to God is not so; every voluntary action depends upon faith in the realizability of its end through a particular means, but not upon faith in God.[3] Secondly, if devotion were identical with faith, then the latter would presuppose another element of faith, and so on to infinity, because devotion is preceded by faith.[4] Thirdly, faith and devotion are declared to be distinct from each other.

Nārada describes belief as a precondition of faith, and faith as a precondition of devotion. First, there is belief (viśvāsa) in God; then this belief is deepened into faith (śraddhā); then this faith is deepened into devotion (bhakti); then there is the realization of God, the dearest.[5] The *Bhāgavata* describes faith as a precondition of attachment (rati), and attachment as a precondition of devotion (bhakti).[6]

2. *Devotion (bhakti)*

Śaṁkara defines unswerving devotion as knowledge. Ānandagiri regards the mind untainted by love and hatred, joy and grief, as the organ of true knowledge, which generates devotion, and which makes the mind firmly established in God. Śrīdharasvāmī regards supreme undivided devotion to God as the effect of integral vision of the Supreme Self as the inner self of the universe. Rāmakaṇṭha also regards it as the fruit of the knowledge of all objects as non-distinct from the essential nature of God.[7] They are Advaita Vedāntists.

Rāmānuja defines devotion as a constant definite recollection

[2] BG., xvii, 2-4. SBG., RKBG., xvii, 2-4.
[3] Naiva śraddhā tu sādhāraṇyāt. SS., i, 24. SSS., i, 24.
[4] Tasyāṁ tattve cānavasthānāt. SS., i, 25. SSS., i, 25; BG., vi, 47.
[5] Ya idaṁ nāradaproktaṁ viśvasiti śraddhatte sa bhaktimān bhavati sa preṣṭhaṁ labhate. NBS., x, 11.
[6] Bhāg., iii, 25, 25.
[7] Avyabhicāriṇī bhaktir jñānam. SBG., xiii, 10. ĀBG., xiii, 9-10. Parameśvare sarvātmadṛṣṭyā ekāntā bhaktiḥ. SrBG., xiii, 10. RKBG., xiii, 10.

of God. Prayer or communion (upāsanā) is a synonym of devotion. Meditation consists in an uninterrupted stream of recollections like a stream of oil. It is certain recollection. Śrīnivāsa, a Rāmānujist, defines devotion as uninterrupted stream of recollections of God. He regards it as meditation (dhyāna), prayer (upāsanā), and love (vedana).[8] Veṅkaṭanātha, another Rāmānujist, defines devotion as a mode of buddhi which is in the nature of delight. Delight is a mode of cognition. Delight in a venerable being is devotion. The knowledge that leads to the realization of God, and that is generated by devotion, is comprised in devotion. Devotion is meditation (dhyāna) which is certain constant recollection of God. Constant recollection consists in continuous thought. Rāmānujists regard feelings as modes of cognition.[9] Varavaramuni, another Rāmānujist, defines devotion as supreme love (niratiśaya-prīti), or as constant recollection of, and desire for communion with, God, or as knowledge of God consisting in supreme love for Him. He regards devotion as the supreme love for God which generates the knowledge of Him, and knowledge of God as the highest love for Him.[10] Thus, Rāmānuja and his followers do not regard devotion as mere feeling or emotion, but as supreme love enlightened by the knowledge of God. They are Viśiṣṭādvaitavādins.

Rūpa Goswāmī, a follower of Caitanya, defines supreme devotion as the service of God with a favourable attitude or love, devoid of desire for all other objects, and unveiled by knowledge and actions.[11] Favourable attitude towards God is love for Him. Hostility towards Him cannot be devotion, being opposed to it. Devotion is free from the knowledge of Brahman devoid of the difference between the individual self (jīva) and the supreme Self, both of which are ontologically real beings according to Caitanya and his followers. But devotion is not free from investigation

[8] Dhruvānusmṛtireva bhaktiśabdenābhidhīyate. RBS., i, 1, 1. YMD., pp. 28-29.

[9] Bhaktiḥ dhīḥ prītirūpa. Mahanīyaviṣaye prītir bhaktiḥ, prītyādayaś-ca jñānaviśeṣāḥ. Bhaktisādhyaṁ prāpakajñānam api bhaktilakṣaṇopetam. TMK., pp. 189, 190, 191.

[10] Nirantara-smṛtyārādhanecchānu-sandhānātmikā bhaktiḥ. VMBG., xviii, 65. Bhaktyā atyartha-prītirūpatām āpannena jñānena. Ibid, ix, 26. Bhaktyā-niratiśaya-prema-rūpayā. VMBG., viii, 10. Ibid, xviii, 55.

[11] Anyābhilāṣitāśūnyaṁ jñāna-karmādyanāvṛtam.
Ānukūlyena kṛṣṇānuśīlanaṁ bhaktir uttamā.
BRS., i, 1, 11.

of the real nature of God who is worshipped. Devotion is free from the performance of daily obligatory duties, occasional duties, specific duties pertaining to castes and stages of life, and prudential duties. But it is not free from the acts of worship of God and service of His devotees. Listening, singing, worship and the like acts should be performed repeatedly. God should be meditated on and discussed frequently. Jīva Goswāmī explains Rūpa Goswāmī's definition of devotion in this manner.[12]

Kṛṣṇadāsa Kavirāja defines devotion as the worship of God with five cognitive organs, five motor organs, and the internal organ, with attachment, and without knowledge and desire. This pure devotion generates ardent love (prema) for God. The *Nāradapañcarātra* defines devotion as the pure service of God, the ruler of the sense-organs, with all the sense-organs without desire for other objects.[13] Kṛṣṇadāsa's definition is an adaptation of Rūpa Goswāmī's definition of devotion. Jīva Goswāmī regards love for God (prīti) as a mode of His essential power of bliss (hlādinīśakti) and consequently in the nature of bliss, which gives supreme bliss to a devotee because it is blissful in nature.

Baladeva Vidyābhūṣaṇa, a follower of Caitanya, discusses the nature of devotion which subjects God to a devotee. (1) It is not in the nature of knowledge and bliss which are modes of sattva (purity) of prakṛti, because God is perfect and not subject to Māyā or prakṛti. An individual self, that is imperfect, has knowledge and bliss, which are modes of sattva of prakṛti (2) Devotion is not in the nature of knowledge and bliss, which constitute the essence of God, because He cannot have an excess (atiśaya) of knowledge and bliss. The contention, that though God is in the nature of bliss, He is said to have excess of bliss, is not valid. (3) Devotion is not in the nature of knowledge and bliss of the individual self (jīva) because they are extremely fragmentary and limited. (4) Devotion is in the nature of knowledge and bliss which inhere in God's powers of knowledge and bliss.[14]

[12] DGS., i, 1, 11.
[13] Sarvopādhi-vinirmuktaṁ tatparatvena nirmalam.
Hṛṣīkeṇa hṛṣikeśasevanaṁ bhaktir ucyate. BRS., i, 1, 12.
CCA., ii, 19, p. 276.
[14] (Bhaktiḥ) bhagavad-vaśīkāra-hetu-bhūtā śaktiḥ hlādinī-sāra-samaveta-saṁvit-sāra-rūpā. Siddhāntaratna, p. 35.

3. *The Nature of Devotion (bhakti)*

Nārada defines devotion as in the nature of supreme love for God. It is single-minded love directed towards God, which is devoid of any desire for wealth, happiness, virtue, and liberation. Love for one's wife, sons and the like is not devotion, for it does not lead to the realization of God. Devotion is in the nature of nectar which makes a devotee immortal as the drinking of nectar makes gods immortal. It breaks the fetters of all sufferings and removes the fear of death.[15] The nature of supreme love for God is indescribable. It can be experienced by a devotee, but cannot be described by him. It is too deep for utterance. It is unique, original, *sui generis,* non-empirical, and transcendental. It is like a dumb person's experience of taste. He can experience all kinds of taste, but cannot express his experience in words. But supreme love for God is manifested in some of its proper abodes. Some devotees endowed with it are found to be suffused with love for all human beings and sentient creation, who are the manifestations of God.[16] Love for God is manifested in love for His creatures. Supreme love for God is devoid of sattva, rajas and tamas, desireless, increases every moment, flows unceasingly, and is experienced in subtler and subtler forms.[17] It is not a modification of purity (sattva), energy (rajas), and inertia (tamas) of the mind, which are the primordial psychical impulses, and, consequently, not perishable: it increases every moment, since it transcends the empirical nature. It springs from God immanent in the individual self as its inner guide, and is directed towards Him, and transcendental. It is continuous and incessant. Though it may be veiled by nescience occasionally, it cannot be destroyed completely. It is experienced in subtler and subtler forms. Its sweetness is infinite and inexhaustible, and can never be experienced in its entirety. It is devoid of all desires for happiness and liberation. Supreme love for God is in the nature of tranquillity and supreme bliss.[18] Disequilibrium and restlessness of the mind spring from the sense of conflict and duality. Devotion is supreme love for God who

[15] Sā tvasmin parama-premarūpā. Amṛta-svarūpāca. NBS., i, 2-3.

[16] Om anirvacanīyaṁ prema-svarūpam. Mūkāsvādanavat. Prakāśyate kvāpi pātre. NBS., vii, 1-3.

[17] Guṇarahitaṁ kāmanārahitaṁ pratikṣaṇa-vardhamānaṁ avicchinnaṁ sūkṣmataram anubhava-rūpam. NBS., vii, 4.

[18] Sāntirūpāt paramānandarūpācca. NBS., viii, 3.

exists equally and entirely in all beings, and so implies love and equality for all beings. Devotion is supreme bliss, and God also is infinite bliss. So devotion generates peace and tranquallity. Devotion is self-proved: it cannot be proved by any other means of knowledge.[19] One who practises the members (aṅga) of devotion, experiences it, and cannot acquire it by any other means. Devotion is the means of devotion; knowledge and works are not the means of devotion. One who has no devotion cannot know it by any other means. Supreme devotion (parā bhakti) is the fruit of all spiritual disciplines. Hence it should be adopted by the aspirants after liberation because it is sure to lead to the realization of God.[20]

Śāṇḍilya defines devotion as supreme attachment to God. It is a mental mode directed towards God. It is different from attachment of worldly persons to external objects of enjoyment. because it is directed towards God and because it is imperishable. Attachment to worldly objects springs from ignorance, whereas attachment to God springs from true knowledge. Devotion is supreme attachment as distinguished from subordinate attachment. It is attachment to God—the universal, infinite and eternal consciousness unlimited by the adjunct of individual nescience limiting the empirical self.[21] It may be argued that attachment (rāga) to God cannot be regarded as devotion, since attachment is an affliction (kleśa) which taints the mind. Śāṇḍilya replies that devotion is attachment to God, and that, consequently, it is not an affliction. All attachment should not be eschewed, but only attachment to worldly objects should be eschewed, because it is repugnant to liberation. Just as all company should not be shunned, but only bad company should be shunned, so all attachment should not be discarded, but only attachment to objects of enjoyment should be discarded.[22] A devotee who has acquired supreme attachment to God achieves immortality. One who lives, moves and has his being in Brahman or God, becomes immortal.[23] Śāṇḍilya's definition of devotion is similar to Nārada's definition.

[19] Pramāṇāntarasyānapekṣatvāt svayaṁpramāṇatvāt. NBS., viii, 2.

[20] Phalarūpatvāt. NBS., iv, 2. Tasmāt saiva grāhyā mumukṣubhiḥ. Ibid, iv, 8.

[21] Sā (bhaktiḥ) parānuraktirīśvare. SS., i, 2. Jīvopādhyanavacchinna-cetana-viṣayiṇī anuraktir eva sā. SSS., i, 1, 2.

[22] YS., ii, 3; SS., SSS., i, 2, 21.

[23] Tatsaṁsthasyāmṛtatvopadeśāt. SS., i, 1, 3. Brahmasaṁstho' mṛtatvam eti. Ch. Up.; SSS., i, 1, 3.

4. *The Characteristics (lakṣaṇa) of Devotion.*

The *Bhāgavata* mentions nine characteristics of devotion: (1) listening to God's glory (śravaṇa), (2) chanting His name and attributes (kīrtana), (3) recollection (smaraṇa) or thought of Him, (4) service to Him (pādasevana), (5) worship of Him (arcana), (6) eulogy of Him by hymns (vandana), (7) servitude to Him (dāsya), (8) friendship for Him (sakhya), and (9) self-dedication to Him (ātmanivedana). It also mentions faith in listening to discourses on Him, attachment to His worship, regard for service to Him, prostration before His image, performing all bodily actions for Him, speaking of His excellence, service to His devotees, enjoying wealth and happiness for Him, renouncing them for Him, renouncing all desires, performing charity, worship, sacrifice, vows, austerities, muttering His name or mystic formula for Him, offering the mind to Him completely without reservation, and knowing God as the indwelling Spirit in all creatures as the characteristics of devotion.[24]

Thus, devotion is the concrete religious consciousness which comprises cognition, feeling, and conation. The knowledge of God as the inner Guide (antaryāmin) of all creatures is the element of cognition. Love of Him as the Master and Friend is the element of feeling. The will attuned and dedicated to Him completely is the element of conation, which is expressed in performing all bodily, verbal, and mental actions for Him. Devotion is enlightened by the knowledge of God as the universal Spirit, and of the universe as His manifestation, enlivened by supreme love for Him, and by deep love for humanity and sentient creation, and activated by completely dedicated will to serve Him and all His creatures. Devotion is the complete transformation of the mind and its orientation towards God—sanctification of the body, life, sense-organs, mind, intellect, and egoism (ahaṁkāra)—conversion of the human personality.

There is a divergence of views among the exponents of devotion on its characteristics. (1) Vyāsa, Parāśara's son, regards devotion as attachment (anurāga) to the worship of God. It is not attachment to objects of enjoyment, which is a hindrance to God's worship. Attachment to the worship of God implies

[24] Bhāg., vii, 5, 23-24; xi, 19, 19-24.

attachment to God. (2) Garga regards devotion as attachment to listening to and chanting God's glory and excellences. (3) Śāṇḍilya regards devotion as constant attachment to the Self (ātmarati), which is an eternal part of God, non-different from Him. The individual self (jīva) suffers on account of his forgetfulness of his essential community of nature with God. (4) Nārada regards devotion as dedication of all one's actions to God and extreme grief on forgetting Him.[25] Dedication of actions to God is not renunciation of them; but it is the performance of them as instruments of God with the consciousness that He is the real doer of his actions. When this consciousness lapses, the devotee feels restless. The milkmaids of Vṛndāvana surrendered all their actions to Kṛṣṇa, God of love incarnate, and suffered intensely in separation from him. (5) Devotion is characterized by the knowledge of majesty of God, who is its object (māhātmyajñāna). God is hostile to conceit and fond of humility.[26] Conceit is the cause of haughtiness, arrogance and self-assertion, which are hindrances to self-surrender to God. So He is hostile to conceit. The sense of one's worthlessness, supportlessness and destituteness produces humility. It generates self-surrender to God who demands complete self-surrender from the devotee. So He is fond of humility. Thus devotion contains humility to God and reverence for Him, who is far superior to the devotee. The devotion which is devoid of the sense of God's superiority is not true. If devotion is not genuine, a devotee cannot feel the sense of 'mineness' in God. A true devotee feels 'I am thine' and 'Thou art mine' in relation to God.[27]

Śāṇḍilya avers that pure devotion is inferred from its signs (liṅga). Svapneśvara explains it thus. Pure devotion characterized by the special characters of strong psychical dispositions cannot be known by perception, like the validity of knowledge. It is inferred from its organic manifestations in the form of shedding tears, bristling of hair, etc. Showing honour (sammāna), excessive regard (bahumāna), delight or love (prīti), pangs of separation (viraha), aversion to all other objects than God (itaravicikitsā), narration of His greatness (mahimakhyāti),

[25] Nāradas tu tadarpitākhilācāratā tadvismaraṇe paramavyākulateti. NBS., iii, 5. Ibid, iii, 1-4.
[26] Īśvarasyābhimānadveṣitvād dainyapriyatvācca. NBS., iv, 3.
[27] Ibid, iii, 6-10.

maintaining one's life for God (tadarthaprāṇasthāna), the sense of one's wife, sons, and property belonging to God (tadīyabhāva), the feeling that all are God's manifestations (sarvatadbhāva), non-hostility towards Him (aprātikūlya), and constant recollection of Him are the characteristics of devotion.[28]

Rūpa Goswāmī mentions the following characteristics of devotion. (1) It destroys afflictions. (2) It gives good. (3) It belittles the importance of liberation. (4) It is extremely difficult of attainment. (5) It is in the nature of intense bliss. (6) It attracts God and subjects Him to a devotee.[29]

(1) Afflictions are demerits (pāpa), seeds of demerits (pāpabīja), and nescience (avidyā). Demerits are of two kinds, viz., (i) demerits which are not yet ripe for bearing fruits (aprārabdha), and which exist in the subtle body of an individual self as potencies of actions, and (ii) demerits which are ripe for bearing fruits (prārabdha) for experiencing which the present body has been born. The *Bhāgavata* asserts that devotion destroys all demerits, vices, and afflictions completely. Listening to God's name, chanting it, obeisance to Him, and recollection of Him destroy all demerits which are ripe for bearing fruits. Penances, gifts, vows, etc., destroy all vices, but cannot destroy their seeds in the form of their potencies (vāsanā), which are destroyed by devotion to God in the form of His worship. The latent potencies (saṁskāra) of vices are called their seeds. Devotion to God destroys nescience (avidyā) which produces egoism and knots of the heart, which the ascetics who have withdrawn their sense-organs from their objects, and their minds from the enjoyment of sentient pleasure, cannot destroy. Devotion to God emerges along with true knowledge (vidyā) and destroys nescience.[30]

(2) Devotion gives good. It gives a devotee love for all creatures and causes them pleasure. It gives him love of all beings, excellent qualities like virtue, knowledge, dispassion, etc., and pleasure. Pleasure is of three kinds: (i) pleasure produced by objects of enjoyment, (ii) bliss of Brahman, and (iii) supreme

[28] SS., SSS., ii, 1, 44.
[29] Kleśaghnī śubhadā mokṣalaghutākṛt sudurlabhā.
Sāndrānanda-viśeṣātmā śrīkṛṣṇākarṣiṇī ca sā.
BRS., i, 1, 17.
[30] BRS., i, 1, 18-26.

bliss of God.[31]. Sentient pleasure is derived from superhuman powers (siddhi), e.g., capacity for becoming light, capacity for becoming large, capacity for getting the objects of desire at any moment, capacity for creating, maintaining and destroying matter and material objects, capacity for subjecting them to one's will, capacity for executing one's will which cannot be thwarted, capacity for assuming any form, and acquiring sovereignty. Devotion gives the pleasure of these supernatural powers, wealth, happiness, virtue and liberation, though a devotee does not seek for them. They come to him unsought as subservient to devotion. If they are sought for, pure devotion cannot be manifested in his mind tainted by this desire. Pure devotion is manifested in a pure mind untainted by all other desires than desire for the pleasure of God. Brahman is inferior to God, because it is unqualified, pure, impersonal, undifferentiated consciousness, existence and bliss. But God is a qualified, personal embodiment of pure bliss and love. Hence the supreme bliss of God is superior to the bliss of Brahman.[32]

(3) Devotion belittles the importance of liberation. Even when a little attachment (rati) to God is produced in a devotee's heart, he does not care a straw for the four ends of life—wealth, happiness, virtue, and liberation, and supernatural powers follow devotion like its handmaids.

(4) Devotion to God is extremely difficult of attainment. It cannot be achieved by spiritual discipline without interest and constancy for a long period of time. God does not grant devotion quickly to an aspirant who practises spiritual discipline with interest and constancy for a long duration. Liberation can be acquired by true knowledge, and earthly and heavenly happiness, by the performance of sacrifices, but devotion to God cannot be acquired by thousands of spiritual disciplines. God grants His devotee liberation but not devotion until he has deep attachment to the cult of devotion.

(5) Devotion to God is in the nature of intense bliss. The bliss of Brahman, if multiplied to infinity, is not even a drop of the ocean of bliss of devotion to God. The bliss of experiencing personal God of infinite love and sweetness is superior to and

[31] Sukhaṁ vaiṣayikaṁ brāhmam aiśvarañceti tat tridhā. BRS., I, 1, 30.
[32] BRS., I, 1, 27-32; Bhāgavata, v, 18, 12.

more intense than that of experiencing impersonal Brahman which is only a ray of His spiritual body.[33]

(6) Devotion attracts God because it subjects Him and His attendants to the will of a devotee who loves Him ardently.[34] The discriminative knowledge of the self as distinct from the mind-body-complex, concentration of the mind on God and absorption in Him, study of the scriptures, austerities and charity cannot subject God to the will of an aspirant so much as intense devotion (ūrjita-bhakti) to Him does. Even slight interest in the cult of devotion reveals to an aspirant the real nature of devotion, which is unintelligible to a person who wrangles with endless arguments.[35]

Jīva Goswāmī, a follower of Caitanya, mentions the following characteristics of love (prīti) for God. (1) It is a mode of the essence of God's essential power of bliss. It is an intense mode of this power.[36] This is its essential characteristic. (2) It is in the form of the cognition, which is in the nature of being favourable to God and full of yearning for Him.[37] Yearning for bringing about the pleasure of God is subordinate to the cognition of being favourable to Him. Love for God is a mental mode of a devotee whose mind is favourably inclined towards Him and intensely yearns for His pleasure.[38] It is not a mode of nescience, or pure essence of the phenomenal mind, but a mode of the non-phenomenal pure essence, because God of infinite sweetness somehow manifests Himself in the devotee's mind in the form of love (prīti) for Him.[39] This is also an essential characteristic of love for God. (3) It is independent of any scriptural injunctions and logical reasonings. It spontaneously emerges from within the mind, and is self-manifest (anapekṣita-vidhiḥ). (4) It fills the mind of a devotee with joy, because it is blissful in its own essential nature. It does not depend upon other conditions for its blissful nature and sweetness (svarasata eva samullasantī).

[33] BRS., i, 1, 35-40.

[34] Kṛtvā hariṁ premabhājaṁ priya-varga-samanvitam.
Bhaktir vaśīkarotīti śrīkṛṣṇākarṣiṇī matā.
BRS., i, 1, 41.

[35] BRS., i, 1, 42-45; Bhāgavata, xi, 14, 20.

[36] Hlādinī-sāra-vṛtti-viśeṣa-svarūpā. Prītisandarbha, section 78.

[37] Bhagavad - ānukūlyātmakatadanugata - tatspṛhādimaya - jñānaviśeṣākārā. Ibid.

[38] Tādṛśa-bhakta-manovṛtti-viśeṣadehā. Ibid.

[39] Amāyika-viśuddha-sattvānavaratollāsād asamorddhva-madhure śrībhagavati katham api cittāvatārāt. Ibid.

(5) Love for God is not determined and limited by other objects (viṣayāntarairanavacchedyā). It is not tainted by the desire for earthly or heavenly happiness and liberation. (6) It does not aim at any other end; it is an end in itself (tātparyāntaram asahamānā). (7) It is sweeter than nectar, the food of gods. Sweetness reaches its acme of excellence in love for God. 'A devotee only can experience this sweetness in his love for God, which is inaccessible to others.'[39a] (8) Love for God is the abode of all virtues (sarvaguṇaikanidhāna-svabhāvā), because devotion destroys all vices. God's essential power of bliss (hlādinīśakti) is manifested in a pure mind purged of all taints and afflictions (kleśa). (9) All covetable ends of life, wealth, happiness, virtue, and liberation, are hand-maids of love for God. Though it does not aim at them, they come of themselves to a devotee (dāsīkṛtāśeṣa-puruṣārtha-sampattikā). (10) Love for God is the only means of producing the pleasure of God by service to Him (bhagavanmanoharaṇaikopāyahārirūpā). All the actions of a devotee are directed towards love for God and service to Him. (11) Love for God produces only one desire to serve God and produce His pleasure, even as a devoted wife's love for her beloved husband produces only one desire to serve him and produce his pleasure (bhagavat-pātivratyavratavaryāparyākulā). (12) A devotee tries to conceal his love for God which he secretly cherishes in his heart; but it is manifested in shedding tears and other organic manifestations, from which it is inferred by others (vāspa-muktādi-vyakta-pariṣkārā). It is characterized by melting of the heart (cittadravatā), which is manifested by bristling of hair, shedding tears, trembling, etc. Formalistic devotion (sādhanabhakti) purifies the mind, and when it is completely purged of its impurities, pure devotion (sādhyabhakti) or love (prīti) is manifested in it. If the mind partly melts, its partial melting is manifested in gooseflesh and the like, but if the mind is not completely purified, love for God is not completely manifested in it. Purification of mind consists in the renunciation of all other ends except service of God. It is directed towards unmotived selfless love for God. These are the extrinsic characteristics of pure devotion.[40]

[39a] Pīyuṣapūrato'pi sarasena svenaiva svadeham sarasayantī. Ibid.

[40] Āśaya-śuddhir nāma anya-tāparyaparityāgaḥ prīti-tātparyañca. Ibid, section 69.

Love for God is self-existent, self-manifest, unconditioned, unmotived and independent. It results in the experience of its sweetness. But a devotee does not care for his own joy due to the experience of the sweetness of his love for God who is the embodiment of unequalled and unsurpassed sweetness.[41]

Baladeva Vidyābhūṣaṇa defines devotion as the essence of bliss and knowledge which are non-different from each other.[42] It is a particular desire for the favour of God and His eternal attendants only, untainted by desire for any other objects. It is a yearning for God only and for no other objects.[43] Devotion is an inseparable attribute in God, but a separable attribute in an individual self. It is the essence of God's power of bliss which constitutes His essential nature. It gives supreme joy to God and the individual self both.[44] Devotion is non-different from God, but different from an individual self devoted to Him.[45] It is the essence of both, and colours their nature, when it is in the nature of attachment, ardent love, pure devotion.[46] Devotees are the heart of God or the objects of His love, and God is the heart of devotees or the object of their love.[47] Pure devotion is called attachment (rati) and ardent love (prema). It increases God's bliss, though He is full of supreme bliss, makes Him experience His essential bliss, and makes His devotees experience it.[48] God is the fruit of knowledge, but devotion is the fruit of devotion because it culminates in the realization of its intense joy. Knowledge gives the reality of God, but devotion gives the experience of its intrinsic bliss which is a pure mode of God's essential power of bliss and knowledge.[49] God is the object of devotion. Devotion is in the nature of intense bliss which cannot exist without God because it is His inseparable attribute. When pure devotion is acquired, God, its object, also is realized. God

[41] Gaudīya Vaiṣṇava Darśana, Vol. IV, Ch. I.

[42] Hlādasaṁvidoḥ samavetayoḥ sāro bhaktiḥ. Siddhāntaratna, i, 40 and Ṭippanī.

[43] Kṛṣṇānyatṛṣṇāśūnyā kṛṣṇamātratṛṣṇā. Ibid, Ṭippanī, i, 40.

[44] Bhagavat-svarūpa-viśeṣabhūta-hlādinyādi-sārātmā bhaktir bhagavatya-pṛthag-viśeṣaṇatayā bhakte ca pṛthag-viśeṣaṇatayā siddhā tayor ānand-ātiśayāya bhavati. Ibid, i. 42.

[45] Bhaktir bhagavato' bhinnā bhaktāt tu bhinnā. Ibid, Ṭippanī, i, 42.

[46] Sā tadubhaya-sārāṁśarūpā rati-premākhyā bhaktiḥ. Ibid, i, 44.

[47] Sādhavo hṛdayaṁ mahyam sādhūnāṁ hṛdayaṁ tvaham. Bhāgavata.

[48] Paramānandamayo'pi yayānandātiśayī bhavati svarūpānandaṁ cānu-bhavati tam anubhāvayati ca bhaktān. Ibid, i, 46.

[49] Jnānaphalaṁ bhagavān bhaktiphalaṁ tu bhaktireva tadviṣayā tasyā evodagrānandatvāt. Ibid, i, 46.

is the supreme end of devotion. Love for God (prema) is regarded as the fifth end of human life by Caitanya and his followers. Devotion does not seek for the four ends of life—wealth, happiness, virtue and liberation.[50]

5. *Devotion and Knowledge*

Some maintain, that knowledge is an indispensable means to devotion, and that devotion cannot be achieved without preceding knowledge.[51] (2) Others maintain, that knowledge and devotion are interdependent on each other.[52] They are complementary to each other; the knowledge of the true nature of God generates devotion to Him; and devotion to God generates true knowledge of Him. (3) Nārada maintains, that devotion is an end in itself, that it is the means as well as the end, and that it is the fruit of all spiritual disciplines. If the members (aṅga) of devotion or devotional acts are repeatedly practised, devotion is attained.[53]

Śāṇḍilya does not regard devotion as knowledge, firstly, because even a person who cherishes hostility towards God has knowledge of Him, but no devotion to Him; secondly, because knowledge is destroyed when devotion emerges; thirdly, because a wise person who has attained the knowledge of God takes refuge with Him—thus knowledge leading to devotion; fourthly, because love springs from knowledge—the sight of beauty, the hearing of excellences, the knowledge of the character of a person generating love for him; fifthly, because the milkmaids of Vṛndāvana attained liberation through supreme love for Kṛṣṇa without knowledge; sixthly, because the knowledge of God is subordinate to supreme attachment to Him; and, lastly, because devotion leads to the recognition (abhijñā) of the nature of God. The knowledge (jñāna) of God generates devotion; and devotion generates recognition dependent on prior knowledge.[54]

But Śāṇḍilya feels the necessity of meditation (yoga) for the culture of devotion. Devotion and knowledge both depend

[50] Bhaktimatāṁ bhaktiviṣayo bhagavān puruṣārthaḥ. Ibid, i, 48.
[51] Tasyā jñānam eva sādhanam ityeke. NBS., iv. 4.
[52] Anyonyāśrayatvam ityanye. Ibid, iv, 5.
[53] Svayaṁphalarūpateti brahmakumārāḥ. NBS., iv, 6.
[54] SS., SSS., i, 1, 4-6, 9, 12-17.

upon concentration of the mind on God. Patañjali speaks of concentration of the mind on God as a means of acquiring trance (samādhi) or complete absorption of the mind in Him. Śāṇḍilya regards it as secondary devotion (gauṇī bhakti) which is a means to supreme attachment to God, which is primary devotion.[55] Śāṇḍilya feels the necessity of knowledge also for the culture of devotion. The cultivation of the intellect should be continued till devotion is enlightened and purified, even as thrashing of paddy should be continued till husks are separated from grains. Devotion is purged of impurities by the exercise of reason in conformity with the teachings of the scriptures.[56] Listening to the Vedic texts, reflection on them, firm conviction, reasoning in harmony with them, sense-restraint, mind-control, endurance of pleasure and pain, withdrawal of the sense-organs from their objects, dispassion for happiness here and hereafter, and desire for liberation should be practised earnestly and diligently till devotion becomes firm, strong, and pure.[57] Thus Śāṇḍilya does not advocate devotion unenlightened by knowledge, but he considers knowledge as subordinate to devotion.

Kāśyapa regards the knowledge of God's sovereignty as conducive to the highest good. He maintains absolute difference between the individual self (jīva) and the Absolute (brahman). Bādarāyaṇa regards the knowledge of the pure self (ātman) or transcendental consciousness, which is the knowledge of the reality, as conducive to liberation. He considers the difference between the individual self and the supreme Self as phenomenal—due to the limiting adjucts only—the former being limited by nescience (avidyā) and its product, a mind-body-complex. Śāṇḍilya regards the knowledge of God's sovereignty and that of the inner self both as conducive to the highest good.[58] The *Bhagavad Gītā* regards the individual self as an eternal part of God.

Advaita Vedāntins regard devotion as inferior to the knowledge of Brahman. God (Īsvara) is a phenomenal appearance of

[55] Īśvarapraṇidhānād vā. YS., i, 23 Yogastūbhayārtham apekṣaṇāt. Gauṇyā tu samādhisiddhiḥ. SS., i, 1, 19-20. SSS., i, 1, 19-20.

[56] Buddhihetupravṛttir āviśuddher avaghātavat. SS., ii, 1, 1.

[57] Tadaṅgānāṁ ca. SS., ii, 1, 2. SSS., ii, 1, 2.

[58] SS., SSS., ii, 3-5. BG., xv, 7.

Brahman conditioned by Māyā or cosmic nescience. Devotion is infected by avidyā, the sense of duality between God and the individual self. Brahman is one undifferentiated pure being, consciousness and bliss unconditioned by cosmic nescience. True knowledge (samyagjñāna) or integral experience (samyaganubhava) apprehends Brahman unaffected by duality, and is, therefore, superior to devotion. Śaṁkara defines supreme devotion as knowledge of the supreme reality, Ātman, or Brahman (paramārthajñanalakṣaṇā), and regards it as necessary for the revelation of truth to a devotee. Śaṁkara defines prayer (upāsanā) as a continuous stream of meditation on the transcendental Ātman or Brahman as unconditioned by cosmic nescience. One who meditates on God as different from his self cannot know the highest truth. But one who has renounced all desires and acquired integral experience (samyagdarśana) of One, who is a true ascetic, and who has universal good will for all beings, directly achieves immortality. This implies that devotion which involves the duality of the individual self and God cannot give the highest truth. Śaṁkara identifies supreme devotion to God with meditation on the supreme Self, Ātman, the Lord of the heart, and being eternally united with Him.[59] Śaṁkara regards subordinate devotion as a prior condition of the intuitive knowledge of Brahman, and identifies supreme devotion with the immediate experience of Brahman. Ānandagiri avers, that one should meditate on Akṣara, the immutable Brahman, with true knowledge (samyagjñana) which has dispelled false empirical knowledge of duality and plurality, and that one who has acquired true knowledge is fit for the realization of God. Ripening of meditation on God or Brahman conditioned by cosmic nescience (māyā) being repeatedly and intensely practised for a long time generates a desire to know the nature of Brahman unconditioned by cosmic nescience, which culminates in the immediate experience of Brahman.[60] Thus devotion which accompanies meditation on God is a propedeutic to true knowledge of Brahman. Veṇkaṭanātha, a Śaṁkarite, also holds the same view. Worship of qualified (saguṇa) Brahman or God with devotion cannot directly bring on liberation because it is generated by the

[59] SBG., xii, 3, 12, 20; ix, 14, 22.
[60] Sopādhikābhidhyāna - paripākān nirupādhikam anusandadhānasya tattva-sākṣātkāra-sambhavāt. ĀBG., xii, 20. Ibid, ix, 34.

knowledge of identity-consciousness, and because this knowledge cannot be acquired without listening to the identity texts, reflection upon their meaning, and firm conviction about its truth. Worship of qualified Brahman or God with devotion leads to meditation on unqualified (nirguṇa) Brahman, which generates through indeterminate trance immediate experience of indeterminate Brahman or Identity-consciousness, and this is liberation. Devotion leads to liberation through true knowledge.[61] Meditation on unqualified Brahman is superior to the worship of God with devotion, because devotion to Him cannot bring on liberation without the intuitive knowledge of unqualified Brahman. By concentrating the mind on God a devotee acquires true knowledge through His grace, and then enters into unqualified Brahman after death. A desireless devotee devoid of the sense of 'I' and 'mine', who concentrates his mind (buddhi) on unqualified Brahman with true knowledge is eternally united with it.[62] Mahādevānanda Sarasvatī avers, that meditation on God generates trance (samādhi) in which a devotee realizes his identity with Him. In trance there is complete absorption of a yogin in the object of meditation.[63] Rāmatīrtha avers, that Brahman is the infinite reality, knowledge and bliss, which is the ontological reality of the empirical world, the individual selves, and God; that until an aspirant annuls the false sense of difference, he cannot realize the highest consciousness of identity; and that consequently devotion, which is infected with the sense of duality of the devotee and God, cannot attain identity consciousness.[64] Madhusūdana Sarasvatī also regards devotion as a prior condition of integral knowledge of Brahman. All spiritual disciplines including supreme devotion purge the mind of all taints and divest it of the knowledge of difference. They generate a stream of cognitions of identity, which are strengthened by listening to the identity-texts, reflection on them and firm conviction, and ultimately end in the manifestation of identity-consciousness or integral experience of Brahman.[65] Devotion to God produces purification of mind, but it is attended with the

[61] *BrGBG.*, xii, 1.
[62] BrGBG., xii, 1 and 14.
[63] ACK., p. 399.
[64] US., Py., p. 127.
[65] *Bhaktyā pareṇa premnā nityayuktāḥ* etena sarvasādhana-nauṣkalyaṁ pratibandhakābhāvāt

empirical knowledge of duality (dvaita). Then listening, reflection, and firm conviction as prescribed by monism lead to the integral knowledge of identity, which manifests supreme bliss.[66] Thus the Advaita Vedāntins consider devotion to be a means to higher knowledge (vidyā). They regard supreme devotion as intuitive experience of Brahman.

The Śaivas also are of the same view. Rāmakaṇṭha defines supreme devotion as the immediate experience of Brahman or pure undifferentiated consciousness and bliss, which is higher knowledge.[67] Devotion is meditation on the nature of Ātman or Brahman, which is in the nature of non-dual pure consciousness.[68] The highest trance (para samādhi) or complete absorption in Brahman is the characteristic of devotion.[69] Rāmakaṇṭha is a Śaiva of Kashmir. The Pāśupata Śaivas of southern India also regard devotion as meditation. Kauṇḍinya defines devotion as meditation.[70] A devotee should have undivided devotion to Śiva, and meditate on Him while sitting, walking, lying, waking, or dreaming, if he seeks for union with Him.[71]

But Caitanya and his followers regard supreme devotion as higher than the knowledge of identity of the individual self and Brahman. They regard God of love as higher than Brahman, pure undifferentiated being, consciousness and bliss, which is a ray of His effulgent spiritual body (tanubhā). They regard pure love for God as a pure mode of His essential power of bliss (hlādinīśakti) which is manifested in the mind of a devotee, which is untainted by desire for happiness and liberation in the form of identity with Brahman. Pure love for God is not veiled by knowledge and action (jñāna-karmādyanāvṛta). Devotion devoid of knowledge is higher than that blended with knowledge. The Bengal Vaiṣṇava's views will be elaborately explained later.

6. *Devotion and Emotions and Passions*

A devotee should direct his emotions and passions—sex-love, anger, conceit and the like—towards God and not towards any

[66] MBG., xii, 6-7 ; ix, 34.

[67] Matsvarūpānubhavarūpām parāṁ kāṣṭhām adhirūḍhā bhaktireva vijñānam. RKBG., ix, 23.

[68] Bhaktirevādvaya - cinmātra - svarūpa - brahma - tattva - bhāvanayā ātmana evopāsanam. RKBG., ix, 27.

[69] Ibid, xviii, 65.

[70] Bhaktir bhāvanā. Pañcārthabhāṣya, ii, 20.

[71] Pāśupatasūtra, ii, 20.

persons.[72] When they are directed towards Him, they are refined, purified and transformed into love for Him. When devotees always divert their sex-love, anger, fear, affection, friendship and other emotions and passions to God from their natural objects, they concentrate their minds on Him, and finally become absorbed in Him. When they cease to identify themselves with their wives, children and property, and always divert their sense of identity to God, finally they attain community of nature with Him, and are united with Him.[73] Many fixed their minds on God because of attachment, aversion, fear, or affection, were purged of their sins, and attained to the supreme status. Grief, joy, fear, hate, greed, delusion, pride and other emotions and passions produce the knowledge of difference, and prevent the knowledge of one God manifesting Himself in many persons and beings.[74] The sense of difference between oneself and others is due to nescience (ajñāna), which generates emotions and passions, and urge deluded persons to injure and kill others. Nescience should be dispelled by the true knowledge of Reality, and emotions should be directed towards God, and transmuted into supreme love for Him, who is the dearest (preṣṭha) to us.[75]

7. *Devotion and Desire*

Supreme devotion is devoid of desire, because it is in the nature of renunciation.[76] Renunciation is the dedication of social duties and religious duties enjoined by the Vedas to God, and the performance of them without any attachment and desire for their fruits in the shape of pleasure.[77] Renunciation is single-minded attachment to God and indifference to the objects of sentient enjoyment, which are repugnant to devotion. Desires are naturally directed towards agreeable objects which are antagonistic to attachment to God. So they should be directed towards God. Attachment to God requires detachment from objects of sensuous pleasure. If social and religious duties are performed

[72] Kāmā-krodhābhimānadikaṁ tasminneva karaṇīyam. NBS., viii, 8.
[73] Kāmaṁ krodhaṁ bhayaṁ sneham aikyaṁ sauhṛdam eva ca.
Nityaṁ harau vidadhato yānti tanmayatāṁ hi te.
Bhāg., x, 29, 15.
[74] Bhāg., vii, 1, 29; x, 4, 26-27.
[75] Bhāg., x, 29, 30; x, 30, 40; x, 46, 5.
[76] Sā (bhaktiḥ) no kāmayamānā mirodharūpatvāt. NBS., ii, 1.
[77] Nirodhastu lokavedavyāpāranyāsaḥ. NBS., ii, 2.

for the pleasure of God, indifference to objects of worldly enjoyment is produced. Hence supreme devotion is desireless, though secondary devotion of the distressed, the inquisitive, and the selfish, is not so.[78] Desires (kāma) should not be suppressed but directed towards, and fulfilled in, God, who alone should be the object of all our desires.[79] When God is worshipped with undivided devotion, He knows the secret desire of His devotee, and gives him of His own accord the divine nature.[80] As a devotee has attachment to God, his desires are directed towards servitude (dāsya) to Him. Desire of a person who has completely given his mind to God no longer remains an impure desire, even as a parched paddy is no longer a seed which may germinate. All desires are destroyed when God rules the heart of a devotee. Only a desireless person can have pure devotion to Him.[81]

Baladeva Vidyābhūṣaṇa (1800 A.D.), a follower of Caitanya, explains the doctrine of supreme devotion expounded in the *Bhāgavata*. Unconditioned and unmediated devotion to God, the supreme Person (puruṣottama), is absolutely desireless and pure.[82] Unmediated devotion is uninterrupted and continuous like a stream of honey. It does not accept liberation in the forms of residence in the abode of God, enjoyment of His sovereignty, proximity to Him, community in nature with Him, and union or identity with Him, even if it is offered by Him. Desireless devotion seeks for loving service of God who is in the nature of bliss. It may be contended, that devotion cannot be desireless, because it desires the bliss which is granted by God pleased with a devotee's devotion through His grace. This contention, Baladeva argues, is not valid, because devotion does not aim at anything other than its object, viz., God, because God who is worshipped is the end of devotion, and because He is in the nature of bliss.[83] His being the end of devotion because He is in the nature of bliss is undisputed. He is the embodiment of the supreme end of the individual self, and gives Himself to His devotee. He is in the nature of bliss and gives bliss or

[78] NBS., ii, 3-5; BG., vii, 16.
[79] NBS., vii, 8.
[80] Bhāg., iii, 13, 49.
[81] Na mayāveśitādhiyāṁ kāmaḥ kāmāya kalpate. Bhāg., x, 22, 26. Ibid, ix, 4, 20; xi, 21, 29, 35.
[82] Ahautukī niṣkāmā viśuddhā. Siddhantaratna, i, 51.
[83] Prakṛte tu bhajanīyo bhagavān eva phalam ānandātmakatvāt. Ibid, i, 52.

Himself to His devotee.[84] It may be further contended, that a devotee's devotion is not desireless because a devotee desires his own pleasure of elation at the pleasure of God awakened by devotion.[85] This contention also is not valid, because the devotees who have acquired pure devotion do not distinctly desire their own pleasure when God is pleased with their devotion, and because they feel God's pleasure as their own pleasure. Further, God is the supreme end of a devotee, the object of his devotion, in the nature of bliss, and fills him with bliss. Hence supreme devotion is desireless.[86]

8. *Devotion and Action*

A living person cannot completely give up all actions, because he cannot maintain his life without actions. Devotion requires renunciation, but renunciation means the resignation of the fruits of actions to God, and not the abandonment of all actions. Whatever we do, whatever we eat, whatever sacrifices we make, whatever we give in charity, and whatever penances we undergo, we should dedicate to God. All actions should be done for God; He alone should be the supreme end of our life and the object of our devotion and love.[87] If all actions are done for God, perfection can be achieved.[88] All actions should be performed without love or hatred and desire for their fruits, and dedicated to God, since they can never bind an agent to empirical life of bondage. This is the message of the *Bhagavad Gītā*.[89]

The *Bhāgavata* also gives the same message. That is real action which pleases God. Whatever actions we do through the body, the sense-organs, the mind (manas), intellect (buddhi), and the soul, we should surrender to God. We should perform our specific duties pertaining to castes and stations in life, and customary social duties, and offer them to God without any desire for fruits.[90] The actions that are done for the pleasure of God with

[84] Bhagavatas tvānandarūpatvāt phalarūpatvaṁ nirvivādam. Evaṁ ca puruṣārtha-mūrtitvātmadātṛtvoktyayo na vyākupyeyuḥ. Ibid, i, 52.

[85] Tenānubhūtena svasukhollāsāt sakāmatvaṁ prāptam. Ibid, i, 53.

[86] Ibid, i, 53-54.

[87] Matkarmakṛt matparamo madbhaktaḥ saṁgavarjitah. BG., xi, 55; BG., xviii, 11; xii, 6; ix, 27; iii, 4-5, 8-9, 19-p0, 30; xii, 10; xviii, 57.

[88] Mad-artham api karmāṇi kurvan siddhim avāpsyasi. BG., xii, 10

[89] BG., v, 10-13; vi, 1-4; ix, 28; xii, 11-12.

[90] Tat karma haritoṣaṁ yat. Bhāg., iv, 29, 49. Ibid, xi, 2, 1.

devotion give rise to true knowledge.[91] The milkmaids of Vṛndāvana lived for God, constantly thought of Him, loved Him as the dearest Lover, did not minister even to their bodily needs for His sake, and were united with Him mentally, who was their Self.[92]

Nārada requires a devotee to dedicate all his actions (tadarpitākhilācārā)—his social and religious duties, and even his soul—to God (niveditātmalokavedaśīla). One can transcend the sense of duality—pleasure and pain—if one performs all actions for God and surrenders their fruits to Him.[93]

Śāṇḍilya observes, that devotion is not in the nature of volition or action, because it does not depend upon it, like knowledge.[94] Just as knowledge depends upon evidence and not upon the knower's will—it cannot be done or undone or altered by him—so primary devotion does not depend upon a devotee's will but upon his secondary devotion.

Baladeva Vidyābhūṣaṇa avers, that though devotion is in the nature of bliss, it appears to be an action (e.g. listening, singing, etc.) in the embodied life because it is related to a devotee's body and sense-organs; that even as sweetness of a fruit is not at first perceived owing to the provocation of bile, but gradually perceived when it is repeatedly tasted, so the nature of devotion is gradually experienced as the essence of bliss through the repeated practice of listening, singing, etc. God is the object of devotion and the supreme end of a devotee. Actions purify the mind: but they cannot bring about the realization of God. Only intuition in the nature of integral knowledge and devotion can directly bring about the realization of God. Thus devotion is preceded by actions in order to generate God-realization.[95]

9. *Devotion and Social and Religious Observances*

The cult of devotion recognizes supreme devotion to God as the primary object of life. We should perform the social duties

[91] Yadatra kriyate karma bhagavat-paritoṣaṇam.
Jñānaṁ yat tadadhīnaṁ hi bhaktiyoga-samanvitam. Bhāg., i, 5, 35

[92] Tā manmanaskā matprāṇā madarthe tyaktadaihikāḥ.
Mām eva dayitaṁ preṣṭham ātmānaṁ manasā gatāḥ.
Bhāg., x, 46, 4.

[93] NBS., iii, 5; vi, 6; viii, 4-5, 8.

[94] Na kriyā kṛtyanapekṣaṇāj jñānavat. SS., i, 7. SSS., i, 7.

[95] Karmaṇaś citta-śuddhau upayogaḥ jñāna-bhakti-rūpāyā vidyāyās tu sākṣātprāptau. Siddhāntaratna, i, 49. Ibid, i, 47-48.

and religious rites which are congenial to devotion to God, and cultivate indifference to those acts which are antagonistic to it. Social and religious observances should be continued till devotion to God becomes firmly established. The sacrifices enjoined by the Vedas, charity, and austerities should be performed without attachment and desire for fruits, for they purify the mind. If the duties inculcated by the scriptures are abandoned, there is a chance of lapsing into impiety and irreligion. Hence social duties ought to be performed until devotion to God is deepened.[96] We should not cherish any thought to upset the social order. We should perform and dedicate our social duties and religious rites to God, and should not abandon them until we are fulfilled in the culture of devotion.[97] But finally we should give up the duties enjoined by the Vedas, when we acquire uninterrupted supreme love for God.[98] We should not unnecessarily revolt against the society, but we should have the courage to be undaunted by the fear of the crowd (janajalpanirbhaya) and to rise above the Vedic prescriptions or scriptural religion.[99]

10. *Devotion and Virtues*

A devotee should cultivate humility, boastlessness, egolessness, harmlessness, fearlessness, truthfulness, non-anger, friendship, tenderness, compassion for all, non-enmity, greedlessness, dispassion, forgiveness, straightness, firmness, non-captiousness, steadiness, buoyancy, spiritedness, sex-restraint, non-stealing, non-hoarding, purity of body and mind, renunciation, charity, endurance, desirelessness, contentment, equipoise of mind, taciturnity, temperance, imperturbability by joy and grief, by love and hatred, by praise and censure, equality towards all beings, indifference to sattva, rajas and tamas and their products, tranquillity, insight into the faults of birth, death, old age and disease, non-affection for wife, sons and house, universal benevolence, study of the scriptures, purity of intuition, shame, and other like

[96] Loke vedeṣu tadanukūlācaraṇaṁ tadvirodhiṣūdāsīnatā. Bhavatu niścayadārḍhyād ūrddhvaṁ śāstrarakṣaṇam. Anyathā pātityśaṅkayā. Loko'pi tāvadeva. NBS., ii, 5-8.

[97] Lokahānau cintā na kāryā niveditātmalokavedaśīlatvāt. Na tadasiddhau lokavyavahāro heyaḥ. NBS., viii, 4-5.

[98] Vedānapi sannasyati kevalam avicchinnānurāgaṁ labhate. NBS., vi, 7.

[99] NBS., vii, 4; x, 10. Jijñāsur api yogasya śabdabrahmātivartate. BG., vi, 44.

virtues.[100] He should cultivate also independence, efficiency, patience, boldness, good character, altruism, gravity, heroism, austerity, strength, hospitality, shame, śama, dama, sense-restraints (yama), and moral observances (niyama). Śama is the steadfast attachment of the intellect to God. Dama is the restraint of the sense-organs. Endurance is tolerance of pain. Contentment is the conquest of sex and greed. Charity is the non-punishment of the offender. Austerity is the renunciation of desires. Heroism is the conquest of the inner nature. Truthfulness is equality towards all and agreeable speech in conformity with truth. Purity is non-attachment to actions. Asceticism is renunciation. Supreme strength is breath control. Shame is moral disapprobation of sins, and recoiling from them. Fortune is independence and other qualities. Learning is the knowledge of non-difference in the self. Foolishness is the sense of identity of the self with the body—its organ. Happiness is the conquest and transcendence of pleasure and pain. Suffering is dependence on desire and pleasure. The human body is the house. The cult of devotion is the true path. The distraction of the mind is the wrong path. The hell is the predominance of tamas. The heaven is the abundance of sattva. Wealth is the excess of good qualities. Poverty is discontent. Mastery is indifference to sattva, rajas, and tamas, and their modes. Slavery is attachment to these guṇas. Supreme devotion to God who is our Friend and Master is the best gain. Sovereignty is community of nature with God. Virtue is desirable wealth. Subordination to the sentient nature is pitiable. Wisdom is the true knowledge of bondage and release.[101]

Compassion is intolerance of others' sufferings, protection of a protegé, and friendship for devotees. Forbearance is the restraint of the mind on the evocation of anger. Renunciation is generosity. Contentment is satisfaction with one's self. Straightness is non-crookedness. Śama is firmness in vows and steadiness of mind. Dama is steadiness of the external sense-organs due to their withdrawal from their proper objets. Equality is indifference to friends and foes. Forbearance is the tolerance of others' offence to oneself. Abstention (uparati) is indifference to achieved gain. Knowledge is the true knowledge of the self and the

[100] BG., ii, 55-19, 64-65, 71; iii, 30; iv, 10, 21-22, 26, 28; vi, 9, 10, 14, 16-17; xii, 13-19; xiii, 7-9, 11; xiv, 25-26; xvii, 16; xviii, 52-54; Bhāg., i, 16, 25-28; xi, 3, 23-26.
[101] Bhāg., xi, 19, 33-44.

Reality, of one's duties at a particular time, in a particular place, under particular circumstances, and intelligence. Dispassion is aversion for objects of pleasure. Mastery is the power of controlling and guiding others. Spiritedness (tejas) is the power of influencing others. Independence is non-subjection to others. Efficiency is skill in actions, cleverness in employing many abilities in extremely complex situations, and proficiency in arts. Patience is the absence of perplexity. Tenderness is softheartedness or the melting of the heart by love. Humility is modesty, respectfulness, and agreeable speech. Good character is rectitude and keeping the company of saints. Gravity is reserve, incommunicativeness, and keeping one's counsel to oneself. Firmness is the absence of fickleness. God's body is made of virtues—truthfulness, sense-control, mind-control, faith, compassion, endurance, austerities, sacrifices, and knowledge of supersensible entities.[102]

11. *Devotion, Sin, and Atonement*

The *Bhāgavata* declares unequivocally that the acts of secondary devotion and primary devotion destroy the taints of the mind produced by sins, purify it, and consume the potencies of actions in the shape of nescience (avidyā). The seeds of sins or nescience cannot be destroyed completely by penances, sex-restraint, control of the sense-organs and the mind (manas), charity, truthfulness, purity of body and mind, restraints (yama), and moral observances (niyama), though they can subdue them temporarily. The potencies of sins remain intact and generate other sins. Penances without faith and devotion cannot purify an aspirant of all his sins and their seeds. But supreme devotion to God can completely destroy all sins, and burn up nescience which is their seed.[103] Devotion destroys sins, even as fire burns a piece of wood into ashes. It destroys nescience and purifies the mind, even as fire destroys the dross of gold. It purifies even a Caṇḍāla of the taint of his low birth.[104] But truthfulness, kindness, austerities, learning, and piety cannot purify a devotee more, because he is already purified by devotion.[105]

[102] Vṛhadvaiṣṇavatoṣiṇī on Bhāg., i, 16, 26-28; Bhāg., x, 5, 41.
[103] Kecit kevalayā bhaktyā vāsudevaparāyaṇāḥ.
Aghaṁ dhunvanti kārtsnyena nīhāram iva bhāskaraḥ.
Bhāg., vi, 1, 15. Ibid, vi, 1, 13-14, 16.
[104] Bhaktiḥ punāti manniṣṭhā śvapākān api sambhavāt. Ibid, xi, 14, 21.
[105] Bhāg., xi, 14, 22, 25.

The secondary acts of devotion—the sight and company of saints, listening to the excellence of God, chanting His name and glory, constant recollection of Him, salutation to Him, worship of Him, etc.—destroy all sins, remove all misery and mental agony, and dispel the darkness of ignorance. They destroy attachment to objects of pleasure, and generate attachment to God. They purify the mind, and produce higher knowledge or intuition (vijñāna), dispassion and primary devotion.[106] These acts involve frequent thought of God, the pure and the Holy, which gradually destroys the contrary thoughts of impurities and sins (pratipakṣa-bhāvanā). Direct efforts to crush them by constantly thinking of them tend to give them a fresh lease of life and strengthen them. But the withdrawal of the mind from them and its concentration on the Holy gradually weaken them because of the lack of sustenance and destroy them.[107]

Śāṇḍilya confirms the teaching of the *Bhāgavata*. The acts of secondary devotion—muttering or chanting the name of God, salutation, worship, prayer, meditation and the like—destroy all sins and impurities of the mind, and purify it.[108] Listening to, and chanting, God's name, and constant recollection of Him are atonements for sins. These acts should be continued till death to atone for heinous sins.[109] Repentance is a mode of atonement for sins. When a sinner repents of his sins, the best form of atonement for his sins is the constant recollection of God. An act of devotion—chanting or recollection—however slight, can destroy great sins. In the cult of devotion all other kinds of atonement are done away with.[110] Thus, devotion is the most powerful atonement for all sins.

12. *Persons eligible for the cult of Devotion.*

All persons, even Caṇḍālas of low birth, are eligible for devotion as they are entitled to the cultivation of the common virtues—non-injury, truthfulness, bodily and mental purity

[106] Nāmasaṁkīrtanaṁ sarvapāpapraṇāśanam. Praṇāmo duḥkhaśamanaḥ. Bhāg., xii, 13, 23. Ibid, x, 48, 31; ix, 9, 6; x, 7, 1-2; xi, 14, 26; xii, 12, 47, 53-54; xii, 3, 51; xi, 14, 22, 25, 26; ii, 5, 18.

[107] YS., ii, 33-34.

[108] Tābhyaḥ pāvitryam upakramāt. SS., ii, 32. SSS., ii, 32.

[109] Smṛtikīrttyoḥ kathādeś cārtau prāyaścittabhāvāt. SS., ii, 46. Ibid, ii, 47.

[110] Laghvapi bhaktādhikāre mahatkṣepakam aparasarvahānāt. SS., ii, 48. SSS., ii, 47-48. Viṣṇupurāṇa, ii, 6, 34.

compassion, faith in God, etc.[111] Svapneśvara adds a condition that they should have a desire to get rid of bondage to the cycle of birth and death. Of all kinds of spiritual discipline, Nārada avers, the cult of devotion is the easiest.[112] It is open to all castes and creeds, women and Śudras, because it is based on firm faith in, and absolute self-surrender to, God. Meditation on the Absolute (braman)—pure transcendental consciousness—demanded by the cult of knowledge, is extremely difficult. But supreme devotion to personal God of love is easy and accessible to all.[113] Among the devotees of God there is no distinction of birth, learning, appearance, family, wealth, vocations and the like, because they all belong to Him.[114]

The *Bhagavad Gītā* preaches the universality and catholicity of the cult of devotion. Even if a person of vile conduct worships God with singleminded devotion, he ought to be regarded as a saint, because his mind is firmly fixed on Him, and because he quickly becomes virtuous and pious, and attains tranquillity. Even persons of vile origin, low caste, and undeveloped intellect —Vaiśyas, Śūdras, and women—attain the supreme status by taking refuge with God.[115] Lord Kṛṣṇa says: "My devotees never perish".[116]

The *Bhāgavata* also throws open the portal of devotion to all irrespective of caste, culture, character, or sex. Even a person of low birth is entitled to the highest status, if he listens to and chants the name of God, thinks of Him and remembers Him. and bows to His image. Even a Caṇḍāla, who sweeps the cremation ground, is superior to a Brāhmaṇa devoid of devotion, if he utters the name of God with faith and devotion.[117] Even a person of low birth is liberated from bondage, if he utters the name of God only once with singleminded devotion. A Caṇḍāla,

[111] Ānindyayonyadhikriyate pāramparyāt sāmānyavat. SS., ii, 50. NBS., x, 5; SSS., ii, 50.

[112] Anyasmāt saulabhyaṁ bhaktau. NBS., viii, 1.

[113] NBS., x, 8; BG., xii, 5.

[114] Nāsti teṣu jāti-vidyā-rūpa-kūla-dhana-kriyādibhedaḥ. Yatas tadīyāḥ. NBS., ix, 6-7.

[115] Api cet sudurācāro bhajate mām ananyabhāk.
Sādhur eva sa mantavyaḥ samyag vyavasito hi saḥ.
Māṁ hi pārtha vyapāśritya ye'pi syuḥ pāpayonayaḥ.
Striyo vaiśyās tathā śūdrās te'pi yānti parāṁ gatim.
BG., ix, 30, 32. Ibid, ix, 31.

[116] Na me bhaktāḥ praṇaśyati. BG., ix, 31.

[117] Aho bata śvapaco' to garīyān yajjihvāgre vartate nāma tubhyam.
Bhāg., iii, 33, 7. Ibid, iii, 33, 6.

who has dedicated his wealth, life, mind, and actions to God, is superior to a Brāhmaṇa, who is endowed with many intellectual and moral qualities, but who is lacking in faith and devotion. A Caṇḍāla devotee purifies his birth and family, but a proud and respected Brāhmaṇa does not. God bestows honour on His devotee. Even savages like Kirātas, Hūnas, Andhras, Pulindas, Pulkasas, Ābhīras, Kaṅkas, Yavanas, Khasas and others of vile conduct are purified by taking refuge with God's devotees. Even the Śūdras, Hūnas, Śavaras, who earn their livelihood by vile actions, transcend cosmic nescience through the acts of devotion.[118] Thus, the *Bhāgavata* unequivocally declares that all persons irrespective of caste, creed, colour, sex, conduct, culture and the like, are eligible for the cult of devotion.

13. *The Cult of Devotion is the highest of all*

The *Bhagavad Gītā* declares: "The yogin is superior to the ascetics, the men of wisdom, and the men of action; and the devotee who, full of faith, and with the inner self abiding in God, worships Him, is most completely united with Him." Those who concentrate their minds on God, and who pray to Him with supreme faith and with their minds united with Him constantly, are most united with Him. Those, who meditate on the imperishable, indefinable, unmanifest, all-pervading, inconceivable, immutable, and immovable, eternal Brahman, withdrawing their sense-organs from their objects, considering and treating all beings as equal, and being engaged in doing good to all creatures, realize the Absolute. But those who meditate on the transcendent impersonal Brahman have to undergo untold sufferings in order to shake off the false sense of identity of the self with the body. It is easier to perform all actions for God and dedicate them to Him, make Him the supreme goal of life, and meditate on, and pray to, Him with an undivided mind, because He is the personal God of love with whom we can hold communion and have personal relation.[119] God delivers them from bondage to birth and death.

The *Bhāgavata* also regards the path of devotion as the best of all kinds of spiritual discipline. Meditation, knowledge,

[118] Bhāg., vii, 9, 10-11; ii, 4, 18; ii, 7, 46.
[119] BG., vi, 46-47; xii, 2-7.

religious rites, study of the scriptures, austerities, and renunciation cannot bring about God-realization so intensely as supreme devotion to God does. No spiritual discipline is more efficacious for worldly men than the cult of devotion to God.[120] It does not require abstruse metaphysical speculation, arduous penances, asceticism and renunciation, abstract knowledge, and complete isolation of the self from the body and the world. But it requires all-consuming love for God, which is imperfectly reflected in all human relations. All human emotions are purified, enriched and fulfilled in God. All works become worship of God, being dedicated to Him. All knowledge is transmuted into knowledge of God in its proper perspective. The whole human life becomes life divine and pulsates with divine energy.

Devotion, Nārada avers, is the best of the three cults of knowledge, action, and devotion undoubtedly. It is easier than the other two paths, and open to all persons irrespective of caste, creed and sex.[121] It is superior to action, knowledge, and meditation, because it is its own fruit. The culture of devotion is necessary for the realization of God, even as personal relationship with a king is necessary for pleasing him. Mere knowledge of his palace is not enough for producing his pleasure; so mere knowledge of God is not enough for pleasing Him. Personal relationship with God should be established through devotion and love: then only He can be realized as God of infinite love, and not as mere Brahman as transcendent Being-Consciousness-Bliss. Hence the path of devotion should be adopted by an aspirant after liberation in the form of the realization of God as infinite love.[122]

14. *Taking Refuge in God* (*Prapatti*)

Taking refuge in God is an essential ingredient of devotion. Persons in quest of knowledge (jñāna) take refuge in God after many births.[122a] Knowledge produces egoism and pride which are impediments to surrender to God. When all endeavours to

[120] Na sādhayati māṁ yogo na sāṁkhyaṁ dharma uddhava.
Na svādhyāyas tapas tyāgo yathā bhaktir mamorjitā.
Bhāg., xi, 14, 20. Ibid, ii, 2, 33.

[121] Trisatyasya bhaktir-eva garīyasī, bhaktir-eva garīyasī. Anyasmāt saulabhyaṁ bhaktau. NBS., x, 8; viii, 1. Ibid, ix, 6.

[122] Sā tu karma-jñāna-yogebhyo'pyadhikatarā. Phalarūpatvāt. NBS., iv, 1-2, Ibid, v, 7-8.

[122a] Bahūnaṁ janmanām ante jñānavān māṁ prapadyate. BG., vii, 19.

achieve knowledge are frustrated, aspirants become humble in spirit and take refuge with God. Cosmic nescience is the māyā of God, which generates ignorance, in the individual selves, of their real nature as distinct from the mind-body-complex composed of essence (sattva), eneregy (rajas), and inertia (tamas) which generate emotions and passions. God's māyā is insurmountable and unconquerable by the individuals' own efforts. Those who take refuge with God can transcend cosmic nescience, ignorance, egoism, delusion and passions.[123] Those who take refuge with God, are purged of attachment, fear, anger and other emotions, purified by knowledge, become full of God, and attain community of nature with Him. He fulfils their spiritual aspirations in accordance with their psychic nature. Those who perform their duties taking refuge with God attain the eternal status through His grace. Those who take refuge with God with all their heart get abiding peace and attain the supreme status. Those who abandon all considerations of virtue and vice, piety and impiety, and take refuge with God only are purified of all sins. Even persons of low birth and vile conduct are purified, and attain the supreme status by taking refuge with God. They become full of divine presence and get undisturbed abiding peace. The *Bhagavad Gītā* regards taking refuge with God (prapatti, śaraṇāgati) as an essential ingredient and a means of devotion.[124]

The *Bhāgavata* also regards taking refuge with God as an essential element in devotion and an indispensable means of it. Devotees should discard scriptural injunctions and prohibitions, desire for sentient pleasure, earthly and heavenly happiness, renunciation and austerities, listening to the scriptures, and take refuge with God, the inner self and guide of all embodied souls, with all their heart. Taking refuge with God only is the most potent and efficacious means of attaining eternal life for embodied selves overcome with threefold sufferings, physical, mental and supernatural. The devotees who take refuge with God are free

[123] Daivi hyeṣā guṇamayī mama māyā duratyayā.
Mām eva ye prapadyante māyām etāṁ taranti te.
BG., vii, 14.

[124] Tam eva śaraṇaṁ gaccha sarvabhāvena bhārata.
Tatprasādāt parāṁ śāntim sthānaṁ prāpsyasi śāśvatam.
BG., xviii, 62.
Sarvadharmān parityajya māmeva śaraṇaṁ vraja.
Ahaṁ tvāṁ sarvapāpebhyo mokṣayiṣyāmi mā śucaḥ.
Ibid, xviii, 66. Ibid, iv, 10, 11; ix, 32.

from debts to human society, ancestors, sages and gods. God destroys the sufferings of those who take refuge with Him.[125] A devotee who takes refuge with God knows 'I am thine' and constantly cherishes this thought in his mind, and experiences bliss.[126]

Śrīnivāsa, a Rāmānujist, regards devotion and taking refuge in God (prapatti) as the only means to liberation. Prapatti is taking refuge in God or throwing oneself on His mercy with firm faith in His protection. It consists in resolution to be favourably inclined towards God and in abandoning hostility towards Him. It consists in self-surrender, self-dedication, or self-giving to God, which is in the nature of a particular kind of knowledge.[127]

The devotees who are penniless and supportless and take refuge in God are prapanna. They are of two classes: (1) those who desire wealth, happiness and virtue, and (2) those who desire liberation. The latter have acquired discrimination between the eternal and the non-eternal because of the company of saints, aversion for the world, detachment, and desire for liberation, are initiated by a competent spiritual guide in the cult of devotion, and, being unable to adopt any other spiritual discipline, and being without any means of livelihood and support, take refuge in God. These aspirants, again, are of two classes: (1) ekāntin and (2) paramaikāntin. Those who desire to acquire other fruits also from God along with liberation are ekāntin. Those who do do not desire to acquire any other fruit except knowledge and devotion from God are paramaikātin. The latter are of two classes: (1) proud and (2) distressed. The former (dṛpta) are those who patiently wait for the moment of death with the firm belief that their accumulated merits and demerits of the past births must be worn out by enjoyments and sufferings of their embodied life. The latter (ārtta) are those who desire every moment of their embodied life to be free from the excruciating pangs of sufferings because they regard them as unbearable.[128]

[125] Bhāg., xi, 5, 42; xi, 12, 15; xi, 19, 9. BRS., i, 2, 200. Prapannārtiharo hariḥ. Ibid., x, 46, 1.

[126] BRS., i, 2, 199.

[127] Nyāsavidyā prapattiḥ. Prapattir nama, ānukūlyasya saṁkalpaḥ prātikūlyasya varjanam. Nyāsaḥ śaraṇāgatiḥ jñānaviśeṣarūpā. YMD., p. 29.

[128] YMD., pp. 34-35.

15. *Surrender of all Actions to God (sarvakarmārpaṇa)*

The *Bhagavad Gītā* regards surrender of all actions to God as an essential ingredient of devotion. All actions should be offered to God, which are performed, without any desire and egoism, and with spiritually illumined mind free from fever of anxiety. Offering of all actions to God mentally does not bind their agents to their fruits. Renunciation of fruits of all actions to God brings supreme peace. All actions dedicated to God make their agents free from bondage to their fruits—happiness and misery. Those who offer all their actions to God, meditate on Him with undivided mind, and are absorbed in Him, are delivered by Him from embodided life. All actions should be offered to God mentally, the mind should be focussed on Him, and He only should be pursued as the goal of life. Such actions lead to the attainment of life eternal through the grace of God.[129]

The *Bhāgavata* also regards dedication of all actions to God as an essential element of devotion. God should be worshipped with all the cognitive and motor sense-organs and mind. All voluntary actions should be performed for the sake of God (tadarthe'khilaceṣṭita). The milkmaids of Vṛndāvana talked about Him, performed all actions for Him, concentrated their minds on Him, and were full of Him.[130] They gave up ministering to their bodily needs for the sake of God, discarded social virtues, fixed their minds on Him, preserved their life for Him, loved Him as the dearest, and realized Him in their hearts.[131] Hence God remembered them always, sustained and protected them; they were objects of His love and eternal attendants who experienced His eternal sport. Nāradā avers, that a devotee should offer all actions regarding the world and religious duties to God, renounce desires for their fruits, and dedicate all actions to Him.[132]

[129] Sarvakarmāṇyapi sadā kurvāṇo madvyapāśrayaḥ.
Matprasādād avāpnoti śāśvataṁ padam avyayam.
BG., xviii, 56. Ibid, xviii, 57; iv, 20; v, 12 & 13; ix, 27 & 28; xii, 6 & 7.

[130] Tanmanaskās tadālāpās tadviceṣṭās tadātmikāḥ. Bhāg., x, 30, 44.

[131] Tā manmanaskā matprāṇā madarthe tyaktā-daihikāḥ.
Māmeva dayitaṁ preṣṭham ātmānaṁ manasā gatāḥ.
Bhāg., x, 46, 4. Ibid, xi, 4, 18-20, 27; x, 80, 4.

[132] NBS., ii, 8; viii, 4, 5, 8.

16. *Dedication of Self to God (ātmanivedana)*

Taking refuge with God and surrender of all actions and their fruits to God pave the way for dedication of one's self to God. The *Bhāgavata* states self-dedication or self-offering as one of the characteristics of devotion. It consists in dedicating one's wife, sons, house, property, all objects of love, and life to God. It consists in dedicating the body, life, sense-organs, and self to God. A person who dedicates his self to God attains community in nature with Him and immortality.[133]

Śāṇḍilya regards preservation of life for God (tadartha-prāṇasthāna), and considering one's wife, children, wealth, property, all objects of love, as belonging to God (tadīyabhāva) as characteristics of devotion. These are included in self-dedication. Bālakṛṣṇa Bhaṭṭa, a Śuddhādvaitavādin, asserts, that dedication of body and self is necessary for pure devotion due to the grace of God (śuddhapuṣṭi-bhakti).[134] This doctrine will be discussed later. Jīva Goswāmī, a follower of Caitanya, explains the text of the *Bhāgavata* mentioned above thus. A person, who has abandoned daily obligatory duties, occasional duties, family duties, and social duties, and who has dedicated his body, sense-organs, mind, self, and all objects of love to God, transcends embodied life, attains immortality, and becomes fit for acquiring God's powers of sovereignty (sārṣṭi). Immortality is the experience of the supreme divine bliss, which makes a devotee fit for the most intimate union with the essential nature of God.[135] Dedication of one's self to God includes offering of the most desired objects and the dearest persons to Him; this brings about infinitude and release. Nārada speaks of a devotee as a person who has dedicated his self to God.[136]

17. *Undivided and Unconditional Love for God (ahaitukī ananyā bhakti)*

The *Bhagavad Gītā* regards undivided devotion as a means to the realization of God, the supreme Person.[137] Unswerving

[133] Niveditātmā amṛtatvaṁ pratipadyamāno mayā ātmabhūyāya kalpate. Bhāg., xi, 29, 34. Ibid, vii, 5, 23; xi, 3, 29.
[134] Sa śuddha-puṣṭi-mārgaḥ yatra sarvabhāvena sarvātmanā dehādeḥ samarpaṇam. PRA., p. 23.
[135] Bhāg., xi, 29, 34; BRS., i, 2, 192; DGS., i, 2, 192.
[136] Bhāg., xi, 11, 41; BRS., i, 2, 197; NBS., viii, 4.
[137] Puruṣaḥ sa paraḥ partha! bhaktyā labhyas tvananyayā. BG., viii, 22

and undivided devotion to God is true knowledge (jñāna),[138] because it is a means to the knowledge of Him. A devotee, who serves, prays to, and worships God with single-minded devotion, completely transcends his psychical nature composed of essence (sattva), energy (rajas), and inertia (tamas) and attains community of nature with Him.[139]

The *Bhāgavata* also describes supreme devotion as undivided devotion (ekāntabhakti). Supreme devotees are tranquil, devoid of attachment, love and hatred, compassionate to all creatures, devoid of enmity, and equal to all. They fix their thoughts on God only (ekāntamati). Undivided devotion to God and constant meditation on Him generate release from embodied life.[140] Supreme devotion is unswerving devotion (achalo bhāvaḥ) or the most intense devotion (tīvrabhakti) to God.[140a]

Rūpa Goswāmī, a follower of Caitanya, defines devotion as a favourable attitude towards God without a desire for any other object (anyābhilāṣitāśūnya). Devotion is undivided love for God. It is pure unconditional love for Him who is its supreme object.[141] It is unconditioned, uncaused, desireless, selfless, supreme love for God. A devotee, who has acquired undivided devotion to God, thinks of Him only, recollects Him only, meditates on Him only, loves Him only, lives for Him only, speaks of Him only, and performs all actions for Him only. His mind is possessed by Him and his whole being is transformed and sanctified by Him. His all thoughts, emotions and volitions are directed towards Him.[142] He lives a divine life.

18. *The Means of Devotion*

Nārada mentions the following as the means (sādhana) of devotion. (1) The renunciation of the objects of enjoyment, and

[138] Mayi cānanyayogena bhaktir avyabhicāriṇī. BG., xiii, 11. Ibid, xviii, 55.

[139] Māṁ ca yo'vyabhicāreṇa bhaktiyogena sevate.
Sa guṇān samatītyaitān brahmabhūyāya kalpate.
BG., xiv, 26.

[140] Ekāntabhaktyā bhagavatyadhokṣaje niveśitātmopararāma saṁsṛteḥ. Bhāg., i, 15, 33. Ibid, i, 15, 47 & 50, xii, 10, 20.

[140a] Bhāg., ii, 3, 10 & 11.

[141] Sarvopādhivinirmuktaṁ tatparatvena nirmalam.
BRS., i, 11, 12. Ibid, i, 1, 11-15.

[142] BG., iii 30; viii, 8 & 14; ix, 13, 14, 22, 27, 34; x, 9; xii, 6, 14, 20; xiii, 11, xiv, 26; xviii, 57: Bhāg., x, 46, 4; xi, 4, 18-20, 27.

of the company of the persons who are engrossed in worldly pleasures is a means to devotion.[143] One who has attachment to worldly objects is absorbed in them; and one who has attachment to God is absorbed in Him. The company of worldly persons produces attachment to objects of pleasure, which is a hindrance to the emergence of devotoion. (2) The company of vicious persons should be shunned by all means. The mind is naturally inclined towards objects of pleasure. This natural inclination is strengthened by evil company. So bad company must be shunned in order to incline the mind towards God. Bad company should be eschewed, because it generates lust, anger, delusion, lapse of memory, destruction of the intellect, and utter ruin. Attachment produces desire; desire being thwarted produces anger; anger produces delusion; delusion produces lapse of memory which generates loss of intelligence; and loss of intelligence generates utter ruin. Lust, anger and delusion produce waves in the mind, which are fanned by bad company into a furious sea agitated by a storm. So bad company must be eschewed. One, who gives up bad company, who keeps the company of saints, and who is devoid of the sense of 'mine' (nirmama), can break the fetters of cosmic nescience (māyā).[144] The distinction between one's self and another springs from egoism due to ignorance of the real nature of the self. When egoism is destroyed on the extinction of ignorance, the sense of difference between one's self and another vanishes.[145] (3) Listening to God's attributes (śravaṇa) from devotees and chanting His name and glory (kīrtana) in their company are the means to the attainment of devotion.[146] Svapneśvara mentions chanting the name of God, fasting and other vows, bowing to God, thinking of Him, meditation on Him, constant recollection of Him, worship of Him, prayer to Him, and dedication of all actions to Him as the means to devotion.[147] These may be performed, Śāṇḍilya avers, simultaneously or successively. Even one of them, if it is powerful, can please God, and bring about supreme devotion. These acts of secondary devotion (gauṇī

[143] Tat tu viṣaya-tayāgāt saṅga-tyāgācca. NBS., v, 2.
[144] NBS., vi, 1-4.
[145] Ajñānaprabhavāhaṁdhiḥ svapareti bhidā yataḥ. Bhāg., x, 4, 26.
[146] Loke'pi bhagavadguṇa-śravaṇa-kīrtanāt. NBS., v, 4.
[147] SSS., ii, 31.

bhakti) are superior to other works, because they generate supreme devotion (parā bhakti), and because they produce other virtues.[148] In fact, supreme devotion cannot be generated by any action; but the acts of secondary devotion destroy the impediments to supreme devotion, and facilitate its emergence.[149] They destroy all sins and taints of the mind, and make it pure; so that devotion, a pure mental mode, may emerge. Listening to, chanting, recollecting, and thinking of, the name and glory of God, and absorption of the mind in Him—the acts of secondary devotion—are conductive to liberation. They produce supreme devotion, which brings about liberation.[150] Vallabha distinguishes between recollecting (smaraṇa) and thinking (cintana). The former is an effortless, spontaneous operation of the mind, while the latter is its voluntary function involving an effort of the will. Vallabha regards meditation (dhyāna) as a kind of thinking, or concentrating the mind on the form of God's image, or on his name while muttering it with a focussed mind.[151] (4) The compassion of saints and a trace of the grace of God are the chief and sure means to the attainment of devotion.[152] The company of saints is inaccessible and unattainable but infallible, since it transmutes a sinner into a saint, even as a touchstone converts iron into gold. It can be acquired through the grace of God only, because there is no difference between God and His devotees.[153]

Bālakṛṣṇa Bhaṭṭa, a follower of Vallabha (1600 A.D.), advocates the doctrine of devotion depending upon the grace of God (puṣṭimārga). Puṣṭi is the grace of God, an attribute of Him, which produdes temporal and non-temporal fruits. It is not perceived by our sense-organs, but inferred from its fruits which are perceptible. It destroys all impediments to the fruition of an aspirant's voluntary efforts. Mahāpuṣṭi is the potent grace of God, which destroys powerful impediments of time (kāla), merits and demerits (karma), and nature (svabhāva),

[148] Iśvaratuṣṭereko'pi balī. Sukṛtajatvāt parahetubhāvācca kriyāsu śreyasyaḥ. SS., ii, 36, 43.

[149] SS., SSS., ii, 29, 32.

[150] Bhāg., (Ch. S. S.), iii, 2, 36.

[151] Aprayatnaś cittavyāpāraḥ smaraṇaṁ, saprayatnaś cittavyāpāraś cintanam. Subodhinī (Ch. S. S.), iii, 2, 36.

[152] Mukhyatastu mahatkṛprayaiva bhagavatkṛpāleśād vā. NBS., v, 5.

[153] Labhyate'pi tatkṛpayaiva. Tasmiṁstajjane bhedābhāvāt. NBS., v, 7-8.

and produces the realization of God.[154] A particular kind of grace of God only generates devotion that leads to the realization of the intrinsic nature of God. It is inferred from devotion which is its effect.[155] (5) The continuous and uninterrupted worship of God is a means to devotion.[156] Worship may be in the form of meditation, prayer, muttering God's name or mystic formula, or the like. If any of these forms of worship be continued uninterruptedly for a long period of time with steadfastness and perseverence, it is sure to generate devotion. (6) One, who lives in a solitary place, who discards the company of persons, who conquers his emotions and passions generated by sattva, rajas and tamas, and who gives up all efforts to maintain his life, transcends cosmic nescience (māyā).[157] Subjection to the guṇas, the innate psychical nature, generates subjection to cosmic nescience. When a person transcends the guṇas by cultivating the neutral attitude of a mere witness (sākṣin) of them without being affected by them, he ceases to be subject to delusion. The guṇas (objects) act upon the guṇas (sense-organs and manas), both of which are in the nature of the not-self. A person should cultivate a neutral attitude towards them; and when he becomes firm in his neutrality, he conquers delusion or false identification of the self with the mind-body-complex. When he takes refuge with God only, the Lord of māyā, he transcends it. When he surrenders himself completely to God and does not make any effort to earn his livelihood, He arranges for his maintenance, and supplies him with the necessaries of life. The Lord of cosmic nescience (māyā) rules in him, and dispels the root ignorance (avidyā) which can no longer fetter him to bondage.[158] (7) One, who renounces actions and their fruits, transcends the sense of duality.[159] Renunciation of actions consists in cultivating the consciousness that God is the real agent of all actions, which arises from the destruction of egoism (ahaṁkāra). Egoism is destroyed, when a person performs all

[154] Mahāpuṣṭitvaṁ balavat - pratibandha - nivṛtti - pūrvaka - svapādāvāpti-sādhakatvam. PRA., p. 16.

[155] Puṣṭiviśesas tu kevalaṁ bhagavat-svarūpa-phalikāṁ bhaktiṁ sādhayati. Bhaktyā kāryarūpayā puṣṭiviśeṣo' numīyate. Ibid, p. 16.

[156] Avyāvṛttabhajanāt. NBS., v, 3. SS., ii, 36.

[157] NBS., vi, 5. BG., ix, 22.

[158] NBS., vi, 5. BG., ix, 22.

[159] Yaḥ karmaphalaṁ tyajati, karmāṇi sannasyati, tato nirdvandvo bhavati. NBS., vi, 6.

actions as an instrument of God, when the divine energy flows in him, when his will pulsates with the Divine Will, when he realizes his freedom of the will as a part of the Divine Freedom. Renunciation of actions does not mean actionlessness. Renunciation of the fruits of actions means surrender of them to God, which are subject to His will. Transcendence of the sense of duality is the blissful state in which there is no sense of one's being an agent of actions, or of experience of their fruits in the form of pleasure and pain. (8) One, who ceases to perform the prudential duties (kāmyakarma) enjoined by the Vedas because he is free from all desires for happiness here and hereafter, and who acquires uninterrupted attachment to God, transcends cosmic nescience undoubtedly, and makes others also transcend it. One should not cease to perform disinterested actions (niṣkāma karma) dedicated to God. One should offer one's self, mind-body-complex, and everything belonging to one, to Him, and love Him with single-minded devotion incessantly. Then only one will break the fetters of māyā, and enable others to do so.[160] (9) An aspirant after devotion should not think of his worldly gain or loss, because he has dedicated himself. his social and religious duties prescribed by the Vedas, and his conduct, to God.[161] He is his only refuge and support in life ; so he is free of all fear and anxiety. He does not worry about Vedic injunctions and prohibitions ; but he performs those actions which he is prompted by God, the Lord of his heart, to do, because he is a conscious instrument of the Divine Will. He does not, therefore, calculate his profit and loss. He has transcended secular consciousness, and been attuned to the Divine Will. (10) An aspirant should not give up his social and religious duties, especially his daily obligatory duties and occasional duties, but should perform them and dedicate their fruits to God, until he is fulfilled in his culture of devotion. Actions are not evil. But egoism or the sense of one's agency of actions and desire for their fruits are evil, and should be discarded.[162] (11) An aspirant should not listen to the character of women, wealthy persons, atheists, and enemies.[163]

[160] Vedān api sannasyati, kevalam avicchinnānurāgaṁ labhate. NBS., vi, 7. Ibid, vi, 8. SSS., ii, 31.

[161] Lokahānau cintā na kāryā niveditātmalokavedaśīlatvāt. NBS., viii, 4.

[162] Na tadasiddhau lokavyavahāro heyaḥ kintu phalatyāgas tat-sādhanaṁ ca kāryam eva. NBS., viii, 5.

[163] NBS., viii, 6.

Listening to the character of women of bad character generates delusion and lust. Listening to the character of wealthy persons produces attachment to wealth. Listening to the character of atheists shakes one's faith in God. Listening to the character of enemies generates hatred. (12) Conceit, boastfulness and the like should be discarded, because the objects of which one boasts, and for which one is conceited, are transitory.[164] (13) An aspirant should dedicate all his actions to God, and direct his passions,—lust, anger, conceit and the like—towards Him, which are then refined, purified and sublimated.[165] (14) An aspirant should not engage in a controversy, because it is unending and often irrelevant, and because it does not lead to the ascertainment of truth.[166] He should not engage in disputation about the Vedas, and take sides in a fruitless controversy. He should not be a sceptic and a dialectician.[167] (15) The scriptures inculcating devotion should be studied and reflected on, and the actions which are enjoined by them as conducive to it should be performed. Thoughts favourable to devotion should be entertained, and actions favourable to it should be performed.[168] (16) An aspirant should not waste a single moment in vain, but pray to, and medidate on, God without thinking of pleasure and pain, gain and loss.[169] Life is short; death may overtake a person at any moment; there is no appropriate or inappropriate time for prayer. Hence no time should be lost in cultivating devotion to God. (17) Non-injury, truthfulness, purity of body and mind, compassion, faith in God, and other virtues conducive to devotion should be cultivated.[170] Malevolence is a hindrance to devotion, and, consequently, should be eschewed. All creatures are the manifestations of God, in whom He is the indwelling Spirit and inner guide. So no injury should be inflicted upon them. Compassion for all creatures should be cultivated. Purity of the mind and purity of the body both are necessary for the culture of

[164] NBS., viii, 7.

[165] Tadarpitākhilācāraḥ san kāma-krodhābhimānādikaṁ tasminneva karaṇīyam. NBS., viii, 8.

[166] Vādo nāvalambyaḥ. Bāhulyāvakāśa-vattvād aniyatatvāt. NBS., x, 1-2.

[167] Bhāg., xi, 18, 30.

[168] Bhaktiśāstrāṇi mananīyāni tadvardhakakarmāṇyapi karaṇīyāni. NBS., x, 3.

[170] NBS., x, 5.

[170] NBS., x, 5.

devotion. Ablutions and other purifying acts are necessary for cleanliness of the body. Restraint of the sense-organs and control of the mind are necessary for purity of the mind. A pure mind cannot exist in an unclean body. God is Truth, and can be attained by unswerving truthfulness. Faith in God is the first step in the culture of devotion. (18) An aspirant should pray to God always without any anxiety with his whole heart.[171] Thoughts of objects of pleasure produce anxiety, and the cessation of such thoughts generates freedom from anxiety, which, in its turn, engenders attachment to, and single-mindedness in, the worship of God.

The *Bhāgavata* prescribes the following means for acquiring devotion: (1) faith in hearing God's name, attributes and actions, (2) chanting them either alone or in a congregation, (3) worshipping Him with constancy, (4) reciting hymns to Him, (5) serving His idol with loving care, (6) adoring and serving His devotees, (7) considering all creatures as His manifestations, (8) performing bodily actions for Him, (9) talking about His excellence, (10) offering one's mind to Him, (11) renouncing all desires, (12) giving up pleasures, enjoyments, and their objects for Him, (13) performing sacrifices, charity, vows, oblations, undergoing penances for Him, (14) muttering His name, and (15) dedication of self to Him. They generate devotion, tranquillity, excess of purity, virtue, knowledge, detachment, supernatural powers, and integral experience of Brahman in the universe.[172] (16) Meditation on Him, (17) serving the spiritual guide, (18) seeing and worshipping God's idol, (19) recollection of Him, (20) taking refuge with Him, (21) humility to Him, and (22) offering all objects acquired to Him also are prescribed as the means of devotion. (23) Servitude (dāsya) and (24) friendship (sakhya) are mentioned as characteristics of devotion along with hearing, chanting, recollection, serving, worship, and hymning.[173]

The *Adhyātmarāmāyaṇa* prescribes the following as the means of devotion: (1) keeping the company of saints, (2) talking about God, (3) chanting His excellence, (4) explaining His

[171] Sarvadā sarvabhāvena niśchintair bhagavān eva bhajanīyaḥ. NBS., x, 6.
[172] Bhāg., xi, 19, 19-27.
[173] Bhāg., vii, 7, 30-31 ; x, 90, 50 ; vii, 9, 9 ; xii, 12, 53-54 ; x, 49, 11-13 ; vii, 5, 23.

message, (5) serving the spiritual guide with sincerity as His medium, (6) practising restraints, observances, etc., and worshipping God daily with constancy, (7) muttering a mystic sound or formula (mantra) symbolizing Him, (8) showing respect to His devotees, thinking all creatures as His manifestations, detachment for objects of pleasure, sense-control, mind-control, etc., and (9) reflection on the nature of the ultimate reality,[174] which is generally prescribed by the monists.

Rāmānuja defines devotion as constant certain recollection of God. The performance of specific duties pertaining to castes and stages of life for the whole life is necessary for devotion to God. Constant certain recollection of God is achieved by taking pure food (viveka), absence of attachment to any object of pleasure (vimoka), frequent practice of concentrating the mind on a good object (abhyāsa), performance of five great sacrifices, e.g. study of the Vedas, performance of sacrifices, charity, austerities, and dispassion (kriyā), practice of virtues (kalyāṇa), e.g. truthfulness, simplicity, compassion, benevolence, non-injury, and successful thoughts, absence of depression (anavasāda) due to grief, and absence of excessive joy (anuddharṣa).[175] Purity of food generates purity of mind, which produces certain recollection that constitutes prayer (upāsanā). Muttering the name of God (japa), fasting, charity, and prayer to God are aids to the knowledge of Brahman. Brahman ought to be sought through penance, celibacy, faith and knowledge. Sense-control, mind-control, listening to the scriptures, and reflection on them are the duties relating to all stages of life. Listening and reflection are the means to the acquisition of knowledge (vidyā). Frequent meditation on God, the object of prayer, is in the nature of a continuous stream of thought (cintā) called bhāvanā. God can be known through devotion which increases purity (sattva).[176]

Śrīnivāsa, a Rāmānujist, regards karmayoga as the performance of unprohibited prudential duties, daily obligatory duties, and occasional duties without any desire for fruits. Worship of God, penance, pilgrimage, charity, and sacrifices should be performed. The disinterested performance of these duties removes impurities of the mind and produces knowledge, and, through it

[174] AR., Araṇyakāṇḍa, x, 22-27.
[175] RBS., i, 1, 1.
[176] RBS., i, 1, 1; iii, 4, 30, 36, 38, 46, 49; YMD., pp. 28-29.

or without it, devotion. Śrīnivāsa regards jñānayoga as reflection on the self as accessory to God and different from the mind-body-complex, a modification of prakṛti, after the mind has been purified by the disinterested performance of the specific duties.[177] He regards karmayoga and jñānayoga as the means of liberation through devotion (bhaktiyoga). He considers the eightfold yoga consisting of sense-restraints (yama), moral observances (niyama), postures (āsana), breath-control (prāṇāyāma), withdrawal of the sense-organs from their objects (pratyāhāra), meditation (dhyāna), concentration of the mind on particular centres of the body (dhāraṇā), and trance (samādhi) to be subsidiary to devotion. God being pleased with a devotee by his devotion and taking refuge in Him gives him liberation. Hence these alone are the means to liberation.[178]

The Mādhva regards truthfulness, benevolence, agreeable speech, study of the scriptures, compassion, longing, faith, charity, delivering the distressed from their misery, preservation of life, and dedication of them to God as the means of liberation. Dedication of the specific duties pertaining to castes and stages of life to Him is the chief means. Liberation,is achieved by appropriate devotion (yogyā bhakti). The ten acts mentioned above constitute appropriate devotion.[178a]

Rūpa Goswāmī mentions the following as the acts conducive to devotion: (1) resorting to a spiritual guide, (2) being initiated and instructed by him in the cult of devotion, (3) serving him with faith and reverence, (4) leading a virtuous life, (5) desire to know the true cult, (6) renunciation of sentient pleasures for the sake of God, (7) residing near the Gaṅgā or a holy river, Dwārakā or a holy place, (8) using the objects which are absolutely necessary for the preservation of life, (9) fasting on the eleventh day of the moon, (10) showing respect to the mother, a peepul tree and the like, which ought be performed by an aspirant at the beginning. The first three acts are the chief ingredients of devotion as a means (sādhanabhakti).[179]

(1) Giving up the company of vicious persons averse to God, (2) not accepting a person who is not eligible as a disciple, (3) not

[177] YMD., p. 28.
[178] YMD., p. 28.
[178a] Bhāgavatatātparya, x, 27, 15, CCA., ii, 9.
[179] BRS., i, 2, 74-77, 82.

entering upon a big enterprise which hinders devotion, (4) not studying parts of many books without understanding and discussion, (5) not feeling misery in the absence of necessary articles or due to loss of them, (6) not being overcome with grief on the death of dear persons, (7) not disregarding other Deities than Kṛṣṇa, (8) non-injury or not causing pain to any creature, (9) not committing flaws in the worship of Kṛṣṇa or in muttering his name, (10) not tolerating hostility towards Kṛṣṇa or his devotees —these ten negative duties are the ingredients of devotion as means (sādhanabhakti). These twenty duties, positive and negative, stated above are the entrance to the realm of devotion.[180]

(1) Bearing the marks of a Vaiṣṇava on the body, (2) writing the name of Kṛṣṇa on the body, (3) bearing the flowers with which Kṛṣṇa is worshipped, (4) dancing before an idol of Kṛṣṇa, (5) falling prostrate on the ground before it, (6) standing up on its arrival, (7) walking behind it in a procession, (8) going to the place where it is kept, (9) walking round it, (10) worshipping it, (11) cleaning its utensils, etc., (12) singing Kṛṣṇa's glory, (13) chanting his name and excellence in the company of others, (14) muttering his name repeatedly, (15) communicating one's thoughts to Kṛṣṇa in thought or words, (16) reciting hymns, (17) eating the food offered to Kṛṣṇa's idol, (18) tasting the water with which its feet have been washed, (19) smelling the incense and the scent of a garland of flowers offered to it, (20) touching it, (21) seeing it, (22) seeing kindled lamps offered to it in the evening, (23) listening to Kṛṣṇa's name, beauty, qualities, and actions, (24) waiting for his grace, (25) remembering his name, form, qualities and actions, (26) meditating on them, (27) servitude, (28) friendship, (29) dedication of self to him, (30) offering articles dear to a devotee to him, (31) performing all actions for him, (32) taking refuge in him with one's whole heart, (33) service of his devotees, (34) tending a tulasī plant dear to him, (35) studying the scriptures (e.g., the *Bhāgavata*), (36) residing at Mathurā, (37) making a festival with his devotees according to his capacity, (38) special adoration of him on a special occasion, (39) making a procession of him on his birth day, (40) faith and intense delight in his worship, (41) discussing the meaning of the *Bhāgavata* with his devotees with delight, (42) keeping the company of the equal

[180] BRS., i, 2, 78-82.

and superior saints, (43) chanting Kṛṣṇa's name in chorus, and residing in the region of Mathurā are the ingredients of devotion as means (vaidhī bhakti). These are the sixty four kinds of worship through the body, sense-organs and mind.[181]

Some of these are discussed here. (1) The company of saints (sādhusaṅga) produces faith in, and devotion to, God, and ultimately release from bondage. An aspirant hears discussion about God from saints, which generates faith in Him, then attachment to Him, and at last devotion to Him. The company of saints destroys all vices and sins, purifies the mind, and produces liberation and God-realization.[182] It produces faith (śraddhā) in God, devotion (bhakti) to Him, ardent love (prema) for Him, and release from bondage to embodied life (saṁsārakṣaya). It produces desire for the realization of God, destruction of ignorance, delusion and egoism, and liberation. A person deluded by ignorance and egoism is incapable of acquiring true knowledge of God and remembering Him. Forgetfulness of God is the cause of bondage; recollection of Him is the cause of its destruction. Faith is produced by the company of saints; faith also induces an aspirant to seek their company, and hear and chant the name, attributes and actions of God. Hearing and chanting destroy all vices and sins. When the mind is purified of all taints, constancy in formalistic devotion is produced. Steadfast formalistic devotion produces interest (ruci) in devotional acts. Interest produces attachment (āsakti), which generates nascent love (rati) for God. Nascent love is intensified into ardent love (prema) for God, which is the abode of transcendent bliss, and the supreme end of human life.[183]

The saints are friends of all creatures and persons, devoid of foes, tolerant, compassionate, tranquil and detached. They forsake their kinsmen and relatives for the sake of God, renounce all observances for Him, take refuge in Him, hear and talk of Him, undergo penances for Him, fix their minds on Him, and cherish undivided devotion to Him. Their company is the door to liberation.[184] They are compassionate, non-violent, truthful

[181] BRS., i, 2, 83-93.

[182] Bhāg., x, 10, 41; x, 51, 54; xi, 2, 30; xi, 12, 16; iii, 25, 25; i. 19, 34.

[183] CCA., ii, ch. 22, 20, 23.

[184] Bhāg., iii, 25, 21-24; v, 5, 2.

blameless, generous, tender, pure, benevolent, tranquil, desireless, unenterprising, constant, self-controlled, temperate, humble, respectful, grave, friendly, wise, efficient, taciturn, unintoxicated, neutral, and destitute of wealth.[185]

The company of restless, foolish, pitiable, lewd, vicious, impious, and worldly pleasure-seekers should be shunned by all means. The company of adulterous persons is the door to bondage and hell. Atheists should be avoided completely. Truthfulness, purity, intelligence, compassion, taciturnity, forgiveness, renown, moral sense, sense-restraint, mind-control and powers born of austerities and meditation are destroyed by the company of sinners. The company of the other sex should be shunned by an aspirant after the supreme status of meditation, knowledge and devotion. Sex-restraint is necessary for the attainment of the highest stage.[186]

Those devotees who worship God, but who do not respect His devotees, and who laugh at, abuse and maltreat them, do not attract His grace, because they are boastful and conceited. But those who worship God and respect His devotees undoubtedly realize Him. The abuse of God's devotees is a much worse sin than the killing of animals. Those persons who worship God with reverence, but who do not respect His devotees, and who are not compassionate to the ignorant, low and sinful, are inferior devotees. God and His devotees are non-different from each other; they are the limbs of His body. He dwells in them, and they dwell in Him. Showing disrespect to devotees and ill-treatment with them destroy the well-being of aspirants.[187]

(2) Hearing (śravaṇa) the name, attributes and actions of God melts the heart, destroys threefold suffering, purifies the mind of all vices, decreases attachment to objects of pleasure, increases attachment to Him, inclines the mind towards Him uninterruptedly, enables it to be concentrated on Him, fills it with bliss, and produces great merits. It generates pure devotion to, and ardent love (prema) for, Him, attracts His grace, subjects Him

[185] CCA., ii, ch. 22.
[186] Bhāg., iii, 31, 33-35; iii, 31, 39. CCA., ii, ch. 22.
[187] CB., iii, ch. 7; ii, 22; ii, 5; Varāha Purāṇa; Haribhaktisudhodaya; Bhāg., x, 5, 46; BG., x, 29.

to a devotee, manifests Him in all beings and objects in the universe, and produces the realization of God.[188]

(3) Chanting God's name (kīrtana) consists in uttering a name which represents Him. Some worship Him by constantly chanting His name in the company of others with their minds focussed on Him, acquire knowledge of Him, and realize Him. Chanting gives intense joy to them and pleases God.[189] His name should be chanted with an undivided mind at all times.[190] There is no restriction of time, place and conditions in chanting God's name. It may be chanted while sitting, walking, eating, breathing, or sleeping, with devotion. Chanting destroys disease, lengthens the span of life, gives happiness, release, and community of nature with God (sarūpatā).[191] Chanting His name constantly destroys intense grief, attachment to objects of pleasure, taints and vices, purifies the mind completely, produces true knowledge of the reality, ardent love for Him, and the realization of Him, and fills the mind with bliss. God, being chanted, meditated on, adored and worshipped, enters into a devotee's mind, dispels its ignorance, reveals Himself quickly to him, and suffuses his mind with His influence.[192] Choral chanting purifies not only the individual minds of the participants in a congregation, but also the group mind of humanity, because thought waves are more subtle and powerful than the subtlest physical waves.[193] Chanting God's name is good both for aspirants and fulfilled (siddha) persons. Those who are desirous of happiness and liberation also should chant it to achieve their ends. Chanting is singing in tunes to the accompaniment of musical instruments.

There is no difference between God and His name, which is an embodiment of His transcendental consciousness and bliss (cidānanda), and which is pure and non-physical. Hence it cannot be perceived, in its spiritual essence, by the physical sense-organs, but it manifests itself to them when it is chanted by a

[188] Bhāg., ii, 4, 24; ii, 2, 36-37; iii, 29, 11-12; iii, 14, 48-50; x, 31, 9-14; x, 7, 2; x, 14, 13-14; x, 53, 37-38; iii, 33, 6; CCA., ii, ch. 9 & 24; CB., ii, ch. 2.

[189] Satataṁ kīrtayanto mām. BG., ix, 14. Ibid, x, 9-10.

[190] Ekena manasā bhagavān kīrtitavyaḥ. SS., BC., p. 176.

[191] Ibid, p. 166.

[192] Sa kīrtyamānaḥ śīghram evāvirbhavatyanubhāvayati ca bhaktān. NBS., x, 7. Bhāg., xii, 4, 52; xii, 12, 47-49; xii, 13, 23; x, 4, 45-50. Padyāvalī, CCA., iii, Ch. 20.

[193] CB., ii, Ch. 23.

devotee. God's name is not a physical sound, but spiritual in nature, being composed of transcendental consciousness (cit) and bliss (ānanda), the essence of Him. It is identical with God and His essence.[194]

Caitanya (1600 A.D.) avers, that God created many names through His infinite grace, and charged them with His infinite powers, which being muttered, chanted and remembered at any time, in any place, and in any condition, generate love for, and realization of, Him. There is no restriction of time, place and condition in muttering and chanting God's names. They should be chanted with an undivided mind, and with humility, endurance, reverence, and devotion. Chanting is better than all sacrifices.[195]

Chanting produces melting of the heart which is expressed in eight spontaneous organic expressions (sāttivika vikāra): gooseflesh, shedding tears, faltering voice, perspiration, change of colour, trembling, inactivity, and insensibility. It is also expressed in breathing quickly, singing, dancing, laughing, crying aloud, rolling on the ground, fainting, stiffening, softening, lengthening, or shortening of the body.[196] All these were found in Caitanya's body while he chanted God's names.

(4) Muttering God's name or a mystic formula representing Him (japa) is the essence of the cult of devotion. A name or a mantra is a concrete symbol, while God's nature as infinite universal consciousness and bliss is an abstract concept. It is much easier to mutter and chant a name and meditate on the meaning of its concept than to meditate on the latter alone. Japa is not mere mechanical repetition of a name, but it is accompanied by faith in its representing God, the pure and the Holy. To repeat His name with faith and devotion is to contact God through mind and spirit. Further, a name or a mantra charged with spiritual power is given to an earnest aspirant by a competent spiritual guide who has experienced the power of God, and who imparts his experience to his disciple through the name.

The sacrifice of muttering is the best of all sacrifices.[197] It

[194] Nāma-cintāmaṇih caitanya-rasavigrahah śuddhaḥ abhinnatvāt nāma-nāminoh. BRS., i, 2, 231. CCA., ii, Ch. 17.

[195] Padyāvalī, CCA., iii, Ch. 20; i, Ch. 3; CB., ii, Ch. 13 & 26. Bhāg., xii, 12, 49.

[196] Bhāg., xi, 2, 40; CB., ii, Ch. 2, 3, 5, 8; iii, Ch. 1, 8; CCA., i, Ch. 7.

[197] Yajñānāṁ japayajño'smi. BG., x, 25.

is of three kinds: audible, inaudible and mental. Inaudible muttering is better than audible muttering; and mental muttering is better than inaudible muttering. An aspirant should mutter a name or a mystic formula of God repeatedly with an undivided mind and meditate on Him for a period of time. Repeated muttering in all times, in all places, in all conditions, produces all powers of spiritual disciplines, destroys all vices, generates ardent love for God, liberation, and God-realization. Muttering God's name saves a person from bondage to embodied life, if he is devoted to God. It does not quickly produce any fruit in an atheist who is engrossed in the pursuit of wealth, bodily pleasures, and wife and children's comforts. Greatness of God's name is incomprehensible by human reason. It should be muttered with faith; then its fruits are experienced.[198]

Haridāsa muttered God's name three hundred thousand times a day from his youth to old age, acquired a supernatural (aprākṛta), spiritual (siddha) body composed of transcendental consciousness (cit) and bliss (ānanda), as Caitanya, his Master, said, and died at his will before him. An earnest devotee dedicates his body to God who spiritualizes it.

Kṛṣṇadāsa Kavirāja (1600 A.D.) avers, that constant muttering of the name of God is the essence of all spiritual disciplines; and that it destroys bondage to embodied life and produces God-realization.[199] Kṛṣṇa's nature or essence and His name are identical; His name (nāma), image (vigraha), and essence (svarūpa) are identical. There is no difference among them; they are embodiments of transcendental consciousness and bliss (cid-ānandarūpa). Transcendental consciousness transcends mental consciousness, and transcendental bliss transcends mental pleasure and joy. Kṛṣṇa is God of love, who is loved by his devotees, and who loves them. His essence and name both are transcendental consciousness and bliss. Hence His name is not perceptible by the sense-organs, but it is self-manifest (svaprakāśa).[200] Here 'Kṛṣṇa' does not mean a historical person. Kṛṣṇadāsa Kavirāja was a follower of Caitanya, and his biographer, who expounded his teachings.

[198] CCA., i, Ch. 7, pp. 57, 59; ii, Ch. 17, pp. 256-57.
[199] CCA., i, Ch. 7, ii, Ch. 24, p. 336; iii, Ch. 3, pp. 390-91.
[200] CCA., ii, Ch. 17; p. 216.

(5) Recollection (smṛti) is bringing about a relation of God to the mind of a devotee by any means.[201] Constant recollection of God destroys the impurities and vices of the mind, increases its purity (sattva) and tranquillity, and generates devotion to Him, knowledge (jñāna), intuition (vijñāna), and detachment.[202] Recollection of God in all times, in all places, and in all conditions, destroys all kinds of sufferings. God is easily realized by one who constantly remembers Him with an undivided mind. One who constantly prays to Him with an undivided mind is always united with Him.[203] Recollection of God depends upon dispassion for earthly objects of pleasure. One whose mind is tainted with attachment to these objects cannot remember God always. Forgetfulness of God is the cause of bondage, and constant recollection of Him is ultimately the cause of release. Those persons, who constantly remember Him, meditate on Him in their hearts, worship Him daily, hear of His excellence, and keep the company of His devotees, easily break the fetters of bondage. Those, who constantly remember Him, and remind others of Him, are filled with joy, and please Him.[204]

(6) Meditation (dhyāna) is thinking of Kṛṣṇa's form, qualities, actions, and being served, deeply.[205] Single-minded attention is the chief means of meditation. There is no restriction of place, time and conditions in meditation.[206] Those persons who meditate on, and pray to, God with single-minded devotion are delivered by Him from the cycle of birth and death. Devotees should meditate on Him with undivided minds after arresting all bodily actions and words which distract them. Those who meditate on Him regularly and constantly are not affected by their actions in their worldly life. Meditation produces endurance of pleasure and pain, of heat and cold, and of hunger and thirst, washes off impurities and vices, and produces devotion, liberation, and God-realization.[207]

(7) God's image or idol should be served and worshipped with

[201] Yathākathañcin manasā sambandhaḥ smṛtiḥ. BRS., i, 2, 173.
[202] Bhāg., xi, 3, 31; xii, 12, 53-54; CCA., ii, Ch. 24.
[203] Ananyacetāḥ satataṁ yo māṁ smarati nityaśaḥ. Tasyāhaṁ sulabhaḥ. BG., viii, 14. Ibid, ix, 22.
[204] CCA., ii, ch. 20; i, ch. 13; AR., YK., viii, 46-47; BG., x, 9.
[205] Dhyānaṁ rūpa-guṇa-krīḍā-sevādeḥ suṣṭhu cintanam. BRS., i, 2, 176. Ibid, i, 2, 177, 180.
[206] SS., BC., pp. 158, 176.
[207] *BG., xii, 6-7; AR., KK., iii, 35; iv, 34.*

etc., to Him, and feeling "I am His servant by all means," which is its essence.[213] Some regard feeling of being a servant of God only as servitude. Others regard the performance of the specific duties pertaining to castes and stages of life, muttering God's name, meditation, etc., for God's pleasure only as servitude. Others regard dedication of the specific duties mentioned above to God as servitude. One who has servitude to God in words, actions and thoughts enjoys embodied release in all conditions.[214]

The performance of the specific duties pertaining to castes and stages of life is not regarded as a member of formalistic devotion by experts in the cult of devotion, though it is regarded as a member by others. These duties should be performed until dispassion for the world and faith in listening to God's excellence are generated.[215] Servitude as a means of formalistic devotion is discussed here.

(11) Friendship (sakhya) is faith and behaving like a friend.[216] Faith and belief are synonymous with each other. But firm belief in God is an ingredient of faith. Friendship for God is included in formalistic devotion (vidhibhakti) which follows the method prescribed by the scriptures. It is included in passionate devotion (rāgānugā bhakti) when it does not follow the method prescribed by them, but when it is actuated by ardent love only.[217] Friendship as a means of formalistic devotion is considered here.

Rūpa Goswāmī opines that knowledge and detachment may be helpful at the time of entering upon the path of devotion, but that they are not members of devotion, because they harden the mind, whereas devotion is very tender in nature. There are three kinds of knowledge: (i) knowledge of the individual self (tvam), (ii) knowledge of Brahman (tat), and (iii) knowledge of their identity (aikya) according to the monist. The third kind of knowledge is hostile to devotion. Knowledge and detachment which do not hinder devotion may be favourable to it in the beginning. Rūpa Goswāmī and Jīva Goswāmī do not consider them to be members (aṅga) of devotion. Knowledge and detachment of a person who has devotion to God are generally not

[213] Dāsyaṁ karmārpaṇaṁ tasya kaiṅkaryam api sarvathā. BRS., i, 2, 181.
[214] Ibid, i, 2, 182-85.
[215] Ibid, i, 2, 244-45.
[216] Viśvāso mitravṛttiś ca sakhyam. BRS., i, 2, 186.
[217] Ibid, i, 2, 189 & 191.

conducive to his welfare. But liberation which is generated by knowledge, and knowledge which is produced by detachment can be achieved through devotion only. Whatever is achieved by the performance of duties, austerities, knowledge, detachment, meditation, charity, and other good works—even heaven, liberation and the abode of Kṛṣṇa—can be easily achieved by pure devotion.[218]

If a person has acquired interest (ruci) in Kṛṣṇa, even his strongest attachment to objects of pleasure is often destroyed. If a detached devotee enjoys objects of pleasure in conformity with devotion to, and interest in, Kṛṣṇa, his detachment is called mixed detachment (yuktavairāgya). Rejection of food and other articles offered to Kṛṣṇa by a person desirous of liberation, who considers them to be natural objects, is called false detachment (phalguvairāgya). It is not a member of formalistic devotion (vaidhī bhakti).[219]

Rūpa Goswāmī does not regard discrimination (viveka), restraints (yama), observances (niyama), etc., as members of formalistic devotioon, because they come of themselves to a devotee. Non-injury, truthfulness, non-thieving, sex-restraint, and non-acceptance of unnecessary gifts are called restraints. Bodily cleanliness and mental purity, contentment, austerities, study of the scriptures, and dedication of all actions to God are called observances. These good qualities come of themselves to a devotee, because they are fruits of devotion to God.[220]

Formalistic devotion, whether its one principal member is practised or whether its many members are practised by a devotee, gives fruition (siddhi) of his spiritual discipline according to his desire. Parīkṣit attained the realization of God through listening to His greatness; Śukadeva, through chanting His name; Prahlāda, through constant recollection of Him; Lakṣmī, through service of Him; Pṛthu, through His worship; Akrura, through reciting His hymns; Hanumān, through servitude; Arjuna, through friendship; and Bali, through offering himself and all his property entirely to Him. Ambarīṣa engaged his vocal organ

[218] Jñāna-vairāgyayor bhakti-praveśāyopayogitā.
Ubhe cittakāṭhinyahetū sukumāra-svabhāveyaṁ bhaktiḥ.
BRS., i, 2, 246-47; DGS., i, 2, 246. Ibid, i, 2, 248-51.
[219] BRS., i, 2, 252-54, 256.
[220] BRS., i, 2, 258-59, 261; YS., ii, 30-32.

in describing His excellence, his hands in cleaning the floor of His temple, his ears in hearing His excellence, his eyes in seeing his image, temple and other signs, his limbs in touching the bodies of his devotees, his nose in smelling the fragrance of the flowers offered to Him, his tongue in tasting the food offered to Him, his legs in walking to the place where his image was worshipped, his head in bowing to it, his mind in meditating on Him, and his desire in serving Him as His servant, and not pursuing earthly enjoyments. Thus he practised many-membered formalistic devotion and realized God. One-membered or many-membered formalistic devotion is always directed towards the acquisition of attachment (rati) to God.[221]

Kṛṣṇadāsa Kavirāja, a Caitanyite, mentions the sixty four members of formalistic devotion stated by Rūpa Goswāmī, and regards (1) keeping the company of saints, (2) choral chanting of his name, (3) listening to the *Bhāgavata,* (4) residing in the region of Mathurā, and (5) doing service to the image of Kṛṣṇa with faith as the principal devotional acts which generate ardent love (prema). Some devotees practise one member, and others practise many members of formalistic devotion and achieve its fruits. A devotee, who practises formalistic devotion in accordance with the injunctions of the scriptures without any desire, is not under moral obligation to discharge his debts to the gods, sages and ancestors by performing sacrifices, studying the Vedas, and by marrying wives and procreating sons. He does not commit sins forbidden by the scriptures voluntarily. He does not atone for his non-voluntary sins, which are purified by God. Knowledge and dispassion are not ingredients of formalistic devotion. Restraints (yama), observances (niyama), etc., come of themselves to him, because they are invariable accompaniments of his communion with God.[222]

[221] BRS., i, 2, 264-66.
[222] CCA., ii, ch. xxii.

CHAPTER XVI

RELIGIOUS EMOTIONS: KINDS OF DEVOTION

1. *The Bhagavad Gītā: Distressed, Inquisitive, Selfish and Wise Devotees*

The *Bhagavad Gītā* mentions four kinds of devotion: (1) devotion of the distressed (ārta), (2) devotion of the inquisitive (jijñāsu), (3) devotion of the selfish (arthārthī), and (4) devotion of the wise (jñānī). The persons seized by robbers, tigers, etc., or attacked with diseases are distressed, who cherish devotion to God for deliverance from their distress. The inquisitive are desirous of knowing the nature of God. The selfish are desirous of wealth and the like. The wise have acquired the knowledge of God.[1] The wise devotee has single-minded devotion to God, and is constantly united with Him; he is superior to the other classes of devotees.[2] All classes of devotees are dear to Him, but the wise devotee is excessively dear to Him, because he is not different from Him. He is non-different from God, concentrates his mind on Him, is absorbed in and united with Him, and firmly established on the path to the highest status.[3] A wise devotee completely surrenders himself to God, and takes refuge with Him after many births, when his intuitive knowledge becomes ripe and he realizes that God is the inner Self of all creatures. One who has realized that all are God is extremely rare.[4] One who has single-minded, undivided, unswerving devotion to God, can have a vision of the cosmic form (viśvarūpa) of God, and a knowledge of His real nature. Devotion of a wise devotee is single-minded supreme devotion (parā bhakti) by which only God, the Supreme Person, can be realized.[5]

The *Mahābhārata* prescribes single-minded devotion, which depends upon the restraint of the sense-organs and the

[1] Ārto jijñāsur arthārthī jñānī ca bharatarṣabha. BG., vii, 16. SBG., vii, 16.

[2] Teṣāṁ jñānī nityayukta ekabhaktir viśiṣyate. BG., vii, 17.

[3] Jñānī tvātmaiva. BG., vii, 18. SBG., vii, 18.

[4] BG., vii, 19. SBG., vii, 19.

[5] BG., viii, 22. Ibid, xi, 54.

concentration of the mind on God and its absorption in Him, as the means of realizing Him. Certainly a devotee with single-minded devotion to God is the best and dear to Him. Single-minded devotion consumes all merits and demerits—which produce happiness in heaven and suffering in hell, and continue the cycle of births and deaths, becomes ripe, and brings about the realization of God. It makes a devotee absolutely pure, free from virtue and vice, endowed with integral knowledge of God as the inner Self of all beings, and constantly united with Him.[6]

2. *The Bhāgavata: Tāmasa, Rājasa, Sāttvika, and Nirguṇa Devotion*

The *Bhāgavata* describes two principal kinds of devotion: (1) devotion actuated by purity (sattva), energy (rajas), and inertia (tamas) of the mind (saguṇa-bhakti), and (2) devotion untainted by these fundamental psychical impulses (nirguṇa-bhakti). The former is of three kinds: (1) devotion impelled by tamas (tāmasa-bhakti), (2) devotion impelled by rajas (rājasa-bhakti), and (3) devotion impelled by sattva (sāttvika-bhakti).

(1) The devotioon of an enterprising person, which is motivated by envy, malevolence and boastfulness (dambha), and which is tainted by the sense of difference, is called tāmasa. The *Bhagavad Gītā* describes boastfulness as a demoniac quality which ought to be eschewed.[7]

Śaṁkara and Śrīdharasvāmī regard dambha as dissimulation of piety, which consists in performing religious rites in order to exhibit one's piety. Rāmakaṇṭha regards it as demonstration of one's religiosity by performing various religious rites without any faith and religious sentiments. Madhusūdana regards dambha as showing off one's piety with the object of gain, distinction or admiration of the people, though one is really impious. Rāmānuja regards dambha as mock piety which consists in the performance of religious rites with the intention of winning popular applause. Hanumān and Nīlakaṇṭha regard dambha as counterfeit ceremonial piety for the purpose of deceiving others. It is

[6] Ekāntabhāvopagatā vāsudevaṁ viśanti te.
Nūnam ekāntadharmo'yaṁ śreṣṭho nārāyaṇapriyaḥ.
MBh., Śāntiparva, ch. 346, 350.

[7] Bhāg., iii, 29, 7-8; BG., xvi, 4.

pretension to piety despite one's impious character. Puruṣottamajī observes that this mock piety is external demonstration of one's religiosity because of the lack of genuine piety in the heart.[8]

(2) The devotion of a person who worships God's image with a sense of difference, being motivated by the acquisition of wealth and other objects of pleasure, is called rājasa. (3) The devotion of a person, who dedicates all his actions to God in order to attain to the state of actionlessness (naiṣkarmya), and who worships God with a sense of difference and without any motive or desire for fruits, is called sāttvika. Devotion impelled by sattva, rajas and tamas is tainted with a sense of difference among God, the devotee, and the act of worship. These are the inferior kinds of devotion—sāttvika devotion being superior to rājasa devotion, and rājasa devotion being superior to tāmasa devotion.[9]

(4) The devotion which is not prompted by the guṇas mentioned above, which is unconditional and immediate love of God, the supreme Person, which is uninterrupted and spontaneous movement of the mind towards Him, like the movement of the water of the Gaṅgā towards the sea, just on hearing of His excellent attributes, and which refuses to accept five kinds of liberation, even if they are offered by Him, and which desires nothing but service to Him. This is the supreme devotion (parā bhakti) through which a devotee transcends the guṇas and attains to community of nature with God, or pure devotion (kevalā bhakti), or single-minded devotion (ekānta bhakti), or the highest devotion (ātyantika bhakti).[10]

The *Bhāgavata* speaks of three classes of devotees—inferior (adhama), mediocre (madhyama), and superior (uttama). (1) An inferior devotee worships God in his image with faith, but does not worship Him in His devotees and other beings. His knowledge of God is limited to an image or idol (arcā) in which He is supposed to abide. (2) A mediocre devotee cherishes love

[8] Dambho dharmadhvajitvam. SBG., NBG., xvi, 4. Antas tadabhāvena bahiḥ dharmaprakaṭanam. ATBG., xvi, 4. SrBG., RKBG., MBG., RBG., HBG., xvi, 4.

[9] Bhāg., iii, 29, 9-10.

[10] Madguṇaśrutimātreṇa mayi sarvaguhāśaye.
Manogatir avicchinnā yathā gaṅgāmbhaso' mbudhau.
Lakṣaṇaṁ bhaktiyogasya nirguṇasya hyudāhṛtam.
Ahaitukyavyavahitā yā bhaktiḥ puruṣottame.
Bhāg., iii, 29, 11-14. Ibid, iii, 29, 13. Cp. AR., UK., vii, 61-67.

(prema) for God, friendship (maitrī) for His devotees, compassion (kṛpā) for the ignorant, and indifference (upekṣā) to his foes. His devotion is manifested in his different attitudes towards different types of persons, and not confined to God's image only; and his devotion to Him is not mere reverence but love. So he is superior to an inferior devotee. (3) A superior devotee sees God in himself and in all creatures, sees them in God and in himself, and sees the divinity of his self.[11] He has integral experience of God in himself and the universe, and supreme love for Him. So he is the best devotee.

The *Bhāgavata* describes the characteristics of the best devotee in the following manner. He is neither elated by the attainment of desired objects nor depressed by the non-attainment of them, regards them all as modifications of Māyā of God, is not deluded by the functions of his body, sense-organs, life, mind, and intellect because of his constant recollection of God, has destroyed the root of ignorance (avidyā), the seed of desires and actions, lives in God only as his abode, has no sense of identity of his self with his body, is not attached to the duties pertaining to his caste and stage of life, does not feel any difference between himself and others, is equal to all beings and calm and tranquil, does not deviate from thinking of God for a single moment, is free of mental anguish by the grace of God, and never forsakes His blessed feet—which destroy heaps of sins—because of intimate love (praṇaya) for Him.[12]

The *Bhāgavata*, we have already seen, describes supreme devotion as the spontaneous and uninterrupted movement of the mind towards God just on hearing of His glory, or as unconditional and immediate love for Him, or as pure single-minded devotion untainted by emotions and passions generated by sattva, rajas and tamas. Supreme devotion is unconditional and unhindered devotion to God, which is the highest virtue of persons, and which attracts His grace, and brings them the highest good.[13]

[11] Sarvabhūteṣu yaḥ paśyed bhagavadbhāvam ātmanaḥ.
Bhūtāni bhagavatyātmanyeṣa bhāgavatottamaḥ.
Bhāg., xi, 2, 45. Ibid, xi, 2, 46-47.

[12] Bhag., xi, 3, 48-55.

[13] Sa vai puṁsāṁ paro dharmo yato bhaktir adhokṣaje.
Ahaitukyapratihatā yayātmā samprasīdati.
Bhāg., i, 2, 6.

3. *Nārada and Śāṇḍilya: Primary and Secondary Devotion*

The *Bhagavad Gītā* describes supreme devotion as enlightened by the knowledge of God, which constantly unites a devotee with Him. A devotee who concentrates his mind on God, adores, worships, and makes obeisance to, Him, and who regards Him as his only goal, is united with Him, and realizes Him. He who performs all actions for God, who seeks Him as his only goal, who is devoid of attachment and enmity, realizes Him. He who dedicates all his actions to God, who lives for Him only, who concentrates his mind on Him, who meditates on, and prays to, Him with an undivided mind, is delivered by Him from the sea of birth and death. He who fixes his mind and intellect on God only will undoubtedly live in Him after death. One who cherishes supreme devotion to God undoubtedly enters into Him. A single-minded devotee is dear to Him. God arranges for the maintenance of his devotee who constantly thinks of Him only, who cherishes single-minded devotion to Him, and who is constantly united with Him. God lives in His devotees, and they live in Him.[14]

The *Bhagavad Gītā*, we have already seen, recognizes four classes of devotees: (1) distressed (ārta), (2) inquisitive (jijñāsu), (3) desirous of ends (arthārthī), and (4) wise (jñānī). Nārada regards the first three kinds of devotion of the distressed, the inquisitive, and the desirous of ends as secondary devotion, and regards the second as superior to the first, and third as superior to the second. He recognizes three other kinds of devotion according as it springs from purity (sattva), energy (rajas), and inertia (tamas) of the mind. He regards sāttvika devotion as superior to rājasa devotion, and rājasa devotion as superior to tāmasa devotion.[15] He regards a God-intoxicated person, who is completely absorbed in God, whose all thoughts, affections, words and actions are directed towards Him, who cherishes single-minded devotion to Him (ekāntin), as the best devotee. He visions God everywhere within and without. Among such single-minded devotees there is no distinction of caste, learning, beauty,

[14] BG., ix, 34; xi. 55; xii, 6-8, 20; xviii, 65, 68; ix, 22, 29.
[15] NBS., vii, 6-7.

lineage, wealth, and avocations, because they all have community of nature with God—being his devotees and eternal portions.[16]

Though devotion is one in its essential nature, it admits of eleven kinds: (1) attachment to the qualities and greatness of God (guṇamāhātmya), (2) attachment to His beauty (rūpa), (3) attachment to His worship (pūjā), (4) attachment to the recollection of Him (smaraṇa), (5) attachment to servitude to Him (dāsya), (6) attachment to friendship for Him (sakhya), (7) attachment to wifehood (kāntā), (8) attachment to parenthood (vātsalya), in relation to Him, (9) attachment to self-dedication to Him (ātmanivedana), (10) attachment to absorption in Him (tanmayatā), and (11) supreme attachment to separation from Him (paramavirahāsakti).[17]

Supreme love (paramaprema) for God is primary devotion. It is undivided single-minded devotion which is absolutely desireless. A single-minded devotee has all-absorbing love for God and apathy for all objects of enjoyment. He takes refuge with God only and abandons all other supports of life. He lives in God and by Him.[18] On attaining such primary devotion, a devotee becomes fulfilled (siddha), immortal (amṛta), and contented (tṛpta). He delights in his Self, sports with his Self, and is contented with his Self. He transcends desire, joy, grief, hate, and endeavour. He neither desires anything, nor grieves for anything, nor hates anybody, nor feels joy on getting anything, nor exerts himself for acquiring any object. Supreme love leads to the realization of God. When God is realized, nothing remains to be attained. The realization of God is the highest stage of fulfilledness and self-realizedness. Supreme love for God is infinite, absolute, and self-complete. When it is acquired, a devotee becomes intoxicated (matta) with God, speechless and mute (stabdha), and self-contented (ātmārāma).[19]

Śāṇḍilya also distinguishes between primary devotion and secondary devotion. The devotions of the distressed (ārta), the inquisitive (jijñāsu), and the selfish (arthārthī) are secondary, and the devotion of the wise (jñānī) is primary. The secondary devotions (gauṇī bhakti) are the means to the acquisition of primary

[16] Bhaktā ekantino mukhyāḥ. Tanmayāḥ. Yatas tadīyāḥ. NBS., ix, 1, 4, 6-7.
[17] NBS., x, 9.
[18] NBS., i, 2; ii, 1, 3, 4.
[19] NBS., i, 4-6.

devotion (parā bhakti). The devotion of the distressed consists in their recollection (smaraṇa) of God, chanting His name and glory (kīrtana), listening to the excellences of God (kathā), making obeisance to Him (namaskāra), etc. The performance of sacrifices, and of the specific duties pertaining to castes and stages of life for the acquisition of knowledge constitutes the devotion of the seekers of knowledge. The devotion for the acquisition of objects is of two kinds: (1) devotion for the acquisition of primary devotion, and (2) devotion for the acquisition of earthly or heavenly happiness. The secondary acts of devotion destroy all sins and purify the mind.[20]

Śāṇḍilya regards single-minded devotion of a devotee to God, the be-all and end-all of his life (ekāntabhāva), as primary devotion (parā bhakti).[21] It is supreme undivided devotion to God, which destroys the intellect absolutely and leads to liberation. Liberation is the realization of the infinite, eternal and absolute bliss of Brahman.[22] The intellect (buddhi) is the limiting adjunct of the individual self, the complete destruction of which brings about liberation.[23]

4. *Madhusūdana: Three Classes of Devotees; Śrīnivāsa: Devotion as Means and Devotion as End*

Madhusūdana, an Advaita Vedāntist, describes three classes of devotees. (1) The best devotees worship God as their inner self, meditate on Him as identical with themselves, and adopt the method of prayer as identity (ahaṁgraha). (2) The mediocre devotees worship a Deity as a symbol of God different from them, and adopt the method of prayer to a symbol (pratīkopāsanā). (3) The inferior devotees worship many deities as different from themselves. They are incapable of prayer as identity and prayer with the help of a symbol; but yet their prayer to many deities is prayer to God, because they sincerely endeavour to transcend the phenomena.[24] The last two classes of devotees are infected with

[20] SS., SSS., ii, 44-49.

[21] Sā ekāntabhāvaḥ. SS., ii, 2, 55. Sā parā bhaktir ekāntabhāvo nānyaḥ. SSS., ii, 2, 55.

[22] Ananyabhaktyā tadbuddhir buddhilayād atyantam. SS., iii, 2, 4.

[23] Parabhaktimātreṇa buddher atyantalaye sati brahmānandāvāptilakṣaṇā muktiḥ. Buddhir jīvopādhiḥ. SSS., iii, 2, 4.

[24] MBG., ix, 15.

the knowledge of difference. Devotion purifies the mind; then knowledge of duality and plurality is known to be false; then intuitive knowledge of identity dawns; then supreme bliss is realized. Worship of personal God (saguṇa brahman) with undivided attention destroys nescience and phenomenal appearances generated by it. The destruction of nescience generates the intuitive experience of indeterminate (nirguṇa) Brahman, which is liberation.[25] Thus Madhusūdana maintains, that supreme devotion (ekānta bhakti) destroys the impediments to true knowledge, and generates integral experience or liberation, and that supreme devotion indirectly leads to liberation through knowledge. Śaṁkara regards supreme devotion as higher knowledge, and identifies them with each other. But, according to Madhusūdana, worship of God with love (prema) destroys the hindrance of dissimilar thoughts, creates a continuous stream of similar thoughts of God, and generates a firm conviction that 'I am Brahman', which produces the integral experience of Brahman, or liberation. Hence supreme devotion (ekānta bhakti) culminates in the higher knowledge or intuitive realization of Brahman.[26]

Rāmakaṇṭha, a Śaivādvaitavādin, regards supreme devotion as of the nature of supreme knowledge. It is the highest excellence of knowledge in the form of the immediate experience of the non-dual supreme self. This supreme devotion which is in the nature of the highest knowledge leads to the knowledge of the supreme Self as the only reality.[27]

Śrīnivāsa, a Viśiṣṭādvaitavādin, describes two kinds of devotion: (1) devotion as means (sādhanabhakti) and (2) devotion as end (phalabhakti). The former is generated by spiritual practice. The latter is produced by the grace of God. Śrīnivāsa describes two classes of devotees: (1) those who practise devotion as means and (2) those who practise devotion as end. Vyāsa and others were of the first kind, while Nātha and others were of the second kind.[28] The first class adopt devotion with its subsidiaries as the means for liberation. The second class practise devotion for its own sake.

[25] MBG., xii, 6.
[26] MBG., ix, 14.
[27] Paramātmādvaita-pratipatti-lakṣaṇā yā jñānasya parā niṣṭhā saiva parā bhaktiḥ. RKBG., xviii, 54. Ibid, xviii, 55, 69.
[28] YMD., pp. 29 and 34.

5. *Bālakṛṣṇa Bhaṭṭa*: *Maryādā bhakti and Puṣṭī bhakti.*

Bālakṛṣṇa Bhaṭṭa, a Vallabhite, mentions two kinds of devotion: (1) maryādābhakti and (2) puṣṭibhakti. The former is directed towards the acquisition of superhuman powers born of meditation, and of liberation and realization of God. The latter is directed towards the realization of the intrinsic nature of God only, and devoid of any other desire for superhuman powers and liberation. It is generated by special favour of God.[29]

Puṣṭibhakti is of four kinds: (1) pravāha-puṣṭi-bhakti, (2) maryādā-puṣṭi-bhakti, (3) puṣṭi-puṣṭi-bhakti, and (4) śuddha-puṣṭi-bhakti. (1) The devotees who have the first kind of devotion are interested in actions conducive to the realization of God, and neither devoid of the sense of 'I' and 'mine' nor transcendent of empirical life (saṁsāra). Pravāha is the stream of worldly life of egoism. (2) Maryādā consists in the performance of those actions which are conducive to the realization of God. It destroys aspirants' attachment to objects of enjoyment and induces them to enter upon the path of renunciation and listen to the excellence and glory of God. The aspirants who adopt maryādābhakti renounce worldly pleasures and listen to discourses on God. (3) Puṣṭi-puṣṭi-bhakti is devotion mixed with knowledge. In this kind of devotion aspirants worship God after acquiring knowledge fit for achieving devotion to God. (4) Śuddha-puṣṭi-bhakti is acquired by aspirants when it is given to them by God through His grace. Pure love (prema) predominates in it, in which aspirants are purified by pure love for God, and sing His glory and worship Him with affection (sneha) only. After they acquire affection, they listen to God's excellence, chant His name, and worship Him with a passion (vyasana). Their affection turns into a passion, and they cannot but perform the acts of devotion. In śuddha-puṣṭi-bhakti pure love is the only means of the realization of God, which dispenses with all kinds of spiritual discipline, and which depends upon His special favour independently of the aspirants' fitness. In it God quickly accepts devotees as their own without considering their fitness. It brings on also earthly happiness and heavenly happiness unsolicited, which are the ends of secular duties and religious duties. It brings about the realization of the

[29] Viśeṣānugrahajanyā yā bhaktiḥ sā puṣṭibhaktiḥ. PRA., p. 17.

essential nature of God.[30] In it a devotee renounces all objects of enjoyment as 'mine' and accepts them as belonging to God. In it a devotee does not obey the injunctions of the society and the scriptures, but seeks for God's pleasure only. He does not desire earthly happiness and happiness in future life, but directs all his actions towards God's pleasure. A female devotee forsakes her husband, sons, relatives and house, and dedicates herself to God, the supreme Person. In it devotional acts of listening to and chanting the name and glory of God generated by intense love (prema) are experienced as supreme bliss. In it there is the experience that intense love for God destroys all hindrances created by time, merits and demerits, and nature, fear of the society, and fear of punishment in future life. Śuddha-puṣṭi-bhakti gives the bliss of the intrinsic nature of God independently of the manifestation of His intrinsic nature. In this kind of devotion establishing bodily, mental and spiritual relationship between an individual embodied self and God is the spiritual discipline, and contact with God through all the sense-organs is its fruit. The relationship is established by the will of God. In it a devotee experiences love for the persons who have established relationship with God, enmity for those who are hostile to Him, and neutrality for those who are indifferent to him. In it a devotee preserves his body for the sake of God, because it belongs to Him. In it no excellence is ever realized in God who is worshipped by a devotee, but God increases love for Him in His worshipper. In the path of puṣṭibhakti God does not give His devotee happiness as the fruit of his worship, but gives him pangs of separation so that he may feel that God suffuses his spirit with divine presence. In it greater bliss is experienced in separation from God than in union with Him, because His sport in numerous forms is experienced by a devotee when he feels the pangs of separation from Him. In it the spiritual discipline (sādhana) is the fruit (phala), and the fruit is the spiritual discipline: the means and the end are identical with each other. Unconditional love (sneha) is the fruit which is to be realized; and it is the means by which the bliss of the intrinsic nature of God is experienced. Unconditional love for God is given by Him through His grace. In this

[30] Sādhanāntara-nirapekṣeṇānugraheṇa yatra laukika-vaidika-siddhiḥ sa śuddha-puṣṭi-bhakti-mārgaḥ. Prabhur jīva-yogyatā-vicāram akṛtvaiva yatra śīghram aṅgīkaroti sa suddha-puṣṭi-bhakti-mārgaḥ. PRA., p. 19. Ibid, pp. 17-18.

cult union with God produces humility (dainya), and not sulks (māna); humility generated by separation from Him brings about the manifestation of God independently of any other conditions. In it a devotee becomes the object of God's recollection: devotion is completely fulfilled when it makes God remember His devotee.[31]

Bālakṛṣṇa Bhaṭṭa avers, that a person is eligible for the cult of puṣṭibhakti, on whom the grace of God descends. God's grace is imperceptible; it is inferred from one's interest (ruci) in this path, which is its effect. A person who acquires interest in this cult is eligible for it. God gives him the company of saints through His grace, and impels him to listen to His excellence and glory and worship Him.

When interest (ruci) in the path of puṣṭibhakti is created in a person, he listens to God's holiness and worships Him. Then God inspires his mind and fills it with His influence; and this divine inspiration purifies his mind. Then listening, chanting and worship are repeated by him, which wash off all impurities of his mind and produce interest (ruci) in God, which is indirect (aparokṣa), because God is not directly experienced at the time. This indirect interest assisted by listening and worship generates subtle devotion (bhāva), which is the seed of devotion. This nascent devotion accompanied with indirect interest and listening and worship bring about the manifestation of God to the devotee's heart.[32] Thus God is directly experienced a little by him. This little experience produces in him a special interest (ruciviśeṣa) in God, which is direct interest (aparokṣa ruci). Nascent devotion (bhāva) is increased by this direct interest and the spiritual discipline of listening, etc., and turned into love (prema). Love for God which destroys attachment to all other objects than God is called affection (sneha). Affection is increased by repeated listening, chanting and worship, and turned into clinging (āsakti) to Him, which produces the experience that the objects which are not related to Him are inimical to love for Him. Clinging to God produces hatred for one's house (gṛhāruci). Aruci is not the absence of interest, or apathy, but the opposite of interest,

Yatra sarvabhāvena sarvātmanā svasmin jīve bhagavat-smṛter viṣayatā sa śuddha-puṣṭi-bhakti-mārgah. PRA., p. 24. Ibid, pp. 19-23.

[32] Sa eṣa bhāvaḥ parokṣarucyā śravaṇādi-sahakṛto' ntar bhagavat-sphūrtiṁ karoti. PRA., p. 25.

or hatred. Nascent devotion (bhāva) in the form of clinging (āsakti) produces the experience that all other objects than God are hostile to love for God. Clinging to God is increased continuously by the appropriate spiritual discipline, and turned into a passion (vyasana), when all bodily functions are thrown away entirely. The clinging to God which attains the stage of a passion is called devotion (bhakti) that consists in serving and worshipping God mentally.[33] It has been called supreme attachment to, or the most intense love for, God. Devotional acts should be performed until a passion for God is acquired. Sometimes intense love (prema) is called clinging (āsakti), and sometimes it is called a passion (vyasana), because they are of the same nature, though the first stage of loving devotion (premabhakti) is called love (prema), its second stage is called clinging (āsakti), and its final stage is called passion (vyasana).[34] This passionate love is described by the *Bhāgavata* as unconditional and immediate love for God.

Passion (vyasana) for God generates the direct knowledge of the presence of God in the universe, which produces intense love for all beings (utkaṭasneha). This stage is called identification of the self with the universe (sarvātmabhāva), when God is manifested to the devotee both in his heart and in the universe. Identification of the self with all beings is undivided devotion,[35] which is the experience of God in all beings. Unconditional genuine love for God is a special kind of devotion which consists in identification of the self with all beings wherein God is the indwelling Spirit.[36] Identification of the self with all beings inculcated by the cult of puṣṭibhakti is included in the erotic sentiment; it is a kind of mystic transcendent erotic sentiment, for which devotees endowed with pure devotion due to the grace of God are eligible.[37]

The final fruit of śuddha-puṣṭibhakti is superhuman power of a devotee in the shape of entering into the eternal sport of

[33] Sā (āsaktiḥ) vyasanaṁ bhāvaṁ prāptā bhaktir mānasī sevā ityucyate. PRA., p. 26.

[34] Prema-paripākāvasthā vyasanam. PRA., p. 27.

[35] Sarvātmabhāva ekāntabhaktiḥ. PRA., p. 31.

[36] Bhagavad-viṣayako nirupadhi-sneho bhakti-viśeṣaḥ sarvātmabhāvaḥ. PRA., p. 31.

[37] Ayaṁ puṣṭimārgīaḥ sarvātmabhāvaḥ śṛṅgāra-rasa-madhyapātī. Etatprāptau suddha-puṣṭi-bhaktānām evādhikāraḥ. PRA., p. 32.

God, whereas formalistic devotion (maryādābhakti) ends in union with God (sāyujya).[38]

6. *Rūpa Goswāmī: Sādhana-bhakti, Bhāva-bhakti and Prema-bhakti*

Rūpa Goswāmī mentions three kinds of devotion: (1) sādhana-bhakti, (2) bhāva-bhakti, and (3) prema-bhakti.[39] (1) The devotion, which is produced by voluntary efforts (e.g., listening, chanting, worshipping, etc.), and which manifests devotion as an end, is called sādhana-bhakti. Bhāva or devotion as an end is not produced, but only manifested by devotion as means, because it is eternally present as a particular mode of God's essential power of bliss in an individual self.[40] Bhāva is the result of a ripe state of devotion as means (sādhana-bhakti); and prema is the result of a riper state of it.

Devotion as means is of two kinds: (1) vaidhī bhakti and (2) rāgānugā bhakti. (1) The devotion as means, which follows the method prescribed by the scriptures (e.g., hearing, chanting, remembering, etc.), and which is not motivated by passionate attachment (rāga), is called formalistic devotion (vaidhī bhakti). The main injunction is the recollection of God, and the main prohibition is forgetfulness of Him. These are obligatory for persons of all castes and stages of life. They achieve the desired ends by performing the acts prescribed by the Vedas and the Sātvata Tantras. Formalistic devotion manifests supreme devotion (parā bhakti).[41]

Persons who have acquired faith (śraddhā) in the worship of God by virtue of the merits born of the company of saints and the like, and who are neither excessively attached to the world nor excessively detached from it, are eligible for formalistic devotion. They are superior, mediocre and inferior. (1) Those who are well-versed in the scriptures, expert in reasoning in conformity with them, and firm in their faith, are the most eligible for formalistic devotion. They are called superior

[38] PRA., pp. 29-30.
[39] Sā bhaktiḥ sādhanaṁ bhāvaḥ premā ceti tridhoditā. HBRS., i, 2, 1.
[40] Kṛtisādhyā bhavet sādhyabhāvā sā sādhanābhidha.
Nitya-siddhasya bhāvasya prākaṭyaṁ hṛdi sādhayatā.
HBRS., i, 2, 2. DGS., i, 2. 2; CB., iii, ch. 3.
[41] BRS., i, 2, 2-5.

devotees. (2) Those who are not well-versed in the scriptures, but who are endowed with faith, are less eligible for formalistic devotion. They are called mediocre devotees. (3) Those who have shallow faith which can be shaken by contradicting arguments are the least eligible for formalistic devotion. They are called inferior devotees. The means of formalistic devotion have already been discussed.[42] Formalistic devotion (vidibhakti) is called by Vallabha and his followers maryādābhakti, because it is motivated by profound faith in the scripture. It does not transcend the limits imposed by them.[43]

7. *Rūpa Goswāmī: Rāgātmikā, Rāgānugā, Kāmarūpā, Sambandharūpā, Kāmānugā and Sambandhānugā bhakti*

(1) Devotion motivated by passionate attachment (rāga) is called loving devotion (rāgātmikā bhakti). It was manifest in the residents of Vṛndāvana, who had passionate attachment to Kṛṣṇa. Rāga consists in being intensely engrossed in its object, in being full of it, and in being spontaneous.[44] There is intense yearning for the obect attended with attachment.

(2) The devotion which imitates passionate attachment of the residents of Vṛndāvana is called rāgānugā bhakti.[45] This devotion is of two kinds: (1) kāmarūpā and (2) sambandharūpā.

(3) Passionate attachment in the form of transcendent amour (kāma) turns the desire for enjoyment into ardent love (prema), because it is expressed in actions which afford pleasure to God only. The sports of the milkmaids of Vṛndāvana were motivated by selfless love for Kṛṣṇa, and not by the selfish desire for their own pleasure as we have already pointed out. Passionate attachment in the form of transcendent amour is a special kind of selfless love for Kṛṣṇa, which attains a certain extraordinary sweetness and actuates sports with them. Hence it is called kāma by the Vaiṣṇavas, though it is not lust. It has become a custom

[42] HBRS., i, 2, 5-8, 22-36.
[43] HBRS., i, 2, 59.
[44] Iṣṭe svārasikī rāgaḥ paramāviṣṭatā bhavet.
Tanmayī yā bhaved bhaktiḥ sātra rāgātmikoditā.
HBRS., i, 2, 62. DSG., i, 2, 62.
[45] Rāgātmikām anusṛtā yā sā rāgānugā.
Ibid, i, 2, 61.

to designate the milkmaids' selfless love as kāma.[46] Even Uddhava and other male devotees of Kṛṣṇa longed to have the milkmaids' love as transcendent amour for Kṛṣṇa.

Kṛṣṇa lived with his step-brother, Balarāma, at the house of Nanda and Yaśodā, his foster-parents, at Vṛndāvana for eleven years after his birth at Mathurā. Then he left for Mathurā and did not return to Vṛndāvana. Kṛṣṇa and Balarāma both were in their late childhood (kiśora), and did not enter upon youth. Parāśara regards ten to fourteen years as kiśora. Kṛṣṇa was not even in the beginning of adolescence. The milkmaids were younger than he was. Hence there could not be sexual relation between Kṛṣṇa and the milkmaids.[47] The Vaiṣṇavas fabricated the fiction that transcendent amour (kāma) was the relation between Kṛṣṇa and the milkmaids for convenience of their method of prayer and worship. They propounded erotic mysticism and endeavoured to sublimate their sex impulse (libido) into holy love for God by meditating on themselves as milkmaids and God of love or Kṛṣṇa as their lover. Some Bengal Vaiṣṇavas were advocates of erotic mysticism. The milkmaids' lust (kāma) for Kṛṣṇa is an absolutely false mental construct of some Vaiṣṇavas.

(4) Passionate attachment (rāgā) in the form of relationship (sambandha) to Kṛṣṇa was entertained by the Vṛṣṇis. Vasudeva's fatherhood and Yaśodā's motherhood in relationship to him were passionate attachment of this kind. Passionate attachments in the form of transcendent amour or selfless love and relationship were, in their essential nature, pure love (prema) only. They existed in the milkmaids, Nanda and Yaśodā who were eternally self-realized souls (nityasiddha).[48]

Passionate attachment predominates in these two kinds of devotion, because it is devoid of the sense of lordship.[49]

[46] Sā kāmarūpā sambhogatṛṣṇām yā nayati svatām.
Āsāṁ premaviśeṣo'yam prāptaḥ kāmapi mādhurīm.
Tattatkrīḍānidānatvāt kāma ityucyate budhaiḥ.
Premaiva goparāmāṇām kāma ityagamat prathām.
Kāmo'tra sveṣṭa-viṣaya-rāgātmaka-prema-viśeṣaḥ. DGS., i, 2, 68. HBRS., i, 2, 68-71.

[47] Ekādaśasamās tatra gūḍhārciḥ sabalo' vasat. Bhāg., iii, 2, 26. Kiśorau shyāmalaś cetau. Ibid, x, 38, 29. Kiśorau nāptayauvanau. Ibid, x, 44, 8. Vṛhatvaiṣṇavatoṣiṇī.

[48] Sambandharūpā govinde pitṛtvādyabhimānitā. HBRS., i, 2, 72. Ibid, i, 2, 74.

[49] Yad aiśyajñānaśūnyatvād eṣāṁ rāge pradhānatā.
Kāma-sambandha-rūpe te prema-mātra-svarūpake.
HBRS., i, 2, 73.

Rāgānugā bhakti, like rāgātmikā bhakti, is of two kinds: (1) kāmānugā and (2) sambhandhānugā. Persons who long for acquiring the rāgātmikā bhakti of the inhabitants of Vṛndāvana are eligible for rāgānugā bhakti. Their longing is generated by hearing of the various kinds of love cherished by the latter for Kṛṣṇa without depending on the authority of the scriptures and favourable reasoning. Formalistic devotion (vaidhī bhakti) depends on the authority of the scriptures and favourable reasoning. Persons are eligible for it until they acquire transcendent love (bhāva).[50] But devotion to Kṛṣṇa, which is sought owing to longing for acquiring transcendent love of the denizens of Vṛndāvana, is rāgānugā bhakti. Those who long to acquire transcendent love of the residents of Vṛndāvana dear to Kṛṣṇa should worship him with their physical and spiritual bodies (siddhadeha) like the latter. Hearing, chanting, etc., which are the members of formalistic devotion, are also the members of ardent devotion.[51]

(5) Kāmānugā bhakti desires to imitate kāmarūpā rāgātmikā bhakti of the milkmaids of Vṛndāvana. It is of two kinds: (1) kāmānugā bhakti which desires to bring about union of the milkmaids of Vṛndāvana with Kṛṣṇa (sambhogecchāmayī); and (2) kāmānugā bhakti which desires to realize the sweetness of the milkmaids' transcendent love for Kṛṣṇa (tadbhāvecchātmikā). Even male persons may desire to acquire their trenscendent love on seeing Kṛṣṇa's image or on hearing of his sports.[52]

(6) Sambandhānugā bhakti consists in a devotees' thinking of, and attributing, his relationship to Kṛṣṇa (e.g., fatherhood, motherhood, friendship, etc.).[53] A devotee may attribute Kṛṣṇa's fatherhood to himself, think of himself as Nanda, his foster-father, and worship his image as such. Or, he may attribute friendship for Kṛṣṇa to himself, think of himself as Subala, and worship his image as such.[54] Some devotees of Kṛṣṇa meditate on him as their husband, son, father, brother, or friend. Devotion imitating transcendent love of the dwellers of Vṛndāvana depends

[50] Vaidha-bhaktyadhikārī bhāvā-virbhāvanāvadhiḥ. HBRS., i, 2, 77. Ibid, i, 2, 74-76.
[51] HBRS., i, 2, 78-81.
[52] HBRS., i, 2, 81-84.
[53] Sambandhānugā bhaktiḥ pitṛtvādi-sambandha-mananā-ropaṇātmika. HBRS., i, 2, 86.
[54] HBRS., i, 2, 87-88.

upon the grace of Kṛṣṇa or his devotees.[55] Vallabha and his followers, Śuddhādvaitavādins, call rāgānugā bhakti puṣṭibhakti, which has already been discussed.

The inhabitants of Vṛndāvana cherished passionate attachment (rāga) to Kṛṣṇa. Deep yearning for the object of love is its essential characteristic (svarūpa lakṣaṇa); and being engrossed in its object is its extrinsic characteristic (taṭastha lakṣaṇa). Devotion inspired by passionate attachment is called rāgātmikā bhakti. Devotion which imitates such attachment is called rāgānugā bhakti. A devotee who practises such devotion at first acquires nascent love (rati), then ardent love (bhāva), and at last passionate love (prema). God becomes subject to passionate love.[56]

The path of knowledge culminates in the manifestation of indeterminate Absolute (Brahman) to an aspirant. The path of meditation results in the manifestation of the supreme Self as the Inner Guide (antaryāmin) to a yogin. Formalistic devotion ends in the transportation of a devotee to Vaikuṇṭha, the abode of Viṣṇu, after death in the body of a comrade of Kṛṣṇa. Devotion inspired by ardent love results in the realization of God incarnate as Kṛṣṇa at Vṛndāvana.[57]

8. *Rūpa Goswāmī: Kinds of Devotion: Devotion inspired by transcendent love (bhāvabhakti): devotion due to intense spiritual discipline, devotion due to the grace of Kṛṣṇa or his devotee, bhāvapratibimba and bhāvachāyā*

Nascent love (bhāva, rati) is a particular mode of the pure essence (śuddhasattva), which resembles a ray of the sun of pure love (prema), and which melts the heart through desires for the realization of God.[58] It is a mode of the pure sattva or God's essential power of consciousness which manifests all objects. It is not a mode of sattva of cosmic nescience.[59] It is eternally present in a devotee dear to God.

[55] Kṛṣṇa-tadbhakta-kāruṇya-mātra-lābhaika-hetukā rāgānugā (bhaktiḥ). HBRS., i, 2, 89. Ibid, i, 2, 90.

[56] CCA., ii, ch. 22.

[57] CCA., ii, ch. 24.

[58] Śuddha-sattva-viśeṣātmā prema-sūryāṁśu-sāmya-bhāk.
Rucibhiś citta-māsṛṇya-kṛd asau bhāva ucyate.
HBRS., i, 3, 1.

[59] Atra śuddhasattvaṁ nāma svaprakāśikā svarūpaśakteḥ saṁvidākhyā vṛttiḥ, na tu māyāvṛtti-viśeṣaḥ. DGS., i, 3, 1.

Nascent love is the first stage of ardent love for God.[60] It is slightly expressed in tears, gooseflesh and other spontaneous organic manifestations (sāttvika-vikāra). Bhāva is nascent love (rati) for God. Though it is self-manifest as a mode of the pure sattva or God's essential power of consciousness, it appears in a mental mode of a devotee, is identified with it, and appears to be an object of apprehension. Though it is in itself in the nature of relish (āsvāda), it becomes a cause of the relish of Kṛṣṇa's sweetness. It is in the nature of bliss because it is a mode of God's essential power of bliss (hlādinī śakti). It is in the nature of relish because it is manifested as an object of apprehension.[61]

Nascent love (bhāva, rati) for God is produced in two ways. (1) It is produced in very fortunate persons by their steadfast practice of hearing, chanting, recollection, meditation, worship and other acts of devotion (sādhanābhiniveśa). (2) It is produced by the grace of Kṛṣṇa or his devotees (kṛṣṇa-tadbhakta-prasāda). Nascent love is mostly produced by the first cause. Nascent love produced by the second cause is rare. (1) The first of these is of two kinds according as it follows the method prescribed by the scriptures (vidhimārga) or the path followed by devotees who imitate passionate attachment of the residents of Vṛndāvana (ragānugāmarga). The steadfast practice of the members of the cult of devotion first produces interest (ruci) in God, then, attachment (āsakti) to Him, and, at last, nascent love (rati) for Him. Rati and bhāva are synonymous. (2) Nascent love produced by constancy in the practice of devotional acts may imitate passionate attachment of the denizens of Vṛndāvana to Kṛṣṇa (rāgānugā).[62]

(2) The nascent love which suddenly emerges without any preceding spiritual discipline is due to the grace of Kṛṣṇa or his devotees.[63] Nascent love produced by the grace of God is of three kinds: (1) nascent love produced by his words (vācika); (2) nascent love produced by his sight (ālokadānaja); and (3) nascent love produced in a devotee's heart (hārdda). Kṛṣṇa said to Nārada, "May you have undivided devotion to me, which gives supreme bliss." These words produced nascent love for

[60] Premnas tu prathamāvasthā bhava ityabhidhīyate. HBRS., i, 3, 1.
[61] HBRS., DGS., i, 3, 4-5.
[62] HBRS., i, 3, 4-7.
[63] Sādhanena vinā yas-tu sahasaivābhijāyate.
Sa bhāvaḥ kṛṣṇa-tadbhakta-prasādaja itīryate. Ibid, i, 3, 9-10.

him in Nārada. The residents of Jāṅgala saw Kṛṣṇa for the first time, were filled with nascent love for him, and could not take away their eyes from him. The grace which is felt by a devotee in his heart is heart-felt (hārdda). Śukadeva felt nascent love for Kṛṣṇa in the womb of his mother without any prior practice of devotional acts, which is generally acquired through them. His nascent love was due to Kṛṣṇa's grace which he felt in his heart. At least, his nascent love for Kṛṣṇa from early childhood was due to his grace which he felt in his heart.

(3) Nascent love for Kṛṣṇa is produced by the grace of his devotee. Prahlāda's natural love for the worship of Kṛṣṇa was produced by the grace of Nārada, his devotee.[64]

Nascent love for God is expressed in a devotee by the following (anubhāva): (1) forbearance (kṣānti), (2) not wasting any time in vain (avyarthakālatvam), (3) detachment (virakti), (4) absence of conceit (mānaśūnyatā), (5) strong expectation (āśābandha), (6) deep yearning (samutkaṇṭhā), (7) interest in chanting Kṛṣṇa's name always, (8) attachment to reciting his excellences, and (9) delight in living in the region inhabited by him. Forbearance is imperturbability of mind in the presence of the causes of mental agitation. A devotee who has nascent love for Kṛṣṇa does not waste a single moment by forgetting him. But he chants his excellence, remembers him, bows to his image, worships him mentally day and night, and offers his whole being to him. Detachment is the absence of attachment to the objects of sentient pleasure, which spontaneously arises without any effort. Detachment is the cause of the absence of attachment to them, which is the effect; the cause and the effect are non-different from each other. A devotee who has nascent love for God does not desire earthly or heavenly happiness or supernatural powers. Such a devotee as thinks of himself as devoid of any excellence, though he is excellent in rank and character, is devoid of conceit. Such a devotee cherishes a strong hope that he will realize God, which sustains him in his life of devotion, though he is not born in a high caste, nor performs his specific duties pertaining to his caste and stage of life, nor practises acts of devotion, nor has knowledge of Brahman, because of his conviction that God shows His grace to worthless persons. Yearning is excessive longing for the attainment of the object of desire,

[64] Ibid, i, 3, 10.

or God. Such a devotee always sings His name and sheds tears. He has attachment to reciting His excellences and delights in living always at Vṛndāvana.[65]

Melting of the heart is the characteristic of nascent love.[66] If it is found in a person desirous of liberation, he has no nascent love for Kṛṣṇa, but its semblance (ratyābhāsa) only, as an expert in devotion recognizes it. A person, who is desirous of happiness and liberation, and who does not practise pure devotion, cannot have nascent love for God.

Apparent nascent love (ratyābhāsa) is of two kinds: (1) reflection (pratibimba) and (2) radiance (chāyā). (1) If apparent nascent love expressed in shedding tears manifests a desire for worldly happiness or liberation without any prior requisite spiritual discipline, it is called a reflection of nascent love for God (rati-pratibimba). An aspirant for earthly enjoyment or liberation sometimes sheds tears while chanting God's name in the company of His devotees because his heart melts, and because his pleased mind catches a reflection of nascent love for God. Hence his apparent nascent love is called a reflection of nascent love.[66a]

(2) The apparent nascent love for God, which slightly resembles pure love for Him, which contains slight spiritual aspiration, which is unsteady, and which removes mental distress, is called radiance of nascent love (rati-chāyā)[67] Even ignorant persons acquire radiance of nascent love for God in the company of His devotees through the acts of hearing, chanting His name, etc. Their radiance of nascent love is suddenly transformed into real nascent love (rati) for God owing to the excessive favour of His devotee. But even the most excellent radiance of nascent love (bhāvābhāsa) gradually decreases and vanishes if His devotee is offended. If a person has intense attachment to desire for liberation, his nascent love (bhāva) becomes apparent (bhāvābhāsa). Or, if he meditates on God as identical with himself (ahaṁgraha), he acquires a false conceit that he is God who

[65] Ibid, i, 3, 12-16; DGS., i, 3, 14-15.

[66] Vyaktaṁ masṛṇatevāntar lakṣyate ratilakṣaṇam.
HBRS., i, 3, 17.

[66a] Aśramābhīṣṭa-nirvāhī rati-laksaṇa-lakṣitaḥ.
Bhogāpavarga-saukhyāṁśa-vyañjakaḥ pratibimbakaḥ.
Ibid, i, 3, 21-22. Ibid, i, 3, 22-23.

[67] Kṣudra-kautūhalamayī cañcalā duḥkha-hāriṇī.
Rateś chāyā bhavet kiñcit tat-sādṛśyā-valambinī.
Ibid, i, 3, 24-25.

ought to be worshipped. Hence an amateurish devotee is sometimes inspired by the feeling that he is God for a moment or a long duration while chanting His name. Sometimes a person is found to acquire nascent love for God suddently without undergoing any spiritual discipline. It is explained by Rūpa Goswāmī in the following manner. His spiritual discipline for the acquisition of nascent love for God was hindered by certain obstacles in his previous birth, which are removed in this birth, and his nascent love surges forth as the fruit of his spiritual discipline in his previous birth.[68]

The nascent love for God, which is very intense, which gives all powers, and which produces transcendent wonder, is produced by the grace of God.[69] If a person, who has acquired nascent love for God through His grace, is found to have some blemish of conduct, we should not find fault with him, because he is fulfilled and not affected by it. Nascent love for God is in the nature of intense bliss, is never quitened because of its ever-increasing desire for enjoying God, and is intensified by many transitory emotions.[70]

9. *Rūpa Goswāmī: Kinds of Devotion: Ardent Love for God (prema) due to nascent love or to His excessive grace: Ardent Love mixed with the knowledge of His lordship or unmixed with it*

When nascent love (bhāva, rati) becomes very intense, melts the heart completely, and generates the sense of 'mine' in the object of love, it becomes ardent love (prema) for God.[71] Devotion as means (sādhanabhakti) generates nascent love; and when it becomes intense, it is transformed into ardent love. Bhīṣma, Prahlāda, Uddhava and Nārada call the feeling of 'mine' in God without that in any other object or person coupled with ardent love (prema) for Him devotion. They identify devotion with intense ardent love for God.

[68] Ibid, i, 3, 26-32. Cp. BG., vi, 41-43.
[69] Lokottara-camatkāra-kārakaḥ sarvaśaktidaḥ.
Yaḥ prathīyān bhaved bhāvaḥ sa tu kṛṣṇa-prasādajaḥ.
Ibid, i, 3, 33-34.
[70] Ibid, i, 3, 34-35.
[71] Samyaṅ-masṛṇitasvānto mamatvāti-śayāṅkitaḥ.
Bhāvaḥ sa eva sāndrātmā budhaiḥ premā nigadyate. Ibid, i, 4, 1.
CCA., ii, ch. 23.

(1) Ardent love for God is produced by nascent love (bhāva) for Him. (2) Ardent love for Him is generated by His excessive favour (atiprasāda). (1) The nascent love for God, which attains supreme excellence, and which is acquired by the constant practice of the principal members of the path of devotion, is called ardent love produced by nascent love (bhāvottha). This kind of nascent love is of two kinds: (*i*) vaidhabhāvottha and (*ii*) rāgānugīyabhāvottha.

(*i*) The ardent love for God which is produced by chanting His name and other acts of devotion is called ardent love produced by formalistic devotion. It is expressed by weeping, crying, singing or dancing owing to the melting of the heart. (*ii*) The ardent love for God which is generated by nascent love imitating the passionate attachment of the residents of Vṛndāvana is called rāgānugīyabhāvottha prema.

(2) The ardent love for God which is evoked by the company of His incarnation is said to be produced by His intense grace (atiprasādottha). The milkmaids of Vṛndāvana did not study the Vedas, nor did they observe any vows, nor did they undergo any austerities; and yet they realized God only through their company of Kṛṣṇa or His intense grace.[71a]

Ardent love produced by excessive grace of God is of two kinds: (*i*) ardent love mixed with the knowledge of His lordship (māhātmyajñānayukta), and (*ii*) ardent love unmixed with any such extrinsic element (kevala). (*i*) The former is very intense and greater than love for all other objects and persons, and brings about liberation in the form of enjoying God's sovereignty (sārṣṭi), which is not achieved by any other means. This kind of ardent love is acquired by the devotees who follow the path prescribed by the scriptures. (*ii*) The latter is called pure (kevala) love, which is uninterrupted devotion permeated by ardent love (prema), which is devoid of any desire, and subjects God to a devotee's will. It is often acquired by those devotees who imitate the ardent love of the inhabitants of Vṛndāvana. If ardent love due to His excessive grace contains even a trace of formalistic devotion, it cannot be pure (kevala) love.

At first a person has faith (śraddhā) in the path of devotion. Then he keeps the company of saints (sādhusaṅga). Then he is engaged in acts of devotion (bhajanakriyā). Then he is purged

[71a] Ibid, i, 4, 2-4.

of many impurities (anarthanivṛtti) such as sins, nescience, afflictions, etc. Then he is engaged in continuous worship without any distraction (niṣṭhā). Then he acquires an intense desire (ruci) for worship with intelligence. Then he gets natural attachment (āsakti) to worshipping God. Then he acquires nascent love (bhāva) for Him. At last he gets ardent love (prema) for Him. The outward behaviour of a person who acquires such ardent love is unintelligible even to those who are proficient in the cult of devotion. One who is intoxicated with pure ardent love for God is immersed in supreme bliss and unconscious of his pleasure and pain which cannot affect one's mind.[72] Pure ardent love is called supreme devotion (parā bhakti) or holy love. It grows more and more intense and becomes successively affection (sneha), sulks (māna), intimacy (praṇaya), passionate attachment (rāga), transcendent attachment (anurāga), transcendent love (bhāva), and supreme holy love (mahābhāva).[73]

10. *Jīva Goswāmī: Rati, Prema, Praṇaya, Māna, Sneha, Rāga, Anurāga and Mahābhāva*

The characteristics of devotion stated by Jīva Goswāmī have already been discussed. The different kinds of impressions (saṁskāra) produced by different kinds of love for God mentioned by him are given here. (1) Nascent love (rati) produces excess of joy, attachment to God, and dispassion for all other objects. (2) Ardent love (prema) produces a firm conviction that God is 'mine'. The strong sense of 'mineness' is the impression produced by it. (3) Intimacy (praṇaya) produces trust which produces the sense of identity with the object of love in body, life and mind. Trust is the impression produced by intimacy, which implies the absence of regard (sambhrama) for God, the object of love, even though He is worthy of regard. (4) When intimacy shows a semblance of crookedness because of the conceit that God is excessively dear to a devotee, it is called sulks (māna). The conceit is the impression produced by sulks. (5) Affection (sneha) produces intense melting of the heart, which generates the absence of contentment even at the sight of the object of love and apprehension of evil from some one, though a devotee

[72] Ibid, i, 4, 5-8; DGS., i, 4, 6-7; CCA., ii, ch. 23.
[73] CCA., ii, ch. 23.

can counteract it. Discontent and apprehension are the impressions produced by affection. (6) The affection, which is in the nature of intense desire for God, is called passionate attachment (rāga). Intense desire to see God is the impression produced by affection. It turns intense sorrow into intense joy on union with God, and intense joy into intense sorrow on separation from Him. (7) Passionate attachment becomes intense and turns into transcendent attachment (anurāga), which makes a devotee experience newer and newer excellences of God every moment. This experience is the impression produced by transcendent attachment. (8) When transcendent attachment is intensified, it produces transcendent wonder (camatkāra), and intoxicates a devotee, it is transformed into supreme holy love (mahābhāva).[74] Transcendent wonder and intoxication are the impressions produced by supreme love. This impression produces intolerance of separation even for a moment during union with God, lengthens a moment into an eon during separation from Him, and generates a sense of insignificance of social codes of morality and religious rites.

11. *Jīva Goswāmī: Stages of the Emergence of Love for God*

(1) *Incomplete manifestation of love for God.*—Love for God aims at the realization of God's sweetness or love only. If it aims at the attainment of any other object, there is incomplete manifestation of it.[75] Incomplete manifestation of love for God is of two kinds: (1) emergence of reflection (ābhāsa) of love; and (2) slight emergence of love. The latter is of two kinds: (*i*) occasional emergence of radiance of love (prīticchavi), and (*ii*) emergence of love (*prīti*).

A yogin who performs eightfold yoga performs also acts of devotion, e.g., hearing, chanting God's name, recollection of, and meditation on, Him. The practice of these acts of devotion produces love for God, which melts his heart, and which is

[74] Prītiḥ khalu bhaktacittam ullāsayati, mamatayā yojayati, visrambhayati, priyatvātiśayena abhimānayati, drāvayati, svaviṣayaṁ prati abhilāṣātiśayena yojayati, pratikṣaṇam eva svaviṣayaṁ navanavatvena anubhāvayati, asamorddhva-camatkāreṇa unmādayati ca. PS., 84, Cp. UNM.

[75] Kevala-tanmādhurya-tātparyatvenaiva prītitve siddhe, tātparyāntarādau sati prīter asamyagāvirbhāva iti siddham. PS., 73.

expressed in gooseflesh, shedding tears, etc. But as he aims at liberation or complete isolation of his self from prakṛti and its modifications including his mind-body-complex, he does not lay stress on devotion, but tries to dissociate his mind from God, because devotion is a form of love (rāga) which is an affliction (kleśa). Therefore in such a yogin there can be no manifestation of genuine love for God, but there is the manifestation of its reflection (ābhāsa). Persons endowed with pure devotion never endeavour to dissociate their minds from God. They do not forsake Him and He does not forsake them.[76] Hence the yogin's melting of the heart is not due to genuine love for God, but to its reflection (prītyābhāsa).

(2) *Occasional manifestation of radiance of love for God (prīticchavi).*—Sometimes radiance of love for God is manifested, where genuine love for Him does not appear.[77] Radiance of love for God dawns on the mind of a devotee who has concentrated it on the excellences of God, but who has not acquired the knowledge of Him and experienced His sweetness. His mind is tinged with His excellences, but he has no knowledge of Him. Temporary attachment to His excellences produces temporary emergence of radiance of love for God.

(3) *Emergence of love for God.*—When a devotee aims at pleasing God primarily, and, at other objects secondarily, love for God dawns on his mind. Here love for God is primary, and love for other objects is secondary.[78] Attachment to other objects is of two kinds: (1) attachment to them, which is almost destroyed, and (2) reflection of attachment to them. When attachment to other objects is almost destroyed, there is the first dawn of love for God. When only a reflection of attachment to other objects is left, there is the manifest emergence of love for God. The dawn of love for God is its incomplete manifestation because attachment to other objects appears occasionally at this stage, though it is extremely feeble. But when there is the manifest emergence of love for God, attachment to other objects

[76] Yo rasagrahaḥ sa tu na tyajati (bhagavantam). Na tu bhagavān api tato' nyathā kuryāt. PS., 73.

[77] Yatra prīti-tātparyābhāvas tatra kadācid udbhavat tacchavimātratvam. PS., 73. Cp. HBRS., i, 3, 24-32.

[78] Yatra tattātparyam anyasaṅgas tu daivāt, tatra tasyā udayāvasthā. Anyasaṅgasya gauṇatvam. PS., 73.

almost disappears, and only a reflection of it remains in the mind.

At the first dawn of love for God, a devotee's attachment to the body disappears, and his non-inury and sense-restraint become natural to him. Attachment to God destroys attachment to the body. Its principal effects are direct experience of God, a strong desire for serving Him, service to Him, and experience of its sweetness. Its secondary effects are non-injury and sense-restraint. At this stage attachment to other objects may reappear.[79]

(4) *Complete manifestation of love for God.*—When there is complete manifestation of love for God, a devotee is not deflected from serving Him by prosperity and adversity. Even though obstacles stand in the way of his worship of God, he regards it as the best means of his real good. When love for God is completely manifested, a devotee is inspired by Him, is filled with supreme bliss, can give peace and bliss to others, and his inspiration persists in all conditions.[80]

There are two stages of the manifest emergence of love for God. In the first stage there is a reflection of engrossment in other objects by chance. In the second stage there is complete absence of engrossment in other objects. Priyavrata had a reflection of engrossment in his wife, sons, house, etc., when he had complete manifestation of love for God, which was unflickering in his mind. Prahlāda had a reflection (ābhāsa) of obstacles which could not deflect him from the path of devotion to God. The obstacles in the path of devotion are of two kinds: (1) obstacles due to offence to some saints; and (2) obstacles due to the will of God. The former are removed by the experience of the consequent sufferings and by the compassion of saints. The latter are removed by the will of God who creates obstacles to enhance His devotees' love for God. Hence the obstacles in the path of devotion are not real but apparent, and not due to a devotee's demerits. In the second stage he becomes unconscious of his pleasure and pain. Śukadeva is an example of this stage of the manifest emergence of love for God.[81]

[79] Bhāg., i, 18, 22; v, 5, 6.
[80] Bhāg., iv, 20, 12; v, 1, 5; PS., 73-76.
[81] PS., 78.

The different degrees of the manifestation of love for God depend upon the different degrees of revelation of the nature of God[82]. Though He is infinite, eternal, complete Being-Consciousness-Bliss, He manifests His sovereignty, beauty, sweetness, etc., to His devotees in different degrees through His essential power of yogamāyā. His attributes are revealed in that degree to a devotee in which they are manifested in a Deity worshipped by him. His love for God also is a mode of God's essential power of bliss, which he acquires from Him. Hence his degree of love for God depends upon the nature of the Deity worshipped by him. The Bengal Vaiṣṇavas regard Kṛṣṇa as the complete manifestation of the essential powers of God, sovereignty, beauty, sweetness and power of giving love for Him. Those devotees who worship Him acquire complete manifestation of love for Him. He has the greatest power of producing ardent love for Him in His devotees. Sweetness of God produces love for Him. Kṛṣṇa is the complete manifestation of God's sweetness. Hence the worship of Him can produce ardent love for Him devoid of His sovereignty.[83]

From the stage of the manifest emergence of devotion onwards devotees attain embodied release (jīvanmukti). They achieve disembodied release (paramamukti) after death, and become comrades of God. His eternal comrades enjoy eternal release.[84]

12. *Five Kinds of Permanent Emotional Disposition of Love for God: Quiet Love, Loving Servitude, Friendly Love, Parental Love and Wifely Love or Extra-nuptial Holy Love*

Baladeva Vidyābhūṣaṇa mentions two kinds of devotion: (1) vidhibhakti and (2) rucibhakti. (1) The former adopts the prescribed path of hearing, chanting, service, worship and the like, and aims at the realization of God of sovereign powers (aiśvarya). (2) The latter is inspired love (ruci) for God, and aims at the realization of God of love (mādhurya). The

[82] Seyam akhaṇḍāpi nijālambanasya bhagavata āvirbhāva-tāratamyena svayaṁ tāratamyenaivāvirbhavati. PS., 78.

[83] Ata eva parama-prema-janakasvabhāvatvam api tasya dṛśyate. PS., 81. CCA., ii, ch. 21; Bhāg., iii, 2, 12.

[84] PS., 73. *Gauḍīya Vaiṣṇava Darśana*, Vol. IV, Ch. 2.

former is formalistic devotion or reverence, whereas the latter is loving devotion. The devotees who cherish love for Him are the dearest to Him. Love may be love for God as Indeterminate Brahman or Supreme Self, love for the master, love for a friend, love for a son, and love for the husband or lover. God attracted by such a devotee's love Himself enters into him. Formalistic devotion is devotion as means, while loving devotion is devotion as end.[85]

Rūpa Goswāmī, Jīva Goswāmī and Kṛṣṇadāsa Kavirāja recognize five kinds of nascent love (rati) for God: (1) quiet love (śāntarati), (2) loving servitude (dāsyarati), (3) friendly love (sakhyarati), (4) parental love (vātsalyarati), and (5) wifely love (madhurarati). These five kinds of love for God are permanent emotional dispositions or sentiments (sthāyibhāva).[86] A sentiment is a dominant emotion which subordinates contrary and non-contrary emotions to itself and shines in its splendour. It exists in the eternal comrades of God at all times. It exists in His devotees who acquire it by spiritual discipline from the time of its emergence onwards. As a mode of God's essential powers of consciousness and bliss nascent love for Him is eternally present in devotees; only it is manifested by spiritual discipline.

Nascent love (rati) for God is of two kinds: (1) principal (mukhyā) and (2) subordinate (gauṇī). (1) Principal nascent love is the first emergence of ardent love (prema) for God, which is a mode of His pure essence. It is not a mode of the phenomenal pure essence of nescience (māyā).[87] (2) Subordinate nascent love for God is a particular emotion which is produced by the excellence of its basic determinant cause, and which is assisted and manifested by nascent love for God, that contracts itself.[88]

Principal nascent love for God is of two kinds: (1) self-developing (svārtha) and (2) other-developing (parārtha). (1) The nascent love for God, which distinctly nourishes itself by non-contrary emotions, and which thwarts itself by contrary emotions, is self-developing. It does not develop non-contrary emotions; nor does it thwart contrary emotions. It acts upon itself, enriches

[85] Siddhāntaratna, ii, 13-14; ii, 49.
[86] Sthāyī bhāvo'tra samproktaḥ śrīkṛṣṇa-viṣayā ratiḥ. BRS., ii, 5, 2. Ibid, ii, 5, 1.
[87] Śuddha-sattva-viśeṣātmā ratir mukhyeti kīrtitā. BRS., ii, 5, 3. DSG., ii, 5, 3.
[88] HBRS., ii, 5, 30.

itself, and weakens itself; it is self-acting. (2) The nascent love for God, which favours and develops other non-contrary and contrary emotions by contracting itself, is other-developing. It does not develop itself, but it develops other non-contrary and contrary emotions; it is other-acting[89] Both self-developing and other-developing varieties of nascent love for God are modes of non-phenomenal pure essence (śuddha-sattva-viśeṣātmā), because they are kinds of principal nascent love (mukhyā rati).

Both these varieties of nascent love are of five kinds: (1) pure (śuddhā), (2) loving servitude (prīti), (3) friendly love (sakhya), (4) parental love (vātsalya), and (5) wifely love (priyatā). Pure nascent love assumes special forms such as loving servitude and the like according to the distinctive natures of the different devotees, even as the bright sun assumes different colours being reflected in crystals of different colours.[90]

Pure nascent love is of three kinds: (1) common (sāmānyā), (2) transparent (svacchā), and (3) quiet (śāntī). Pure nascent love (śuddhā rati) is expressed in trembling, closing the eyes, opening them, and the like. (1) Common nascent love is found in ordinary devotees who are attracted towards God, which does not assume any special form mentioned above. (2) Transparent nascent love assumes different special forms in different pure devotees, who come in contact with different adepts in spiritual disciplines and undergo them according to their instructions, and whose minds are not yet fixed on a particular relish (āsvāda). (3) Quiet nascent love is found in devotees in whom tranquillity (śama) prevails, who know God as indeterminate Brahman or Supreme Self, who renounce attachment to objects of pleasure, who concentrate their minds on Brahman, and who experience the bliss of the Ātman or Self. Quiet nascent love often abounds in tranquillity, and is devoid of the sense of 'mine' for God.[91] It is love for Him as the Lord, and mixed with the knowledge of His sovereignty. It is love mixed with knowledge (jñānamiśrā bhakti). The knowledge of the essential nature of God only is manifested in it. The

[89] HBRS., ii, 5, 3-5.
[90] Śuddhā prītis tathā sakhyaṁ vātsalyaṁ priyatetyasau.
Vaiśiṣṭyaṁ pātravaiśiṣṭyād ratireṣo-pagacchati. HBRS., ii, 5, 6-7.
[91] Prāyaḥ śama-pradhānānāṁ mamatā-gandha-varjitā.
Paramātmatayā kṛṣṇe jātā śāntī-ratir matā.
HBRS., ii, 5, 14-15. Ibid, ii, 5, 13.

knowledge of relationship to Him is not manifested in it, because He is not known as the embodiment of love. Quiet love for God is not characterized by the sense of 'mine' (mamatā) for the same reason.[92]

(1) Loving servitude (prīti, dāsya rati) is nascent love for God as worthy of being worshipped, which produces a conceit in a devotee that he is inferior to Him, and that he is a fit object of His favour, which produces attachment to Him, and which destroys attachment to other objects.[93] Attachment to God and dispassion for other objects are the common characteristics of quiet love and loving servitude. But in the latter there is a desire to serve and please God because it is characterized by the sense of 'mine', whereas in the former there is neither the sense of 'mine' nor a desire for service.

(2) Friendly love (sakhya rati) is in the nature of trust because it produces a conceit in a devotee that he is equal to Him, which is devoid of the sense of inferiority to Him. It is expressed in laughter, cutting jokes and the like.[94] It is characterized by the sense of 'mine' and equality. It is devoid of reverence for God and free from restraint and reserve. The sense of equality is its special characteristic.

(3) Parental love (vātsalyarati) for God produces a conceit in a devotee that he or she is father or mother of God, and that He is a child to be brought up, protected and favoured. Nascent love for God, which is full of affection, tenderness and compassion, is called parental love. It is expressed in bringing up, benediction, caressing, etc.[95]

(4) Wifely love (madhurarati, priyatā) produces a conceit in a devotee that he or she is God's beloved woman and that He is his or her lover. It is the cause of mutual enjoyment of God and the devotee. A devotee has wifely love for God, and He has love for His devotee; the latter is the excitant cause of the

[92] CCA., ii, ch. 19.

[93] Svasmād bhavanti ye nyūnās te' nugrāhyā harer matāḥ.
Ārādhyatvātmikā teṣāṁ ratiḥ prītir itīritā. Tatrās-aktikṛd anyatra prītisaṁhāriṇī hyasau. HBRS., ii, 5, 23-24.

[94] Sāmyād viśrambharūpaiṣāṁ ratiḥ sakhyam ihocyate.
HBRS., ii, 5, 25.

[95] Anugrahamayī teṣāṁ ratir vātsalyam ucyate.
HBRS., ii, 5, 26. Ibid, ii, 5, 27.

former. Wifely love for God is expressed in sweet words, side-long glances, knitting the brow, smile, etc.[96]

Different devotees have different kinds of nascent love for God because of their congenital or prenatal impressions (vāsanā). The five kinds of nascent love are not of equal relish (svāda). Loving servitude is superior to quiet love. Friendly love is superior to loving servitude. Parental love is superior to friendly love. Wifely love is superior to parental love. Quiet love is devoid of the sense of 'mine'. But the other four kinds of nascent love are characterized by the sense of 'mine', which becomes more and more intense in friendly love, parental love, and wifely love. Quiet love cannot be blended with the other kinds of nascent love. But the latter have the qualities of quiet love, viz., steadfast devotion to God and dispassion for objects of pleasure, whereas quiet love is devoid of the qualities of loving servitude, etc. Loving servitude can be blended with friendly love. It can be blended with parental love also. Wifely love cannot be blended with parental love.[97] Five kinds of nascent love (rati) for God may be pure (kevalā) or mixed (saṁkulā).

Quiet love may develop into ardent love (prema); loving servitude, into passionate attachment (rāga); friendly love, into initial transcendent attachment (anurāga); parental love, into final transcendent attachment (anurāga anta); and wifely love, into supreme holy love (mahābhāva).[98]

[96] Mitho harer mṛgākṣyāś ca sambhogasyādi-kāraṇam.
Madhurāparaparyāyā priyatākhyoditā ratiḥ.
HBRS., ii, 5, 27-28.

[97] HBRS., ii, 5, 15-22; PS., 84.

[98] CCA., ii, ch. 24.

(ālambana vibhāva) of the religious sentiment of nascent love, the former being its object and the latter, its abode. Kṛṣṇa is God incarnate and the best of all heroes, who is the repository of all excellences in all times. He is beautiful, ever-new, charming, strong, spirited, very young, truthful, sweet-tongued, learned, intelligent, clever, efficient, grateful, pure, self-controlled, steady, forgiving, grave, buoyant, generous, pious, heroic, compassionate, respectful, benign, humble, happy, renowned, influential, popular, prosperous, eloquent, ready-witted, diplomatic, proficient in many languages, firm in vows, well-versed in the scriptures, endowed with a keen insight into times, places, persons and circumstances, equal to all, possessed of keen moral reason, noble, fascinating to women, worshipped by all, possessed of all auspicious signs, and controlled by ardent love. He is a protector of his protegés, a friend of his devotees, a refuge of saints, a doer of good to all, a genius, and the supreme Person (puruṣottama) endowed with all powers of lordship and excellent qualities in their fulness. Some of these qualities exist in some persons in minute quantity. But all of them exist in infinite quantity in him.[3] He is omniscient, omnipotent, completely realized, and manifested in millions of universes. He is the embodiment of infinite being, consciousness and bliss, and invested with inconceivable powers. He is greater than Brahmā, Viṣṇu and Śiva, the creator, the preserver, and the destroyer of the world. He is the seed of all divine incarnations (avatārāvalībīja).[4] He attracts the hearts of all in the three worlds, and amazes all with his unequalled and unexcelled beauty and charm. He is the object of the religious sentiment.

Kṛṣṇa's devotees are endowed with ardent love for him; their minds are constantly focussed on him; their hearts are full of passionate attachment to him. They are endowed with many excellent qualities which have already been stated. They are either aspriants (sādhaka) or adepts (siddha). The devotees, who have acquired nascent love for God, whose minds are not yet completely purged of all their impurities, and who are fit for realizing him, are aspirants. The devotees whose actions are

[3] Ete paripūrṇatayā bhānti tatraiva puruṣottame. HBRS., ii, 1, 26-27. Ibid, ii, 1, 13-17; 19-25.

[4] Sadā-svarūpa-saṁprāptaḥ sarvajño nitya-nūtanaḥ.
Saccidānanda-sāndrāṅgaḥ sarva-siddhi-niṣevitaḥ.
Avicintya-mahāśaktiḥ koṭi-brahmāṇḍa-vigrahaḥ.
HBRS., ii, 1, 30-31. Ibid, ii, 1, 32, 34.

always directed towards God, whose minds are free from all taints, and who always experience the relish of the joy of ardent love for Him, are adepts. The adepts are either those who have acquired their status (sampraptasiddhi) or those who are eternally fulfilled (nityasiddha). The former have acquired their status either by spiritual disciplines (sādhana) or by the grace (kṛpā) of God. The latter are endowed with supreme love for God and eternal bliss. The devotees are, again, divided into five classes: (1) quiet (śānta), (2) servants (dāsa), sons (suta), etc., (3) friends (sakhi), (4) elders (guru), and (5) beloved women (preyasī). Kṛṣṇa's qualities, actions, toilette, smile, physical beauty, tinkling of his anklets, sound of his flute, his foot-prints, place of his residence, his devotees, his birth-day, etc., are the excitant cause of the religious sentiment of nascent love. Kṛṣṇa's qualities are of three kinds, physical, verbal and mental. Young age, beauty, ornaments, tenderness, etc., are his physical qualities. His infancy (kaumāra) from the first year to the fifth year is the excitant cause of the religious sentiment of parental love (vatsala-rasa). His childhood (pauganda) from the sixth year to the tenth year and sports are the excitant cause of the religious sentiment of friendly love (sakhyarasa). His later childhood and early adolescence (kaiśora) from the eleventh year to the sixteenth year are the excitant cause of all religious sentiments of devotion including loving servitude (dāsyarasa) and extranuptial holy love (madhurarasa). His age from the seventeenth year onwards constitutes his youth (yauvana). His actions are games, sports, dance in a circle (rāsalīlā) with comrades, and the like. His qualities and actions are the excitant causes of the religious sentiments of devotion.[5] His qualities constitute his essence, but when they are meditated on as different from it, they become the excitant causes of the religious sentiments of devotion. When they are meditated on as his essence, they are the basic determinant causes of these sentiments.

The ensuant causes of the religious sentiments of devotion are the organic manifestations from which the various kinds of nascent love for God are inferred.[6] Dancing, rolling on the ground, singing, shouting, stretching out the limbs, yawning, deep breathing, hiccough, laughing loudly, foaming at the mouth,

[5] HBRS., ii, 1, 68, 72, 74, 76-78, 102-109, 113-22, 136.
[6] Anubhāvāstu cittastha-bhāvānām avabodhakāḥ. Ibid., ii, 2, 1.

sudden outcry, indifference to people, and the like are the ensuant causes (anubhāva). The voluntary organic manifestations are called udbhāsura. The spontaneous organic expressions are called sāttvikabhāvas. The mind affected by nascent love for God and the kindred emotions is called sattva. The organic expressions of such a mind are called sāttvikabhāvas. The mind affected by the emotions mentioned above acts upon life which agitates the body, and produces trembling, perspiration, gooseflesh, faltering voice, shedding tears, change of colour, inactivity and insensibility. Singing, yawning, etc., are called śīta. Dancing, rolling on the ground, etc., are called kṣepaṇa. Sāttvikabhāvas are snigdha, digdha and rukṣa. Snigdha sāttvikabhāvas are primary (mukhya), when they are spontaneous organic expressions of the mind affected by any one of quiet nascent love (śāntarati), loving servitude (dāsyarati), friendly love (sakhyarati), parental love (vātsalyarati), and wifely love (madhurarati). Such sāttvikabhāvas are secondary (gauṇa), when they are spontaneous organic expressions of nascent love blended with mirth, anger, wonder, or the like emotion. The former indicate a direct relation between a devotee and God, while the latter indicate an indirect relation between them. The sāttvikabhāvas are called digdha, when the mind of a devotee, who has acquired nascent love for God, is affected by emotions other than primary or secondary nascent love but following it. The sāttvikabhāvas are called rukṣa, when the mind of a person, who is like a devotee, and who is devoid of nascent love for God, is affected by wonder and other emotions on hearing of His charming and wonderful qualities and actions.[7] The different degrees of their intensity singly or jointly have already been explained. Nascent love for God is the principal cause of all joy and transcendent wonder, which are the characteristics of the religious sentiments of devotion, without which the spontaneous organic expressions cannot produce transcendent wonder.[8]

Rūpa Goswāmī discusses the nature of apparent spontaneous organic expressions (sāttvikābhāsa) in order to discriminate genuine organic manifestations from them. They are not really spontaneous organic expressions of nascent love (rati) for God, but they

[7] Ibid, ii, 2, 1-4; ii, 3, 1-10. Ibid, ii, 3, 14-37.
[8] Sarvānanda-camatkārahetur bhāvo varo ratiḥ.
Ete hi tadvinābhāvān na camatkāritāśrayāḥ. Ibid, ii, 3, 32-33.

appear to be so. They are of four kinds: (1) produced by apparent nascent love (ratyābhāsabhāva) or reflection (pratibimba) or radiance (chāyā) of nascent love; (2) produced by apparent sattva (sattvābhāsabhāva), (3) produced without apparent sattva (niḥsattva), and (4) produced by contrary emotions (pratīpa).[9] (1) When an aspirant after liberation, who generally practises meditation, sheds tears by hearing and chanting God's name and excellence, he manifests apparent organic expression because he has a reflection of nascent love for Him. (2) When the mind of a person, which is naturally tender, is affected by the semblance of joy, wonder and other emotions, he has apparent sattva (sattvābhāsa), and its organic expressions produced by it (sattvābhāsabhāva). Joy, wonder, etc., which emerge from nascent love for God are genuine; but they are apparent when they do not emerge from it.[10] A Mīmāṁsaka who performs sacrifices prescribed by the Vedas, and who is an atheist and devoid of devotion, sheds tears on hearing devotional songs. His shedding tears is an apparent organic expression produced by apparent sattva. (3) When the mind of a person, which is naturally unstable, inwardly hard but outwardly soft, is affected by the semblance of joy, wonder and other emotions, or who practises emotional expressions, he has gooseflesh, tears, etc., even without apparent sattva. The mind is tender (ślatha) when it is soft both within and without, whereas it is unstable (picchila), when it is hard within and soft without. A tender mind is affected by apparent emotions, but an unstable mind is not affected by them. But there are apparent organic expressions (sāttvikābhāsa) in both. When they are manifested without apparent sattva, they are called devoid of sattva (niḥsattva).[11] Those who are hard within and hard without cannot have organic expressions, e.g., shedding tears, bristling of the hair, etc., through practice. Those persons, whose minds are naturally tender or unstable, often have apparent emotional expressions in a congregation in which many devotees chant the name of God together. Those, whose minds are naturally tender, can have apparent

[9] Ibid, ii, 3, 38-39. Rateḥ pratibimbatve chāyātve ca sati ratyābhāsabhavatvam. DGS., ii, 3, 39.

[10] Mudvismayādyābhāsamātrākrānta-cittatve sattvābhāsabhavatvam. Ibid, ii, 3, 39. Ibid, ii, 3, 41-42.

[11] Mudvismayābhāśasyāpi antarasparśe bahirapi asparśe niḥsattvatvam. DGS., ii, 3, 39. HBRS., DGS., ii, 3, 42-43.

emotional expressions elsewhere. (4) The enemies of God have contrary emotional expressions (pratīpa) under the influence of anger, fear, etc. These also are apparent organic expressions. Here anger, fear, etc., are excited in relation to God.

The transitory emotions and states emerge out of, and merge in, the permanent emotional dispositions or sentiments, and nourish, develop and strengthen them into religious sentiments (bhaktirasa) in co-operation with the basic determinant cause, the excitant cause, the ensuant cause, and the spontaneous organic expressions. Nascent love (rati) for God is the primary sentiment (sthāyibhāva). Anger, fear, wonder and the like are subordinate to it. The thirty three transitory emotions and states discussed already are the accessory states (vyabhicāribhāva) of the religious sentiments Rūpa Goswāmī, Jīva Goswāmī and Viśvanātha Cakravartī's views about their nature and origin have already been explained.[12].

2. *The Quiet Religious Sentiment (Śāntabhaktirasa)*

The permanent sentiment of quiet nascent love for God is made relishable in persons endowed with tranquillity by the determinant cause, the excitant cause, the ensuant cause, and transitory emotions, and transformed into the quiet religious sentiment.[13] Pure nascent love for God is of three kinds: (1) common, (2) transparent, and (3) quiet. Common nascent love and transparent nascent love cannot be developed into religious sentiments, because the former is not distinct and the latter is not stable. Only quiet nascent love can be developed into the quiet religious sentiment which is called by Jīva Goswāmī noetic religious sentiment (jñānabhaktirasa), because it contains the elements of devotion and knowledge.[14] The bliss of the quiet devotees is often like that of experiencing indeterminate Brahman, which is less intense than the bliss of experiencing God, who is the embodiment of infinite being, consciousness and bliss and other excellent attributes. The slight experience of the essential

[12] Viśeṣeṇābhimukhyena caranti sthāyinaṁ prati.
Unmajjanti nimajjanti sthāyinyamṛta-vāridhau.
Ibid, ii, 4, 1-3. Ibid, ii, 4, 1-6; ii, 5, 2. Ibid, ii, 3, 43-44.

[13] Vibhāvādyaiḥ śamināṁ svādyatāṁ gataḥ sthāyī śāntiratiḥ śāntabhaktirasaḥ. HBRS.. iii, 1, 4.

[14] DCS., iii, 1, 4; PS., 203.

nature of God as manifested in an image is the principal determinant cause of the quiet religious sentiment, whereas the experience of His excellent attributes and actions is that of the religious sentiment of loving servitude. The quiet religious sentiment is inferior to the religious sentiment of loving servitude, and the bliss of the former is inferior to that of the latter. But the bliss of the quiet religious sentiment is superior to that of the experience of indeterminate Brahman.[15]

God, the embodiment of infinite being-consciousness-bliss, Infinite Self, indeterminate Brahman, transcendent of cosmic nescience and its products, is the object and determinant cause (viṣayālambana) of the quiet religious sentiment, and the quiet devotees are the abodes (āśrayālambana) of this sentiment. The quiet devotees are those who have acquired nascent love for God through His or His devotees' grace. They are either ātmārāma or tāpasa. The former were immersed in the bliss of experiencing indeterminate Brahman, and acquired nascent love for God through His grace. The latter worship God without renouncing desire for liberation because of their conviction that liberation is unhindered by impediments through devotion only. The former are contented with, and delight in, Brahman, while the latter are saints who have firm faith in the cult of devotion to God, and who acquire a ray of quiet nascent love for Him through the excessive grace of His devotees and yogins absorbed in Brahman. God is personal while Brahman is impersonal. Theists regard God as superior to Brahman which is a ray of His spiritual body.[16]

Listening to the principal Upaniṣads, residing in a solitary place, manifestation of a particular mode of the mind, discrimination of the nature of reality, predominance of the power of knowledge, company of the wise devotees, discussion of the nature of Brahman with the experts in the knowledge of the Upaniṣads, etc., are the extraordinary excitant causes of the quiet religious sentiment. The smell of tulasī leaves offered to an image of a divine incarnation, the sound of a conchshell, a holy mountain, a holy forest, a holy place, reflection on the transitoriness of the objects of enjoyment, and the destruction of all things by time,

[15] Prāyaḥ svasukhajātīyaṁ sukhaṁ syād atra yoginām.
Kintvātma-saukhyam aghanaṁ ghanaṁ tvīśamayaṁ sukham.
HBRS., DGS., iii, 1, 5. Ibid, iii, 1, 6.

[16] HBRS., iii, 1, 7-13.

etc., are the ordinary excitant causes of the quiet religious sentiment.

The absence of hatred for the atheists, the absence of excessive regard for God's dear devotees, regard for the extermination of embodied life and for embodied release, independence, egolessness, etc., are the extraordinary mental consequents of the quiet religious sentiment. Fixing the eyes on the tip of the nose, walking with eyes fixed on a short space ahead, assuming the bodily attitude of wisdom, silence, actions of a saint who does not observe the rules of purity, etc., are the extraordinary bodily expressions of the quiet religious sentiment. Yawning, stretching out the limbs, instructing about devotion, obeisance to an image of a divine incarnation, reciting hymns, etc., are the ordinary bodily expressions of the quiet religious sentiment. All spontaneous organic expressions except insensibility are the sāttvikabhāvas of this religious sentiment. They are in a kindled condition (jvalita), and not in a blazing condition (dīpta), in the bodies of the yogins devoid of egoism. Self-abasement, contentment, joy, ascertainment, recollection, dejection, eagerness, agitation, conjecture, etc., are its accessory emotions and states.[17]

Quiet nascent love (śantarati), which is the basic permanent sentiment of the quiet religious sentiment, is of two kinds: (1) moderate (samā) and (2) intense (sāndrā). The former is evoked by the experience of God in the state of a yogin's trance in which his mind devoid of any mode is modified into Brahman on hearing of His excellence. The latter is evoked by the direct experience of God in his indeterminate trance because of the complete destruction of his nescience (avidyā). The bliss of the latter is more intense than that of the former.

Quiet religious sentiment (sāntabhaktirasa) is of two kinds: (1) indirect or mediate (pārokṣya) and (2) direct or immediate (sākṣātkāra). The former is due to the experience of God mediated by austerities and meditation. The latter is due to the direct experience of God who is the dearest as the inner supreme Self of a devotee. One who is devoted to the pursuit of the knowledge of Brahman may acquire nascent love for God through His grace. His series of impressions of knowledge being weakened by God's compassion, he becomes fond of the bliss of the religious sentiment of devotion. Vilvamaṅgala was at first an aspirant after

[17] Ibid, iii, 1, 13-24.

the intuitive realization of Brahman, and then acquired wifely love for God through His grace, like Śukadeva. The bliss of the experience of God is superior to that of the experience of Brahman, which is an incomplete manifestation of Him.[18]

Tranquillity (śama), which is said to be the permanent basic sentiment of the quiet religious sentiment, is imperturbability of the mind, which is not expressed in organic manifestations. Hence the Rhetoricists deny the existence of the quiet religious sentiment. But Rūpa Goswāmī observes, that quiet nascent love (śāntarati) can be the basic permanent sentiment of the quiet religious sentiment. Tranquillity is unswerving fixation of the intellect on God, which is not possible without quiet nascent love.[19] Tranquillity (śama) is abiding in the essential nature of the self, which is devoid of attachment to objects of pleasure. Quiet nascent love is love of a person with a tranquil mind for God. He is the embodiment of infinite and eternal bliss, and the object of quiet nascent love. There cannot be constant concentration of the mind on God without quiet nascent love for Him, which is transformed into the quiet religious sentiment by the appropriate determinant, excitant and ensuant causes. The quiet religious sentiment is free from pleasure and pain, hatred and envy, partiality and egoism. Some regard contentment (dhṛti) as its basic permanent sentiment. Others regard self-abasement (nirveda) as its basic sentiment. Some regard the quiet religious sentiment as the only æsthetic sentiment, and the other æsthetic sentiments as its different forms. If self-abasement is due to the knowledge of the reality, it may be the basic sentiment of the quiet religious sentiment. But if it is due to the loss of cherished objects or the advent of a calamity, it is not the basic sentiment of the quiet religious sentiment, but its accessory emotion.[19a]

3. *The Religious Sentiment of Loving Servitude (Prītabhaktirasa, Dāsyabhaktirasa)*

The loving regard of devotees for God being made relishable by the appropriate determinant cause, the excitant cause, the

[18] Ibid, iii, 1, 25-26.
[19] Tanniṣṭhā durghaṭā buddher etāṁ śāntiratiṁ vinā. Ibid, iii, 1, 29. Ibid, iii, 1, 28.
[19a] Ibid, iii, 1, 29-33; ii, 5, 13-14; NSAG., NS., pp. 334-40.

ensuant cause, and accessory emotions is transformed into the religious sentiment of loving servitude.[20] It is of two kinds: (1) the religious sentiment of loving servitude (sambhrama-prītarasa) and (2) the religious sentiment of loving regard (gaurava-prītarasa). (1) In the former the person to be favoured by God is a servant (dāsa) or a devotee who regards himself as a servant of God who is his master. (2) In the latter the person to be favoured by God is to be brought up like a child (lālya). In the former there is the sentiment of awe or reverence for God as master who maintains and protects his devotee as a servant. In the latter there is the sentiment of loving regard for God as father who brings up and fondles a devotee as a child. The Śaivas regard God as father, and the Śāktas regard God as mother.

(1) In the religious sentiment of loving servitude (sambhrama-prītarasa) a devotee thinks himself to be a servant of God, and entertains loving regard (prīti) mingled with awe or reverence (sambhrama). This permanent sentiment is transformed into the religious sentiment of loving servitude by the appropriate determinant cause, the excitant cause, the ensuant cause, and the accessory emotions. God and His devotees who worship Him as His servants are the basic determinant cause of this religious sentiment. God as the creator of countless worlds, invested with inconceivable and superhuman powers, the seed of all divine incarnations, eternally self-fulfilled, supremely adorable, omniscient, omnipotent, morally perfect, compassionate, the protector of the protegés, the best friend of the devotees, and subject to love, and invested with the powers of lordship is its determinant cause. God is the object (viṣaya), and devotees are the abodes (āśraya) of this sentiment.

God's servants are of four classes: (1) trusted (praśrita), (2) obsequious (nideśavaśavartin), (3) faithful (viśvasta), and (4) humble (vinamra) on account of the knowledge that God is the master. Trusted servants are those devotees who think themselves as appointed by God to perform some duties. Obsequious servants are those devotees who are ready to execute His commands. Faithful servants are faithful in the execution of his commands. Humble servants are submissive to Him due to

[20] Ātmocitair vibhāvādyaiḥ prītir āsvādanīyatāṁ.
Nītā cetasi bhaktānāṁ prītabhaktiraso mataḥ.
Ibid, iii, 2, 3. Ibid, iii, 2, 4.

their knowledge of His superiority. They are called appointed (adhikṛta) servants, dependent (āśrita) attendants, comrades (pāriṣada), and followers (anuga) respectively. The dependent servants are of three classes: (1) those who have taken refuge with God for protection (śaraṇya); (2) those who were aspirants after the knowledge of indeterminate Brahman, who relinquished their desire for liberation, and who have taken refuge with God of unequalled and unexcelled love and grace (jñānicara); and (3) those who were formerly attached to His worship, but who are now devoted to His service (sevāniṣṭha). Among the three classes of the devotees who think themselves to be God's servants there are three subclasses: (1) those who are eternally realized (nityasiddha), (2) those who have achieved realization (siddha), and (3) those who are aspirants after realization of God (sādhaka).[21]

Bowing to the image of an incarnation of God, eating the food offered to it, the company of His devotees, etc., are the extraordinary excitant cause of the religious sentiment of loving servitude. Listening to His supreme excellence, the sight of His image, the smelling of the fragrance of the flowers offered to it, and the like are its ordinary excitant cause. Execution of the commands of His devotees, friendship for them without a trace of envy, devoted service to His image and devotees, etc., are its extraordinary ensuant cause. Regard for His devotees who think themselves to be His friends, renunciation of the objects of sentient pleasure, etc., are its ordinary ensuant cause. All sāttvikabhāvas are its spontaneous organic expressions. Joy, pride, contentment, self-abasement, dejection, misery, anxiety, recollection, apprehension, ascertainment, eagerness, fickleness, conjecture, agitation, shame, inactivity, stupor, insanity, dissimulation, awakening, dream, fatigue, sickness, and death-like condition are its accessory emotions and states. The remaining nine transitory emotions and states, e.g., intoxication, languor, terror, epilepsy, lethargy, fierceness, revenge, envy, and sleep do not nourish this religious sentiment appreciably. In the religious sentiment of union with God joy, pride and contentment are the accessory emotions. In the religious sentiment of separation from Him fatigue, sickness and death-like condition are the accessory states.

[21] Ibid, iii, 2, 5-17, 29-30

The remaining eighteen transitory emotions are the accessory emotions in both.[22]

Awe or trembling of the heart with adoration owing to the knowledge of God being the master mingled with regard is the basic permanent sentiment in the religious sentiment of loving servitude.[23] This subconscious emotional disposition is roused to consciousness by the sight of an image of a divine incarnation, listening to his excellence, etc., gradually increases in intensity and becomes ardent love, affection and passionate attachment. Regard blended with awe (sambhramaprīti) is called ardent love when it is devoid of apprehension of decreasing and firmly rooted in the mind. Showing a passion for God, etc., are its external manifestations. When ardent love becomes very intense and melts the heart, it becomes affection. Its mental consequent is intolerance of separation from God for a single moment. Affection becomes passionate attachment when even pain is experienced as pleasure owing to the direct experience of God or manifestation of Him in the heart, or the experience of His grace, and attempts are made to please Him even at the cost of life when the least relationship with Him is established.[24] The appointed and dependent servants often acquire ardent love; comrades achieve affection; and some comrades and followers attain passionate attachment.

The religious sentiment of loving servitude (sambhramaprīta-rasa) is of two kinds: (1) the absence of union with God (ayoga) and (2) union with Him (yoga). In the former a servant who feels separation from Him, always thinks of Him, remembers His excellences, and thinks of the means of uniting with Him. The absence of union (ayoga) is of two kinds: (2) yearning for union with God which has not yet been experienced (utkaṇṭhita), and (2) separation from Him after union with Him (viyoga). Eagerness, misery, self-abasement, anxiety, fickleness, insanity, inactivity, and stupor are the accessory emotions and states in yearning for union. Heat of the body, emaciation, wakefulness,

[22] Ibid, iii, 2, 30-39.

[23] Sambhramaḥ prabhutā-jñānāt kampaś cetasi sādaraḥ.
Anenaikyaṁ gatā prītiḥ sambhramaprītir ucyate.
Ibid, iii, 2, 40.

[24] Hrāsaśaṅkācyutā baddhamūlā premeyam ucyate.
Sāndraś cittadravaṁ kurvan premā sneha itīryate.
Snehaḥ sa rāgo yena syāt sukhaṁ duhkham api sphuṭam.
Ibid, iii, 2, 44-46.

blankness of the mind, discontent, inactivity, sickness, insanity, fainting, and death-like condition are the transitory emotions and states in separation. Blankness of the mind is its instability. Discontent is the absence of attachment to all things. These are also the accessory states of the ordinary sentiment of separation from the lover.

Union with God (yoga) is of three kinds: (1) fulfilment (siddhi), (2) satisfaction (tuṣṭi) and coresidence (sthiti). (1) Yearning for a devotee's union with God is called fulfilment. (2) Separation after union with Him is called separation. Union with God after separation is called satisfaction. (3) Living in the company of God is called coresidence. Serving the image of a divine incarnation with great care and attention whenever there is an opportunity, and the like are the expressions of union with God. Some who are ignorant of the relish of loving servitude for God regard it as a bhāva which cannot be developed into a religious sentiment.[25] Rūpa Goswāmī rejects this view because the *Bhāgavata* clearly recognizes it as a religious sentiment.[26] A bhāva is an emotion which cannot be developed into an æsthetic or religious sentiment (rasa).

(2) Those devotees who consider themselves as children of God who brings them up and fondles them have regard for Him blended with filial love. When it is nourished by the appropriate determinant cause, the excitant cause, the ensuant cause and the accessory emotions, it is transformed into the religious sentiment of loving regard (gauravaprītirasa).[27]

The devotees who consider themselves as children of God are the abodes (āśraya) of the religious sentiment of loving regard. God as the father endowed with great intelligence, great strength, great renown, who is the most venerable superior, maintainer, protector and fondler, is the object (viṣaya) of this religious sentiment. Both these are its determinant cause. Parental love of God, etc., are its excitant cause. Sitting on a low seat before an image of a divine incarnation, following his path of conduct,

[25] Kecid asyā rateḥ kṛṣṇabhaktyāsvāda-bahirmukhāḥ.
Bhāvatvam eva niścitya na rasāvasthatāṁ jaguḥ.
Ibid, iii, 2, 61-62. Ibid, iii, 2, 49-56; 57-60.

[26] Bhāg., xi, 3, 32; vii, 7, 34.

[27] Lālyābhimāninām kṛṣṇe syāt prītir gauravottarā.
Sā vibhāvādibhiḥ puṣṭā gauravaprīta ucyate.
Ibid, iii, 2, 64-65.

relinquishing wanton actions, shouldering his burden, etc., are the expressions of the religious sentiment of loving regard. Obeisance, excessive silence, reserve, humility, executing his commands even at the cost of life, looking downward, steadiness, refraining from coughing, laughing, etc., are the expressions of the religious sentiment of loving servitude. In both sentiments of loving servitude and loving regard the knowledge of God's lordship and majesty is the predominant element.[28] Inactivity, horripilation, perspiration, etc., are the spontaneous organic expressions of the religious sentiment of loving regard. Joy, self-abasement and other transitory emotions which are the accessory states of the religious sentiment of loving servitude are also the accessory states of this religious sentiment.

Loving regard for God as father or the like who brings up His devotees as children blended with the feeling of His superiority because of the conceit of one's bodily relationship with Him is the permanent emotional disposition of the religious sentiment of loving regard.[29] It is eternally present in some devotees. It is gradually intensified, acquires certain specific characters, and is transformed into ardent love, affection, and passionate attachment. Each of these is of two kinds: (1) the absence of union (ayoga) and (2) union (yoga). The former is of two kinds: (1) yearning for union (utkaṇṭhita) and (2) separation after union (viyoga). The latter is of three kinds: (1) fulfilment (siddhi), (2) satisfaction (tuṣṭi), and (3) coresidence (sthiti) as explained above.[30]

4. *The Religious Sentiment of Friendly Love (Preyobhaktirasa)*

The permanent emotional disposition of friendship is made relishable by the appropriate determinant cause, the excitant cause, the ensuant cause and the transitory emotions, and is transformed into the religious sentiment of friendly love.[31] A divine

[28] Ubhayeṣāṁ sadārādhyadhiyaiva bhajatām api.
Sevakānām ihaiśvarya-jñānasyaiva pradhānatā.
Ibid, iii, 2, 69. Ibid, iii, 2, 65-67.

[29] Dehasambandhitāmātrād gurudhīratra gauravam.
Tanmayī lālake prītir gauravaprītir ucyate.
Ibid, iii, 2, 76-77. Ibid, iii, 2, 75.

[30] Ibid, iii, 2, 78-79.

[31] Sthāyī bhāvo vibhāvādyaiḥ sakhyam ātmocitair iha.
Nītaś citte satāṁ puṣṭim rasa preyān udīryate.
Ibid, iii. 3, 1.

incarnation, who is mighty, learned, efficient, compassionate, heroic, intelligent, forgiving, popular, diplomatic, happy and prosperous, is the object (viṣaya) of this religious sentiment. The devotees, who consider themselves as his friends of equal age, endowed with similar qualities, unreserved in their behaviour, and extremely confident, are its abodes (āśraya). Both these are the determinant cause of the religious sentiment of friendship. Among the devotees who think themselves as friends some are eternally self-realized, some are self-realized through spiritual discipline, and others are aspirants after self-realization. The young age, beauty, amiable deportment, sports, etc., of a divine incarnation are the excitant cause of this religious sentiment. Immobility, perspiration, horripilation, shedding tears, choked voice, pallor, etc., are its spontaneous organic expressions. All transitory emotions except fierceness, terror and indolence in relation to God are its accessory states. In separation all transitory emotions except intoxication, joy, pride, sleep and contentment are its accessory states. In union all transitory emotions except fatigue, sickness, misery, epilepsy and death-like condition are its accessory states.[32]

Friendship is love between two persons who are almost equal, which is in the nature of mutual confidence and devoid of reverence. Confidence is due to deep trust without any reserve. A devotee's friendly love for God is the permanent emotional disposition of the religious sentiment of friendship. This friendly love gradually increases in intensity and becomes intimacy, ardent love, affection and passionate attachment.[33] Intimacy (praṇaya) is the friendly love which is not blended with a trace of reverence even when its object is distinctly worthy of reverence. The religious sentiment of friendship also is of two kinds: (1) the absence of union and (2) union. The former is of two kinds: (1) yearning for union and (2) separation. The latter is of three kinds: (1) fulfilment, (2) satisfaction and (3) coresidence as explained above. Only persons who cherish friendly love for God can feel the religious sentiment of friendship with the assistance of the determinant cause, the excitant cause, the ensuant cause and the accessory states. The ten conditions stated above

[32] Ibid, iii, 3, 2-6, 23, 27, 51-54.
[33] Vimukta-sambhramā yā syād viśrambhātmā ratir dvayoḥ.
Prāyaḥ samānayoratra sā sakhyaṁ sthāyiśabdabhāk.
Ibid, iii, 3, 54-55. Ibid, iii, 3. 56-57.

occur in separation. In the religious sentiment of friendship God or a divine incarnation and the devotee are supposed to feel the same kind of emotion for each other, whereas in the religious sentiments of loving servitude and parental love they feel different kinds of emotion for each other. Hence the devotees who think themselves as friends of God regard the religious sentiment of friendship as the best of all kinds of religious sentiments. It produces transcendent wonder in their minds. The transitory emotions in separation are the same as those in the religious sentiment of loving servitude.[34]

5. *The Religious Sentiment of Parental Love (Vatsalabhaktirasa)*

The permanent emotional disposition of parental love for God is evoked and nourished by the appropriate determinant cause, the excitant cause, the ensuant cause and the accessory emotions, and transformed into the religious sentiment of parental love.[35] God is the object (viṣaya) of this religious sentiment. The devotees, who consider themselves as fathers or mothers, and a divine incarnation as their child, are its abode (āśraya). Kṛṣṇa, who is dark in complexion, graceful in features, beautiful, tender, sweet-tongued, simple, shy, modest, respectful and generous, is the object and determinant cause of his elders' religious sentiment of parental love. He is not known as the abode of prowess and lordly powers. His elders regarded as superiors and teachers are the abodes of this religious sentiment. Nanda, Kṛṣṇa's foster-father, Yaśodā, his foster-mother, Vasudeva, his father, and Devakī, his mother, are his elders who are the abodes of the religious sentiment of parental love for him. His infancy, beauty, dress, pranks, prattle, smile, sports, etc., are its excitant cause. Smelling his head, rubbing his body with hands, blessing, commanding, tending, fondling, giving good advice, kissing, embracing, calling him by name, etc., are its expressions. Immobility, shedding tears, faltering voice, oozing out of milk from the breasts, etc., are its spontaneous organic expressions. All the transitory emotions, which nourish the religious sentiment of loving servitude, and epilepsy are the accessory states of the religious

[34] Ibid, iii, 3, 57-61.
[35] Vibhāvādyaistu vātsalyaṁ sthāyī puṣṭim upāgataḥ.
Eṣa vatsalatāmātraḥ prokto bhaktiraso budhaiḥ.
Ibid, iii, 4, 1.

transformed into the religious sentiment of holy love.[38] It is a mysterious incomprehensible religious sentiment, because it is not in harmony with the life of renunciation. It is a transcendent, disembodied, sefless, holy love for Kṛṣṇa based on sublimated, purified eros as has already been explained. Though he did not enter upon adolescence and was in his late childhood (kaiśora), he was looked upon by young unmarried and married milkmaids as their lover, who cherished selfless holy love for him. Some male and female devotees worship God as their lover, and think themselves as the young milkmaids who dedicated their whole being to Kṛṣṇa.

Kṛṣṇa as invested with unequalled and unsurpassed beauty, love, grace and sweetness is the object (viṣya). Or God of infinite love and sweetness is its object. The young milkmaids, who loved Kṛṣṇa as their lover with all-consuming, undivided love, were the abodes of the religious sentiment of holy love. Or, the devotees, who worship God as their lover, are its abode (āśraya). Both the object and the abode are the determinant cause of this religious sentiment. The sound of Kṛṣṇa's flute, etc., are its excitant cause. Sidelong glances, smile, etc., are its ensuant cause. Gooseflesh, shedding tears, choked voice, trembling heart, etc., are its spontaneous organic expressions. All transitory emotions and states except indolence and fierceness are its accessory states. Extra-conjugal holy love (madhurarati) is the basic permanent emotional disposition of this religious sentiment. Extra-conjugal holy love between Rādhā and Kṛṣṇa was never interrupted by any other similar or dissimilar emotions.

The religious sentiment of extra-conjugal holy love is of two kinds: (1) union (sambhoga) and (2) separation (vipralambha). The religious sentiment of separation is of many kinds: (1) incipient love before union (pūrvarāga), (2) the sulks (māna), (3) sojourn in a distant land (pravāsa), etc. Their nature has already been explained in connection with the erotic sentiment and emotions derived from love. Rūpa Goswāmī regards the religious sentiment of extra-conjugal holy love as the best sentiment of devotion. It is called the bright sentiment (ujjvalarasa), pure sentiment (śucirasa), sentiment of wifely love (kāntārasa),

[38] Ātmocitair vibhāvādyaiḥ puṣṭiṁ nītā satāṁ hṛdi.
Madhurākhyo bhaved bhaktiraso' sau madhurā ratiḥ.
Ibid, iii, 5, 1. Ibid, iii, 5, 2.

erotic sentiment (śṛṅgārarasa) of devotion. These are the five principal religious sentiments of devotion (bhaktirasa).[39]

7. *The Subordinate Religious Sentiments of Devotion (Gauṇabhaktirasa)*

There are seven subordinate religious sentiments: (1) ludicrous religious sentiment, (2) marvellous religious sentiment, (3) heroic religious sentiment, (4) pathetic religious sentiment, (5) furious religious sentiment, (6) terrible religious sentiment, and (7) odious religious sentiment. These are illustrated by Rūpa Goswāmī by the relation of Kṛṣṇa to his devotees.

(1) Love for Kṛṣṇa blended with mirth (hāsarati) is evoked by the appropriate determinant cause and the excitant cause, nourished by the ensuant cause and the accessory emotions and states, and turned into the comic sentiment of devotion (hāsya-bhaktirasa). Kṛṣṇa or a person who is related to him as the object (viṣaya) and determinant cause of this religious sentiment. A person related to Kṛṣṇa acts in relation to him, and is its object as related to him. Generally old persons and children are the abodes (āśraya) of this religious sentiment. But sometimes even superior persons are its abodes owing to the extraordinary character of its determinant and excitant causes. When Kṛṣṇa, an infant, was frightened at the sight of decrepit and fierce-looking Nārada and refused to come to him, he burst into a laughter. Here the former was the object, and the latter, the abode, of the ludicrous sentiment of devotion. Unusual dress and uncommon activities of Kṛṣṇa are its excitant cause. Throbbing of the nose, the checks, and the lips, etc., are its ensuant cause. Joy, indolence, dissimulation, etc., are its accessory emotions and states. Nascent love for Kṛṣṇa with mirth is the permanent emotional disposition which is developed into this sentiment. It is of six kinds: (1) smita, (2) hasita, (3) vihasita, (4) avahasita, (5) apahasita and (6) atihasita. Their nature has already been explained in connection with the ludicrous sentiment (hāsyarasa).[40]

(2) Love for Kṛṣṇa blended with wonder (vismayarati) is evoked and rendered relishable by the appropriate determinant cause, the excitant cause, the ensuant cause and accessory emotions,

[39] Ibid, iii, 5, 3-11. UNM., i, 2-6.
[40] Ibid, iv, 1, 5-10. Ibid, iv, 1, 12-15.

and converted into the marvellous sentiment of devotion (adbhuta-bhaktirasa). Kṛṣṇa, the cause of superhuman actions, is the object (viṣaya) of this religious sentiment. His devotees of all kinds are its abodes (āśraya). His particular actions which excite wonder are its excitant cause. Expansion of the eyes, immobility, horripilation, shedding tears, etc., are its ensuant cause. Agitation, joy, inactivity, etc., are its accessory states. Love with wonder due to Kṛṣṇa's superhuman actions is its permanent emotional disposition.

The marvellous sentiment of devotion is of two kinds: (1) perceptual and (2) inferential. (1) The former is due to the visual perception, or auditory perception, or the chanting of Kṛṣṇa's superhuman actions. (2) The latter is due to the inference of his superhuman powers from certain miraculous phenomena perceived. His superhuman actions do not produce wonder in his foes who cherish hatred for him. The least wonderful actions of him produce wonder in his dearest friends, which increases the excellence of their love for him.[41] The marvellous sentiment of devotion, Jīva Goswāmī observes, which is found in persons devoid of love for Kṛṣṇa, evoked by his wonderful actions, is a mere imitation of it. It cannot be excited in a person, if he has no nascent love for him. Love for Kṛṣṇa is the basis of this secondary religious sentiment.[42]

When Kṛṣṇa revealed his cosmic form (viśvarūpa) to Arjuna in the battle-field of Kurukṣetra, he experienced the marvellous sentiment of devotion, because he had transcendent wonder blended with supreme bliss. It was evoked by Kṛṣṇa, the basic determinant cause, his cosmic form, the excitant cause, and nourished by horripilation, obeisance, etc., the ensuant cause and sāttvikabhāvas, and by ascertainment of duty, contentment, joy, conjecture, etc., as the accessory states, and transformed into the marvellous sentiment of devotion. Arjuna's nascent love for Kṛṣṇa blended with wonder was the basic permanent emotional disposition of this religious sentiment.[43]

(3) Love for Kṛṣṇa blended with courage (utsāharati) is evoked by the appropriate determinant cause and the excitant cause,

[41] Ibid, iv, 2, 1-7.
[42] Ajāta-prītināntu tatsambandhena ye vismayādayo bhāvāstadīyaraśāśca dṛśyante, te' tra tadanukāriṇa eva jñeyāḥ. PS., 174.
[43] MBG., xi, 14.

nourished by the ensuant cause and the accessory emotions, and transformed into the heroic sentiment of devotion (vīrabhaktirasa). There are four kinds of heroes: (1) a fighting hero (yuddhavīra), (2) a generous hero (dānavīra), (3) a merciful hero (dayāvīra), and (4) a pious hero (dharmavīra). Kṛṣṇa and his devotees of these four kinds are the basic determinant cause (ālambana vibhāva) of the heroic sentiment of devotion. All devotees may have courage. A friend or a dear friend, who engages in a battle for Kṛṣṇa's pleasure, is a fighting hero, and the latter is his opponent. If Kṛṣṇa is a spectator, then his another friend is an opponent. The fights between Kṛṣṇa and his friend, or between his friends for his pleasure, are mere play, and not real. Sometimes persons, who are heroes by nature, show wonderful courage in fighting among their friends. The opponent's bragging, flourishing his arms, daring his adversary to fight, showing prowess, taking up weapons, etc., are the excitant cause of the heroic sentiment of devotion. Self-glorification, roaring, bragging, jumping, desire to fight even in a helpless condition, not flying away from the battle-field, giving assurance of safety to the frightened, etc., are its ensuant cause. All kinds of sāttvikabhāvas are its spontaneous organic expressions. Pride, agitation, contentment, shame, ascertainment, joy, dissimulation, revenge, impatience, envy, recollection, etc., are its accessory states. Nascent love for Kṛṣṇa or the like with courage to fight (yuddhotsāharati) is its permanent emotional disposition. It is either artificially produced by one's powers or by one's assistants. Or, it is inherent in one's nature and manifested by one's powers or by one's assistants. Courage to fight is intense desire to win.[44]

In the heroic sentiment of devotion a friend of Kṛṣṇa is the opponent, and not his enemy. His enemy is the basic determinant cause of the furious sentiment of devotion, because he infuriates his devotees. The heroic sentiment of devotion differs from the furious sentiment of devotion in that the former is devoid of the redness of the eyes due to the absence of anger, while the latter is attended with redness of the eyes due to the presence of anger.[45]

[44] Ibid, iv, 3, 1-11.
[45] Suhṛdeva pratibhaṭo vīre kṛṣṇasya na tvariḥ.
Sa bhakta-kṣobhakāritvād raudre tvālambano rase.
Ibid, iv, 3, 12-13.

Generous heroes are of two kinds: (1) a generous hero who gives all to Kṛṣṇa (bahuprada). and (2) a generous hero who renounces even objects which are difficult of attainment when they are offered to one (upasthitadurāpārthatyāgī). (1) A devotee who suddenly gives all his wealth to Kṛṣṇa for his pleasure is bahuprada. The sight of a fit object of gift, etc., are the excitant cause of this religious sentiment of a generous hero. Giving more than what is sought for, smiling speech, firmness, generosity, patience, etc., are its ensuant cause. Conjecture, eagerness, joy, etc., are its accessory emotions and states. Nascent love for Kṛṣṇa blended with courage to make gifts (dānotsāharati) is its basic permanent emotional disposition. It is a strong and firm desire to give away one's wealth. A generous hero who gives all is of two kinds: (*i*) a generous hero who gives all his wealth to begging Brāhmins for Kṛṣṇa's prosperity (ābhyudayika), and (*ii*) a generous hero who gives all his dear objects which are impregnated with the sense of 'I' and 'mine' to Kṛṣṇa (tatsampradānaka). Such a hero's gift is of two kinds: (*a*) prītidāna and (*b*) pūjādāna. His gift of wealth with loving regard to Kṛṣṇa in the form of a relative is prītidāna. His gift of wealth to Kṛṣṇa in the form of a Brāhmin is pūjādāna. (2) A devotee who does not accept even liberation in the form of powers of sovereignty offered by Kṛṣṇa is a generous hero who renounces even objects, which are difficult of attainment and which are offered to him. Kṛṣṇa's grace, talks, smile, etc., are the exciting cause of this kind of religious sentiment. Firmness in the delineation of his excellences, etc., are its ensuant cause. Excess of contentment is its accessory emotion. The courage to renounce is a strong desire to renounce even sovereignty offered by Kṛṣṇa.

A devotee who offers his body in pieces to Kṛṣṇa in the disguise of a distressed person owing to his compassionate heart is called a merciful hero (dayāvīra). A devotee, who depends only on the excessive grace of Kṛṣṇa, who does not depend on any other person. and who cherishes the most intense love for the former, is called a heroic comrade. The manifestation of the distress of a distressed person, etc., are the exciting cause of this kind of religious sentiment. A merciful devoted hero's deliverance of the distressed person from his distress even at the cost of his life, speaking words of comfort, assurance of safety, firmness, etc., are its ensuant cause. Impatience, ascertainment, joy, etc., are its accessory states. Nascent love for Kṛṣṇa blended with courage to show mercy to the distressed (dayotsāharati) is the basic permanent emotional disposition underlying this religious sentiment. Courage which evokes mercy for the distressed is called courage for mercy.

Rūpa Goswāmī distinguishes between the religious sentiment of a generous hero (dānavīrabhaktirasa) and that of a merciful hero (dayāvīrabhaktirasa). In the former a devotee knows a disguised form of Kṛṣṇa to be in his real nature, and makes gifts for Kṛṣṇa's pleasure or welfare, while in the latter a devotee does not know a disguised form of Kṛṣṇa to be Kṛṣṇa, and makes gifts to him out of compassion—his nascent love for Kṛṣṇa being naturally manifested as compassion when the latter is found in distress even in a disguised form. Vopadeva and others do not consider the religious sentiment of a merciful hero to be a distinct sentiment of devotion.

A devotee who always practises acts of piety for Kṛṣṇa's pleasure, and who is often quiet and tranquil, is called a pious hero (dharmavīra). Hearing of the instructions of the scriptures, etc., are the exciting cause of the religious sentiment of a pious hero. Moral conduct, faith in God, tolerance, restraints, etc., are its ensuant cause. Ascertainment, recollection, etc., are its accessory states. Nascent love for Kṛṣṇa with courage to perform acts of piety is the basic permanent emotional disposition (dharmotsāharati) underlying this religious sentiment. Courage to perform acts of piety with devotion is called courage for piety. Sacrifice, worship, meditation, offerings to sacrificial fire, etc., for Kṛṣṇa are the acts of piety. Some do not regard the religious sentiment of a pious hero as a distinct sentiment of devotion.[46]

(4) Nascent love for Kṛṣṇa blended with grief (śokarati) is evoked and nourished by its appropriate determinant cause, excitant cause, ensuant cause, and accessory emotions and states, and transformed into the pathetic sentiment of devotion (karuṇa bhaktirasa). Kṛṣṇa, though a receptacle of uninterrupted supreme bliss, supposed to be distressed for the time being by a devotee due to his excessive ardent love for him, is the object (viṣaya) of this religious sentiment. Kṛṣṇa's dear ones also similarly distressed, or the kinsmen and relatives of his devotees devoid of the bliss

[46] Ibid, iv, 3, 12-39, 41.

of devotion to him, are the objects of this sentiment of devotion. The three kinds of devotees who perceive the three kinds of objects stated above are its abodes (āśraya). Both the objects and the abodes are its basic determinant cause. Kṛṣṇa's form, attributes, actions, etc., or those of his dear ones, or of the kinsmen and relatives of his devotees are its excitant cause. Dryness of the mouth, lamentation, looseness of the limbs, laboured breathing, crying out, falling on the ground, striking the ground, striking the chest, etc., are its ensuant cause. Eight kinds of sāttvikabhāvas are its spontaneous organic expressions. Inactivity, self-despisement, languor, misery, anxiety, dejection, impatience, fickleness, insanity, death-like condition, indolence, epilepsy, sickness, stupor, etc., are its accessory emotions and states. Nascent love for Kṛṣṇa blended with grief is its permanent emotional disposition. It is love which is partly modified by the presence of grief in the mind.[47]

Mirth, etc., can be evoked without nascent love, but grief cannot be evoked without it. Greater or less intensity of grief depends upon greater or less intensity of nascent love for the person who excites grief. Grief and love are inseparable. This is the distinctive characteristic of the pathetic sentiment of devotion.[48]

Kṛṣṇa is the embodiment of supreme bliss, the highest good, and sovereignty, and cannot therefore be touched by any evil or harm. So there cannot be any apprehension of evil in regard to him. But apprehension of harm to him evokes the emotion of grief. How is this possible? The knowledge of the lordship of Kṛṣṇa is not veiled by nescience (avidyā), but by the religious sentiment due to excessive love for Kṛṣṇa.[49] God has six powers of sovereignty: knowledge, power, strength, lordship, heroism and spiritedness. These are the special powers of sovereignty. But they are divided into two common powers: (1) supreme lordship (parama-aiśvarya) and (2) supreme sweetness (parama-mādhurya). The former evokes fear, awe, etc., while the latter excite intrest in God's form, attributes and actions, which produces ardent

[47] Ibid, iv, 4, 1-8.
[48] Ratyā sahāvinābhāvāt kāpyetaśya viśiṣṭatā.
Ibid, iv, 4, 10. Ibid, iv, 4, 9-10.
[49] Kṛṣṇaiśvaryādyavijñānaṁ kṛtaṁ naiṣām avidyayā.
Kintu premottara-rasa-viśeṣeṇaiva tat kṛtam.
Ibid, iv, 4, 11.

love (prema) for Him. Relation of God to His essential bliss is His essential nature. The experience of His essential nature and supreme lordship is veiled by a devotee's ardent love for Him, and not by his nescience.[50] Grief being evoked by the distress of Kṛṣṇa manifests his supreme bliss and assumes an indescribable state of joy veiled by the experience of adventitious pain. Hence the pathetic sentiment of devotion produces transcendent wonder and joy.[51]

(5) Nascent love for Kṛṣṇa blended with anger (krodharati) is evoked and nourished by the appropriate determinant cause, the excitant cause, the ensuant cause and accessory emotions and states, and transformed into the furious sentiment of devotion (raudrabhaktirasa) in the heart of a devotee. Kṛṣṇa, his well-wishers and foes are its objects (viṣaya). When Kṛṣṇa is its object, his female friends, old milkmaids, etc., are its abodes (āśraya). When his well-wishers and foes are its objects, all kinds of devotees are its abodes. When some harm is done to a female friend by his negligence, he is the object of her furious sentiment of devotion. When an old milkmaid's anger is evoked by him because her daughter-in-law is attracted towards him, he is the object of her furious sentiment of devotion. When his well-wishers become negligent in taking care of him, they are the objects of the sentiment. When the actions of his foes evoke anger in his devotees, the former are the objects of the latter's sentiment. When an enemy of a devotee hinders the latter's relation to Kṛṣṇa and evokes his anger, the former is the object of his furious sentiment of devotion.[52]

Kṛṣṇa's well-wishers (hita) are of three classes: (1) negligent, (2) rash, and (3) jealous. (1) When a protector of Kṛṣṇa deviates from his duty of protection owing to his preoccupation with some other work, he is negligent. (2) When a well-wisher of Kṛṣṇa sends him to a dangerous place, he is rash. (3) When a well-wisher of Kṛṣṇa is overcome by strong jealousy, he is jealous.

Hostile persons (ahita) are of two classes: (1) one's own foes and (2) Kṛṣṇa's foes. (1) The former hinder one's relation to Kṛṣṇa. (2) The latter are Kṛṣṇa's antagonists. Śiśupāla, Kṛṣṇa's foe, excites anger blended with love in Bhīma, who is Kṛṣṇa's friend.

[50] DGS., iv, 4, 11. [51] HBRS., DGS., iv, 4, 12.
[52] Ibid, iv, 5, 1-3; PS. 167.

Kṛṣṇa's well-wishers' or foes' ironical laughter, insinuation, glances, disregard, etc., are the excitant cause of the furious sentiment of devotion. Pressing the palms, grinding the teeth, biting the lips, striking the arms, eyeing crookedly, hanging down the head, quick breathing, shaking the head, bloodshot eyes, chiding, knitting the eye-brows, keeping silence, throbbing of the lips, frowning hard, etc., are its ensuant cause. All sāttvikabhāvas are its spontaneous organic expressions. Agitation, inactivity, pride, self-despisement, stupor, fickleness, envy, fierceness, revenge, fatigue, etc., are its accessory emotions and states. Nascent love for Kṛṣṇa blended with anger is the permanent emotional disposition underlying this sentiment. It is of three kinds: (1) anger evoked by the foes (kopa), (2) anger excited by the friendly persons (manyu), and (3) anger evoked by a friend in women (roṣa). The second kind of anger (manyu) is of three kinds: (i) anger excited by superior persons, (ii) anger roused by equal persons, and (iii) anger evoked by inferior persons. Kopa is expressed by pressing the palms, manyu, by keeping silence, and roṣa, by pale redness of the corners of the eyes. Manyu is not assisted by nascent love for Kṛṣṇa. Kopa evoked by foes is natural. Anger without being assisted by nascent love for Kṛṣṇa is not transformed into the furious religious sentiment.[53] The anger of the female friends of Kṛṣṇa who worship him with extranuptial holy love does not attain stability like that of the old milkmaids and his other female friends. Even in the anger evoked by foes, nascent love for Kṛṣṇa is the permanent sentiment and anger towards the foes is the accessory emotion which fosters it. The transitory emotions in which fierceness predominates nourish the furious sentiment of devotion which has foes for its object; those in which revenge predominates foster the religious furious sentiment which has friends for its object; those in which envy predominates develop the religious furious sentiment which has the lover for its object.[53a] When nascent love for Kṛṣṇa is veiled by anger, it is called krodharati; love is relished and transformed into the religious furious sentiment with the assistance of anger. Śiśupāla, a foe of Kṛṣṇa, has no nascent love for Kṛṣṇa, and consequently his anger roused by his enmity cannot be converted

[53] Krodho rativinābhāvānna bhaktirasatāṁ vrajet.
Ibid, iv, 5, 19. Ibid, iv, 5, 5-18.

[53a] DGS., iv, 5, 15.

into the religious furious sentiment; his anger is a natural emotion.

(6) Nascent love for Kṛṣṇa blended with fear (bhayarati) is evoked by the appropriate determinant cause and the excitant cause, nourished by its ensuant cause and accessory emotions and states, and transformed into the terrible sentiment of devotion (bhayānakabhaktirasa). Kṛṣṇa and terrible beings are its objects (viṣaya). Kṛṣṇa excites the terrible religious sentiment in his guilty and pitiable friends. Demons and other terrible beings excite this religious sentiment in Kṛṣṇa's friends, who see, hear, or remember great harm being done to him by them, and who apprehend his harm owing to love for him. Frowns, etc., of the terrible beings who are the objects and determinant causes are the excitant cause of the terrible sentiment of devotion. Dryness of the mouth, hard breathing, looking backward, concealing oneself, searching for a secure place, crying out, reeling, etc., are its ensuant cause. All sāttvikabhāvas except shedding tears are its spontaneous organic expressions. Terror, unsteadiness, agitation, misery, dejection, stupor, epilepsy, apprehension, death-like condition, etc., are its accessory emotions and states. Nascent love for Kṛṣṇa blended with fear (bhayarati) is the permanent emotional disposition underlying the terrible religious sentiment. It is not produced in persons other than those, who have nascent love for Kṛṣṇa, and who are favoured by him.[54] It is generally produced in those women and children, who have nascent love for Kṛṣṇa, and who are favoured by him.

(7) Nascent love for Kṛṣṇa blended with disgust (jugupsārati) is evoked and nourished by the appropriate determinant cause, the excitant cause, the ensuant cause and the accessory emotions and states, and transformed into the odious sentiment of devotion. Here nascent love for God is veiled by disgust for filthy objects. Kṛṣṇa is the object (viṣaya) of this religious sentiment. The quiet devotees who have taken refuge with him are its abodes (āśraya). Those devotees who have not yet attained proximity to God also are its abodes. The perception of filthy objects, etc., are its exciting cause. Spitting, narrowing the mouth, covering the nose, running away, etc., are its ensuant cause. Trembling, horripilation, perspiration, etc., are its spontaneous organic expressions.

[54] Etadālambanā bhītiḥ kevala-prema-śāliṣu. Ibid, iv, 6, 9. Ibid, iv, 6, 1-11.

Languor, fatigue, insanity, stupor, self-despisement, misery, dejection, unsteadiness, inactivity, etc. are its accessory emotions and states. Nascent love for Kṛṣṇa blended with disgust is its permanent emotional disposition. Disgust is either due to discrimination or natural. A particular devotee who has acquired nascent love for Kṛṣṇa, feels disgust for his body due to discrimination. All persons feel disgust for impure and filthy objects, which is therefore natural. A devotee who has acquired nascent love for Kṛṣṇa has always a well-purified mind which is agitated and repelled by the least loathsome object. Hence his odious religious sentiment is assisted by his nascent love for Kṛṣṇa.[55]

Rūpa Goswāmī describes the comic religious sentiment, the heroic religious sentiment, the pathetic religious sentiment, the furious religious sentiment, the terrible religious sentiment, the marvellous religious sentiment, and the odious religious sentiment as the subordinate or secondary religious sentiments (gauṇabhaktirasa) after his predecessors who dealt with the ordinary æsthetic sentiments (prākṛtarasa). In reality, these are the accessory states of the five genuine religious sentiments of quiet love, loving servitude, friendship, parental affection, and wifely love or extranuptial holy love.[56]

8. *Harmony and Conflict among the Religious Sentiments*

Some religious sentiments are in harmony with other religious sentiments. Some religious sentiments are in conflict with other religious sentiments. The religious sentiments which assist, nourish and strengthen other religious sentiments are friendly towards them. Those religious sentiments which antagonise, contract and weaken other religious sentiments are hostile to them. Just as there are harmony and conflict among the æsthetic sentiments, so there are harmony and conflict among the religious sentiments.

Rūpa Goswāmī describes harmony and conflict among the religious sentiments in the following manner. The religious sentiment of loving servitude, the odious religious sentiment, the

[55] Labdha-kṛṣṇa-rater eva suṣṭhu pūtaṁ manas sadā.
Kṣubhyatyahṛdyaleśe'pi tato'syāṁ ratyanugrahaḥ.
Ibid, iv, 7, 7-8. Ibid, iv, 7, 1-6.

[56] Pañcaiva śāntādyā bhaktirasāḥ. Hāsādayaḥ prāyo vyabhicāritāṁ vibhrati. Ibid, iv, 7, 9-10. Ibid, iv, 7, 8-9.

religious sentiment of a pious hero, and the marvellous religious sentiment are friendly to the religious sentiments of loving servitude, friendship, parental affection, and wifely love or extranuptial love. The religious sentiment of wifely love or extranuptial love, the religious sentiment of a fighting hero and the furious religious sentiment are hostile to the quiet religious sentiment.

The odious religious sentiment, the quiet religious sentiment and the religious sentiments of a generous hero and a pious hero are friendly to the religious sentiment of loving servitude. The religious sentiment of wifely love or extranuptial holy love, the religious sentiment of a fighting hero produced directly by the relation to Kṛṣṇa, and the similar furious sentiment are hostile to it.

The religious sentiment of wifely love or extranuptial holy love, the comic religious sentiment, and the religious sentiment of a fighting hero directly produced by the relation to Kṛṣṇa are friendly to the religious sentiment of friendship. The religious sentiment of parental affection, the odious religious sentiment, the furious religious sentiment, and the terrible religious sentiment directly produced by the relation to Kṛṣṇa are hostile to it.

The comic religious sentiment, the pathetic religious sentiment, and the terrible religious sentiment excited by demons, etc., are friendly to the religious sentiment of parental affection. The religious sentiments of wifely love or extranuptial holy love, loving servitude, and the religious sentiment of a fighting hero evoked by the relation to Kṛṣṇa, and the similar furious religious sentiment are hostile to it.

The comic religious sentiment and the religious sentiment of friendship are friendly to the religious sentiment of wifely love or extranuptial holy love. The religious sentiment of parental affection, the odious religious sentiment, the quiet religious sentiment, the furious religious sentiment, and the terrible religious sentiment are hostile to it. Rūpa Goswāmī does not accept the view of some thinkers that the religious sentiments of a fighting hero and a pious hero are friendly to this religious sentiment, and that the other religious sentiments are hostile to it.

The odious religious sentiment, the religious sentiment of wifely love or extranuptial holy love, the religious sentiment of friendship, and the religious sentiment of parental affection are friendly to the comic religious sentiment. The pathetic religious sentiment and the terrible religious sentiment are hostile to it.

The heroic religious sentiment and the religious sentiments of quiet love, loving servitude, friendship, parental love, and wifely love or extranuptial holy love are friendly to the marvellous religious sentiment. The furious and the odious religious sentiments are hostile to it. Jīva Goswāmī observes, that they can produce transcendent wonder because they are religious sentiments (bhaktirasa), but that they conflict with the religious sentiment of wonder due to the perception of other marvellous objects.[57]

The marvellous religious sentiment, the comic religious sentiment, and the religious sentiments of friendship and loving servitude are friendly to the herioc religious sentiment. The terrible religious sentiment is hostile to it. Some regard the quiet religious sentiment also as hostile to it.

The furious religious sentiment due to the recollection of the persecution of one's dear ones and the religious sentiment of parental affection are friendly to the pathetic religious sentiment. The comic religious sentiment, the marvellous religious sentiment, and the religious sentiment of union (sambhoga) with the lover are hostile to it.

The pathetic religious sentiment and the heroic religious sentiment are friendly to the furious religious sentiment. The comic religious sentiment, the terrible religious sentiment, and the religious sentiment of wifely love or extranuptial holy love are hostile to it.

The odious religious sentiment and the pathetic religious sentiment are friendly to the terrible religious sentiment. The heroic religious sentiment, the religious sentimnt of wifely love or extranuptial holy love, the comic religious sentiment, and the furious religious sentiment are hostile to it.

The quiet religious sentiment, the comic religious sentiment, and the religious sentiment of loving servitude are friendly to the odious religious sentiment. The religious sentiments of wifely love or extranuptial holy love and friendship are hostile to it. The other religious sentiments also which are known to be in

---

[57] Alaukika-vastvantarānubhava-jāta-camatkārasya bhīṣaṇa-bībhatsitayor anubhavena vighātaḥ syāt. Tayoḥ svataś camatkārakaratvaṁ na niṣidhyate. DGS., iv, 8, 9.

conflict with it by reason are hostile to it. The religious sentiments which are neither friendly nor hostile to the other religious sentiments are neutral to them. They neither foster and strengthen them nor contract and weaken them.[58]

A religious sentiment is made very relishable when it is blended with friendly religious sentiments.[59] When two friendly religious sentiments are blended with each other, very often their equality cannot be ascertained. One of them becomes a predominant whole (aṅgin), and the other becomes a subordinate part (aṅga) of it. When a primary religious sentiment or a secondary religious sentiment is the predominant whole, its friendly religious sentiment becomes its subordinate part. Many religious sentiments may combine into a principal religious sentiment or a subordinate religious sentiment. Whatever religious sentiment, principal or subordinate, is the most relishable, is the predominant whole, while the other religious sentiments which foster and strengthen it as its accessory states are its subordinate parts. The other Rhetoricists also assert, that the principal æsthetic sentiment is the stable whole (aṅgin), and that the other æsthetic sentiments which nourish and strengthen it are its transitory parts (aṅga).[60] The subordinate religious sentiments excited by slight determinant causes nourish and strengthen the principal religious sentiment which is the predominant whole (aṅgin), and are merged in it. Sometimes a subordinate religious sentiment evoked by a strong determinant cause is fostered and developed by its principal religious sentiment which is contracted and weakened by it, and becomes the predominant whole (aṅgin); but the principal religious sentiment which becomes its subordinate part is not merged in it. The principal religious sentiment, which becomes the predominant whole, is developed and strengthened by the similar and the dissimilar sentiments and makes them its subordinate parts. If the religious sentiments which are the subordinate parts of a religious sentiment which is a predominant whole can contribute to the excellence of its relish, then only the task of their being its subordinate parts is

[58] HBRS., iv, 8, 1-15.
[59] Suhṛdā miśraṇam samyag āsvādyaṁ kurute rasam.
Ibid, iv, 8, 15.
[60] So'ṅgī sarvātigo yaḥ syān mukhyo gauṇo' thavā rasaḥ.
Sa evāṅgaṁ bhaved aṅgipoṣī saṁcāritāṁ vrajan.
Ibid, iv, 8, 22.

fulfilled. If they fail to do so, their combination with it becomes fruitless. If there is no relation of being fostered and fostering between two religious sentiments, there can be no relation of a whole and a part between them.[61] The religious sentiments, which are friendly to some other religious sentiment, nourish and strengthen it, when they blend with it. But the religious sentiments, which are hostile to some other religious sentiment, make it disrelishable.[62] The religious sentiment of parental love becomes very disrelishable, when it is blended with a trace of the religious sentiment of wifely love. Disrelish due to the hostility of the religious sentiments often turns into a mutilated religious sentiment (rasābhāsa).

Sometimes a religious sentiment blending with its hostile religious sentiment does not become disrelishable. If another religious sentiment intervenes between two such religious sentiments, the former does not become disrelishable. If two such religious sentiments are evoked by different objects (viṣaya), or exist in different abodes (āśraya), they do not produce disrelish. But if two principal religious sentiments—one being hostile to the the other—having different objects or existing in different abodes blend with each other, they produce disrelish. But if the hostile religious sentiment is a subordinate religious sentiment, the principal religious sentiment will not become a disrelish by blending with it, if they have different objects or exist in different abodes.[63] Two religious sentiments which are hostile to each other can blend with each other harmoniously, if they are subordinate parts of another predominating religious sentiment, which is nourished and developed by them.[64] The religious sentiment of extranuptial holy love of Rādhā and Kṛṣṇa does not become disrelishable, if hostile religious sentiments blend with each other in superexalted supreme holy love. Sometimes the blending of all religious sentiments in Kṛṣṇa, the supreme person of inconceivable powers, becomes relishable.[65]

[61] Ibid, iv, 8, 23-27.
[62] Janayatyeva vairasyaṁ rasānāṁ vairiṇā yutiḥ.
Ibid, iv, 8, 28. Ibid, iv, 8, 29.
[63] Viṣayāśrayabhede ca gauṇena dviṣatā saha.
Ityādiṣu na vairasyaṁ vairiṇor janayed yutiḥ.
Ibid, iv, 8, 32-33. Ibid, iv, 8, 31, 34.
[64] Aṅgayor aṅginaḥ puṣṭau bhaved ekatra saṅgatiḥ.
Ibid, iv, 8, 36.
[65] Ibid, iv, 8, 38-39.

9. *Apparent Religious Sentiments* (*Rasābhāsa*): *Uparasa, Anurasa and Aparasa*

Rūpa Goswāmī defines apparent religious sentiments as those which are mutilated or devoid of some of their characteristics.[66] They are of three kinds: (1) uparasa, (2) anurasa, and (3) aparasa. Uparasas are superior; anursas are mediocre; and aparasas are inferior.

The five principal religious sentiments of quiet love, loving servitude, friendly love, parental love, and wifely love or extra-nuptial holy love, and the seven subordinate religious sentiments, viz., the comic sentiment, the marvellous sentiment, the heroic sentiment, the furious sentiment, the terrible sentiment, the pathetic sentiment, and the odious sentiment, become uparasas, when they are mutilated or deformed by their basic permanent emotional dispositions, determinant causes, excitant causes, ensuant causes, and accessory emotions and states. The uparasas are incomplete flavours.

The quiet religious sentiment becomes an incomplete flavour, when a devotee is absorbed in Brahman, identifies the entire universe, its effect, with it completely, or when there is excess of disgust for the body, or of discrimination between self and not-self. The religious sentiment of loving servitude becomes an incomplete flavour, when a devotee who regards himself as Kṛṣṇa's servant shows impertinence before him, or despises his devotees, or sees greater excellence in some other Deity than Kṛṣṇa, his own worshipped Deity, or when he transcends the limits of servitude. The religious sentiment of friendship becomes an incomplete flavour, when only Kṛṣṇa feels friendly love for a devotee who does not feel it for him, when the latter disregards Kṛṣṇa's other friends, or when he fights with them very often. The religious sentiment of parental affection becomes an incomplete flavour, when a superior of Kṛṣṇa knows him to be of excessive power, or when he does not take adequate care of him. or when he shows excessive compassion to him. The religious sentiment of wifely love or extranuptial holy love becomes an incomplete flavour, when either the lover or the beloved woman only cherishes such love for the other, or when the latter cherishes love for many lovers. Here complete absence of love is meant.

[66] Vikalā rasā eva rasābhāsāḥ. Ibid, iv, 9, 1.

Such religious sentiment does not become an incomplete flavour, when there is prior absence of wifely love or extranuptial holy love. Some opine that, such religious sentiment becomes an incomplete flavour, also when the lover cherishes equal love for many beloved women. But when he cherishes different degrees of love for them according to their love in different degrees, such religious sentiment does not become an incomplete flavour.

The religious sentiments become incomplete flavours, when their determinant causes or ensuant causes are deformed. The deformity of the determinant causes is attributed to the basic permanent emotional dispositions. The violation of customary morality, vulgarity, and impertinence are called by the experts the deformity of the ensuant causes. The subordinate religious sentiments also become incomplete flavours.[67]

The five principal religious sentiments and the seven subordinate religious sentiments become after-flavours (anurasa), when they are produced by the determinate causes, etc., which are devoid of any relation to Kṛṣṇa. Even when the quiet religious sentiment and the seven subordinate religious sentiments evoked by the determinate causes, etc., bearing relation to Kṛṣṇa are manifested in neutral persons, they become after-flavours (anurasa), which are false imitations of the religious sentiments.

When the comic religious sentiment, etc., are evoked by Kṛṣṇa and his antagonist as their objects and determinant causes, they become tainted flavours (aparasa). Jarāsandha, an enemy of Kṛṣṇa, laughed, when he saw Kṛṣṇa running away from a distance. The former had a tainted comic religious sentiment. But a devotee of Kṛṣṇa would have the pure comic religious sentiment at the sight of both. The other subordinate religious sentiments become tainted flavours in a similar manner. Sometimes excellent apparent religious sentiments (rasābhāsa) are called religious sentiments (rasa) by some experts.[68]

10. *The Religious Sentiment of Devotion (bhaktirasa) is Transcendental (alaukika)*

(1) Devotion or nascent love (rati) for God is a mode of His essential power of transcendental consciousness and bliss. It is in the nature of non-phenomenal pure essence (śuddha-sattva-

[67] Ibid, iv, 9, 2, 9, 11, 15. [68] Ibid, iv, 9, 20-24.

viśeṣātmā), which is not a mode of cosmic nescience (māyā) which is composed of unconscious essence (sattva), energy (rajas) and tamas (inertia). Śuddha sattva is not an unconscious mode of māyā, but in the nature of transcendental consciousness. Nascent love for God is in the nature of transcendental bliss (ānandarūpa) also. It is a property of the supermind which is not an evolute of cosmic nescience, and which is free from nescience (avidyā) and insentience. If it were an attribute of the insentient mind, which is an evolute of cosmic nescience, it would not be transformed into the religious sentiment of devotion.[69]

Nascent love for God is the permanent emotional disposition (sthāyibhāva) of the religious sentiment of devotion (bhaktirasa), as we have already explained. Once it dawns on the heart of a person, it does not disappear, though it may increase and decrease at times. It is not produced but manifested by favourable conditions. It subordinates similar and dissimilar emotions to itself, and predominates over them. It is manifested in quiet love, loving servitude, friendly love, parental love, and wifely love or extra-nuptial holy love. The bliss of nascent love for God is more intense than the bliss of Brahman experienced by a yogin. The permanent sentiment of nascent love is manifested by the grace of God when nescience (avidyā) that veils it is destroyed by the company of His devotees.

There is an eternal urge in the individual self (jīva) for union with the universal Self or God of love, which is at the root of its unhappiness. Finite loves cannot make it perfectly happy; they are imperfect manifestations of its deep-lying innate love for God, which is unconscious, subconscious, half-conscious, or conscious. God, or Kṛṣṇa, a perfect incarnation of God, according to Caitanya and his followers, is the embodiment of all kinds of religious sentiments (akhila-rasāmṛtamūrti). He excites different religious sentiments in different devotees according to their different permanent emotional dispositions.[70] Nascent love for God being transcendental, the religious sentiment of devotion also is transcendental.

[69] Śuddha-sattva-viśeṣātmā ratiḥ. HBRS., ii, 5, 3. Ratir ānanda-rupaiva. Ibid, ii, 1, 10. Hlādinīsāravṛttiviśeṣasvarūpā bhāgavatī prītiḥ. PS., 78. Sāmājikānāṁ śuddhasattvaṁ na māyāvrttirūpam, api tu cidrūpam eva. Viśvanātha cakravartī's commentary on AK., v, 3.

[70] Ibid, i, 1, 1.

(2) God, or Kṛṣṇa, who is the infinite being-consciousness-bliss, who is possessed of unequalled and unsurpassed excellence, and who is completely free from insentient matter, is the object (viṣaya) and determinant cause (ālambana vibhāva) of the religious sentiment of devotion. Because its object-determinant cause is transcendental, it is transcendental.[71]

(3) God's comrades are the abodes (āśraya) and determinant cause of nascent love, who are like Him. His eternal comrades are parts or concrete embodiments of His essential power (svarūpaśakti), and therefore transcendental. His comrades who have acquired community of nature with Him through spiritual discipline, are not ordinary worldly persons, because their bodies are composed of pure sattva, which is not a mode of cosmic nescience. Therefore the religious sentiment of devotion, which is experienced by God's comrades who are like Him, is transcendental.[72]

(4) The attributes, actions, etc., of God, or His incarnation, the excitant cause of the religious sentiment of devotion, constitute His essential nature, and are composed of transcendental consciousness and bliss. Kṛṣṇa's dress, ornaments, flute, etc., are composed of transcendental consciousness and bliss untainted by cosmic nescience. They are not mere natural objects though they appear to be so to the unregenerate and unenlightened sense-organs, because they are not the modifications of cosmic nescience. The place of Kṛṣṇa's residence, his devotees, offerings to him, and the scriptures delineating his excellence are composed of transcendental consciousness (cinmaya). Those things which are related to him belong to him and partake of his transcendental nature.[73] There are certain objects, e.g., clouds, etc., which neither constitute his essence nor are related to him, but they excite nascent love for God at times. Jīva Goswāmī calls them adventitious excitant cause. They also acquire the transcendent condition because they being inspired by God's powers excite the recollection of Kṛṣṇa in his devotees who cherish nascent love for him because of their resemblance to his complexion. They cannot excite nascent love for God without being

[71] Ālambana-kāraṇasya śrībhagavato' samorddhvātiśayi-bhagavattvād eva siddham. PS., 111.
[72] Tat-parikarasya ca tattulyatvād eva. PS., 111.
[73] Uddīpana-kāraṇānāṁ tadīyānāñca tadīyatvāt. PS., 111.

inspired by His powers.[74] The excitant cause of the religious sentiment of devotion being transcendental, the latter is transcendental.

(5) Just as the determinant and excitant causes of the religious sentiment of devotion are transcendental, so its ensuant cause (anubhāva) or expressions of nascent love for God are transcendental. Dancing, rolling on the ground, crying loudly, singing, dancing etc., voluntary expressions, and shedding tears, perspiration, gooseflesh, etc., spontaneous organic expressions of loving devotion, are transcendental and full of superhuman influence. They are excited by the transcendental determinant and excitant cause, and induce a similar emotion in other devotees. They are not found in common worldly persons.[75] The organic expressions of devotional love being transcendental, the religious sentiment of devotion is transcendental.

(6) Self-abasement and other accessory emotions and states which nourish and develop the religious sentiment of devotion are transcendental, because they are not found in ordinary human beings forgetful of God.[76] When Kṛṣṇa disappeared from the place of circular dance, the milkmaids fainted and had lapse of memory and mental bewilderment owing to separation from their dearest lover.[77] Such accessory states are not found in ordinary human beings, and so they are transcendental. The accessory emotions of the religious sentiment of devotion being transcendental, the latter is transcendental.

Nascent love (rati) for God is transformed into the religious sentiment of devotion, because it has fitness for being converted into the latter by its intrinsic blissful nature (svarūpayogyatā), because the determinant, excitant and ensuant causess of the latter have fitness for exciting it (parikarayogyatā), and because the abode of the latter being endowed with the innate permanent emotional disposition of nascent love has fitness for feeling the religious sentiment (purusayogyatā)[77a] Of all its causes, nascent love for God is its most predominant cause. Kavikarṇapūra

[74] Āgantukā api tacchaktyupavṛṁhitatvena sādṛśyāt tatsphūrtimayatvena ālaukikīṁ daśām āpluvanti. PS., 111.

[75] Kāryarūpāḥ pulakādayo' pi alaukikāḥ. PS., 111.

[76] Nirvedādyāḥ sahāyāś cālaukikāḥ. PS., 111.

[77] PS., 345-46; Bhāg., x, 46, 5.

[77a] Sāmagrī tu rasatvāpattau trividhā svarūpayogyatā parikarayogyatā puruṣayogyatāca. PS., *Gauḍīya Vaiṣṇava Darśana*, Vol. V., ch. IX.

regards its determinant cause as the efficient cause, its accessory emotions as the auxiliary cause, its basic emotional disposition of nascent love as the inherent cause, its particular modification as the noninherent cause, and the ensuant cause as the effect, of the religious sentiment. Its causes cannot produce it, but they can manifest it.[78] Kavikarṇapūra is an advocate of the doctrine of manifestation (abhivyativāda). But sometimes he speaks of the transformation of the permanent emotional dispositions into the æsthetic sentiments. Kṛṣṇadāsa Kavirāja advocates the doctrine of modification (pariṇāmavāda), and holds that the permanent emotional disposition of nascent love for God is modified by the determinant and other causes into the religious sentiment of devotion. Rūpa Goswāmī avers, that nascent love for God being made relishable by the determinant cause, etc., assumes an intensely blissful and wonderful character.[79] Jīva Goswāmī also agrees with Rūpa Goswāmī in advocating the doctrine of transformation. According to him the determinant cause generates the incipient condition of being converted into the religious sentiment of loving devotion in nascent love for God; the accessory emotions and states activate nascent love well; the ensuant cause actually transforms nascent love into the religious sentiment. The distinctive character of nascent love for God imparts its distinctiveness to Him, the object-determinant cause, excitant cause, ensuant cause, etc., of the religious sentiment. Though the causes are different from one another, they are identified with one another, and transform nascent love into the religious sentiment of devotion with transcendent bliss and wonder.[80]

11. *Jīva Goswāmī's denial of Æsthetic or Dramatic Sentiments and their Transcendental nature*

Jīva Goswāmī denies the transcendental nature and the character of rasa of the so-called æsthetic or dramatic sentiments for the following reasons:

(1) Ordinary love is a particular mental mode of a worldly person, whose mind is composed of sattva, rajas and tamas, which

[78] Sthāyī samavāyikāraṇam ālambanoddīpanavibhāvau nimittakāraṇam. Sthāyino vikāraviśeṣo' samavāyi-kāraṇam rasābhivyakte reva bhavati, na tu rasasya. AK., v, 1. Ibid, v.

[79] HBRS., ii, 1, 10-11; CCA., ii, ch. 23; PS., 110.

[80] Kāraṇādi-sphūrtiviśeṣavyakta-sphūrtiviśeṣā tanmilitā bhagavat-prītis tadīya-prīti-rasa-maya ucyate. PS., 110.

are evolutes of cosmic nescience (māyā). The mental mode is empirical, and consequently finite and limited in time and space, and with origin and end. What is finite and temporal cannot be in the nature of bliss; the infinite only is bliss.[81] Ordinary love (rati) cannot be turned into an æsthetic sentiment (rasa) which is said to be in the nature of bliss (ānandamaya) and transcendent wonder (lokottara-camatkāra-prāṇa).[82]

(2) Ordinary love, though not in the nature of bliss, may be said to be turned into the blissful æsthetic sentiment in conjunction with the determinant cause, etc. Jīva Goswāmī argues, that the determinant cause, etc., being finite and limited, are not in the nature of bliss, and that, consequently, they cannot turn ordinary love into a blissful æsthetic sentiment.[83]

(3) Ordinary love is slightly in the nature of pleasure which ends in pain.[84] It is desire for enjoyment of sentient pleasure. An individual turns his mind away from God and directs it to external objects of pleasure owing to ignorance and so suffers from pain of embodied life. Sentient pleasure is always attended with sentient pain. Real pleasure or bliss emerges from the destruction of sentient pleasure and pain which arise from desire for enjoyment.[85] When tranquillity (śama) emerges in the mind, sentient pleasure and pain are destroyed. Tranquillity is steadfast devotion of the mind to God.[86] When the mind is turned away from sentient pleasure and pain and constantly fixed on God who is infinite bliss, a devotee feels bliss.

(4) The human body is the source of sentient pleasure and pain, and it is full of loathsome ingredients, viz., flesh, bone, blood, stool, urine, phlegm, flatulence, bile, etc. So the determinant cause, etc., cannot turn ordinary love into an æsthetic sentiment characterized by transcendent wonder and bliss. They can always produce the odious sentiment only.[87]

[81] Nālpe sukham asti. Bhūmaiva sukham. Chānd. Up., vii, 23, 1.
[82] SDP., iii, 2.
[83] Laukikasyaiva vibhāvādeḥ rasajanakatvaṁ na śraddheyam PS., 110.
[84] Laukikasya ratyādeḥ sukharūpatvaṁ yathākathañcid eva. Vastuvicāre duḥkha-paryavasāyitvāt. PS., 110.
[85] Sukhaṁ duḥkha-sukhātyayaḥ duḥkhaṁ kāmasukhāpekṣā. Bhāg., xi, 19, 41. CCA., ii, ch. 20.
[86] Śamo manniṣṭhatā buddheḥ. Bhāg., xi, 19, 36.
[87] Tajjanakatve sarvatra bībhatsa-janakatvam eva sidhyati. PS., 110. Bhāg., x, 60, 45.

(5) An embodied self, which is subject to birth and death, disease and grief, is the object and abode of ordinary love. Hence its ordinary love, which is inconstant and discontinuous, cannot be a permanent emotional disposition (sthāyibhāva); nor can it be turned into a blissful æsthetic sentiment (rasa).

Jīva Goswāmī denies the nature of rasa and transcendental character of the æsthetic or dramatic sentiments. He regards the religious sentiment of loving devotion (bhaktirasa) only as a transcendental sentiment. His view seems to be unwarranted.

Madhusūdana, though a monist, regards both dramatic or æsthetic sentiments and religious sentiments as of the nature of rasa. God, who is in the nature of supreme bliss, Himself enters into a devotes's mind, is experienced by him, becomes a permanent emotional disposition, and then is transformed into the religious sentiment.[88] A beloved woman and other objects which are the determinant causes of the æsthetic sentiments, are the effects of God, who is the embodiment of infinite consciousness and bliss. But though He is their cause, He is not experienced in them because He is veiled by cosmic nescience. Hence they also can enter into the mind of an appreciative connoisseur, and be converted into æsthetic sentiments.[89] The object-consciousness is known when the veil of cosmic nescience is removed, and is manifested in the mind as a permanent emotional disposition, which is converted into an æsthetic sentiment. It is inferior to a religious sentiment because in the former only object-consciousness (viṣayacaitanya) tainted with insentient matter is manifested whereas in the latter full consciousness and bliss of an individual self (pramātṛ-caitanya), are manifested.[90] Madhusūdana's view seems to be rational in the sense that both æsthetic sentiments and religious sentiments are experienced by ordinary persons.

[88] Bhagavān paramānanda-svarūpaḥ svayam eva hi.
Manogatas tadākāra-rasatām eti puṣkalam.
Bhaktirasāyana, i, 10.

[89] Kāntādiviṣayepyasti kāraṇaṁ sukha-cid-ghanam.
Kāryākāratayā bhedepyāvṛtaṁ māyayā svataḥ.
Ibid, i, 11.

[90] Ibid, i, 13. *Gaudīya Vaiṣṇava Darsana*, Vol. v, ch. 7.

Chapter XVIII

ATTENTION

1. *The Nature of Attention*

Vācaspatimiśra defines attention as one-pointedness of the mind.[1] It is conation or mental activity. Viśvanātha also defines attention as the act of focussing the mind on one object to the exclusion of other objects.[2] It involves selection and rejection. It selects one desirable object and rejects other undesirable objects. In it the mind is fixed on one proper object and withdrawn from other improper objects.[3] Selection is the positive aspect of attention and rejection is its negative aspect. A person is attentive, Śaṁkara avers, when his mind is focussed on a proper object, and he is inattentive when his mind is not controlled and fixed on a proper object, but dispersed on improper objects.[4] Attention is the fixation of the mind (manas) and an external sense-organ on a proper object without wavering.[5] In sensory attention there is adjustment of a proper sense-organ to its object along with the concentration of the mind (manas) on it. Ānandagiri also points out the positive and negative aspects of attention and defines it as the fixation of the mind on one proper object and its withdrawal from all other improper objects.[6] The mind is attentive when it is devoid of distraction.[7]

When the mind is not impelled by rajas and tamas, it becomes attentive. Rajas is the cause of restlessness and activity. Tamas is the cause of lethargy, inadvertence, bewilderment and sleep. Sattva is the cause of calmness, stability, knowledge, and

[1] Ekāgram ekatānam. TV., i, 1.
[2] Praṇidhānaṁ cittaikāgryam. NSV., iii, 2, 34.
[3] praṇidhānaṁ manaso viṣayāntara-sañcāra-vāraṇam. NSV., iii, 2, 44.
[4] Yuktamanāḥ samanaskaḥ. Amanaskaḥ apragṛhīta-manaskaḥ. SB., Kaṭha Up., i, 3, 7-8.
[5] Yadaiva bāhyāntaḥkaraṇānāṁ sthirā dhāraṇā, tadānīm eva niraṅkuśam apramattatvam. Ibid, ii, 3, 11.
[6] Sarvebhyo viṣayebhyo pratyāhṛtya ekasmin viṣaye samādhānam. ĀBG., vi, 12.
[7] Ekāgraṁ vikṣepa-rahitaṁ manaḥ. SrBG., vi, 12.

transparence of the mind. When sattva predominates over rajas and tamas in the mind, it becomes stable.[8]

Attention requires the inhibition of the actions of the mind, of the body, and of the vocal organs, which distract the mind. All other actions of the mind which divert it from attending to a proper object should be arrested. All verbal actions should be inhibited. All movements of the body should be stopped. The body and the mind should be oriented towards the object attended to. Attention requires adjustment of the mind and a proper sense-organ to an object, when it is sensory.[9]

Buddhaghoṣa mentions the following characteristics of attention. (1) In attention the range of consciousness becomes narrow. The greater is the attention, the more narrow is its range. (2) Attention makes the object of consciousness distinct. The greater is the attention, the more distinct is the consciousness of the object. (3) Attention leads to the growth, fulfilment and perfection of the factor of enlightenment. (4) Attention leads to serenity because it entails the absence of distraction.[10]

According to the *Bhagavadgītā*, the external sense-organs are controlled by the mind (manas), and it is controlled by the self (ātman). Only a self-controlled self can control the mind which is by nature extremely restless and distracting.[11] An uncontrolled self cannot control the restless mind.[12] Attention is the essence of meditation (yoga).

Bhaṭṭa Akalaṅka avers, that the mind constantly shifts from one object to another: it shifts from a substance to its mode, from one word to another word, from a bodily movement to a speech, from a speech to a thought, and so on. This constant shifting of attention from one object to another can be arrested by the concentration of attention on one object.[13] Mobility of the mind can be arrested by the fixation of attention.

Pūjyapāda also describes the nature of attention as the fixation of the mind on one desirable object and its withdrawal from

[8] BG., vi, 12; vi, 26; MBG., vi, 12; ĀBG., BrGBG., xviii, 52.
[9] Yata-vāk-kāya-mānasaḥ dhyānābhimukhīkṛta-kāya-vāṅ-mano-vṛttiḥ. RBG., xviii, 52.
Yata-cittendriya-kriyaḥ. BG., vi, 12.
[10] POP., ch. iii, 26; iv, 52, 59.
[11] Manasaivendriya-grāmaṁ viniyamya samantataḥ. BG., vi, 24. Vaśyātmanā yatatā (yogaḥ) śakyaḥ. Ibid, vi, 36.
[12] Asaṁyatātmanā yogo duṣprāpaḥ. BG., vi, 36.
[13] TRV., p. 356.

other undesirable objects. Thinking of many objects involves oscillation of attention. When this oscillation is arrested, and the mind is fixed on one object, it becomes attentive and one-pointed.[14] Pūjyapāda calls the knowledge of an object without oscillation of attention, which is manifested like an unflickering flame of a lamp, meditation, which is the arrest of diversion of the mind to irrelevant objects.[15]

Attention involves the adjustment of the whole organism to the object attended to—its attentive attitude. It involves the adjustment of an appropriate sense-organ to the object. It involves the adjustment of the mind (manas) to the object.[16]

2. *The Determinants of Attention*

Attention requires the removal of all distractions which divert the mind from a desirable object. It requires the inhibition of the distracting bodily movements, of vocal functions, and of mental activities. Concentration of the mind and the sense-organs on a desirable object is called a penance (tapas). Attention requires calmness of the mind undisturbed by emotions such as love, hatred, fear, etc., which agitate it. Movements of the body distract attention, and, consequently, should be inhibited. Attention requires an undisturbed, unagitated, motionless body. These are the negative conditions of attention.[17]

The intensity of a stimulus (tīvratā-paṭute) acting upon a sense-organ is a determinant of sensory attention. The roar of a thunder acting upon the auditory organ, or a fire in contact with the tactual organ, quickly attracts the attention of a person even when he is asleep or preoccupied with some other object, and produces a sensation in him suddenly. Thus the intensity of a stimulus is a determinant of sensory attention.[18] In non-voluntary sensory attention the sense-object-intercourse is the principal cause of perception. But there is also the mind-sense-organ-

[14] Nānārthāvalambanena cintā parispandavatī. Ekasmin niyamaḥ ekāgracinta-nirodhaḥ. SS., ix, 27; p. 260.

[15] Jñānam evāparispandamānaṁ dhyānam. Cittavikṣepatyāgago dhyānam. SS., ix, 27; p. 260: SS., ix, 20; p. 257.

[16] YMP., i, 23.

[17] MBG., vi, 13; xviii, 52; SBG., vi, 14., ĀBG., vi, 27.

[18] Suptānāṁ vyāsakta-manasāṁ ca ghana-garjitādinā śrotra-sannikarṣād vahnyādinā tvak-sannikarṣācca drāg eva jñānotpatter indriyārtha-sannikarṣasya prādhānyam. NSV., ii, 1, 24.

intercourse as well as the self-mind-intercourse, though there is neither volition nor concentration of the mind on the object[19] Probably it means that minimal attention is a necessary precondition of consciousness, while concentration of attention is necessary for clear and distinct consciousness. The strength of an object consists in its intensity, which is the object of the sense-object-intercourse, and not the object of the intercourse of the self with the mind.[20] The strength of the stimulus is an objective condition of sensory attention.

Interest is a subjective condition of attention. A song attracts attention because it is interesting and desired for its own sake.[21] Interest produces desire to know an object. The desire to hear a song is also a subjective condition of attention to it.

The absence of preoccupation of the mind with another object is a subjective condition of attention. Śakuntalā's preoccupation with the thought of Duṣyanta, her lover, was the cause of her inattention to the entreaty of the saint, Durvāsā. If the mind is preoccupied with another object, it cannot attend to an object. Attention depends upon the absence of preoccupation. A sudden and strong stimulus may break in upon the consciousness of a person whose mind is preoccupied with another object.[22]

Habit is a subjective condition of attention. It requires the practice of controlling the mind (mano-nigrahāvṛtti) and fixing it on a proper object and withdrawing it from other improper objects. Habit is the repetition of the similar cognitions of an object in a certain stage of the mind and the arrest of the emergence of dissimilar cognitions.[23]

The mind inclined towards an object cannot be fixed on it owing to the lapse of mind-control (dhṛti) which prevents it from attending to undesirable objects. The power of controlling the

[19] Asati praṇidhāne saṅkalpe cāsati supta-vyāsakta-manasāṁ yad indriyārtha-sannikarṣād utpadyate jñānam, tatra manaḥsaṁyogo'pi kāraṇam. NBh., ii, 1, 27.

[20] Tasya prābalyaṁ tīvratā-paṭute, taccārtha-viśeṣa-prābalyam indriyārtha-sannikarṣa-viṣayam. NBh., ii, 1, 27.

[21] Arthaviśeṣasya gītādeḥ- prābalyāt bubhutsitatvād gītādi-śravaṇam. NSV., ii, 1, 27.

[22] Artha-viśeṣa-prābalyāddhi supta-vyāsakta-manasāṁ jñānotpattir ekadā bhavati. NBh., ii, 1, 27.

[23] Abhyāso nāma cittabhūmau kasyāñcit samāna-pratyayāvṛttiś cittasya. SBG., vi, 35. Vijātīya-pratyayāntaritā. ĀBG., vi, 35.

mind and preventing its dispersion is a subjective condition of attention[24]

Emotions are the subjective conditions of attention. Love impels a person to attend to a beloved person. Hate prompts a person to attend to a hated enemy. Anger moves a person to attend to a person who thwarts his desire. Fear actuates a person to attend to a terrible animal or person or object that evokes the emotion. Grief prompts a person to attend to the loss of a cherished object, or the death of a dear person. Greed impels a person to attend to covetable objects. Envy prompts a person to attend to real or imaginary faults in another's excellence. Pride moves a person to attend to his real or imaginary superior qualities, e.g. noble birth, wealth, learning, beauty, youth, etc. Thus emotions motivate attention.[25]

Emotions sometimes divert attention to undesirable objects. Distraction is dispersion of the mind over improper objects, which can be overcome by the habit of discerning their faults and by cultivating dispassion for them. The habit of attention to proper objects can be facilitated by cultivating the counter habit of inattention to improper objects, which depends upon the frequency of discerning their transitoriness, consequential painfulness, and repugnance to moral excellence and tranquillity.[26] The mind which is naturally restless subordinates the body and the sense-organs to other undesirable objects which agitate the whole psycho-physical organism, and prevents it from being adjusted to a desirable object.[27] It can be controlled by habit and dispassion.

Desire (kāma) and aversion (dveṣa) spring from love and hate. Desire is the active tendency of the mind to appropriate its object. Aversion is the active tendency of the mind to avoid, remove, or destroy its object. Desire is evoked by a favourable object. Aversion is excited by a harmful object. Desire prompts the mind to attend to an agreeable object. Aversion impels it to attend to a disagreeable object. Thus desire and aversion also are the subjective conditions of attention. Sometimes they

[24] Viṣaya-pravaṇaṁ sattvaṁ dhṛtibhraṁśān na śakyate. Niyantum ahitād arthād dhṛtir hi niyamātmikā. CS., iv, 1, 100.

[25] BG., ii, 56, 62, 64; iii, 31, 32; iv, 10; v, 23, 26, 28; vi, 9.

[26] Mano durnigrahaṁ calam vairāgyeṇa ca gṛhyate. BG., vi, 35. Vairāgyaṁ nāma bhogeṣu doṣa-darś-anābhyāsāt vaitṛṣṇyam. Vikṣeparūpaḥ pracāraś cittasya nirudhyate. SBG., vi, 35.

[27] Cañcalaṁ hi manaḥ sarīram indriyāṇi ca paravaśīkaroti. SBG., vi, 34. BG., vi, 35; SBG., ĀBG., vi, 35.

motivate attention to undesirable objects and cause distraction, which can be overcome gradually by cultivating the habits of attending to desirable objects and discerning the faults of their improper objects.[28] Desire and aversion should be uprooted with their subconscious impressions (vāsanā) or potencies by reflecting on the faults of their improper objects.

When the mind is diverted to undesirable objects because of the prenatal potencies of actions, or demerits acquired in the previous births, it should be gradually concentrated on the self with the aid of mind-control. The distracted mind should not be suddenly withdrawn from the distracting objects, because that is not conducive to the health of the mind.[29] Congenital predisposition is a subjective condition of attention. It is called a potency of actions in the previous birth in Indian psychology. When it determines attention to undesirable objects, the mind should be gradually withdrawn from them with patience by repeated practice, because innate predisposition is very powerful.[30]

Bhaṭṭa Akalaṅka avers, that attention or concentration of the mind depends on the following conditions: (1) a congenial environment, which is neither too hot nor too cold, which is free from the scorching sun and rain, which is not infested by wild beasts, birds and reptiles,—that divert the internal organ and the external sense-organs to improper objects; (2) a favourable posture of the body; (3) inhaling and exhaling slowly and steadily; (4) inhibition of distracting bodily actions; (5) suppression of attachment, aversion and delusion; (6) fixation of the mind without wavering on a desirable object; and (7) suppression of lethargy, sleep, attachment, sex-love, grief, mirth, fear, doubt, desire and aversion.[31] Brahmadeva avers, that fixation of the mind on a desirable object depends on (1) dispassion, (2) freedom from love and hatred, (3) conquest of distractions, e.g., heat, cold, hunger, thirst, etc., (4) freedom from desire and aversion, and (5) a

[28] BG., ii, 71; iii, 34, 37, v, 23, 28; 18, 24. Yoga-pratikūlān sarvān kāmān savāsanāṁ styaktvā manasaiva viṣaya-doṣa-darśinā indriyasamūhaṁ viśeṣeṇa niyamya yogo yoktavyaḥ. SrBG., vi, 24.

[29] Yadi tu prāktana-karma-saṁskāreṇa mano vicalet tarhi dhāraṇayā sthirīkuryāt śanaih, abhyāsa-krameṇa na tu sahasā. SrBG., vi, 25. ĀBG., vi, 25.

[30] Sahasā viṣayebhyaḥ sakāśād uparame manaso na svāsthyaṁ sambhavati. ĀBG., vi, 25.

[31] TRV., ix, 44, p. 356.

dispassionate desire to know the nature of the object. The true knowledge of the object attended to is the effect of attention.[32]

3. *Distraction*

When a person's mind is not withdrawn from objects of sentient pleasure owing to restlessness of the sense-organs and concentrated on a desirable object, he has a distracted mind, which is scattered on many undesirable objects.[33] The mind is restless and unstable owing to the faults (doṣa) such as love and hatred which are due to false knowledge. Instability of the mind (manas) is due to its constituent rajas.[34]

The different stages of the mind from the standpoint of the practice of yoga have already been discussed. In the extremely unsteady (kṣipta) stage the mind always flits from object to object, being impelled by rajas which causes restlessness. But in the state of distraction (vikṣipta) the mind becomes occasionally steady despite its great instability.[35] The mind becomes attentive when it is one-pointed or focussed on one object. The more sattva predominates over rajas and tamas, the more attentive the mind becomes.[36]

Patañjali mentions disease, mental lethargy, doubt, inadvertence, inertia, non-withdrawal of mind, illusion, instability of the mind, and restlessness as the causes of distraction.[37] Vyāsa explains the nature of these causes. (1) Disease is disharmony of phlegm, bile and flatulence, overfunctioning, underfunctioning, and injudicious correlation, of the sense-organs, and indigestion of food eaten. (2) Mental lethargy is the absence of activity of the mind. (3) Doubt is uncertain knowledge of an object in the shape of two alternatives: 'Is it this or that?' (4) Inadvertence is nonperformance of the actions which are necessary for achieving trance. (5) Inertia is disinclination of the mind to act due to the excess of inertia (tamas) and lethargy of the body due to the

[32] DSV., 57, p. 207.
[33] Indriyalaulyāt anuparataḥ anekāgramanāḥ vikṣiptacittaḥ. SB., Kaṭha Up., i, 2, 24.
[34] ĀBG., vi, 26; SrBG., vi, 26; xviii, 54.
[35] Vikṣiptam kṣiptād viśiṣṭam. Viśeṣo' sthema-bahulasya kādācitkaḥ sthemā. TV., i, 1. IPC., p. 347.
[36] TV., i, 2. Ekāgram ekatānam. TV., i, 1.
[37] YS., i, 30. YBh., i, 30.

excess of phlegm, bile and flatulence. (6) Non-withdrawal of the mind from the enjoyment of sensible objects of pleasure is a condition of distraction. (7) Illusion is false perception of one object as another. (8 Non-stability of the mind is non-attainment of the stage of trance or complete absorption of the mind in its object. (9) Restlessness is the unsettled state of the mind in which it is scattered over many undesirable objects. Non-stability is a negative state, while restlessness is a positive state of the mind. These are the causes of distraction.

Distraction (vikṣepa) can be overcome by reflecting upon the faults of undesirable objects which divert the mind from the desirable object on which it ought to be focussed, and by cultivating dispasion (vairāgya). (1) The mind distracted by desire and experience of pleasure should be controlled by habit (abhyāsa). Experience of pleasure is attained either through the external sense-organs or through mental reflection. Habits are of two kinds: habit of attention and habit of inattention.[38] Habit of attention is due to repeated concentration of the mind on a desirable object in conformity with the performance of daily obligatory and occasional duties.[39] Habit of inattention is the arrest of the activities of the mind concerning undesirable objects.[40] (2) Inattention is constant mobility of attention (cittapracāra), which is accompanied by agitation of vital forces (prāṇaspandana). Constant practice is necessary for the suppression of it. Breath-control (prāṇāyāma) is conducive to the conquest of distraction. (3) Innate potencies of actions (vāsanā) of previous births is a cause of inattention or attention to improper objects. (4) Dispassion which destroys potencies of actions can overcome distraction. What is called congenital interest in modern psychology is attributed to prenatal potencies of actions (vāsanā) in Indian psychology. These can be completely destroyed by dispassion.[41]

Restrain the mind (manas), Gauḍapāda observes, from the objects of desire by reflecting on their ultimately painful nature.[42]

[38] Abhyāsaḥ sajātīya-pratyaya-pravāhaḥ vijātīya-pratyayāntaritaḥ. MBG., viii, 8. SrBG., viii, 8.

[39] RBG., xviii, 52; ĀBG., SrBG., MBG., vi, 26; MBG., SrBG., RBG., viii, 8; SBG., ĀBG., vi, 35.

[40] SB., Kaṭha Up., iii, 2, 11.

[41] MBG.. vi, 35.

[42] Duḥkhaṁ sarvam anusmṛtya kāma-bhogān nivartyayet. Māṇḍ Up., Kārikā, iii, 43. SB., iii, 43.

Śaṁkara avers, that the mind can be diverted from them by the repeated practice of dispassion (vairāgya). If the mind is diverted again and again to objects of pleasure, arrest its diversion by repeated efforts of will. If the mind is engrossed in objects of enjoyment, reflect on their faults (doṣa), e.g., transitoriness and consequential painfulness, concentrate it on a desirable object, and attain absorption in it. When the mind is absorbed in it without flickering, do not allow it to be diverted again to objects of desire. Gauḍapāda states these means of overcoming distraction.[43] Śaṁkara also reiterates these means in conformity with the teachings of the *Bhagabad Gītā*, and asserts, that distraction can be overcome by the repetition of the knowledge of the real nature of the undesirable objects of attention, and by the practice of dispassion.[44]

Habit is formed by repeated efforts to concentrate the mind (manas) on one object. An effort of will consists of the following: (1) energy to restrain the mind which is naturally inclined to turn outward to different objects; (2) quick action without wasting time over its feasibility or unfeasibility; and (3) patience and perseverence in fixing the mind on a proper object with conviction in its success. If it is practised for a long period of time without long intervals with faith and devotion, a firm habit of fixation of the mind is formed.[45] If there are long intervals of discontinuity in the practice, the habit cannot be formed. If there is lack of faith and devotion, the habit cannot be formed. If distractions occur very often during the practice, the habit cannot be formed. If love, hate and other emotions agitate the mind very often, the habit cannot be formed. Then the subconscious impressions of the fixation of attention are weakened by the subconscious impressions of diversion of the mind.[46]

The stream of mental modes is naturally inclined towards the objects of pleasure. Rāmānanda Yati avers, that it can be withdrawn from them by habit and dispassion. (1) Habit consists in the repetition of voluntary efforts to concentrate the mind on a

[43] Laye sambodhayec cittaṁ vikṣiptaṁ śamayet punaḥ.
Sakaṣāyaṁ vijānīyāt samaprāptaṁ na cālayet.
Mānd. Up., Kārikā, iii, 44.

[44] Jñānābhyāsa-vairāgya-dvayopāyena manaḥ yojayet. SB., Mānd. Up., Kārikā, iii, 44.

[45] Sa tu dhīrghakāla-nairantarya-satkārā-sevito dṛḍhabhūmiḥ. YS., i, 14. YSC., i, 14. YSC., i, 13.

[46] YSC., i, 14, 23.

desirable object, free from the modes of rajas and tamas. If a strong habit is formed by repetition of concentration of the mind for a long period of time with faith, its deep subconscious impression is not overcome by the subconscious impression of inattention, and facilitates the fixation of attention on a desirable object.[47] (2) Dispassion generates discriminative knowledge of the self as distinguished from the mind-body-complex. It facilitates the concentration of the mind on the self. But without repetition and formation of a habit of attention the mind may lapse into sleep and distraction.[48]

Diversion of attention to irrelevant objects is due to emotions and passions. These can be controlled by cultivating the habit of feeling friendship for all persons, compassion for the distressed persons, joy for the virtuous persons, and neutrality for the vicious persons, and by frequent meditation on the transitoriness of the world and the objects of enjoyment, and on the transitoriness, unsubstantiality, painfulness and impurity of the body. Distraction of attention is overcome by cultivating dispassion, which is generated by meditating on the real nature of the body, and by renouncing attachment to the objects of pleasure.[49]

4. *Physiological and Psychical Correlates of Distraction and Means of overcoming Distraction*

Patañjali mentions pain, mental agitation, bodily movements, and inhalation and exhalation as the accompaniments of distraction (vikṣepa).[50] Vyāsa explains pain as bodily, mental and supernatural suffering. Bodily pain is due to disease and the like. Mental pain is due to frustration of desire, etc. Supernatural pain is due to harm done by supernatural beings. All sentient beings make voluntary efforts to remove pain and its cause. Mental agitation is due to the thwarting of a desire. Bodily movements are due to rheumatism and other diseases. Quick inhalation and exhalation are the correlates of distraction. They are hindrances to concentration of the mind on a desirable object. They can be counteracted by the following means.[51]

[47] YMP., i, 13 and 14.
[48] YMP., i, 12.
[49] Kāya-svabhāva-cintanād viṣaya-rāga-nivṛtter vairāgyam upajāyate. SS., vii, 12; p. 205. TASar., iv, 73.
[50] YS., i, 31.
[51] YBh., i, 31.

(1) Distractions can be overcome by cultivating the habit of focussing the mind on one object. The mind should be frequently withdrawn from irrelevant and undesirable objects and focussed on relevant and desirable objects.[52] The mind may be repeatedly fixed on an agreeable object, or any other object, to cultivate the habit (abhyāsa) of attention. First attention should be fixed on a gross object, and then on a subtle object. First attention should be focussed on an external physical object, then on a percept, an image, an idea, or a concept. Attention may be fixed on the idea of God. It may be focussed on a centre of the body, e.g., the tip of the nose, the middle of the eye-brows, the centre of the throat, or the like.

(2) Transparence and one-pointedness of the mind can be achieved by cultivating love for all happy persons, compassion for all distressed persons, joy for all virtuous persons, and indifference to all vicious persons. Thus rajas and tamas will be suppressed, and sattva will predominate over them and make the mind one-pointed.[53]

(3) Stability of the mind can be achieved by regulation of inhalation and exhalation (prāṇāyāma). Irregularities of breathing are physiological correlates of distraction. When these are regularized by the daily practice of breath-control, distraction can be easily overcome.[54]

(4) Stability of the mind can be achieved by concentrating it on the sattva of the intellect in the heart, when it becomes luminous and destitute of rajas and tamas. Rajas makes the mind restless; tamas veils its knowledge and luminosity. Sattva makes it luminous and manifests its knowledge.[55]

(5) Stability of the mind can be achieved by concentrating it on the mind of a yogin free from attachment to all objects. The company of saints makes the mind free from agitation and excitement, and tends to make it one-pointed.[56]

(6) One-pointedness of the mind can be achieved by

[52] Tatpratiṣedhārtham ekatattvābhyāsaḥ. YS., i, 32. Vikṣepa-pratiṣedhārtham ekatattvāvalambanaṁ cittam abhyaset. YBh., i, 32.

[53] Evaṁ bhāvayataḥ śuklo dharma upajāyate, tataś ca cittaṁ prasīdati, prasannam ekāgraṁ sthitipadaṁ labhate. YBh., i, 33. YS., i, 33.

[54] Prāṇāyamaḥ manasaḥ sthitiṁ sampādayet. YBh., i, 34. YS., i, 34.

[55] Hṛdaya-puṇḍarīke asmitāyāṁ samāpannaṁ cittaṁ nistaraṅgaṁ bhavati. YBh., i, 36. YS., i, 36.

[56] Vīta-rāga-cittālambanoparaktaṁ cittaṁ sthitipadaṁ labhate. YBh., i, 37. YS., i, 37.

concentrating it on an agreeable object uninterruptedly for a certain duration daily. It is easy to concentrate the mind on the photo of a beloved person, or the like. When one-pointedness of it is achieved in regard to it, it can be transferred to other desirable objects.[57] The mind can be fixed on the image of Śiva, Rāma, or Kṛṣṇa, who is worshipped by a person because such a Deity or a divine incarnation satisfies his deepest spiritual aspirations. When a habit of concentration of the mind is formed with regard to such an object, it can be transferred to other desirable objects.[58]

(7) Stability of the mind can be achieved by concentrating it on the beautiful image of a Deity that flashes in it in a dream, or on the dream-image of a saint, or on the happiness that emerges in dreamless sleep in which sattva predominates.[59]

(8) The habit of fixation of the mind can be easily formed by the repeated muttering of the mystic sound *'Aum'* or *'Om'* and meditating on God represented by it.[60]

(9) Stability of the mind can be achieved by cultivating dispassion for all objects of pleasure. Dispassion can be acquired by discerning faults of these objects, which consist in the fact that they ultimately yield pain and hinder the attainment of the highest good. Dispassion is the fruit of discrimination between self and not-self.[61] Supreme dispassion for all objects composed of essence (sattva), energy (rajas), and inertia (tamas) and different from the self can be acquired by cultivating the habit of concentrating the mind on the self and acquiring discriminative knowledge.[62]

Until the mind is purged of love, hate, envy and other impurities, it cannot be effectively focussed on a desirable object. In order to eradicate these impurities of the mind, one should cultivate the habits, of friendship or good will (maitrī) for all persons, of compassion (karuṇā) for distressed persons, of glandness (muditā) at virtuous persons, and of indifference (upekṣā) to

[57] Yadevābhimataṁ tadeva dhyāyet, tatra labdhasthitikam anyatrāpi sthipadaṁ labhate. YBh., i, 39. YS., i, 39.

[58] YMP., i, 39.

[59] Svapna-nidrā-jñānālambanaṁ vā. YS., i, 38. YMP., i, 38.

[60] Tajjapas tadartha-bhāvanam. YS., i, 28. YBh., i, 28.

[61] Viṣaya-vitṛṣṇasya vairāgyam. YS., i, 15. Viṣaye vitṛṣṇasya cittasya viṣaya-doṣa-darśinaḥ prasaṁkhyānabalāt vairāgyam. YBh., i, 15.

[62] Tat paraṁ puruṣakhyāteḥ guṇa-vaitṛṣṇyam. YS., i, 16.

vicious persons.[63] The cultivation of these virtues destroys envy, malevolence, jealousy, hatred and other taints of the mind, and generates pure virtue and pre-eminence of sattva in it. When the mind becomes pure, transparent and tranquil, it easily becomes steady and one-pointed. A tranquil mind is easily concentrated on a desirable object.[64]

5. *Attention and Perception*

The perceptual activity involves attention. Alertness or set is a condition of attention. An appropriate sense-organ should be preadjusted to the object of attention. A traveller tests the stability of a bamboo bridge before he mounts on to it. Attention is exploratory,[65] while perception is discovery. Attention is a preliminary step to perception.

Some draw a distinction between indeterminate perception and determinate perception. The former is the first impression of an object as 'something'—a simple apprehension, a 'knowledge of acquaintance'. The latter is a 'knowledge about' an object invested with common and distinctive attributes, and thus involves assimilation and discrimination. The former requires minimal attention, whereas the latter requires a greater degree of attention. Determinate preception involves apperception or assimilation of a new impression to the apperception-mass or the system of knowledge already acquired. It is the self that perceives an object with the help of the external sense-organs and manas, the internal organ. The manas and the external sense-organs are unconscious and so incapable of perceiving an object. It is the self that attends, with the help of manas and the external sense-organs, to an external object. Attention carries the stimulus from the object to the self and rouses consciousness. It brings the stimulus to the focus of consciousness and produces a distinct impression or perception of it. Thus voluntary attention is preparatory to determinate perception.[66]

Bhāsarvajña defines attention as investigation into the nature

[63] YSB., i, 33.
[64] YMP., i, 34.
[65] *Questions of King Milinda*, I, pp. 172-73.
[66] IPC., Vol. I, ch. 2.

of an object by reflcting upon it in all its aspects.[67] Thus attention explores the nature of an object and paves the way for perception which discovers it.

The Jaina recognizes four stages of ordinary perception: (1) avagraha, (2) īhā, (3) avāya, and dhāraṇā. Just after peripheral stimulation there is simple apprehension of an object in a general way (darśana), which apprehends its general features (sattāmātra), and not its particular features. Just after simple apprehension there is the perception of an object with its general and some special features (avagraha). It excites a desire (īhā) to know more distinctive qualities of it. Then there is definite prception (avāya) which ascertains the real nature of it. Then there is retention (dhāraṇā) of the perception. Determinate perception of an object involves assimilation and discrimination which depend upon voluntary attention.[68]

6. *Attention and Recollection*

A person fixes his attention on the idea of an object with a desire to remember it and recalls it after the lapse of some time as the result of his fixation of attention on it.[69] Sometimes an object is recalled quickly and sometimes it is recalled after some delay. When it is recalled after some delay, attention is fixed on the series of relevant thoughts which are associated with it, and recalls it to consciousness. The self fixes its manas on the relevant thoughts, excludes it from the irrelevant thoughts with the intention to remember an object, and recalls it after some delay, and not suddenly.[70] The manas does not remember an object because it is unconscious. It is the self that remembers an object with the help of manas.[71] Thus active recollection depends upon voluntary attention.[72] Attention to an idea or image is ideational attention.

[67] Prabandhena anucintanaṁ praṇidhānam. NSār., p. 38.
[68] IPC., pp. 108-09; SS., i, 15; PK., 40; TDTV., 40; TASār., ii, 10-12.
[69] Susmūrṣayā khalvayaṁ manaḥ praṇidadhānaḥ cirād api kañcid arthaṁ smarati. NBh., iii, 2, 29.
[70] Susmūrṣayā cāyaṁ manaḥ praṇidadhānaś cirād api kañcid arthaṁ smarati, nākasmāt. NBh., iii, 2, 32. Yadā cireṇ, tadā susmūrṣayā manasi dhāryamāṇe cintāprabandhe sati kasyacid arthasya liṅgabhūtasya cintanaṁ smṛtihetur bhavati. Ibid, iii, 2, 31. NSV., iii, 2, 31.
[71] Jñatvañca manaso nāsti, jñānapratiṣedhāt. Ibid, iii, 2, 32.
[72] IPC., Vol. I, pp. 394-95.

7. *Attention and Consciousness*

Attention is a precondition of clear, distinct, discriminative consciousness. When the self does not focus the manas on an object through a sense-organ, it has an indistinct impression of it. But when it fixes the manas on the object through an appropriate sense-organ, it has a distinct impression of it. The more it attends to the object, the more distinct its impression becomes. The mode of the internal organ (antaḥkaraṇa) or manas, according to the Sāṁkhya-Yoga and the Vedānta, is modified into the form of the object attended to, and becomes one with it. Meditation (dhyāna) which is a form of concentration of manas is the uninterrupted stream of the similar cognitions of an object to the exclusion of dissimilar cognitions of other objects. Trance (samādhi) is the complete absorption of the manas in the object of attention when there is no consciousnenss of distinction between the knowing self, the mental mode of knowing, and the known object. The object only flashes forth in consciousness, divested of all association with its name and concept and correlates.[73]

Aniruddha defines meditation as reflection on an object with a focussed mind.[74] The object reflected on colours the manas or its mode; the mental mode is modified into its form. The self, which is really detached, erroneously thinks the mental mode tinged with its object and modified into its form, as its own state owing to egoism (abhimāna). The transference of the form of the object to its apprehending mental mode is wrongly attributed to the self owing to the attribution of egoism to the self. Transference is not real.[75] Aniruddha defines trance as meditation in which the manas is objectless and its mode being tinged by its object is suppressed.[76]

When the manas is focussed on an object, the self gets a distinct cognition of it and becomes unconscious of other objects. A person engaged in making an arrow with a focussed mind fails to perceive a king with his army marching on a nearby road.

[73] Pratyayaikatānatā dhyānam. YS., iii, 2. Tadevārthamātranirbhāsaṁ svarūpaśūnyam iva samādhiḥ. YS., iii, 3. YBh., iii, 2-3. YCM., 354, 379.

[74] Ekāgratayā viṣaya-cintanaṁ dhyānam. SSV., vi, 24.

[75] Abhimānaḥ ātmanyahaṁkārādhyāsād uparāgādhyāsaḥ. SSV., vi, 28. Uparāgo na tāttvikaḥ. Ibid, vi, 27.

[76] Nirviṣayaṁ vā mano dhyānam. Samādhāvatra dhyānaśabdaḥ. Uparāgo viṣayavāsanā. Tannirodhaḥ samādhau. SSV., vi, 24-26. SPS., vi, 25.

So a person with a fixed mind does not deviate from the state of absorption in its object. One-pointedness of the mind should be cultivated with great care because it is conducive to the ascertainment of truth.[77]

8. *Attention and Interest and Desire*

Attention depends upon interest. Our sense-organs are assailed by a multitude of stimuli in the environment at the same time. We do not attend to them all. But we attend to that object which evokes our interest. We attend to a song and the like because they excite our interest and because we desire to hear them. Here attention is motivated by interest and desire.[78] If there are many interests in the mind, the most predominant one pushes the others in the background, renders them subconscious, dominates the field of consciousness and determines attention to a proper object.[79]

Pūjyapāda mentions the following steps in the process of perception. In the first stage (avagraha) an object is perceived in its general outline. In the second stage the self has a desire (īhā) to know its particular qualities if it excites interest in the self. In the third stage (avāya) the self attends to its particular qualities and acquires a certain and definite knowledge of the object with all its distinctive qualities.[80] This definite and distinct perception of an object with its general and particular qualities presupposes interest, desire, and attention.

But in attention, Nemicandra asserts, the self should be divested of all desires for other objects, and the mind (manas) should be concentrated on the desirable object only without wavering. The self should have interest in, and desire for, that object only to the exclusion of others. Attention to it is sustained by interest and desire.[81]

[77] Iṣukāravannaikacittasya samādhihāniḥ. SPS., iv, 14. SSV., iv, 14. Cittaikāgratā tattvajñānāyādaraṇīyā. SSM., iv, 14.

[78] Artha-viśeṣasya gītādeḥ prābalyāt bubhutsitatvād gītādi-śravaṇam. NSV., ii, 1, 27.

[79] C. R. Jain: *Jaina Psychology*, p. 16.

[80] Viṣaya-viṣayi-sannipāta-samayānantaram ādyagrahaṇam avagrahaḥ. Avagṛhīte'rthe tadviśeṣākāṅkṣaṇam īhā. Viśeṣa-nirjñānād yāthātmyāvagamanam avāyaḥ. SS., i, 15, pp. 62-63.

[81] DS., DSV., 55.

9. *Attention and Inhibition*

The self can inhibit the agitation of any of the impulses that torment it by refusing to be dominated by it. It can withdraw attention from all external objects when the sense-organs no longer operate on them. When it fixes attention on one object, there is the cessation of sensory activity in regard to all other objects. The self can be intensely conscious of one object at a time. When it is intensely conscious of one object, it is unconscious of all other objects.[82]

Attention involves inhibition, because it consists in the complete withdrawal of the mind (manas) from the improper objects which are hindrances to its concentration on its proper object.[83] When the mind is withdrawn from the external objects of the sense-organs, over which it exercises its control, the sense-organs are automatically withdrawn from them, even as the bees fly away from an object when the queen bee flies away from it.[84]

Attention involves the inhibition, of the movements of the body, of the actions of the vocal organs, of the functions of the sense-organs, and of the other operations of the manas, which distract it. It requires the cessation of the distracting actions—bodily, sensory, and mental.[85]

Attention involves the partial inhibition of even such non-voluntary actions like inhalation and exalation. In attention we hold our breath and appear neither to inhale nor exhale. When we perform an action which involves an effort of will, e.g., producing fire by rubbing two sticks together, or running a race, or bending a stiff bow and stringing it, we partly arrest our inhalation and exhalation. When we make an important speech, we seem to control our breath. The *Chāndogya Upaniṣad* gives these examples.[86] Two voluntary actions cannot be performed with attention at the same time. But a voluntary action can be

[82] *Jaina Psychology*, pp. 41-42.

[83] Samādhi-pratyanīkārthebhyaḥ samantāc cetaso vyāvartanaṁ pratyāhāraḥ. NSār., p. 39.

[84] Cittanirodhe cittavat niruddhānīndriyāṇi. YBh., ii, 54.

[85] Tatraikāgraṁ manaḥ kṛtvā yatacittendriyakriyaḥ.
BG., vi, 12.

[86] Tasmād aprāṇannanapānan vācam abhivyāharati. Ch. Up., i, 3, 3. Ato yānyanyāni vīryavanti karmāṇi yathāgner manthanam ājeḥ saraṇam dṛḍhasya dhanuṣa āyamanam aprāṇannanapānaṁ stāni karoti. Ch. Up., i, 3, 5. Ranade: *The Constructive Survey of Upanishadic Philosophy*, pp. 114-15.

performed with attention along with non-voluntary actions, e.g., inhalation and exhalation, which are automatic actions. A voluntary action can be performed with attention along with a habitual action also. The Upaniṣadic thinker ignored these psychological truths when he made these statements.

10. *Attention and eightfold Yoga*

Patañjali defines yoga as the complete suppression of the mental modes, which can be achieved by the practice of the eightfold yoga consisting of sense-restraints (yama), moral observances (niyama), breath-control (prāṇāyama), withdrawal of the mind (manas) from the objects of the sense-organs (pratyāhāra), fixed postures of the body (āsana), fixation of the mind on the navel, the heart, the throat, and other vital centres of the organism (dhāraṇā), meditation (dhyāna), and absorption or trance (samādhi). Fruition in the arresting of mental modes is facilitated by the habitual performance of one's specific duties pertaining to caste and stage of life.

According to the Sāṁkhya, meditation consists in the suppression of rajas which produces restlessness. When sattva predominates over rajas and tamas in the manas, it becomes free from attachment, mobility, and inertia, and becomes steady and meditative.[87] Fruition in the suppression of mental functions can be achieved by dispassion and habit. It can be attained by the transparence of discriminative knowledge which constitutes supreme dispassion. The Sāṁkhya-Yoga, like the Advaita Vedānta, identifies supreme dispassion (paravairāgya) with supreme knowledge (parajñāna). The former regards the discriminative knowledge of the self (ātman) as distinguished from the mind-body-complex as supreme knowledge, whereas the latter regards the intuitive knowledge of Brahman as distinct from the phenomenal world and the empirical selves (jīva) as supreme knowledge. The Sāṁkhya does not believe in Brahman or God. The Yoga believes in the existence of God, but it does not regard the realization of God as the supreme end of life. It regards meditation on God and dedication of all duties to Him as the means of the total suppression of mental modes and the

[87] Rāgāpahatir dhyānam. SPS., iii, 30. Rāgāt rajoguṇāc calitatvaṁ, tadapahatir niścalitatvaṁ dhyānam. SSV., iii, 30. SPS., SSV., iii, 31-35.

discriminative knowledge (vivekajñāna) of the self (ātman) which is different from God. Fruition in the suppression of mental modes can be achieved by repetition of meditation.[88] Concentration of the mind can be acquired by cultivating tranquillity (śama) and eschewing love and hate. Dispassion cannot be attained by enjoyment, but by discerning faults in its objects, which ultimately lead to painful consequences.[89]

Patañjali also regards habit and dispassion as the means of the total suppression of mental modes.[90] The nature of habit and dispassion according to the Yoga has already been explained.

Vidyānandi Svāmī, a Jaina thinker, regards yoga as not the complete suppression of the mental modes, as Patañjali thinks, but as the fixation of the mind on an object in order to acquire a stable knowledge of it.[91] Stable knowledge is definite, distinct and unwavering like the unflickering flame of a lamp. It is the effect of attention or focussing the mind on an object.[92]

[88] Vairāgyād abhyāsācca. SPS., iii, 36. Vairāgyāt parāj jñāna-prasāda-mātrāt. Abhyāsāt paunaḥpunyena dhyānāt. SSV., iii, 36. SPB., vi, 31.

[89] SSM., iv, 13; iv, 26; SPS., SSV., iv, 28.

[90] Abhyāsa-vairāgyābhyāṁ tannirodhaḥ. YS., i, 12.

[91] Sthirajñānātmakaś cittanirodho notra saṁgataḥ. TSV., ix, 27, 2; p. 497.

[92] Ibid, ix, 27, 6, pp. 498-99.

CHAPTER XIX

NON-VOLUNTARY AND VOLUNTARY ACTIONS

1. *Non-voluntary Actions and Voluntary Actions*

Praśastapāda divides efforts (prayatna) into two kinds: (1) vital actions prompted by life and (2) voluntary actions initiated by desire and aversion.[1] Vital effort is preceded by life, and inferred from inhalation and exhalation of a sleeping person, and from the conjunction of the internal organ (manas) with another sense-organ on awaking from sleep. It is produced by the conjunction of the self with the internal organ, which depends upon a merit of the self.[2] Vital effort of the self in a region of the body in which there is no external sense-organ is the cause of inhalation and exhalation during sleep, and of the conjunction of the internal organ with another sense-organ on awaking from sleep. An unseen agency (adṛṣta) is not the cause of these two phenomena, because they are inferred to be produced by an effort.[3] When there is no possibility of another cause, an unseen principle (adṛṣṭa) is assumed to be the cause of a certain phenomenon. The vital effort (prayatna) is produced by the conjunction of the self with the internal organ, which depends upon the self's particular merit or demerit. The self is its inherent cause, its conjunction with the internal organ is its non-inherent cause, and its particular merit or demerit is its efficient cause.[4] Śaṁkara regards inhalation, exhalation, yawning, sneezing, hunger, thirst, trembling, etc., as the acts of vital force (prāṇa).[5] They are non-voluntary actions. They are automatic and reflex actions in the language of modern psychology. They carry on the life of the organism, and are not actuated by volition. They are different from voluntary actions, which are prompted by desire and

[1] Prayatno dvividho jīvana-pūrvakaḥ icchā-dveṣa-pūrvakaśca. PBh., Benaras, Saṁvat 1941, p. 349.

[2] Asya jīvanapūrvakasya ātmamanasoḥ saṁyogād dharmā-dharmāpekṣād utpattiḥ. PBh., pp. 349-50.

[3] Nādṛṣṭasyaivātra kāraṇatvam, anumānena prayatna-kāryatvopa-labdheḥ. Vyomavatī, pp. 628-29.

[4] Vyomavatī, Ch. S. S., 1930, pp. 628-29.

[5] VCM., 104.

aversion, and which are consciously adapted to the attainment of desired objects or to the avoidance of undesired objects.

Śrīdhara observes, that non-voluntary vital acts are produced by life (prāṇa) which consists in the contact of the self with the internal organ (manas) brought about by merit and demerit which are the results of voluntary actions in a previous birth.[6] Life consists in the contact of the self endowed with a body and invested with the potencies of its maturing past actions with the internal organ. Life is the cause of vital actions such as inhalation and exhalation during sleep. They are the effects of an effort (prayatna) because they are actions. All actions proceed from an effort. Vital actions during sleep cannot proceed from desire and aversion which are conscious mental acts. But during sleep there is no consciousness at all. Hence the vital actions during sleep are the effects of an effort of vital energy. They not only regulate the process of respiration during sleep, but also bring about the contact of the internal organ with an external sense-organ, which is inferred from the perception of objects.

Śaṅkaramiśra regards the random movements of a child's hands and feet as non-voluntary actions prompted by vital energy, and not consciously adjusted to the appropriation of a beneficial object, or to the avoidance of an injurious object, which, consequently, do not generate merits or demerits.[7] There are bodily movements of a person in deep sleep or swoon, which are not prompted by volitions or consciousness. They are, therefore, non-voluntary and non-moral.[8] Kaṇāda regards voluntary actions as actions which are prompted by desire or aversion, or by attachment to enjoined actions or by aversion to prohibited actions, and which produce merits or demerits.[9] Desire and aversion are the springs of voluntary actions, produce merits and demerits through them, and bind the self to the cycle of births and deaths.

The actions actuated by desire lead to the attainment of the good. The actions actuated by aversion lead to the rejection of

[6] Dharmādharmāpekṣa ātmamanasoḥ saṁyogo jīvanam. NK., p. 263.

[7] Bālakasya yadyapi kara-caraṇādi-cālanaṁ prayatna-pūrvakam eva tathāpi hitāhita-prāpti-parihāra-phalakaṁ na bhavati, na vā puṇya-pāpa-hetuḥ. VSU., v, 1, 11.

[8] Yatnābhāve prasuptasya calanam. VS., v, 1, 13. Prasuptasya caitanyābhāva-daśām upalakṣayati tena mūrchitasya jīvato'caitanye'pi vāyukṛtaṁ calanam. VSU., v, 1, 13.

[9] Icchā-dveṣa-pūrvikā dharmādharmayoḥ pravṛttiḥ. VS., vi, 2, 14. VSU., vi, 2, 14.

the evil. They are consciously willed and purposive actions involving deliberation and choice. They also maintain the equilibrium of the body.[10] This function of voluntary actions is not recognized by modern psychology.

The two kinds of volition which produce positive voluntary action (pravṛtti) and negative voluntary action (nivṛtti) are objects of mental perception. But life or vital effort which produces vital actions (jīvanayoniprayatna) is not an object of mental perception or sensuous perception.[11]

2. *Instinctive Actions*

Early Buddhism recognizes three primal cravings, viz., (1) will-to-live (bhavatṛṣṇā), (2) sex-instinct (kāmatṛṣṇā), and (3) craving for wealth and power (vibhavatṛṣṇā). Jainism mentions four instincts, viz., (1) food-seeking instinct (āhāra), (2) instinct of fear or flight (bhaya), (3) sex-instinct (maithuna), and (4) instinct of appropriation (parigraha). Jayasenācārya traces these instincts (saṁjñā) to intense delusion (moha). Delusion is false knowledge of not-self as self. The sex-instinct serves the biological end of race-preservation. The other three instincts serve the biological end of self-preservation. They are different from the modifications of the pure consciousness of the self and veil the experience of supersensuous happiness which is inherent in the self. They are psychical sinful influxes (bhāvapāpāsrava) and produce physical sinful influxes (dravyapāpāsrava). They can be arrested by restraint (saṁvara).[12]

Amṛtacandrasūri mentions these four instincts which are common to men and other animals. They are possessed even by animals endowed with one sense-organ. They are the common effects of the infra-atomic karma-particles called cāritramoha which veil the self's character. They are too intense and overpowering to be guided by the knowledge of good and evil.[13]

Pūjyapāda defines the sex-instinct as intense craving for union of man and woman for each other, who are possessed by the modifications of attachment owing the emergence of delusion

[10] Itarastu hitāhita-prāpti-parihāra-samarthasya vyāpārasya hetuḥ śarīravidhārakaśca. PBh., p. 628. Ch. S. S., 1930.
[11] TK., p. 17; TBh., p. 27; BhP., 149.
[12] PK., 141; TDTV., 140; Bālabodhinī, 140.
[13] Āhārasya bhayasyāpi saṁjñā syan maithunasya ca. Parigrahasya cetyevaṁ bhavet saṁjñā caturvidhā. TASār., ii, 36.

veiling their character. The sex-union is due to modes of attachment, and produces the pleasure of the sex-organ. A person under the influence of lust kills animals, tells lies, misappropriates others' property, and commits other immoral actions. Amṛtacandrasūri describes sex-union as due to the excess of lust, which is the strongest delusion. It is called abrahma because it makes one forget the nature of the self completely.[14]

Vidyānandisvāmī discusses the nature of sex-union which is the expression of the sex-instinct. It is not an action of man and woman, because it is not joint cooking of man and woman. It is not a modification of sex-love which is expressed in man and woman's mutual embrace of their bodies, because it is also the expression of sex-love of one of them through the same act. It is an action of body and mind, which satisfies the craving for sex-union of man and woman both. It may be the sight of a woman's body, the hearing of a woman's sex-love, the touch of her body, the recollection of a past sex-act, etc., which are due to desire for sex-union. A person devoid of self-control only is under the influence of lust. But a completely self-controlled person has conquered the sex-instinct.[15]

Amṛtacandrasūri defines the instinct of appropriation as the sense of 'mine' in any object.[16] Vidyānandisvāmī defines appropriation as the act of preserving one's mental and material possessions, and the like.[17] Pūjyapāda defines appropriation as taking possession of precious articles like cattle, gems, pearls, etc., acquisition, preservation, and improvement, of property. It is the external manifestation of the desire to appropriate objects which excite attachment. A person who has acquired right knowledge, right perception, and right character, and who is not subject to delusion, is free from the desire to appropriate things. Desire to kill animals, desire to tell lies, desire to steal, desire for sex-union, etc., spring from the desire for appropriation. Desire for acquisition, possession, preservation and improvement of property springs from the desire for appropriation.[18]

[14] Maithunaṁ madanodrekād abrahma parikīrtitam. TASār., iv, 77; SS., vii, 16.

[15] Tathā maithunam abrahma pramattasyaiva tat punaḥ. Pramādarahitānāṁ hi jātucit tadasambhavaḥ. TSV., vii, 16, 1.

[16] Mamedam iti saṁkalparūpā mūrcchā parigrahaḥ. TASār., iv, 77.

[17] Bāhyābhyaṁtaropadhi-saṁrakṣaṇādi-vyāpṛtir mūrcchā. TSV., vii, 17; p. 463.

[18] SS., vii, 17, pp. 207-08.

The *Bṛhadāraṇyaka Upaniṣad* mentions three primal desires: (1) sex-desire (puttraiṣaṇā) or desire for sons, (2) desire for wealth (vittaiṣaṇā) or desire for appropriation, and (3) desire for happiness here and hereafter (lokaiṣaṇā).[19]

Patañjali regards the instinctive fear of death (abhiniveśa) as an expression of the instinct of will-to-live. Every person has the instinctive fear of death. It is the negative aspect of the primal will-to-live. The desire for future life and transmigration is an expression of will-to-live. The instinctive fear of death is due to the recollection of the painful experience of many deaths in the past.[20] Even learned persons have fear of death like ignorant persons. It is an expression of the desire for the continuance of one's life. The will-to-live is the strongest primal desire or instinct.

3. *Is the New-born Child's drinking Mother's Milk Instinctive?*

Gotama (200 B.C.) speaks of a new-born child's congenital desire for taking his mother's breast, and ascribes it to the recollection of the habit of taking food to satisfy his hunger in his previous birth.[21] It is found that persons pressed by hunger have desire for food due to the recollection of the habit of taking food to appease their hunger. The new-born child had a past body; and he formed the habit of taking food when he was hungry. His innate desire to drink his mother's milk when he is hungry is due to his recollection of his habitual taking food in his past birth.[22] Vātsyāyana (400 A.D.) explains Gotama's aphorism in this manner. Viśvanātha (1700 A.D.) avers, that the new-born child's desire for his mother's milk is due to his prenatal habit of taking food to apease his hunger. He acquired the experience that taking food satisfied his hunger and was conducive to his good. He retained the experience in the form of a subconscious impression, which is revived by an unseen agency which produced his life and impels him to take his mother's breast.

[19] iii, 5, i; iv, 4, 22.

[20] Maraṇatrāsaḥ pūrva-janmānubhūtaṁ maraṇa-duḥkham anumāpayati. YBh., ii, 9.

[21] Pretyāhārābhyāsa-kṛtāt stanyābhilāṣāt. NS., iii, 1, 22.

[22] Kṣut-pīḍitaḥ pūrvābhyastam āhāram anusmaran stanyam abhilaṣati. NBh., iii, 1, 22.

Therefore his drinking his mother's milk is due to the recollection of its being a means to his pleasure.[23]

The new-born child's congenital desire to drink his mother's milk is not like the blooming and closing of a lotus flower, because it is not a mere vital act, but a mental act. Nor is it like the attraction of a piece of iron to a magnet, because it is not a physical act.[24]

Śaṅkaramiśra (1500 A.D.) also ascribes the new-born child's drinking his mother's milk to his inference that it is a means to his good or pleasure. The inference is due to the recollection of the invariable concomitance of taking food and getting pleasure due to the appeasement of hunger. This recollection is due to the revival of the subconscious impression of the past experience in the previous birth.[25] Thus Śaṅkaramiśra concedes the new-born child the power of conscious reflection, recollection and inference which are denied by modern psychology. Thus the Nyāya and the Vaiśeṣika explain a new-born child's drinking his mother's milk as due to his cognition or recollection of its being a means to his good or pleasure because of the revival of his prenatal subconscious impression retained in his self with a subtle body despite its transmigration to another gross body. This theory may be compared with Wundt's theory of instincts as due to lapsed intelligence that our instincts were intelligent and voluntary actions in our remote ancestors, from which intelligence and volition lapsed in the course of racial evolution, though he did not believe in transmigration.

But the Prābhākara maintains, that a new-born child remembers that the milk of his mother's breast ought to be drunk. His recollection is produced by the subconscious impression of it in his previous birth revived by the unseen principle (adṛṣṭa). Then he drinks the milk of his mother's breast. He does not know the invariable concomitance that drinking milk is conducive to his good.[26] He criticizes the Nyāya view thus. The Naiyāyika

[23] Jātamātrasya yaḥ stanyābhilāṣaḥ, sa tāvad āhārābhyāsa-janitaḥ; janmāntarīṇāhareṣṭa - sādhanatādhī - janya - jīvanādṛṣṭodbodhita - saṁskārādhīneṣṭa-sādhanatā-smaraṇena hi bālaḥ stanyapāne pravartate. NSV., iii, 1, 22.

[24] NS., iii, 1, 20 & 23.

[25] Nahi saṁskarodbodham antareṇa vyāptismṛtiratra, na ca tām antareṇeṣṭasādhanatānumitir na ca tām antareṇa stanyapānādau pravṛttiḥ. KR., p. 133.

[26] Bālasya vyāptyagraheṇādyā pravṛttiḥ jīvanādṛṣṭodbodhita-janmāntara-saṁskāra-janyāt stanapānaṁ kāryam iti smaraṇāt. TCS., p. 133.

maintains that a new-born child's first act of drinking his mother's milk is produced by his knowledge that it is a means to his good.

The stream of births is beginningless. A new-born child with his parched throat feels pain and remembers pleasure by the law of contrast. Then he remembers that the act of drinking milk gives pleasure, and that it is capable of being done by his volition, because there is a direct relation between the act of drinking milk and getting pleasure. He does not remember that the act of drinking his mother's milk is a means to his good, as the Naiyāyika maintains, because there is no direct relation between them. The cognition that the action ought to be done is the cause of the voluntary action of drinking mother's milk. The recollection of the fact that drinking mother's milk is a means to the child's good is not the cause of the voluntary action. When a new born child first drinks his mother's milk, he has no knowledge of its being a means to his good, because there are no causal conditions of such a cognition. Hence the cognition that an action ought to be done is the cause of the first voluntary action and the subsequent voluntary actions. That an action ought to be done implies that it can be done by one's volition.[27]

4. *The New-born Child's Emotions*

Gotama speaks of a new-born child's congenital joy, fear and grief due to the recollection of actions repeatedly performed in the previous birth.[28] He feels joy when he gets an object of desire. He feels grief when he is deprived of an objct of desire. He feels fear when he encounters a dreadful object. Vātsyāyana avers, that his first emotions are due to the recollection of the similar experiences in his past birth. They are produced by causes; they cannot be produced without any cause; they are produced by the recollection of the similar experiences acquired in his previous birth, and not by any other cause.[29] A new-born child feels attachment to those objects which gave him pleasure

[27] Tena stanapāne kāryatva-jñānād eva pravṛttiḥ. Ādya-pravṛttau kāryatva-jñānaṁ prayojakoṁ klṛptam agre'pi tadeva pravartakaṁ klṛptatvāt. TCS., pp. 138-39.

[28] Pūrvābhyasta-smṛtyanubandhāt jātasya harṣa-bhaya-śoka-sampratipatteḥ. NS., iii, 1, 19.

[29] Harṣādayo vikārāḥ nimittād bhavitum arhanti, na nimittam antareṇa; na cānyat pūrvābhyastasmṛtyanubandhāt nimittam astīti. NBh., iii, 1, 21. Ibid, iii, 1, 19.

in his past birth. Attachment is evoked by the thought of the objects which afforded him pleasure in the past birth.[30] Śaṅkaramiśra observes, that a new-born child feels the emotions of joy, fear, and grief, which are inferred from his smile, trembling, and crying respectively due to the recollection of his similar emotions in his past birth, and that his recollection is due to the revival of their subconscious impressions retained in his self by an unseen agency which produces his life and associates his self with a new body. The series of births is beginningless.[31] Thus Vātsyāyana and Śaṅkaramiśra credit a new-born child with the powers of remembering, thinking and reasoning[32] which are denied by modern psychology.

Milk oozes out of the udders of a cow for nourishment of her calf. This action is not unconscious and automatic. The cow's maternal love for her calf and desire to give it her milk prompts its oozing out; and the calf also draws it out by efforts of volition. Hence oozing out of milk is not an unconscious physiological action, but a conscious action preceded and initiated by an emotion and a desire.[33] Śaṁkara offers this explanation of the oozing out of milk from a cow's udders for the nourishment of her calf.

5. *Emotional Expressions*

We have already discussed the nature of emotional expressions (anubhāva) elaborately, which are non-voluntary actions. Some of them are spontaneous organic expressions of emotions (sāttvikabhāva). Others are the expressions of emotions, which are preceded by the thought of these actions (udbhāsura). Trembling, perspiration, gooseflesh, pallor, faltering voice, inactivity, insensibility, etc., are spontaneous organic expressions of emotions. Laughing, crying, dancing, running, rolling on the ground, etc., are preceded by the ideas of these actions.[34]

[30] Jātasyāpi pūrvānubhūtārtha-cintana-kṛto rāgaḥ. NBh., iii, 1, 27. Ibid, iii, 1, 25.

[31] Jātamātrasya bālakasya smita-kampa-ruditair anumitānāṁ harṣa-bhaya-śokānāṁ pūrva-janmānubhūta-nimitta-smṛtim antareṇānupapatteḥ. KR., p. 38.

[32] NBh., iii, 1, 27; KR., p. 38.

[33] Cetanāyāḥ dhenvāḥ snehecchayā payasaḥ pravartakatvopapatteḥ vatsa-coṣaṇena ca payasa ākṛṣyamānatvāt. SBS., Poona, 1918, ii, 2, 3.

[34] HBRS., ii, 3, 1-2; CCA., ii, ch. 23.

They are not consciously adapted to the attainment of the good and the rejection of the evil, and are not voluntary and purposive actions.

6. *Desire, Desire to Act, Aversion, Volition, and Voluntary Action*

Praśastapāda defines desire as a craving for the attainment of one's own good, or of another's good, which is not yet attained.[35] It is a yearning for the attainment of an unattained object. It is not only egoistic but altruistic also. It is produced by the conjunction of the self with manas, which depends on pleasure, or recollection. The conjunction of the self with manas is the non-inherent cause of desire; the self is its inherent cause. Desire is a quality of the self and inheres in it. It is the cause of effort of will, recollection, merit and demerit.[36]

Viśvanātha, a Neo-Naiyāyika, divides conation into three kinds: (1) a positive volition (pravṛtti) to realize the good, (2) a negative volition to avoid or reject the evil (nivṛtti), and (3) vital actions including automatic actions and reflex actions due to the vital effort (jīvanayoniprayatna).[37] The first and the second are volitions proper including conscious choice and freedom. The third kind is conation but not volition, because it does not depend upon one's freedom and conscious choice.

Viśvanātha divides desire into two kinds: (1) desire for an end, and (2) desire for a means. The end is pleasure and the absence of pain. The cognition of the end is the cause of the desire for an end. An end can induce a person to perform a voluntary action, if it is desired by him as existing in his self as an object of his desire. It is the object of a person's desire which does not depend upon any other desire.[38] Desire for a means depends upon the desire for an end, because a means is a means to the realization of an end. The cognition of a means as conducive to the realization of an end is the cause of a desire for a means.[39] A means is not in itself an object of a person's desire.

[35] Svārthaṁ parārthaṁ vā'prāpta-prārthanecchā. PBh., p. 625. Vyomavatī, p. 626.
[36] PBh., p. 625.
[37] Pravṛttiśca nivṛttiśca tathā jīvanakāraṇam. BhP., 149.
[38] Itarecchānadhīnecchāviṣayatvam. SM., p. 467. BhP., 146.
[39] Upāyecchāṁ pratīṣṭasādhanatā-jñānaṁ kāraṇam. SM., p. 467.

Viśvanātha defines desire to act (cikīrṣā) as desire to perform a voluntary action, which is qualified by the cognition that it can be accomplished by one's volition.[40] Desire to act is desire to perform an action, which can be done by one's volition, and which is known to be capable of being accomplished by one's volition, because of the experience 'I shall accomplish by cooking'.[41] (1) The cognition of an action being capable of being accomplished by one's volition, and (2) the cognition of its being conducive to one's good are the positive conditions of desire to act.[42] There can be no desire to produce rain because it cannot be accomplished by one's volition. (3) The cognition of the action entailing a stronger evil is a negative condition of desire to act; it is a counteracting cause of cikīrṣā. Hence there is no desire to eat rice mixed with honey and poison.[43] Eating rice is conducive to one's good. Eating rice with honey is conducive to one's greater good. But eating rice mixed with poison is known to be a means to one's death. So the cognition of eating rice mixed with honey and poison entailing a stronger evil counteracts the action. It is a negative condition of the desire to act; its absence is necessary for the desire.

Some hold that a stronger aversion is a counteracting cause of a desire to act,[44] or that the cognition of its not producing a stronger evil is a cause of desire to act.[45] They maintain, that the cognition of an action being a means to a stronger evil is not a counteracting cause of a desire to act, but that not being productive of a stronger evil is its cause, because a person has a desire to act immediately after having the cognition of an action being capable of being accomplished by his volition, and the cognition of its being a means to his good, though he has no cognition of its not being productive of a stronger evil. If the cognition of the action being productive of a stronger evil were the cause of a desire to act, then in the action stated above there could not be a desire to act.[46]

[40] Cikīrṣā kṛtisādhyatvaprakārecchā. BhP., 147.
[41] Kṛtisādhyatva-prakārikā kṛtisādhya-viṣayiṇīcchaā cikīrṣā. SM., p. 468.
[42] Cikīrṣāṁ prati kṛtisādhyatājñānaṁ iṣṭasādhanatājñānaṁ ca kāraṇam. SM., p. 468.
[43] Balavaddviṣṭasādhanatājñānaṁ pratibandhakam ato madhuviṣa-sampṛktānna-bhojane na cikīrṣā. SM., p. 469.
[44] Balavaddveṣaḥ pratibandhaka ityanye. SM., p. 469.
[45] Balavadaniṣṭājanakatva-jñānaṁ kāraṇam. SM., pp. 469-71.
[46] Dinakarī on SM., p. 470.

Śaṁkara mentions bodily desires (dehavāsanā), desires for not-self (anātmavāsanā), egoistic desires (ahaṁvāsanā), altruistic or social desires (lokavāsanā), religious desires (śāstravāsanā), and spiritual desires (divyavāsanā) or desires for the self (ātmavāsanā) or the supreme self (parmātmavāsanā). Desires for the good (sadvāsanā, sadbhāvavāsanā) are desires for the self or the supreme self. He speaks of complexes of desires (vāsanāgranthi). Desires (kāma) spring from ignorance (avidyā) and produce actions (karma). These desires are desires for not-self or desires for the evil (durvāsanā.) Empirical pleasure arises from the fulfilment of them. Trancendental bliss arises from the extermination of them.[47]

Aversion is recoiling from an evil or pain. It is the opposite of desire. Viśvanātha avers, that the cognition of an action being a means to one's evil is the cause of aversion.[48] The cognition of an action being a means to a strong evil is the cause of aversion to a means of pain; and the cognition of its being a means to a greater good is a counteracting cause of this kind of aversion.[49] Hence there is no aversion to cooking food which entails intermediate pain, because the pleasure of eating food and consequent health are a greater good than the pain of cooking food.

Viśvanātha analyses a positive volition (pravṛtti) to realize a good into the following elements: (1) a desire to act (cikīrṣā) or perform a voluntary action, (2) the cognition that it can be done by one's volition (kṛtisādhyatājñāna), (3) the cognition that it is means to one's good (iṣṭasādhanatājñāna), (4) the absence of the cognition that it is productive of a stronger evil (balavad-aniṣṭānanubandhitva-jñānābhāva), and (5) the perception of the materials of the action (upādāna-pratyakṣa).[50]

A negative volition (nivṛtti) is aimed at the avoidance or rejection of an evil. Viśvanātha regards aversion or the cognition of an action as a means to one's evil or pain as the cause of a negative volition.[51] It is proved by the method of agreement

[47] VCM., 274-76, 317, 319, 327, 335, 364 & 528.

[48] Dviṣṭa-sādhanatā-buddhir bhaved dveṣasya kāraṇam. BhP., 149.

[49] Duḥkhopāya-viṣayakaṁ dveṣaṁ prati balavaddviṣṭa-sādhanatājñānaṁ kāraṇam. Balavadiṣṭa-sādhanatā-jñānaṁ pratibandhakam. SM., p. 471.

[50] Cikīrṣā-kṛiti-sādhyeṣṭa-sādhanatva-matis-tathā. Upādānasya cādhyakṣaṁ pravṛttau janakaṁ bhavet. BhP., 150-51.

[51] Nivṛttistu bhaved dveṣād dviṣṭa-sādhanatā-dhiyaḥ. BhP., 151. SM., pp. 491-92.

in presence and agreement in absence. Where there is aversion or the cognition of an action being conducive to one's harm, there is a negative volition. Where there is no aversion or cognition of an action being conducive to one's harm, there is no negative volition.

The Prābhākara analyses a voluntary action into the following steps: (1) the cognition that an action ought to be done (kāryatājñāna), (2) a desire to perform the action (cikīrṣā) which implies that it can be accomplished by one's volition (kṛtisādhyatājñāna), (3) the act of volition (pravṛtti, kṛti), (4) the bodily effort (ceśṭā) which is the expression of the volition, and (5) the bodily action (kriyā) which produces a change in the external world.

The Prābhākara regards the cognition that an action ought to be done as the cause of a voluntary action. This cognition depending upon a desire to do the action is its cause. The voluntary action does not depend upon any other condition.[52]

The desire to do an action is produced by the cognition that it can be accomplished by one's volition because there is the law that desire is produced by the cognition whose qualification (prakāra) is its own qualification.[53] The desire to act is the desire to perform an action. Its qualification is its capability of being accomplished by one's volition. Hence the cognition of the action being capable of being accomplished by one's volition is the cause of the voluntary action through the desire to act.

The Prābhākara Mīmāṁsaka regards the cognition that an action ought to be done as produced by the representation of the thing as specifying the self which appropriates it and identifies itself with it as the cause of a voluntary action.[54] The self identifies itself with the idea of the action that ought to be done, and exerts its volition to execute it. The cognition that an action *ought* to be done (kārya) implies that it *can* be done by one's free will (kṛtisādhya). A voluntary action implies freedom of the will. Viśvanātha explains the Prābhākara doctrine in this manner.

Gāgābhaṭṭa explains it thus. The Prābhākara regards the

[52] Kāryatājñānaṁ pravartakam iti guravaḥ. Jñānasya pravṛttau jananīyānāṁ cikīrṣātiriktaṁ nāpekṣitam asti. SM., pp. 471-72.

[53] Sā (cikīrṣā) kṛtisādhyatā-jñāna-sādhyā icchāyāḥ sva-prakāra-prakārakadhīsādhyatva-niyamāt. SM., p. 472.

[54] Svaviśeṣaṇavattā-pratisandhāna-janya-kāryatājñānasya pravartakatvāt. SM., pp. 472-73.

cognition that an action ought to be done, which is inferred from the representation of the act as specifying the self as the determining cause of a voluntary action through a desire to do the action. He does not regard the cognition that an action is a means to one's good and the cognition that the action does not produce a stronger evil as the determining cause of a voluntary action.[55] The cognition that an action ought to be done and is capable of being done by one's volition is a sufficient cause of a voluntary action.

Gāgābhaṭṭa distinguishes two kinds of kāryatājñāna: (1) 'This action *can* be done by me'; and (2) 'this action *must* be done by me'.[56] The first cognition refers to the capability of an external object or action being accomplished by one's volition, and is not the cause of a voluntary action. The second cognition due to the cognition of an action being conducive to one's good and the cognition of its not being productive of a stronger evil, is the cause of a volition and a voluntary action through a desire to act.[57] Here 'due to' (janya) means 'inferred from' (anumita). This cognition that 'this action must be done by me' is appropriated by the self; it identifies itself with the cognition which specifies the self; the cognition is known as a qualification of the self which freely resolves on doing the action.[58] In prudential duties directed towards the fulfilment of a desire, the desire for a fruit is the qualification which specifies the self. In daily obligatory duties purity and life at the time are the qualifications of the self.[59] The self is the agent commanded by a scriptural or secular injunction to act.

The Naiyāyika regards the cognition that an action is conducive to the agent's good as the essential element in the cause of a volition. The Prābhākara, on the other hand, regards the cognition that an action ought to be done and can be done by his

[55] Atra guravavaḥ. Svaviśeṣaṇavattā-pratisandhānajanya-kāryatājñānasyaiva cikīrṣādvārā pravṛtti-hetutvam neṣṭasādhanatva-balavad-aniṣṭānanubandhitva-jñānayorapi. Bhāṭṭacintāmaṇi, Benares, 1933, p. 63.

[56] Kāryatājñānaṁ dvividhaṁ, mayedaṁ kartuṁ śakyata ityevaṁ rūpaṁekam, mamedam avaśyaṁ kāryam ityevaṁ rūpaṁ dvitīyam. Ibid, p. 63.

[57] Tatrādyaṁ padārtha-niṣṭha-yogyatā-gamyam iti na pravṛttiṁ prati hetuḥ. Dvitīyaṁ tu sveṣṭa-sādhanatva-balavad-aniṣṭānanubandhitva-jñāna-janyam iti cikīrṣādvārā pravṛttiṁ prati hetuḥ. Ibid, p. 63.

[58] Idam eva sva-viśeṣaṇavattā-pratisandhāna-janyatvam. Ibid, p. 63.

[59] Svaṁ niyojyaḥ, tadviśeṣaṇaṁ kāmye phalakāmanā, nitye śuci-tatkālajīvitvādi. Ibid, p. 63.

volition as the essential element in the cause of a volition. He does not deny the cognition of an action being conducive to one's good in a prudential duty (kāmyakarma); but he regards it as proving that it ought to be done and can be done by one's volition. The Naiyāyika does not regard the representation of the cognition of the desired object as conducive to one's good as specifying one's self as a determinant of a volition. But the Prābhākara regards the self's appropriation of the desire for the object qualifying it as the essential element in the cause of a volition in regard to a prudential duty. He denies the need of the cognition of any desired object being conducive to one's good in a volition in regard to a daily obligatory duty (nityakarma). But the element of self-reference is indispensable in such a volition also. The self appropriates the idea of the action and determines to perform it.

The cognition that an action ought to be done and can be done which is produced by the representation of it as specifying the self is the common property in all cases of volition. It is inferred from the cognition of an action being conducive to one's good, the cognition that it does not entail a stronger evil, and the cognition of one's purity and living at the time, and is the cause of a volition as the cognition that an action ought to be and can be done. The cognitions from which it is inferred are sometimes present and sometimes absent. This view is in conformity with the parsimony of hypotheses.[60]

Jānakīnātha explains the Prābhākara view thus. The cognition that an action ought to be done and can be done by one's volition due to the cognition of one's being qualified by purity is the cause of a volition in regard to a daily obligatory duty. The cognition that an action ought to be done and can be done by one's volition due to the cognition of the action being conducive to one's good, or occurring simultaneously with this cognition, is the cause of a volition in regard to prudential duties. The cognition, that an action can be done by one's volition, in general is the cause of a volition in general.[61]

[60] Evaṁ ceṣṭasādhanatva-balavad-aniṣṭānanubandhitva-śucitatkāla-jīvitva-jñāna-janyānāṁ kāryatā-jñānānaṁ kāryatājñānatvena anugatānāṁ pravṛttau hetutvam iti lāghavam. Ibid, p. 64.

[61] Nitye śaucādimattva-pratisandhāna-janyaṁ kāryatājñānaṁ pravartakam. Anyatra ceṣṭasādhanatā-jñāna-janyam iṣṭasādhanatājñāna-kālinaṁ vā kāryatājñānaṁ hetuḥ, pravṛttisāmānye ca kṛtisādhyatā-jñāna-samānyam. NSM., Saṁvat 1972, Benares, pp. 250-51.

The Prābhākara regards the representation of the action as specifying the self as the cause of the cognition that it ought to be done and can be done by its volition. The Naiyāyika does not recognize any causal relation between the cognition of an action being conducive to one's good and the cognition of its capability of being accomplished by one's volition. He regards both the cognitions as having the same object.[62]

Jānakīnātha states the ancient Nyāya view thus. The cognition that an action can be done by one's volition having for its object the action which is known as a means to one's good is the cause of a volition, because it has the merit of simplicity. The cognition that an action can be done by one's volition, which is produced by the cognition that it is conducive to one's good, is not the cause of a volition.[63]

7. *The Prābhākara view of the Cause of a Volition*

Rāmānujācārya (1800 A.D.), a Prābhākara, states the Prābhākara view of the cause of a voluntary action and criticizes the Nyāya view in *Tantrarahasya*. It is maintained, that a volition is produced by the cognition that an action is conducive to one's good, and that it is not produced by the cognition that an action ought to be done and can be done by one's volition. So it is said: "Even a dull person does not engage in an action without aiming at an end". The end is the fruit or result aimed at.

This view is not tenable for the following reasons. A person does not exert his volition to eat past food which was a means of the appeasement of hunger. He does not eat present food which is a means to his good, when his hunger is gratified. A child does not exert his volition to acquire a kingdom which has been predicted by an expert palmist, though he knows it to be conducive to his good. A person does not make any effort to produce rain or the sun, though he knows them to be the means to his good. Past food, present food, future rain, etc., are conducive to one's good, but not capable of being accomplished by one's volition. Hence being conducive to one's good is different

[62] S. K. Maitra: *The Ethics of the Hindus*, C. U., 1925., p. 62.

[63] Atra jarannaiyāyikāḥ. Iṣṭasādhanatā-viṣavakaṁ kṛtisādhyatājñānam eva lāghavāt pravartakam. Na tviṣṭasādhanatājñāna-janya-kāryatājñānādi gauravāt. NSM., p. 252.

from being capable of being done by one's volition.[64] The cognition that an action can be done by one's volition is the cause of a volition, but the cognition that an action is a means to one's good is not the cause of a volition. But the capability of an action being done by a volition (kāryatva), which is in the nature of an exertion, depends upon its being a means to the realization of its end; it is directly capable of being done. There is a difference between capability of being done by one's volition and being conducive to one's good, though both are directed to the realization of the same end. Capability of being done by one's volition, on which its existence depends, is the principal cause of a volition. The realization of an end, which depends upon a volition, is not the chief moving cause of a volition. The realization of an end depends upon an action which is its means.[65] There is no positive volition with regard to pain or an object of pain. But there is a positive volition with regard to pleasure or an object of pleasure. The knowledge of an action, which is a means to pleasure, being capable of being done by one's volition, depends upon its being a means to pleasure, not independently of it. So the knowledge of an action being conducive to one's good is not the chief incentive to a volition. All persons know pleasure as an object to be accomplished by their volitions independently of its being a means to any other end. Hence capability of being done by one's volition is the direct incentive to a volition, and not being a means to one's good. The former is different from the latter.[66]

A voluntary action can be known by perception or inference. A volition is apprehended by mental perception. The capability of an action being accomplished by a volition is known by inference. When a person is induced to perform a voluntary action by an injunction, the knowledge that it is capable of being accomplished by his volition is an incentive to it, and not the knowledge that it is conducive to his good.[67] Imperative sentences indicate that some actions ought to be done and are capable of

[64] Tenānyā kāryatā, anyā ceṣṭa-sādhanatā. TR., p. 63.

[65] Phalaṁ pratyupāyatvaṁ phala-sādhanatvaṁ, kṛtiṁ prati pradhānatvaṁ tadadhīnasattākatvaṁ ca kāryatvaṁ, na tu kṛtyadhīnasiddhimātram. TR., p. 63.

[66] Tena sādhanatottīrṇā kāryatā, na tviṣṭasādhanataiva. TR., p. 63.

[67] Vākyamūla-pravṛttāvapi kāryatā-jñānam eva pravṛtti-prayojakaṁ, na tviṣṭasādhanatājñānam. TR., p. 63.

being done. Vedic injunctions indicate that some actions ought to be done because they realize the Moral Law (apūrva) and are categorical imperatives. The Moral Law ought to be accomplished because it is an Ought, and not because it is a means to an end or pleasure. Daily obligatory duties (e.g., ablution, prayer, etc.) and occasional duties (e.g., bath during eclipse) ought to be performed because they are imperative, and not because they are means to some ends. Hence those who maintain that the Moral Law (apūrva) ought to be accomplished because it is a means to an end are refuted. The Moral Law ought to be accomplished because it is a categorical imperative—an unconditional command.

The knowledge of a desire, it may be argued, is the cause of a positive volition, which is indicated by an injunctive sentence. The Prābhākara refutes it thus. Desire, no sooner than it is produced, is the cause of a volition; desire as known is not its cause. Let it be so. An injunctive sentence, which is spoken to a superior, equal, or inferior person, in the form of a request, an invitation, or a command, and which does not indicate what ought to be done and can be done by a volition, may be said to be the the cause of a volition. This argument is invalid, because what ought to be done or can be done by a volition takes the forms of a request, an invitation, or a command. An injunction regarding prudential duties may be said to be a means to an ulterior end or happiness. This argument is wrong, because the end as known by an agent and qualifying him is not the chief cause of a volition, but because a Moral Law is known to be of the nature of Ought, which ought to be obeyed for itself.[68] An end is a qualification of the enjoined self, and cannot be accomplished by the self unrelated to it. But the Moral Law or Ought, which is in the nature of a command, ought to be accomplished in itself, not as a qualification of the enjoined self.[69] A Moral Law enjoins a self to accomplish it, because it is obligatory in its nature. The obligatory character of the Moral Law is the chief determinant of a positive volition. Or the knowledge of the Moral Law that ought to be accomplished is the cause of a positive action. In other words, the cognition that something

[68] Maivaṁ, na hi niyojya-viśeṣaṇatayā pratipannasya tasya prādhānyaṁ, kiṁ tu svataḥsādhyatayā pratipannasya niyogasyaiva. TR., p. 64.

[69] Na hyasmanmate phalasya bhāvyatvaṁ, kiṁ tvapūrvasyaiva. Phalaṁ tu niyojya-viśeṣaṇam. Na hi tasya bhāvyatayā' nvayaḥ, apūrvasya bhāvyasya svato labdhatvāt. TR., p. 64.

ought to be done and can be done (kāryatājñāna) is the cause of a positive volition.

8. *Gaṅgeśa's exposition of the Prābhākara's view of the cause of a Voluntary Action*

Gaṅgeśa, the founder of the Navya Nyāya school, states the Prābhākara's view and arguments supporting it in the following manner. The Prābhākara maintains, that the cognition that an action can be done by one's volition is the cause of a voluntary action.[70] The cognition produces a volition through a desire to act. If despite the presence of a desire to act, the voluntary action is not produced, the delay in its production is due to the absence of some other cause. The desire to act is the desire for an action which can be done by one's volition, and which is known as being capable of being done by one's volition.[71] It occurs in such as form as 'I shall accomplish this by cooking'. The desire to act is due to the cognition that the action can be done by one's volition, because the cognition of a desire is the cause of a desire.[72] So a person exerts his volition for cooking which can be done by his volition. The cognition that an action is a means to one's good without the cognition that it can be done by one's volition, is not the cause of a voluntary action, because then there would be a desire to act even when an action is known to be incapable of being done by one's volition.[73] The cognition that an action cannot be done by one's volition cannot be said to be the counteracting cause of a voluntary action, because the inclusion of the absence of this counteracting cause in the cause of a voluntary action would contain a larger number of elements and thus violate the parsimony of hypotheses.[74] Otherwise, the cognition that an action cannot be done by one's volition, the

[70] Kāryatva-jñānaṁ pravartakam iti guravaḥ. TCS., B.I., Calcutta, 1901, pp. 6-7.

[71] Cikīrṣa ca kṛtisādhyatva-prakārikā kṛtisādhya-kriyā-viṣayecchā. TCS., pp. 14-15.

[72] Sā (cikīrṣā) svakrtisādhyatā-jñānasādhyā icchāyāḥ svaprakāraka-dhīsādhyatva-niyamāt. TCS., p. 16.

[73] Na tviṣṭasādhanatā-jñāna-sādhyā svakṛtyasādhye cikīrṣāpatteḥ. TCS., p. 18.

[74] Svakṛtyasādhyatva-jñānaṁ pratibandhakam iti cet, na, tadabhāvakā-raṇatve gauravāt. TCS., p. 18.

cognition that it is a means to one's evil or pain, the cognition that it is worthy of rejection, and the cognition that it cannot produce the desired fruit, would be the counteracting causes of the desire to act, and the cognition that an action can be done by one's volition would be the cause of a voluntary action.[75]

Sondaḍa contends, that a desire to act is due to the cognition that the action is a means to one's good as in the desire for rain. This contention is invalid, because the desire 'I shall do the action through my volition' like the desire 'I shall cook food with fire' is experienced before the act of volition, and therefore incapable of being denied. Though desire is possible in an act of volition, the desire to act is not the cause of a voluntary action, but the desire which can be fulfilled by one's volition is its cause, because a cognition, a desire to act, and a volition are experienced to have the same object. A person knows a jar to be made, desires to make it, and makes it.[76]

It may be contended, that if cikīrṣā be a desire to act by one's volition, then it will not vanish if desired cooking is done by another person's volition, because the desire to do an action by one means (e.g., by one's volition) is not counteracted by getting the desired fruit by some other means (e.g., by another person's volition), as the desire to acquire wealth by accepting gifts is not counteracted by acquiring wealth through love. This contention is wrong, because when the object of one's desire is attained, the desire for it is destroyed, and when the desire for an end is destroyed, the desire for its means also vanishes, since the desire for an end is the cause of a desire for a means.[77] If another person cooks rice, cooking and rice both are accomplished. If some other cooked rice is desired, then the desire to cook will persist. Rather, the desire to act will not vanish, if the realization of the end of a desire and the destruction of the desire for an end be not said to be the counteracting causes of the desire to act, because its end has not been realized.[78] If

[75] Anyathā svakṛtyasādhyatvāniṣṭa-sādhanatvopakṣaṇīyatva-niṣphalatva-jñānaṁ pratibandhakaṁ kriyājñānam eva pravartakaṁ kalpyeta. TCS., pp. 23-24.

[76] Iṣṭasādhanatvena vṛṣṭāviva kṛtavicchāsambhave'pi kṛtīcchā na pravartikā, kintu svakṛtisādhyecchaiva, jñāna-cikīrṣa-kṛtīnām eka-viṣayatvānubhavāt. TCS., pp. 26-27.

[77] Na, sva-viṣaya-siddhatvasya phalecchā-vicchedasya copāyecchā-virodhitvāt. TCS., pp. 27-28.

[78] Pratyutāsiddhatvāt kṛtāvevecchā na vicchidyeta yadi kṛti-viṣaya-siddhatva-phalecchā-vicchedau na virodhinau. TCS., p. 32.

wealth is acquired by love, the desire for acquiring greater wealth is not destroyed, because its end is not realized, and because the desire for the end still persists. If a person has desire for mere wealth, his desire for wealth by accepting gifts is destroyed when he acquires wealth through love, because the end of his desire (e.g., mere wealth) has been realized. A common desire is destroyed when any of its object is attained.[79] Otherwise, the desire for wealth can never be destroyed, because all wealth can never be acquired.

In fact, the Prābhākara concludes, there are the cognition that an action can be done by one's volition, and the cognition that the action is a means to one's good in the cognition that the volition which is favourable to a voluntary action is a means to one's good.[80] A volition produces voluntary action; a voluntary action produces a fruit which is desired. A volition produces a desired fruit through a voluntary action. Therefore, there is a desire in an action which can be done by one's volition, just as there is a desire in a volition due to the cognition that a volition which is favourable to a voluntary action is a means to one's good. Hence a desire to act is invariably preceded by the cognition that it can be done by one's volition.[81] Wherever there is a desire to act, there is the cognition that the action can be done by one's volition. Hence a desire to act is the cause of a volition,—as the desire to act which has an object which is identical with the object of the volition, not as a desire for the volition,—because if the desire to act and the volition have different objects, it violates the parsimony of hypotheses. The desire to act is about the same object about which there is a volition.[82]

It may be contended, that a volition is the object of a desire to act, and that cooking is the object of a volition, and that, therefore, the desire to act and the volition have different objects. This contention is not valid, because there is a desire for an object through that character through which it is known

[79] Kiñcid-viśeṣa-siddhyaiva hi sāmānyecchā-vicchedaḥ. TCS., pp. 33-34.

[80] Vastutastu kriyānukūlā kṛtir iṣṭopāya iti jñāne kriyāyāḥ kṛtisādhyatvam iṣṭopāyatvaṁ ca bhātam. TCS., pp. 35-36.

[81] Cikīrṣāyāṁ kṛtisādhyatva-prakāra-naiyatyam. TCS., p. 37.

[82] Ataḥ kṛti-samāna-visaya cikīrṣātvena cikīrṣayāḥ kṛti-kāraṇatvam, na tu kṛtīcchātvena bhinna-viṣayatayā gauravāt. TCS., pp. 37-40.

to be conducive to one's good.[83] There will be a desire for cooking known to be conducive to one's good, as capable of being done by one's volition, as there is a desire for rain in one's field when such rain is known to be conducive to one's good. Just as there is no desire for rain, through a desire to act, in the object of a volition, so there is no desire for rain, though there is a desire to act in the object of volition.[84] If it be urged that a different set of causal conditions is operative there, this is not possible. It would be possible if cooking as capable of being done by one's volition were the cause of cooked rice. But it is not the cause of cooked rice, because that would violate the parsimony of hypotheses. Cooking as cooking is the cause of cooked rice. That cooking is not done without a volition is a different matter.

If it be argued, that the desire 'I shall do this by my volition' like the desire 'I shall do this by fire' is due to the cognition that the action is a means to my good, then the cognition that the action can be done by one's volition is the cause of a volition, like the cognition that the action can be done by fire.[85]

If dependence on a desire to act which is experienced be said to be a special determinant of a volition, then there can be no effort of will in the vital acts due to the vital effort (jīvanayoni-prayatna), because they are not dependent on a desire to act. If dependence on a desire to act be not a special determinant of a volition, then there may be an effort of will in vital acts due to a vital effort according to the Naiyāyika, who regards the cognition that an action can be done by one's volition, and the cognition that an action is a means to one's good as the causes of a voluntary action.[86] If dependence on a desire to act be a mark (upalakṣaṇa) of a volition, then there may be a volition in vital acts, because there is no generic property of all volitions. But there is no effort of will in vital acts. If dependence on a desire to act be a qualification (viśeṣaṇa) of a volition, then the

[83] Yena rūpeṇa yasyeṣṭasādhanatvaṁ tena prakāreṇa tatrecchā. TCS., p. 40.

[84] Kṛtau kṛtiviṣaye vā cikīrṣāyāṁ na vṛṣṭīcchā. TCS., p. 40. TCR., p. 40.

[85] Tarhi tatra vahni-sādhyatā-jñānavad atrāpi kṛtisādhyatva-jñānaṁ kāraṇam āvaśyakam. TCS., p. 41.

[86] Kṛtau cānubhava-siddha-cikīrṣādhīnatvaṁ viśeṣaḥ tena prāṇa-pañcaka-sañcāre jīvanayonikṛtisādhye na pravṛttiḥ. TCS., pp. 41-44.

cognition of a desire to act is the cause of both a desire to act and a vountary action, and that violates the parsimony of hypotheses.

Further, the cognition that an action can be done by one's volition which depends on a desire to act has been said to be the cause of a voluntary action. A volition depends upon a desire to act; cooking depends upon a volition. The voluntary action of cooking is due to the cognition that cooking can be done by one's volition. There is capability of being done by a desire to act in a volition; and there is capability of being done by one's volition in cooking. Therefore a volition is a means to cooking. Hence a volition is both a means and an end at the same time. A means is an accomplished fact (siddha). An end is a realizable and non-existent object (sādhya). Therefore, there cannot be the cognition of cooking being capable of being done by one's violition which depends on a desire to act, because the same object cannot be a means and an end both at the same time.[87]

This argument is wrong, because there is a particular volition, which is distinguished from a vital action due to the vital effort, which is perceived through the internal organ, and which is marked by a desire to act, of which a desire to act is a cause. Desire to act is the cause of a volition distinguished from vital acts due to the vital effort. Dependence on a desire to act is the common property, which is the mark (upalakṣaṇa) of all particular volitions.[88] Being produced by a desire to act is the mark of a volition. It is a character of a volition in the form of a voluntary action, and not of any other volition. The cognition of a volition as volition is the cause of particular volitions as distinguished from vital acts due to the vital effort.[89] The cognition that an action can be done by a volition is the cause of a voluntary action.[90]

It may be urged, that a volition cannot be a qualification (viśeṣaṇa) of what is realizable by it (sādhya) because the volition

[87] Cikīrṣā-sādhyāvasthāyaḥ kṛteḥ siddhāvastha-sādhanatva-virodhena kṛtisādhyatā pākādau na jñāyeta. TCS., p. 46.

[88] Cikīrṣādhīnatvenānugatena kṛtiviśeṣāṇām upalaksyāṇām anugatatvamapi. TCS., pp. 47-48.

[89] Jīvanayoniyatna-vyāvṛtta-kṛtiviśeṣāṇāṁ kṛtitvena jñānaṁ kāraṇam. TCS., p. 49.

[90] Tathā ca pravṛttitvarūpeṇa pravṛtti-sādhyatā-jñānaṁ pravṛttau hetuḥ. TCR., p. 49.

does not exist at the time, that what is non-existent cannot be a qualification, that a volition is produced after the cognition that an action can be done by one's volition, that it does not exist before the cognition stated above, and that therefore a volition cannot be a qualification of what is realizable by a volition. If a volition be said to exist before the cognition that an action can be done by one's volition, then the fallacy of mutual dependence is committed: the cognition that an action can be done by one's volition depends upon a volition; and a volition depends upon the cognition that an action can be done by one's volition.[91] A volition cannot be said to be a mark (upalakṣaṇa) of what is realizable by a volition, because then it is not a distinguishing attribute, and leads to an unwarranted stretch of its application.

This argument is wrong, because a volition must be a qualification (viśeṣaṇa) of the cognition that an action can be done by one's volition, since it is an object of the cognition, and because a volition is a mark (upalakṣaṇa) of what is realizable by a volition, since it indicates its character.[92] Otherwise, the Naiyāyika also would meet the same difficulty. The object of desire (iṣṭa) cannot be a qualification of the cognition that an action is conducive to one's good, because desire does not exist at the time. Nor is it a mark of the cognition stated above, because then it is not a distinguishing property, and leads to an unwarranted stretch of its application, because the cognition that an action is conducive to onee's good or evil may be the cause of a voluntary action. Further, in that case, the cognition of a mark (liṅga) or reason (hetu) would be the cause of an inference even when the mark is non-existent.[93]

It may be contended, that if dependence upon a desire to act be the cause of a voluntary action, then there may be a desire to act in labour which involves intermediate pain, because that labour also can be done by one's volition dependent on a desire to act.[94]

[91] Nanu kṛtisādhye na kṛtir viśeṣaṇam asattvāt, sattve vā kṛtau satyāṁ jñānaṁ jñāne ca kṛtir ityanyonyāśrayaḥ. TCS., p. 49.

[92] Na, kṛtir hi jñāne viṣayatayā viśeṣaṇam eva sādhye ca paricāyakatayopalakṣaṇam. TCS., pp. 49-50.

[93] Anyathā iṣṭasādhane' pīṣṭaṁ na viśeṣaṇam asattvāt nopalakṣaṇam atiprasaṅgāt, liṅgajñānādau vā kā gatiḥ. TCS., p. 50.

[94] Nanvevaṁ śrame'pi cikīrṣā syāt tasyāpi cikīrṣādhīna-kṛitisādhyatvāt. TCS., p. 50.

The Mīmāṁsaka replies, that the labour is produced by the acts of eating, etc., and that it is not produced by a volition dependent on a desire to act, because it is not the object of a desire to act, and because a volition is the cause of the mere object of a desire to act, which is different from the perception of its destruction caused by it.[95]

Some contend that, as the act of going is not accomplished by the volition which is dependent upon the desire to eat, so the act of labour is not accomplished by the volition which is dependent upon the desire to eat. This contention is not valid for the following reason. When a person makes an effort of volition (kṛti) to lift a heavy weight owing to illusion, which cannot be executed by his volition, he has a volition before he undergoes labour, though he cannot lift the heavy weight. Likewise, when a person bound by an iron chain makes an effort of volition to move owing to illusion, he has a volition before he undergoes labour, though he cannot move. In both these cases, a volition must be regarded as the cause of the labour, because no action (e.g., lifting a heavy weight or movement) has been done. Therefore, an action caused by a volition is not the cause of labour.[96]

It may be argued, that labour is due to an action in the motor nerves. Then the following difficulty arises: the rule that a volition is the cause of an action, which is the object of a desire to act, and which is different from the perception of destruction caused by a volition, is violated in the case of pleasure. Pleasure is not an object of a desire to act which is the cause of a volition, and yet it is produced by a volition. A volition is produced by a desire to act which has a means for its object; it is not produced by a desire to act which has pleasure for its object.[97]

Some contend, that labour cannot be produced by a volition dependent on a desire to act, because then labour could be produced by an effort of volition due to aversion also. This

[95] Śramastu bhojanādi-kriyā-sādhyo na tatkṛtisādhyaḥ acikīrṣitatvāt kṛteḥ svadhvaṁsa-sākṣātkārātirikte cikīrṣā-viṣaya-mātre janakatvāt. TCS., pp. 51-52.

[96] Kṛtau satyāṁ kriyānutpāde'pi śramānubhavāt kṛtereva kāraṇatvāt. Na tu tajjanya-kriyāyāḥ. TCS., p. 52.

[97] Na hi sukhaṁ kṛtikāraṇa-cikīrṣā-viṣayaḥ, upāya-cikīrṣā-janyā hi kṛtiḥ na tu sukha-cikīrṣā-janyā. TCS., pp. 52-53.

contention is not valid for the following reason. The killing of an enemy is conducive to one's good. So it is produced by a volition dependent on a desire to act, because aversion cannot be the cause of a positive voluntary action. But aversion to an enemy is proved by the experience 'I hate the enemy'.

Labour can be produced by a volition as a volition, and not as a volition dependent on a desire to act. If a volition dependent on a desire to act were the cause of labour, which is not an object of the desire to act, then there would be no such rule that eating, an object of a desire to act, is produced by a volition, and that going, which is not an object of a desire to act, is not produced by a volition, and that going also, like labour, would be produced by a volition dependent on a desire to act. But eating is produced by a particular volition dependent on a desire to act; it is not produced by a mere volition because it is not produced by a vital effort.[98]

It may be argued, that labour is not produced by a volition which has eating for its object, but that it is produced by a vital effort which is produced simultaneously with eating. This argument is invalid. A volition as a volition cannot produce labour, because a vital effort cannot produce labour, because any other volition cannot produce labour, and because even despite the presence of the vital effort a person, who does not lift a heavy weight or do any other such act, does not experience labour. Therefore, the vital effort is not the cause of labour; just as eating is produced by a volition which has eating for its object according to the Naiyāyika and the Prābhākara both, so it must be admitted that the intermediate labour involved in eating also is produced by a volition which has eating for its object because there is no other alternative.[99]

It may be argued, that a sleeping person's labour inferred from his perspiration, etc., is produced by his vital effort. This argument is wrong, because perspiration, etc., are produced by other causes than labour. Otherwise, a person in a waking condition also, may also experience labour though he is completely inactive, because he has the vital effort at the time.

[98] Bhojanādiśca cikīrṣādhīna-kṛti-viśeṣāt, sa hi kṛtimātraṁ vyabhicarati jīvanayonikṛtes tadanutpādāt. TCS., p. 55.

[99] Bhojanādivat śrama-viśeṣānām api bhojanādi-kṛtisādhyatvam ananyagatikatvāt. TCS., p. 56.

That labour may be produced by a volition is the opponent's contention. This contention is not valid, because a volition dependent on one's desire is the cause of a voluntary action. Labour is always produced by a volition dependent on a desire for some other object. There can be no desire for labour, because it is in the nature of pain.[100] Labour is the intermediate act which is involved in a voluntary action which realizes another object. Labour is produced by a volition which seeks to realize another object (e.g., cooked rice). So there is no volition in regard to labour.[101]

Some maintain, that dependence on one's desire to act is the qualification of a volition. But that violates the parsimony of hypotheses, because desire to act contains a greater number of elements than a desire.[102]

Some Mīmāṁsakas maintain, that 'having an end' is a property of a volition. Labour cannot be produced by a volition qualified by having an end, because it is not the object of a desire to act, but because it can be produced by a volition as volition. An object of a desire to act only can be produced by a volition qualified by having an end. Hence all voluntary actions are painful and involve labour, because labour is produced by mere volition.[103]

According to some Mīmāṁsakas, capability of being produced by one's volition only is a determining condition of a desire to act. But, according to the Naiyāyika, (1) capability of being produced by a volition, (2) being a means to one's good, (3) pleasure, and (4) the absence of pain are the determining conditions of a desire to act. The cognitions of these are the causes of a desire to act. According to some Mīmāṁsakas, (1) pleasure and (2) the absence of pain are the determining conditions of a desire; the cognitions of pleasure and the absence of pain are the causes of a desire.[104] Desire for pleasure produced by rain is directed towards rain also as its object. There is no

[100] Svecchādhīnatvasya kṛtiviśeṣaṇatvāt, śramaśca niyamato' nyecchādhīna-kṛti-sādhyaḥ śrame duḥkhatvenecchā-virahāt. TCS., pp. 56-57.

[101] Ata evānyecchā-janya-kṛti-sādhyatvena śramo nāntarīyaka ityucyate. TCS., pp. 57-58.

[102] Sva-cikīrṣādhīnatvaṁ tu na kṛtau viśeṣaṇaṁ gauravāt. TCS., p. 58.

[103] Tadviśiṣṭa-kṛti-sādhyaśca na śramaḥ acikīrṣitatvāt kintu kṛtimātra-sādhyaḥ. Ata eva kaṣṭaṁ karmetyanubhavo lokānām. TCS., pp. 60-61.

[104] Icchā-prayojakantu mama sukhatvaṁ duḥkhābhāvatvaṁ ceti dvayam. TCS., p. 62.

desire for rain as a means to one's pleasure, because being a means is contradictory to a desire.[105] If a desire is known to be a means to one's good, then it is both a means and an end. But this is not possible because they are contradictory to each other. A means is an accomplished fact, but an end is a realizable object. So a means cannot be an end. Rain is not yet existent, and, consequently, cannot be a means, and there can be no cognition of it as a means to one's good. But, according to the Naiyāyika, (1) pleasure, (2) the absence of pain, and (3) being a means to pleasure are the determining conditions of a desire; and the cognitions of these are its causes.

Though eating poison can be effected by a volition, there is no desire to eat it, because it is known to be productive of a stronger evil (e.g., death). Therefore, some argue, that a volition must be specified by the qualification of being produced by a desire to act;[106] so that the cognition that an action can be done by a volition produced by a desire to act is the cause of a voluntary action. Eating poison cannot be done by a volition produced by a desire to act. So there is no voluntary action of eating poison.

This argument is not valid. If this were so, eating poison could not be effected by a volition, because it is not produced by the vital effort. So the qualification 'being produced by a desire to act', is useless. This qualification is added to a volition in order to exclude the vital effort and a negative voluntary action. The vital effort and a volition not to do an action cannot produce eating poison. Hence the qualification is useless.[107]

The Naiyāyika argues, that the cognition of eating poison being capable of being done by a volition due to a desire to act occurs owing to the illusion of its being conducive to one's good, because capability of being done by a volition is due to a cognition of it. This applies to the worship of a Buddhist temple also. A voluntary action follows from the cognition of its being capable of being done by a volition, though, in reality, it is not capable of being done by a volition. In fact, a voluntary action may occur, even if there is a counteracting cause (e.g., the cognition of

[105] Na tviṣṭasādhanatvena tatrecchā sādhanatvasyecchā-virodhitvāt. TCS., pp. 62-63.

[106] Kṛtau cikīrṣā-janyatvaṁ viśeṣaṇam iti kaścit. TCS., p. 63.

[107] Evaṁ hi viṣabhakṣaṇaṁ kṛtisādhyam eva na syāt jīvanayonikṛtes tasyānutpatter iti vyarthaṁ viśeṣaṇam. TCS., pp. 63-64.

the action not being conducive to one's good), owing to the cognition that it is capable of being done by a volition. A person, who is full, also may exert his volition to eat food for the same reason. The cognition here means the recollection of the action being done by one's volition in the past.[108]

It may be contended, that the apprehension (anubhava) of an action being capable of being done by one's volition, which is different from the recollection of it, is the cause of a voluntary action, because if a cognition common to apprehension and recollection were the cause of a voluntary action, then a person would exert his volition to eat poison owing to the recollection of his action being done by a volition. Here the action being capable of being done by one's volition would not be inferred from the cognition of the action being conducive to one's good, or from the statement of a reliable person. This contention is not valid, because, in fact, if eating poison be capable of being done by one's volition, then it may be inferred from some other reason, or from the statement of a reliable person. There can be no voluntary action from the apprehension of an action being capable of being done by a volition, which is inferred from a false reason (liṅga), or from a false verbal statement. There is a voluntary action here; but there is no cognition that the action can be done by one's volition, which is the cause of a voluntary action according to the Prābhākara, because he does not admit the existence of an illusion, which he regards as non-apprehension of the distinction between a presentative element and a representative element.[109]

The Prābhākara replies, that this contention is not valid, because the cognition that an action can be done by one's volition being inferred from the cognition of its specifying the self is the cause of a voluntary action.[110] A particular action known as specifying the self is the cause of a voluntary action.[111] A person does not eat poison or worship a Buddhist temple, because he has no knowledge that the action is conducive to his good, and because he has no knowledge that it can be done by his volition due to the knowledge that it is conducive to his good, as he does

[108] TCS., TCR., p. 64.
[109] TCS., pp. 65-66. IPC., pp. 282-83.
[110] Maivaṁ, svaviśeṣaṇavattā-pratisandhāna-janyaṁ hi kāryatājñānaṁ pravartakam. TCS., pp. 67-68.
[111] Sa ca kāryaviśeṣaḥ puruṣa-viśeṣāvagataḥ pravṛttihetuḥ. TCS., p. 71.

not perform such an action in the state of illusion.[112] A person who is full, does not eat food, because he is devoid of desire for eating food, and because he has no knowledge that the action is conducive to his good, from which he may infer that he can do it by his volition.[113]

Some maintain, that there can be the cognition that labour can be done by one's volition due to the cognition of the self's living, and that, therefore, the qualificaton 'distinct from life' should be added to 'specifying the self'. This view is wrong, because labour is not capable of being done by one's volition dependent on the self's desire, and because, consequently, a person does not exert his volition to labour.[114]

Others maintain, that the cognition that an action can be done by one's volition, inferred from its being a means to one's good, is the cause of a voluntary action. This view is wrong, because daily obligatory duties are not conducive to one's good or pleasure.[115]

It may be contended, that the cognition that an action can be done by one's volition, which knows it to be conducive to one's good, and which does not entail a stronger evil, like eating poison, is the cause of a voluntary action, because it contains a smaller number of elements than the cognition that an action can be done by one's volition due to the cognition of its specifying the self. It may be contended further, that a desire to act in regard to a means is due to the cognition of its being a means to one's good, because it is a desire for a means, like desire for rain which is a means to one's pleasure. In desire to act in regard to enjoyment of pleasure, which is an end, there is no desire for a means. Therefore, the cognition of an action being a means to one's good or pleasure is not the cause of a desire to act in regard to enjoyment of pleasure.

This contention is not tenable, because 'being produced by the cognition of an action specifying the self' is absent from the desire to act in regard to enjoyment of pleasure, and is therefore not its

[112] Saṁjātā-bādhasya ca viṣabhakṣaṇe caitya-vandane ca bhrama-daśāyām iva neṣṭasādhanatā-jñānam asti yena tajjanya kāryatā-jñānāt pravarteta. TCS., pp. 71-72.

[113] Tṛptasya ca kāmanā-viraheṇa iṣṭasādhanatājñānābhāvāt na tathā bodhaḥ. TCS., p. 72.

[114] Tanna, śrame svecchādhīna-kṛtisādhyatvābhāvāt. TCS., p. 78.

[115] Iṣṭasādhanatā-liṅgakam kāryatājñānaṁ pravartakam ityapare, tanna, nitye tadabhāvāt. TCS., p. 78.

determining condition, because being conducive to one's good is the determining condition of a desire to act in regard to a means of a positive voluntary action, and because it is not the determining condition of a desire to act in regard to the enjoyment of pleasure.[116]

It may be argued, that a volition in regard to the enjoyment of pleasure arises from the desire to act in regard to a means, and that both the views are vitiated by the same difficulty. This argument is not valid, because the same object cannot be known to be a means to one's good and an end to be realized by a volition, because they are contradictory to each other.[117] The Prābhākara view that the cognition of an action being capable of being done by one's volition due to the cognition of its being a means to one's good, is the cause of a voluntary action, is not vitiated by this difficulty. But the Nyāya view that the cognition of an action being capable of being done by one's volition, which knows the action to be a means to one's good, is vitiated by this difficulty. An end (sādhya) which is unrealized can be realized by a volition. A realized end cannot be realized by a volition. A means is an accomplished fact. A non-existent means cannot produce an effect.[118]

If cooking is known to be both unrealized and realized, existent and non-existent, then it can be known as an end and a means. But the same object cannot be known by the same person to be a means and an end at the same time.[119]

It may be argued, that the same object may be a means and an end, which are not contradictory to each other, and that there is no need of their cognitions which are contradictory to each other. This argument is wrong, because then cooking would always be a means and an end, if it were a means and an end at any time. Cooking cannot be said to be a means and an end at different times, because cooking cannot be known without

[116] Na, tavāpi sva-viśeṣaṇa-dhī-janyatvā-bhāvena tatra tasyāprayojakatvāt. Kṛti-hetu-cikīrṣāyām tat prayojakaṁ. TCS., p. 81.

[117] Maivaṁ sādyatva-sādhanatvayor-virodhenāikatra jñātum aśakyatvāt. TCS., pp. 81-82.

[118] Asiddhāvasthasya hi sādhyatvaṁ siddhatā-daśāyaṁ tadabhāvāt, siddhatā-daśāyaṁ ca sādhanatvam asiddhāvasthāvataḥ kāryānutpatteḥ. TCS., p. 82.

[119] Tathā ca pākāder asiddhatva-siddhatva-jñāne sādhyatva-sādhanatva-grahaḥ. Na caikam ekenaikadā siddham asiddhaṁ ca iti jñāyate. TCS., pp. 83-84.

knowing it to be an existent means and a non-existent end. Cooking cannot be known to be capable of being done by one's volition without knowing its limitor (avacchedaka). Therefore, cooking is related to a means and an end qualified by different times.[120] But if cooking is said to be known to be a present end and a future means, then the invariable concomitance of a means and an end cannot be known, because the present object and the future object are different and have no common property, and because they have no common property which may be denoted by a word, the objects cannot be denoted by it.[121]

It may be argued, that a desire to act is due to the cognition that an action is a means to one's good, which is accomplished by a volition; so that there is no contradiction between a means and an end. This argument is wrong, because none desire to do what is already accomplished, and because there is no cognition of an object accomplished by a volition before a volition occurs.[122]

It may be argued, that cooking is not a means to an end (e.g., cooked rice), because it is said to be a means to one's good as capable of being accomplished by one's volition, and that it will be a means to one's good when it will be accomplished by a volition. This argument is invalid, because cooking has not been said to be a means to the end (e.g., cooked rice) as capable of being accomplished by a volition; because, therefore, capability of being accomplished by a volition, which is future and different from a past volition and a present volition, is the determining condition of a desire to act; because such an end (sādhya) is contradictory to a means (sādhana); and because a means being an accomplished fact, the cognition of an object being a means is contradictory to a desire, since no one has a desire for an accomplished fact. Thus the view that the cognition of being a means to one's good as the cause of a desire for a means is the cause of a desire for rain, is refuted. The cognition of an object being a means is contradictory to its being an object of desire. Therefore, the cognition of rain being a means to one's good

[120] Tasmāt samayopādhika eva tadubhayasambandhaḥ pāke. TCS., pp. 85-86.

[121] Na, īdānīm-agrima-padārthayor nānātvād ananugamena vyāptya-grahāt. TCS., p. 86.

[122] Na ca kṛtitaḥ siddham iṣṭasādhanam itijñānāt cikīrṣā, na hi siddhaṁ kaścit cikīrṣati, kṛteḥ pūrvaṁ kṛtitaḥ siddham itijñānābhāvācca. TCS., pp. 86-87.

cannot be the cause of the desire for rain. Rain is not in itself a good or object of desire. How, then, can there be a desire for rain? The cognition of good or pleasure which is produced by rain is the cause of the desire for rain. The cognition of rain being a means to good or pleasure is not the cause of the desire for rain.

Pleasure and the absence of pain are the ends. The means of pleasure and the means of the absence of pain are the means.[123] Others maintain, that an end (uddeśya), which may be described as the common element of pleasure and the absence of pain, and their means, is the determining condition of desire for these three objects, that the character of an end is different from these three objects, because there is a common cause of a common effect, and that such an end, known to be different from pain and the means of pain, is the determining condition of a desire to act in regard to pleasure and the means of pleasure. The character of an end, or the common property of pleasure, the absence of pain, and their means, is not contradictoriness to pain, because pleasure and pain are not contradictory to each other, since they can exist at the same time in the same person, and since pain and its cause do not coexist in effort (yatna) at the same time in the same person.[124]

This view is wrong, because even in the absence of the knowledge of such an end (uddeśya) desire is produced by the knowledge of pleasure, and because pleasure would not be an end in itself, if desire were produced after the knowledge of pleasure when there was the knowledge of an end. That is an end in itself which being known produces a desire for it. Further, if pleasure were the cause of a desire, a common property might be assumed in pleasure. But pleasure etc., are not the causes of a desire, because pleasure etc., are future or non-existent. Only an existent object can be a cause. But the cognition of pleasure, etc., is the cause of a desire.[125]

But it may be argued, that pleasure, etc., as existing in the knowledge of pleasure, etc., is the determining condition of a desire. This argument is wrong, because just as the character of

[123] TCS., pp. 87-90.
[124] TCS., pp. 90-92.
[125] Tanna. Tadajñāne'pi sukhatva-jñānād icchotpatteḥ. Kiñcānugata-dharma-kalpanāpī kāraṇe. Na ca sukhādi icchā-kāraṇam, anāgatatvāt, kintu tadavagamaḥ. TCS., pp. 92-93.

an end is said to be produced where there are the cognitions of pleasure, the absence of pain, and their means, so desire may be said to be produced where there are the cognitions of pleasure, etc. There is no need of the character of an end being produced here. After a volition has occurred, cooking effected by a volition may occur; but it cannot occur without a prior volition. Cooking accomplished by a volition cannot occur before a volition.[126]

It may be contended, that even when a voliltion is destroyed and cooking is present, it is not an effect of the volition, or it is not qualified by the character of being accomplished by the volition, because the volition is already destroyed. How can a person desirous of cooking know it to be qualified by the character of being accomplished by a volition, because the volition is destroyed when cooking comes into existence?

This contention is wrong, because the cognition of an object (e.g., cooking) being capable of being accomplished by a volition is a determining condition, which is known to be a means to one's good, and because there is no invariable concomitance of what is qualified by being capable of being accomplished by a volition and a means to one's good.[127]

It may be contended, that there can be no cognition of cooking being capable of being accomplished by a volition, because it involves mutual dependence. After cooking is accomplished by a volition there can be the perception of its being accomplished by a volition. Again, after the perception of cooking being accomplished by a volition there can be a volition. It may be further contended, that when cooking is effected by a volition, there can be neither a desire to act nor a volition in regard to cooking, because it has already been effected.

This contention is not valid for the following reason. 'Cooking is capable of being produced by my volition, because it is a means to my good, which cannot be effected without my volition, or because it is a means to my good without depending upon a supernatural cause, etc., like my eating'.[128] This inference

[126] TCS., pp. 93-95.

[127] Na, yadvṛtti-kāmya-sādhanatvaṁ tatra kāryatābuddheḥ prayojakavāt, na tu kāryātā viśiṣṭasya kāmya-sādhanateti vyāptiḥ. TCS., pp. 96-97.

[128] Na, pāko matkṛtisādhyaḥ matkṛtiṁ vinā asattve sati madiṣṭa-sādhanatvāt daivādya-nadhīnatve sati madiṣṭa-sādhanatvād vā madbhojana-vad ityanumānāt. TCS., pp. 97-106.

is based upon the invariable concomitance that the action (e.g., cooking), which is the means of a person's good at a particular time, which cannot be realized without his volition at the time without the means of his good, without which he cannot have the cognition that the action is capable of being done by his volition, is capable of being done by him.[129] This invariable concomitance is supported by the fact that a non-existent object cannot be a means to one's good. 'Not being productive of a stronger evil' should be added to the reason as a qualification in order to account for the fact that a person does not eat rice mixed with honey and poison. There is no vyabhicāra in a past cooking, because there was capability of being accomplished by a volition in it in a past time, though it is not present in it at the present time, because the capability of being accomplished by a volition is present in a past cooking in a general way, or as a limitor (avacchedaka) of it, and because there is no desire for the rice which was cooked in the past, or because such rice is not a means to one's good. Where there is no probandum (sādhya) even in the presence of the probans (hetu), a fallacious reason called vyabhicāra is committed.

Hence a person afflicted with the intense heat of the summer does not bathe in a tank when he has been drenched by rain, because he has the knowledge that his desired contact with water has been brought about by rain without his volition. There is no voluntary action here, because there is the absence of the cognition that the action can be done by one's volition owing to the absence of the reason 'without my volition'. When an action is not possible without his volition, a person exerts his volition to perform it.

Some maintain, that a person, who regards the mere cooling of the heat as his good, does not know that bathing in a tank is a means to his good, because it has been brought about by a shower of rain without his volition. This view is wrong, because mere contact of water with one's body is a means to the cooling of the heat of the summer. The contact with water, which is a means of the cooling of heat, is present in bathing in a tank; so it may produce the voluntary action of bathing. If contact

[129] Svakṛtisādhyatājñānaṁ yasya yadiṣṭasādhanaṁ yatkṛtiṁ vinā yadā na sambhavati tat tadā tatkṛtisādhyam iti vyāpteḥ, asiddhasyeṣṭasādhanatvābhāvāt. TCS., pp. 106-107.

with water be not admitted in bathing in a tank, then rain also cannot be a means of contact with water. But bathing in a tank also can bring about contact with water.[130]

Being a means to one's good cannot be a reason of its being capable of being effected by one's volition, because there is no reason of the cognition of an object (e.g., cooked rice) being capable of being produced by one's volition before the occurrence of the volition, like cooking.[131]

The Naiyāyika contends, that if this be so, then let the cognition that an action is a means to one's good, which is a reason (liṅga) of its being effected by a volition, be the cause of a voluntary action, because it is prior to the latter and its invariable and necessary antecedent.[132] The argument that the cognition that an action can be done by a volition is the cause of a voluntary action because it contains a smaller number of elements, is wrong, because there is no proof for inferring that an action can be done by a volition, and because both being a means to one's good and being capable of being done by a volition do not exist before a voluntary action. If they are said to be absent together before a voluntary action owing to the presence of the counteracting causes of the inference of the action being capable of being done by a volition, that is not possible, because in the cognition of the reason the action being capable of being done by a volition is not manifested, and because consequently it cannot be a reason of a desire to act in regard to that. Therefore, the cognition of some other reason also cannot be the cause of a voluntary action.[133]

It may be contended, that the past cooking or the present cooking being not the subject (pakṣa) of inference of its being capable of of being done by a volition, because its being so is contradicted by experience, nor the future cooking being the subject, because it is non-existent and not the locus of the reason, the genus of cooking existing in a future cooking is the subject of inference, because it is a genus, like the genus of cow. This contention is wrong, because there is no evidence for the genus

[130] TCS., pp. 107-10.

[131] Kāryasādhanatvañca kṛtisādhyatve na liṅgaṁ pākādivad odanāderapi pravṛtteḥ pūrvaṁ kṛtisādhyatva-jñāne hetvabhāvāt. TCS., p. 110.

[132] Nanevaṁ liṅgajñānam eva pravartakam astu prāthamikatvāt āvaśyakatvācca. TCS., p. 111.

[133] TCS., pp. 111-12.

of cooking existing in a future cooking being capable of being produced by a volition. Mere cooking cannot be said to be the subject of inference, because mere cooking is the genus of cooking which cannot be produced by a volition, and because there is no reason for its being so. If all acts of cooking are the subject of inference, then produced cookings cannot be produced by a volition, and future acts of cooking being non-existent, they are not the abodes of the probans. It may be argued, that cooking, which is neither past, nor present nor future, is the subject of inference, and that cooking in general being capable of being done by a volition is not contradicted by perception. This argument is wrong, because only an existent object is a subject of inference, because an inference of an object (sādhya) known to be existent is contradicted by experience, and because if the inference is about a mere existent object, then it cannot produce a desire to act and a volition in regard to such an existent object.

It may be argued, that a desire to act and a volition in regard to a future non-existent object is produced by the cognition that an action can be done by a volition, which is common to past and present objects, and that a desire to act and a volition are produced by such a cognition as does not know whether the act is past or present. This argument is wrong, because there is no cognition of that kind of capability of being done by a volition, which is the object of the desire to act, and because therefore the cognition of another kind of capability of being done by a volition would produce the desire to act. Then let the cognition of the reason (liṅga), or of being a means to one's good, be the cause of a voluntary action, because it is prior to the cognition of the probandum (sādhya), or capability of being done by a volition.[134]

Some later Prābhākaras maintain, that the cognition that 'this action is capable of being done by my volition' is not the cause of a voluntary action, because there can be neither perception nor inference of a future object, but that a person knows that he has the capacity for doing an action which he has seen in another person, and then exerts his volition to perform the

[134] TCS., pp. 112-15.

action.[135] Thus a person knows that another person, who is desirous of cooked rice, who has the knowledge of its means, and who has got uncooked rice and other materials, can effect cooking by his volition, and knows that he is like such a person, and then exerts his volition to cook rice. Thus the cognition that an action is capable of being done by another's volition is the cause of a voluntary action in regard to cooking done by another person. In regard to one's own cooking one's cogntion of one's self being specified by the qualification which is the determining condition of the capability of the action being done by one's volition is its cause.[136] Therefore, a person does not exert his volition to eat poison or worship a Buddhist temple, because he has no knowledge of its being a means to his good, which is the cause of his knowledge of his capacity for effecting the action by his volition. Likewise a person, who is desirous of satisfying his hunger, knows that eating is capable of being done by a volition, and exerts his volition to eat food. But a person, who has satisfied his hunger, does not know his desire for satisfying his hunger, and so does not exert his volition to eat food.[137]

Some still later Prābhākaras add the qualification 'not entailing a stronger evil' to 'that a person knows that he has the capacity for doing an action which he has seen in another person'.[138] A person does not eat poison or worship a Buddhist temple, because he knows that it can be done by his volition, which entails a stronger evil.

The object of a voluntary action (e.g., cooking) is known in a general way, not determined by time. The future cooking is produced by the power of a volition. The desire to act has for its object cooking and the like undetermined by time. It has not for its object such a form as 'I shall accomplish a future object'.[139]

[135] Navīnāstu mamedaṁ kṛtisādhyam itijñānaṁ na pravartakam anāgata-viṣaye pratyakṣānumānayor asambhavāt, kintu yādṛśasya puruṣasya kṛtisādhyaṁ yad dṛṣṭaṁ tādṛśatvam ātmanaḥ pratisandhāya tatra pravartate. TCS., pp. 139-40.

[136] Anyakṛtapāke kṛtisādhyatājñānam ātmanaḥ pāke kṛtisādhyatva-prayojaka-viśeṣaṇavattva-jñānaṁ ca pravartakam. TCS., p. 140.

[137] TCS., pp. 140-41.

[138] Atinavīnāstu yādṛśasyetyādau avigītatvaṁ tatkṛtau viśeṣaṇam āhuḥ. TCS., p. 141.

[139] Pravṛtti-viṣayaśca sāmānyataḥ kālāsambhinnaḥ pākādir jñāyate, pravṛtti-mahimnā cānāgata-pāka-siddhiḥ, cikīrṣā ca kālāsambhinna-viṣayā na tu bhāvinaṁ kṛtyā sādhayāmītyākāraiveti. TCS., pp. 142-43.

9. *Gaṅgeśa's (Nyāya) Criticism of the Prābhākara view of the Cause of a Voluntary Action*

Gaṅgeśa (1200 A.D.) gives an elaborate criticism of the Prābhākara doctrine of the cause of a voluntary action in *Tattvacintāmaṇi* and states the Nyāya view that the cognition that an action is capable of being done by one's volition, which knows that it is conducive to one's good, and that it does not entail a stronger evil, is the cause of a voluntary action, because it is in conformity with the parsimony of hypotheses. Mathurānātha observes, that the cognition stated above is the cause of a desire to act in regard to a means (upāyacikīrṣā).[140] Gaṅgeśa avers, that the cognition of the self being specified by the knowledge that the action is a means to one's good, which can be done by the self's volition, and which does not entail a stronger evil, is not the cause of a voluntary action, because it assumes a larger number of elements and thus violates the parsimony of hypotheses.[141] The argument that there is a contradiction between an existent means and a non-existent end is invalid, because there is no contradiction between a means and an end undetermined by time.[141a] We have an experience that cooking which is non-existent is an end, and that cooking as existent is a means, both being taken as undetermined by time. The same object being a means as well as an end at the same time involves a contradiction. There is a contradiction between capability of being done by one's volition determined by a particular time and being a means to one's good determined by the same time, because there is a rule that they cannot exist in the same object at the same time. There is no contradiction between a mere means undetermined by time and an end, or between a means determined by some other time and an end. Though a means may exist at some other time, the means in general does exist. The absence of a genus implies the absence of a species: the absence of a jar implies the absence of a blue jar. But the absence of a species does not imply the absence of a genus: the absence of a blue jar does not imply the absence of

[140] Viṣabhakṣaṇādi-vyāvṛttaṁ kṛtisādhyatvajñāne iṣṭasādhanatvaṁ viṣayatayāvacchedakaṁ lāghavāt. TCS., p. 144. TCR., p. 144.

[141] Na tu svaviśeṣaṇa-vattā-pratisandhānajanyatvaṁ gauravāt. TCS., p. 144. TCR., p. 144.

[141a] Na ca siddhāsiddhāvasthayoḥ sādhyatva-sādhanatvayor virodhaḥ, nirviśeṣitayor avirodhāt. TCS., p. 145.

a jar. Non-existence determined by some other time is contradictory to existence determined by the same time, because the former indicates the absence of its existence at the same time. Non-existence determined by some other time is not contradictory to mere existence. If it were contradictory to mere existence, then the absence of existence could exist at some other time. But, in fact, it does not exist at some other time. If existence and non-existence undetermined by time were contradictory to each other, then the same cooking would be either existent or non-existent, and it could not be existent and non-existent at different times. But it is non-existent at one time and existent at a different time.[142]

The Nyāya does not maintain, that the cognition of an action being a means to one's good determined by that time, qualified by its capacity for being done by one's volition determined by that time, is the cause of a desire to act, or of a volition, so that there may be a contradiction between the means and the end.[143] 'One should perform a sacrifice called vājapeya'. In this instance, when the sacrifice is in the state of a means, it is existent, and, consequently, it is not an end at the time, because there is a contradiction between its being a means and an end at the same time. In a prior state the sacrifice is an end. There is no contradiction between its being a means at one time and an end at another time. Because the sacrifice is an existent means, it is not contradictory to its being an end. In fact, it is a means and an end at different times.[144]

It is contended, that the means and the end, which are contradictory to each other, are apprehended in the same locus, at the same time, in its different parts of space, even as contact with a monkey and the absence of contact with a monkey, which are contradictory to each other, are apprehended in a tree, at the same time, in its different parts. It is further contended, that an action being capable of being done by a volition and its being a means to one's good are apprehended in the same locus at different times is not valid, because there is no reason (liṅga)

[142] Nirviśeṣitayor virodhe ca siddhatvāsiddhatvayoscānyataradeva pākādau syānna tu samaya-bhede'pyubhayam. TCS., p. 147.

[143] Na ca tadā kṛtisādhyatve sati tadeṣṭasādhanatvajñānaṁ pravartakaṁ. TCS., p. 147.

[144] Na tu karaṇasya siddhatvena sādhyatva-virodhaḥ yāga-svarūpe tayoḥ sattvāt. TCS., p. 148.

for that statement, and that capability of an action being done by a volition and its being a means to one's good exist in the same locus, at the same time, in its different parts of space.

This contention is not valid, because it has already been stated that there is no contradiction between an end and a means at different times. The absence of contradiction means the absence of non-existence in the same locus, at the same time, in its same part of space. A means is an accomplished or existent object; an end is an unaccomplished or non-existent object. Though they are existent and non-existent respectively, there is no contradiction between them at different times, because the same object (e.g., a sacrifice) is known as an end and a means at different times, and consequently proved by a valid means of knowledge.[145] Hence just as there is a contradiction between contact with a monkey and the absence of contact with a monkey in a tree in the same part of space (deśa), so there is a contradiction between an object being a means and it being an end at the same time. Therefore the same object is not known to be an end and a means at the same time. It is wrong to argue, that the same object (e.g., cooking) cannot be known as an end and a means. Further, if the end and the means are contradictory to each other, then according to the Prābhākara also, that an action can be done by one's volition cannot be inferred from the action being a means to one's good, because there can be no knowledge of the invariable concomitance of the probans (hetu) with the probandum (sādhya), since they are not known to coexist in the same locus, being contradictory to each other. There can be no inference because the invariable concomitance between the probans and the probandum is not known. When the invariable concomitance is not proved, either contradicted reason (bādha) or unproven reason (svārupāsiddhi) is committed; the former fallacy arises when the probandum does not exist in the subject (pakṣa) of inference; the latter fallacy is committed when the probans does not exist in the subject.[146]

The Prābhākara may argue, that 'the capability of an action being done by my volition at the present time' is the

[145] Na, sādhyatva-sādhanatvayor avirodhasyoktatvāt, evaṁ siddhatvāsiddhatvayor bhāvābhāvarūpatve'pi na virodhaḥ ekadharmigatvena mānasiddhatvāt. TCS., pp. 150-51.

[146] TCS., pp. 151-52.

probandum, that 'the action being a means to my good at a future time' is the probans, that 'what is a means to my good at a future time without depending on an unseen principle (daiva), etc., is capable of being done by my volition at the present time' is the invariable concomitance, and that the probans and the probandum are known as occurring at different times. This argument is wrong, because the invariable concomitance between the probans and the probandum cannot be known because of the absence of a common property between the present probandum and the future probans, which are different objects.[147] Just as the same act of cooking is not known to be an end and a means at the same time, so, in the other instance, the probandum and the probans are not known at the same time. If 'capability of being done by one's volition at the present time' and 'being a means to one's good at a future time' are said to be known, then let the cognition of being a means to one's good at a future time,—it being capable of being done by one's volition at the present time,—be the cause of a voluntary action according to the Naiyāyika.[148]

Nor can it be argued, that the cognition that an action can be done by one's volition is inferred from the cognition that the action is a means to a desired end, because one's pleasure or desired end does not arise from non-existent cooking since after knowing the existence of cooking, its producing one's pleasure is known, because after knowing its non-existence its being capable of being done by one's volition is known, and because consequently there is a contradiction between an existent means and a non-existent end here also. Further, there cannot be a desire to act (cikīrṣā) in regard to pleasure due to the absence of the cognition that an action can be done by one's volition· being inferred from the cognition oı one's self being specified by the cognition of a desire.[149] The desire to act cannot arise from the mere cognition that an action can be done by one's volition, because then one who has the knowledge that the action entails

[147] Idānīm-agrima-padārthayor nānātvād anugatarūpābhāvena vyāpter agrahāt. TCS., p. 152.

[148] Pratītau vā mamāpīdānīṁ kṛtisādhyatve satyagre iṣṭasādhanam iti jñānaṁ pravartakam astu. TCS., p. 153.

[149] Api ca sva-viśeṣaṇa-dhī-janya-kāryatā-jñānābhāvāt sukhe kathaṁ cikīrṣā. TCS., p. 154.

a stronger evil may have a desire to act in regard to eating poison.

It may be contended, that the cognition that an action can be done by one's volition, inferred from the cognition of one's self being specified by its desire for the action, is the cause of a desire to act, that when the cognition of pleasure, the cause of a desire, knows that the action can be done by one's volition, there is a desire to act in regard to pleasure, or that when there are the cognition of pleasure and the cognition that the action can be done by one's volition, and that if there is only the cognition of pleasure, which does not know that an action can be done by one's volition, there is only a desire (icchā). This contention is not valid. Then let the cognition of the cause of a desire, which knows that an action can be done by one's volition, be the cause of a desire to act in regard to pleasure, and of a desire to act in regard to a means of pleasure, because it is in conformity with the parsimony of hypotheses. Just as the cognition of pleasure is the cause of a desire, so the cognition of a means of pleasure is the cause of a desire. Hence it is better to regard the cognition of the cause of a desire, which knows that the action which fulfils the desire can be done by one's volition as the cause of a desire to act, because it contains both the cognitions.[150] Therefore, the cognition of cooking being a means to one's good or pleasure, which knows that cooking can be done by one's volition, is the cause of the desire to act in regard to cooking. Because the cognition of rain being a means to one's pleasure does not know that rain can be done by one's volition, there can be no desire to act in regard to rain, but there can be only a desire for rain. The cognition of pleasure, the cause of a desire, which knows that the action which brings about pleasure can be done by one's volition, is the cause of a desire to act.[151] Otherwise there would be no desire to act after the cognition of pleasure. In fact, a desire to act in regard to a means (e.g., cooking) is produced by the cognition that the means is conducive to one's pleasure, because it is a desire for a means

[150] Ityeva sukha-tadupāya-cikīrṣā-kāraṇam astu lāghavāt, sukhatva-jñānavad iṣṭasādhanatā-jñānasyāpīcchākāraṇatvāt. TCS., p. 155.

[151] Sukha-cikīrṣāyām icchākāraṇa-jñāne kṛtisādhyatā-viṣayake cikīrṣā-janakatvāvadhāraṇāt. Anyathā tatra cikirṣānutpatteḥ. TCS., pp. 155-56.

like the desire for rain.[152] In the desire for rain there is the cognition that it is a means to one's pleasure, though there is no cognition that rain can be produced by one's volition. The desire for rain is a desire for a means; so it is produced by the cognition that it is a means to one's pleasure.

It may be contended, that there can be a desire to act in regard to a means (e.g., cooking), though there is no cognition of its being conducive to one's pleasure, and that therefore the inference mentioned above is devoid of favourable reasoning. This contention is not valid, because that the cognition of the means being conducive to one's pleasure is the cause of a desire for a means is proved by the method of agreement in presence and agreement in absence: when there is the cognition of the means being conducive to one's pleasure, there is a desire for means; and when there is no cognition of the means being conducive to one's pleasure, there is no desire for a means. Because rain is not pleasure or good in itself, there can be no desire for rain, if there is no cognition of its being a means to one's pleasure. Because a desire for a means is different from a desire for pleasure, it is necessary to assume a different cause for it, since there is no hindrance to such an assumption. The cognition of an object being a means to ones' pleasure is a specific cause of a desire for a means.

It may be contended, that a desire for a means is not produced by the cognition of its being conducive to one's pleasure, but that a desire for a means which is not a desire to act, or desire which is not a desire to act, is produced by the cognition of an object being a means to one's pleasure. This contention is wrong, because it violates the parsimony of hypotheses, and because there is no cognition of a means being conducive to one's pleasure in a desire for pleasure, which is a desire other than a desire to act.

Then it is necessary to regard the cognition of an object being conducive to one's pleasure, which knows that it can be produced by one's volition, as the cause of a desire to act. But the mere cognition of an object being a means to one's pleasure without the cognition that the means can be brought about by one's volition, is not the cause of a desire to act, because a

[152] Vastutas tu upāya-cikīrṣā iṣṭasādhanatā-jñāna-sādhyā upāyecchātvāt vṛṣṭīcchāvat. TCS., pp. 156-57.

specific effect cannot be produced without a specific cause. The cognition that an action (e.g., cooking) can be done by one's volition is a necessary element in the cause of a desire for what can be effected by one's volition.[153] Therefore, it must be admitted that a new-born child has the cognition that drinking mother's milk is conducive to his pleasure when he makes an effort to drink it, because the cognition of a means being favourable to one's pleasure is the specific cause of a desire for a means. We should assume a cause on the basis of causes and effects observed in our experience.[154]

It may be contended, that a means contradicts a desire, because a means is an existent object, and because an existent object cannot be an object of a desire; and that desire for rain is produced by the cognition of pleasure produced by rain. This contention is wrong, because there is no contradiction between a means and a desire inasmuch as there is no contradiction between existence and non-existence which are unspecified by time.[155] Existence and non-existence determined by the same time are not the characters of a means and a desire, which are not known also as existent and non-existent respectively at the same time. There is no contradiction between a means and a desire, because they are taken in a general way unspecified by particular times.

The argument, that ones' desire for rain is produced by the cognition that it is conducive to one's pleasure, is not valid, because in this view also there is a contradiction between existence and non-existence. Rain must be admitted to be existent (siddha), since a non existent object cannot produce one's pleasure; and rain must be admitted to be non-existent in order to fulfil the desire for it, because there can be no desire for an existent object. When there is rain, there is ones' good (e.g., crops); and when there is no rain, there is no good. The method of agreement in presence and agreement in absence proves that the existence of rain produces one's good (e.g., crops). This

[153] Kṛtisādhyatājñānaṁ vihāya iṣṭasādhanatājñānamātram na cikīrṣopadhāyakam. TCR., p. 159.

[154] Ata eva stana-pāna-pravṛtta vapyupāecchā-kāraṇatvena gṛhītasyeṣṭa-sādhanatva-jñānasyāpi kalpanaṁ dṛṣṭānurodhitvāt kalpanāyāḥ. TCS., p. 159.

[155] Na, nirviśeṣitayoḥ siddhatvāsiddhatvayor avirodhenecchāsādhanatvayor avirodhāt. TCS., pp. 160-61.

cognition is produced by the existence of rain. Further, the injunctive sentence 'one shohuld make a circle' which is a Buddhist rite, may be valid testimony, because there is no impediment to its conveying its meaning, because, according to the Prābhākara, the cognition that an action can be done by one's volition due to a desire to act is the cause of a voluntary action, which is not contradicted here.

The cognitions of the cognitions that an action can be done by another person's volition, that he has a desire for cooked rice, and that he knows the action to be a means to his pleasure, are not the causes of a voluntary action, because this view violates the parsimony of hypotheses. Nor are the cognitions, of the cognition that one has desire for cooked rice, and of the cognition that one knows that the action is conducive to one's pleasure, are not the causes of a voluntary action for the same reason. But the cognition that 'an action is a means to my good', 'the action being capable of being done by my volition' is the cause of 'my voluntary action', because this view is in conformity with the parsimony of hypotheses.[156] It has already been said how there can be no contradiction between an existent means and a non-existent end. It has also been said how there can be the cognition that a future cooking can be done by one's volition. Furthermore, a person exerts his volition to paint a picture imagined by himself after knowing that it can be done by his volition, and that it is a means to his good ; and in youth a person exerts his volition to perform sexual acts owing to the maturation of his sex-impulse after knowing that he can perform the action, and that it is conducive to his pleasure. Hence a cognition that an action can be done by one's volition and that it is conducive to one's good or pleasure, is the cause of a voluntary action.

How can a person desire 'I shall perform the action by my volition' after knowing that another person can perform it by his volition, in regard to an object which is already existent? He cannot have such a desire, because there can be no desire for an existent object, and because there can be no knowledge of a non-existent object.

It may be contended, that a desire for a non-existent object, which can be done by one's volition, is known from the

[156] Kintu matkṛtisādhyatve sati madiṣṭasādhanatājñānam eva lāghavāt. TCS., p. 163.

cognition that an existent object can be produced by one's volition; because a desire is by nature for a non-existent object, and because there is the relation of cause and effect between a cognition and a desire to act which are known in a similar manner, and because there is no relation of causality between a cognition and a desire to act in regard to the same object, since it violates the parsimony of hypyotheses. A cognition of a future object in a general manner is the cause of a desire to act in regard to it. It may be argued, that the cognition of pleasure is the cause of a desire for pleasure, because a cognition and a desire are cause and effect respectively as known in a similar manner, because a desire is for a future non-existent object, and because there is no cognition of a non-existent object.

This argument is invalid, because there is the cognition of a future non-existent object in a general way, which produces a desire for such a non-existent object, as has already been pointed out.[157] Let it be so. Yet let the cognition of an action being a means to one's pleasure be the distinguishing qualification of the cognition of the action being capable of being done by one's volition, because the cognition of an action being capable of being done by one's volition, which is known as conducive to one's pleasure, contains a smaller number of elements than the cognition of an action being a means to one's own pleasure, or to another's pleasure, and the cognition of the desire for a fruit, and because there is no evidence to prove that the cognition of the cognition of an action being conducive to one's pleasure and the cognition of the desire for a fruit are the causes of a voluntary action. If there were evidence for this, its violation of the parsimony of hypotheses would be tolerated.[158]

The Neo-Prābhākaras maintain, that the cognition that an action can be done by one's own volition, is the cause of a voluntary action.[159] Therefore, a peasant does not exert his volition to produce rain, which cannot be produced by his volition. They maintain further, that the cognition that an action can be done by one's volition is the principal cause of a voluntary action, and that a desire as existent is the auxiliary

[157] Na, asiddha-viṣayecchānurodhenānāgatajñānopāyasya darśitatvāt. TCS., p. 165.
[158] TCS., p. 165.
[159] Navyāstu svakṛtisādhyatājñānam eva pravartakam. TCS., p. 166.

cause of it,—the knowledge of desire being not necessary.[160] The former is the principal cause of a desire to act also, and the latter is the auxiliary cause of a desire to act also. A person, who has the knowledge that eating poison entails a stronger evil, has no desire for eating poison, because he has no cognition that the action is a means to his pleasure, which is the cause of a desire. A person does not exert his volition to eat past food, because he has no desire for past food. Because a person's hunger has been satisfied, he has no desire for past satisfaction of hunger due to the absence of the knowledge that eating is a means to his pleasure.[161]

It may be contended, that if being an object of desire is an auxiliary cause of a voluntary action, then there cannot be a voluntary action in regard to cooking, because there cannot be a desire for cooking, since it is not in itself an object of desire. This contention is not valid, because there can be a desire for cooking, since it is known to be a means to one's good.[162]

It may be contended, that the cognition that an action is a means to one's pleasure, which is known to be capable of being done by one's volition, is the cause of a desire to act, because an object of desire (iṣṭatva) is known from the knowledge of its being a means to one's pleasure, which occurs first, on which it depends. This contention is not valid, because there is a desire to act in regard to pleasure, though it is not a means to pleasure, because the cognition that pleasure can be produced by one's volition is the cause of the desire to act in regard to pleasure, and because being a means to pleasure is not its cause.[163] Though there are agreement in presence and agreement in absence between cooking and the cognition of its being a means to one's pleasure, they are rendered ineffective by its being an object of desire, because there being agreement in presence and agreement in absence between cooking and being an object of desire, its being an object of desire is the cause of

[160] Svakṛtisādhyatājñāna-viṣaye iṣṭatvasya svarūpasataḥ pravṛttau sahakāritvāt. TCS., p. 166.

[161] TCS., pp. 166-67.

[162] Iṣṭasādhanatvajñānena tasyāpīṣṭatvāt. TCS., p. 167.

[163] Na, iṣṭasādhanatvābhāve'pi bhoge cikīrṣātvāt tasyāṁ svakṛtisādhyatvajñāne satīṣṭatvam eva kāraṇaṁ natviṣṭasādhanatvaṁ vyabhicārāt. TCS., p. 167.

a voluntary action in regard to it. This being so, there can be a voluntary action in regard to pleasure, because pleasure is an object of desire.

This argument is invalid, because there can be a voluntary action in regard to pleasure after the cognition that pleasure is a means to the enjoyment of pleasure according to those who regard the cognition that an action is a means to one's pleasure as the cause of a voluntary action. The objection as to a voluntary action in regard to enjoyment of pleasure holds good in both the doctrines. It is a fact that there is a desire to act in regard to pleasure. But it may be objected, that there can be no volition in regard to pleasure, because there is always a volition in regard to a non-existent action (e.g., cooking), the means of which are existent. This objetion holds good in both the doctrines.[164] Hence the cognition that an action can be done by one's volition is the principal cause of a voluntary action; and the cognition that an action is an object of desire is its auxiliary cause.[165] This is the position of the Neo-Prābhākaras.

Gaṅgeśa replies, that this contention of the Neo-Prābhākaras is not valid for the following reason. It is known for certain, that the cognition that an object is a means to one's pleasure is the cause of a desire for a means, and that a desire does not produce a desire for itself—that a desire for cooking does not produce a desire for cooking.[166]

But why does a person, who has obtained cooked rice, not exert his volition to cook rice? He does not do so, because he has no desire for cooked rice, and because mere cooked rice is already existent. Likewise, a person does not exert his volition to eat past food, because he has no desire for past food.

But why does not a child exert his volition to acquire a kingdom, which has been predicted by an expert palmist, though he knows that the action can be done by his volition and that it is a means to his pleasure? He does not do so, because a future kingdom is non-existent, because a voluntary action is

[164] Sukhe cikīrṣā bhavatyeva kṛtistu na bhavati kṛteḥ siddhavṛttyasiddha-kriyāviṣayatva-niyamāditi cet tulyam. TCS., pp. 168-69.

[165] Tasmāt svakṛtisādhyatvaṁ vidhiḥ iṣṭatvaṁ sahakāri. TCS., p. 169.

[166] Iṣṭasādhanatājñānasy opāyecchāyāṁ hetutvāvadhāraṇāt tasyās-tajjanyatvaniyamād icchāyāḥ svaviṣayecchānutpādakatva-niyamāt. TCS., pp. 169-70.

always in regard to an existent object, and because he has no knowledge of the means of acquiring the future kingdom.[166a] When he knows the means of acquiring a kingdom, he does exert his volition to worship a god, etc. This argument is invalid, because there being no desire to act in regard to an existent object, there can be no volition in regard to a sacrifice and the like, and because worship of a god, etc., also being non-existent, there can be no volition in regard to it. Further, the objection to the acquisition of a future kingdom in youth from the knowledge that the action can be done by one's volition, and the knowledge that it is a means to one's pleasure, is futile in the instance that if there be no knowledge of the means of acquiring a kingdom, there can be no voluntary action in regard to it.

It may be argued, that the cognition that an action can be done by one's volition, the cognition that it is a means to one's pleasure, and the cognition of the means of realizing one's good, are not the causes of a voluntary action, because this view violates the parsimony of hypotheses, and because these cognitions have different objects. This argument is invalid for the following reason. In youth the person does exert his volition to acquire a kingdom. But in childhood he does not exert his volition to acquire it, because he knows that he cannot execute it by his volition, or because he knows that he cannot execute it without performing the means of acquiring the kingdom, even as a person does not perform the voluntary action of cooking, because he knows that cooking cannot be done by his volition without uncooked rice, which is the means of cooked rice. But a person does engage in worshipping a god, etc., after knowing that he can execute the means of getting a kingdom by his volition, and that the action is a means to his pleasure.[166b]

That the action does not produce greater pain than the intermediate pain which is indispensable for producing the object of desire, should be added as a qualification of the action being a means to one's pleasure. The absence of the knowledge of the qualification mentioned above is not the cause of a

[166a] Bhāvirājyasyāsiddhatvāt pravṛtteḥ siddha-viṣayatva-niyamāt rājyopāyāparicayācca. TCS., pp. 171-72.
[166b] TCS., pp. 166-73.

voluntary action, because it violates the parsimony of hypotheses.. But the qualification itself as qualifying the cognition of the action being a means to one's good is the cause of a voluntary action, because it is in conformity with the parsimony of hypotheses.[167] Therefore, a person does not eat rice mixed with honey and poison.

If this be so, then there can be no voluntary action which involves greater labour if the object of desire can be attained by another voluntary action which involves less labour. That an action does not entail a stronger evil cannot be a qualification (viśeṣaṇa), because sometimes expense of immense wealth and great labour involved in a voluntary action are not esteemed to be a stronger evil, and because sometimes even a little pain involved in a voluntary action is esteemed to be a stronger evil. Hence 'entailing a stronger evil' is not restricted to a particular class of voluntary actions. An evil cannot be said to be stronger than a good, because 'greater intensity' of evil cannot be restricted to a particular class of objects.[168] A pious and virtuous person sometimes commits immoral actions knowing them to be immoral because of the obscuration of his knowledge that they lead to hell by the great intensity of his lust or hatred.[169] Adultery is due to the great intensity of lust. Killing an enemy is due to the great intensity of hatred.

Udayayna (1050 A.D.) maintains, that the knowledge that an action is a means to one's good is the cause of a voluntary action,. and that an injunctive sentence conveys the intention of a reliable person, which induces a person to perform a voluntary action which he knows to be conducive to his good through the the injunction.[169a] Udayana says: "A voluntary action is an expression of a volition; a volition (kṛti) is due to a desire (icchā), or a desire to act (cikīrṣā). A desire to act is due to the knowledge that it can be done by one's volition, and that it is a means to one's good. An injunction conveys the knowledge that the

[167] Iṣṭasādhane ceṣṭotpattināntarīyaka-duḥkhādhika-duḥkhājanakatvaṁ viśeṣaṇaṁ, na tu tajjñanābhāvaḥ kāraṇaṁ, kintu tadeva viṣayatayā kāraṇatāvaccedakaṁ lāghavāt. TCŚ., pp. 174-90.

[168] TCS., pp. 193-94, 196-97.

[169] Āstikasya niṣiddhatvena jñāte'pi pravṛttiḥ rāga-dveṣayor utkaṭatvena naraka-sādhanatva-jñāna-tirodhānāt. TCŚ., p. 197.

[169a] Ācāryāstu pravartakam iṣṭasādhanatājñānam eva liṅarthastvāptābhiprāyo lāghavāt. TCS.. pp. 284-85.

enjoined action is a means to one's good".[170] Haridāsa (1500 A.D.) observes, that a desire to act is due to the cognition that action can be done by one's volition and that it is conducive to one's good, and that an injunction conveys the intention of a reliable person, from which its being a means to one's good is inferred.[171] Haridāsa and Vardhamāna (1250 A.D.) regard desire as existing as the cause of a voluntary action, and not desire as known, as its cause.[172]

10. *Viśvanātha's exposition of the Prābhākara view of the Cause of a Volition*

The Prābhākara regards the cognition that an action ought to be done and can be done by a volition (kāryatājñāna) as the cause of a volition through a desire to do it. The Nyāya maintains that the cognition that something is conducive to one's good is the cause of a voluntary action. This view is wrong, because if it were valid, then a person would exert his volition to bring down the moon, which is conducive to his good, though it is incapable of being accomplished by his volition. If the Nyāya urge, that the cognition of the action being incapable of being accomplished by one's volition is the counteracting cause of a volition, that is not tenable, because that would violate the parsimony of hypotheses. The hypothesis of the cognition, that an action is capable of being accomplished by one's volition, being the cause of a volition, contains a smaller number of elements than the hypothesis that the cognition that an action is conducive to one's good, qualified by the absence of the counteracting cause, in the form of the cognition that the action is incapable of being accomplished by one's volition. If the Nyāya consider the cognition of an action being incapable of being accomplished by one's volition to be the counteracting cause of a volition, then he regards the cognition of the action being conducive to one's good, qualified by the absence of the counteracting cause, as the cause of a volition, and that contains

[170] Pravṛttiḥ kṛtirevātra, sā cecchātaḥ, yataśca sā.
Tajjñānaṁ, viṣayas tasya vidhistajjñāpako'tha vā.
NKS., v, 6.

[171] Cikīrṣā krtisādhyatveṣṭa-sādhanatā-jñānāt. Iṣṭasādhanatvānumāpaka āptābhiprāyo vidhipratyayārthaḥ. Ṭīkā, p. 75.

[172] Icchāyāḥ svarūpasatyā eva pravrttihetutvāt. Ibid, p. 76. Na cecchā jñātā prayatna-jananī. kintu sattayā. NKSP., v, p. 82.

cannot be produced simultaneously, because being an end and being a means are contradictory to each other. An end is realizable; a means is an accomplished object. The same action cannot be known to be an end to be realizable by one's volition and an accomplished means to one's good by the same person at the same time.

The Naiyāyika concludes, that the cognition of an action being capable of being done by one's volition, the cognition of it being conducive to one's good, and the cognition of its not entailing a stronger evil, having the same object, are the causes of a volition; or that the cognition that an action can be done by one's volition, which is known to be a means to one's good, and which is known not to entail a stronger evil, is the cause of a volition, because it has the merit of simplicity. So it is wrong to argue that the cognition that an action can be done by one's volition and the cognition that it is a means to one's good occur at different times.[174] There is no contradiction between 'being a means' and 'being an end', because there is no contradiction between the cognition of an action being a means to one's good at one time and the cognition of its being capable of being accomplished by one's volition at a different time, and because the cognition of an action being a means to one's good and an end to be realized by one's volition unspecified by time can occur at the same time. Viśvanātha summarizes the arguments stated by Gaṅgeśa on behalf of the Prābhākara.

11. *Viśvanātha and Jānakīnātha's exposition of the Nyāya view of the Cause of a Volition*

The Nyāya maintains, that the cognition of an action being conducive to one's good, the cognition of its being capable of being accomplished by one's volition, and the cognition of its not producing a stronger evil, at the present time, are the causes of a positive volition.[175] A child does not make any effort to acquire a kingdom to which he is entitled in youth, because its acquisition is incapable of being accomplished by his volition at the time. A person whose hunger is satisfied does not eat food,

[174] Lāghavena balavad-aniṣṭānanubandhīṣṭasādhanatve sati kṛiti-sādhyatājñānasya tatra hetutvāt. SM., p. 476.

[175] Idānīṁtan eṣṭasādhanatvādi-jñānaṁ pravartakam. SM., p. 477.

because he has no cognition that eating food is conducive to his good at the time. A person whose mind is perverted by wrath eats poison, because he has the cognition that the action does not entail a stronger evil (e.g., death) at the time. A person commits adultery or kills an enemy, because his knowledge that such an immoral action leads to hell is eclipsed by his excessive lust or hatred at the time. A person has no desire to produce rain, sun, etc., because he has no knowledge that rain can be produced by his volition. Nor has he any volition in regard to them for the same reason. But he has a mere desire for rain, etc., because he has the knowledge that they are conducive to his good. A person has no volition in regard to vital acts due to the vital effort, because he cannot produce them by his volition. The Naiyāyika maintains, that a scriptural injunction conveys the knowledge that an enjoined action is capable of being done by one's volition, being conducive to one's good, and not being productive of a stronger evil.[176]

Jānakīnātha also summarizes Gaṅgeśa's arguments in stating the Nyāya view of the cause of a volition. The cognition that an action can be done by one's volition, it being known to be conducive to one's good and not productive of a stronger evil, is the cause of a positive volition. A scriptural injunction means that an enjoined action is capable of being accomplished by one's volition, being conducive to one's good, and being not productive of stronger evil. This is the Nyāya view.[177]

It may be urged, that there is no cognition that an action is conducive to one's good in regard to a daily obligatory duty. This argument is invalid, because there is the knowledge that such an action leads to heaven or the avoidance of the sin of omission. It may be urged, that if a daily obligatory duty is done by a person actuated by a desire for its fruit, then it ceases to be non-empirical (nitya) and becomes prudential (kāmya). This contention is beside the mark, because the Nyāya does not regard that action as non-empirical, which is not dependent on the desire for a fruit; because it regards that action as non-

[176] Balavad-aniṣṭānanubandhitva-viśiṣṭeṣṭasādhanatve sati kṛtisādhyatvaṁ vidhyarthaḥ. SM., p. 484.

[177] Balavad-aniṣṭānanubandhī-ṣṭasādhanatve sati kṛtisādhyatva-viṣayakaṁ jñānaṁ pravartakam. Vidhyartho'pi balavad-aniṣṭānanubandhīṣṭasādhanatve sati kṛtisādhyatvam. NSM., pp. 254-55.

empirical, the non-performance of which produces a sin of ommission; and because this character remains intact even if such a duty is performed with a desire for the avoidance of a sin of ommission. It cannot be urged, that there can be no volition in regard to a daily obligatory duty, when there is no desire for a fruit, because such a duty is known to be conducive to one's good, and therefore this knowledge can produce a volition.[178]

12. *Gāgābhaṭṭa's criticism of the Nyāya view and exposition of the Bhāṭṭa view of the Cause of a Volition*

The Nyāya regards the cognition that an action is conducive to one's good, the cognition that it can be accomplished by one's volition, and the cognition that it does not produce a stronger evil, as the causes of a volition, because in the absence of any of them the desire to perform it is not produced. An injunctive sentence has the power of conveying these three meanings.

Gāgābhaṭṭa contends, that an injunctive sentence does not directly mean that an action can be accomplished by one's volition; but that it means that a volition is favourable to a sacrifice that is enjoined, which implies that it can be accomplished by the enjoined person's volition. Similarly, an injunction does not directly mean that the action is conducive to his good, which is implied by the knowledge that the sacrifice that is enjoined is a means to the attainment of heaven, which is his good. The action cannot be known to be conducive to his good, unless he knows it to be a means to the attainment of heaven. A person desirous of heaven performs the Jyotiṣṭama sacrifice. He knows that the sacrifice is a means to the attainment of heaven, and that consequently it is conducive to his good. If he knew that it was not a means to the attainment of heaven, he would not perform it. Likewise, an injunction does not directly mean that an action does not produce a stronger evil. It is implied by the injunction which is praised. That the action does not entail a stronger evil is known, when it is known that there is the absence of greater intermediate pain in the form of fatigue, exertion, etc., in the process of realizing the good. Further, in the knowledge of a person desirous of heaven and

[178] NSM., pp. 252-53.

having a volitiin to perform the sacrifice, which is a means to his good, which can be done by his volition, and which does not entail a stronger evil, his volition is known as a substantive (viśeṣya) and the other elements as its qualifications (prakāra).[179]

The Bhāṭṭa Mīmāṁsaka maintains, that the denotative power residing in words is the meaning of an injunction, and that this is the inciting cause of a volition.[180] Volitions are of two kinds: (1) dependent on one's freedom, and (2) dependent on another's will. (1) The cognition of an action conducive to one's good, the cognition of its being capable of being accomplished by one's volition, and the cognition of its not entailing a stronger evil, are the inciting causes of the first kind of volition. So far the Bhāṭṭa agrees with the Naiyāyika. (2) The cognition of being directed by the command of the king, the preceptor, etc., is the inciting cause of the second kind of volition.[180a] The commands of the king, the preceptor, etc., are not individually the moving causes of volitions, because each of them is not found to cause all volitions. But the cognition of the moving power residing in one's volition is the cause of a volition.[181] It takes such forms as 'the king moves me to perform the voluntary action', 'the Moral Law moves me to perform the voluntary action', etc. Moving power is a particular activity of a person or an entity, which is favourable to another person's volition.[182] It is a command of a conscious person, e.g., a king or the like. A supernatural activity inhering in a Vedic injunction, which regulates its denotative power, is the cause of a volition of an enjoined person, because the Vedas are unconscious and have no speaker. The Mīmāṁsaka does not believe in God who is regarded as the creator of the Vedas by the Naiyāyika. The denotative power of a scriptural injunction is the cause of an enjoined person's volition, even as the command of a king or the like is cause of another's volition.[183]

[179] Bhāṭṭacintāmaṇi, pp. 67-68.

[180] Abhidhaiva śabdaniṣṭhā pravartanarūpā vidhyarthaḥ. Ibid, p. 68.

[180a] Pravṛttir dvedhā svecchādhīnā parādhīnā ca. Tatrādvāyām iṣṭasādhanatvādidhiḥ kāraṇam. Antyāyām rājagurvāder ājñā-preraṇādidhiḥ. Ibid, p. 68.

[181] Kiṁ tu icchādi-niṣṭha-pravartanātva-prakāraka-jñānaṁ hetuḥ. Ibid, p. 68.

[182] Pravartanā ca para-pravṛttya-nukūla-vyāpāra-viśesaḥ. Ibid, p. 68.

[183] Vede vaktur abhāvād acetanasya vedasyābhidhāniyāmakaḥ kaścic-chabda-samaveto'laukikaḥ. Pravṛttiḥ vidher abhidhājñānād iti. Ibid, p. 68.

13. *The Nature and Kinds of the End or Motive (Prayojana)*

Gotama defines an end or motive as that which induces the self to act.[184] Motive is the idea of the end which moves the self to act. That object which is to be attained or avoided by the self, and for the attainment or avoidance of which it adopts means, is the end or motive, because it is the cause of a voluntary action.[185] This is Vātsyāyana's interpretation. Motives are the final causes of voluntary actions, while faults (doṣa), attachment, aversion and deulsion, are their efficient causes.[186]

Viśvanātha mentions four motives: (1) the pursuit of pleasure, (2) the avoidance of pain, (3) the pursuit of the means to pleasure, and (4) the avoidance of the means of pain. Of these the first two are the principal motives, and the last two are the subordinate motives. The first two are the ends in themselves, and are desired for their own sake. They are objects of a desire which is independent of any other desire.[187] Keśavamiśra recognizes only two kinds of motives: (1) the attainment of pleasure, and (2) the removal of pain. All voluntary actions are actuated by these two motives. All seek pleasure and shun pain.[188]

Dharmarājādhvarīndra defines a motive as the end of an action which being known by the self excites a desire in it for its attainment.[189] A motive is represented by the self, chosen by it, and sought to be attained by it. It moves the self to exert its volition for its attainment. The idea of an end which moves the self to act is called a motive. Dharmarājādhvarīndra mentions two kinds of ends, principal and subordinate. Pleasure and the removal of pain are the principal motives. The means to the attainment of pleasure and the means to the removal of pain are the subordinate motives. The principal motive is the object of a desire which does not depend upon the desire of any other object. It is an end in itself, and not a means to any other end. The subordinate motive is the object of a desire

Yam adhikṛtya pravartate, tat prayojanam. NS., i, 1, 24.
NBh., i, 1, 24.
NS., NBh., iv, 1, 2-3.
NSV., i, 1. 24; BhP., 146; SM., p. 467.
TBh., p. 31.
Yad avagataṁ sat svavṛttitayā iṣyate tat prayojanam. VP., p. 406.

which depends upon the desire of some other object. It is not an end in itself but a means to some other end.[190]

It may be asked how a pleasure which is not yet attained can move the self to act. It is replied that a future pleasure is known by the self by inference based on memory and imagination. It is represented by the self, and becomes a part of it as an idea, and thus excites a desire in it in such a form as 'May this pleasure be mine'. A future pleasure which is not represented by the self cannot excite a desire in it. Wealth, sons and the like become objects of desire when they are known by the self as means to the attainment if pleasure. They become indirectly related to the self when they are represented by it. That object is the motive of a particular self which is known to be capable of being attained by it, and excites a desire in it for its attainment. The pleasure of a king cannot be the motive of a poor person, because it is not represented by him as capable of being attained by him, and because it does not excite a desire in him for its attainment. When the attainment of a pleasure is beyond the reach of a person, it never becomes the object of his desire.[191]

14. *The Conditions of Overt Action*

Overt action is the outer expression of the inner volition. The muscular action of a hand, for instance, is the effect of the contact with the self and its volition.[192] The organism and its parts are its inherent cause (samavāyi kāraṇa), the contact with the self is its non-inherent cause (asamavāyi kāraṇa), and volition is its efficient cause (nimitta kāraṇa). So it is said, "The self is the cause of a desire; a desire is the cause of a volition; a volition is the cause of bodily exertion; and bodily exertion is the cause of an overt action".[193] A person who exerts his will can raise his hand; this bodily action is not possible without his volition and contact of his self with his manas.

[190] Maṇiprabhā on VP., p. 408.
[191] Śikhāmaṇi and Maṇiprabhā on VP., pp. 406-7.
[192] Ātmasaṁyoga-prayatnābhyāṁ haste karma. VS., v, 1, 1.
[193] Ātmajanyā bhaved icchā, icchājanyā bhavet kṛtiḥ.
Kṛtijanyā bhavec ceṣṭā tajjanyaiva kriyā bhavet.
VSV., v, 1, 1. VSB., v, 1, 1.

15. *Kinds of Actions*

Caraka defines an action as the effort of the vocal organs, manas, and body.[194] The mental act of willing, its expression in language, and its expression in a bodily action are the three kinds of acts. Language is recognized as a distinct kind of action as it mediates between the inner act of volition and the outer act of the body.

Gotama also metions three kinds of actions: (1) verbal, (2) mental, and (3) physical.[195] Verbal actions consist in speaking words; physical acts pertain to the body; and mental actions pertain to the mind. Verbal actions should be included in bodily actions. Hence there are two kinds of actions, mental and physical. Resolution is the mental stage of a voluntary action. Sometimes it is expressed in language, and sometimes in a muscular action of the body and brings about a change in the environment.

Śivāditya mentions three kinds of actions from the moral standpoint: (1) moral actions, (2) immoral actions, and (3) neutral actions. Moral actions are those which are enjoined by the Vedas. Immoral actions are those which are forbidden by them. Neutral actions are those which are devoid of any moral worth.[196]

Patañjali mentions four kinds of actions: (1) white, (2) black, (3) white and black, and (4) neither white nor black. The actions of the yogins who have destroyed all afflictions (kleśa) are neither white nor black and produce neither merits nor demerits, because they have been dedicated to God, and because their fruits have been renounced. The afflctions are nescience, egoism, attachment, aversion, and fear of death. White actions are austerities, study of the scriptures, meditation, muttering of the mystic sound *Om*, etc., which produce merits. Black actions are killing animals, etc., which produce demerits. The performance of sacrifices by killing animals and paying fees to Brāhmaṇas is black and white and produces merits and demerits. The Nyāya and the Mīmāṁsā do not regard the killing of animals in a sacrifice enjoined by the Vedas as a sin. But the Sāṁkhya and Patañjali regard it as a sin.[197]

[194] Karma vāṅmanaḥ-śarīra-pravṛttiḥ. CS., i, 11, 33.
[195] Pravṛttir vāg-buddhi-śarīrārambhaḥ. NS., i, 1, 17.
[196] Prayatno'pi vihita-niṣiddhodāsīna-viṣayaḥ. SP., p. 26.
[197] YS., iv, 7, YBh., iv, 7.

16. *The Psychical Elements in a Volition*

Desire, a condition of a positive volition, and aversion, a condition of a negative volition, have already been explained. Rāmakaṇṭha defines kāma as resolution for the attainment of an object of desire due to attachment to it.[198]

Determination (utsāha) is an essential psychical element in a volition, which precedes a voluntary action. Madusūdana describes it as a resolution of the mind in the form 'I must do this'. He regards utsāha as the determinate knowledge of such a resolution to execute a voluntary action.[199] Puruṣottamajī defines utsāha as endeavour to execute a purposive action with the knowledge that it is the best course in a particular situation.[200] Rāmānuja and Veṅkaṭanātha regard utsāha as readiness of the mind filled with energy to perform a voluntary action.[201] Śaṁkara and Śrīdharasvāmī regard it as enterprise (udyama). Hanumān and Vedāntadeśika Veṅkaṭanātha regard utsāha as effort of will or volition (prayatna).[202]

Ascertainment of duty in a complex situation is another important psychical element in a voluntary action. Madhusūdana regards non-delusion (asaṁmoha) as an act of volition preceded by the determination of duty when the mind has to choose between alternative possibilities. It is an act of volition after deliberation and determination of duty when complex circumstances demanding adequate comprehension and moral evaluation present themselves to a person. Śaṁkara regards non-delusion as an act of volition preceded by determination of duty when the mind is tossed in doubt and oscillates between alternative courses of action in a complex situation. Śrīdharasvāmī regards non-delusion as the absence of mental perplexity, which produces a voluntary action in regard to duties with discrimination and unagitated mind.[203]

Rāmānuja defines dhṛti as determination of duty even in

[198] Kāmaṁ rāga-nimittakam iṣṭaviṣayeṣu saṁkalpam. RKBG., xviii, 53.

[199] Utsāha idam ahaṁ kariṣyāmi eveti niścayātmikā buddhiḥ. MBG., xviii, 26. NBG., xviii, 26.

[200] Utsāha uttamatva-jñānena udvamaḥ. ATBG., xviii, 26.

[201] Utsāha udyukta-cetastvam. RBG., xviii, 26. BrGBG., xviii, 26.

[202] SBG., SrBG., HBG., RBTC., xviii, 26.

[203] SBG., x, 4; RBG., x, 4; SrBG., x, 5. Asaṁmohaḥ pratyutpanneṣu boddhavyeṣu kartavyeṣu cāvyākulatayā vivekena pravṛttiḥ. MBG., x, 4.

great danger.[204] It is ascertainment of duty in a complex situation without intellectual confusion. Rāmānuja defines dhṛti also as the power of enduring unavoidable pain without flinching until a task undertaken is accomplished.[205] Madhusūdana defines dhṛti as a mental mode which is the cause of not giving up a task undertaken in spite of hindrance. Rāmānuja also defines dhṛti as the power of finishing a task undertaken, brushing aside all obstacles.[206]

Firmness or resolution (sthairya) is an essential element in a voluntary action. Śaṁkara defines firmness in spiritual discipline as determination in the pursuit of liberation. Rāmānuja also defines it as unswerving determination in spiritual pursuits. Śrīdharasvāmī defines it as unflinching devotion (ekaniṣṭhatā) to the realization of the highest good. Madhusūdana defines it as repeated endeavours with unflagging zeal in the pursuit of liberation in spite of many kinds of hindrances. These definitioss imply that firmness is steadfast determination in the pursuit of a chosen end or good. Rāmakaṇṭha regards constancy as the absence of fickleness in performing one's duties by arresting the flaw of doubt. It implies a clear moral insight into one's duty in a concrete complex situation and determination in the performance of it.[207]

Constancy (acāpala) is an element in a voluntary action. It is allied to determination. Rāmakaṇṭha defines constancy as the absence of fickleness. Fickleness is instability in a critical situation. Constancy is the absence of negligence is the performance of obligatory duties. Śaṁkara regards steadiness as the arrest of all useless activities of the motor organs, and fickleness as useless activity of the organs of the body. Śrīdharasvāmī also defines steadiness as the inhibition of useless movements.[208]

Dexterity (dākṣya) is necessary for performing a voluntary action efficiently. Śaṁkara regards dexterity as an effort of volition to perform an action suddenly to master a complex situation. When a person has to perform an action suddenly, a

[204] Dhṛtir mahatyām api āpadi kṛtyakartavyatāvadhāraṇam. RBG., xvi, 3.

[205] Ārabdhe karmaṇi yāvat samāptim avarjanīya-duḥkha-dhāraṇaṁ dhṛtiḥ. RBG., xviii, 26.

[206] MBG., xviii, 26; RBG., xviii, 43.

[207] SBG., SrBG., MBG., RKBG., xiii, 7.

[208] SBG., SrBG., xvi, 2.

dexterous person does not lose his nerve but energizes and acts without being perturbed in the least. This quality is called dexterity. Rāmānuja defines dexterity as the power of performing all actions completely.[209] Śrīdharasvāmī regards dexterity as efficiency in all actions. Madhusūdana defines it as the power of undertaking and accomplishing all actions, which have to be performed quickly, without any perplexity in complex situations.[210]

Negligence stands in the way of performing one's duty at the proper time. The *Bhagavad Gītā* regards negligence as an effect of tamas or inertia of mind. Śaṁkara defines it as non-performance of duties in time. Ānandagiri regards it as non-performance of a duty by a person who desires to perform it but cannot do so owing to his mind being preoccupied with some other action. Śrīdharasvāmī identifies pramāda with inattention. Madhusūdana identifies it with non-discrimination or inability to ascertain the real nature of things, which counteracts the effect of sattva or purity of mind, viz., right cognition.[211] Rāmakaṇṭha regards negligence as the absence of discrimination of the right means and the right ends. Śaṁkara traces negligence to attachment for worldly objects of pleasure, e.g., children, cattle and the like.[212]

Carefulness is favourable to the performance of one's duty at the proper time. Carefulness (apramāda) in the performance of duties is due to one's freedom from subjection to objects of pleasure. It is due to the conquest of sensibility.[213]

Procrastination is an impediment to the performance of one's duty at the proper time. Rāmakaṇṭa defines procrastination as the habit of making delay in performing actions which ought to be done quickly. Śaṁkara and Śrīdharasvāmī assert that a procrastinate person has always a contented nature, and does not think of performing an action, which ought to be done to-day or tomorrow, due to the predominance of tamas in his mind.

[209] Dākṣyaṁ sarva-kriyā-nirvṛti-sāmarthyam. RBG., xviii, 43; SrBG., xviii, 43; SBG., xviii, 43.

[210] Dākṣyaṁ sahasā pratyutpanneṣu kāryeṣu avyāmohena pravṛttiḥ. MBG., xviii, 43.

[211] BG., SBG., SrBG., MBG., xiv, 8.

[212] RKBG., xiv, 8; SB., Muṇḍ. Up., iii, 4.

[213] ABG., ii, 45.

Ānandagiri and Madhusūdana attribute procrastination to constant apprehension of evil consequences that may arise from the performance of an action.[214]

[214] RKBG., SBG., SrBG., ĀBG., MBG., xviii, 28.

INDEX

Abhijalpa, 337
Abhimāna, 490
Abhinavagupta, 138, 170-72, 290, 308, 313, 317
Abhisārikā, 350
Ābhyudayika, 457
Absence of, hatred, 129; longing, 119-20; pain, 520-21, 526; the sense of mine, 125; union, 449-50, 452
Absolute pleasure, 66
Abstention, 375
Accessory states, 207-75, 270-71; kinds of, 209-71; nature of, 207-09
Acquisition, 91
Acyutarāya, 184, 188, 192, 202, 205, 216, 220, 221, 232, 263, 267, 269
Actionlessness, 407
Adbhuta bhaktirasa, 454-55
Ādhāra cakra, 7
Ādhibhautika pain, 76
Ādhidaivika pain, 76
Adhīrā, 343
Ādhyātmika pain, 76
Adoration of God, 394
Adṛṣṭa, 387, 495, 500
Advaita Vedānta, 98-99, 133, 366, 369
Æsthetic enjoyment, 163-70
Æsthetic sentiment, 163-74; comic, 298-99; denial of, 473-75; erotic, 290-98; furious, 302-03; heroic, 303-05; kinds of, 285-321; nature of, 163-70; odious, 306-07; of devotion, 316-18; of parental affection, 315; origin of, 170-74; painful, 319; pathetic, 299-301; pleasant, 318-19; quiet, 307-15; terrible, 305
Affected repulse, 348
Affection, 326-27; for God, 415, 427; honey-like, 327; melted-butter-like, 327
Affliction, 360
Agitation, 233-36
Ahaṁgraha, 411, 424
Ahaṁkāra, 388
Ahiṁsā, 139, 390, 394
Ājalpa, 338
Ājñā cakra, 7, 9
Ājñāvahā nāḍī, 10
Ākāśa cakra, 8
Akaṣāya emotions, 161
Alaṅkāra, psychology of, 164-351
Ālaṅkārikas, 277, 284
Amaradāsa, 67
Amorous flutter, 346
Amṛtacandra Sūri, 37, 63, 497, 498
Anahata cakra, 7, 9-10
Ānandagiri, 60, 102, 104-05, 107-11, 114-16, 120-22, 124-26, 129, 131, 133, 135-36, 138-40, 142-45, 147, 149-54, 221, 353, 367, 476, 556-57
Ānandatīrtha, 108, 120, 134, 139, 149, 152
Anger, 92, 95, 99, 110-13, 161, 191-96
Aniruddha, 21, 34-35, 72, 80, 490
Annaṁbhaṭṭa, 57, 73
Anticipatory pleasure, 64
Anubhāva, 285-87
Anuddharṣa, 392
Anurāga, 330-31, 427-28, 435
Anurasa, 468-69
Anxiety, 116-17, 223-24
Aparasa, 468-69
Apperception, 488
Apprehension, 212-14
Appropriation, 92-95, 497-98
Ardent love for God, 395, 404, 408, 425-27
Arrogance, 348
Atonement, 376-77
Attachment, 24, 50, 94, 96, 99, 102-03; to God, 395
Attention, 476-94; and consciousness, 490-91; and desire, 491; and inhibition, 492-93; and interest, 491; and perception, 488-89; and recollection, 489; and yoga, 493-94; determinants of, 478-82; habit of, 483; nature of, 476-78
Ātyantika bhakti, 407
Avagraha, 489, 491
Avāya, 489, 491
Aversion, 91-100, 504-05
Avidyā, 23, 25-26, 28-29, 31, 35-37, 40, 59, 66, 77, 97-99, 114
Awaking, 267-68
Ayoga, 449

Bādarāyaṇa, 366
Bain, 188, 204, 206, 315
Baladeva Vidyābhuṣaṇa, 102, 105, 109, 111, 352, 355, 364, 371, 373, 431-32
Bālakṛṣṇa Bhaṭṭa, 384, 387, 413-17
Bashfulness, 348
Benevolence, 137-38, 392-93
Bhaktirasa, 436-75, 469-73
Bhaktiyoga, 393